The Lost Cause

by

E. A. Pollard

A facsimile of the original 1867 edition

Bonanza Books
New York

Eng.ᵈ by H.B.Hall,N.Y.

Jeffⁿ. Davis

JEFFERSON DAVIS

Engraved expressly for the Lost Cause by E.A.Pollard.

THE LOST CAUSE;

𝔄 𝔑𝔢𝔴 𝔖𝔬𝔲𝔱𝔥𝔢𝔯𝔫 ℌ𝔦𝔰𝔱𝔬𝔯𝔶 𝔬𝔣 𝔱𝔥𝔢 𝔚𝔞𝔯 𝔬𝔣 𝔱𝔥𝔢 ℭ𝔬𝔫𝔣𝔢𝔡𝔢𝔯𝔞𝔱𝔢𝔰.

COMPRISING

A FULL AND AUTHENTIC ACCOUNT OF THE RISE AND PROGRESS OF THE LATE SOUTHERN CONFEDERACY—THE CAMPAIGNS, BATTLES, INCIDENTS, AND ADVEN-TURES OF THE MOST GIGANTIC STRUGGLE OF THE WORLD'S HISTORY.

DRAWN FROM OFFICIAL SOURCES, AND APPROVED BY THE MOST DIS-TINGUISHED CONFEDERATE LEADERS.

BY

EDWARD A. POLLARD, OF VIRGINIA,

EDITOR OF THE RICHMOND "EXAMINER" DURING THE WAR.

WITH NUMEROUS SPLENDID STEEL PORTRAITS.

SOLD ONLY BY SUBSCRIPTION.

𝔑𝔢𝔴 𝔜𝔬𝔯𝔨:

E. B. TREAT & CO., PUBLISHERS.

BALTIMORE, MD.: L. T. PALMER & CO. ST. LOUIS, MO.: I. S. BRAINERD. LOUISVILLE, KY.: GEO. B. FESSENDEN & CO. AUGUSTA, GA., and AUBURN, ALA.: GEO. W. LOYD. CHARLESTON, S. C.: ROBERT WILSON. MEMPHIS, TENN.: J. B. SUTTON. HOUSTON, TEXAS: J. F. FULLER. JAS. H. HUMMEL, NEW ORLEANS, LA.

1867.

Library of Congress Catalog Card Number: 74-25666
All rights reserved.
This edition is published by Bonanza Books
a division of Crown Publishers, Inc.
c d e f g h
Manufactured in the United States of America

INTRODUCTION.

THE facts of the War of the Confederates in America have been at the mercy of many temporary agents; they have been either confounded with sensational rumours, or discoloured by violent prejudices: in this condition they are not only not History, but false schools of present public opinion. By composing a severely just account of the War on the basis of cotemporary evidence—ascertaining and testing its facts, combining them in compact narrative, and illustrating them by careful analyses of the spirit of the press, not only in this country, but in Europe, the author aspires to place the history of the War above political misrepresentations, to draw it from disguises and concealments, and to make it complete in three departments: the record of facts; the accounts of public opinion existing with them; and the lessons their context should convey or inspire. These three are the just elements of History. If the author succeeds in what he proposes, he will have no reason to boast that he has produced any great literary wonder; but he will claim that he has made an important contribution to Truth, and done something to satisfy curiosity without "sensation," and to form public opinion without violence.

The author desires to add an explanation of the plan of composition he has pursued in the work. It is impossible to write history as an intelligible whole, and to secure its ends, without preserving a certain *dramatic unity* in the narrative. It is by such unity that the lesson of history is conveyed, and its impression properly effected; and to do this it becomes necessary to discard from the narrative many small incidents, either epi-sodal in their nature, or of no importance in the logical chain of events. With this view, the author has paid but little attention to small occur-rences of the war which in no way affected its general fortunes, and has measured his accounts of battles and of other events by the actual extent of their influence on the grand issues of the contest. Instead of a con-fused chronological collection of events, he has sought to prepare for the reader a compact and logical narrative that will keep his attention close to the main movement of the story, and put instruction as to causes hand in hand with the information of events.

CONTENTS.

CHAPTER I.

CHAPTER II.

CHAPTER V.

CHAPTER VI.

CHAPTER VII.

CHAPTER VIII.

CHAPTER IX.

C H A P T E R   X .

C H A P T E R   X I .

CHAPTER XIV.

CHAPTER XVII.

CHAPTER XVIII.

CHAPTER XXI.

CHAPTER XXII.

CHAPTER XXIII.

CHAPTER XXIV.

CHAPTER XXV.

CHAPTER XXVI.

CHAPTER XXVII.

CHAPTER XXVIII.

CHAPTER XXIX.

CHAPTER XXX.

CHAPTER XXXI.

CHAPTER XXXII.

CHAPTER XXXIII.

CHAPTER XXXIV.

CHAPTER XXXV.

CHAPTER XXXVI.

CHAPTER XXXVII.

CHAPTER XXXVIII.

CHAPTER XXXIX.

CHAPTER XL.

CHAPTER XLI.

CHAPTER XLII.

CHAPTER XLIII.

CHAPTER XLIV.

ILLUSTRATIONS.

CHAPTER I.

THERE is nothing of political philosophy more plainly taught in history
than the limited value of the Federal principle. It had been experimented upon in various ages of the world—in the Amphictyonic Council,
in the Achæan league, in the United Provinces of Holland, in Mexico, in
Central America, in Columbia, and in the Argentine republic; in all
these instances the form of government established upon it had become
extinct, or had passed into the alternative of consolidation or anarchy and
disintegration. Indeed, it is plain enough that such a form of government
is the resource only of small and weak communities; that it is essentially
temporary in its nature; and that it has never been adopted by States
which had approached a mature condition, and had passed the period of
pupillage. It is not to be denied that the Federal principle is valuable in
peculiar circumstances and for temporary ends. But it is essentially not

permanent; and all attempts to make it so, though marked for certain periods by fictitious prosperity and sudden evidences of material activity and progress, have ultimately resulted in intestine commotions and the extinction of the form of government. What, indeed, can be more natural than that the members of a confederation, after they have advanced in political life and become mature and powerful, should desire for themselves independence and free action, and be impatient of a system founded on their early and past necessities!

Coleridge, the acute English scholar and philosopher, once said that he looked upon the American States as " splendid masses to be used by and by in the composition of two or three great governments." For more than a generation past it was considered by a party in America, as well as by intelligent men in other parts of the world, that the American Union, as a confederation of States, had performed its mission, and that the country was called to the fulfilment of another political destiny.

And here it is especially to be remarked that those statesmen of the South, who for more than thirty years before the war of 1861 despaired of the continuation of the Union, were yet prompt to acknowledge its benefits in the past. There could be no dispute about the success of its early mission; and no intelligent man in America dared to refer to the Union without acknowledging the country's indebtedness to it in the past. It had peopled and fertilized a continent; it had enriched the world's commerce with a new trade; it had developed population, and it was steadily training to manhood the States which composed it, and fitting them for the responsibility of a new political life. The party that insisted at a certain period that the interests of the Southern States demanded a separate and independent government, simply held the doctrine that the country had outlived the necessities of the Union, and had become involved in the abuses of a system, admirable enough in its early conception, but diverted from its original objects and now existing only as the parent of intolerable rivalries, and the source of constant intestine commotions.

With reference to these abuses, it must be remarked here that although the Federal principle was the governing one of the American Union, yet such Union was not purely a confederation of States; it was mixed with parts of another system of government; and that the subordination of the Federal principle to these produced many additional causes of disruption, which plainly hurried the catastrophe of separation and war.

But before coming to the subject of these abuses, it will be necessary to determine the true nature and value of the Union. We must go back to an early period of American history; we must explore the sources of the great political parties in the country; and we must enumerate among the causes of disunion not only the inherent weakness of the Federal principle, but those many controversies which aided and expedited the result, and in which the true idea of the Union was violated, the government distorted to the ends of party, and faction put in the place of a statesmanship that sought long but in vain to check its vile ambition and avert the final result.

When the thirteen colonies in North America resolved to throw off the yoke of Great Britain, committees of correspondence were established in each colony. In May, 1774, after Lord Dunmore dissolved a patriotic Virginia House of Burgesses, eighty-nine of its members met at the Raleigh Tavern, in Williamsburg, and, among other acts, recommended that all the colonies should send deputies to a General Congress, to watch over the united interests of all, and deliberate upon and ascertain the measures best adapted to promote them.

On the 4th of July, 1776, the Congress published a Declaration of Independence. It declared that the colonies were " free and independent States," thus asserting their separate State sovereignty, and expressly negativing the idea of consolidation, held by New Hampshire, who on the 15th of June, 1776, voted that the Thirteen United Colonies ought to be declared " a free and independent State."

At this time the only common agent of the States was a Congress which really had no legislative power. Its action was generally wise, and therefore cheerfully acquiesced in and made efficient by the principals. But as the war continued, its pressure became heavier ; men, money, and supplies were needed ; and often the resolutions of Congress were either wholly neglected or positively repudiated by the States. It became apparent that the common agent must be clothed with actual power, and this could only be done by an express agreement between the States, whereby each should bind itself to observe certain rules, and obey certain regulations adopted to secure the common safety.

It was thus that the first Confederation of the American States—the articles of which were adopted by the several States in 1777—originated in the necessities of the war waged by them against Great Britain for their independence. A common danger impelled them to a close alliance, and to the formation of a confederation, by the terms of which the colonies, styling themselves States, entered " *severally* into a firm league of friendship with each other for their common defence, the security of their liberties, and their mutual and general welfare, binding themselves to assist each other against all force offered to or attacks made upon them or any of them, on account of religion, sovereignty, trade or any other pretence whatever."

In order to guard against any misconstruction of their compact, the several States made explicit declaration, in a distinct article, that " *each* State *retains its* sovereignty, freedom and independence, and every power, jurisdiction, and right which is not by this confederation *expressly delegated* to the United States in Congress assembled."

The objects and character of this confederation or union were thus distinctly defined. Under its terms the war of the Revolution was successfully waged, and resulted in the treaty of peace with Great Britain in 1783, by the terms of which the several States were, *each by name*, recognized to be independent.

As the Confederation originated in the necessities of the war against Great Britain, it was these necessities which determined its character and measured its powers. It was something more than a military alliance; for it was intended to unite the resources of the States, to make a common financial fund, and to " secure the public credit at home and abroad." Partial and imperfect as was the union it established, it accomplished a great historical work, and dated an important era; it supplied what scarcely anything else could have supplied—a political bond between colonies suddenly erected into sovereign States; it was the stepping stone to a firmer association of the States, and a more perfect union. In this sense are to be found its true offices and value. Lines of exasperated division had been drawn between the colonies; the sharp points of religious antagonism had kept them at a distance; the natural difficulties of intercourse and the legislative obstructions of trade had separated them; differences of government, contrast of manners, diversity of habits had contributed to the estrangement; and in these circumstances a bond of union, however slightly it held them, was important as the initial of their political association, and was educating them for the new and enlarged destiny dated with their independence.

We have implied that the Confederation was a bond of very partial and imperfect effect. It practically existed not more than two years; although its nominal term in history is eight years. It was debated for nearly five years. It was not consummated until 1781. It was full of glaring defects; it had no power to enforce the common will of the States; it had no jurisdiction of individuals; it had but a mixed and confused power over foreign relations, and the treaties it might make were dependent on commercial regulations of the different States. Having outlived the prime necessity that originated it during the war, its cohesive powers gradually gave way; it yielded to the impressions of new events; and it is remarkable that the association formed under it and entitled a " Perpetual Union " was practically terminated by the uninterrupted free will of the States which composed it.

A convention of delegates assembled from the different States at Philadelphia in May, 1787. It had been called by Congress " for the sole and express purpose of *revising* the Articles of Confederation, and reporting to Congress and the several legislatures such alterations and provisions therein, as shall, when agreed to in Congress, and confirmed by the States, render the Federal Constitution adequate to the exigencies and the preservation of the Union." This was the Convention that erected the two famous political idols in America : the Constitution of 1789 and the Union formed under it, and entitled itself to the extravagant adulation of three generations as the wisest and best of men.

This adulation is simply absurd. The language in the call of the Convention was singularly confused. The men who composed it were common flesh and blood, very ignorant, very much embarrassed, many of them unlettered, and many educated just to that point where men are silly, visionary, dogmatic and impracticable.

Hildreth, the American historian, has made a very just remark, which describes the cause of the unpopularity of his own compositions. He says : " In dealing with our revolutionary annals, a great difficulty had to be encountered in the mythic, heroic character above, beyond, often wholly apart from the truth of history, with which, in the popular idea, the fathers and founders of our American Republic have been invested. American literature having been mainly of the rhetorical cast, and the Revolution and the old times of the forefathers forming standing subjects for periodical. eulogies, in which every new orator strives to outvie his predecessors, the true history of those times, in spite of ample records, illustrated by the labors of many diligent and conscientious inquirers, has yet been almost obliterated by declamations which confound all discrimination and just appreciation in one confused glare of patriotic eulogium." *

---

* We find in 1866, even after the experience of the war, President Johnson declaring that the authours of the Constitution were *divinely inspired ;* that " they needed and obtained a wisdom superiour to experience." This is silly extravagance, if not worse. We shall see that there was one element of originality and of great virtue in the Constitution ; but *apart from this,* the sober student of history, looking over three generations of fierce political conflict in America, must be struck by the enormous defects and omissions of an instrument that has shared so much the undue admiration of mankind.

In another work the authour has enumerated in the paragraphs quoted below the defective texts of the Constitution :

" It is impossible to resist the thought, that the framers of the Constitution were so much occupied with the controversy of jealousy between the large and the small States that they overlooked many great and obvious questions of government, which have since been fearfully developed in the political history of America. Beyond the results and compromises of that jealousy, the debates and the work of the Convention show one of the most wonderful blanks that has, perhaps, ever occurred in the political inventions of civilized mankind. They left behind them a list of imperfections in political prescience, a want of provision for the exigencies of their country, such as has seldom been known in the history of mankind."

" A system of negro servitude existed in some of the States. It was an object of no solicitude in the Convention. The only references in the Constitution to it are to be found in a provision in relation to the rendition of fugitives ' held to service or labour,' and in a mixed and empirical rule of popular representation. However these provisions may imply the true status of slavery, how much is it to be regretted that the Convention did not make (what might have been made so easily) an explicit declaration on the subject, that would have put it beyond the possibility of dispute, and removed it from even the plausibility of party controversy ! "

The Constitution formed by this Convention, although singularly deficient—and so far from being esteemed by American demagogueism as "almost of Divine authority," actually one of the loosest political instruments in the world—contained one admirable and novel principle, which grew out of the combination of circumstances in the debate. One party in the Convention plausibly contended that its power was limited to a mere revision and amendment of the existing Articles of Confederation, and that it was authorized to add nothing to the Federal principle. Another party favoured the annihilation of the State governments. A third party stood between these extremes, and recommended a "national" government in the sense of a supreme power with respect to certain objects common between the States and committed to it. But when on this third plan the question of representation arose, it was found that the large States insisted upon a preponderating influence in both houses of the National Legislature, while the small States insisted on an equality of representation in each house; and out of this conflict came the mixed representation

"For many years the very obvious question of the power of the General Government to make 'internal improvements' has agitated the councils of America : and yet there is no text in the Constitution to regulate a matter which should have stared its authours in the face, but what may be derived, by the most forced and distant construction, from the powers of Congress 'to regulate commerce,' and to ' declare war,' and ' raise and support armies.' "

"For a longer period, and with a fierceness once almost fatal to the Union, has figured in the politics of America ' the tariff question,' a contest between a party for revenue and a party for protective prohibitions. Both parties have fought over that vague platitude of the Constitution, the power of Congress ' to regulate commerce ;' and in the want of a more distinct language on a subject of such vast concern, there has been engendered a controversy which has progressed from the threshold of the history of the Union up to the period of its dissolution."

"With the territorial possessions of America, even at the date of the Convention, and with all that the future promised in the expansion of a system that yet scarcely occupied more than the water-slopes of a continent, it might be supposed that the men who formed the Constitution would have prepared a full and explicit article for the government of the territories. That vast and intricate subject—the power of the General Government over the territories, the true nature of these establishments, the status and political privileges of their inhabitants—is absolutely dismissed with this bald provision in the Constitution of the United States :

" ' New States may be admitted by Congress into this Union.'—ART. iv., SEC. 3."

In addition to these flagrant omissions of the Constitution may be observed a fault, which it was sought to correct in the Constitution of the Confederate States, and which has latterly grown much upon public attention. It is that defective construction of the Cabinet, which excludes all the ministers of the government from any participation in the legislative councils. The practical consequences of this defective organization of the government is, that the relations between the Executive and Congress have gradually descended to a *back-door* communication, in which the Executive has lost its dignity, and American politics been severely scandalized. The relations of the British ministry to Parliament are such that a vote of censure, any night, may change the administration of public affairs. There is no such faculty of adaptation in the American system. If there is a variance between the Executive and Congress, the former communicates with its partisans in that body through the back-door and lobby, and the practical consequences are bribery, corruption, and all sorts of devious and unworthy appliances to the legislation of the country.

of *the people* and *the States*, each in a different house of Congress; and on this basis of agreement was reared the Constitution of the United States of America.

The great novelty of this Constitution—the association of the principle of State sovereignty with a common government of delegated powers acting on *individuals* under specifications of authority, and thus, therefore, not merely a Federal league—is scarcely to be esteemed as an *a priori* discovery, and to be ascribed, as American vanity would have it, to the wisdom of our forefathers. The mixed representation of the people and the States originated, as we have seen, in a jealousy sprung in the Convention, and is better described as the fruit of an accident than the elaborate production of human wisdom. It was a compromise. It simply extricated the Convention from a dead-lock of votes between the large and the small States as to the rule of representation. But it was of immense importance as the initial and necessary measure of the combination of State sovereignty with the simple republic. There is reason to suppose that the framers of the Constitution did not fully comprehend the importance of the great political principle on which they had stumbled, with its long train of consequences, and that, as often happens to simple men, they had fallen upon a discovery, of the value of which they had but a dim apprehension.

The principle involved in the measure of the Convention referred to was more fully and perfectly developed in the Amendments, which were the fruit of the legislative wisdom of the States, not of that of the Convention, and were designed to give a full development and a proper accuracy to what was certainly ill-performed work in it. The following Amendments were embodied in the official declarations of at least six of the States, coupled with their ratification of the Constitution, and made by them the conditions precedent to such ratification.

"The enumeration in the Constitution, of certain rights, shall not be construed to deny or disparage others retained by the people.

"The powers not delegated to the United States by the Constitution, nor prohibited by it to the States, are reserved to the States respectively, or to the people.

The Union, thus constituted, was not a consolidated nationality. It was not a simple republic, with an appendage of provinces. It was not, on the other hand, a mere league of States with no power to reach individuals. It was an association of sovereign States with a common authority qualified to reach *individuals* within the scope of the powers delegated to it by the States, and employed with subjects sufficient to give it for certain purposes the effect of an American and national identity.

At the separation from the British Empire, the people of America preferred the establishment of themselves into thirteen separate sovereignties, instead of incorporating themselves into one. To these they looked up for the security of their lives, liberties, and properties. The Federal government they formed to defend the whole against foreign nations in time of war, and to defend the lesser States against the ambition of the larger. They were afraid of granting power unnecessarily, lest they should defeat the original end of the Union ; lest the powers should prove dangerous to the sovereignties of the particular States which the Union was meant to support, and expose the lesser to being swallowed up by the larger.

The articles of the first Confederation had provided that " the Union shall be perpetual." Notwithstanding this, as we have seen, another convention subsequently assembled which adopted the present Constitution of the United States. Article VII. provided that " the ratifications of nine States shall be sufficient for the establishment of this Constitution, between the States ratifying the same." In effect, this Constitution was ratified at first by only a portion of the States composing the previous Union, each at different dates and in its sovereign capacity as a State, so that the second Union was created by States which " seceded " from the first Union, three of which, in their acts of ratification, expressly reserved the right to secede again. Virginia, in giving her assent to the Constitution, said : " We, the delegates of the people of Virginia, duly elected, etc., etc., do, in the name and in behalf of the people of Virginia, declare and make known that the powers granted under the Constitution, being derived from the people of the United States, may be resumed by them whenever the same shall be perverted to their injury or oppression." The State of New York said that " the powers of Government may be re-assumed by the people whenever it shall become necessary to their happiness." And the State of Rhode Island adopted the same language.

The reader of American history must guard his mind against the errour that the Union was, in any sense, a constitutional revolution, or a proclamation of a new civil polity. The civil institutions of the States were already perfect and satisfactory. The Union was nothing more than a convenience of the States, and had no mission apart from them. It had no value as an additional guaranty of personal liberty, nor yet for its prohibitions of invasion of individual rights. These had been declared with equal clearness and vigour five centuries before in the Great Charter at Runnymede, had been engrafted upon the Colonial Governments, and were the recognized muniments of American liberty.

The novelty and value of the Federal Constitution was the nice adjustment of the relations of the State and Federal Governments, by which they both became co-ordinate and essential parts of one harmonious system ; the nice arrangement of the powers of the State and Federal Governments, by which was left to the States the exclusive guardianship of their domestic affairs, and of the interests of their citizens, and was granted to the Federal

Government the exclusive control of their international and inter-State relations; the economy of the powers of the States with which the Federal Government was endowed; the paucity of subjects and of powers, withdrawn from the States, and committed to the Federal Government. It was the recognition of the idea of Confederation—the appreciation of the value of local self-government. It was the recognition that the States were the creators and their powers were inherent, and that the Federal Government was the creature and its powers were delegated.

The two great political schools of America—that of Consolidation and that of State Rights—were founded on different estimates of the relations of the General Government to the States. All other controversies in the political history of the country were subordinate and incidental to this great division of parties. We see, at once, how it involved the question of negro-slavery in the South. The agitation of this question was a necessity of the Consolidation doctrine, which was mainly the Northern theory of the government; for duty being the correlative of power, the central government at Washington was responsible for the continuance or existence of slavery in proportion to its power over it. On the other hand, the State Rights party assented to the logical integrity of the proposition that if the government had been consolidated into one, slavery might have been abolished, or made universal throughout the whole; but they claimed that the States had retained their sovereignty, for the reason, among others, that they desired to avoid giving any pretext to the General Government for attempting to control their internal affairs; and they, therefore, contended that the Northern party could with no more reason assail the domestic institutions of the South than they could attack the similar institutions of Cuba and Brazil.

The difference between the State Rights and Consolidation schools may be briefly and sharply stated. The one regarded the Union as a compact *between* the States: the other regarded the Union as a national government set up *above and over* the States. The first adopted its doctrine from the very words of the Constitution; the seventh article for the ratification of the Constitution reading as follows:

" The ratification of the *Conventions of nine States* shall be sufficient for the establishment of this constitution BETWEEN *the States* so ratifying the same."

The great text of the State Rights school is to be found in the famous Kentucky and Virginia Resolutions of 1798. These resolutions are properly to be taken as corollaries drawn from those carefully-worded clauses of the Constitution, which were designed to exclude the idea that the separate and independent sovereignty of each State was merged into one common government and nation. The Virginia resolutions were drawn up by Mr. Madison, and the Kentucky resolutions by Mr. Jefferson. The first Kentucky resolution was as follows :

"1st. *Resolved*, That the several States comprising the United States of America, are not united on the principle of unlimited submission to their general government, but that by compact under the style and title of a Constitution for the United States, and of amendments thereto, they constituted a general government, for special purposes, delegated to that government certain definite powers, reserving each State to itself, the residuary mass of right to their own self-government ; and that whensoever the general government assumes undelegated powers, its acts are unauthoritative, void, and of no force ; that to this compact each State acceded, as a State, and is an integral party ; that this government created by this compact, was not made the exclusive or final judge of the extent of the powers delegated to itself, since that would have made its discretion and not the Constitution the measure of its powers; but that as in all other cases of compact among parties having no common judge, each party has an equal right to judge for itself, as well of infractions as of the mode and measure of redress."

The most formidable conflict between these two schools of politics took place during the memorable tariff controversy of 1831–'2, in which Daniel Webster of Massachusetts and John C. Calhoun of South Carolina, the most remarkable antitypes of Northern and Southern statesmanship, joined in debate, explored the entire field of controversy, searched every feature and principle of the government, and left on record a complete and exhausting commentary on the whole political system of America.

Mr. Calhoun was logician enough to see that the Kentucky and Virginia Resolutions involved the right of Secession. But he was not disposed to insist upon such a remedy. He lived in a time when, outside of his own State, there was a strong sentimental attachment to the Union ; and he would have been a reckless politician, who would then have openly braved popular passion on this subject. Indeed Mr. Calhoun professed, and perhaps not insincerely, an ardent love for the Union. In a speech to his constituents in South Carolina, he declared that he had "never breathed an opposite sentiment," and that he had reason to love the Union, when he reflected that nearly half his life had been passed in its service, and that whatever public reputation he had acquired was indissolubly connected with it.

It was the task of the great South Carolina politician to find some remedy for existing evils short of Disunion. He was unwilling, either to violate his own affections or the popular idolatry for the Union ; and at the same time he was deeply sensible of the oppression it devolved upon the South. The question was, what expedient could be found to accommodate the overruling anxiety to perpetuate the Union, and the necessity of checking the steady advance of Northern aggression and sectional domination in it. Mr. Calhoun did succeed in accommodating these two considerations. He hit upon one of the most beautiful and ingenious theories in American politics to preserve and perfect the Union, and to introduce into it that principle of adaptability to circumstances, which is the first virtue of wise governments. He proposed that in cases of serious dispute between any State and the General Government, the matter should be referred to a convention of all the States for its final and conclusive determination. He thus proposed, instead of destroying the Union, to erect over it an august guardianship, and instead of bringing it to the tribunal of popular passion, to arraign it only before the assembled sovereign States which had created it.

Mr. Calhoun abundantly explained his doctrine. "Should," said he, "the General Government and a State come into conflict, we have a higher remedy : the power which called the General Government into existence, which gave it all of its authority, and can enlarge, contract, or abolish its powers at its pleasure, may be invoked. The States themselves may be appealed to, three-fourths of which, in fact, form a power, whose decrees are the Constitution itself, and whose voice can silence all discontent. The utmost extent then of the power is, that a State acting in its sovereign capacity, as one of the parties to the constitutional compact, may compel the government, created by that compact, to submit a question touching its infraction to the parties who created it." He insisted with plain reason that his doctrine, so far from being anarchical or revolutionary, was "the only solid foundation of our system and of the Union itself." His explanation of the true nature of the Union was a model of perspicuity, and an exposition of the profoundest statesmanship. In opposition to a certain vulgar and superficial opinion, that the State institutions of America were schools of provincialism, he held the doctrine that they were in no sense hostile to the Union, or malignant in their character ; that they interpreted the true glory of America ; and that he was the wisest statesman who would constantly observe "the sacred distribution" of power between the General Government and the States, and bind up the rights of the States with the common welfare.

It is a curious instance of Northern misrepresentation in politics and of their cunning in fastening a false political nomenclature upon the South, that the ingenious doctrine of Mr. Calhoun, which was eminently conservative, and *directly addressed to saving the Union*, should have been entitled "Nullification," and its author branded as a Disunionist. Unfortunately, the world has got most of its opinions of Southern parties and men from the shallow pages of Northern books ; and it will take it long to learn the lessons that the system of negro servitude in the South was not "*Slavery ;*" that John C. Calhoun was not a "*Disunionist ;*" and that the war of 1861, brought on by Northern insurgents against the authority of the Constitution, was not a " *Southern rebellion.*" Names are apparently slight things; but they create the first impression; they solicit the sympathies of the vulgar; and they often create a cloud of prejudice which the greatest exertions of intelligence find it impossible wholly to dispel. But it is not the place here to analyze at length the party terms of America; and the proper definition of the words we have referred to as falsely applied to the South will appear, and will be easily apprehended in the general argument and context of our narrative.

CHAPTER II.

ALTHOUGH the American Union, as involving the Federal principle, contained in itself an element ultimately fatal to its form of government, it is not to be denied that by careful and attentive statesmanship a rupture might have been long postponed. We have already briefly seen that, at a most remarkable period in American history, it was proposed by the great political scholar of his times—John C. Calhoun—to modify the Federal principle of the Union and to introduce an ingenious check upon its tendencies to controversy—a measure that might long have extended the term of the Union, and certainly would have realized a very beautiful idea of political association.

But we must notice here another cause of disunion that supervened upon that of Federal incoherence, and rapidly divided the country. It was that Sectional Animosity, far more imposing than any mere discord of States, inasmuch as it put in opposition, as it were, two distinct nations on a geographical line, that by a single stroke divided the country, and thus summarily effected what smaller differences would have taken long to accomplish.

We have elsewhere briefly referred to the divisions of population between the Northern and Southern States, marked as they were by strong contrasts between the characters of the people of each. Had these divisions existed only in a contracted space of country, they might have resulted in nothing more than the production of parties or the formation of classes. But extending as they did over the space of a continent, these divisions ceased to be political parties or classes of one community, and really existed in the condition of distinct communities or nations. A recent English writer has properly and acutely observed : " In order to master the difficulties of American politics, it will be very important to realize the fact that we have to consider, not the action of rival parties or opposing interests within the limits of one body politic, but practically that of two distinct communities or peoples, speaking indeed a common language, and united by a federal bond, but opposed in principles and interests, alienated in feeling, and jealous rivals in the pursuit of political power."

No one can read aright the history of America, unless in the light of a North and a South : two political aliens existing in a Union imperfectly defined as a confederation of States. If insensible or forgetful of this theory, he is at once involved in an otherwise inexplicable mass of facts, and will in vain attempt an analysis of controversies, apparently the most various and confused.

The Sectional Animosity, which forms the most striking and persistent feature in the history of the American States, may be dated certainly as far back as 1787. In the Convention which formed the Constitution, Mr. Madison discovered beneath the controversy between the large and small States another clashing of interests. He declared that the States were divided into different interests by other circumstances as well as by their difference of size ; the most material of which resulted partly from climate, but principally from the effects of their having or not having slaves. " These two causes," he said, " concurred in forming the great division of interests in the United States ; " and " if any defensive power were necessary it ought to be mutually given to these two sections." In the South Carolina Convention which ratified the Constitution, Gen Pinckney spoke of the difference between the inhabitants of the Northern and Southern States. He explained: "When I say Southern, I mean Maryland and the States southward of her. There, we may truly observe that nature has drawn as strong marks of distinction in the habits and manners of the people, as she has in her climates and productions."

There was thus early recognized in American history a political North and a political South; the division being coincident with the line that separated the slave-holding from the non-slave-holding States. Indeed, the existence of these two parties and the line on which it was founded was recognized in the very frame-work of the Constitution. That provision of this instrument which admitted slaves into the rule of representation (in the proportion of three-fifths), is significant of a conflict between North and South; and as a compact between the slave-holding and non-slave-holding interests, it may be taken as a compromise between sections, or even, in a broader and more philosophical view, as a treaty between two nations of opposite civilizations. For we shall see that the distinction of North and South, apparently founded on slavery and traced by lines of climate, really went deeper to the very elements of the civilization of each; and that the Union, instead of being the bond of diverse States, is rather to be described, at a certain period of its history, as the forced alliance and rough companionship of two very different peoples.

When Gen. Sullivan complained to Washington that there was a party in New England opposed to his nomination as minister of war, because they considered he had " apostatized from the true New England faith, by sometimes voting with the Southern States," he declared thus early the true designs of the North to get sectional control of the government.

The slavery question is not to be taken as an independent controversy in American politics. It was not a moral dispute. It was the mere incident of a sectional animosity, the causes of which lay far beyond the domain of morals. Slavery furnished a convenient line of battle between the disputants; it was the most prominent ground of distinction between the two sections; it was, therefore, naturally seized upon as a subject of controversy, became the dominant theatre of hostilities, and was at last so conspicuous and violent, that occasion was mistaken for cause, and what was merely an incident came to be regarded as the main subject of controversy.

The institution of slavery, as the most prominent cause of distinction between the civilizations or social autonomies of North and South, was naturally bound up in the Sectional Animosity. As that animosity progressed, the slavery question developed. This explains, indeed, what is most curious in the political history of slavery—namely that the early part of that history is scarcely more than an enumeration of dates and measures, which were taken as matters of course, and passed without dispute. The Fugitive Slave Law of 1793 was passed without a division in the Senate, and by a vote of forty-eight to seven in the House. Louisiana and Florida, slave-holding territories, were organized without agitation. Kentucky, Tennessee, Mississippi and Alabama were admitted into the Union without any question as to their domestic institutions. The action of Congress, with respect to the north-west territory, was based upon a *pre-existing* anti-slavery ordinance, and had no significance. There was nothing or but little in the early days of the Union, to betoken the wild and violent controversy on slavery, that was to sweep the country like a storm and strew it with scenes of horrour.

With the jealousy of Southern domination came the slavery agitation; proving clearly enough its subordination to the main question, and that what was asserted as a matter of conscience, and attempted to be raised to the position of an independent controversy, was but part of or an attachment to an animosity that went far below the surface of local institutions. The Hartford Convention, in 1814, which originated in jealousy of the political power of the South, proposed to strike down the slave representation in Congress, and to have the representation conformed to the number of free persons in the Union. A few years later, the country was more distinctly arrayed into two sectional parties, struggling for supremacy with regard to the slavery question. The legislation on the admission of Missouri in 1820, by which the institution of slavery was bounded by a line of latitude, indicated the true nature of the slavery controversy, and simply revealed what had all along existed : a political North and a political South. It was here that we find the initial point of that war of sections which raged in America for forty years, and at last culminated in an appeal to arms. The Missouri legislation was the preliminary trace of disunion. "A geographical line," wrote Mr. Jefferson, "coinciding with a marked principle, moral and political, once conceived and held up to the angry passions of men will not be obliterated ; and every new irritation will make it deeper and deeper."

The North naturally found or imagined in slavery the leading cause of the distinctive civilization of the South, its higher sentimentalism, and its superior refinements of scholarship and manners. It revenged itself on the cause, diverted its envy in an attack upon slavery, and defamed the institution as the relic of barbarism and the sum of all villainies. But, whatever may have been the defamation of the institution of slavery, no man can write its history without recognizing contributions and naming prominent results beyond the domain of controversy. It bestowed on the world's commerce in a half-century a single product whose annual value was two hundred millions of dollars. It founded a system of industry by which labour and capital were identified in interest, and capital therefore protected labour. It exhibited the picture of a land crowned with abundance, where starvation was unknown, where order was preserved by an unpaid police ; and where many fertile regions accessible only to the labour of the African were brought into usefulness, and blessed the world with their productions.

We shall not enter upon the discussion of the moral question of slavery. But we may suggest a doubt here whether that odious term " slavery," which has been so long imposed, by the exaggeration of Northern writers, upon the judgment and sympathies of the world, is properly applied to that system of servitude in the South which was really the mildest in the world ; which did not rest on acts of debasement and disenfranchisement, but elevated the African, and was in the interest of human improvement ; and which, by the law of the land, protected the negro in life and limb, and in many personal rights, and, by the practice of the system, bestowed upon him a sum of individual indulgences, which made him altogether the most striking type in the world of cheerfulness and contentment. But it is not necessary to prolong this consideration.* For, we repeat, the slavery question was not a moral one in the North, unless, perhaps, with a few thousand persons of disordered conscience. It was significant only of a contest for political power, and afforded nothing more than a convenient ground of dispute between two parties, who represented not two moral theories, but hostile sections and opposite civilizations.

In the ante-revolutionary period, the differences between the populations of the Northern and Southern colonies had already been strongly developed. The early colonists did not bear with them from the mother-country to the shores of the New World any greater degree of congeniality than existed among them at home. They had come not only from different stocks of population, but from different feuds in religion and politics. There could be no congeniality between the Puritan exiles who established themselves upon the cold and rugged and cheerless soil of New England, and the Cavaliers who sought the brighter climate of the South, and drank in their baronial halls in Virginia confusion to roundheads and regicides.

In the early history of the Northern colonists we find no slight traces

* It may not be improper to note here a very sententious defence of the moral side of slavery occurring in a speech delivered, in 1856, by Senator Toombs of Georgia, in the Tremont Temple at Boston. It is briefly this : " The white is the superior race, and the black the inferior ; and subordination, with or without law, will be the status of the African in this mixed society ; and, therefore, it is the interest of both, and especially of the black race, and of the whole society, that this status should be fixed, controlled, and protected by law."

The whole ground is covered by these two propositions : that subordination is the necessary condition of the black man ; and that the so-called " slavery " in the South was but the precise adjustment of this subordination by law.

of the modern *Yankee;* although it remained for those subsequent influences which educate nations as well as individuals to complete that character, to add new vices to it, and to give it its full development. But the intolerance of the Puritan, the painful thrift of the Northern colonists, their external forms of piety, their jaundiced legislation, their convenient morals, their lack of the sentimentalism which makes up the half of modern civilization, and their unremitting hunt after selfish aggrandizement are traits of character which are yet visible in their descendants.* On the other hand, the colonists of Virginia and the Carolinas were from the first distinguished for their polite manners, their fine sentiments, their attachment to a sort of feudal life, their landed gentry, their love of field-sports and dangerous adventure, and the prodigal and improvident aristocracy that dispensed its stores in constant rounds of hospitality and gaiety.

Slavery established in the South a peculiar and noble type of civilization. It was not without attendant vices; but the virtues which followed in its train were numerous and peculiar, and asserted the general good effect of the institution on the ideas and manners of the South. If habits of command sometimes degenerated into cruelty and insolence; yet, in the greater number of instances, they inculcated notions of chivalry, polished the manners and produced many noble and generous virtues. If the relief of a large class of whites from the demands of physical labour gave occasion in some instances for idle and dissolute lives, yet at the same time it afforded opportunity for extraordinary culture, elevated the standards of

---

* It appears that in the revolutionary war Gen. Washington acquired a singular insight into the New England character. From his camp at Cambridge, in 1775, he wrote, in a private letter to Richard Henry Lee, an account of the New England part of his army, that reminds one of incidents of 1861–'5. We append an extract from this letter, which remained for many years in the Lee family, and was only brought to light during the recent war:

"* * * I submit it, therefore, to your consideration, whether there is, or is not, a propriety in that resolution of the Congress which leaves the ultimate appointment of all officers below the rank of general to the governments where the regiments originated, now the army is become Continental? To me, it appears improper in two points of view—first, it is giving that power and weight to an individual Colony which ought of right to belong to the whole. Then it damps the spirit and ardour of volunteers from all but the four New England Governments, as none but their people have the least chance of getting into office. Would it not be better, therefore, to have the warrants, which the Commander-in-Chief is authorized to give *pro tempore*, approved or disapproved by the Continental Congress, or a committee of their body, which I should suppose in any long recess must always sit? In this case, every gentleman will stand an equal chance of being promoted, according to his merit: in the other, all offices will be confined to the inhabitants of the four New England Governments, which, in my opinion, is impolitic to a degree. I have made a pretty good slam among such kind of officers as the Massachusetts Government abounds in since I came to this camp, having broken one colonel and two captains for cowardly behaviour in the action on Bunker's Hill, two captains for drawing more provisions and pay than they had men in their company, and one for being absent from his post when the enemy appeared there and burnt a house just by it. Besides these, I have at this time one colonel, one major, one captain, and two subalterns under arrest for trial. In short, I spare none, and yet fear it will not all do, as these people seem to be too inattentive to everything but their *interest*."

scholarship in the South, enlarged and emancipated social intercourse, and established schools of individual refinement. The South had an element in its society—a landed gentry—which the North envied, and for which its substitute was a coarse ostentatious aristocracy that smelt of the trade, and that, however it cleansed itself and aped the elegance of the South, and packed its houses with fine furniture, could never entirely subdue a sneaking sense of its inferiority. There is a singularly bitter hate which is inseparable from a sense of inferiority; and every close observer of Northern society has discovered how there lurked in every form of hostility to the South the conviction that the Northern man, however disguised with ostentation, was coarse and inferiour in comparison with the aristocracy and chivalry of the South.

The civilization of the North was coarse and materialistic. That of the South was scant of shows, but highly refined and sentimental. The South was a vast agricultural country; waste lands, forest and swamps often gave to the eye a dreary picture; there were no thick and intricate nets of internal improvements to astonish and bewilder the traveller, no country picturesque with towns and villages to please his vision. Northern men ridiculed this apparent scantiness of the South, and took it as an evidence of inferiority. But this was the coarse judgment of the surface of things. The agricultural pursuits of the South fixed its features; and however it might decline in the scale of gross prosperity, its people were trained in the highest civilization, were models of manners for the whole country, rivalled the sentimentalism of the oldest countries of Europe, established the only schools of honour in America, and presented a striking contrast in their well-balanced character to the conceit and giddiness of the Northern people.

Foreigners have made a curious and unpleasant observation of a certain exaggeration of the American mind, an absurd conceit that was never done asserting the unapproachable excellence of its country in all things. The Washington affair was the paragon of governments; the demagogical institutions of America were the best under the sun; the slip-shod literature of the country, the smattered education of the people were the *foci* of the world's enlightenment; and, in short, Americans were the lords of creation. De Tocqueville observed: "the Americans are not very remote from believing themselves to belong to a distinct race of mankind."

But it is to be remarked that this boastful disposition of mind, this exaggerated conceit was peculiarly *Yankee*. It belonged to the garish civilization of the North. It was Daniel Webster who wrote, in a diplomatic paper, that America was "the only great republican power." It was Yankee orators who established the Fourth-of-July school of rhetoric, exalted the American eagle, and spoke of the Union as the last, best gift to man. This *afflatus* had but little place among the people of the South. Their civilization was a quiet one; and their characteristic as a people has always been that sober estimate of the value of men and things, which, as in England, appears to be the best evidence of a substantial civilization and a real enlightenment. Sensations, excitements on slight causes, fits of fickle admiration, manias in society and fashion, a regard for magnitude, display and exaggeration, all these indications of a superficial and restless civilization abounded in the North and were peculiar to its people. The sobriety of the South was in striking contrast to these exhibitions, and was interpreted by the vanity of the North as insensibility and ignorance, when it was, in fact, the mark of the superiour civilization.

This contrast between the Northern and Southern minds is vividly illustrated in the different ideas and styles of their worship of that great American idol—the Union. In the North there never was any lack of rhetorical fervour for the Union; its praises were scunded in every note of tumid literature, and it was familiarly entitled "the glorious." But the North worshipped the Union in a very low, commercial sense; it was a source of boundless profit; it was productive of tariffs and bounties; and it had been used for years as the means of sectional aggrandizement.

The South regarded the Union in a very different light. It estimated it at its real value, and although quiet and precise in its appreciation, and not given to transports, there is this remarkable assertion to be made: that the *moral* veneration of the Union was peculiarly a sentiment of the South and entirely foreign to the Northern mind. It could not be otherwise, looking to the different political schools of the two sections. In the North, the doctrine of State Rights was generally rejected for the prevalent notion that America was a single democracy. To the people of the North the Union was therefore a mere geographical name, a political designation which had no peculiar claims upon their affection. In the South the Union was differently regarded. State Rights was the most marked peculiarity of the politics of the Southern people; and it was this doctrine that gave the Union its moral dignity, and was the only really possible source of sentimental attachment to it. The South bowed before neither an idol of gain, nor the shadow of a name. She worshipped that picture of the Union drawn by John C. Calhoun: a peculiar association in which sovereign States were held by high considerations of good faith; by the exchanges of equity and comity; by the noble attractions of social order; by the enthused sympathies of a common destiny of power, honour and renown. But, alas! this picture existed only in the imagination; the idea of Mr. Calhoun was never realized; and the South, torn from its moral and sentimental attachment to the Union, found that it had no other claims upon its affection.

To understand how the Union became a benefit to the North and resulted in the oppression of the South, it is only necessary to compare the two sections in the elements of prosperity, and to explore the sources of those elements as far as they can be traced within the domain of the Union.

CHAPTER III.

MATERIAL DECLINE OF THE SOUTH IN THE UNION.—SHIFTING OF THE NUMBERS AND ENTER-
PRISE OF THE COUNTRY FROM THE SOUTHERN TO THE NORTHERN STATES.—VIRGINIA'S
RANK AMONG THE STATES AT THE TIME OF THE REVOLUTION.—COMMERCIAL DISTRESS
OF THE STATES AFTER THE REVOLUTION.—HOW NEW ENGLAND SUFFERED.—THE SOUTH
THEN RECKONED THE SEAT OF FUTURE EMPIRE.—THE PEOPLE AND STRENGTH OF AMERICA
BEARING SOUTHWARDLY.—EMIGRATION TO THE SOUTH.—KENTUCKY AND THE VALES
OF FRANKLAND.—VIRGINIA'S PROSPERITY.—HER EARLY LAND SYSTEM.—THE CHESA-
PEAKE.—ALEXANDRIA.—GEORGE WASHINGTON'S GREAT COMMERCIAL PROJECT.—TWO
PICTURES OF VIRGINIA: 1789 AND 1829.—AN EXAMPLE OF THE DECLINE OF THE SOUTH
IN MATERIAL PROSPERITY.—THIS DECLINE NOT TO BE ATTRIBUTED TO SLAVERY.—ITS
TRUE CAUSES.—EFFECT OF THE LOUISIANA PURCHASE ON THE TIDES OF EMIGRATION.—
UNEQUAL FEDERAL LEGISLATION AS A CAUSE OF THE SECTIONAL LAPSE OF THE SOUTH
IN THE UNION.—THE KEY TO THE POLITICAL HISTORY OF AMERICA.—A GREAT DEFECT
OF THE AMERICAN CONSTITUTION.—POPULATION AS AN ELEMENT OF PROSPERITY AND
POWER.—HOW THIS WAS THROWN INTO THE NORTHERN SCALE.—TWO SECTIONAL MEAS-
URES.—COMPARISONS OF SOUTHERN REPRESENTATION IN CONGRESS AT THE DATE OF THE
CONSTITUTION AND IN THE YEAR 1860.—SECTIONAL DOMINATION OF THE NORTH.—A
PROTECTIVE TARIFF.—"THE BILL OF ABOMINATIONS."—SENATOR BENTON ON THE
TARIFF OF 1828.—HIS RETROSPECT OF THE PROSPERITY OF THE SOUTH.—HISTORY OF
THE AMERICAN TARIFFS.—TARIFF OF 1833, A DECEITFUL COMPROMISE.—OTHER MEAS-
URES OF NORTHERN AGGRANDIZEMENT.—INGENUITY OF NORTHERN AVARICE.—WHY THE
SOUTH COULD NOT USE HER DEMOCRATIC ALLIANCE IN THE NORTH TO PROTECT HER
INTERESTS.—THIS ALLIANCE ONE ONLY FOR PARTY PURPOSES.—ITS VALUE.—ANALYSIS
OF THE DEMOCRATIC PARTY IN THE NORTH.—THE SOUTH UNDER THE RULE OF A NU-
MERICAL MAJORITY.—ARRAY OF THAT MAJORITY ON A SECTIONAL LINE NECESSARILY
FATAL TO THE UNION.—WHEN AND WHY THE SOUTH SHOULD ATTEMPT DISUNION.

IT is not unusual in countries of large extent for the tides of population and enterprise to change their directions and establish new seats of
power and prosperity. But the change which in little more than a
generation after the American Revolution shifted the numbers and enterprise of the country from the Southern to the Northern States was so
distinctly from one side of a line to the other, that we must account such
the result of certain special and well-defined causes. To discover these

causes, and to explain that most remarkable phenomenon—the sharply-defined transfer of population, enterprise, and commercial empire from the South to the North—we shall pass rapidly in review a number of years in the history of the American States.

About the revolutionary period Virginia held the front rank of the States. Patrick Henry designated her as " the most mighty State in the Union." " Does not Virginia," exclaimed this orator, " surpass every State, in the Union in the number of inhabitants, extent of territory, felicity of position, in affluence and wealth ? " Her arms had been singularly illustrious in the seven years' war ; and no State had contributed to this great contest a larger measure of brilliant and patriotic service. James Monroe, himself a soldier of the Revolution, declared : " Virginia braved all dangers. From Quebec to Boston, from Boston to Savannah she shed the blood of her sons."

The close of the Revolution was followed by a distress of trade that involved all of the American States. Indeed, they found that their independence, commercially, had been very dearly purchased : that the British Government was disposed to revenge itself for the ill-success of its arms by the most severe restrictions on the trade of the States, and to affect all Europe against any commercial negotiations with them. The tobacco of Virginia and Maryland was loaded down with duties and prohibitions ; the rice and indigo of the Carolinas suffered similarly ; but in New England the distress was out of all proportion to what was experienced in the more fortunate regions of the South, where the fertility of the soil was always a ready and considerable compensation for the oppression of taxes and commercial imposts. Before the Revolution, Great Britain had furnished markets for more than three-fourths of the exports of the eight Northern States. These were now almost actually closed to them. Massachusetts complained of the boon of independence, when she could no longer find a market for her fish and oil of fish, which at this time constituted almost wholly the exports of that region, which has since reached to such insolence of prosperity, and now abounds with the seats of opulence. The most important branch of New England industry—the whale fisheries—had almost perished ; and driven out of employment, and distressed by an unkind soil, there were large masses of the descendants of the Puritans ready to move wherever better fortune invited them, and the charity of equal laws would tolerate them.

In these circumstances it is not surprising that, in the early stages of the Federal Republic, the South should have been reckoned the seat of future empire. There was a steady flow of population from the sterile regions of the North to the rich but uncultivated plains of the South. In the Convention that formed the Constitution Mr. Butler, a delegate from New England, had declared, with pain, that " the people and strength of America were evidently bearing southwardly and southwestwardly." As the sectional line was then supposed to run, there were only five States on the southern side of it : eight on the northern. In the House of Representatives the North had thirty-six votes ; the South only twenty-nine. But the most persistent statement made in favour of the Constitution in Virginia and other Southern States, was, that though the North, at the date of this instrument, might have a majority in the representation, the increase of population in the South would, in the course of a few years, change it in their favour. So general and imposing was the belief that the Southern States were destined to hold the larger share of the numbers and wealth of America. And not without reason was such a prospect indulged at this time. The people of New England were then emigrating to Kentucky, and even farther to the South and Southwest. In vain the public men of the North strove to drive back the flow of population upon the unoccupied lands of Maine, then a province of Massachusetts. Land was offered there for a dollar an acre. But the inducement of even such a price was insufficient to draw the emigrant to the inhospitable regions of the Penobscot. There was the prosperous agriculture to tempt him that had made Virginia the foremost of the British colonies. There were the fertile and undulating prairie lands of Kentucky to invite and reward his labours. There were the fruitful vales of Frankland—a name then given to the western district of North Carolina—to delight his vision with the romances of picturesque prosperity. To these regions the Northern emigration flowed with steady progress, if not with the rapidity and spirit of a new adventure.

Virginia did not need the contributions of numbers or of capital moving from the North after the Revolution, to make her the foremost State of the Union. She was already so. In 1788, her population was estimated at more than half a million, and her military force at fifty thousand militiamen. Her early land system, in which the soil was cultivated by tenants, and thus most effectively divided for labour, had put her agricultural interest far above that of the other States, and during the colonial period had drawn to her borders the best class of population in America—that of the yeomanry of England. The Chesapeake was the chosen resort of the trader. Alexandria, then the principal commercial city of Virginia, was thought to hold the keys to the trade of a continent. The election of George Washington to the Presidency of the United States interrupted him in a project, by which he hoped to unite the Bay of Chesapeake, by her two great arms, the James and Potomac rivers, with the Ohio, and eventually to drain the commerce of the Lakes into the same great basin, and, extending yet further the vision of this enterprise, to make Alexandria the eastern depot of the fur trade. Everywhere was blazoned the prosperity of Virginia ; and, indeed, in coming into the

Union, many of her public men had said that she sacrificed an empire in itself for a common concern.

Of the decline of the South, after the early periods of the government, in population and industry, Virginia affords the most striking example. To show the general fact and to illustrate especially the decline of that State, we may take two pictures of Virginia, placing an interval between them of scarcely more than one generation of men.

At the time of the adoption of the Constitution, Virginia was in the heyday of prosperity. Her system of tenant farms spread before the eye a picture of thrifty and affluent agriculture. In 1800 she had a great West Indian and a flourishing European trade. She imported for herself and for a good part of North Carolina and, perhaps, of Tennessee. She presented a picture in which every element of prosperity combined with lively effect.

In 1829 it was estimated in her State Convention that her lands were worth only half what they were in 1817. Her slave property had proportionally declined, and negro men could be bought for one hundred and fifty dollars each. Her landed system had become extinct. Regions adapted to the growth of the grasses were converted into pasture lands. The busy farms disappeared; they were consolidated to make cattle-ranges and sheep-walks. Where once the eye was entertained with the lively and cheerful scenes of an abundant prosperity it looked over wasted fields, stunted forests of secondary growth of pine and cedar, and mansions standing partly in ruins or gloomily closed in tenantless silence.

The contrast between such prosperity and such decay, witnessed in every part of the South, though not perhaps to the extent displayed in Virginia, and taking place within a short and well-defined period of time, demands explanations and strongly invites the curiosity of the historical inquirer. And yet the explanation is easy when we regard obvious facts, instead of betaking ourselves to remote and refined speculations after the usual fashion of the curious, with respect to striking and remarkable phenomena.

It has been a persistent theory with Northern writers that the singular decline of the South in population and industry, while their own section was constantly ascending the scale of prosperity, is to be ascribed to the peculiar institution of negro slavery. But this is the most manifest nonsense that was ever spread on the pages of history. Negro slavery had no point of coincidence with the decline referred to; it had existed in the South from the beginning; it had been compatible with her early prosperity extending over the period of the Constitution; it had existed in Virginia when Virginia was most flourishing. But the fallacy of the anti-slavery argument is not only apparent in the light of the early history of America: examples in other parts of the world emphasize it, and add to the illustration. Cuba and Brazil are standing examples of the contributions of negro slavery to agricultural wealth and material prosperity; while on the other hand Jamaica affords the example of decline in these respects from the very abolition of this institution of labour.

The true causes of that sectional lapse, in which the South became by far the inferiour part of the American Union in every respect of material prosperity, will naturally be looked for in the peculiar history of that Union. We shall make this discovery of adequate causes in not more than two prominent considerations, having reference to the geographical and political history of the American States.

1. The Louisiana Purchase, although opposed by the North, on the ground that it was an acquisition to the territorial and political power of the South, was mainly instrumental in turning the scale of population as between the two sections. It opened the Mississippi River; turned the tide of emigration to its upper branches; opened a new empire—the Northwest, soon to become known as " the Great West; " and drew to these distant fields much of the numbers and wealth that had before tended to the South and Southwest for the rewards of enterprise.

2. But by far the more important cause of that decline we have marked in the South was the unequal legislation of Congress and the constant discrimination of the benefits of the Union as between the two sections of the country.

And here in this consideration it is not too much to say that we find the key to the whole political history of America. The great defect of the American Constitution was that it rested too much power upon the fluctuating basis of *population*. In the Convention that formed this instrument there were Southern members who made light of the Northern majority in representation. They thought the next census would set all right. But the Northern party understood the advantage of getting the control of the government in the outset; they strained every nerve to gain it; and they have never since relinquished it.

Population, where the soil is not too densely peopled, and yields a good average of production, is the obvious source of national wealth, which, in turn, increases population. This great productive power was thrown into the Northern scale. By the two measures, of the exclusion of slavery from the Territories and the interdiction of the slave trade, Congress turned the tides of population in favour of the North, and confirmed in the Northern majority the means of a sectional domination.

What effect this turn in the population had upon the political power of the South in the Union is at once seen in the startling changes of her representation in the lower house of Congress. The population of the South had, of course, largely increased, since the date of the Revolution; but it had not been able to keep up with the changes in the ratio of representation. This had been at first 33,000; in the census of 1860, it was raised to 127,381. In the first House of Representatives, Virginia had ten members to six from New York; the proportion under the last census was, Virginia eleven to New York thirty. South Carolina, which originally had one-thirteenth of the popular representation in Congress, would only return, under the census of 1860, four members in a house of two hundred and thirty-three. The representative power in the North had become enormously in excess, and whenever it chose to act unanimously, was capable of any amount of oppression upon the rival section.

Under this sectional domination grew up a system of protections and bounties to the North without parallel in the history of class legislation and of unequal laws in a common country. Virginia had accepted the Constitution in the hope that the General Government, having " power to regulate commerce," would lift the restrictions from her trade. This consideration was held out as a bribe for votes in the Convention. She was bitterly disappointed. In the Virginia Convention of 1822, Mr. Watkins Leigh declared: " Every commercial operation of the Federal Government, since I attained manhood, has been detrimental to the Southern Atlantic slaveholding, planting States."

The South had no protection for her agriculture. At the time of the adoption of the Constitution, the manufacturing interest was a very unimportant one in the country. But manufactures soon became a prominent and special branch of industry in the North; and a course of sectional legislation was commenced to exact from the South a large portion of the proceeds of her industry, and bestow it upon the North in the shape of bounties to manufacturers and appropriations in a thousand forms. " Protection " was the cry which came up from every part of the North. Massachusetts, although unwilling to be taxed on the importation of molasses, wanted protection for the rum she made from it, and contended that it should be fenced in by high duties from a competition with the rum of Jamaica. Pennsylvania sought protection for her manufactures of steel and her paper mills. Connecticut had manufactures of woollens and manufactures of cordage, which she declared would perish without protection. New York demanded that every article should be protected that her people were able to produce. And to such clamours and demands the South had for a long time to submit, so helpless indeed that she was scarcely treated as a party to common measures of legislation. The foundation of the *protective* tariff of 1828—" the bill of abominations," as it was styled by Mr. Calhoun—was laid in a Convention of Northern men at Harrisburg, Pennsylvania; and from this Convention were excluded all sections of the country intended to be made tributary under the act of Congress.

Of the tariff of 1828 Senator Benton remarked: " The South believed itself impoverished to enrich the North by this system; and certainly an unexpected result had been seen in these two sections. In the colonial state the Southern were the richer part of the colonies, and they expected to do well in a state of independence. But in the first half century after independence this expectation was reversed. The wealth of the North was enormously aggrandized; that of the South had declined. Northern towns had become great cities, Southern cities had decayed or become stationary; and Charleston, the principal port of the South, was less considerable than before the Revolution. The North became a money-lender to the South, and Southern citizens made pilgrimages to Northern cities to raise money upon their patrimonial estates. The Southern States attributed this result to the action of the Federal Government—its double action of levying revenue upon the industry of one section of the Union and expending it in another—and especially to its protective tariffs."

Again, contrasting the condition of the South then with what it had been at the Revolutionary period, the same Senator remarked: "It is a tradition of the colonies that the South had been the seat of wealth and happiness, of power and opulence; that a rich population covered the land, dispensing a baronial hospitality, and diffusing the felicity which themselves enjoyed; that all was life, and joy, and affluence then. And this tradition was not without similitude to the reality, as this writer can testify; for he was old enough to have seen (after the Revolution) the still surviving state of Southern colonial manners, when no traveller was allowed to go to a tavern, but was handed over from family to family through entire States; when holidays were days of festivity and expectation long prepared for, and celebrated by master and slave with music and feasting, and great concourse of friends and relations; when gold was kept in chests, after the downfall of Continental paper, and weighed in scales, and lent to neighbours for short terms without note, interest, witness, or security; and when petty litigation was at so low an ebb that it required a fine of forty pounds of tobacco to make a man serve as constable. The reverse of all this was now seen and felt—not to the whole extent which fancy or policy painted, but to extent enough to constitute a reverse, and to make a contrast, and to excite the regrets which the memory of past joys never fails to awaken."

The early history of the tariff makes a plain exhibition of the stark outrage perpetrated by it upon the Southern States. The measure of 1816 had originated in the necessities of a public revenue—for the war commenced against England four years before had imposed a debt upon the United States of one hundred and thirty millions of dollars. It was proposed to introduce into this tariff the *incidental* feature of "protection;" and it was argued that certain home manufactures had sprung up during the exigencies of the war, which were useful and deserving, and that they were likely to lapse under the sudden return of peace and to sink under foreign competition. A demand so moderate and ingenious the South was not disposed to resist. Indeed, it was recommended by John C. Calhoun himself, who voted for the bill of 1816. But the danger was in the precedent. The principle of protection once admitted maintained its hold and enlarged its demands; it was successively carried farther in the tariffs of 1820, '24, and '28. And in 1831, when it was shown by figures in Congress that the financial exigencies that had first called the tariff into existence had completely passed away, and that the government was, in fact, collecting about twice as much revenue as its usual expenditures required, the North still held to its demands for protection, and strenuously resisted any repeal or reduction of the existing tariff.

The demand of the South at this time, so ably enforced by Calhoun, for the repeal of the tariff, was recommended by the most obvious justice and the plainest prudence. It was shown that the public debt had been so far diminished as to render it certain that, at the existing rate of revenue, in three years the last dollar would be paid, and after three years there would be an annual surplus in the treasury of twelve or thirteen millions. But the North was insensible to these arguments, and brazen in its demands. The result of this celebrated controversy, which shook the Union to its foundations, was a compromise or a modification of the tariff, in which however enough was saved of the protective principle to satisfy for a time the rapacity of the North, and that through the demagogical exertions of Henry Clay of Kentucky, who courted Northern popularity, and enjoyed in Northern cities indecent feasts and triumphs for his infidelity to his section.

But the tariff of 1833 was a deceitful compromise, and its terms were never intended by the North to be a final settlement of the question. In 1842 the settlement was repudiated, and the duties on manufactures again advanced. From that time until the period of Disunion the fiscal system of the United States was persistently protective; the South continued to decline; she had no large manufactures, no great cities, no shipping interests; and although the agricultural productions of the South were the basis of the foreign commerce of the United States, yet Southern cities did not carry it on.

Nor was the tariff the only measure of Northern aggrandizement in the Union. Besides manufactures, the North had another great interest in navigation. A system of high differential duties gave protection to it; and this, of course, bore with peculiar hardship on the Southern States, whose commodities were thus burdened by a new weight put upon them by the hand of the General Government. In tariffs, in pensions, in fishing bounties, in tonnage duties, in every measure that the ingenuity of avarice could devise, the North exacted from the South a tribute, which it could only pay at the expense and in the character of an inferiour in the Union.

But in opposition to this view of the helplessness of the South and her inability to resist the exactions of the North, it may be said that the South had an important political alliance in the North, that she was aided there by the Democratic party, and that she thus held the reins of government during the greater portion of the time the tariffs alleged to be so injurious to her interests existed. And here we touch a remarkable fact in American politics. It is true that a large portion of the Democratic party resided in the North, and that many of the active politicians there pretended to give in their adhesion to the States Rights school of politics. But this Democratic alliance with the South was one only for party purposes. It was extravagant of professions, but it carefully avoided trials of its fidelity; it was selfish, cunning, and educated in perfidy. It was a deceitful combination for party purposes, and never withstood the test of a practical question. The Northern Democrat was always ready to contend against the Whig, but never against his own pocket, and the peculiar interests of his section. The moment economical questions arose in Congress, the Northern Democrat was on the side of Northern interests, and the Southern ranks, very imposing on party questions, broke into a scene of mutiny and desertion. It was indeed the weak confidence which the South reposed in the Democratic party of the North that more than once betrayed it on the very brink of the greatest issues in the country, and did more perhaps to put it at disadvantage in the Union than the party of open opposition.

It was through such a train of legislation as we have briefly described that the South rapidly declined in the Union. By the force of a numerical majority—a thing opposed to the American system, properly understood—a Union, intended to be one of mutual benefits, was made a conduit of wealth and power to the North, while it drained the South of nearly every element of material prosperity.

It is true that the numerical majority of the North the South held long in check by superior and consummate political skill. Party complications were thrown around the Sectional Animosity. But it was easy to see that some time or other that animosity would break the web of party; and that whenever on sectional questions the North chose to act in a mass, its power would be irresistible, and that no resource would be left for the South than to remain helpless and at mercy in the Union or to essay a new political destiny. We shall see that in the year 1860 the North did choose to *act in a mass*, and that the South was thus and then irresistibly impelled to the experiment of Disunion.

CHAPTER IV.

THE SECTIONAL EQUILIBRIUM.—HOW DISTURBED IN 1820.—CONTEST ON THE ADMISSION OF TEXAS.—COMPROMISE MEASURES OF 1850.—DECLARATION OF A "FINALITY."—PRESIDENT PIERCE'S ADMINISTRATION.—THE KANSAS-NEBRASKA BILL.—REPEAL OF "THE MISSOURI COMPROMISE."—ORIGIN OF THE REPUBLICAN PARTY IN THE NORTH.—COMPOSITION AND CHARACTER OF THIS PARTY.—AMAZING PROGRESS OF THE ANTI-SLAVERY SENTIMENT IN THE NORTH.—NEW INTERPRETATION OF THE KANSAS-NEBRASKA BILL BY SENATOR DOUGLAS.—INTENDED TO COURT THE ANTI-SLAVERY SENTIMENT.—DOCTRINE OF "NON-INTERVENTION" IN THE TERRITORIES.—THE "DRED SCOTT DECISION."—THE KANSAS CONTROVERSY.—THE LECOMPTON CONVENTION.—THE TOPEKA CONSTITUTION.—PRESIDENT BUCHANAN'S POSITION AND ARGUMENTS.—OPPOSITION OF SENATOR DOUGLAS.—HIS INSINCERITY.—THE NORTHERN DEMOCRATIC PARTY DEMORALIZED ON THE SLAVERY QUESTION.—DOUGLAS' DOCTRINE OF "POPULAR SOVEREIGNTY."—"A SHORT CUT TO ALL THE ENDS OF BLACK REPUBLICANISM."—DOUGLAS AS A DEMAGOGUE.—THE TRUE ISSUES IN THE KANSAS CONTROVERSY.—IMPORTANT PASSAGES IN THE CONGRESSIONAL DEBATE.—SETTLEMENT OF THE KANSAS QUESTION.—DOUGLAS' FOUNDATION OF A NEW PARTY.—HIS DEMAGOGICAL APPEALS.—THE TRUE SITUATION.—LOSS OF THE SECTIONAL EQUILIBRIUM.—SERIOUS TEMPER OF THE SOUTH.—THE JOHN BROWN RAID.—IDENTITY OF JOHN BROWN'S "PROVISIONAL CONSTITUTION AND ORDINANCES" WITH THE SUBSEQUENT POLICY OF THE REPUBLICAN PARTY.—CURIOUS FORESHADOW OF SOUTHERN SUBJUGATION.—THE DESCENT ON HARPER'S FERRY.—CAPTURE AND EXECUTION OF BROWN.—HIS DECLARATION.—NORTHERN SYMPATHY WITH HIM.—ALARMING TENDENCY OF THE REPUBLICAN PARTY TO THE ULTRA ABOLITION SCHOOL.—"THE HELPER BOOK."—SENTIMENTS OF SIXTY-EIGHT NORTHERN CONGRESSMEN.—THE CONCEIT AND INSOLENCE OF THE NORTH.—AFFECTATION OF REPUBLICANS THAT THE UNION WAS A CONCESSION TO THE SOUTH.—HYPOCRISY OF THIS PARTY.—INDICATIONS OF THE COMING CATASTROPHE OF DISUNION.—THE PRESIDENTIAL CANVASS OF 1860.—DECLARATIONS OF THE DEMOCRATIC PARTY.—THE CHARLESTON CONVENTION.—SECESSION OF THE SOUTHERN DELEGATES.—THE DIFFERENT PRESIDENTIAL TICKETS.—ELECTION OF ABRAHAM LINCOLN.—ANALYSIS OF THE VOTE.—HOW HIS ELECTION WAS A "SECTIONAL" TRIUMPH.—OMINOUS IMPORTANCE OF IT IN THAT VIEW.—ARGUMENTS FOR SUSTAINING LINCOLN'S ELECTION.—SEWARD'S ARGUMENT IN THE SENATE.—LINCOLN'S ELECTION A GEOGRAPHICAL ONE.—HOW THERE WAS NO LONGER PROTECTION FOR THE SOUTH IN THE UNION.—THE ANTI-SLAVERY POWER COMPACT AND INVINCIBLE.—ANOTHER APOLOGY FOR LINCOLN'S ELECTION.—FALLACY OF REGARDING IT AS A TRANSFER OF THE ADMINISTRATION IN EQUAL CIRCUMSTANCES FROM THE SOUTH TO THE NORTH.—HOW THE SOUTH

THE wisest statesmen of America were convinced that the true and
intelligent means of continuing the Union was to preserve the sectional
equilibrium, and to keep a balance of power between North and South.
That equilibrium had been violently disturbed, in 1820, at the time of the
Missouri Compromise. The relative representations of the North and
South in the United States Senate were then so evenly balanced that it
came to be decisive of a continuance of political power in the South
whether Missouri should be an addition to her ranks or to those of her
adversary. The contest ended, immediately, in favour of the South; but
not without involving a measure of proscription against slavery.

Another struggle for political power between the two sections occurred
on the admission of Texas. The South gained another State. But the
acquisition of Texas brought on the war with Mexico; and an enormous
addition to Northern territory became rapidly peopled with a population
allured from every quarter of the globe.

On the admission of California into the Union, the South was persuaded to let her come in with an anti-slavery Constitution for the
wretched compensation of a reënactment of the fugitive slave law, and
some other paltry measures. The cry was raised that the Union was in
danger. The appeals urged under this cry had the usual effect of recon-
ciling the South to the sacrifice required of her, and embarrassed anything
like resistance on the part of her representatives in Congress to the compromise measures of 1850. South Carolina threatened secession; but
the other Southern States were not prepared to respond to the bold and
adventurous initiative of Southern independence. But it should be stated
that the other States of the South, in agreeing to what was called, in severe
irony, the Compromise of 1850, declared that it was the last concession
they would make to the North; that they took it as a "finality," and
that the slavery question was thereafter to be excluded from the pale of
Federal discussion.

In 1852 Franklin Pierce was elected President of the United States.
He was a favourite of the State Rights Democracy of the South; and it
was hoped that under his administration the compromise measures of 1850
would indeed be realized as a "finality," and the country be put upon
a career of constitutional and peaceful rule. But a new and violent agitation was to spring up in the first session of the first Congress under his
administration.

The Territory of Nebraska had applied for admission into the Union.
Mr. Stephen A. Douglas, Senator from Illinois, reported from the Com-

mittee on Territories a bill which made two Territories—Nebraska and Kansas—instead of one, and which declared that the Missouri Compromise Act was superseded by the compromise measures of 1850, and had thus become inoperative. It held that the Missouri Compromise act, "being inconsistent with the principles of *non-intervention by Congress with slavery* in the States and Territories as recognized by the legislation of 1850, commonly called the Compromise Measures, is hereby declared inoperative and void; it being the true intent and meaning of this act not to legislate slavery into any Territory or State, nor to exclude it therefrom, but to leave *the people thereof* perfectly free to form and regulate their domestic institutions, subject only to the Constitution of the United States." The bill passed both houses of Congress in 1854.

The Kansas-Nebraska bill, involving as it did the repeal of the Missouri Compromise, was taken by the South as a sort of triumph. The latter measure, being viewed as an act of proscription against the South, was justly offensive to her; although indeed the repeal was scarcely more than a matter of principle or sentiment, as the sagacious statesmen of the South were well aware that the States in the Northwest were likely, from the force of circumstances, to be settled by Northern people, and to be thus dedicated to their institutions.* But it was then supposed that the phraseology of the Kansas-Nebraska bill was not liable to misconstruction; and that when it was declared that the people of the Territories were to determine the question of slavery, it meant, of course, that they were to do so in the act of forming a State Constitution and deciding upon other institutions of the State as well as that of slavery.

In the North, the repeal of the Missouri Compromise was the occasion of a furious excitement. Mr. Douglas was hung in effigy in some of their towns, execrated by Northern mobs, and even threatened with violence to his person. The anti-slavery sentiment of the North was rapidly developed in the excitement; a new party was organized with reference to the question of slavery in the Territories; and thus originated the famous Republican party—popularly called the Black Republican party—which was indeed identical with the Abolition party in its sentiment of hostility to slavery, and differed from it only as to the degree of indirection by which its purpose might best be accomplished. This party comprised the great mass of the intellect and wealth of the North. It was also the

---

* As a general rule the South could not compete with the North in the race of emigration to new countries. Nor was it her interest, being a sparsely settled and agricultural country, to do so. A recent English commentator on the American Union (Mr. Spence) well observes: ' It is an unfortunate result of the complex politics of the Union that the political instinct of the South is driven to oppose its material interest. It must expand while the North expands, or succumb. It cannot seek expansion from choice or interest, but is driven to it by the impulse of political self-preservation."

Protectionist party. Its leaning was in favour of strong government, and whatever there might be of aristocracy in the North belonged to it.

The new party sprung at once into an amazing power. In the Presidential canvass of 1852, which had resulted in the election of Mr. Pierce, John P. Hale, who ran upon what was called the "straight-out" Abolition ticket, did not receive the vote of a single State, and but 175,296 of the popular vote of the Union. But upon the repeal of the Missouri Compromise, Abolitionism, in the guise of "Republicanism," swept almost everything before it in the North and Northwest in the elections of 1854 and 1855; and in the Thirty-first Congress, Nathaniel Banks, an objectionable Abolitionist of the Massachusetts school, was elected to the speakership of the House.

In the mean time, the language of the Kansas-Nebraska bill was the subject of no dispute. No one supposed that from this language there was to originate an *afterthought* on the part of Mr. Douglas, and that, by an ingenious torture of words, this measure was to be converted into one to conciliate the anti-slavery sentiment of the North, and to betray the interests of the South. This afterthought was doubtless the consequence of the rapid growth of the Black Republican party, and the conviction that the Democratic party in the North could only recover its power by some marked concession to the sectional sentiment now rapidly developing on the subject of slavery.

It should be noticed here that the doctrine of "non-intervention," which prohibited Congress from interfering with the question of slavery in the Territories, had been affirmed by a judicial decision in the Supreme Court of the United States. In the famous "Dred Scott case," a negro demanded his freedom on the ground of legal residence beyond the latitude of 36° 30′ N.—the line of the Missouri Compromise. The Supreme Court pronounced that Congress had no power to make that law; that it was therefore null and void; and declared "that the Constitution recognizes the right of property in a slave, and makes no distinction between that description of property and other property owned by a citizen;" and further, that every citizen had the clear right to go into any Territory, and take with him that which the Constitution recognized as his property.

So far the rights of the South in the Territories were thought to be plain; the design of the Black Republican party to exclude slavery therefrom by the Federal authority had been pronounced unconstitutional by the highest judicial authority in the country; and the Kansas-Nebraska bill was thought to be a plain letter, which taught that slavery was the subject of exclusive legislation by States, or by Territories *in the act of assuming the character of States*. But the South only stood on the threshold of a new controversy—another exhibition of the ingenuity of the anti-slavery sentiment to assert itself in new methods and on new issues.

THE KANSAS CONTROVERSY.

What is known as the Kansas Controversy was a marked era in the political history of the Union. It illustrated most powerfully the fact that the slavery question really involved but little of moral sentiment, and indicated a contest for political power between two rival sections.

When Mr. Buchanan came into the Presidential office, in 1857, he at once perceived that the great point of his administration would be to effect the admission of Kansas into the Union, and thus terminate a dispute which was agitating and distracting the country. In September, 1857, the people of the Territory had called a Convention at Lecompton to form a Constitution. The entire Constitution was not submitted to the popular vote; but the Convention took care to submit to the vote of the people, for ratification or rejection, the clause respecting slavery. The official vote resulted: For the Constitution, with slavery, 6,226; for the Constitution, without slavery, 509. Under this Constitution, Mr. Buchanan recommended the admission of Kansas into the Union; and indeed he had reason to hope for it in view of the principles which had governed in his election.

The argument on the other side was that the entire Constitution had not been submitted to the people, and that the principle of "popular sovereignty" had been invaded by the Convention, in not representing all the voters of the Territory, and in not submitting the entire result of their labours to a vote of the people. The Anti-Slavery or Free State party had also their Constitution to advocate, an instrument framed in 1855, at Topeka, which had been submitted to the people, and ratified by a large majority of those who voted. But the facts were that scarcely any but Abolitionists went to the polls; and it was notorious that the Topeka Constitution was the fruit of a bastard population that had been thrown into the Territory by the "Emigrant Aid Societies" of New England.

In his first message to Congress, Mr. Buchanan surveyed the whole ground of the controversy. He explained that when he instructed Gov. Walker of Kansas, in general terms, in favour of submitting the Constitution to the people, he had no other object in view beyond the all-absorbing topic of slavery; he considered that under the organic act —known as the Kansas-Nebraska bill—the Convention was bound to submit the all-important question of slavery to the people; he added, that it was never his opinion, however, that, independently of this act, the Convention would be bound to submit any portion of the Constitution to a popular vote, in order to give it validity; and he argued the fallacy and unreasonableness of such an opinion, by insisting that it was in opposition to the principle which pervaded our institutions, and which was every day carried into practice, to the effect that the people had the right to delegate to representatives, chosen by themselves, sovereign power to frame Constitutions, enact laws, and perform many other important acts, without the necessity of testing the validity of their work by popular approbation.

These views appeared reasonable enough. But Mr. Buchanan found that they were opposed by many members of Congress who had actively supported him in his canvass, and chief and leader among them the distinguished author of the Kansas-Nebraska bill, Mr. Douglas. This man had assembled an opposition under the captivating term of "popular sovereignty;" but these words had a certain narrow and technical party meaning, and covered a remarkable and ingenious design upon the power and interests of the South.

It had long been evident to intelligent observers that the Northern Democratic party, of which Mr. Douglas some time ago had been the acknowledged leader, was becoming demoralized on the slavery question. This party had formerly acted with the South for political power. In the depression of that power and the rapid growth of the anti-slavery party in the North, it had no hesitation in courting and conciliating the ruling element. This disposition was accommodated by the controversy which had taken place between Mr. Douglas and the administration of Mr. Buchanan. The anti-slavery sentiment in the North was conciliated by the partisans of the former in adopting a new principle for the government of the Territories, which was to allow the people to determine the question of slavery *in their Territorial capacity*, without awaiting their organization as a State, and thus to risk the decision of the rights of the South on the verdict of a few settlers on the public domain. This doctrine was violently entitled by Mr. Douglas "popular sovereignty;" but it was more justly described by Gov. Wise of Virginia, as "a short cut to all the ends of Black Republicanism."

It is thus seen that Mr. Douglas had tortured the language of the Kansas-Nebraska bill into the sense that the unorganized population of a Territory might decide the question of slavery as against the State interests of the South; thus indicating to the North that this measure might quite as easily and readily exclude slavery as the intervention of Congress, the right of which the Black Republican party claimed.

Mr. Douglas was an able and eloquent demagogue. He imposed his doctrine upon the minds of not a few of the Southern people by the artfulness of its appeals to the name of a principle, which had none of the substance of justice or equality. He raised in Congress what was called the Anti-Lecompton party, pledged to the exclusion of Kansas under the Lecompton Constitution, and insisting on the right of Territorial legislation on the subject of slavery. For six months the Kansas question occupied Congress, and held the country in anxiety and suspense. It was a contest for political power between North and South. The mere industrial interests or morals of slavery had nothing to do with it.

The sum of the controversy was that the South struggled for the principle of equality in the Territories, without reference to the selfish interests of slavery, and even with the admission of the hopelessness of those interests in Kansas; while the North contended for the narrow selfish, practical consequence of making Kansas a part of her Free-soil possessions. This was evident in the debates in Congress. At one stage of the discussion, Mr. English, of Indiana, asked the question: " Is there a Southern man here who will vote against the admission of Kansas as a Free State, if it be the undoubted will of the people of that Territory that it shall be a Free State—if she brings here a Constitution to that effect ?"—and there was a general response " Not one " from the Southern side of the House. At another period of the debate, Mr. Barksdale of Mississippi put the question to Black Republican members whether they would vote for the admission of Kansas into the Union with a Constitution tolerating slavery " if a hundred thousand people there wished it." Mr. Giddings of Ohio replied that he " would never vote to compel his State to associate with another Slave State." Mr. Stanton, his colleague, added : " I will say that the Republican members of this House, so far a I know, will never vote for the admission of any Slave State north of 36° 30'."

The result of the dispute was the report of a bill for the admission of Kansas, which became a law in June, 1858, and substantially secured nearly all that the North had claimed in the matter. The people were authorized to form a new Constitution. Kansas did not come into the Union until nearly three years afterwards, just as it was going to pieces ; and then it came in with an anti-slavery Constitution, and President Buchanan, consistently, signed the bill of admission.

But the trouble did not end with the solution of the Kansas difficulty. The true character of that event, and the debates which had attended it in Congress, convinced the South that it could hardly expect, under any circumstances, the addition of another Slave State to the Union. The pernicious doctrines of Mr. Douglas were used to erect a party which, while it really pandered to the anti-slavery sentiment of the North, imposed upon the South by cheap expressions of conservatism, and glozed statements of its designs. Mr. Douglas proclaimed his views to be in favour of non-intervention by Congress on the subject of slavery ; he avowed his continued and unalterable opposition to Black-Republicanism ; his principles were professed to be " held subject to the decisions of the Supreme Court "—the distinction between judicial questions and political questions being purposely clouded; and his friends, with an ingenious sophistry that had imposed upon the South for thirty years with success, insisted that the support of Stephen A. Douglas was a support of the party in the North which had stood by the South amid persecution and defamation.

But it was evident to reflecting minds that, either by the policy of the Black Republican party, or the shorter device of the Douglas Democracy for the government of the Territories, the sectional equilibrium of the Union was lost. A disposition was shown to calculate the real value of a Union which, by its mere name and the paraphrases of demagogues, had long governed the affections of the people, but in which, it was now seen, the South must constantly descend in political power; in which she paid a tribute to the North in unequal taxations and in the courses of trade, estimated by a Northern writer at two hundred millions of dollars a year; and in which she was constantly enduring insult, occupied the position of an inferiour, and was designated as the spotted and degraded part of America.

THE JOHN BROWN RAID.

Other events were to repeat and enlarge the shock given to the Union by the Kansas controversy. In October, 1859, occurred the famous John Brown raid into Virginia, in which an old man, who had obtained in Kansas the notoriety of a horse-thief and an assassin, invaded the State of Virginia at Harper's Ferry with a band of outlaws, declared his purpose to free the slaves, and commenced with a work of blood the first acts of sectional rebellion against the authority of the United States. It seems that this man, who had the singular combination of narrow sagacity, or cunning with visionary recklessness that is often observed in fanatics, had, in 1858, summoned a convention in West Canada, in which he proposed to substitute a plan of action entitled "Provisional Constitution and Ordinances" for all other governments then in existence in the United States.

This fanatical instrument has a very curious interest from its general similitude to that "plan of action" which was afterwards adopted by the Government at Washington in its great war upon the South, and its subsequent programme of subjugation.

The main point of the preamble of John Brown's Constitution was to announce the fact that the new government especially contemplated the accession of "the proscribed, oppressed, and enslaved" people of the United States. And this, and the qualification for membership in a following article, intimated that not sex, colour, age, political or social condition would be at all considered against any one.

The powers of the central Congress were defined in this instrument after the strictest school of Consolidation ; and the existence of the States was nowhere practically acknowledged.

In article 17 we find the following provision :

"It shall be the duty of the President and Secretary of State to find out, as soon as possible, the real friends, as well as enemies of this organization in every part of the country ; to secure among them inn-keepers, private postmasters, private mail contractors, messengers and agents, through whom may be obtained correct and regular information constantly."

The remaining articles of the Constitution develop a plan to build up on the ruins of existing laws and institutions a despotism, in which the " enemies of the government " are to be deprived of their capacity to do further evil by the loss of their liberty and property, while the loyal citizens are to form a sort of aristocratic fraternity, whose patriotic duty it will be to punish disloyalty at all hours and upon all occasions " promptly and effectually," and " without the formality of a complaint." The confiscation of the property of all slaveholders and " other disloyal persons " is directed ; and here, too, we find prescribed oaths of neutrality and allegiance, registering, &c.

This curious foreshadow of the policy of the North, which was to supplant the Constitution of the United States, originated in a convention of thirty-five fanatics, of whom ten where white men and the remaining twenty-five negroes of various shades of colour. John Brown, having thus prefaced his expedition into Virginia, collected a small company of insurgents, black and white, on a farm he had rented near Harper's Ferry, hoping that, as he invaded Virginia, the blacks would flock to his standard, and be armed there with the pikes and rifles he had provided for his recruits.

At half past ten o'clock, Sunday night, 17th October, 1859, the Potomac was crossed, and, proceeding with military method, the party seized first the watchman guarding the railroad bridge at Harper's Ferry, and, posting pickets at certain points, occupied the arsenal and armory building. A white confederate, named Cook, went out in command of a party for the purpose of getting black recruits from the adjoining estates of slaveholders. He arrested Col. Lewis Washington in his house, and brought in some other hostages in the persons of prominent citizens. In the meanwhile, Brown's pickets from time to time arrested and brought into his presence all who, from motives of curiosity or otherwise, had ventured within his military lines. These were retained as prisoners in one of the armory buildings. The pickets having captured one of the watchmen on the bridge, when the one who was to relieve him made his appearance, they challenged him. He, alarmed, at once retreated without obeying their command to stand. Finding words of no avail, the outlaws fired upon the fugitive, and brought him to the ground. Upon examining their victim, they discovered that he was a mulatto and mortally wounded.

About three o'clock in the morning, the Baltimore train arrived. This was halted for two or three hours, and finally, after much expostulation, allowed to pass. The news soon reached Washington; and Col. Robert E. Lee, then lieutenant-colonel of the Second Cavalry, was despatched to command the regular troops concentrating at Harper's Ferry. Accompanied by his aid, Lieut. J. E. B. Stuart—afterward the world-renowned cavalry chief of Lee's Army of Northern Virginia—he set out on a special train, and sent a telegraphic despatch to the U. S. Marines, in advance of him, directing them what to do. Other troops—the militia from Virginia and Maryland—had promptly reached the scene, and when Col. Lee arrived during the night, were awaiting his orders to act. He immediately placed his command within the armory grounds, so as to completely surround the fire-engine house where the insurgents had taken refuge. In it, Brown and his party had confined Col. Washington, Mr. Dangerfield, and some other citizens whom they had surprised and captured the night before; and therefore to use the cannon upon it now would be to endanger the lives of friends as well as foes.

Accordingly, at daylight, Col. Lee took measures to attempt the capture of the insurgents, if possible, without bloodshed. At seven in the morning he sent his aid, Lieut. Stuart, to summon them quietly to surrender, promising only protection from violence and a trial according to law. Brown refused all terms but those which he had more than once already asked for, namely: "That he should be permitted to pass out unmolested with his men and arms and prisoners, that they should proceed unpursued to the second toll-gate, when they would free their prisoners, and take the chances of escape." These concessions were, of course, refused.

At last, perceiving all his humane efforts to be of no avail, Col. Lee gave orders for an attack. A strong party of marines advanced by two lines quickly on each side of the door. When near enough, two powerful men sprung between the lines, and, with heavy sledge-hammers, attempted to batter down the doors, but failed. They then took hold of a ladder some forty feet long, and, advancing on a run, brought it with tremendous effect upon the door. At the second blow it gave way, and immediately the marines rushed to the breach as a volley from within came right upon them. One man, in the front, fell mortally wounded, and sharp and rapid was the firing from within from the insurgents, now driven to desperation. The next moment the gap was widened, and the marines poured in. As Lieut. Stuart entered the door, a voice cried out, "I surrender." Brown said, "One man surrenders, give him quarter!" and at the same time fired his piece.   The next moment Stuart's sword had entered his skull, and the desperate outlaw was stretched bleeding.   The other insur-gents were quickly secured ; and the liberated citizens, who had held up their hands to designate themselves to the marines, and thus escape their fire, were hailed with shouts of congratulation as they passed out of the building.

While suffering from a wound supposed to be mortal, Brown made the following admissions to Governor Wise of Virginia : " I never had more than twenty-two men about the place at one time ; but had it so arranged, that I could arm, at any time, fifteen hundred men with the following arms : two thousand Sharp's rifles, two hundred Maynard's revolvers, one thousand spears.   I would have armed the whites with the rifles and revolvers, and the blacks with the spears ; they not being sufficiently familiar with other arms.   I had plenty of ammunition and provisions, and had a good right to expect the aid of from two to five thousand men, at any time I wanted them.   Help was promised me from Maryland, Kentucky, North and South Carolina, Virginia, and Canada. The blow was struck a little too soon.   The passing of the train on Sunday night did the work for us ; that killed us.   I only regret that I have failed in my designs ; but I have no apology to make or concession to ask now. Had we succeeded, when our arms and funds were exhausted by an increasing army, contributions would have been levied on the slaveholders, and their property appropriated to defray expenses and carry on the war of freedom."

On the 2d of December, 1859, having been tried at Charleston, Vir-ginia, and condemned, Brown was conducted to the gallows, and there, in sight of the beautiful country, a portion of which he had hoped one day to possess, he suffered the extreme penalty of the law.   He died with the unnatural firmness of a fanatic—but as many in the North interpreted it, with the exalted courage of a martyr.

It had been said in some Northern newspapers that the John Brown raid and its expiation would have a good effect in opening the eyes of the people to the crime and madness of Abolition doctrines.   But subsequent events were quite to the contrary.   The Northern elections of the next month showed no diminution in the Black Republican vote.   The mani-festations of sympathy for John Brown could not be contained, and took place openly in many of the Northern cities and towns.   Upon the day appointed for his execution, a motion for adjournment, out of respect to the sacredness of the day, was lost in the State Senate of Massachusetts by only three votes ; while in many of the towns the bells of the churches were tolled, and congregations assembled to consecrate the memory of their hero.   The body was carried to North Elba in New York, and after it was consigned to the grave, many of the New England clergy allotted

John Brown an apotheosis, and consigned his example to emulation as one not only of public virtue, but of particular service to God.

But a much graver series of events was to show the real sympathy of the North with John Brown's "plan of action," and to attest the rapid tendency of the Black Republican party to the worst schools of Abolition. At the meeting of Congress in December, 1859, the Black Republicans nominated to the speakership of the House Mr. Sherman of Ohio, who had made himself especially odious to the South, by publicly recommending, in connection with sixty-eight other Republican Congressmen, a fanatical document popularly known as "*Helper's Book.*" This publication, thus endorsed by Black Republicans, and circulated by them in the Northern elections, openly defended and sought to excite servile insurrections in the South; and it was with reason that the entire Southern delegation gave warning that they would regard the election of Mr. Sherman, or of any man with his record, as an open declaration of war upon the institutions of the South; as much so, some of the members declared, as if the John Brown raid were openly approved by a majority of the House of Representatives.

This book, which even Mr. Seward, the leader of the Black Republican party, had recommended, along with others, urged the North to exterminate slavery, and at once, without the slightest compensation, in language of which the following is a specimen, addressed to the Southerners: "Frown sirs; fret, foam, prepare your weapons, threaten, strike, shoot, stab, bring on civil war, dissolve the Union; nay, annihilate the solar system, if you will—do all this, more, less, better, worse—anything; do what you will sirs—you can neither foil nor intimidate us; our purpose is as fixed as the eternal pillars of heaven; we have determined to abolish slavery, and—so help us God—abolish it we will!"

Some other extracts from this infamous book we may place here to indicate its character, and the importance of the act of the Black Republican party in endorsing it as a campaign document: "Slavery is a great moral, social, civil, and political evil, to be got rid of at the earliest practicable period. . . . . Three-quarters of a century hence, if the South retains slavery, which God forbid! she will be to the North what Poland is to Russia, Cuba to Spain, and Ireland to England. . . . . Our own banner is inscribed—No coöperation with slaveholders in politics; no fellowship with them in religion; no affiliation with them in society; no recognition of pro-slavery men, except as ruffians, outlaws, and criminals. . . . . We believe it is, as it ought to be, the desire, the determination, and the destiny of the Republican party to give the death-blow to slavery. . . . . In any event, come what will, transpire what may, the institution of slavery must be abolished. . . . . We are determined to abolish slavery at all hazards—in defiance of all the opposition, of whatever nature, it is possible for the slaveocrats to bring against us. Of this they may take due notice, and govern themselves accordingly. . . . . It is our honest conviction that all the pro-slavery slaveholders deserve to be at once reduced to a parallel with the basest criminals that lie fettered within the cells of our public prisons. . . . . Compensation to slave-owners for negroes! Preposterous idea—the suggestion is criminal, the demand unjust, wicked, monstrous, damnable. Shall we pat the blood-hounds for the sake of doing them a favour? Shall we feed the curs of slavery to make them rich at our expense? Pay these whelps for the privilege of converting them into decent, honest, upright men?"

Such was the language, endorsed by sixty-eight Northern Congressmen, applied to the South: to that part of the Union indeed which was the superiour of the North in every true and refined element of civilization; which had contributed more than its share to all that had given lustre to the military history of America, or the councils of its senate; which, in fact, had produced that list of illustrious American names best known in Europe: Washington, Jefferson, Madison, Monroe, Jackson, Marshall, Clay, Calhoun, Scott, and Maury.

The fact was that insult to the South had come to be habitual through every expression of Northern opinion; not only in political tirades, but through its lessons of popular education, the ministrations of its church, its literature, and every form of daily conversation. The rising generation of the North were taught to regard the Southerner as one of a lower order of civilization; a culprit to reform, or a sinner to punish. A large party in the North affected the insolent impertinence of regarding the Union as a concession on the part of the North, and of taunting the South with the disgrace which her association in the Union inflicted upon the superiour and more virtuous people of the Northern States. There were no bounds to this conceit. It was said that the South was an inferiour part of the country; that she was a " plague-spot; " that the national fame abroad was compromised by the association of the South in the Union; and that a New England traveller in Europe blushed to confess himself an American, because nearly half of the nation of that name were slaveholders. Not a few of the Abolitionists made a pretence of praying that the Union might be dissolved, that they might be cleared, by the separation of North and South, of any implication in the crime of slavery. Even that portion of the party calling themselves Republicans, affected that the Union stood in the way of the North. Mr. Banks, speaker of the House in the Thirty-first Congress, was the author of the coarse jeer—" Let *the Union slide;* " and the New York *Tribune* had complained that the South " could not be *kicked* out of the Union."—We shall see in the light of subsequent events how this Northern affectation for disunion was a lie, a snare to the South, and a hypocrisy unparalleled in all the records of partisan animosity.

It would have been more or less than human nature if the South had not been incensed at expressions in which her people were compared with "mad-dogs"—with "small-pox, as nuisances to be abated," or classed with gangs of "licensed robbers," "thieves," and "murderers." But it was not only the wretched ribaldry of the "Helper Book" that was the cause of excitement; the designs there declared of war upon the South, and recommended by an array of Black Republican names, were the occasion of the most serious alarm. It is true that Mr. Sherman, the "Helper Book" candidate for the speakership of the House, was finally withdrawn, and one of his party, not a subscriber to the book, elected. But the fact remained that more than three-fourths of the entire Northern delegation had adhered to Mr. Sherman for nearly two months in a factious and fanatical spirit. Such an exhibition of obstinate rancour could not fail to produce a deep impression on the South; and the early dissolution of the Union had now come to be a subject freely canvassed in Congress and in the country.

We have thus, in a rapid summary of political events from 1857 to 1860—the Kansas controversy, the John Brown raid, and the "Helper Book" *imbroglio*—enabled the reader to discover and combine some of the most remarkable indications of the coming catastrophe of Disunion. In the historical succession of events we shall see that occurrence rapidly and steadily advancing, until at last the sharp and distinct issue of a sectional despotism was forced upon the South, and war precipitated upon the country.

The Democratic party of the South had coöperated with the Democratic party of the North in the Presidential canvass of 1856, upon the principles of the platform adopted by the National Democratic Convention assembled in Cincinnati, in June of that year. They expressed a willingness to continue this coöperation in the election of 1860, upon the principles of the Cincinnati platform; but demanded, as a condition precedent to this, that the question of the *construction* of this platform should be satisfactorily settled. To this end, the Democratic party, in several of the Southern States, defined the conditions upon which their delegates should hold seats in the National Convention, appointed to meet at Charleston, on the 23d of April, 1860. The Democracy in Alabama moved first and adopted a series of resolutions, the purport of which was afterwards embodied in the instructions administered by some of the other Cotton States to their delegations to the National Convention.

The most important of these resolutions were as follows:

"*Resolved*, That the Constitution of the United States is a compact between sovereign and co-equal States, united upon the basis of perfect equality of rights and privileges.

"*Resolved, further*, That the Territories of the United States are common property, in which the States have equal rights, and to which the citizens of any State may rightfully emigrate, with their slaves or other property, recognized as such in any of the States of the Union, or by the Constitution of the United States.

" *Resolved, further*, That the Congress of the United States has no power to abolish slavery in the Territories, or to prohibit its introduction into any of them.

" *Resolved, further*, That the Territorial Legislatures, created by the legislation of Congress, have no power to abolish slavery, or to prohibit the introduction of the same, or to impair by unfriendly legislation the security and full enjoyment of the same within the Territories; and such constitutional power certainly does not belong to the people of the Territories in any capacity, before, in the exercise of a lawful authority, they form a Constitution, preparatory to admission as a State into the Union; and their action in the exercise of such lawful authority certainly cannot operate or take effect before their actual admission as a State into the Union."

When the Convention met at Charleston two sets of resolutions were represented :

I.

" *Resolved*, That the platform at Cincinnati be reaffirmed with the following resolutions :

" *Resolved*, That the Democracy of the United States hold these cardinal principles on the subject of slavery in the Territories : First, that Congress has no power to abolish slavery in the Territories. Second, that the Territorial Legislature has no power to abolish slavery in any Territory, nor to prohibit the introduction of slaves therein, nor any power to exclude slavery therefrom, nor any power to destroy and impair the right of property in slaves by any legislation whatever.

*　　*　　*　　*　　*　　*　　*　　*

II.

" *Resolved*, That the platform adopted by the Democratic party at Cincinnati be affirmed, with the following explanatory resolutions :

" *First*. That the government of a Territory, organized by an act of Congress, is provisional and temporary; and, during its existence, all citizens of the United States have an equal right to settle with their property in the Territory, without their rights, either of person or property, being destroyed or impaired by Congressional or Territorial legislation.

" *Second*. That it is the duty of the Federal Government, in all its departments, to protect, when necessary, the rights of persons and property in the Territories and wherever else its constitutional authority extends.

" *Third*. That when the settlers in a Territory, having an adequate population, form a State Constitution, the right of sovereignty commences, and being consummated by admission into the Union, they stand on an equal footing with the people of other States; and the State thus organized, ought to be admitted into the Federal Union, whether its Constitution prohibits or recognizes the institution of slavery."

The Convention refused to accept either of the foregoing resolutions, and adopted, by a vote of 165 to 138, the following as its platform on the slavery question :

"1. *Resolved*, That we, the Democracy of the Union, in Convention assembled, hereby declare our affirmance of the resolutions unanimously adopted and declared as a platform of principles by the Democratic Convention at Cincinnati, in the year 1856, believing that Democratic principles are unchangeable in their nature, when applied to the same subject-matters; and we recommend as the only further resolutions the following:

"Inasmuch as differences of opinion exist in the Democratic party as to the nature and extent of the powers of a Territorial Legislature, and as to the powers and duties of Congress under the Constitution of the United States, over the institution of slavery within the Territories:

"2. *Resolved*, That the Democratic party will abide by the decisions of the Supreme Court of the United States on the questions of constitutional law."

This platform being unsatisfactory to the Southern delegates, a body of them seceded, and called a new Convention at Baltimore, on the 18th of June. The Cotton States all withdrew from the Charleston Convention; but the Border States remained in it, with the hope of effecting some ultimate settlement of the difficulty. But the reassembling of the Convention at Baltimore resulted in a final and embittered separation of the opposing delegations. The majority at Charleston exhibited a more uncompromising spirit than ever; and Virginia, and all the Border Slave States, with the exception of Missouri, withdrew from the Convention, and united with the representatives of the Cotton States, then assembled in Baltimore, in the nomination of candidates representing the views of the South. Their nominees were John C. Breckinridge of Kentucky for President, and Joseph Lane of Oregon for Vice-President.

The old Convention, or what remained of it, nominated Stephen A. Douglas of Illinois for President, and Benjamin Fitzpatrick of Alabama for Vice-President. The latter declining, Herschel V. Johnson of Georgia was substituted on the ticket.

A Convention of what was called the "Constitutional Union" party met in Baltimore on the 9th of May, 1860, and nominated for President and Vice-President John Bell of Tennessee and Edward Everett of Massachusetts. Their platform consisted of a vague and undefined enumeration of their political principles, as, "The Constitution of the Country, the Union of the States, and Enforcement of the Laws."

The National Convention of the Black Republican party was held at Chicago in the month of June. It adopted a platform declaring freedom to be the "normal condition" of the Territories; and protesting especial attachment to the Union of the States. The Presidential ticket nominated by the Convention was, Abraham Lincoln of Illinois for President, and Hannibal Hamlin of Maine for Vice-President.

The great majority of the Southern Democracy supported the Breckinridge ticket; it was the leading ticket in all the Slave States except Missouri; but in the North only a small and feeble minority of the Democratic party gave it their support.   In several States, the friends of Douglas, of Breckinridge, and of Bell coalesced, to a certain extent, with a view to the defeat of Lincoln, but without success, except in New Jersey, where they partially succeeded.

The result of the contest was, that Abraham Lincoln received the entire electoral vote of every free State, except New Jersey, and was, of course, elected President of the United States, according to the forms of the Constitution.

The entire popular vote for Lincoln was 1,858,200 ; that for Douglas, giving him his share of the fusion vote, 1,276,780 ; that for Breckinridge, giving him his share of the fusion vote, 812,500 ; and that for Bell, including his proportion of the fusion vote, 735,504.   The whole vote against Lincoln was thus 2,824,874, showing a clear aggregate majority against him of nearly a million of votes.

The analysis of the vote which elected Mr. Lincoln showed plainly enough that ˙ was a *sectional* triumph ; and it was in view of that ominous fac , rather than in any less important resentment, or with any especial reference to the declaration of principles in the Chicago platform, that the South proposed to repudiate for herself the result of the election, and to go out of a Union now plainly converted into a means of deliberate sectional oppression.

There has been much loose and plausible protest against this course of the South, in which it has been said that it was essentially revolutionary and refractory ; that Mr. Lincoln had been elected according to the forms of the Constitution by a majority of the electoral college, and that the South was bound by honour and in precedent to submit to the result of an election legitimately and constitutionally accomplished.   This view was pronounced by Mr. Seward, in the Senate of the United States.   " Was the election illegal ? " he asked.   " No ; it is unimpeachable.   Is the candidate personally offensive ?   No ; he is a man of unblemished virtue and amiable manners.   Is an election of President an unfrequent or extraordinary transaction ?   No ; we never had a Chief Magistrate otherwise designated than by such election, and that form of choice is renewed every four years.   Does any one even propose to change the mode of appointing the Chief Magistrate ?   No ; election by universal suffrage, as modified by the Constitution, is the one crowning franchise of the American people.   To save it they would defy the world."

But it was surprising to find a man of Mr. Seward's pretension to statesmanship using such a loose and superficial argument to sustain an election, the sectional significance of which, kept out of view, was really the important point, and, of itself, terminated the constitutional existence of the Union.

True, Mr. Lincoln was the choice of the majority of the electoral college. But his election was almost purely geographical. The South had sustained a defeat, not at the hands of a party, but at those of the Northern power. Every Northern State but New Jersey had voted for Mr. Lincoln ; every Southern State had voted against him. He was not known as a statesman, whose name might therefore be one of national significance ; he was known only as a partisan, and the election of such a man in such a character was plainly to declare war against the other side.

In the face of this sectional triumph there was plainly no protection for the South in the future. There was none in power ; for the superiour political strength of the North was now beyond dispute. There was none in public opinion ; for that, all the political history of America showed, was the slave of the majority. There was none in the courts ; for the Dred Scott decision had been denounced in the Chicago platform as a dangerous heresy, and the doctrine upon which Mr. Lincoln had been elected had been actually declared illegal by the supreme judicial authority of the country.

In Congress the Northern States had 183 votes ; the South, if unanimous, 120. If then the North was prepared to act in a mass its power was irresistible ; and the election of Mr. Lincoln plainly showed that it was prepared so to act and to carry out a sectional design. The anti-slavery power in the North was now compact and invincible. A party opposed to slavery had organized in 1840, with about seven thousand voters ; in 1860, it had polled nearly two million votes, and had succeeded in electing the President of the United States. The conservative party in the North had been thoroughly corrupted. They were beaten in every Northern State in 1860, with a single exception, by the avowed enemies of the South, who, but a few years ago, had been powerless in their midst. The leaders of the Northern Democratic party had, in 1856 and in 1860, openly taken the position that freedom would be more certainly secured in the Territories by the rule of non-intervention than by any other policy or expedient. This interpretation of their policy alone saved the Democratic party from entire annihilation. The overwhelming pressure of the anti-slavery sentiment had prevented their acceding to the Southern platform in the Presidential canvass. Nothing in the present or in the future could be looked for from the so-called conservatives of the North ; and the South prepared to go out of a Union which no longer afforded any guaranty for her rights or any permanent sense of security, and which had brought her under the domination of a section, the designs of which, carried into legislation, would destroy her institutions, and even involve the lives of her people.

Such was the true and overwhelming significance of Mr. Lincoln's election to the people of the South. They saw in it the era of a sectional domination, which they proposed to encounter, not by *revolution*, properly so called, not by an attempt to recover by arms their constitutional rights in the Union, but simply to escape by withdrawal from the confederation, and the resumption of their original character of independent States.

But again it was urged by the apologists of Mr. Lincoln's election that such escape of the South from its results was unfair, in view of the fact that during most of the preceding period of the Union, the South had held in its hands the administration at Washington, and had but little reason now to complain that it had passed to those of the rival section.

This view was not without plausibility, and yet as fallacious as that which appealed to the prescriptive rule of majorities in America. The South had held political power at Washington for a long time; but that power threatened nothing in the North, sought nothing from it, desired to disturb nothing in it. It had no aggressive intent: it stood constantly on the defensive. It had no sectional history: it was associated with a general prosperity of the country. "Do not forget," said Senator Hammond of South Carolina, when Mr. Seward boasted in the United States Senate that the North was about to take control at Washington,—"it can never be forgotten—it is written on the brightest page of human history— that we, the slaveholders of the South, took our country in her infancy, and, after ruling her for sixty out of seventy years of her existence, we shall surrender her to you without a stain upon her honour, boundless in prosperity, incalculable in her strength, the wonder and the admiration of the world. Time will show what you will make of her; but no time can ever diminish our glory or your responsibility."

When the South held power, it was only to the North a certain absence from office, a certain exclusion from patronage. But when the North was to obtain it, acting not as a party, but a people united on a geographical idea, it was something more than a negative evil or disappointment to the South; it was the enthronement at Washington of a sectional despotism that threatened the institutions, the property, and the lives of the people of the Southern States. Power in the hands of the South affected the patronage of a political party in the North. Power in the hands of the North affected the safety and happiness of every individual in the South.—It was simply determined by the South to withdraw from a game where the stakes were so unequal, and where her loss would have been ruin.

CHAPTER V.

THE telegraph had no sooner announced the election of Abraham Lincoln President of the United States than the State of South Carolina prepared for a deliberate withdrawal from the Union. Considering the argument as fully exhausted, she determined to resume the exercise of her rights as a sovereign State; and for this purpose her Legislature called a Convention. It assembled in Columbia on the 17th of December, 1860. Its sessions were held in a church, over which floated a flag bearing the device of a palmetto tree, with an open Bible at its trunk, with the inscription: "God is our refuge and strength, a very present help in time of trouble, therefore will we not fear, though the earth be removed and though the mountains be carried into the sea; the Lord of Hosts is with us—the God of Jacob is our refuge."

On the 18th the Convention adjourned to Charleston, and on the 20th of December passed the memorable ordinance of Secession, concluding that "the Union now subsisting between South Carolina and other States, under the name of 'The United States of America' is hereby dissolved." The ordinance was passed by a unanimous vote. A ceremony was appointed for the signing in public of the roll of parchment on which the ordinance was engrossed. The public procession entered St. Andrew's Hall in order: the President and members of the Convention coming first, followed by the President and members of the Senate, and the Speaker and House of Representatives. Their entry was greeted by loud and prolonged cheers from the spectators; the proceedings were commenced with prayer; the Attorney-General of the State then announced that the ordinance had been engrossed by order of the Convention, and the parchment roll was signed by the members who were called successively to the table. When all had signed, the parchment was raised in the sight of the assemblage, and when the President announced the State of South Carolina an Independent Commonwealth, the whole audience rose to their feet, and with enthusiastic cheers testified their sense of the thrilling proclamation.

A few days after this event a memorable event occurred in Charleston harbour. On the 26th of December Major Anderson, who was in command of the Federal forces there, evacuated Fort Moultrie, spiking the guns and burning the gun carriages, and occupied Fort Sumter with a view of strengthening his position. This movement was effected as a surprise under cover of night. The place in which Major Anderson had now taken refuge was pronounced by military critics to be well-nigh impregnable. Fort Sumter was a small work; but as strong as could well be conceived. It was a modern truncated pentagonal fort, rising abruptly out of the water at the mouth of Charleston harbour, three and a half miles from the city. The foundation was an artificial one, made of chips of granite firmly imbedded in the mud and sand, and so well constructed that it had cost half a million of dollars, and consumed ten years of labour. When Major Anderson occupied the fortification, it was so nearly completed as to admit the introduction of its armament. The walls were of solid brick and concrete masonry, sixty feet high, and from eight to twelve

feet in thickness, and pierced for three tiers of guns on the northern, eastern, and western sides. These guns commanded the harbour, thus giving
the Federal garrison the power to arrest the shipping bound to and from
the port, and to assume an attitude of hostility inconsistent with the safety
of that part of the State of South Carolina.

In the mean time the event of South Carolina's formal withdrawal from
the Union was treated by the North generally with derision. Northern
newspapers scoffed at her; Northern pictorials abounded with caricatures
of Palmetto chivalry; secession cockades, it was said, would soon pass out
of fashion, and, on the appearance of the first United States regiment in
Charleston harbour, would be found as scarce as cherries in the snow.
But what was most remarkable in the treatment of the event by the
Northern newspapers and politicians was, that they all united in affecting
the most entire and ready willingness that South Carolina, and as many
Slave States as chose to accompany her should go out of the Union whenever they pleased. This affectation, which was half insolence and half
hypocrisy, was heard everywhere in the North. As long, indeed, as the
North apprehended no serious consequences, and from its very vanity
refused to entertain the idea that the South had any means or resources
for making a serious resistance to the Federal authority, it easily afforded
to ridicule the movement of South Carolina; to compare her to a " spoilt
child," wandering from the fold of a " paternal government;" and to
declare that there was really no design to coerce her or her sister States,
but rather pleasure at the separation. " Let the prodigal go," exclaimed
one of the political preachers of the North. A God-speed was added by
Mr. Greeley, of the New York *Tribune*. And yet a few months later,
and these men and their followers were in agonies of anxiety and parox-
ysms of fury to reclaim what they then called the " rebel " States, declaring that their cities should be laid in ashes, and their soil sown with blood;
while the benevolent *Tribune* drew from its imagination and hopes a picture, not of the returned prodigal, but of punished " rebels " returning
home to find their wives and children cowering in rags, and Famine sitting at the fireside.*

---

* (From the New York *Tribune* of Nov. 26, and Dec. 17, 1860.)

" We hold with Jefferson to the inalienable right of communities to alter or abolish forms of
government that have become oppressive or injurious, and if the Cotton States shall become satisfied that they can do better out of the Union than in it, we insist on letting them go in peace. The
right to secede may be a revolutionary one, but it exists nevertheless, and we do not see how one
party can have a right to do what another party has a right to prevent. Whenever a considerable
section of our Union shall deliberately resolve to go out, we shall resist all coercive measures designed to keep it in. We hope never to live in a Republic whereof one section is pinned to the
residue by bayonets. . . . . If ever seven or eight States send agents to Washington to say,
We want to go out of the Union,' we shall feel constrained by our devotion to human liberty, to
say, ' Let them go !' And we do not see how we could take the other side, without coming in

But had the Northern people really been candid and just in their professed willingness to let the South go, they might have found, alike in the political precedents of the country and in the sound reason of its states men, ample grounds for such a disposition. The doctrine of State secession was no new thing in the North. The right of it had been reserved by the State of New York, on her adoption of the Federal Constitution. The exercise of such right had been threatened on four separate occasions by the State of Massachusetts. She had threatened to secede from the Union, with reference to the adjustment of the State debts; again, on account of the Louisiana Purchase; thirdly, because of the war of 1812–'14, when, as Mr. Jefferson said, "four of the Eastern States were only attached to the Union like so many inanimate bodies to living men;" and fourthly, on the annexation of Texas, when her Legislature actually resolved in advance that this event would be good cause for the dissolution of the Union. With reference to the Louisiana Purchase, and the bill to admit into the Union the Territory of Orleans, under the name of Louisiana, Mr. Quincy, of Massachusetts, had placed on record in Congress a definition of the remedy of secession; for, at the instance of members, he had put in writing, and placed on the desk of the House of Representatives, the following proposition: "If this bill passes, it is my deliberate opinion that it is virtually a dissolution of this Union; that it will free the States from their moral obligations, and, as it will be the right of all, so it will be the duty of some, definitely to prepare for a separation—amicably, if they can; violently, if they must."

But it is not necessary to make here any discussion or recrimination on the subject of State secession. For the South claimed a double justification of her withdrawal from the Union; and in putting it on the alternative of that right of self-government proclaimed in the American Declaration of Independence, and existing in all republican systems, she could claim its recognition from the highest sources, both of official and popular authority in the North.

Indeed, the President-elect, Mr. Lincoln, had, at another period of his public life, made this remarkable declaration: " Any people, anywhere, being inclined and having the power, have the right to rise up and shake

direct conflict with those rights of man which we hold paramount to all political arrangements, nowever convenient and advantageous."

(From the same, of May 1, 1861.)

"But, nevertheless, we mean to *conquer* them [the Confederate States], not merely to *defeat*, but to *conquer*, to *subjugate them*. But when the rebellious traitors are overwhelmed in the field, and scattered like leaves before an angry wind, *it must not be to return to peaceful and contented homes !* They must find *poverty* at their firesides, *and see privation in the anxious eyes of mothers, and the rags of children.* The whole coast of the South, from the Delaware to the Rio Grande, *must be a solitude.*

off the existing Government, and form a new one that suits them better. Nor is this right confined to cases where the people of an existing Government may choose to exercise it. Any portion of such people that can, may revolutionize, putting down a minority intermingled with or near about them, who may oppose them."

On the eve of hostilities the New York *Tribune* declared: "Whenever portion of this Union, large enough to form an independent, self-sustaining nation, shall see fit to say authentically to the residue, 'We want to get away from you,' we shall say—and we trust self-respect, if not regard for the principle of self-government, will constrain the residue of the American people to say—Go!'"

At a later period, Mr. Seward, then President Lincoln's Secretary of State, used the following language to Mr. Adams, the United States Minister at London: "For these reasons he [Mr. Lincoln] would not be disposed to reject a cardinal dogma of theirs [the Secessionists], namely, that the Federal Government could not reduce the seceding States to obedience by conquest, even although he were disposed to question that proposition. But in fact the President willingly accepts it as true. Only an imperial or despotic government could subjugate thoroughly disaffected and insurrectionary members of the State. This Federal Republican system of ours is, of all forms of government, the very one most unfitted for such a labour."

It was in the face of this plain and abundant record that the North, as we shall hereafter see, prepared to make upon the seceded Southern States a war the most terrible in modern annals, and the most monstrous of Christian times. But we must return here to the course of events immediately following the secession of South Carolina.

There could be no doubt of the disposition of all the Cotton States to accompany South Carolina in her withdrawal from the Union, and to make common cause with her. But there was some hesitation as to the time and mode of action; and in Georgia especially there was a strong party in favour of holding a conference of all the Southern States before taking the decisive and irrevocable step. The influence of Alexander H. Stephens was not only given to this party in Georgia, but betrayed a design to keep the State in the Union. He had made a speech of great ingenuity, to show that the cause of the Union was not yet hopeless, that all honourable means should be used to save it—that, notwithstanding the election of Mr. Lincoln, the Northern States might yield to a determined admonition from the South. But to this art of the demagogue there were plain and forcible replies. Mr. Howell Cobb urged that delay was dangerous, and that the Legislature ought to pass an act of secession to be ratified by the people; Mr. Toombs insisted that all hope of justice from the North was gone, and that nothing remained but separation, and, if necessary, war to maintain the rights of the South; and while the discussion was going on, the Mayor of Savannah had already pledged fifty thousand Georgians to rally to the aid of South Carolina, if needed.

It was impossible for any checks of authority or arts of the demagogue to restrain the popular sentiment in the Cotton States that clamoured to follow the example of South Carolina. On the 7th day of January, 1861, the State of Florida seceded from the Union. Mississippi followed on the 9th day of the same month; Alabama on the 11th; Georgia on the 20th; Louisiana on the 26th; and Texas on the 1st of February. Thus, in less than three months after the announcement of Mr. Lincoln's election, all the Cotton States had seceded from the Union.

They had done more than this. They had secured all the forts, arsenals, and government places lying within their territory, with the exception of Fort Sumter in Charleston harbour, and Fort Pickens near Pensacola. At this latter place was to occur a history somewhat similar to that of Sumter.

Here was a fine bay; a splendid navy yard; and the principal depot of the Gulf fleet. In the beginning of 1861, a small military force was stationed there in charge of the forts. These forts were, Fort McRae, on the main land, with a lagoon behind it, and guarding one side of the harbour; Fort Barancas, directly facing the entrance of the harbour, and Fort Pickens on the other, or east side of the harbour entrance. This latter was on the extremity of the long, low, sandy Santa Rosa Island, which stretched away to the eastward, and formed an excellent breakwater to the bay. The navy yard was about a mile inside the bay, beyond Fort Barancas, and was thus in an admirably safe position.

The seizure of these places was earnestly and instantly advised by Senator Yulee, of Florida, in private letters written from his seat in the United States Senate. Fort Barancas and McRae, with the navy yard, were at once surrendered by the naval commandant; but Lieut. Slemmers, not approving such a course, secretly crossed over to Fort Pickens, as Major Anderson did from Moultrie to Sumter, and there stationed himself, while the ingenuity and enterprise of the government at Washington were to be taxed for his reinforcement.

The scene of secession was now to be transferred to Washington. On the 21st of January, 1861, an impressive and memorable event occurred in the Senate of the United States. On that day, resignations of certain distinguished Senators were announced, in consequence of the secession of their States. Even the Republican Senators treated the occasion with respect; the chamber was pervaded by an air of solemnity; and the galleries were crowded by a vast concourse of spectators, the intelligent of whom recognized in the scene transpiring before their eyes the ceremony of the first serious disintegration of the authority at Washington.

The Senators who withdrew on this day were Mr. Jefferson Davis, of Mississippi, Messrs. Fitzpatrick and Clay, of Alabama, and Messrs Yulee and Mallory, of Florida. Most of them made temperate and courteous speeches in announcing the fact and occasion of their resignation. Mr. Davis, although at the time much prostrated by ill health, made a speech of remarkable force and dignity; and turning to different members, declared that he was the type of the general feelings of his constituents toward theirs; that he felt no hostility to them; that he went thence unencumbered by the remembrance of any injury received; but he said, if the North had resolved on hostile relations towards the seceded States, then " we will invoke the God of our fathers, who delivered them from the power of the lion, to protect us from the ravages of the bear; and thus, putting our trust in God and in our own firm hearts and strong arms, we will vindicate the right as best we may."

Mr. C. C. Clay of Alabama was more violent. In severing his connection with the Senate, he took occasion to make out a very full bill of indictment against the Republican party, and to recount the grievances that impelled the South to separate herself from the Union. A portion of his speech is interesting here as the historical statement on the side of the South of the causes and necessity of Disunion, made by one of her leading statesmen, and reflecting much both of the intelligence and passion of his countrymen. He said:

" It is now nearly forty-two years since Alabama was admitted into the Union. She entered it, as she goes out of it, while the Confederacy was in convulsions, caused by the hostility of the North to the domestic slavery of the South. Not a decade, nor scarce a lustrum, has elapsed, since her birth, that has not been strongly marked by proofs of the growth and power of that anti-slavery spirit of the Northern people which seeks the overthrow of that domestic institution of the South which is not only the chief source of her prosperity, but the very basis of her social order and state polity. It is to-day the master-spirit of the Northern States, and had, before the secession of Alabama, of Mississippi, of Florida, or of South Carolina, severed most of the bonds of the Union. It denied us Christian communion, because it could not endure what it styles the moral leprosy of slaveholding; it refused us permission to sojourn, or even to pass through the North, with our property; it claimed freedom for the slave if brought by his master into a Northern State; it violated the Constitution and treaties and laws of Congress, because designed to protect that property; it refused us any share of lands acquired mainly by our diplomacy and blood and treasure; it refused our property any shelter or security beneath the flag of a common government; it robbed us of our property, and refused to restore it; it refused to deliver criminals against our laws, who fled to the North with our property or our blood upon their hands; it threatened us, by solemn legislative acts, with ignominious punishment if we pursued our property into a Northern State; it murdered Southern men when seeking the recovery of their property on Northern soil; it invaded the borders of Southern States, poisoned their wells, burnt their dwellings, and murdered their people; it denounced us by deliberate resolves of popular meetings, of party conventions, and of religious and even legislative assemblies, as habitual violators of the laws of God and the rights of humanity; it exerted all the moral and physical agencies that human ingenuity can devise or diabolical malice can employ to heap odium and infamy upon us, and to make us a by-word of hissing and of scorn throughout the civilized world. Yet we bore all this for many years, and might have borne it for many more, under the oft-repeated assurance of our Northern friends, and the too fondly cherished hope that these wrongs and injuries were committed by a minority party, and had not the sanction of the majority of the people, who would, in time, rebuke our enemies, and redress our grievances.

" But the fallacy of these promises and folly of our hopes have been too clearly and conclusively proved in late elections, especially the last two Presidential elections, to permit us to indulge longer in such pleasing delusions. The platform of the Republican party of 1856 and 1860 we regard as a libel upon the character and a declaration of war against the lives and property of the Southern people. No bitterer or more offensive calumny could be uttered against them than is expressed in denouncing their system of slavery and polygamy as "twin relics of barbarism." It not only reproaches us as un- christian and heathenish, but imputes a sin and a crime deserving universal scorn and universal enmity. No sentiment is more insulting or more hostile to our domestic tran- quillity, to our social order, and our social existence, than is contained in the declaration that our negroes are entitled to liberty and equality with the white man. It is in spirit, if not effect, as strong an incitement and invocation to servile insurrection, to murder, arson, and other crimes, as any to be found in abolition literature.

" And to aggravate the insult which is offered us in demanding equality with us for our slaves, the same platform denies us equality with Northern white men or free negroes, and brands us as an inferiour race, by pledging the Republican party to resist our entrance into the Territories with our slaves, or the extension of slavery, which—as its founders and leaders truly assert—must and will effect its extermination. To crown the climax of insult to our feelings and menace of our rights, this party nominated to the Presidency a man who not only endorses the platform, but promises, in his zealous sup- port of its principles, to disregard the judgments of your courts, the obligations of your Constitution, and the requirements of his official oath, by approving any bill prohibiting slavery in the Territories of the United States.

" A large majority of the Northern people have declared at the ballot-box their ap- proval of the platform and the candidates of that party in the late Presidential election. Thus, by the solemn verdict of the people of the North, the slaveholding communities of the South are ' outlawed, branded with ignominy, consigned to execration, and ulti- mate destruction.' "

" Sir, are we looked upon as more or less than men? Is it expected that we will or can ex- ercise that god-like virtue which ' beareth all things, believeth all things, hopeth all things; endureth all things ; ' which teaches us to *love our enemies, and bless them that curse us ?* Are we devoid of the sensibilities, the sentiments, the passions, the reason, and the instincts of mankind? Have we no pride of honour, no sense of shame, no reverence of our ances- tors, no care of our posterity, no love of home, or family, or friends? Must we confess our baseness, discredit the fame of our sires, dishonour ourselves, degrade our posterity, abandon our homes, and flee from our country, all for the sake of the Union? Must we agree to live under the ban of our own Government? Must we acquiesce in the inaugu- ration of a President, chosen by confederate, but unfriendly, States, whose political faith constrains him, for his conscience and country's sake, to deny us our constitutional rights, because elected according to the forms of the Constitution? Must we consent to live under a Government which we believe will henceforth be controlled and administered by those who not only deny us justice and equality, and brand us as inferiours, but whose avowed principles and policy must destroy our domestic tranquillity, imperil the lives of our wives and children, degrade and dwarf, and ultimately destroy, our State? Must we live, by choice or compulsion, under the rule of those who present us the dire alternative of an 'irrepressible conflict' with the Northern people, in defence of our altars. and our fireside, or the manumission of our slaves, and the admission of them to social and political equality? No, sir, no! The freemen of Alabama have proclaimed to the world that they will not; and have proved their sincerity by seceding from the Union, and hazarding all the dangers and difficulties of a separate and independent station among the nations of the earth."

Mr. Jefferson Davis had resigned from the Senate of the United States to encounter a responsibility and accept a trust the greatest of modern times. Public opinion in all the seceded States had long designated him as the leader of their new destinies. A convention of delegates from the then six seceded States assembled in Congress at Montgomery, Alabama, on the 4th of February, 1861, for the purpose of organizing a provisional government. This body adopted a Constitution for the Confederate States on the 8th of February. On the 9th of February, Congress proceeded to the election of a President and Vice-President, and unanimously agreed upon Jefferson Davis, of Mississippi, for President, and Alexander H. Stephens, of Georgia, for Vice-President.

The framers of the new government at Montgomery studiously adhered, in the main features of their plan, to the Washington model; but the Constitution adopted by them differed in some particulars from that of the United States. And it is to be remarked that at every point of difference it made an undoubted improvement, or corrected some acknowledged evil of former times. The Confederate Constitution absolutely prohibited the over-sea slave-trade; that of the United States did not. It permitted cabinet ministers to take part in the discussions of Congress. It prohibited bounties or duties to foster any branch of industry. After a specified time the post-office was required to cover its own expenses. No extra compensation was to be paid to any contractor. The President was to hold office for six years, and was not to be reëligible. The subordinate government officers were not to be removed by the President without a report to the Senate giving his reasons. The right of property in slaves and that of taking them into any Territory were expressly stated; but in this, it was claimed that no new principle was adopted or laid down, which did not already exist in the Constitution of the old Union.

The choice of President was thought at the time to be quite as fit and admirable as the other work of the Convention. But of this, the most serious doubts were hereafter to arise. Jefferson Davis, the President of the Confederate States, was a name that was associated with much that was brilliant and honourable in the history of the old government. He had served that government in the field and in council. He had received a military education at West Point; had served in the Mexican War, at the head of a regiment of volunteer riflemen, winning distinction at Monterey and Buena Vista; and had been called to the cabinet of President Pierce, as Secretary of War; in the administration of which office he increased the strength of the United States army, proposed to abolish the permanent staff-organization for one of details on staff-duty, and sent to the Crimea a commission to report upon the state of the science of war, and the condition of European armies. He re-entered political life as a Senator in Congress. In that highest school of debate in America, he was distinguished for a style of polished and graceful oratory; and speaking in moderate rhetorical figures, and in subdued tones, he was never the flaming fanatic or popular exhorter, but just the speaker to address with agreeable effect a small assembly of intelligent and cultivated persons.

Mr. Davis was a man whose dignity, whose political scholarship, whose classical and lofty expressions, whose literary style—unexcelled, perhaps, in the power of *statement* by any cotemporary model,—whose pure morals, well-poised manners and distinguished air, were likely to adorn the high station to which he had been raised, and calculated to qualify him, in many striking respects, as the representative of the proud and chivalrous people of the South. But these accomplishments concealed from the hasty and superficial view defects of character which were most serious, indeed almost vital in their consequences, and which were rapidly to be developed in the course of his administration of the new government. His dignity was the mask of a peculiar obstinacy, which, stimulated by an intellectual conceit, spurned the counsels of equal minds, and rejected the advice of the intelligent, while it was curiously not inconsistent with a complete subserviency to the smallest and most unworthy of favourites. His scholarship smelt of the closet. He had no practical judgment; his intercourse with men was too distant and constrained for studies of human nature; and his estimate of the value of particular men was grotesque and absurd. The especial qualifications of a great leader in the circumstances in which Mr. Davis was placed would have been strong and active common-sense, quick apprehension, knowledge of men, and a disposition to consult the aggregate wisdom of the people, and to gather the store of judgment from every possible source of practical advice within its reach. Mr. Davis had none of these plain qualities. He had, instead of these, certain elegant and brilliant accomplishments, which dazzled the multitude, confused the world in its judgment of his merits, and gave him a singular reputation, in which admirers and censors were strangely mingled : one party, looking at a distance, extravagant in its praise, the other, having a nearer view, unlimited in its condemnation.

But we must reserve a fuller estimate of President Davis' character for other periods in our narrative. While the formidable events we have just been relating—that of the secession of seven Southern States, and their erection of a new government—were taking place, there were on foot measures of pacification, to which attention must be given as well as to measures of hostility. These measures looking towards peace involve the action of the Congress of the United States; the action of States outside of Congress; and certain strange proceedings on the part of the Federal Executive, which were undoubtedly influential in determining the question of peace or war.

In the early part of the session of the United States Congress, a hope of pacification had been generally indulged by the country, and was largely shared by some of the Southern members. Even after the secession of South Carolina, Southern members, who made violent Disunion speeches on the floor of Congress, yet entertained in their private conversation a prospect of adjustment, and confidentially advised their constituents not to sell their city lots in Washington, or dispose of their property interests in the Northern States. But as the session progressed it became evident that no concessions were to be expected from Congress; that the temper of the Republican party was unyielding and insolent; that it was not impressed with any serious danger, and even in the event of a crisis, was confident of subduing the South with such expedition and decision as to make an issue of arms rather to be desired than otherwise. Indeed, the *ultimatum* of the Republican party was distinctly enough announced in resolutions offered by Mr. Clarke of New Hampshire, which passed both houses of Congress. These resolutions declared that the provisions of the Constitution were already ample enough for any emergencies; that it was to be obeyed rather than amended; and that an extrication from present dangers was to be looked for in strenuous efforts to preserve the peace, protect the public property, and enforce the laws, rather than in new guaranties for peculiar interests, compromises for particular difficulties, or concessions to unreasonable demands. Under this surface of smooth words, the proposition was plain that the demands of the South were unreasonable, and not to be allowed, and were to be resisted to the extremities of coercion and war.

Committees in both houses had been appointed to consider the state of the Union. Neither committee was able to agree upon any mode of settlement of the pending issue between the North and the South. The Republican members in both committees rejected propositions acknowledging the right of property in slaves, or recommending the division of the Territories between the slaveholding and non-slaveholding States by a geographical line.

On the 18th of December, 1860, Mr. Crittenden of Kentucky had introduced in the Senate a series of resolutions which contained a plan of compromise, which it was long hoped would be effected, and which for months continued a topic of discussion in Congress. The features of this plan may be briefly indicated. It sought to incorporate into the Constitution the following propositions :

1. That south of a certain geographical parallel of latitude, Congress, or a Territorial Legislature, shall have no power to abolish, modify, or in any way interfere with slavery in the Territories.

2. That Congress shall have no power to abolish slavery in the District of Columbia ;

3. Or in the forts, arsenals, dock-yards, or wherever else the Federal Government has exclusive jurisdiction.

4. That in case of the failure to arrest any alleged " fugitive from service," from violence to the officer of the law, or intimidation of his authority, the community where such failure took place shall be compelled to pay the value of such alleged fugitive to the owner thereof, and may be prosecuted for that purpose and to that effect.

The fate of this measure was significant enough of the views and temper of the Republican party, if any additional evidence of these had been needed. In the Senate it was voted against by every Republican senator ; and again, every Republican in that body voted to substitute for Mr. Crittenden's propositions the resolutions of Mr. Clarke, to which reference has already been made.

In the House, certain propositions moved by Mr. Etheridge, which were even less favourable to the South than Mr. Crittenden's, were not even entertained, on a vote of yeas and nays ; and a resolution giving a pledge to sustain the President in the use of force against seceding States was adopted by a large majority.

It is remarkable that of all the compromises proposed in this Congress for preserving the peace of the country, none came from Northern men ; they came from the South, and were defeated by the North ! The " Crittenden Compromise " (for a geographical limit within which to *tolerate*, not establish slavery in the Territories) was, as we have seen, the principal feature of these pacific negotiations ; it was considered fully capable to reconstruct the Union ; it had even the adhesion or countenance of such influential leaders of Secession as Toombs, of Georgia, and Jefferson Davis, the future President of the Southern Confederacy ; it constituted under the circumstances the only possible existing hope of saving the Union. But, unfortunately for the peace of the country, the North deliberately defeated it.

While the door of Congress was thus closed to peace, there was outside of it a remarkable effort at conciliation, which testified to the popular anxiety on the subject. The action of the States was invoked. Commissioners from twenty States, composing a "Peace Conference," held at the request of the Legislature of Virginia, met in Washington on the 4th of February, and adjourned February 27th. All the Border Slave States were represented. Most of the delegates from these States were willing to accept the few and feeble guaranties of the Crittenden proposition. The ultimate result was the recommendation of a project to Congress which, in detail, was less favourable to the South than that contained in Mr. Crittenden's resolutions, but generally identical with it in respect of running a geographical line between the slaveholding and non-slaveholding territories, and enforcing the provisions of the Fugitive Slave Law. One curious additional feature was that no territory should in the future be acquired by the United States, without the concurrence of the Senators from the Southern States and those from the Northern States. But it is useless to go into the details of the report of the Peace Commissioners; for it never received any steady or respectful consideration in either house of Congress. In the Senate it was summarily voted down by a vote of twenty-eight to seven; and the House, on a call of yeas and nays, actually refused to receive it.

There was an evident disposition on the part of the so-called Border Slave States to avoid a decisive step. To this hesitation the North gave a significance which it did not really possess. It is true that Tennessee and North Carolina decided against calling a State Convention; but this action implied simply that they were awaiting the results of the peace propositions to which they had committed themselves. The State of Virginia, which had distinguished herself by a conspicuous effort to save the Union—for it was on the unanimous invitation of her Legislature that the Peace Conference had been assembled—had called a State Convention in the month of January. It was elected on the 4th of February; and the Northern party found singular gratification in the circumstance that a majority of Union men was returned to an assembly so critical.

There is no doubt the Convention of Virginia was sincerely anxious by every means in its power to restore the Union. But the party in favour of secession was steadily strengthening in view of the obstinate front presented by the Black Republican party in Congress. Delegates who had been returned as Union men, were afterwards instructed to vote otherwise. Petersburg, Culpepper, Cumberland, Prince Edward, Botetourt, Wythe, and many other towns and counties, held meetings and urged prompt secession. The action of the Federal authorities was daily becoming more irritating and alarming. A garrison was thrown into Fort Washington on the Potomac; and it was observed that guns were being mounted on the parapet of Fortress Monroe, and turned inland upon the very bosom of Virginia.

However Virginia might have lingered, in the hope that the breach that had taken place in the Union might be repaired by new constitutional guaranties, there could be no doubt, in view of her record in the past, that whenever the issue of war was made, whenever the *coercion* of the seceded States should be attempted, she would then be on the side of Southern Independence, prompt to risk all consequences. The Federal government could not have been blind to this; for the precedents of the State were well known. The Resolutions of '98 and '99, originated by Mr. Jefferson, constituted the text-book of State-Rights, and vindicated and maintained the right and duty of States suffering grievances from unjust and unconstitutional Federal legislation, to judge of the wrong as well as of " the mode and measure of redress." At every period of controversy between Federal and State authority, the voice of Virginia was the first to be heard in behalf of State Rights. In 1832-'33, the Governor of Virginia, John Floyd, the elder, had declared that Federal troops should not pass the banks of the Potomac to coerce South Carolina into obedience to the tariff laws, unless over his dead body; and a majority of the Legislature of Virginia had then indicated their recognition of the right of a State to secede from the Union. At every stage of the agitation of the slavery question in Congress and in the Northern States, Virginia declared her sentiments, and entered upon her legislative records declarations that she would resist the aggressive spirit of the Northern majority, even to the disruption of the ties that bound her to the Union. In 1848, she had resolved, in legislative council, that she would not submit to the passage of the Wilmot proviso, or any kindred measure. From the date of the organization of the Anti-Slavery party, her people, of all parties, had declared that the election of an abolitionist to the Presidency would be a virtual declaration of war against the South. The Legislature that assembled a few weeks after Mr. Lincoln's election, declared, in effect, with only four dissenting voices, that the interests of Virginia were thoroughly identified with those of the other Southern States, and that any intimation from any source, that her people were looking to any combination in the last resort other than union with them, was unpatriotic and treasonable.— In view of a record so plain and explicit, it was madness to suppose that the Convention of 1861 entertained any desire to cling to the Union other than by constitutional guaranties, or that Virginia would hesitate for a moment to separate from that Union whenever it should actually undertake to subjugate her sister States of the South.

We have seen that there was but little prospect of peace in the proceedings of Congress, or in the action of the people, outside of Congress, through the forms of State authority. The conduct of the Federal Executive afforded no better prospect; indeed, instead of being negative in its results, it did much to vex the country and to provoke hostility.

The policy of Mr. Buchanan was unfortunately weak and hesitating—

an attempt at ambidexterity, in which he equally failed to conciliate the Secessionists and pacify their designs, or to make any resolute effort to save the Union. He had, in his message to Congress, denounced secession as revolutionary; and although he was clear in the constitutional proposition that there was no right of "coercion" on the part of the Federal Government, yet he did but little, and that irresolutely, to put that Government in a state of defence, in the event of violence on the part of the seceded States. This timid old man—a cautious, secretive politician, who never felt the warmth of an emotion, and had been bred in the harsh school of political selfishness—attempted to stand between two parties; and the result was embarrassment, double-dealing, weak and despicable querulousness, and, finally, the condemnation and contempt of each of the parties between whom he attempted to distribute his favours.

It is true that Mr. Buchanan was over-censured by the North for his failure to reinforce the garrisons of the Southern forts. When Gen. Scott, on the 15th of December, 1860, recommended that nine Federal fortifications in the Southern States should be effectively garrisoned, there were only five companies of Federal troops within his reach; and he could only have intended in proposing such an impracticable measure to make a certain reputation rather as a politician than as a general. Again, when, six weeks later, Gen. Scott renewed this recommendation, the fact was that the whole force at his command consisted of six hundred recruits, obtained since the date of his first recommendation, in addition to the five regular companies. The army of the United States was still out of reach on the remote frontiers; and Gen. Scott must have known that it would be impossible to withdraw it during mid-winter in time for this military operation.

But while Mr. Buchanan's course in refusing to distribute a thousand men among the numerous forts in the Cotton States, as well as Fortress Monroe, is, in a measure, defensible against Northern criticism, for such a proceeding would have been an exhibition of weakness instead of strength, and, at the time, a dangerous provocation to the seceded States, yet, in this same matter, he was about to commit an act of perfidy, for which there can be neither excuse nor disguise. He had refused to reinforce Fort Moultrie in Charleston Harbour, for the reason that it might provoke and alarm the Secession party, and disturb the movements in Congress and in the country then looking towards peace. But, for the same reason, he gave the distinct and solemn pledge that he would permit the military *status quo* in Charleston Harbour to remain unless South Carolina herself should attempt to disturb it. No language could be more explicit than that in which this pledge was conveyed.

The official instructions made on the 11th of December to Major Anderson, then in command of Fort Moultrie, ran as follows:

" You are aware of the great anxiety of the Secretary of War that a collision of the troops with the people of the State shall be avoided, and of his studied determination to pursue a course with reference to the military force and forts in this harbour, which shall guard against such a collision. He has, therefore, carefully abstained from increasing the force at this point, or taking any measures which might add to the present excited state of the public mind, or which would throw any doubt on the confidence he feels that South Carolina will not attempt by violence to obtain possession of the public works or interfere with their occupancy. The smallness of your force will not permit you, perhaps, to occupy more than one of the three forts, but *an attack on or attempt to take possession of either one of them will be regarded as an act of hostility*, and you may *then* put your command into either of them which you may deem most proper to increase its power of resistance."

On the day previous to the date of these instructions, the South Carolina delegation had called on the President ; the distinct object of their visit being to consult with him as to the best means of avoiding a hostile collision between their State and the Federal Government. At the instance of Mr. Buchanan, their communication was put in writing, and they presented him the following note :

" In compliance with our statement to you yesterday, we now express to you our strong conviction that neither the constituted authorities, nor any body of the people of the State of South Carolina, will either attack or molest the United States forts in the harbour of Charleston, previously to the action of the convention ; and we hope and believe not until an offer has been made through an accredited representative to negotiate for an amicable arrangement of all matters between the State and Federal Government, provided that no reinforcements be sent into these forts, and *their relative military status shall remain as at present.*"

Yet we have seen how this military *status* was disturbed by Major Anderson's removal to Fort Sumter, an act which greatly strengthened his position, which put him from an untenable post into what was then supposed to be an impregnable defence, which changed the *status*, quite as much so as an accession of numerical force, and which, to the State of South Carolina, could have none other than a hostile significance. Mr. Buchanan was reminded of his pledge, and asked to order Major Anderson back to Fort Moultrie. He refused to do so. Mr. Floyd, of Virginia, the Secretary of War, in view of the President's violation of faith, and the atempt to make him a party to it, withdrew from the cabinet in a high state of indignation ; and thus was accomplished the first act of Mr. Buchanan's perfidy on the eve of war.

The second was soon to follow. After determining not to order Anderson back to Fort Moultrie, President Buchanan determined to take another step—actually to send troops to Sumter. Under his direction the War Department chartered a steamer called the "Star of the West," which sailed from New York on the 5th of January, 1861, having on board two hundred and fifty soldiers, besides stores and munitions of war. A specious plea was originated for this expedition, and it was declared that its purpose was to provision a "starving garrison." When the vessel appeared off Charleston Harbour, on the 9th of January, heading in from the sea, and taking the channel for Sumter, a battery at Point Cummings on Morris Island opened upon her at long range. Not daring to penetrate the fire, the Star of the West ran out to sea with all speed; and the soldiers on board of her were subsequently disembarked at their former quarters on Governour's Island.

When the result of this expedition was known, Mr. Buchanan affected surprise and indignation at the reception given the Federal reinforcements, and declared that the expedition had been ordered with the concurrence of his Cabinet. Mr. Jacob Thompson of Mississippi, who yet remained in the Cabinet, repelled the slander, denounced the movement as underhanded, and as a breach not only of good faith towards South Carolina, but as one of personal confidence between the President and himself, and left the Cabinet with expressions of indignation and contempt.

Mr. Buchanan's administration terminated with results alike fearful to the country and dishonourable to himself. He retired from office, after having widened the breach between North and South, and given new cause of exasperation in the contest; obtaining the execrations of both parties; and going down to history with the brand of perfidy. When he ceased to be President on the 4th of March, 1861, seven Southern States were out of the Union; they had erected a new government; they had secured every Federal fort within their limits with two exceptions—Sumter and Pickens; they had gathered not only munitions of war, but had obtained great additions in moral power; and although they still deplored a war between the two sections as "a policy detrimental to the civilized world," they had openly and rapidly prepared for it. Fort Moultrie and Castle Pinckney had been occupied by the South Carolina troops; Fort Pulaski, the defence of the Savannah, had been taken; the Arsenal at Mount Vernon, Alabama, with twenty thousand stand of arms, had been seized by the Alabama troops; Fort Morgan, in Mobile Bay, had been taken; Forts Jackson, St. Philip, and Pike, near New Orleans, had been captured by the Louisiana troops; the Pensacola Navy-Yard and Forts Barrancas and McRae had been taken, and the siege of Fort Pickens commenced; the Baton Rouge Arsenal had been surrendered to the Louisiana troops; the New Orleans Mint and Custom-House had been taken; the Little Rock Arsenal had been seized by the Arkansas troops;

and on the 18th of February, Gen. Twiggs had transferred the military posts and public property in Texas to the State authorities.

It is remarkable that all these captures and events had been accomplished without the sacrifice of a single life, or the effusion of one drop of blood. It was, perhaps, in view of this circumstance, that people lingered in the fancy that there would be no war. Yet the whole country was agitated with passion; the frown of war was already visible; and it needed but some Cadmus to throw the stone that would be the signal of combat between the armed men sprung from the dragon's teeth.

CHAPTER VI.

A LARGE portion of the Northern people have a custom of apotheosis, at least so far as to designate certain of their public men, to question whose reputation is considered bold assumption, if not sacrilegious daring. But the maxim of *de mortuis nil nisi bonum* does not apply to history. The character of Abraham Lincoln belongs to history as fully as that of the meanest agent in human affairs ; and his own declaration, on one occa sion, that he did not expect to "escape" it is sure to be verified, now or hereafter.

We have already stated that Mr. Lincoln was not elected President of the United States for any commanding fame, or for any known merit as a statesman. His panegyrists, although they could not assert for him a guiding intellect or profound scholarship, claimed for him some homely and substantial virtues. It was said that he was transparently honest. But his honesty was rather that facile disposition that readily took impressions from whatever was urged on it. It was said that he was excessively amiable. But his amiability was animal. It is small merit to have a Falstaffian humour in one's blood. Abraham Lincoln was neither kind nor cruel, in the proper sense of these words, simply because he was destitute of the higher order of sensibilities.

His appearance corresponded to his rough life and uncultivated mind. His figure was tall and gaunt-looking; his shoulders were inclined forward; his arms of unusual length; and his gait astride, rapid and shuffling. The savage wits in the Southern newspapers had no other name for him than "the Illinois Ape."

The new President of the United States was the product of that partizanship which often discovers its most "available" candidates among obscure men, with slight political records, and of that infamous demagogueism in America that is pleased with the low and vulgar antecedents of its public men, and enjoys the imagination of similar elevation for each one of its own class in society. Mr. Lincoln had formerly served, without distinction, in Congress. But among his titles to American popularity were the circumstances that in earlier life he had rowed a flat-boat down the Mississippi; afterwards been a miller; and at another period had earned his living by splitting rails in a county of Illinois. When he was first named for the Presidency, an enthusiastic admirer had presented to the State Convention of Illinois two old fence-rails, gaily decorated with flags and ribbons, and bearing the following inscription: "Abraham Lincoln, the Rail Candidate for President in 1860.—Two rails from a lot of 3,000, made in 1830, by Thos. Hanks and Abe Lincoln." The incident is not mentioned for amusement: it is a suggestive illustration of the vulgar and silly devices in an American election.

Since the announcement of his election, Mr. Lincoln had remained very retired and studiously silent in his home at Springfield, Illinois. Expectations were raised by the mystery of this silence; his panegyrists declared that it was the indication of a thoughtful wisdom pondering the grave concerns of the country, and likely to announce at last some novel and profound solution of existing difficulties; and so credulous are all men in a time of anxiety and embarrassment, and so eager to catch at hopes, that these fulsome prophecies of the result of Mr. Lincoln's meditations actually impressed the country, which awaited with impatience the opening of the oracle's lips.

Never was a disappointment so ludicrous. No sooner did Mr. Lincoln leave his home on his official journey to Washington, than he became profuse of speech, entertaining the crowd, that at different points of the railroad watched his progress to the capital, with a peculiar style of stump oratory, in which his Western phraseology, jests, and comic displays amused the whole country in the midst of a great public anxiety. He was reported to have been for months nursing a masterly wisdom at Springfield ; he was approaching the capital on an occasion and in circumstances the most imposing in American history ; and yet he had no better counsels to offer to the distressed country than to recommend his hearers to "keep cool," and to assure them in his peculiar rhetoric and grammar that "nobody was hurt," and that there was "nothing going wrong." The new President brought with him the buffoonery and habits of a demagogue of the back-woods. He amused a crowd by calling up to the speaker's stand a woman, who had recommended him to grow whiskers on his face, and kissing her in public ; he measured heights with the tall men he encountered in his public receptions ; and, as part of the ceremony of the inauguration at Washington, he insisted upon kissing the thirty-four young women who, in striped colours and spangled dresses, represented in the procession the thirty-four States of the Union. These incidents are not improperly recorded : they are not trivial in connection with a historical name, and with reference to an occasion the most important in American annals.

At Philadelphia, where Mr. Lincoln was required to assist in raising a United States flag over Independence Hall, he was more serious in his speech than on any former occasion in his journey. In his address was this language : " that sentiment in the Declaration of Independence which gave Liberty, not alone to the people of this country, but, I hope, to the world for all future time. It was that which gave promise that, in due time, the weight would be lifted from the shoulders of all men." These words were supposed to be aimed at the institution of negro slavery in the South. With reference to them a Baltimore newspaper said : " Mr. Lincoln, the President elect of the United States, will arrive in this city, with his suite, this afternoon by special train from Harrisburg, and will proceed, we learn, directly to Washington. It is to be hoped that no opportunity will be afforded him—or that, if it be afforded, he will not embrace it—to repeat in our midst the sentiments which he is reported to have expressed yesterday in Philadelphia." This newspaper paragraph and some other circumstances equally trivial were made the occasion of an alarm that the new President was to be assassinated in Baltimore, or on his way to that city. The alarm was communicated to Mr. Lincoln himself. He was in bed at the time in Harrisburg. He at once determined to leave by a special train direct to Washington. Not satisfied with thus avoiding Baltimore, his alarm took the most unusual precautions. The telegraph wires were put beyond the reach of any one who might desire to use them. His departure was kept a profound secret. His person was disguised in a very long military cloak; a Scotch plaid cap was put on his head; and thus curiously attired, the President of the United States made his advent to Washington. "Had he," said the Baltimore *Sun*, "entered Willard's Hotel with a 'head-spring' and a 'summersault' and the clown's merry greeting to Gen. Scott, 'Here we are,' the country could not have been more surprised at the exhibition." *

Mr. Lincoln's nervous alarm for his personal safety did not subside with his arrival in Washington. General Scott, who was in military command there, had already collected in the capital more than six hundred regular troops, and had called out the District militia, to resist an attempt which would be made by an armed force to prevent the inauguration of President Lincoln and to seize the public property. He insisted upon this imagination; he pretended violent alarm; he had evidently made up his mind for a military drama, and the display of himself on the occasion of Mr. Lincoln's inauguration. His vanity was foolish. A committee of the House of Representatives investigated the causes of alarm, heard the General himself, and decided that his apprehensions were unfounded. But he would not be quieted. He communicated his fears to Mr. Lincoln to such effect, that for some time before and after his inauguration soldiers were placed at his gate, and the grand reception-room of the White House was converted into quarters for troops from Kansas, who, under the command of the notorious Jim Lane, had volunteered to guard the chamber of the President.

Inauguration-day passed peacefully and quietly, but was attended by an extraordinary military display. Troops were stationed in different parts of the city; sentinels were posted on the tops of the highest houses and other eminences; the President moved to the Capitol in a hollow square of cavalry; and from the East portico delivered his inaugural address with a row of bayonets standing between him and his audience.

The address was such an attempt at ambidexterity as might be expected from an embarrassed and ill-educated man. It was a singular mixture. The new President said he was strongly in favour of the mainten-

---

* The silly or jocose story of the intended assassination was, that a party of Secessionists had plotted to throw the train of cars on which Mr. Lincoln was expected to travel to Baltimore, down a steep embankment, and this project failing, to murder him in the streets of Baltimore. But Mr. Lincoln left his wife and children to take the threatened route to Baltimore, and to risk the reported conspiracy to throw the cars from the track; and it turned out that they arrived safe at their journey's end, and without accident of any sort.

ance of the Union and was opposed to Secession; but he was equally against the principle of coercion, provided the rights of the United States government were not interfered with. He gave a *quasi* pledge not to appoint Federal officers for communities unanimously hostile to the authority of the Union; he appeared to proceed on the supposition that the South had only to be disabused of her impressions and apprehensions of Northern hostility; in one breath he exclaimed: "we are not enemies but friends;" in another he made the following significant declaration:

"The power confided to me *will be used to hold, occupy, and possess the property and places belonging to the Government*, and collect the duties and imposts; but, beyond what may be necessary for these objects, there will be no invasion, no using of force against or among the people anywhere."

The address was variously received, according to the political opinions of the country, and made decided friends in no quarter. Mr. Lincoln's own party was displeased with it; and the Republican newspapers declared that its tone was deprecatory and even apologetic. The Northern Democrats had no violent disapproval to express. The Border Slave States, which yet remained in the Union, were undetermined as to its meaning, but regarded it with suspicion. In fact it was with reference to these that Mr. Lincoln was embarrassed, if he was not actually at this time balancing between peace and war. If coercion was attempted towards the seceded States, the Border Slave States would go out of the Union, and the country would be lost. If a pacific policy was adopted, the Chicago platform would go to pieces, and the Black Republican party would be broken into fragments.

There is reason to believe that for some weeks after Mr. Lincoln's inauguration there was a serious pause in his mind on the question of peace or war. His new Secretary of State, Mr. Seward, at the New England Dinner in New York, had confidently predicted a settlement of all the troubles "within *sixty days*"—a phrase, by the way, that was to be frequently repeated in the course of four long years. Mr. Horace Greeley testifies that on visiting Washington some two weeks or more after Mr. Lincoln's inauguration, he was "surprised to see and hear on every hand what were to him convincing proofs that an early collision with the 'Confederates' was not seriously apprehended in the highest quarters." If there was really an interval of indecision in the first days of Mr. Lincoln's administration, it was rapidly overcome by partisan influences, for his apparent vacillation was producing disaffection in the Black Republican party, and the clamour of their disappointment was plainly heard in Washington.

In the seceded States the inaugural address had been interpreted as a menace of war. This interpretation was confirmed by other circumstances than the text of Mr. Lincoln's speech. In every department of the public service there had been placed by the new President violent abolitionists and men whose hatred of the South was notorious and unrelenting. The *Pennsylvanian*, a newspaper published in Philadelphia, said : " Mr. Lincoln stands to-day where he stood on the 6th of November last, *on the Chicago Platform*. He has not receded a single hair's breadth. *He has appointed a Cabinet in which there is no slaveholder—a thing that has never before happened since the formation of the Government ;* and in which there are but two nominally Southern men, and both bitter Black Republicans of the radical dye. Let the Border States ignominiously *submit* to the Abolition rule of this Lincoln Administration, if they like ; but *don't let the miserable submissionists pretend to be deceived.* Make any base or cowardly excuse but this."

But whatever may have been the just apprehensions of the Confederate Government at Montgomery, it exhibited no violent or tumultuous spirit, and made the most sedulous efforts to resist the consequence of war. There can be no doubt of the sincerity and zeal of its efforts to effect a peaceable secession, and to avoid a war which it officially deplored as " a policy detrimental to the civilized world."

As early as February, prior even to the inauguration of Mr. Lincoln, the Confederate Congress had passed a resolution expressive of their desire for the appointment of commissioners to be sent to the Government of the United States, " for the purpose of negotiating friendly relations between that government and the Confederate States of America, and for the settlement of all questions of disagreement between the two governments upon principles of right, justice, equity, and good faith."

In pursuance of this resolution, and in furtherance of his own views, Mr. Davis deputed an embassy of commissioners to Washington, authorized to negotiate for the removal of the Federal garrisons from Forts Pickens and Sumter, and to provide for the settlement of all claims of public property arising out of the separation of the States from the Union. Two of the commissioners, Martin Crawford of Georgia, and John Forsythe of Alabama, attended in Washington, arriving there on the 5th of March. They gave only an informal notice of their arrival, with a view to afford time to the President, who had just been inaugurated, for the discharge of other pressing official duties in the organization of his administration, before engaging his attention in the object of their mission. On the 12th of March, they addressed an official communication to Mr. Seward, Secretary of State, explaining the functions of the embassy and its purposes.

Mr. Seward declined to make any official recognition of the commissioners, but very readily consented, for purposes which the sequel demonstrated, to hold verbal conferences with them, through the friendly inter mediation of Judge Campbell of Alabama. Through this gentleman, the commissioners, who had consented to waive all questions of form, received constant assurances from the Government of the United States of peaceful intentions, of the determination to evacuate Fort Sumter; and further that no measures, changing the existing *status*, prejudicially to the Confederate States, especially at Fort Pickens, were in contemplation; but that, in the event of any change of intention on the subject, notice would be given to the commissioners.

It was confidentially explained to the commissioners that to treat with them at that particular juncture might seriously embarrass the administration of Mr. Lincoln with popular opinion in the North; and they were recommended to patience and urged to confidence by assurances which keener diplomatists than these ill-chosen representatives of the Confederacy might have had reason to doubt.

But, at last, at the opportune time, this game with the commissioners was to be terminated. Dull and credulous as they were, their attention was, at last, attracted to the extraordinary preparations for an extensive military and naval expedition in New York, and other Northern ports. These preparations, commenced in secresy, for an expedition whose destination was concealed, only became known when nearly completed, and on the 5th, 6th, and 7th April transports and vessels of war, with troops, munitions, and military supplies, sailed from Northern ports bound southwards. Alarmed by so extraordinary a demonstration, the commissioners requested the delivery of an answer to their official communication of the 12th March, and thereupon received, on the 8th April, a reply dated on the 15th of the previous month, from which it appeared that during the whole interval, whilst the commissioners were receiving assurances calculated to inspire hope of the success of their mission, the Secretary of State and the President of the United States had already determined to hold no intercourse with them whatever; to refuse even to listen to any proposals they had to make, and had profited by the delay created by their own assurances, in order to prepare secretly the means for effective hostile operations.

Of this remarkable deception, and the disreputable method by which it had been obtained, President Davis justly and severely remarked, in a message to the Confederate Congress: "The crooked paths of diplomacy can scarcely furnish an example so wanting in courtesy, in candour, and directness, as was the course of the United States Government towards our commissioners in Washington."

While the Confederate commissioners were thus being hoodwinked and betrayed, the reinforcement of Sumter was the subject of constant Cabinet consultation at Washington, held in profound secresy from the public, and surrounded by an air of mystery that gave occasion for the most various rumours. Gen. Scott had advised the President that, in his military judgment, it had become impracticable to reinforce Fort Sumter, on account of the number of batteries erected by the Confederates at the mouth of the harbour; that an entrance from the sea was impossible. But Mr. Lincoln, and especially one member of his Cabinet, Mr. Blair, were firm in their refusal to evacuate the fort. It now became the concern of the government to avoid the difficulty of military reinforcements by some artifice that would equally well answer its purposes. That artifice was the subject of secret and sedulous consultation, that extended through several weeks.

About the last of March, Capt. Fox, of the Federal Navy, was sent to Charleston by the government, and stated that his object was entirely pacific. He was, by a strange credulity, allowed to visit the fort and to communicate with Major Anderson. His real object was to carry concealed despatches to Major Anderson, and to collect information with reference to a plan for the reinforcement of the garrison. On his return to Washington he was called frequently before President Lincoln and his Cabinet to explain his plan for reinforcing the fort, and to answer the objections presented by Gen. Scott and the military authorities. The project involved passing batteries with steamers or boats at night at right angles to the Confederate line of fire, and thirteen hundred yards distant —a feat which Capt. Fox argued was entirely practicable, and that many safe examples of it had been furnished by the Crimean War.

In this conflict of counsels the Washington administration hesitated. Mr. Lincoln, at one time, although with bitter reluctance, agreed that the fort should be evacuated, if the responsibility of the act could be thrown on the preceding administration of Mr. Buchanan. A leading article for a New York paper had been prepared, the proof-sheet of which was submitted to Mr. Lincoln and approved. In this, the ground was taken that the evacuation was an absolute military necessity, brought about by treason on the part of Mr. Buchanan, who, it was insisted, might have reinforced and supplied the garrison, but not only failed to do so, but purposely left it in such condition as to force his successor in office to encounter the ignominy of yielding it up to the Southerners. This same article lauded Mr. Lincoln's pacific policy, saying: " Had war—not peace —been his object,—*had he desired to raise throughout the mighty North a feeling of indignation which in ninety days would have emancipated every slave on the continent, and driven their masters into the sea*—if need be, he had only to have said—" Let the garrison of Fort Sumter do their duty, *and perish beneath its walls:* and on the heads of the traitours and rebels and slavery propagandists be the consequences."

And yet the horrible alternative depicted here and indicated as the means of rousing the North to a war of extermination upon slavery and slave-owners, was eventually and deliberately adopted by Mr. Lincoln. The point with the government was to devise some artifice for the relief of Fort Sumter, short of open military reinforcements, decided to be impracticable, and which would have the effect of inaugurating the war by a safe indirection and under a plausible and convenient pretence. The device was at last conceived. On the afternoon of the 4th of April, President Lincoln sent for Capt. Fox, and said he had decided to let the expedition go, but he would send a messenger from himself to the authorities at Charleston, declaring that the purpose of the expedition was only to *provision* the fort, peaceably or forcibly, as they might decide for themselves.

Meanwhile the dalliance with the Confederate commissioners—the part of the artifice allotted to Secretary Seward—was kept up to the last moment. At one time Mr. Seward had declared to Judge Campbell, who was acting as an intermediary between the Secretary and the commissioners, that before a letter, the draft of which Judge Campbell held in his hand, could reach President Davis at Montgomery, Fort Sumter would have been evacuated. Five days passed, and instead of evacuating, Major Anderson was busy in strengthening Sumter! A telegram from Gen. Beauregard informed the commissioners of this. Again Judge Campbell saw Mr. Seward, and again, in the presence of a third party, received from him assurances that the fort was to be evacuated, and was authorized by him to state to the commissioners, that " the government will not undertake to supply Fort Sumter, without giving notice to Governor Pickens." This was on the 1st of April. On the 7th, Judge Campbell again addressed Mr. Seward a letter, alluding to the anxiety and alarm excited by the great naval and military preparations of the government, and asking whether the peaceful assurances he had given were well or ill founded. Mr. Seward's reply was laconic: " Faith as to Sumter fully kept: *wait and see!* " On the very day that Mr. Seward uttered these words, the van of the Federal fleet, with a heavy force of soldiers, had sailed for the Southern coast !

THE REDUCTION OF FORT SUMTER.

On the 3d of March President Davis had commissioned P. G. T. Beauregard, then Colonel of Engineers in the Confederate service, Brigadier-general, with official directions to proceed to Charleston, and assume command of all the troops in actual service in and around that place. On arriving there he immediately examined the fortifications, and undertook the construction of additional works for the reduction of Fort Sumter, and the defence of the entrances to the harbour.

On three sides, formidable batteries of cannon and mortars bore upon the Fort. On the south, at a distance of about twelve hundred yards, was Cumming's Point on Morris' Island, where three batteries had been completed, mounting six guns and six mortars. Farthest off of these, was the Trapier battery, built very strongly with heavy beams and sand-bags, and containing three eight-inch mortars; next the " iron battery," covered over with railroad bars, and having thick iron plates to close the embrasures after the guns were fired. Nearest to Sumter was the " Point battery," a very large and strong work, containing three ten-inch mortars, two forty-two pounders and a rifled cannon. From these works, a long line of batteries stretched down the sea side of Morris' Island, commanding the ship channel, and threatening a terrible ordeal to the Federal vessels, should they attempt to enter. Nearly west of Sumter, on James' Island, was Fort Johnson, where a strong battery of mortars and cannon was erected. On the northeast was Fort Moultrie, ready with Columbiads, Dahlgren guns, mortars, and furnaces for red-hot shot. In the cove near the western end of Sullivan's Island, was anchored a floating battery, constructed of the peculiarly fibrous palmetto timber, sheathed with plate iron, and mounting four guns of heavy calibre.

On the 8th day of April a message was conveyed to Gov. Pickens of South Carolina, by Lieut. Talbot, an authorized agent of the Federal Government. It was as follows :

" I am directed by the President of the United States, to notify you to expect an attempt will be made to supply Fort Sumter with provisions only, and that if such attempt be not resisted, no effort to throw in men, arms, or ammunition will be made, without further notice, or in case of an attack upon the fort."

The long suspense was over; the Federal fleet was approaching the coast. The message was telegraphed by Gen. Beauregard to Montgomery, and the instructions of his Government asked. Mr. Walker, the Confederate Secretary of War, replied, that if there was no doubt as to the authorized character of the messenger, Beauregard should at once demand the evacuation of Sumter, and if refused, should proceed to reduce it. The demand was made at two o'clock of the 11th April. Major Anderson replied : " I have the honour to acknowledge the receipt of your communication demanding the evacuation of this Fort, and to say in reply thereto, that it is a demand with which I regret that my sense of honour and of my obligation to my Government prevent my compliance." Nothing was left but to accept the distinct challenge of the Federal Government to arms. A little past three o'clock in the morning of April 12th, Gen. Beauregard communicated by his aides with Major Anderson, notifying him that " he would open the fire of his batteries on Fort Sumter in one hour from that time."

At 4.30 A. M., the signal shell was fired from Fort Johnson. The fire from Fort Johnson was quickly followed by that of Moultrie, Cumming's Point, and the floating battery. The incessant flash of the ordnance made a circle of flame, and the bursting of bombs over and in Fort Sumter became more and more constant as the proper range was obtained by the artillerists.

Fort Sumter did not reply until seven o'clock. About that hour, it poured a well-directed stream of balls and shell against Moultrie, the floating battery, and the work on Cumming's Point. The fire continued throughout the day. Towards evening it became evident that that of the Confederates was very effective. The enemy was driven from his barbette guns; several of them were disabled; the parapet walls had crumbled away; deep chasms had opened below; the embrasures of the casemates had been so shattered as no longer to present a regular outline; the chimneys and roofs of the houses were in ruins.

While this bombardment was going on, a portion of the Federal fleet had reached the rendezvous off Charleston. It attempted to take no part in the fight. The only explanation of this extraordinary conduct of the naval expedition is found in a curious account from the pen of Capt. Fox himself. He writes: "As we neared the land, heavy guns were heard, and the smoke and shells from the batteries which had just opened fire on Sumter were distinctly visible. I immediately stood out to inform Capt. Rowan, of the Pawnee, but met him coming in. He hailed me and asked for a pilot, declaring his intention of standing into the harbour and sharing the fate of his brethren of the army. I went on board, and informed him that I would answer for it, that *the Government did not expect any such gallant sacrifice,* having settled maturely upon the policy indicated in the instructions to Capt. Mercer and myself."

Early in the morning of the 13th, all of the Confederate batteries re-opened upon Fort Sumter, which responded vigorously for a time, directing its fire specially against Fort Moultrie. At eight o'clock A. M., smoke was seen issuing from the quarters of Fort Sumter; upon this, the fire of the Confederate batteries was increased, as a matter of course, for the purpose of bringing the enemy to terms as speedily as possible, inasmuch as his flag was still floating defiantly above him. Fort Sumter continued to fire from time to time, but at long and irregular intervals, amid the dense smoke, flying shot, and bursting shells. The Confederate troops, carried away by their naturally generous impulses, mounted the different batteries, and at every discharge from the fort, cheered the garrison for its pluck and gallantry, and hooted the fleet lying inactive just outside the bar.

A little past one o'clock a shot from Moultrie struck the flag-staff of Sumter, and brought down the ensign. At this time the condition of

Sumter and its garrison, had become desperate; the interiour was a heap of ruins; the parapet had been so shattered that few of its guns remained mounted; the smoke was packed in the casemates so as to render it impossible for the men to work the guns; the number of the garrison was too small to relieve each other; incessant watching and labour had exhausted their strength. The conflagration, from the large volume of smoke, being apparently on the increase, Gen. Beauregard sent three of his aides with a message to Major Anderson, to the effect that seeing his flag no longer flying, his quarters in flames, and supposing him to be in distress, he desired to offer him any assistance he might stand in need of. Before his aides reached the fort, the Federal flag was displayed on the parapets, but remained there only a short time, when it was hauled down, and a white flag substituted in its place.

The fort had surrendered. The event was instantly announced in every part of Charleston by the ringing of bells, the pealing of cannon, the shouts of couriers dashing through the streets, and by every indication of general rejoicing. " As an honourable testimony to the gallantry and fortitude with which Major Anderson and his command had defended their posts," Gen. Beauregard not only agreed that they might take passage at their convenience for New York, but allowed him, on leaving the fort, to salute his flag with fifty guns. In firing the salute, a caisson exploded, which resulted in mortal injuries to four of the garrison. This was the only loss of life in the whole affair. It appeared indeed that a Divine control had made this combat bloodless; and that so wonderful an exemption might have invited both sections of America to thoughts of gratitude and peace.*

But it was not to be so. The fire of the war first drawn at Sumter produced an instant and universal excitement in the North. It convinced the people of that section that there was no longer any prospect of recovering the Southern States by the cheap policy of double and paltering speeches. From the madness of their conviction, that they could no longer hope to accomplish their purposes by peaceful deceits and amusements of compromise, there was a sudden and quick current of public sentiment in the North towards the policy of coercion, with the most instant exertions to effect it.

The battle of Sumter had been brought on by the Washington Govern-

* The North has been famous for cheap heroes in this war. Major Anderson was one of the earliest. When he arrived in the North from Sumter, he was greatly lionized, and travelled around the country feasting and speech-making. He was promoted to the rank of brigadier-general, and appointed to command the forces then gathering in Kentucky for the Western campaign. But he unexpectedly resigned; probably because he was unwilling to put in jeopardy his easily acquired reputation, or perhaps because, as he had once despatched from Sumter to Washington, " his heart was not in the war."

ment by a trick too dishonest and shallow to account for the immense display of sentiment in the North that ensued. The event afforded indeed to many politicians in the North a most flimsy and false excuse for loosing passions of hate against the South that had all along been festering in the concealment of their hearts. That action suddenly convinced them that the South was really resolved to separate ; it disconcerted their hopes and plans of seducing her back into the Union by false and temporizing speeches ; it utterly disappointed the Northern expectation that the South was not really in earnest, and that " all would come out right " by a little hypocrisy and affectation on the Northern side ; it snapped as a rotten net their vile and cheap schemes of getting the South back into the Union by art and deceit ; and men, finding no longer any purpose for concealment, threw aside their former professions, quickly determined to coerce what they could not cozen. This was the whole explanation of the Northern " reaction " at the occurrence at Sumter.

There now ensued in the North a sort of crusade against the South, the passion, the fury, and blasphemy of which it is almost impossible to describe. The holiness of this crusade was preached, alike, from the hustings and the pulpit. Dr. Tyng, a celebrated minister of New York, assembled certain " roughs " and marauders of that city, known as " Billy Wilson's men," presented them Bibles, and declared that in carrying fire and sword into the rebellious States, they were propitiating Heaven, and would go far to assure the salvation of their souls.* In most of the

---

* As an evidence of the contrast of spirit between the Christian churches, North and South, with reference to the war, we may place in juxtaposition here certain remarkable cotemporary expressions of sentiment emanating from two of the most conspicuous Episcopal divines of the country—Bishop Meade of Virginia, and Doctor Tyng of New York.

The report of the first venerable Diocesan to the Episcopal Convention of Virginia, on the eve of the war, was replete with Christian sentiment befitting the occasion. He wrote : " *I have clung with tenacity to the hope of preserving the Union to the last moment.* If I know my own heart, could the sacrifice of the poor remnant of my life have contributed in any degree to its maintenance, such sacrifice would have been cheerfully made. But the developments of public feeling and the course of our rulers have brought me, *slowly, reluctantly, sorrowfully,* yet most decidedly, to the painful conviction that notwithstanding attendant dangers and evils, we shall consult the welfare and happiness of the whole land by separation. And who can desire to retain a Union which has now become so hateful, and by the application of armed force, which, if successful, would make it tenfold more hateful, and soon lead to the repetition of the same bloody contests ?

" In connection with this civil and geographical separation in our country, and almost necessarily resulting from it, subjects of some change of the ecclesiastical relations of our Diocese must come under consideration. There is a general and strong desire, I believe, to retain as much as possible of our past and present happy intercourse with those from whom we shall be in other matters more divided. A meeting is already proposed for this purpose in one of the seceded States, whose plans, so far as developed, I will submit to the consideration of this body at its present session.

" I cannot conclude without expressing the earnest desire that the *ministers and members of our Church, and all the citizens of our State, who are so deeply interested in the present contest, may conduct it in the most elevated and Christian spirit, rising above unworthy and uncharitable imputations*

Northern cities men were forced to wear badges of "loyalty," and every house required to hang out the Federal flag as a signal of patriotism, and an evidence of their support of the war. This peculiarly Yankee exhibition in flags pervaded nearly every square mile of country, and was carried even into the sanctuary. Pulpits were dressed with the Stars and Stripes; Sunday-school children wore the colours of the Federal ensign; the streets were rubicund with the bunting; and even in distant parts of the country flags floated from gate-posts and tops of trees, as evidences of "loyal" sentiments and marks for protection against "vigilance committees." This singular exhibition of "Union" sentiment was not a mere picturesque affair; it was attended with fearful riots and violence, and the man who refused to display a piece of bunting was treated as a criminal and outlaw, pursued by mobs, and threatened with death.

Into this crusade against the South all parties and sects and races were strangely mingled. Old contentions and present animosities were forgotten; Democrats associated with recreants and fanatics in one grand league, for one grand purpose; foreigners from Europe were induced into the belief that they were called upon to fight for the "liberty" for which they had crossed the ocean, or for the "free homesteads" which were to be the rewards of the war; and all conceivable and reckless artifices were resorted to to swell the tide of numbers against the South.

But what was most remarkable in this display of popular fury was its

on all who are opposed. Many there are equally sincere, on both sides, as there ever have been in all the wars and controversies that have been waged upon earth; though it does not follow that all have the same grounds of justice and truth on which to base their warfare.

"Let me, in conclusion, commend to the special prayers all those who have now devoted themselves to the defence of our State. From personal knowledge of many of them, and from the information of others, there is already, I believe, a large portion of religious principle and genuine piety to be found among them. I rejoice to learn that in many companies not only are the services of chaplains and other ministers earnestly sought for and after, but social prayer-meetings held among themselves. Our own Church has a very large proportion of communicants among the officers of our army, and not a few among the soldiers. Let us pray that grace may be given them to be faithful soldiers of the Cross, as well as valiant and successful defenders of the State."

About the same time, Dr. Tyng addressed a public meeting in New York, with reference to the war. He said he would not descend to call it civil warfare. He would not meet pirates upon the deck, and call it warfare. He would hang them as quick as he would shoot a mad dog. [Cheers.]

There was one road to peace, and that was absolute and entire subjection. [Cheers.] He did not mean the subjection of the South, but of the riotous mob which there had control of affairs. The sword of justice was the only pen that could write the final treaty. Referring to the troops that had been raised, the speaker asked who ever saw such an army as has been gathered in our land? He would not except the rare birds of Billy Wilson's Regiment. He might venture to say of them that their salvation might be in the very consecration they have made of themselves to their country. [Cheers.] Twenty-three thousand Bibles had been given to the troops who go to fight for their country; did anybody believe there were five hundred copies in the army of renegades who are meeting them in the contest? It would scald and singe their polluted hands. We had every cause to be proud of our army. They are worthy of the Bible. How their names will glisten in glory!

sudden and complete absorption of the entire Democratic party in the North, which had so long professed regard for the rights of the Southern States, and even sympathy with the first movements of their secession. This party now actually rivalled the Abolitionists in their expressions of fury and revenge. They not only followed the tide of public opinion, but sought to ride on its crest. Daniel S. Dickinson of New York, who had enjoyed the reputation of a "Northern man with Southern principles," became the fiercest advocate of the war, and consigned his former friends in the South to fire and sword. Edward Everett of Massachusetts, who, a few months ago, had declared that the Southern States should be permitted to go out of the Union in peace, became an apostle of the war, and exhausted his famous rhetoric in preaching the new gospel of blood.* These men were types of their party. In the early stages of Secession, it had been said that such was the sympathy of New York with the movement, that the Southern States would be able to recruit several regiments for their military service. Now in that city a newspaper office was threatened with a mob, because it had dared to criticise the defence of Sumter; and Democratic orators—among them a man named John Cochrane, who had made his reputation and modelled his manners by playing toady to Southern members in Congress—harangued the multi-

---

* In a letter published in the newspapers of the day, Mr. Everett wrote:

"It was my opinion that, if they [the Cotton States] would abstain from further aggression, and *were determined to separate, we had better part in peace.* But the wanton attack on Fort Sumter (which took place not from any *military necessity,* for what harm was a single company cooped up in Charleston harbour, able to do to South Carolina? but for the avowed purpose of ' stirring the blood of the South, and thus bringing in the Border States), and the subsequent proceedings at Montgomery have wholly changed the state of affairs. The South has *levied an unprovoked war* against the Government of the United States, the mildest and most beneficent in the world, and has made it the duty of every good citizen to rally to its support."

The excuse of the Sumter attack served other Democrats, beside Mr. Everett, as a convenient handle for hypocrisy and falseness. To be used as such, of course, it had to be put in a convenient shape of words. Mr. Everett speaks of it as "a wanton attack." How wanton on the part of the South—how even evitable on her part, when the Administration made the direct challenge, which the South had forewarned the Government at Washington that it would be constrained to accept? This was a simple question; but it presented the whole issue of the Sumter complication, and severely indicates where the responsibility for the collision lies.

There is a wretched argument in Mr. Everett's statement above, which, wretched as it is, may be reversed against himself. He says that there was no "military necessity" for the possession of the fort by South Carolina, as it was able to do her no harm. Then, in what respect greater was the military necessity for the Government to retain it, if it was so powerless to control or to affect the seceded State?

It was no question of military necessity. The Government at Washington wanted the fort as an appanage of its sovereignty. So did South Carolina. And its possession by the latter was but the incident of the separation, which Mr. Everett says he had recommended! It was but the logical and legitimate conclusion of his own policy! Why should he complain that South Carolina should be in possession—and even bloodless possession—of the fort, which very fact was but the essential and inevitable carrying out of his own early recommendation of her separate sovereignty!

tude, advising them to " crush the rebellion," and, if need be, to drown the whole South in one indiscriminate sea of blood.

This giving way of the Democratic party to the worst fanaticism of the North, proved beyond doubt that it was wholly unreliable, entirely un-trustworthy as the friend of the South, and, as Senator Brown of Missis sippi had designated it in the last Congress, hopelessly " *rotten.*" But it proved something more than this. It proved that remarkable want of virtue in American politics, common in a certain degree, to all parts of the country. It was another illustration of the fact which runs through the whole of the political history of America, that in every election where one party greatly preponderates, or in every decisive exhibition of a majority, the minority is absorbed and disappears ; principle is exchanged for expe-diency ; public opinion becomes the slave of the larger party ; and public men desert the standards of conviction to follow the dispensations of patronage, and serve the changes of the times.

President Lincoln did not hesitate to take immediate advantage of the " reaction " in the North. Two days after the boodless battle of Sumter, he issued his proclamation to raise seventy-five thousand troops, usurping the power and discretion of Congress to declare war by a shallow, verbal pretence of calling them out under the act of 1795, which only contem-plated the raising of armed *posses* " in aid of the civil authorities." *

Even in this conjuncture, the President still hesitated to unmask his real intentions of a war of subjugation, still embracing the hope of keeping the Border States " loyal " to his Government. On the very day of the

---

* The following is a full copy of this important paper :

" Whereas, the laws of the United States have been for some time past, and now are, opposed, and the execution thereof obstructed, in the States of South Carolina, Georgia, Alabama, Florida, Mississippi, Louisiana, and Texas, by combinations too powerful to be suppressed by the ordinary course of judicial proceedings, or by the powers vested in the marshals by law : now, therefore, I, Abraham Lincoln, President of the United States, in virtue of the power in me vested by the Con-stitution and the laws, have thought fit to call forth the Militia of the several States of the Union to the aggregate number of 75,000, in order to suppress said combinations, and to cause the laws to be duly executed.

" The details for this object will be immediately communicated to the State authorities through the War Department. I appeal to all loyal citizens to favor, facilitate, and aid, this effort to main-tain the honour, the integrity, and existence, of our national Union, and the perpetuity of popular government, and to redress wrongs already long enough endured. I deem it proper to say that the first service assigned to the forces hereby called forth will probably be to repossess the forts, places, and property which have been seized from the Union.; and in every event the utmost care will be observed, consistently with the objects aforesaid, to avoid any devastation, any destruction of, or interference with property, or any disturbance of peaceful citizens of any part of the country ; and I hereby command the persons composing the combinations aforesaid, to disperse and retire peace ably to their respective abodes, within twenty days from this date.

" Deeming that the present condition of public affairs presents an extraordinary occasion, I do hereby, in virtue of the power in me vested by the Constitution, convene both houses of Congress. The Senators and Representatives are, therefore, summoned to assemble at their respective chambers

attack on Sumter, he made the most pacific protests to the Virginia Commissioners, who were then visiting him;—the President then threatening no other retaliation for the capture of Sumter than the withdrawal of the mails from the seceded States. But Virginia was not to be easily deluded. Two days after the interview of her Commissioners with President Lincoln, her people were reading his call for a land force of seventy-five thousand men; and almost instantly thereafter, the proud and thrilling news was flashed over the South that Virginia had redeemed the pledges she had given against coercion, and was no longer a member of the Federal Union, but in a new, heart-to-heart, defiant union with the Confederate States of the South.

The ordinance of secession on the part of Virginia was met by signs of discontent in some thirty or forty counties in the western part of the State. But despite this distraction, her example was not without its influence and fruit. North Carolina, Tennessee, and Arkansas followed the leadership of Virginia, in what may be called *the second* secessionary movement of the States—which, made as it was, in the immediate presence of war, and led by Virginia in the face of the most imposing, actual, and imminent dangers to herself, showed a courage and devotion of a degree not permitted to be exhibited by the first movement of the Cotton States. History will not allow the real leadership of Virginia in the glory of the movement for freedom to be disputed by South Carolina. Where all are confessed brave, and where opportunities only have differed for exhibitions of devotion, it is only in the historical spirit, and not in that of invidiousness, that the fact is claimed for Virginia of a supreme manifestation of devoted courage and leadership.

The people of Virginia had not long to wait to see verified the interpretation that that State had given to Mr. Lincoln's policy, as one of coercion and subjugation of the South, and of unauthorized war upon its citizens. He increased his levies by repeated proclamations, until more than two hundred thousand men in the North were put under arms. He exchanged his former pretext for calling out troops to repossess the Southern forts. He induced his new forces to believe that they were only intended for the defence of his capital. He did not hesitate, however, to occupy Maryland with troops, to increase the garrison and subsidiary

at twelve o'clock, noon, on Thursday, the fourth day of July next, then and there to consider and determine such measures as, in their wisdom, the public safety and interest may seem to demand.

"In witness whereof, I have hereunto set my hand, and caused the seal of the United States to be affixed.

"Done at the City of Washington, this fifteenth day of April, in the year of our Lord, one thousand eight hundred and sixty-one, and of the independence of the United States the eighty-fifth.

"By the President,   "ABRAHAM LINCOLN.

"WILLIAM H. SEWARD, *Secretary of State*."

forces at Fortress Monroe to more than twelve thousand men, and to establish systems of despotism in Maryland and Missouri, by the disarming of citizens, military arrests, the suspension of the *habeas corpus*, and the striking down of the liberties of the people by a licentious soldiery.

Before the fall of Sumter, the Confederate Government at Montgomery had perfected its organization, and was quietly awaiting events. There could be no doubt of the confidence of the people in its mission. It had called for a slight loan—only five millions of dollars; but the proposals amounted to eight millions, and not one of them was below par. It had appointed three commissioners to England, France, Russia, and Belgium, instructed to ask the recognition of the Confederate States as a member of the family of nations.

The guns of Sumter gave a new animation to the Government and produced an excitement in the South that in volume and effect well responded to the fury of the North. President Davis, at once, Congress being out of session, called upon the States for volunteers for the public defence. He also published a proclamation inviting applications for privateering service, in which private armed vessels might aid the public defence on the high seas under letters of marque and reprisal granted by Congress. The popular reply to these measures was enthusiastic. In every portion of the country, there was exhibited the most patriotic devotion to the common cause. Transportation companies freely tendered the use of their lines for troops and supplies. The presidents of the railroads of the Confederacy assembled in convention, and not only reduced largely the rates heretofore demanded for mail service, and conveyance of troops and munitions, but voluntarily proffered to receive their compensation at these reduced rates in the bonds of the Confederacy, for the purpose of leaving all the resources of the Government at its disposal for the common defence. Requisitions for troops were met with such alacrity that the numbers tendering their services, in every instance, greatly exceeded the demand. On the 29th of April, President Davis wrote to the Confederate Congress then convoked by him: " There are now in the field at Charleston, Pensacola, Forts Morgan, Jackson, St. Philip and Pulaski, nineteen thousand men, and sixteen thousand are now *en route* for Virginia.—It is proposed to organize and hold in readiness for instant action, in view of the present exigencies of the country, an army of one hundred thousand men."

On the 20th day of May the seat of the Confederate Government was removed from Montgomery, Alabama, to Richmond, Virginia. It was clear enough that this latter State was to be the grand theatre of the war on land.

The first concern of Virginia after secession was not to raise troops: these were abundant; but to select a commander whose skill and name might obtain universal confidence in the commonwealth, and befit the heroic and momentous occasion. Lieut.-Col. Robert E. Lee, a son of the famous Harry Lee, of the Revolution, and descended from a family conspicuous for two hundred years in Virginia, had resigned his commission in the United States Army, immediately on learning of the secession of his State. He had done so, protesting an attachment to the Union, but putting above that a sense of duty, that would never allow him to take part against his State, and " raise his hand against his relatives, his chil dren, his home." This sentiment of duty was expressed in very noble terms in the letter which tendered his resignation. The man who, some years ago, had written in a private letter to his son at college, " *Duty* is the sublimest word in our language," was now in his own life to attest the sentiment, and give its example; and when we find him in his farewell letter to Gen. Scott, referring to " the struggle it had cost him " to sep- arate himself from the Federal service, we are prepared for the touching and noble declaration of his wife : " My husband has wept tears of blood over this terrible war ; but he must, as a man of honour and a Virginian, share the destiny of his State, which has solemnly pronounced for inde- pendence."

Governor Letcher was not slow in nominating Lee Major-General in command of all the military forces in Virginia. The nomination was unanimously confirmed by the Convention. Gen. Lee was conducted to the State House ; there was an imposing ceremony of reception ; the trust reposed in him was announced in a glowing speech from the Chair. In the excitement and elation of the occasion, his reply was singularly solemn and beautiful. He said :

" Mr. President and gentlemen of the Convention : Profoundly im- pressed with the solemnity of the occasion, for which I must say I was not prepared, I accept the position assigned me by your partiality. I would have much preferred, had your choice fallen upon an abler man. Trusting in Almighty God, an approving conscience, and the aid of my fellow- citizens, I devote myself to the service of my native State, in whose behalf alone, will I ever again draw my sword."

But a few days after the secession of Virginia, she was a great camp. It was popularly estimated that in the early summer there were within her borders forty-eight thousand men under arms. The valleys and hills swarmed with soldiers ; the rush to arms could scarcely be contained ; the alternative was not who should go to the war, but who should stay at home. Two merchants had fought in Richmond, because one had re- proached the other for being in his store, when nearly everybody in the city was following the drum, and companies were actually begging to be accepted into service. It is no wonder that Gen. Lee made a very unpopu- lar and just remark : that the volunteer spirit of the country should be in a measure checked and moderated, and that he threw cold water on a rabble who hurrahed him at a railroad station, by telling them they had better go home.

Gen. Lee's first task was to organize and equip the military forces that were from every direction flowing in upon his charge. The military council at the State House, Richmond, consisting of Governor Letcher, Lieut.-Gov. Montague, Lieut. M. F. Maury, of the Navy, Gen. Lee and others, was in almost constant session. The raw material promptly brought forward was to be effected for speedy service. The quartermaster and commissary departments were to be organized, to enable the immediate concentration of troops upon the borders of the State, wherever the movements of the enemy might demand the presence of troops. In fact, Gen. Lee had now all the duties of a minister of war to discharge, in addition to those more immediate of general-in-chief. And yet all these duties were executed with a rapidity and effect, and an easy precision of manner that may be said, at the outset of the war to have secured Lee's reputation as an unrivalled organizer of military forces, and thus early to have indicated one conspicuous branch of his great mind.

On the 6th of May, Virginia was admitted into the Southern Confederacy; and her forces then forming part of the entire Confederate Army, Lee's rank was reduced to that of Brigadier-General. In that position he was to remain for some time in comparative obscurity, while the more conspicuous names of Beauregard and others were to ride the wave of popular favour.

CHAPTER VII.

IT is to be remarked that Virginia did not secede in either the circumstances or sense in which the Cotton States had separated themselves from
the Union. She had no delusive prospects of peace to comfort or sustain
her in the decisive step she took. She did not secede in the sense in which
separation from the Union was was the primary object of secession. On
the contrary, her attachment to the Union had been proved by the most

untiring and noble efforts to save it; her Legislature originated the Peace Conference, which assembled at Washington in February, 1861; her representatives in Congress sought in that body every mode of honourable pacification; her Convention sent delegates to Washington to persuade Mr. Lincoln to a pacific policy; and in every form of public assembly, every expedient of negotiation was essayed by Virginia to save the Union. When these efforts at pacification failed, and the Government at Washington drew the sword against the sovereignty of States and insisted on the right of coercion, it was then that Virginia appreciated the change of issue, and, to contest it, found it necessary to withdraw from the Union. Her act of secession was subordinate; it was a painful formality which could not be dispensed with to contest a principle higher than the Union, and far above the promptings of passion and the considerations of mere expediency.

It takes time for popular commotions to acquire their meaning and proper significance. A just and philosophical observation of events must find that in the second secessionary movement of the Southern States, the war was put on a basis infinitely higher and firmer in all its moral and consitutional aspects; that at this period it developed itself, acquired its proper significance, and was broadly translated into a contest for liberty.

It was in this changed view of the contest and on an issue in which force was directly put against the sentiment of liberty, that the Border States followed the lead of Virginia out of the Union. The particular occasion of the movement was not so much the fire at Sumter as the proclamation of Mr. Lincoln to raise forces, the only purpose of which could be the subjugation of the South. In this proclamation the issue was distinctly put before the Border States; for Mr. Lincoln called upon each of them to furnish their quotas of troops for a war upon their sister States. The unnatural demand was refused in terms of scorn and defiance. Gov. Magoffin of Kentucky replied that that State " would furnish no troops for the wicked purpose of subduing her sister Southern States." Gov. Harris of Tennessee notified Mr. Lincoln that that State " would not furnish a single man for coercion, but fifty thousand if necessary for the defence of her rights." Gov. Ellis of North Carolina telegraphed to Washington : " I can be no party to this wicked violation of the laws of the country, and to this war upon the liberties of a free people." Gov. Rector of Arkansas replied in terms of equal defiance, and declared " the demand is only adding insult to injury ; " and Gov. Jackson showed an indignation surpassing all the others, for he wrote directly to Mr. Lincoln : " Your requisition in my judgment is illegal, unconstitutional, and revolutionary, and, in its objects, inhuman and *diabolical*." The only Southern State that did not publicly share in this resentment, and that made it an occasion of official ambiloquy, was Maryland. Her Governor, Thomas

Holladay Hicks, had advised that the State should occupy for the present a position of " neutrality ; " and while he amused the country with this absurd piece of demagogueism, and very plainly suggested that in the approaching election of congressmen, the people of Maryland might determine their position, it is equally certain that he gave *verbal* assurances to Mr. Lincoln that the State would supply her quota of troops, and give him military support.

The indications of sentiment in the Border States soon ripened into open avowals. Tennessee seceded from the Union on the 6th of May ; on the 18th day of May the State of Arkansas was formally admitted into the Southern Confederacy ; and on the 21st of the same month, the sovereign Convention of North Carolina, by a unanimous vote, passed an ordinance of secession. This latter State, although slow to secede and accomplish formally her separation from the Union, had acted with singular spirit in giving early and valuable evidence of sympathy with the Southern cause. Under the orders of her Governor, Fort Macon, near Beaufort, was seized on the 15th of April, and promptly garrisoned by volunteers from Greensborough and other places. Fort Caswell was also taken, and on the 19th the Arsenal of Fayetteville was captured without bloodshed, thus securing to the State and the South sixty-five thousand stand of arms, of which twenty-eight thousand were of the most approved modern construction.

Virginia had taken the decisive step, and passed her ordinance of secession on the 17th day of April. It became an immediate concern to secure for the State all the arms, munitions, ships, war stores, and military posts within her borders, which there was power to seize. Two points were of special importance : one was the Navy Yard, at Gosport, with its magnificent dry-dock—its huge ship-houses, shops, forges, ware-rooms, rope-walks, seasoned timber for ships, masts, cordage, boats, ammunition, small arms, and cannon. Besides all these treasures, it had lying in its waters several vessels of war. The other point was Harper's Ferry on the Potomac River, with its armory and arsenal, containing about ten thousand muskets and five thousand rifles, with machinery for the purpose of manufacturing arms, capable with a sufficient force of workmen, of turning out twenty-five thousand muskets a year.

Movements to secure these places and their advantages were only partially successful. In two days a large force of volunteers had collected at Harper's Ferry. The small Federal force there requested a parley ; this was granted ; but in a short time flames were seen to burst from the armory and arsenal ; the garrison had set fire to the arms and buildings, and escaped across the railroad bridge into Maryland. The Virginia troops instantly rushed into the buildings. A large number of the arms were consumed, but about five thousand improved muskets in complete order, and three thousand unfinished small arms, were saved. The retreat-

ing garrison had laid trains to blow up the workshops, but the courage
and rapid movement of the Virginians, extinguished them, and thus saved
to their State the invaluable machinery for making muskets and rifles.

On the succeeding day preparations were made by the Federals for
the destruction of the Navy Yard at Gosport, while reinforcements were
thrown into Fortress Monroe. The work of destruction was not as fully
completed as the enemy had designed ; the dry-dock, which alone cost
several millions of dollars, was but little damaged ; but the destruction
of property was immense. All the ships in the harbour, excepting an old
dismantled frigate, the United States, were set fire to and scuttled. But
the Merrimac, a powerful steam frigate of twenty-six hundred tons, new,
fully equipped, and nearly ready for sea, was only partially destroyed, and
became, as we shall hereafter see, a famous prize of the Confederacy.

At this time it was expected that Maryland would emulate the heroic
example of Virginia, and cast her fortunes with that of the Confederacy.
But two days after the secession of Virginia occurred a memorable collision in the streets of Baltimore ; and the first blood of Southerners was
shed on the soil of Maryland. When it became certain that Northern
troops were to be assembled for the purpose of invading the seceded
States, the indignation of the people of Maryland, and especially of Baltimore, could not be restrained. It being known that a body of volunteers
from Massachusetts were coming through the city, on the 19th of April,
a fierce and determined purpose to resist their passage was aroused. As
several hundred of these volunteers, sixty of whom only were armed and
uniformed, were passing through the city in horse-cars, they found the
track barricaded near one of the docks by stones, sand, and old anchors
thrown upon it, and were compelled to attempt the passage to the depot,
at the other end of the city, on foot. A body of citizens got in front of the
troops, checked their advance, shouting, threatening, taunting them as
mercenaries, and uttering loud cheers for the Southern Confederacy.
A Confederate flag was displayed by some of the crowd. Stones were
thrown by some of the citizens ; two soldiers were struck down, and many
others severely hurt. At this time the troops presented arms and fired.
Several citizens fell dead, others were wounded, and falling, were borne
off by those near them. Fury took possession of the crowd ; up to this
time they had used no weapons more deadly than stones, but now revolvers
were drawn and fired into the column of troops, and men were rushing in
search of fire-arms. The firing on both sides continued in quick succession of shots from Frederick to South streets. Several of the citizens fell,
but, undismayed, they pressed the soldiers with an incessant and heavy
volley of stones. The troops were unable to withstand the gathering
crowd ; they were bewildered by their mode of attack ; they pressed along
the streets confused and staggering, breaking into a run whenever there

was an opportunity to do so, and turning at intervals to fire upon the citizens who pursued them.

Harassed and almost exhausted, the troops at length reached Camden station. But here the fight continued without intermission ; stones were hurled into the cars with such violence that the windows and panelling were shattered ; the soldiers' faces and bodies were streaming with blood, and they could only protect themselves by lying down or stooping below the windows. Taunts clothed in the most fearful language, were hurled at them ; men pressed up to the windows of the car, presenting knives and revolvers, and cursing up in the faces of the soldiers ; and for half a mile along the track there was a struggling and shouting mass of human beings —citizens piling the track with obstructions, and policemen removing them as fast as possible. In the midst of the excitement, amid hootings, shouts, and curses, the train moved off ; and as it passed from the depot a dozen muskets were fired into the crowd, the volley killing a well-known merchant, who was taking no part in the fight, and was standing as a spectator at some distance from the track.

In this irregular combat two soldiers were killed and several severely wounded ; while, on the other side, the casualties were more serious—nine citizens killed and three wounded. A terrrible excitement ensued in Baltimore, and continued for weeks. The bridges on the railroad leading to the Susquehanna were destroyed ; the regular route of travel was broken up ; and large bodies of Northern troops were thus diverted from the railroad lines, and placed in the necessity of being carried in transports to Annapolis. Mass meetings were held in Baltimore, and speeches of defiance made to the Government at Washington. The city council appropriated five hundred thousand dollars for the avowed purpose of putting the city in a state of defence, but with the farther intent on the part of many, that instant measures should be taken to relieve the State from Federal rule.

But this rule was steadily encroaching upon Maryland, and strengthening itself beyond the hope of successful resistance. Each day Southern sentiment became more timid and equivocal, as the Federal power commenced to display itself. The Legislature of Maryland at last put the State in an attitude of indefinite submission. It passed resolutions protesting against the military occupation of the State by the Federal Government, and indicating sympathy with the South, but concluding with the declaration : " Under existing circumstances, it is inexpedient to call a sovereign Convention of the State at this time, or take any measures for the immediate organization or arming of the militia."

Baltimore was rapidly brought under the yoke. By a concerted movement of the Federal authorities, Col. Kane, the marshal of police, was arrested ; the Police Board suspended ; a provost-marshal appointed, and

Baltimore brought under the law of the drum-head. The municipal police were disbanded, and a reign of terror threatened to establish itself in what was already a condition of anarchy. The writ of *habeas corpus* was suspended; the houses of suspected persons were searched; blank warrants were issued for domiciliary visits; and the mayor and members of the police board were arrested, and, without a trial, imprisoned in a military fortress. In other parts of the State, the inauguration of "the strong government" steadily progressed. And so thoroughly effective was it that in less than a month after the Baltimore riot, Maryland was raising her quota of troops under Mr. Lincoln's proclamation, and Governor Hicks had openly called for four regiments of volunteers to assist the Northern Government in its now fully declared policy of a war of invasion and fell destruction upon the South. But the history of such a change has to be read in the light of many circumstances. Disarmed; not even allowed to retain its militia organization; planted with troops; subjected to an infamous and degraded sway; cozened and betrayed by its Governor; divided within itself; its citizens separated by long-exasperated lines of prejudice; its press exhausting itself to envenom the differences of men; "suspicion poisoning his brother's cup;" corruption chaffering in public market-places for the souls of men; and crime and outrage recognizable only before the tribunal of Despotism, it is not wonderful that Maryland became the easy prey of a Government that scrupled at no means of success and spared no opportunity for the perversion of the principles of men.

Whether the easy subjugation of Maryland persuaded the people of the North that the war was to be a slight task, or whether that opinion is to be ascribed to their own insolent vanity, it is very certain that they entered upon the war with a light estimation of its consequences and with an exhibition of passion, rant and bombast, such, perhaps, as the world has never seen in similar circumstances. The Government at Washington shared, or encouraged for its own purposes, the vulgar opinion that the war was soon to be despatched. It either believed, or affected to believe, that the Southern States would be reduced in a few months. But it is to be remarked that the Federal Government had a particular purpose in reducing, in popular opinion, the importance of the contest. It desired to attract volunteers by the prospects of short service and cheap glory; and it was especially anxious to guard against any probability of recognition by England or France of the new Confederacy, and to anticipate opinion in Europe by misrepresenting the movements of the Southern States as nothing more than a local and disorganized insurrection, incidental to the history of all governments, and unworthy of any serious foreign attention. It was in this view Mr. Lincoln had framed his proclamation, calling for an army of seventy-five thousand men. He took especial pains to model this paper after a Riot Act : to style sovereign States " unlawful combinations ; " and to " command the persons composing the combinations aforesaid, to disperse and retire peaceably to their respective abodes within twenty days."

But something more remarkable than this grotesque anticipation of a four years' war, was to emanate from the statesmanship at Washington. On the 4th of May, Mr. Seward, Secretary of State, wrote a letter of instructions to Mr. Dayton, the recently appointed minister to France, designed as a circular notice to the European courts, which, as a tissue of misrepresentation and absurdity, and an exhibition of littleness in a politician's cast of the future, is one of the most remarkable productions of the political history of the war. In this document the Federal Secretary of State urged that Mr. Dayton could not be " too decided or too explicit " in assuring the French Government that there was no idea of the dissolution of the Union ; and that the existing commotion was only to be ranked among the dozen passing changes in the history of that Union. He concluded : " Tell M. Thouvenel, then, with the highest consideration and good feeling, that the thought of a dissolution of this Union, peaceably or by force, has never entered into the mind of any candid statesman here, and it is high time that it be dismissed by statesmen in Europe." Yet at the time this was penned eight millions of Mr. Seward's countrymen had decided on a dissolution of the Union, and the gathering armies of the South were within a few miles of the Federal capital.

Meanwhile the action of the European Governments with reference to the war was thought to be indecisive, and was still the subject of a certain anxiety. The British Government and the French Emperor, although they regarded and ranked the Confederate States as belligerents, proclaimed a strict neutrality in the war, and closed their ports to the armed vessels and privateers of either of the belligerents. The British House of Commons had deemed it necessary to adjourn the discussion of American affairs by the indefinite postponement of Mr. Gregory's notice of a motion on the subject. That gentleman had sought to defend his motion for the recognition of the Southern Confederacy in a letter in the London *Times*, of a power and ingenuity calculated to affect public opinion, and putting the question to the people of England and of France in every possible aspect. He pointed out the reasons of his advocacy of the recognition of the new Confederate republic in several particulars : as an effectual blow at the slave trade, " mainly carried on by ships sailing from Northern ports and floated by Northern capital ; " as an amelioration of the condition of slavery ; as a means of peace and unrestricted commerce ; as a just retaliation upon the " Morrill " tariff, the successful issue of Northern policy, against which the South had protested ; and as the vindication of the right of a people to assert their independence. Mr.

Gregory concluded with the strong conviction that the interests of France and England were identical in the American question, and that "the recognition by these two great Powers of the Southern Confederacy would cause the war party in the North to pause before plunging their countrymen deeper into the sad struggle."

The idea promulgated at Washington of a ninety days' commotion was readily taken up by the Northern press, and was made the occasion of a volume of conceit, that was amusing enough in the light of subsequent events. Not a paper of influence in the North appeared to comprehend the importance of the impending contest; and the commentary of rant, passion, and bombast upon it exceeded all known exhibitions of the insane vanity of the Northern people.

" The rebellion " was derided in a style which taxed language for expressions of contempt. The New York *Tribune* declared that it was nothing " more or less than the natural recourse of all mean-spirited and defeated tyrannies to rule or ruin, making, of course, a wide distinction between the will and power, for the hanging of traitours is sure to begin before one month is over." " The nations of Europe," it continued, " may rest assured that Jeff. Davis & Co. will be swinging from the battlements at Washington, at least, by the 4th of July. We spit upon a later and longer deferred justice."

The New York *Times* gave its opinion in the following vigorous and confident spirit: " Let us make quick work. The 'rebellion,' as some people designate it, is an unborn tadpole. Let us not fall into the delusion, noted by Hallam, of mistaking a ' local commotion ' for a revolution. A strong active ' pull together ' will do our work effectually in thirty days. We have only to send a column of twenty-five thousand men across the Potomac to Richmond, and burn out the rats there; another column of twenty-five thousand to Cairo, seizing the cotton ports of the Mississippi; and retaining the remaining twenty-five thousand, included in Mr. Lincoln's call for seventy-five thousand men, at Washington, not because there is need for them there, but because we do not require their services elsewhere."

The Philadelphia *Press* declared that " no man of sense could, for a moment, doubt that this much ado-about-nothing would end in a month." The Northern people were " simply invincible." " The rebels," it prophesied, " a mere band of ragamuffins, will fly, like chaff before the wind, on our approach."

The West was as violent as the North or East, quite as confident, and valorous to excess. The Chicago *Tribune* insisted on its demand that the West be allowed to fight the battle through, since she was probably the most interested in the suppression of the rebellion and the free navigation of the Mississippi. " Let the East," demanded this valorous sheet, " get out of the way; this is a war of the West. We can fight the battle, and successfully, within two or three months at the furthest. Illinois can whip the South by herself. We insist on the matter being turned over to us."

It is no wonder that, with the prospect of a short war extended from Washington and enlivened by pictures of cheap glory in the newspapers, the rage for volunteering in the North should have been immense. Going to the war "for three months" (the term of the enlistment of volunteers) was looked upon as a sort of holiday excursion, and had peculiar attractions for the firemen, the rowdies, and "roughs" of the Northern cities, from which brutal material it was boasted that the North would gather the most terrible and invincible army that ever enacted deeds of war. Many of these men adopted the Zouave costume to add to the terrours of their appearance; and a company of them actually went through the ceremony of being sworn in a public hotel in New York to "cut off the heads of every d—d Secessionist in the war." Such exhibitions of brutal ferocity were told with glee and devoured with unnatural satisfaction by the Northern people. If the rowdies were in constant scenes of disorder and violence before they were marched away—if Ellsworth's and Billy Wilson's men did knock down quiet citizens and plunder stores in New York and Washington, the story was merrily told even in the communities where these outrages were committed; for these displays were taken as proofs of desperate courage, and the men so troublesome and belligerent towards quiet citizens were indicated as the terrible and ruthless crusaders who were to strike terrour to the simple armies of the South, and win the brightest and bloodiest laurels on the field of battle.

But it was not only the vagrant and unruly classes of the great and vicious cities of the North that flocked to the standards of the war. The most quiet citizens could not resist the temptation of entering a race for cheap glory. The North was full of martial rage. The war spirit pervaded not only the holiday volunteer soldiers of the cities, but the country people, the shoemakers and cobblers of New England and the coal-heavers of Pennsylvania. Governor Dennison, of Ohio, telegraphed to Washington, offering thirty thousand troops. Governor Weston, of Indiana, received offers showing that the same numbers were ready to come forward in his State. Governor Curtin, of Pennsylvania, was equally liberal in his assurances to Washington. Massachusetts and New York were pressing with offers of men and money for "the three months' war."

But while the North was making such insolent and giddy exhibitions on the threshold of the war, it must be confessed that, on the part of the South, there was also very imperfect appreciation of the impending crisis, and of the extent and solemnity of the adventure in which the Confederate States were to embark.

In the first stages of the dispute the Southern leaders had declared that there would be no war; that the mere act of secession would exact from the North all that was claimed, and prove in the end a peaceful experiment. Heated orators in Charleston exclaimed that there would be no conflict of arms, and that they would be willing to drink all the blood shed in the contest.

Again, when the Confederate Government was established at Montgomery the idea still prevailed that secession had the countenance of a large party in the North, and that the Black Republicans would find it impossible to get up a war in front of hostile States and in face of a partisan opposition at home. This idea had especial hold of the mind of President Davis. It has been thought a little strange that in the frame of the new government there should be such little originality; that it should have exhibited so few ideas of political administration higher than the Washington routine; and that the Montgomery statesmen and legislators should have fallen into an almost servile copy of the old Federal Constitution. This has been accounted for by the circumstance that the new administration of the affairs of the South naturally fell into the hands of old Washington politicians, who were barren of political novelty. But there is a more direct and especial explanation. It was expected that the assimilation of the Montgomery Constitution to that of the United States with some especial additions developing the democratic view and construction of that latter instrument would have the effect of conciliating, or, at least, of neutralizing the Democratic party in the North. In the addres on the occasion of his inauguration, President Davis took especial pains t declare that the seceded States meditated a change only of the constituent parts, not the system of the government; and he distinctly referred to the expectation that, with a Constitution differing only from that of their fathers, in so far as it was explanatory of their well-known intent, freed from sectional conflicts, the States from which they had recently parted might seek to unite their fortunes with those of the new Confederacy. Indeed, so far did this conceit go, that it was proposed in some of the newspapers of the day—among them the New York *Herald*, then the affected friend of the South—that the Union should be " reconstructed " by the accession of the Northern States to the Montgomery Constitution, excluding perhaps the New England States, as odious to both parties in the reconstruction.

But no sooner did these silly prospects of amicable association with Northern Democrats end and war blaze out at Sumter, than a new delusion took possession of the Confederate leaders. This was that the war would be decided speedily, and its history be compassed in a few battlefields. It had been a theme of silly declamation that " the Yankees " would not fight; and so-called statesmen in the South expounded the doctrine that a commercial community, devoted to the pursuit of gain, could never aspire to martial prowess, and were unequal to great deeds of arms. But if these orators had considered the lessons of history they would have found that commercial communities were among the most pugnacious and ambitious and obstinate of belligerents, and might have traced the discovery through the annals of Carthage, Venice, Genoa, Holland, and England.

Another idea was that the victory of the South was to be insured and expedited by the recognition of the new Government by the European Powers. "Cotton," said the Charleston *Mercury*, "would bring England to her knees." The idea was ludicrous enough that England and France would instinctively or readily fling themselves into a convulsion, which their great politicians saw was the most tremendous one of modern times. But the puerile argument, which even President Davis did not hesitate to adopt, about the power of "King Cotton," amounted to this absurdity: that the great and illustrious power of England would submit to the ineffable humiliation of acknowledging its dependency on the infant Confederacy of the South, and the subserviency of its empire, its political interests and its pride, to a single article of trade that was grown in America!

These silly notions of an early accomplishment of their independence were, more than anything else, to blind and embarrass the Confederate States in the great work before them. Their ports were to remain open for months before the blockade, declared by Mr. Lincoln, could be made effective; and yet nothing was to be imported through them but a few thousand stand of small arms, when, in that time, and through those avenues, there might have been brought from Europe all the needed munitions of war. Immense contracts were to be offered the Government, only to be rejected and laughed at. Golden opportunities were to be thrown away, while the Confederate authorities still persuaded themselves that the war was to be despatched by mere make-shifts of money, and a sudden rush of volunteers to arms.

It is a curious speculation how to explain that two belligerents, like the North and South, could have shown such blindness and littleness of mind in entering upon the mighty and tremendous contest which was to ensue, and which had, in fact, become obvious and inevitable. But it is said that the Governments and leaders of each party only shared the general popular opinion on each side, as to the rapid decision of the war. This excuse is imperfect. Those who are put in authority and in the high places of government are supposed to have peculiar gifts, and an education and training suited to the art of governing and advising men; they should be able to discern what the populace does not often see. Prescience is the specialty of the statesman; and because a populace is blind, that is no excuse for his defect of vision. For the false view obtaining at Washington and at Montgomery in the opening of the war, there is a very curt and quite sufficient explanation. It is that there was really but little states-manship in America, and that much which passed current under that name was nothing more than the educated and ingenious demagogueism, which reflects vividly the opinions of the masses, and acts out the fancies of the hour. It does seem indeed almost incredible that public men at Washington and at Montgomery could have observed the crisis, without considering the resources and the temper of each section ; for each of these elements in the contest showed plainly enough that it was to be one of immense extent and indefinite duration.

It will be interesting here to make a brief statement of the resources of the United States about the time of the war, and to show how they were divided between the two belligerents.

The census of the United States, of 1860, showed a population of more than thirty-one millions. A web of railroads, the wonder of the world, stretched from the Atlantic Ocean to the Missouri River ; and the most important of these had been constructed within the last thirty years, for in 1830 there was but one railway connecting the great Lakes with tide-water. The total extent of these railroads was more than thirty thousand miles. Their tonnage per annum was estimated at thirty-six million tons, valued at about four thousand millions of dollars. Such was the huge internal commerce of the United States. Their manufactures formed an enormous fund of wealth ; they represented an annual product of two thousand millions of dollars. In the census of 1860, we have, as the total assessed value of real estate and personal property in the thirty-four States and Territories the monstrous sum of sixteen thousand millions of dollars.

But of population, of internal improvements, of manufactures, and of all artificial wealth the North held much the larger share. She had a population of twenty-three millions against eight millions in the South. The North had manufacturing establishments for all the requirements of peace and war. She had the advantages of an unrestrained commerce with foreign nations. She had all the ports of the world open to her ships ; she had furnaces, foundries, and workshops ; her manufacturing resources compared with those of the South were as five hundred to one ; the great marts of Europe were open to her for supplies of arms and stores ; there was nothing of material resource, nothing of the apparatus of con-quest that was not within her reach ; and she had the whole world wherein to find mercenary soldiers and a market for recruits.

Yet one fact is to be admitted here, which may strike many readers with surprise, and which furnishes a subject of curious reflection, with reference to what we shall hereafter see of the management of their re-sources by the Confederates. This remarkable fact is that about the beginning of the war the South was richer than the North in all the *necessaries* of life. It is sufficient to compile certain results from the census of 1860 to show this: Of live stock (milch cows, working oxen, other cattle, sheep and swine) in the Northern States there were two to each person; in the Southern States, five to each person. Of wheat each person in the Northern States reckoned six bushels; each *white* person in the Southern States about as much. Of Indian corn, each person in the Northern States reckoned twenty-eight bushels; while in the Southern States each white person reckoned fifty-one bushels, and white and black together stood for thirty-five bushels per head.

But the South entered the war with only a few insignificant manufactories of arms and materials of war and textile fabrics. She was soon to be cut off by an encircling blockade from all those supplies upon which she had depended from the North and from Europe in the way of munitions of war, clothing, medicines, etc. She was without the vestige of a navy; while, on the water, the North was to call into existence a power equivalent to a land force of many hundred thousand men.

It had been feared that in the haste of preparation for the mighty contest that was to ensue, the South would find herself poorly provided with arms to contend with an enemy rich in the means and munitions of war. But in respect of small arms, at least, she found herself amply furnished. Mr. Floyd, the Secretary of War under Mr. Buchanan's administration, had taken occasion to transfer to the different arsenals at the South more than one hundred thousand muskets. This proceeding was long a favorite theme of reproach and censure in the North, and was most unjustly taken as a proof of incipient treason in Mr. Buchanan's Cabinet. It was certainly an important assistance to the South (although this contribution of arms was really less than was due her); for without it she would have been hurried into the war with the few and very imperfect arms purchased by the States, or owned by the citizens.*

---

* For years the accusation clung to Secretary Floyd that he improperly and fraudulently supplied the South with these muskets, and "*the story of the stolen arms*" was perpetuated in every variety of Yankee publication. It is strange indeed, as ex-President Buchanan remarks in a recent printed defence of his Administration, "to what extent public prejudice may credit a falsehood, not only without foundation, but against the clearest official evidence." Let us see how the facts reduce this story of fraud and "treason:" In December, 1859, Secretary Floyd had ordered the removal of *one-fifth* of the old percussion and flint-lock muskets from the Springfield Armory, where they had accumulated in inconvenient numbers, to five Southern arsenals. The United States had, on hand, say 500,000 of these muskets; 115,000 includes all transferred to the Southern arsenals. And this order of distribution was made, almost *a year before* Mr. Lincoln's election, and several months before his nomination at Chicago. Again, in 1860, the aggregate of rifles and muskets distributed was 10,151, of which the Southern and Southwestern States received only 2,849, or between *one-third and one-fourth of the whole number*. It thus appears that the Southern and Southwestern States received much less in the aggregate, instead of more than the quota of arms to which they were justly entitled under the law for arming the militia. Could the force of misrepresentation further go than to torture from these facts the charge that Mr. Buchanan's Secretary of War had fraudulently sent public arms to the South for the use of the insurgents! Yet this is but one example of that audacity and hardy persistence in falsehood displayed in all Northern publications concerning the war.

But it may be said here generally that against the vast superiority of the North in material resources and in the apparatus of war, the South had a set-off in certain advantages, not appreciable perhaps by superficial observers, but which constitute a most important element in a true historical estimate of the match between the two belligerents. The coarse popular opinion in the North was that the superiority of numbers would give it an overwhelming preponderance of strength. But something more than numbers makes armies; and war is not a duel, a single contest despatched according to an established routine. The South had a superiour animation in the war. She stood on the defensive; and should thus have been able to put against the invading force two enemies: the opposing army and the people. She had, also, on her side one single advantage which should have been decisive of the contest—an advantage which no numbers could really surmount, or skill effectively circumvent. That advantage was *space*. It had been the victor in many former wars When Napoleon invaded Russia, he won battles, he obtained the very object of his march; but *space* defeated him—the length of the march from Warsaw to Moscow ruined him. When Great Britain attempted to subdue only that part of America that borders the Atlantic, *space* defeated her; her armies took the principal cities, New York, Philadelphia, Charleston, Savannah, Richmond; but victories were barren of result, the Continental troops, dispersed in the country, were easily re-assembled, the lines of military occupation existed only on paper, and the process of conques became one of hopeless repetition, and was at last abandoned in despair.

In an intelligent view of the precedents of history it might safely be predicted that the South, fighting on its own soil, and for it, and occupying a territory of more than 728,000 square miles in extent, and in which the natural features of the country, in mountain, river, and swamp, were equivalent to successive lines of fortification, would be victor in the contest, however unequally matched in men and the material of war, *unless the management of her affairs should become insane, or her people lose the virtue of endurance.*

CHAPTER VIII.

SOME weeks after the secession of Virginia, Mr. Lincoln is said to have
remarked that he "would soon get the wolf by the ears." He probably
meant in this figure of the backwoodsman that he would soon secure the
two important passages into Virginia: that along the Orange and Alexandria and Central Railroads towards Richmond, and that along the water
avenue of the James.

On the 24th of May Alexandria was occupied by the Federals, the Virginia forces evacuating the town, and falling back towards Manassas Junction. The invasion was accomplished under the cover of night. It was attended by an incident which gave a lesson to the enemy of the spirit he was to encounter, and furnished the first instance of individual martyrdom in the war. On one of the hotels of the town, the Marshall House, there was a Confederate flag flying. The proprietor of the hotel, Mr. Jackson, captain of an artillery company in his town, had deliberately declared that under any circumstances he would defend that flag with his life, and had been deaf to the advice of his neighbours not to make his house, by this display, a sign for the enemy's attack. The flag could be seen from a window of the White House in Washington. As a company of Fire Zouaves, at the head of which was Col. Ellsworth, a *protégé* of Mr. Lincoln, entered the town in the gray of the morning, their commander swore that he would have the flag as his especial prize. He was attended in his adventure by a squad of his men. Having found his way into the hotel, he got through a trap-door to its top, where he secured the obnoxious ensign; but descending the ladder he found facing him a single man in his shirt sleeves, with a double-barrel gun in his hands. "Here is my trophy," exclaimed Ellsworth, displaying the flag on his arm. "And you are mine," replied Jackson, as he quickly raised his gun, and discharged its contents into the breast of the exultant Federal. Another moment and the brave Virginian was stretched by the side of his antagonist a lifeless corpse; for one of Ellsworth's men had sped a bullet through his brain, and another had thrust a bayonet into his breast as he was in the act of falling.

In the low country of Virginia, in the vicinity of Fortress Monroe, an affair occurred on the 10th of June, which, though it is not to be ranked as a decisive engagement, was certainly a serious and well-timed check to the enemy in this direction. A Federal column, exceeding four thousand men, moved out from Fortress Monroe in the direction of Great Bethel, a church which stood about nine miles on the road leading south from Hampton. The position here had been entrenched by Gen. J. B. Magruder, who had in his command about eighteen hundred men. It was designed by the enemy to attack the Confederates in their front, while another portion of the column should cross the creek, which ran here, some distance below, and attempt to get into the Confederate work through a gorge which was supposed to be open. The attack in front was easily repulsed, as the Federals never dared to advance from the woods which obscured their position; and when the 1st North Carolina Regiment was ordered forward, the enemy actually broke before this small force got within sixty yards of their position. The column that had crossed the creek advanced with cheers, supposing that they had turned the Confed erate position; but a volley of musketry put them to flight, and the officer who led them, Major Winthrop, was killed by the bullet of a North Carolina rifleman, as he in vain attempted to rally his men to the charge. The loss of the Confederates in this affair was one man killed and seven wounded; that of the enemy, by their own acknowledgment, was thirty killed and more than one hundred wounded. In the little experience of war on both sides the action of Bethel was rated as a famous battle, and was paraded through many columns of the newspapers. The cotemporary estimate of its importance is ludicrous enough in the light of subsequent events, and in comparison with those monuments of carnage, which were hereafter to appear on the fields of Virginia.

The comparative pause of warlike excitement after the affair of Bethel, and the apparent lull of hostilities, while, in fact, both Governments were making active preparations for the contest, was marked by some interesting demonstrations of public opinion in the North. It might have been noticed in this time, that public attention in the North was measurably turned from military movements to the financial aspects of the war, and to the provisions which the Northern Congress was so soon to be called upon to make, in order to meet present exigencies. A considerable portion of the Northern press appeared to show the same diversion of attention; and their tone might have been noticed to have become decidedly more healthy and prudent in leaving for a time the grosser excitements of war to ponder the vital concerns of the debts, taxes, burdens, and losses consequent upon hostilities.

Some time ago, an ominous growl from Wall street had reached the ear of the Government at Washington. The discontent had since slowly and steadily manifested itself. Combinations were spoken of among Northern capitalists to terminate the war; to grant no more loans or aids to the Government; and to overrule the programme of the politicians at Washington by the superiour power of their money and their commercial interest. The estimates of the Government had indeed become frightful. The cost of the war was rated at ten million dollars a week. Besides this, Congress was to be called upon to make a current annual appropriation for ordinary expenditures and interest on the debt, of at least one hundred and fifty millions of dollars, which indispensable estimate—however the war might be pushed for a time on credit—there could be no possible way of meeting unless by modes of direct taxation, in income taxes, excises, etc.

The Northern Government had the most serious reasons to distrust the Wall street combination, and to put itself out of the power of capitalists, who were plainly aggrieved by the prospect, that was now being steadily developed, of a long and expensive war. A Cabinet council was called, and Mr. Secretary Chase proposed a new plan of national loan. It was to make a direct appeal to the *people* to provide means for the prosecution of the war. Outside of the Cabinet, at whose board the plan was reported to have been well received, it met with the most strenuous objections.

In these distresses and embarrassments of the Government, the bellicose elements of the North, resenting all prospects of peace, became more exacting than ever, and even accusatory of the authorities at Washington. The more violent New York papers demanded a vigorous military movement on the part of the Government before the meeting of Congress. They accused the Administration of supineness of policy and uncertainty of purpose; and they, even, did not hesitate to charge that the President and his Cabinet were conniving with "the rebels," and had consented to become parties to a negotiation for peace. These heated and ungenerous expressions did not stop here. Personalities were freely indulged in. The President was vilely abused for not having recalled Mr. Harvey, the minister to Portugal, because he had corresponded with the South Carolina authorities during Mr. Buchanan's administration; and Gen. Scott, who was sacrificing for the Northern objects of the war, all that remained to him of the years and honours of a long life, was not spared from an atrocious libel charging him with having offered premiums to "treason" in procuring the restoration to the United States service and the promotion to a lieutenant-colonelcy of Major Emory, a Marylander, who had formerly resigned his command on the Indian frontier.

These dissatisfied utterances, although they may have been but little annoying, personally, to the Government, were significant of other most serious troubles to be apprehended in the conduct of the war. They gave evidence of a sentiment in the North, at once fanatical and formidable, resolved to push the war beyond the avowed objects of the Government, and to resist any termination of it short of the excision or abolition of slavery in the South. This sentiment had, in fact, already become clamorous and exacting. A war short of the abolition of slavery was denounced as a *farce*, and its mission of defending the Union was openly exchanged in the mouths of fanatics for that of achieving "the rights of humanity."

In the mean time indications were obvious enough of the common intention of the belligerents to make the first great battles of the war in Virginia. Here was to open the first great chapter of Carnage—on a theatre at once wide and brilliant;—filled with the array of armies of two powerful peoples, which brought from their wealth and long seasons of prosperity all that could invest war with destructive power and dramatic display;—occupying a territory noble and inspired in historical memories —the name of which, "*Virginia*," had ever been a word of magic pride throughout the breadth and length of a continent;—and engaging in the issues of its imposing drama the liberties, or, at least, the *independence* of more than eight millions of men.

On the lines of the Potomac, Gen. Scott had gathered one of the largest armies that had ever been seen in America. Nothing was left undone to complete its preparations; in numbers it was all that was desired; and it was provided with the best artillery in the world. All the regulars east of the Rocky Mountains, to the number of several thousand, collected since February, in the city of Washington, from Jefferson Barracks, from St. Louis, and from Fortress Monroe, were added to the immense force of volunteers that had been brought down to the lines of the Potomac. The following is the estimate of the force of this army at this time, obtained from official sources: Fifty-five regiments of volunteers, eight companies of regular infantry, four of marines, nine of regular cavalry, and twelve batteries, forty-nine guns. It was placed at the command of Gen. McDowell, who came to this important post of action with the reputation of the greatest and most scientific general in the North, but who was to run, indeed, a very short career of Yankee popularity.

On the Confederate side, preparations for the coming contest were quite as busy, if not so extensive. At the beginning of June, Gen. Beauregard was in consultation with President Davis and Gen. Lee, at Richmond, while, by means of couriers, they held frequent communication with Gen. Johnston, then in command near Harper's Ferry. The result was, that a military campaign was decided upon, embracing defensive operations in North Virginia and the Shenandoah Valley, and the concentration of an army, under Beauregard, at the Manassas Gap railroad junction, and in the immediate locality. The position taken by Gen. Beauregard was one of great strength; and probably no better for defensive purpose could be found in the whole State of Virginia. It was about midway between the eastern spur of the Blue Ridge and the Potomac below Alexandria; the right wing stretched off towards the waters of the Occoquan through a wooded country; the left was a rolling table-land readily commanded from the successive elevations until it broke into a rough and intricate country that no army could pass without the greatest difficulty. The intervening country was commanded by Beauregard's army so perfectly that there was scarcely a possibility of its being turned. A small stream, called Bull Run, ran in this locality, nearly from west to east, to its confluence with the Occoquan River, about twelve miles from the Potomac, and draining a considerable scope of country, from its source in Bull Run Mountain, to within a short distance of the Potomac at Occoquan. At Mitchell's Ford, the stream was about equi-distant between Centreville and Manassas, some six miles apart. There were a number of other fords; but the banks of the stream were rocky and steep.

Gen. Beauregard was fresh from the glories of Sumter. A brief account of this man, who was, indeed, the central figure in the early period of the war, will be interesting here. He was now forty-five years old. His family was of French extraction, and had settled in Louisiana in the reign of Louis XV. In 1838, he was graduated at West Point, taking the second honours in a class of forty-five. He entered the Mexican war as a lieutenant, obtained two brevets in it, the last that of major; and was subsequently placed by the Government in charge of the construction of some public buildings at New Orleans, as well as the fortifica tions on and near the mouth of the Mississippi. About the beginning of the year 1861, he was appointed superintendent of the Military Academy at West Point; but the appoinment was revoked within forty-eight hours by President Buchanan, for the spiteful reason, as is alleged, that Senator Slidell of Louisiana, the brother-in-law of the nominee, had given offence by a secession speech at Washington. Subsequently, Major Beauregard resigned his commission in the service of the United States, and was appointed by Gov. Moore of Louisiana, Colonel of Engineers in the Provisional Army of the South; from which position, as we have seen, he was called by President Davis to the defence of Charleston.

Gen. Beauregard was singularly impassioned in defence of the cause which he served. He hated and despised " the Yankee; " and it must be confessed was the author of some silly letters in the early part of the war, deriding the power of the enemy. That the South would easily whip the North was his constant assertion, even if the first " had for arms only pitch-forks and flint-lock muskets." Of the army which Gen. Scott was marshalling on the borders of Virginia, he wrote that the enemies of the South were " little more than an armed rabble, gathered together hastily on a false pretence, and for an unholy purpose, with an octogenarian at its head ! "

Beauregard's personal appearance could scarcely escape notice. He was a small, brown, thin man, with features wearing a dead expression, and hair prematurely whitened. His manners were distinguished and severe, but not cold; they forbade intimacy; they had the abruptness without the vivacity of the Frenchman; but they expressed no conceit, and were not repulsive. He had ardour, a ceaseless activity, and an indomitable power of will. His notions of chivalry were somewhat stilted, and he had fought his first battle with an interchange of courtesies that induced a Frenchman to exclaim in Paris: " *Quelle idée chevalresque! On voit que vous avez profité, vous autres Américains, de l'exemple Français. Ce Général Beauregard port un nom Français!* "

It is not to be wondered that Gen. Beauregard, with the eclat of the first victory of the war, and the attractions of a foreign name and manners, should have been the ladies' favourite among the early Southern generals. He was constantly receiving attentions from them, in letters, in flags, and in hundreds of pretty missives. His camp-table was often adorned with presents of rare flowers, which flanked his maps and plans, and a bouquet frequently served him for a paper weight. There was perhaps a little tawdriness about these displays in a military camp; but Gen. Beauregard had too much force of character to be spoiled by hero-worship, or by that part of popular admiration, the most dangerous to men intent on great and grave purposes—the flattery and pursuit of women.

Beauregard's army in Northern Virginia was then known as the Army of the Potomac. In the latter part of July, its effective force was enumerated as 21,833 men and twenty-nine guns. But there was within reach of it the Army of the Shenandoah, numbering little less than nine thousand men.

This latter force was commanded by Gen. Joseph E. Johnston, a native of Virginia, who had distinguished himself in the Mexican war, and at the commencement of the present hostilities was at the head of the quartermaster's department in the United States Army with the rank of brigadier-general. Of the operations of his army in the Shenandoah Valley it is necessary to make a brief sketch, as these operations were a necessary part of the early campaign of the Potomac, and an obvious prelude to the great battle of the 21st July we are proceeding to relate.

In the latter part of May, Gen. Johnston assumed command of the Army of the Shenandoah, and, after a complete reconnoissance of Harper's Ferry and environs, he decided that the place was untenable, and, therefore, determined to withdraw his troops to Winchester. At this time Gen. Patterson was advancing, with a strong force, from Pennsylvania and Maryland into Virginia, and it was supposed that an attempt would be made by that general to form a junction in the Shenandoah Valley with Gen. McClellan, then advancing towards Winchester from the western parts of Virginia. To prevent this junction Gen. Johnston abandoned Harper's Ferry, on the 13th of June, after first burning the railroad bridge and such buildings as were likely to prove most useful to the enemy.

The Confederates retired to Winchester, but had scarcely arrived there when information was obtained that the Federals were still advancing; and Gen. Jackson—afterwards known as the immortal "Stonewall" Jackson—with his brigade, was sent to the neighbourhood of Martinsburg, to aid Stuart's cavalry in destroying what they could of the Baltimore and Ohio Railroad stock, and thus check the enemy's movements. On the 2d of July, however, Patterson succeeded in crossing the Potomac at Williamsport; the river being scarcely waist-deep there. Jackson fell back to Falling Waters, on the main road to Martinsburg, a running fire being kept up. A detachment of Federal troops was then sent forward to reconnoitre, and Jackson was encountered in a position where he had formed his men in line of battle, with four guns directly on the turnpike along which the enemy was advancing. For half an hour Jackson succeeded in maintaining his ground; but, at last, was compelled to fall back slowly, and finally to retire, when about to be outflanked, scarcely losing a man, and bringing off forty-five prisoners.

Jackson having rejoined the main army under Johnston, at Winchester, Patterson fell back towards the river. The design of this Federal commander appears to have been little more than a series of feints to detain Johnston in the Valley of the Shenandoah, and to prevent the union of his forces with those of Beauregard, then strongly encamped on the plains of Manassas. But the design was transparent to Johnston, and, indeed, was turned upon the enemy, for the more skilfully executed feint movement of Johnston completely deceived the enemy to the last moment.

But while Johnston was thus keeping in check Patterson's column at the head of the Shenandoah Valley, an important event, and one of no little disaster to the Confederate cause, was to occur in Northwestern Virginia—as was designated that portion of the State beyond the western ridges of the Alleghany Mountains. It was designed by the Federal Government not only to secure this region, but to use it as a base from which to project columns of invasion into the Valley of Virginia and the rich counties of the Southwest.

THE AFFAIR OF RICH MOUNTAIN.

An army under Gen. George B. McClellan was to be used for this purpose. Its advanced regiments had already penetrated far in upon the line of the Baltimore and Ohio Railroad; had driven a small force from Philippi; had occupied that town and Grafton, and had pushed forward, by country roads, from Wheeling and the Ohio River to Buckhannon, in Upshur County. The movements of McClellan were now directed towards Beverley, with the object of getting to the rear of Gen. Garnett, who had been appointed to the command of the Confederate forces in Northwestern Virginia, and was occupying a strong position at Rich Mountain, in Randolph County.

But the unskilful distribution of the Confederate forces and their inadequate numbers contributed to the success of the enemy. The strength of Gen. Garnett's command was less than five thousand infantry, with ten pieces of artillery, and four companies of cavalry. The disposition of these forces was in the immediate vicinity of Rich Mountain. Col. Pegram occupied the mountain with a force of about sixteen hundred men and some pieces of artillery. On the slopes of Laurel Hill, Gen. Garnett was intrenched with a force of three thousand infantry, six pieces of artillery and three companies of cavalry.

The plans of the enemy promised a complete success. Gen. Rosecrans, with a Federal column of about three thousand men, was to gain, by a difficult march through the mountain, Pegram's left and rear, while McClellan attacked in front with five thousand men, and a number of pieces of artillery. On the 11th of July, before daybreak, Rosecrans' column was in motion. The path up the mountain was rugged and perplexed beyond all expectation; the weather was uncertain; often heavy showers of rain poured down for hours, and when the clouds broke, the sun appeared and filled the air with heat. Through the laurel thickets, clambering up ravines, slipping from stones dislodged and earth moistened by the rain, the Federals toiled up the mountain. As they advanced through the forest, the Confederate artillery posted on the top of the mountain, opened upon them, but with little effect, as their lines were concealed by the trees and brushwood. After some sharp skirmishing, Rosecrans threw out his men on either flank, with the view of surrounding the small Confederate force. Finding himself with three thousand of the enemy in his rear, and five thousand in his front, Col. Pegram endeavored to escape with his command after a small loss in action. Six companies of infantry succeeded in escaping; the other part of the command was surrendered as prisoners of war.

As soon as Gen. Garnett heard of the result of the engagement at Rich Mountain, he determined to evacuate Laurel Hill, and retire to Huttonsville by the way of Beverley. But this plan was disconcerted by a failure to block the road from Rich Mountain to Beverley; and Gen. Garnett was compelled to retreat by a mountain road into Hardy County. The retreat was a painful one, and attended with great suffering; the pursuing enemy fell upon the rear of the distressed little army at every opportunity; and at one of the fords on Little Cheat River four companies of a Georgia regiment were cut off, and Gen. Garnett himself was killed by one of the enemy's sharpshooters.

The results of the engagements on the mountain and of the pursuit of the retreating army was not very considerable in killed and wounded— probably not a hundred on the side of the Confederates. But they had lost nearly all of their artillery, more than a thousand prisoners, and almost the entire baggage of the command, portions of which had been used in blocking the road against the enemy's artillery.

But this early disaster to the Confederate cause was soon to be more than retrieved on a broader and more interesting theatre, and by one of the most decisive and dramatic victories of the war; and to the direction of these important operations our narrative now takes us in the regular succession of events.

On the 18th of July, a despatch reached Gen. Johnston at Winchester, that the great Northern army was advancing on Manassas. He was immediately ordered to form a junction of his army with that of Beauregard, should the movement in his judgment be deemed advisable.

The " Grand Army," as the Northern newspapers entitled it, was at last ready to move, and only after a period of impatience on the part of the Northern people, that was clamorous and insolent with the assurance of victory. " On to Richmond " had been the cry of Northern newspapers for weeks ; extreme parties in the Federal Congress urged an immediate advance ; and it was thought to be so easy an enterprise to press forward and plant the stars and stripes in the Capitol Square of Richmond, that men wondered why Gen. Scott, who directed the military movements from Washington, did not at once grasp the prize within his reach, complete his reputation, and despatch the war. At last it was given out in Washington that the Grand Army was ready to move ; and that Richmond would be occupied probably in ten days. It was an occasion of peculiar hilarity, and the prospect of a triumphal entry of the Federal arms into Richmond was entertained with every variety of public joy. Politicians prepared carriage-loads of champagne for festal celebration of the victory that was to be won ; tickets were printed and distributed for a grand ball in Richmond ; a stream of visitors to the battle-field set out from Washington, thronged with gay women and strumpets going to attend " the Manassas Races ; " and soon in the rear of McDowell's army was collected an indecent and bedizened rabble to watch the battle from afar. Such an exhibition of morbid curiosity or of exultant hate has seldom been witnessed in the history of the civilized world.

THE BATTLE OF MANASSAS.

The great contest of arms was to be preceded by an affair which, however intended, proved of some importance. On the 18th of July, the enemy made a demonstration with artillery in front of Gen. Bonham's brigade, which held the approaches to Mitchell's Ford. Meanwhile, he was advancing in strong columns of infantry, with artillery and cavalry on Blackburn's Ford, which was covered by Gen. Longstreet's brigade. Before advancing his infantry, the enemy maintained a fire of rifle artillery for half an hour ; then he pushed forward a column of over three thousand infantry to the assault. Twice the enemy was foiled and driven back by the Confederate skirmishers and Longstreet's reserve companies. As he returned to the contest, Longstreet, who commanded only twelve hundred bayonets, had been reinforced with two regiments of infantry and two pieces of artillery. Unable to effect a passage of the stream, the enemy's fire of musketry was soon silenced, and the affair became one of artillery. Gradually his fire slackened, and his forces were drawn off in evident confusion. Sixty of his dead were found on the field. The Confederate casualties were unimportant—fifteen killed and fifty-three wounded.

Whatever the significance of this affair—whether or not it was intended as a mere " reconnoissance in force," according to the enemy's account—it was considered as a prelude to an important battle, and, in the artillery duel, which it had brought on, had given the Confederates great confidence in this unexpectedly brilliant arm of their service.   Two days passed without any military event.   But on the night of the 20th of July it was evident that the enemy was in motion.   As the lights around Centreville seemed to die out about midnight, low murmuring noises reached the Confederate out-posts, as if large bodies of men were marching towards the Stone Bridge, where the extreme left of Beauregard's army rested.   The bumping of heavy wagons and artillery was distinctly audible, and words of command could be faintly heard in the still night.

The sun of the 21st of July rose with more than usual splendour.   It was a calm Sabbath morning.   The measured sounds of artillery told that both armies were on the alert.   Smoke curling away from the cannon's mouth rose slowly into the air ; glistening masses of troops could be seen on the distant landscape, and far away in the west rose the dark outline of the Blue Ridge, which enclosed, as an amphitheatre, the woods and hollows, the streams and open spaces of Manassas Plain.

The night before the battle Gen. Beauregard had decided to take the offensive.   Gen. Johnston had arrived during the day, but only with a portion of the Army of the Shenandoah ; five thousand of his men having been detained on the railroad for want of transportation.   It was determined that the two forces, less than thirty thousand effective men of all arms, should be united within the lines of Bull Run, and thence advance to the attack of the enemy, before Patterson's junction with McDowell, which was daily expected.   But a battle was to ensue, different in place and circumstances from any previous plan on the Confederate side.

The Confederate army was divided into eight brigades, stretching for eight or ten miles along the defensive line of Bull Run.   The right of the line was much stronger than the left, in position and numbers ; the extreme left at Stone Bridge being held by Colonel Evans with only a regiment and battalion.   It had been arranged by McDowell, the Federal commander, that the first division of his army, commanded by Gen. Tyler, should take position at Stone Bridge, and feign an attack upon that point, while the second and third divisions were, by routes unobserved by the Confederates, to cross the run, and thus effect a junction of three formidable divisions of the grand army, to be thrown upon a force scattered along the stream for eight miles, and so situated as to render a concerted movement on their part impracticable.

A little after sunrise the enemy opened a light cannonade upon Col

Evans' position at Stone Bridge. This continued for an hour, while the main body of the enemy was marching to cross Bull Run, some two miles above the Confederate left. Discovering, to his amazement, that the enemy had crossed the stream above him, Col. Evans fell back. As the masses of the enemy drew near, military science pronounced the day lost for the Confederates. They had been flanked by numbers apparently overwhelming. That usually fatal and terrible word in military parlance—"*flanked*"—may be repeated with emphasis.

It is true that Col. Evans, who had held the position at Stone Bridge, where the enemy's feint was made, had discovered the nature of that demonstration in time to form a new line of battle, as the main body of the enemy emerged from the "Big Forest," where it had worked its way along the tortuous, narrow track of a rarely-used road. But the column that crossed Bull Run numbered over sixteen thousand men of all arms. Col. Evans had eleven companies and two field-pieces. Gen. Bee, with some Georgia, Alabama, and Mississippi troops, moved up to his support. The joint force was now about five regiments and six field-pieces. That thin line was all that stood between sixteen thousand Federals and victory. It is wonderful that this small force of Confederates should have, for the space of an hour, breasted the unremitting battle-storm, and maintained for that time odds almost incredible. But they did it. It was frequently said afterwards by military men in Richmond, that the Confederates had been whipped, but that the men, in the novelty of their experience of a battle-field, "did not know it."

But at last the blended commands of Bee and Evans gave way before the surging masses of the enemy. The order for retreat was given by General Bee. The Confederates fell back sullenly. Their ranks were fast losing cohesion; but there was no disorder; and, at every step of their retreat, they stayed, by their hard skirmishing, the flanking columns of the enemy. There were more than five-fold odds against them. The enemy now caught the idea that he had won the day; the news of a victory was carried to the rear; the telegraph flashed it to all the cities in the North, and before noon threw Washington into exultations.

General Bee had a soldier's eye and recognition of the situation. The conviction shot through his heart that the day was lost. As he was pressed back in rear of the Robinson House, he found Gen. Jackson's brigade of five regiments ready to support him. It was the timely arrival of a man who, since that day, never failed to be on the front of a battle's crisis, and to seize the decisive moments that make victories. Gen. Bee rushed to the strange figure of the Virginia commander, who sat his horse like marble, only twisting his head in a high black stock, as he gave his orders with stern distinctness. "General," he pathetically exclaimed, "they are beating us back." "Then, sir," replied Jackson, " we'll give them the bayonet." The words were as a new inspiration. Gen. Bee turned to his over-tasked troops, exclaiming, " There are Jackson and his Virginians standing like a *stone-wall*. Let us determine to die here, and we will conquer."

In the meantime, where were the Confederate Generals—Beauregard and Johnston? They were four miles away. Gen. Beauregard had become involved in a series of blunders and mishaps, such as had been seldom crowded into a single battle-field. In ignorance of the enemy's plan of atttack, he had kept his army posted along Bull Run for more than eight miles, waiting for his wily adversary to develop his purpose to him. He had, at an early hour of the morning, determined to attack with his right wing and centre on the enemy's flank and rear at Centreville, with precautions against the advance of his reserves from the direction of Washington. Even after his left flank had been so terribly engaged, he supposed that this movement would relieve it ; and in his official report of the action, he writes : " by such a movement, I confidently expected to achieve a complete victory for my country by 12 o'clock, M."

It was half-past ten in the morning, when Gen. Beauregard learned that his orders for an advance on Centreville had miscarried. He and Gen. Johnston had taken position on a commanding hill, about half a mile in the rear of Mitchell's Ford, to watch the movements of the enemy. While they were anxiously listening there for sounds of conflict from the Confederate front at Centreville, the battle was bursting and expending its fury upon their left flank. From the hill could be witnessed the grand diorama of the conflict. The roar of artillery reached there like protracted thunder. The whole valley was a boiling crater of dust and smoke. The enemy's design could be no longer in doubt ; the violent firing on the left showed, at last, where the crisis of the battle was ; and now immense clouds of dust plainly denoted the march of a large body of troops from the Federal centre.

Not a moment was now to be lost. It was instantly necessary to make new combinations, and these the most rapid, to meet the enemy on the field upon which he had chosen to give battle. It was evident that the left flank of the Confederates was being overpowered. Dashing on at a headlong gallop, Gens. Beauregard and Johnston reached the field of action, in the rear of the Robinson House, just as the commands of Bee and Evans had taken shelter in a wooded ravine, and Jackson's brigade had moved up to their left, to withstand the pressure of the enemy's attack. It was a thrilling moment. Gen. Johnston seized the colours of the 4th Alabama regiment, and offered to lead the attack. Gen. Beauregard leaped from his horse, and turning his face to his troops, exclaimed : " I have come here to die with you."

In the meantime the Confederate reserves were rapidly moving up to support the left flank. The movement of the right and centre, begun by Jones and Longstreet, was countermanded. Holmes' two regiments and a battery of artillery of six guns, Early's brigade and two regiments from Bonham's brigade, with Kemper's four six-pounders were ordered up to support the left flank. The battle was re-established; but the aspect of affairs was yet desperate in the extreme. Confronting the enemy's attack Gen. Beauregard had as yet not more than sixty-five hundred infantry and artillerists, with but thirteen pieces of artillery, and two companies of cavalry. Gens. Ewell, Jones (D. R.), Longstreet and Bonham had been directed to make a demonstration to their several fronts, to retain and engross the enemy's reserves and forces on their flank, and at and around Centreville. Gen. Johnston had left the immediate conduct of the field to Beauregard, and had gone in the direction of the Lewis House, to urge reinforcements forward.

The battle was now to rage long and fiercely on the plateau designated by the two wooden houses—the Henry and Robinson House—which stood upon it. Gen. Beauregard determined to repossess himself of the position, and formed his line for an assault; his right rushed to the charge, while his centre, under Jackson, pierced that of the enemy. The plateau was won, together with several guns; but the enemy threw forward a heavy force of infantry, and again dispossessed the Confederates. It was evident that the latter were being slowly overpowered by the weight of numbers. A force, estimated at twenty thousand infantry, seven companies of cavalry, and twenty-four pieces of artillery were bearing hotly and confidently down on their position, while perilous and heavy reserves of infantry and artillery hung in the distance.

It was now about two o'clock in the afternoon. Fortunately the reinforcements pushed forward, and directed by Gen. Johnston to the required quarter, were at hand just as Gen. Beauregard had ordered forward a second effort for the recovery of the disputed plateau. The brigade of Holmes and another were put in the line. Additional pieces of artillery came dashing up, and a new inspiration seemed to be caught by the Confederates. The line swept grandly forward; shouts ran along it; and steadily it penetrated the fire of the enemy's artillery. The whole open ground was again swept clear of the enemy; but it was strewn with the evidences of a terrible carnage. Gen. Bee had fallen near the Henry House, mortally wounded. A little further on, Col. Bartow, of Georgia had fallen, shot through the heart—and one of the bravest and most promising spirits of the South was there quenched in blood. But the tide of fortune had changed; the plateau was now firmly in our possession; and the enemy, driven across the turnpike and into the woods, was visibly disorganized.

But there were to be three stages in the battle of Manassas. We have already described two : the enemy's flank movement and momentary victory, and the contest for the plateau. The third was now to occur ; and the enemy was to make his last attempt to retrieve the fortune of the day.

His broken line was rapidly rallied. He had re-formed to renew the battle, extending his right with a still wider sweep to turn the Confederate left. It was a grand spectacle, as this crescent outline of battle developed itself, and threw forward on the broad, gentle slopes of the ridge occupied by it clouds of skirmishers ; while as far as the eye could reach, masses of infantry and carefully-preserved cavalry stretched through the woods and fields.

But while the Federals rallied their broken line, under shelter of fresh brigades, and prepared for the renewal of the struggle, telegraph signals from the hills warned Gen. Beauregard to "look out for the enemy's advance on the left." At the distance of more than a mile, a column of men was approaching. At their head was a flag which could not be distinguished ; and, even with the aid of a strong glass, Gen. Beauregard was unable to determine whether it was the Federal flag, or the Confederate flag—that of the Stripes or that of the Bars. " At this moment," said Gen. Beauregard, in speaking afterwards of the occurrence, " I must confess my heart failed me. I came, reluctantly, to the conclusion that, after all our efforts, we should at last be compelled to leave to the enemy the hard-fought and bloody-field. I again took the glass to examine the flag of the approaching column ; but my anxious inquiry was unproductive of result—I could not tell to which army the waving banner belonged. At this time all the members of my staff were absent, having been despatched with orders to various points. The only person with me was the gallant officer who has recently distinguished himself by a brilliant feat of arms—General, then Colonel, Evans. To him I communicated my doubts and my fears. I told him that I feared the approaching force was in reality Patterson's division ; that, if such was the case, I would be compelled to fall back upon our reserves, and postpone, until the next day, a continuation of the engagement."

Turning to Col. Evans, the anxious commander directed him to proceed to Gen. Johnston, and request him to have his reserves collected in readiness to support and protect a retreat. Col. Evans had proceeded but a little way. Both officers fixed one final, intense gaze upon the advancing flag. A happy gust of wind shook out its folds, and Gen. Beauregard recognized the Stars and Bars of the Confederate banner ! At this moment an orderly came dashing forward. " Col. Evans," exclaimed Beauregard, his face lighting up, " ride forward, and order General Kirby Smith to hurry up his command, and strike them on the flank and rear ! "

It was the arrival of Kirby Smith with a portion of Johnston's army left in the Shenandoah Valley, which had been anxiously expected during the day; and now cheer after cheer from regiment to regiment announced his welcome. As the train approached Manassas with some two thousand infantry, mainly of Elzey's brigade, Gen. Smith knew, by the sounds of firing, that a great struggle was in progress, and, having stopped the engine, he had formed his men, and was advancing rapidly through the fields. He was directed to move on the Federal left and centre. At the same time, Early's brigade, which had just come up, was ordered to throw itself upon the right flank of the enemy. The two movements were made almost simultaneously, while Gen. Beauregard himself led the charge in front. The combined attack was too much for the enemy. The fact was that his troops had already been demoralized by the former experiences of the day; and his last grand and formidable array broke and crumbled into pieces under the first pressure of the assault. A momentary resistance was made on a rising ground in the vicinity of what was known as the Chinn House. As the battle surged here, it looked like an island around which flames were gathering in all directions. The enemy was appalled. He had no fresh troops to rely on; his cannon were being taken at every turn; lines were no sooner formed than the Confederates broke them again; they gave way from the long-contested hill; the day was now plainly and irretrievably lost.

As the enemy was forced over the ridge or narrow plateau, his former array scattered into flight, spreading each moment, until the fields were soon covered with the black swarms of flying soldiers. But into this general and confused rout a singular panic penetrated, as by a stroke of lightning, and rifted the flying army into masses of mad and screaming fugitives. As the retreat approached Cub Run bridge, a shot from Kemper's battery took effect upon the horses of a team that was crossing; the wagon was overturned in the centre of the bridge, and the passage obstructed; and at once, at this point of confusion, the Confederates commenced to play their artillery upon the train carriages and artillery wagons, reducing them to ruins. Hundreds of flying soldiers were involved in the common heap of destruction; they dashed down the hill in heedless and headlong confusion; the main passage of retreat was choked; and for miles the panic spread, flying teams and wagons confusing and dismembering every corps, while hosts of troops, all detached from their regiments, were mingled in one disorderly rout. Vehicles tumbled against each other; riderless horses gallopped at random; the roar of the flight was heard for miles through clouds of dust; and as the black volume of fugitives became denser, new terrours would seize it, which called for agonizing efforts at extrication, in which horses trampled on men, and great wheels of artillery crushed out the lives of those who fell beneath them.

It was not only at Cub Run bridge that the retreat had been choked. Fugitive thousands rushed across Bull Run by the various fords, and horse, foot, artillery, wagons, and ambulances were entangled in inextricable confusion. Clouds of smoke and dust marked the roads of retreat, and rolled over the dark green landscape in the distance. Where the roads were blocked, some of the troops took to the fields and woods, throwing away their arms and accoutrements; and from the black mass of the rout might be seen now and then a darting line of figures in which panic-stricken men and riderless horses separated from the larger bodies, and fled wildly through the country. Even the sick and wounded were dragged from ambulances; red-legged Zouaves took their places; men in uniform mounted horses cut out of carts and wagons. Never was there such a heterogeneous crowd on a race-course. Soldiers, in every style of costume; ladies, who had come with opera-glasses to survey the battle; members of Congress and governors of States, who had come with champagne and after-dinner speeches to celebrate a Federal victory; editors, special correspondents, telegraph operators, surgeons, paymasters, parsons —all were running for dear life—disordered, dusty, powder-blackened, screaming or breathless in the almost mortal agonies of terrour.

For three miles stretched this terrible diorama of rout and confusion, actually without the pursuit or pressure of any enemy upon it! The Confederates had not attempted an active pursuit. The only demonstration of the kind consisted of a dash by a few of Stuart's and Beckham's cavalry, in the first stages of the retreat, and a few discharges of artillery at Centreville, where the Confederates had taken a gun in position. The cry of "cavalry" was raised, when not a Confederate horseman was within miles of the panic-stricken fugitives, who did not abate their mad struggle to escape from themselves, or cease their screams of rage and fright, even after they had passed Centreville, and were heading for the waters of the distant Potomac.

Over this route of retreat, now thronged with scenes of horrour, there had passed in the morning of the same day a grand army, flushed with the hopes of victory, with unstained banners in the wind, and with gay trappings and bright bayonets glistening through the green forests of Virginia. A few hours later, and it returns an indescribable rout—a shapeless, morbid mass of bones, sinews, wood and iron, throwing off here and there its *nebula* of fugitives, or choking roads, bridges, and every avenue of retreat; halting, struggling, and thrilling with convulsions at each beat of artillery that sounded in the far distance, and told to the calm mind that the Confederates had rested on their victory.

It was not until the sight of the Potomac greeted the fugitives that their terrours were at all moderated. Even then they were not fully assured of safety, or entirely dispossessed of panic. At Alexandria, the rush of troops upon the decks of the river boats nearly sunk them. At Washington the railroad depot had to be put under strong guard to keep off the fugitives, who struggled to get on the Northern trains. They were yet anxious to put a greater distance between themselves and the terrible army, whose vanguard, flushed with victory and intent upon planting its flag on the Northern capitol, they aready imagined on the banks of the Potomac, within sight of their prize, and within reach of their revenge.

But the Confederates did not advance. The victorious army did not move out of the defensive lines of Bull Run. It is true, that within the limits of the battle-field, they had accomplished a great success and accumulated the visible fruits of a brilliant victory. They had not only defeated the Grand Army of the North, but they had dispersed and demoralized it to such an extent, as to put it, as it were, out of existence. With an entire loss in killed and wounded of 1,852 men, they had inflicted a loss upon the enemy which Gen. Beauregard estimated at 4,500, in killed. wounded, and prisoners ; they had taken twenty-eight pieces of artillery and five thousand small arms ; and they had captured nearly all of the enemy's colours. But the Confederates showed no capacity to understand the extent of their fortunes, or to use the unparalleled opportunties they had so bravely won. At any time within two weeks after the battle, Washington might have fallen into their hands, and been taken almost as an unresisting prey. Patterson had only ten thousand men before the battle. His army, like the greater part of McDowell's, was composed of three months' men, who refused to re-enlist, and left for their homes in thousands. The formidable hosts that had been assembled at Washington were fast melting away, some slain, many wounded, more by desertion, and yet more by the ending of their terms of enlistment and their persistent refusal to re-enter the service. On the Maryland side, Washington was then very inadequately defended by fortifications. The Potomac was fordable above Washington, and a way open to Georgetown heights, along which an army might have advanced without a prospect of successful resistance. It needed but a march of little more than twenty miles to crown the victory of Manassas with the glorious prize of the enemy's capital.

But the South was to have its first and severest lesson of lost opportunity. For months its victorious and largest army was to remain inactive, pluming itself on past success, and giving to the North not only time to repair its loss, but to put nearly half a million of new men in the field, to fit out four extensive armadas, to open new theatres of the war, to perfect its " Anaconda Plan," and to surround the Confederacy with armies and navies whose operations extended from the Atlantic border to the western tributaries of the Mississippi.

CHAPTER IX.

THE victory of Manassas proved the greatest misfortune that could
have befallen the Confederacy. It was taken by the Southern public as the
end of the war, or, at least, as its decisive event. Nor was this merely a

vulgar delusion. President Davis, after the battle, assured his intimate friends that the recognition of the Confederate States by the European Powers was now certain. The newspapers declared that the question of manhood between North and South was settled forever; and the phrase of " one Southerner equal to five Yankees " was adopted in all speeches about the war—although the origin or rule of the precise proportion was never clearly stated. An elaborate article in " De Bow's Review " compared Manassas with the decisive battles of the world, and considered that the war would now degenerate into mere desultory affairs, preliminary to a peace. On the whole, the unfortunate victory of Manassas was followed by a period of fancied security, and of relaxed exertions on the part of the Southern people highly dangerous and inauspicious. The best proof of this inactivity is to be found in the decrease of enlistments by volunteers.

There are to be found in the politics and literature of the Confederacy at this time, some very singular indications of the exaggerated and foolish confidence which took place upon the event of Manassas. So certain, after this event, was supposed to be the term of Confederate existence, that politicians actually commenced plotting for the Presidential succession, more than six years distant. Mr. Hunter of Virginia about this time left Mr. Davis' Cabinet, because it was said that he foresaw the errours and unpopularity of this Administration, and was unwilling by any identification with it to damage his chances as Mr. Davis' successor in the Presidential office. Gen. Beauregard was already designated in some quarters as the next Confederate President; and the popular nominee of an honour six years hence, wrote a weak and theatrical letter to the newspapers, dated " Within Hearing of the Enemy's Guns," and declaring: " I am not either a candidate, nor do I desire to be a candidate, for any civil office in the gift of the people or Executive." There was actually a controversy between different States as to the location of the capital of a Government, the existence of which they could not understand was yet imperilled by war. The controversy went so far that the city council of Nashville, Tennessee, appropriated $750,000 for a residence for the President of the Southern Confederacy, as an inducement to remove the capital there.

It is remarkable that the statesmen of Richmond did not observe the singular temper of the authorities at Washington, on the news of their defeat at Manassas. On the very day that Washington was crowded with fugitives from the routed army, the Federal Congress legislated calmly and patiently throughout; and the House of Representatives, passed unanimously the following resolution :

" *Resolved,* That the maintenance of the Constitution, the preservation of the Union, and the enforcement of the laws, are sacred trusts which must be executed ; that no disaster shall discourage us from the most ample performance of this high duty; and that we pledge to the country and the world the employment of every resource, national and individual, for the suppression, overthrow, and punishment of rebels in arms."

While the South reposed on the laurels of Manassas, the active and elastic spirit of the North was at work to repair its fortunes. It accomplished wonders. It multiplied its armies; it built navies with infuriate energy; it recovered itself from financial straits which distant observers thought hopeless; a few weeks after the battle of Manassas it negotiated a loan of one hundred and fifty millions of dollars, at a fraction above the legal interest of New York; in short, its universal mind and energy were consolidated in its war upon the South. There is no more remarkable phenomenon in the whole history of the war than the display of fully-awakened Northern energy in it, alike wonderful in the ingenuity of its expedients and in the concentrated force of its action. At every stage of the war the North adopted the best means for securing specific results. It used the popularity of Fremont to bring an army into the field. It combined with the science of McClellan, Buell, and Halleck, such elements of popularity as could be found in the names of Banks, Butler, and Baker. It patronized the great ship-brokers and ship-owners of New York to create a navy. The world was to be astonished soon to find the North more united than ever in the prosecution of the contest, and the proportions of the war so swollen as to cover with its armies and its navies the frontiers of half a continent.

While these immense preparations were in progress in the North, and while the South indulged its dreams of confidence, there was a natural pause of large and active operations in the field. The months of summer and early fall following the battle of Manassas are barren of any great events in the history of the war. But within this period there occurred two campaigns, remarkable for other circumstances than decisive influence, taking place on widely separated theatres, and yet much alike in their features of discursive contest. These were the campaigns in the distant State of Missouri and in the mountainous regions of Western Virginia.

THE MISSOURI CAMPAIGN.

The politics of Missouri had always been strongly Southern. As early as 1848–'9, when the North was evidently intent upon excluding the South from the territory obtained in the Mexican war—acquired principally by the blood of Southern soldiers—the Legislature of Missouri passed resolutions affirming the rights of the States, as interpreted by Calhoun, and pledging Missouri to " co-operate with her sister States in any measure they might adopt " against Northern encroachments. On opposition to these resolutions, Mr. Benton was defeated for the United States Senate; and they remained on the statute-book of Missouri unrepealed to the date of the war.

In the last Presidential campaign, Missouri, under one of those apparent contradictions or delusions not uncommon in American politics, gave her vote for Douglas. This result was obtained chiefly through the influence of Sterling Price, who had formerly been Governour of the State, had previously represented her in Congress, and was a man of commanding influence with his party.

Price and his party were strongly attached to the Union, and hoped that it might be perpetuated with safety and honour to the South. Of the Convention called in January, 1861, not a single member was yet ready to avow the policy of secession; and Price himself, who had been returned as a Union man without opposition, was elected its president.

But the Federal authorities in Missouri did not show that prudence which the occasion called for; they did nothing to conciliate the disposition of the Convention; and as events marched onward, the designs of the Washington Government were too plainly unmasked, to leave any doubt with the people of Missouri of the fate prepared for them.

In the city of St. Louis there had been several collisions between the citizens and Federal soldiery; and those anxious to keep the peace of the State had reason to fear that these riots would be the inaugurating scenes of revolution. On the 10th of May, 1861, Capt. (afterwards General) Lyon of the Federal army, had compelled the unconditional surrender of a brigade of Missouri militia, encamped under the State law. This high-handed proceeding was attended by other outrages. All the arms and ammunition in St. Louis were seized; houses were searched; and a line of military posts extended around the city, gave evidence of a reign of terrour.

About this time, Sterling Price, having been commissioned by Gov. Jackson of Missouri as major-general, proceeded to consult with Gen. Harney, of the Federal forces, as to the best mode of " restoring peace and good order to the people of the State, in subordination to the laws of the General and State Governments." In view of the riotous demonstrations at St. Louis, Price, having " full authority over the militia of the State," undertook, with the sanction of the Governour, to maintain order; and Gen. Harney declared that he had no intention of using the military at his command, to cause disturbance. Both recommended the citizens to keep quiet, and attend to their ordinary occupations.

But soon after this, Gen. Harney was removed by orders from Washington. Gen. Price continued to busy himself with the duties of his command, and on the 4th of June, issued an address, in which he declared that the people of Missouri should exercise the right to choose their own position in any contest which might be forced upon them, unaided by any military force whatever. He referred to a report of the intention of the Federal authorities to disarm those of the citizens of Missouri who did not agree in opinion with the Administration at Washington, and put arms in the hands of those who in some localities of the State were supposed to sympathize with the views of the Federal Government; and he added: "The purpose of such a movement could not be misunderstood, and it would not only be a palpable violation of the agreement referred to, and an equally plain violation of our constitutional rights, but a gross indignity to the citizens of this State, which would be resisted to the last extremity." In the conclusion of his address he wrote: "The people of Missouri cannot be forced, under the terrours of a military invasion, into a position not of their own free choice. A million of such people as the citizens of Missouri were never yet subjugated, and if attempted, let no apprehension be entertained of the result."

On the 13th of June, 1861, Gov. Jackson issued his proclamation calling for fifty thousand volunteers. Price appointed nine brigadier-generals. These preparations were large on paper; but the brigadiers had no actual force at their command; and even, if men were not lacking, arms and ammunition were; and as for military training and discipline, there had been for years no military organization, and not even a militia muster in Missouri. It was thus poorly prepared for the contest that the State of Missouri, separated from her confederates and alone, showed a heroism almost unexampled in history in spurning the plea of "helplessness," and confronting the entire power of the North, at a time indeed when Northern newspapers were declaring that she was but as a mouse under the lion's paw.

The first development of the campaign on the part of Gen. Price was to issue orders to the several brigadiers just appointed, to organize their forces as rapidly as possible, and push them forward to Booneville and Lexington. His ulterior design was, having collected at Lexington volunteers from the whole region accessible to it, to march down to the extreme southwest part of the State where subsistence was abundant; where opportunity might be had to organize his army; and where he expected to be joined by Confederate forces from Arkansas under the command of Brig.-Gen. McCulloch.

No serious thought was entertained of giving battle at Booneville. About eighteen hundred Missourians were assembled in camp near there; and not more than one-third of them were armed. They had not a piece of artillery; and their small arms were generally of a very imperfect kind, including single-barrelled shot-guns and rifles. On the 20th of June, Gen. Lyon, with a well-appointed Federal force about three thousand strong, debarked near Booneville. The six hundred armed Missourians, ander command of Col. Marmaduke, were posted in loose order in a wood along a wheat-field not far from the water's edge. Seeing no reasonable hope of holding his position against a column of Federals advancing with eight pieces of artillery, Col. Marmaduke ordered his little force to retreat. The men refused to obey the order; and received the advancing enemy with a close volley, under which more than a hundred fell killed and wounded. But the shock of the encounter, as the enemy came on, was too much for the thin and irregular line of these desperately brave men, and they were soon scattered in flight. Their loss was inconsiderable—three men killed, and twenty-five or thirty wounded; and they had given to the enemy his first lesson of the courage and adventure of the "rebel militia" of Missouri.

After the singular affair of Booneville, Gov. Jackson, who had taken the field, commenced to retire his small force towards Warsaw; intending to effect a junction with Price, and to continue with him the line of march to the southwestern angle of the State. This was effected on the night of the 3d of July; the column from Lexington forming a junction with Jackson's forces in Cedar County. The plan of campaign was now to get as far as possible from the line of the Missouri River, which gave facilities for attack to the enemy, who could bring forward overwhelming numbers before Gen. Price could possibly organize his forces in this vicinity and throw them in fighting posture.

The very night of the junction of the two columns, an order was issued for the report and organization of the entire force. Two thousand men reported to Brig.-Gen. Rains, six hundred to Brig.-Gen. Slack, and about five hundred each to Brig.-Gens. Clark and Parsons; making an entire force of about thirty-six hundred men. This, then, was the Patriot Army of Missouri. It was a heterogeneous mixture of all human compounds, and represented every condition of Western life. There were the old and the young, the rich and poor, the high and low, the grave and gay, the planter and labourer, the farmer and clerk, the hunter and boatman, the merchant and woodsman. At least five hundred of these men were entirely unarmed. Many had only the common rifle and shot-gun. None were provided with cartridge-boxes or canteens. They had eight pieces of cannon, but no shells, and very few solid shot or rounds of grape and canister. Rude and almost incredible devices were made to supply these wants: trace-chains, iron-rods, hard pebbles, and smooth stones were substituted for shot; and evidence of the effect of such rough missiles was to be given in the next encounter with the enemy.

On the 4th of July, with his motley, ill-provided, brave army, Gen. Jackson, then in command, took up his line of march for the Southwest, where he hoped to join McCulloch. In the mean time, however, Gen. Sigel, with a column of Federals three thousand in number, had been sent out from St. Louis on the southwestern branch of the Pacific Railroad to Rolla, and had arrived at the town of Carthage, immediately in Jackson's front, thus threatening him with battle in the course of a few hours. About ten o'clock in the morning of the 5th of July, the Missourians approached a creek within a mile and a half of the enemy, whose forces in three detachments were admirably posted upon the brow of a hill.

The first important encounter of arms in Missouri was now to take place. Gen. Jackson found great difficulty in forming his line of battle and in deploying his cavalry under the constant fire of Sigel's batteries. Gen. Sigel had assured his men that there would be no serious conflict; he had remarked that the Missourians were coming into line like a worm-fence, and that a few grape and canister thrown into their midst would soon involve them in confusion and put them to flight. But he was terribly undeceived. When it was found impossible, on account of the rawness of their horses, to get the cavalry in position under fire, the order was given for the infantry to charge the enemy; the cavalry to come up at the same time in supporting distance. They advanced at the double-quick with a shout. The Federals retreated across Bear Creek, a wide and deep stream, destroying the bridge over which they had crossed. They still continued their retreat along the bank of the creek, for the distance of a mile or more, and formed behind a skirt of timber.

The Missourians had to cross an open field; they were exposed to a raking fire before they could reach the enemy's cover. A number of the cavalry dismounted, and acted with the infantry, so as to put in active use all the small arms brought upon the field. They rushed towards the skirt of timber, and opened vigorously upon the enemy across the stream, who returned the fire with spirit. For the space of an hour the fire on each side was incessant and fierce. At last, the Missourians threw a quantity of dead timber into the stream, and commenced crossing in large numbers, when the enemy again abandoned his position, and started in the direction of Carthage, eight miles distant. A running fight was kept up all the way to Carthage. Here the enemy again made a stand, forming ambuscades behind houses, wood-piles, and fences. After a severe engagement there of some forty minutes, he retreated under cover of night in the direction of Rolla; never halting until the next day, about forty miles from the field of battle, over twelve of which he had been pursued by men, whom Gen. Sigel had expected to capture, almost without a fight.

The results of the day were greatly encouraging and gratifying to the Missourians. These raw and poorly-armed men had driven a well-disciplined enemy from three different positions. Their own loss was probably not more than fifty killed and one hundred and fifty wounded; that of the enemy, who had suffered greatly in his retreat, about three times as large. No wonder that with this experience of the fighting qualities of the people against whom they had to contend, the Federal commanders in Missouri were awakened to a sense of the magnitude of the work before them.

The day succeeding this engagement, Gen. Price, who had hitherto been detained from active command by a severe sickness, arrived at Carthage, accompanied by Brig.-Gen. McCulloch of the Confederate forces, and Maj.-Gen. Pearce of the Arkansas State troops, with a force of nearly two thousand men. These timely reinforcements were hailed with great joy ; and the patriot army was alike animated by the appearance of their beloved commander, and the assurance, which McCulloch's presence gave them, of the friendly feeling and intention of the Confederate Government.

The next day the forces at Carthage, under their respective commands, took up their line of march for Cowskin Prairie, near the boundary of the Indian Nation. Here they remained for several days, organizing and drilling ; Gen. Price still continued to receive reinforcements ; and the whole numerical strength of the command was now rated about ten thousand. With this force, although yet imperfectly armed, it was decided to venture on the offensive ; and it having been ascertained that the Federal commanders, Lee, Sturgis, Sweeny, and Sigel, were about to form a junction at Springfield, it was determined by Price, McCulloch, and Pearce, to march upon that place, and attack the enemy where he had taken his position in force.

When the army reached Crane Creek, about thirty miles from Springfield, a consultation was held as to their future course. Gen. Price earnestly advocated an advance. Gen. McCulloch doubted its prudence. He looked with great concern on the large proportion of undisciplined men in Price's command ; he regarded the unarmed men as incumbrances ; and he concluded that the unorganized and undisciplined condition of both wings of the army suggested the wisdom of avoiding battle with the disciplined enemy upon his own ground and in greatly superiour numbers. Gen. Price resented the idea of the nature of the materials under his command, and assured McCulloch that when the time of battle came, these untaught and headstrong men would fight together and with a resolution which would spurn defeat. He requested the Confederate commander to loan a number of arms from his command for the use of such Misssouri soldiers as were unarmed, believing that, with the force at his command, he could whip the enemy. This McCulloch refused, and still declined the responsibility of ordering an advance of the whole command.

But in the midst of this hesitation Gen. McCulloch received a general order from Gen. Polk, commander of the Southwestern division of the Confederate army, to advance upon the enemy in Missouri. Another council was called. McCulloch exhibited the order he had received, and offered to march at once upon Springfield, upon condition that he should have the chief command of the army. The question of rank was one of no little embarrassment. Price was a Major-General in the State service. McCulloch was a Brigadier-General in the Confederate service. If the State troops were merely militia, and Price a General of Militia, the question was at once settled—McCulloch would have been entitled to precedence. But the Missourians, with much show of reason, contended that their State had assumed an independent attitude, and by her laws, as a sovereign, had raised an army which was on a regular military footing, and therefore their Major-General was entitled to command.

The question was solved by Price in a noble and patriotic spirit. He relinquished his post to McCulloch, expressing himself in substance as follows: "I seek not distinction; I am not fighting for that; but in the defence of the liberties of my countrymen. It matters little *what* position I hold. I am ready to surrender, not only the command, but my life as a sacrifice to the cause." That his services and his presence among the men should not be lost, he took a subordinate position in the forthcoming contest. McCulloch assumed chief command, and Price was a division general under him; and thus the army marched forward to meet the foe.

THE BATTLE OF OAK HILL.

On the 7th of August, McCulloch reached a camp three miles from Wilson's Creek, and twelve miles from Springfield. His command was thus composed: the Missouri forces numbered eight thousand, of whom only about six thousand were armed; the Confederate troops were three thousand two hundred, coming from Louisiana, Texas, and Arkansas; and there were eighteen hundred Arkansas State troops under General Pearce. The total effective force was thus about eleven thousand, of whom nearly six thousand were mounted; and it had fifteen pieces of artillery.

General Lyon had assembled at Springfield an effective army of nearly ten thousand men, consisting of his own and Col. Totten's forces from Booneville and St. Louis, and the troops heretofore acting under Gens. Sigel and Sturgis and Col. Sweeny. About two thousand were "home guards," of Missouri, the rest were United States regulars and volunteers from the Northwestern States. Their artillery consisted of sixteen pieces —several batteries being of the regular service.

On the 9th of August McCulloch moved up to Wilson's Creek, intending to advance upon the enemy at Springfield. But Lyon had anticipated him, and was already moving in three heavy columns. The next morning before sunrise, the enemy had succeeded in obtaining the position he desired; and McCulloch, who was quietly taking breakfast at the time, was surprised by his couriers announcing that the enemy were in sight and in great force, and had gained both sides of his camp.

On the right Gen. Sigel had already opened a heavy fire. By muffling the wheels of his cannon, he had succeeded, under cover of the night, in getting positions near McCulloch's camp, and now poured into it a severe and destructive fire. Gen. Lyon led the attack on the left.

Reinforcements were rapidly hurried in the direction of Sigel's attack. Gen. McCulloch sent forward Col. Hebert's Louisiana Volunteers and McIntosh's mounted Arkansians, who, moving to the left, gained a position along a fence enclosing a cornfield. Here McIntosh dismounted his men, and the two regiments rapidly advanced in the face of a galling fire. A terrible conflict of small arms ensued. Undismayed, breasting a deadly fire, the gallant men of these regiments leaped the fence, and drove the enemy before them back upon his main body. But still Sigel's artillery continued to play with damaging effect. A battery, commanded by Capt. Reid, was brought up to oppose it. Seizing the critical moment, Gen. McCulloch placed himself at the head of two companies of a Louisiana regiment near him, and marching to the right, drew rapidly upon the adverse guns. At the same time, McIntosh and Hebert, with their men, came up, and with a loud cheer, they rushed upon the enemy's cannoniers, driving them from their guns. This gallant charge swept everything before it; five guns were taken; and nothing could now arrest the tide of success on the right. Sigel fell back in confusion, and lost his last gun in a retreat which had now become irretrievable.

Having cleared their right and rear, it became necessary for the Confederate forces to direct all their attention to the centre, where Gen. Lyon was pressing upon the Missourians with all his strength. To this point McIntosh's regiment, Churchill's regiment on foot, Gratiot's regiment, and McRae's battalion were rapidly moved. Along the whole line of the hill, upon which the enemy was posted, a terrible fire of musketry was now kept up. The roar of the battle was tremendous, bursting along two opposing lines which swept for miles over the rolling fields. Masses of infantry fell back and again marched forward. The summit of the hill was covered with the dead and wounded. Totten's battery on the enemy's side did fearful execution. With the loss of many men and horses, the Federal battery, after a fierce engagement with Woodruff's, was with difficulty withdrawn. Part of it was again planted where it swept the front—part was masked to meet an advance. At this moment, when the fortunes of the day yet hung in doubt, two regiments of Gen. Pearce's command were ordered forward to support the centre. Reid's battery was also brought up and the Louisiana regiment was again called into action on the left of it. The enemy was now evidently giving way.

Gen. Lyon had marked the progress of the battle with deep anxiety.

He saw that his men were unable to advance against the sheet of fire before them, and he marked with desperate concern the huge chasms in his lines where his torn regiments had given way. He had already been wounded in the leg, and a bullet had cut the scalp of his head. His horse was shot under him. Bloody and haggard, he turned to one of his officers, and said : " I fear the day is lost—I will lead the charge." Remounting and riding rapidly to the front, he said simply to the nearest regiments, " Forward, men : I will lead you." He had advanced but a little way, when two small rifle-balls, or buckshot, pierced his breast. He reeled in his saddle, and fell dead from his horse.*

The Federal line pushed forward, but after a brief encounter was evidently staggered. McCulloch and Price threw forward nearly all their reserves. Totten's dreadful battery at last fell back. Missourians, Arkansians, Louisianians, and Texans pressed forward. The Federal centre gave way ; the wings were forced to the rear ; and with one wild yell, the Southerners broke upon their disordered ranks, pushing them back, and strewing the ground with their dead. The order to retreat was given, and soon the enemy's infantry columns, artillery, and wagons, were seen in the distance among the hills, rapidly making their way towards Springfield, defeated and driven from the field.

The Federal loss could not have been less than two thousand in killed and wounded ; three hundred prisoners were taken, and six pieces of artillery. Gen. McCulloch officially stated his loss as two hundred and sixty-five killed and eight hundred wounded. More than half of this loss was among the Missourians commanded by Price.

After the brilliant victory of Oak Hill—which for a time freed the whole of Southwestern Missouri from Federal rule—it unfortunately fell out that McCulloch and Price could not agree upon a plan of campaign.

---

* Maj.-Gen. Nathaniel Lyon was a native of Connecticut, and had served in the regular army of the United States. He was an exception to the politics of that army ; for he was an undisguised and fanatical Abolitionist. He entered the United States army as second lieutenant in 1841, and was subsequently brevetted captain. He arrived in St. Louis in April, 1861, having been sent from a post far in the Southwest to stand a court-martial on the charge of peculation. Here his great activity in suppressing the excitement of Southern feeling, seizing the arsenal, erecting defences around the city, and disarming Southern sympathizers, recommended him to notice in the North and at Washington ; and he rapidly rose from the rank of captain to that of major-general in two months. He was undoubtedly an able and dangerous man : one who appreciated the force of audacity and the value of quick decision. He was small in stature, wiry, active, of dark complexion : brave, to a fault ; and an excellent, though restless and ambitious officer. For several days before the battle in which he lost his life, he is said to have been a prey to uneasiness and disappointment, which brought upon his face a troubled look, observed by all around him. To one of his staff he said gloomily, that he " believed in presentiments," and could not rid himself of the idea that the coming battle would result disastrously. After he was dead, it was remarked that the same troubled look he had borne for days clung to his countenance in death. The fall of this man was undoubtedly a serious loss to the Federals in Missouri.

The former therefore took the responsibility of withdrawing the Confederate forces, and retired with his army to the frontiers of Arkansas. Late in August, Gen. Price, abandoned by the Confederate forces, took up his line of march for the Missouri River, with an armed force of about five thousand men, and seven pieces of cannon. He, however, continued to receive reinforcements from the north side of the Missouri River. On the 7th of September he encountered a force of irregular Federal troops under the notorious Lane and Montgomery, at a place called Drywood, some fifteen miles east of Fort Scott. Defeating and brushing this force from his path, Price threw a small garrison into Fort Scott, and pressed on towards Lexington, the main object of his movement.

In the meantime the active and adventurous demonstrations of Brig.-Gen. Harris, in Northern Missouri, had made an important diversion of the enemy in favour of Gen. Price. Although surrounded by enemies, and within their reach from many points, Gen. Harris had secretly organized a force, and by the rapidity of his movements produced the impression that he was stronger than he really was ; the result of which was that he had diverted several thousand men from the support of Gen. Lyon, and held them north of the river until after the battle of Oak Hill, thus making an important contribution to the issue of that contest. On the 10th of September, Gen. Harris crossed the Missouri at Artien Creek. Recruits in bodies of ten, fifty, and a hundred constantly joined him, and when he effected a junction with Gen. Price, he added nearly three thousand effective men to a force already consisting of more than six thousand.

Some weeks previous, Gen. Fremont had arrived to take chief command of the Western Department. He had reached St. Louis, and military preparations were immediately carried on with renewed vigour. He assumed his command with great ostentation ; and his displays of garish splendour in his camp were such that some of the Northern newspapers were provoked to say that he resembled more an Eastern satrap than an American commander. But the most remarkable event with which he inaugurated his authority was a proclamation, issued at St. Louis, on the 30th of August. In this remarkable fulmination of authority he declared that, in his judgment, the public safety and the success of the Federal arms required " unity of purpose without let or hindrance to the prompt administration of affairs ; " therefore he proclaimed martial law through the whole State of Missouri, and asserted that the lines of his army of occupation extended from Leavenworth, by way of the posts of Jefferson City, Rolla, and Ironton, to Cape Girardeau on the Mississippi ; all persons within these lines, taken with arms in their hands, were to be tried by court-martial, and shot if found guilty ; he furthermore proclaimed, that the property, real and personal, of persons who took up arms against the United States, or who should be proved to have taken part with their enemies in the field, should be confiscated, and *their slaves should be freemen.*

This proclamation was vastly pleasing to a large and rapidly-growing party in the North, who recognized the extinction of negro slavery in the South as an essential object of the war. It was an ingenious idea, too, to make of slavery a party-coloured crime—sinful in the "rebel," but blameless in the Union man. The brutality of the proclamation, too, was refreshing; for there were already many in the North who believed that their fellow-countrymen should be shot, and this in the name of the Union, for the simple crime that as citizens of the State of Missouri they obeyed the orders of the lawful authority of their State.

But the Government at Washington was not yet prepared for these lengths of the war; and it is a curious commentary on the future of Mr. Lincoln's policy with respect to the extinction of slavery, that Fremont's proclamation was distinctly disavowed and instantly overruled by him.

But while Fremont was thus indulging his political fanaticism, he was strangely inattentive to the course of military events in Missouri. Lexington, upon which Gen. Price was now directing his march, was feebly defended. It was only when it was seriously threatened that Col. Mulligan moved up from Jefferson City with his Irish brigade, and found himself with an insufficient garrison, and but little time to strengthen his works, confronted and encompassed by an army of more than ten thousand men.

THE SIEGE OF LEXINGTON.

On the 12th of September, Gen. Price approached Lexington. In the midst of the straggling town there was a large brick building known as the College Building. Col. Mulligan had planned an earthwork ten feet high, with a ditch eight feet wide, enclosing the College, with a large area capable of holding a garrison of ten thousand men. As Price approached the town a sharp affair occurred with the enemy's outposts, and at one time a general engagement was threatened. Taking advantage of the smoke, Gen. Rains prepared to lead a column to the assault of the breast-works at an angle which was apparently weakly defended. But the movement was discovered by the enemy, who rallied in force to the threatened point. Kneeling down to shelter themselves, with levelled muskets and fingers upon the triggers, the Federals were silent as death. The Missourians advanced at a rapid run. When within a hundred yards of the breastworks, the smoke lifted, a line of fire flashed along the entrenchments, and five hundred muskets launched their bullets against the advancing ranks. But with a presence of mind inspired by their habits, the Missourians dropped at the flash, and, instantly rising, again rushed forward. Again they met a fire which was more destructive. Finding that a surprise was hopeless, and that the Federals were assembling a large part of their artillery at the threatened point, the column of attack was withdrawn.

Discovering, at the close of the day, that his ammunition, the most of which had been left behind in the march from Springfield, was nearly exhausted, and that his men, most of whom had not eaten anything in thirty-six hours, required rest and food, General Price withdrew from the town and encamped. His ammunition wagons having been at last brought up, and large reinforcements having come in, he again moved into the town on the 18th, and commenced the final attack upon the enemy's works.

Col. Mulligan bore himself with the bravery characteristic of an Irishman, and worthy of a better cause. When summoned to surrender, he replied: "If you want us, you must take us." The garrison had not sufficient supplies of water within their entrenchments, and were compelled to resort to the river, nearly half a mile distant, under the constant fire of skirmishers. Large bodies had to fight their way to the water, and bloody conflicts ensued. As a detachment of the Missouri troops, under command of Col. Rives, were passing down the bank of the river to capture a steamboat lying under the enemy's guns, a fire was opened upon him from a building known as Anderson's House, standing on the summit of the bluff, and designated as a hospital by the white flag over it. There were in the building at the time twenty-four sick; but it contained also a large body of armed soldiers. Indignant at the perfidy which directed this attack, several companies from Gen. Harris' and the fourth division rushed up the bank, leaped over every barrier, and speedily overpowered the garrison. The important position thus secured was within one hundred and twenty-five yards of the enemy's entrenchments.

Early in the morning of the 19th September, the roar of cannon and rattle of musketry again resounded through the hills around the beleaguered camp. The garrison suffered much from thirst. The pressure of the assault was incessant and bloody. Cannon surrounded them on three sides, and, occupying positions of command, poured out constant torrents of shot, shell, stones, fragments of iron,—every missile that could be found and used for battering and death.

On the 20th, Gen. Price caused a number of bales of hemp to be transported to the river heights, where movable breastworks were speedily constructed out of them. The demonstrations of the artillery, and particularly the continued advance of the hempen breastworks, attracted the attention and excited the alarm of the enemy. Several daring attempts were made to drive back the assailants. At one time, in extreme desperation, a cavalry assault was made by the Illinois mounted men upon one of the Missouri batteries; but the assailants were terribly cut up with grape and buckshot, and retreated in confusion to the entrenchments.

Col. Mulligan had received two painful wounds. After having once ordered down a white flag which some of the "home guards," had displayed, he, at last, convinced of the hopelessness of his situation, determined on a surrender. He did so, only after fifty-two hours of continuous fighting. Immediately Gen. Price issued an order, that the forces under Col. Mulligan, having stacked their arms, "were not to be insulted by word or act, for they had fought like brave men." Mulligan, having given up his sword, had it immediately returned to him by Gen. Price, who said he "could not see a man of his valour without his sword." The brave captive was afterwards treated with true chivalric courtesy by Gen. Price, who induced him and his wife to become his guests, and entertained them with all the hospitality at his command.

The entire loss of the Missourians in this series of engagements was but twenty-five killed and seventy-two wounded. The enemy's loss was considerably larger, and, though never officially reported, was estimated by their own narratives as amounting to five hundred in killed and wounded. The visible fruits of the victory were considerable. The Missourians captured five colonels, a hundred and nineteen other commissioned officers, and thirty-five hundred non-commissioned officers and privates, five cannon, two mortars, over three thousand muskets, rifles and carbines, about seven hundred and fifty horses, a quantity of ammunition, and more than one hundred thousand dollars worth of commissary stores. There was also recovered about $900,000 of coin of which the Lexington Bank had been robbed, in accordance with Fremont's instructions, which Gen. Price ordered to be immediately restored to its owners.

The capture of Lexington and the bold and brilliant movements of the Missouri patriots in other parts of the State—among them the operations in Southeastern Missouri of the partisan Jeff. Thompson and his "Swamp Fox Brigade"—excited rage and alarm in the Washington administration. Gen. Fremont, who was severely censured for not having reinforced Mulligan, hoped to recover his position by activity and success; he put himself at the head of the army, and advanced towards Jefferson City, sending back the promise that he would overwhelm Price. It was at this period that Gen. Price found his position one of the greatest emergency. He had received intelligence that the Confederate forces, under Gens. Pillow and Hardee, had been withdrawn from the southeastern portion of the State. Gen. McCulloch had retired to Arkansas. Gen. Price was left with the only forces in Missouri to confront an enemy sixty thousand strong; he was almost entirely without ammunition: and he was beset with other difficulties and embarrassments. A large number of his men had volunteered in haste, and hied to the camps with hardly a change of clothing. Many were naturally anxious to return to their homes. The difficulty of maintaining a wagon train sufficient to support so large an army was seriously felt. Thus surrounded by circumstances of the most painful and unlooked-for misfortune, Gen. Price was compelled not only to make a retrograde movement, but, also, to disband a considerable portion of his forces.

With his army thus diminished, Gen. Price commenced his retreat about the 27th of September. With Sturgis on the north side of the river, Lane on the west, and himself on the east, Fremont expected to cut off and capture the entire force of the Missourians. This Price adroitly prevented by sending out cavalry as if intending to attack each of the enemy separately, and so covering his retreat. This retreat was executed in a most admirable manner, and amidst numerous obstacles. The Osage river was crossed in two flat-bottomed boats, constructed for the occasion by the Missouri soldiers; and then Price moved to Neosho, on the Indian frontier of the State. Here the Legislature had assembled, and here Price again formed a junction with McCulloch, at the head of 5,000 men. It was at this time the State Legislature at length passed the Ordinance of Secession, and Gen. Price had the satisfaction of firing a hundred guns to celebrate the event.

From Neosho Price and McCulloch fell back to Cassville and Pineville, on the southern borders of the State. At Pineville, Price made preparation to receive Fremont, determined not to abandon Missouri without a battle. But just at this juncture news came that Fremont had been superseded as commander of the Federal forces. His course had given great offence at Washington; and Attorney-General Bates had declared that it would be "a crime" to keep him in command. It was said that his vanity had become so insolent that he paid no regard whatever to acts of Congress, the orders of his superiours, the usages of the service, or the rights of individuals; and that he was surrounded by a band of contractors, and, in partnership with them, plundered the public funds without mercy. On such persistent representations the order at Washington was at last given for his removal and the appointment of Gen. Hunter in his place.

Fremont had obtained intimation that such an order was on the way from Washington. He took singular pains to prevent it from reaching him. He had two body-guards, one of whites and one of Indians. He gave strict orders that no one should be admitted through the inner lines surrounding his headquarters, except by his direct orders. Notwithstanding his precautions, one of the three military messengers sent from St. Louis, by address and stratagem succeeded in gaining admission, and, making his way to Fremont's presence on the night of the 7th of November, delivered to him the fatal missive which concluded his career.

This event had the effect of demoralizing the Federal forces to such an extent that an immediate retreat was thought advisable by the acting officers in command. The degraded General showed symptoms of rebellion. The Dutch were greatly attached to him ; signs of mutiny were shown by these adherents ; for a time open revolt was threatened ; but Fremont's subordinates, Sigel and Asboth, positively refused to sustain him, and the army was ordered to retreat from Springfield. The Federals accordingly left that town in the direction of Rolla, and were pursued by Gen. Price to Osceola. From Osceola, Gen. Price fell back to Springfield, to forage his army and obtain supplies. Both armies having thus drawn off, we may leave here for the present the history of the Missouri campaign.

Notwithstanding the adverse termination of this campaign with respect to the occupation of Missouri, it had alreay accomplished much ; it had given an exhibition of spirit and resource without a parallel in equal circumstances ; and it constitutes the most remarkable and brilliant episode of the war. It was a chapter of wonders. Price's army of ragged heroes, had marched over eight hundred miles ; it had scarcely passed a week without an engagement of some sort ; it was tied down to no particular line of operations, but fought the enemy wherever he could be found ; and it had provided itself with ordnance and equipments almost entirely from the prodigal stores of the Federals. The hero of Missouri started on his campaign without a dollar, without a wagon or team, without a cartridge, without a bayonet-gun. When he commenced his retreat, he had about eight thousand bayonet-guns, fifty pieces of cannon, four hundred tents, and many other articles needful in an army, for which his men were almost exclusively indebted to their own strong arms in battle.

This campaign was little less than a puzzle to military critics. Price managed to subsist an army without governmental resources. He seldom complained of want of transportation. His men were never demoralized by hunger. They would go into the cornfield, shuck the corn, shell it, take it to the mill, and bring it into camp, ground into meal. Or, if they had no flour, they took the wheat from the stack, threshed it themselves, and asked the aid of the nearest miller to reduce it to flour. Price proved that such an army could go where they pleased in an agricultural country. His men were always cheerful. They frequently, on the eve of an engagement, danced around their camp-fires with bare feet and in rag costumes, of which it was declared " Billy Barlow's dress at a circus would be decent in comparison." Price himself wore nothing on his shoulders but a brown-linen duster ; and this and his white hair streaming on the battle-field made him a singular figure. Despite the exposure and hardship of this campaign, the most remarkable fact remains to be recorded : that in its entire course not more than fifty men died from disease.

Such a record of courage, of expedient and of endurance, has no known parallel in the war. It settled forever the question of Missouri manhood. It did more than this : it proved that the spirit of the native and true population of Missouri was strongly Southern, and that it needed nothing but organization and opportunity for its triumph.

THE WESTERN VIRGINIA CAMPAIGN.

The campaign in Western Virginia, which was mostly cotemporary with that of Missouri, and very similar to it in its discursive character, unfortunately did not partake of its brilliancy. With but little compensation, either in the prestige of arms, or in the fruits of single victories, it surrendered to the enemy a country of more capacity and grandeur than perhaps any other of equal limits on the American continent ; abounding in immense forests, possessed of almost fabulous mineral resources, offering to the manufacturer the vastest water-power in the world, and presenting in its deposits of coal and salt, fields of inexhaustible enterprise and wealth.

In the month of June, Brigadier-General Wise of Virginia was sent into the Kanawha Valley ; it being supposed that by his rare and characteristic enthusiasm he would be able to rally the people of this region to the support of the State. He established his headquarters at Charleston, and succeeded in raising a brigade of twenty-five hundred infantry, seven hundred cavalry and three batteries of artillery. With subsequent reinforcements his command amounted to four thousand men. It was obvious enough that with this small force, his situation was extremely critical. The enemy had already landed considerable forces at Parkersburg and Point Pleasant on the Ohio River, and was rapidly using his superiour facilities for raising troops in the populous States of Ohio and Indiana, and his ample means of transportation by railroad through those States and by the navigation of the Ohio and Kanawha Rivers, to concentrate a large force in the lower part of the Kanawha Valley.

After some desultory movements, and a brilliant affair on Scary Creek, in Putnam County, where Col. Patton with a small force repulsed three Federal regiments, Gen. Wise prepared to give battle to the Federal forces, which, under the command of Gen. Cox, had been largely increased, and which were steadily advancing up the Valley, both by land and water. But the conflict was not to occur. A more formidable danger, from a different direction, menaced the Confederates. The disaster at Rich Mountain—the surrender of Pegram's force, and the retreat northward of Garnett's army, had withdrawn all support from the right flank, and, indeed, from the rear of Gen. Wise. He was in danger of being cut off in the rear by several roads from the northwest, striking the Kanawha road at various points between Lewisburg and Gauley Bridge. The danger seemed to him so pressing, that he fell back immediately with his entire force, first to Gauley Bridge and thence to Lewisburg, reaching the latter place about the 1st of August, and after a retreat which was necessarily much disordered, on account of his meagre means of transportation.

Within a few weeks after Gen. Wise fell back to Lewisburg, the Confederate cause in Western Virginia received the aid of a very effective body of men. John B. Floyd, who had been at one time Governor of Virginia, and afterwards Secretary of War under President Buchanan, was commissioned a brigadier-general in the Confederate army, and had succeeded in raising a command of three regiments of infantry and a battalion of cavalry. This force was intended for service in Western Virginia, and Gen. Floyd soon decided, with the approval of the War Department, that the defence of the Kanawha Valley was the object of first importance. He accordingly advanced to the White Sulphur Springs, nine miles east of Lewisburg, and held conferences with Gen. Wise. An advance towards the Gauley was promptly determined on, but the two bodies, under their commanders, moved at different times, and with perfectly distinct organizations, though within supporting distance.

Gen. Floyd moved first, and for some days skirmished vigorously with Cox's troops, which were in force at Gauley Bridge and in the neighbourhood of the "Hawk's Nest," a picturesque and majestic monument of wooded rocks, rising a thousand feet from the river road, at a point ten miles below the mouth of the Gauley. Gen. Wise having come up, the joint Confederate forces now approached nearer the enemy, skirmishing with various success. But while thus occupied, it was ascertained that another foe threatened their flank.

Col. Tyler, commanding the Seventh Ohio Regiment, of nearly thirteen hundred men, was approaching the Gauley River at Carnifax Ferry, about five miles south of Summerville, in Nicholas County, and twenty-four miles above Gauley Bridge. His movement was therefore on the right flank of the Confederates, and had he succeeded in crossing the river and reaching their rear, he would have cut their communications with Lewisburg. Gen. Floyd at once determined to cross the river at Carnifax Ferry and encounter this movement of the enemy. He at once put his brigade in motion, taking with him a part of Wise's cavalry; that commander remaining with the larger body of his troops at Pickett's Mills in Fayette County, so as to hold the turnpike, and guard against any aggressive movement of Cox, which might have embarrassed that against Tyler.

The enterprise of Gen. Floyd was thoroughly successful. Having crossed the Gauley, he, on the morning of the 26th of August, fell upon Tyler at a place called Cross Lanes; defeated and dispersed his force; and inflicted upon him a loss of about two hundred in killed, wounded, and prisoners.

After the affair of Cross Lanes, Gen. Floyd proceeded to strengthen his position on the Gauley. Owing to an unfortunate want of concert between Wise and himself, these two Confederate forces in Western Virginia were separated by a deep and rapid river; and Floyd himself was unable to attempt a movement against Cox. He was far from his depot of provisions in Lewisburg, and being unprovided with adequate transportation, it would have been rash to have ventured forward on the north of the river. Knowledge of this situation of affairs was not lost upon the enemy. Gen. Rosecrans—a name which was hereafter to become familiar on more important theatres of the war—commanded the Federal forces between Buckhannon and Cheat Mountain. He at once conceived the idea of overwhelming the Confederates on both sides of the Gauley, and accordingly moved rapidly down the road leading from Weston to Summerville, with at least nine thousand men and several heavy batteries of artillery.

Gen. Floyd was in a bend of Gauley River, very near Carnifax Ferry. On the 10th of September, Rosecrans, by a rapid march of sixteen miles, threw his entire force about Floyd's entrenchments, and commenced a vigorous attack. The force of Floyd's command did not exceed seventeen hundred and fifty men. But his flanks were well protected by precipices or cliffs heavily wooded; and from three o'clock until nightfall his centre, protected by an imperfect earthwork, sustained an assault from an enemy five times his numbers, made with small arms, grape, and round-shot, from howitzers and rifled cannon. As the sun was sinking, Rosecrans ordered a final and desperate charge. His troops pressed rapidly forward to short musket range; the Southern lines were wrapped in fire; a thousand bullets darted into the adverse ranks, and for a few moments the carnage was appalling. The Federals fell back, and returned no more to the assault. The ground was covered with hundreds of their dead and wounded. The Confederates had not lost a man killed and not more than twenty wounded.

During the night, Gen. Floyd crossed the river by means of two ferry-boats and a hastily constructed bridge of logs. He had accomplished a brilliant success in the check and lesson he had already given the enemy; and knowing Rosecrans' superiority of numbers, and fearing for his own communications in his rear, he determined to withdraw to Wise's camp, and unite the two commands.

It appears that when Floyd had first learned of Rosecrans' advance, he had despatched orders to Gen. Wise for reinforcements, and that he failed to procure them. He wrote to the War Department at Richmond that he could have beaten the enemy, if these reinforcements had come up when ordered; that if he could have commanded the services of five thousand men, instead of eighteen hundred, which he had, he could have opened the road directly into the Valley of the Kanawha. He indicated the urgent necessity of shaping the command in that region of country so as to ensure unity of action,—the condition of success in all military operations.

In a few days Rosecrans crossed the Gauley with his army, and as the force opposing them was superiour in numbers, Floyd and Wise fell back deliberately towards Sewell's Mountain. New differences now developed themselves between these two leaders, which disturbed that unity of action so much desired. After reaching Sewell's Mountain, Gen. Floyd held a council of his officers, and determined to fall back still further, to Meadow Bluff, eighteen miles west of Lewisburg. Gov. Wise followed him only as far as the eastern slope of the mountain, where he proceeded to strengthen his position, which he named Camp "Defiance."

At this pause in military operations in the Kanawha Valley, it will be convenient to note the events which had occurred further north in this Western region of Virginia, and to observe the movements of the Confederate army there under the command of a man whose star was to be singularly obscured before it mounted the zenith of fame—Gen. Robert E. Lee.

After the retreat of Gen. Garnett from Rich Mountain, and the death of that officer, Gen. Lee was appointed to succeed him, and, with as little delay as possible, repaired to the scene of operations. He took with him reinforcements, making his whole force, in conjunction with the remnant of Gen. Garnett's army, about sixteen thousand men. The roads in this part of the country were deep in mud and horrible with precipices. By patience and skill, Gen. Lee advanced with his army across the Alleghany range, and deliberately approached the enemy in Randolph County.

Rosecrans was then the ranking officer of the Federal troops in Northwestern Virginia ; but Gen. Reynolds held the approaches to Beverly with a force estimated at from ten to twelve thousand men. The larger part of these were strongly entrenched at a point at the junction of Tygart's Valley River and Elk Run, which post was called by the Federals " Elk Water." The remainder held the pass at the second summit of Cheat Mountain, on the best road from Staunton to Parkersburg. The mountain had three well-defined summits. The second presented the greatest advantages for fortification, and here the enemy had built a powerful fort or block-house in the elbow of the road, flanked by entrenchments of earth and logs, protected by dense abattis on every side, and rendered inaccessible, in two directions, by the steep and rugged walls of the mountain.

Having approached the enemy, Gen. Lee directed careful reconnoissances to be made of all his positions. Col. Rust, of the 3d Arkansas Regiment, made what afterwards proved to be a very imperfect reconnoissance of the enemy's position on Cheat Mountain, and reported that it was perfectly practicable to turn it and carry it by storm. Gen. Lee at once issued his orders for a united movement upon the forces of the enemy, both at Elk Water and on Cheat Mountain. After great labour and the endurance of severe hardships on the mountain spurs, where the weather was very cold, Gen. Lee succeeded in getting below the enemy at Elk Water, placing other portions of his forces on the spurs of the mountain immediately east and west of the enemy, and marching another portion of his troops down the river close to the enemy. The forces were thus arranged in position for making an attack upon the enemy at Elk Water, and remained there for some hours, waiting the signal from Col. Rust's attack on Cheat Mountain.

That officer, with fifteen hundred troops, chiefly his Arkansas men, had turned the Cheat Summit Fort, and was now in its rear. But he saw at once that his former reconnoissance had been deceptive. The fortified post was literally unapproachable, by reason of thick abattis of felled trees, with branches and undergrowth densely interlaced, extending from the block-house nearly half a mile down the rugged sides of the mountain. Col. Rust gave no signal for the advance, awaited by the forces at Elk Water; he thought his enterprise hopeless, and withdrew his troops. Gen. Lee, informed of the miscarriage of this part of his plan, abandoned the whole of it, and retired his command without any results whatever.

The failure to dislodge the enemy from Cheat Mountain, and thus re lieve Northwestern Virginia, was a disappointment to the Southern public, whose expectations had been greatly raised by vague rumours of Lee's strategy and plans. It was thought, too, that this distinguished commander might have realized some results of his well-matured plan, if, despite of the disconcert of Rust, he had risked an attack upon the enemy's position at Elk Water, which a portion of his forces had surrounded. But regrets were unavailing now; danger was imminent in another quarter. Learning by couriers of the union of Rosecrans and Cox, and of their advance upon Wise and Floyd, Gen. Lee decided at once to reinforce the Southern armies on the line of Lewisburg. He reached Gen. Floyd's camp at Meadow Bluff, on the 20th of September, and after conferring with him for two days, joined Gen. Wise at Sewell Mountain, on the 22d. The experienced eye of Lee saw at once that Wise's position was very strong, and capable of arresting a very heavy hostile force. He accordingly ordered forward his troops to the spot, and extended the defensive works already planned.

Meanwhile Gen. Rosecrans, with fifteen thousand men, advanced, and took possession of the top of Big Sewell Mountain, skirmishing with the forward troops of the Wise brigade. Gen. Lee daily expected an attack, and was prepared for it. His force was now quite equal to that of the enemy. He was within sight of him; each apparently awaiting an attack from the other. But the opportunity of a decisive battle in Western Virginia was again to be lost. On the night of the 6th of October, Rosecrans' troops moved to the rear in the dark, and the next morning, when the Confederates looked out from their camp, the whole of the threatening host that had confronted them for twelve days before, was gone. Gen. Lee made no attempt to pursue them. It was said that the mud, the swollen streams, and the reduced condition of his artillery horses made pursuit impracticable.

But one incident of success was to occur in a campaign of so many disappointments. When Gen. Lee withdrew from the Cheat Mountain region, he left Gen. H. R. Jackson with twenty-five hundred men to hold his position on the Greenbrier River. On the 3d of October, the enemy, about four thousand strong, attacked Jackson's position. A severe artillery engagement occurred, in which Jackson could not bring more than five pieces in action to return the fire of the enemy's eight. Masses of infantry were then thrown forward on Jackson's right and front, marching up the wooded sides of a hill that rose from the river. The location of the hill was such that they could not fire effectively until they crossed the river ; and as they attempted to form and deploy, in order to a charge, the 12th Georgia Regiment fired several rapid volleys of musketry into them, which instantly checked their advance. At the same time, Shumaker's guns were directed to the point in the woods in which they were known to be crowded, and completed their discomfiture by playing upon them with destructive effect. The regiments on the hill-side retreated rapidly, and soon the whole force of the enemy's infantry, artillery, and cavalry was moving in a confused mass to the rear. His loss in the engagement in killed and wounded was estimated at from two hundred and fifty to three hundred. The loss of the Confederates was officially reported as six killed and thirty-one wounded.

The approaching rigours of winter terminated the campaign in Western Virginia ; or it may be said to have been virtually abandoned by the Richmond authorities. Gen. Lee, who had shed such little blood in the campaign, and obtained such indifferent reputation in mountain warfare, was appointed to take charge of the coast defences of South Carolina and Georgia. Gen. Wise was ordered to report to Richmond, and was subsequently assigned to important duty in North Carolina. Gen. Floyd lingered in the mountains ; had some desultory affairs with the enemy ; subsequently retired to Southwestern Virginia ; and from there was transferred by the Government to the now imposing theatre of war in Tennessee and Kentucky.

Thus ended the effort of the Confederate authorities to reclaim the larger portion of Western Virginia. We have put in a brief space its narrative of military events ; for, after all, it was a mere series of local adventures, compared with other operations of the war.

CHAPTER X.

THE new Federal Congress, pursuant to the summons of President Lincoln, met in Washington on the 4th of July. The event was the occasion of a new development of the Northern policy, and a remarkable enlargement of the operations of the war.

In his message, Mr. Lincoln announced a great political discovery. It was that all former statesmen of America had lived, and written, and labored under a great delusion; that the States, instead of having created the Union, were its *creatures;* that they obtained their sovereignty and independence from it, and never possessed either until the Convention of 1787. This singular doctrine of consolidation was the natural preface to a series of measures to strengthen the Government, to enlarge the Executive power, and to conduct the war with new decision, and on a most unexpected scale of magnitude.

President Lincoln had already instituted certain remarkable measures of war. He had published his proclamation declaring the ports of the

Southern Confederacy in a state of blockade, and denouncing any molesta tion of Federal vessels on the high seas as *piracy*, having reference to let ters of marque issued by the Confederate authority. He had prohibited all commercial intercourse with the States composing the new confedera tion. And although he insisted on referring to the belligerent powers in the flippant and unimportant words of "persons engaged in disorderly proceedings," he had found it advisable, as early as the 3d of May, in addition to his first requisition for seventy-five thousand men to operate against these disorderly persons, to call for forty-odd thousand additional volunteers to enlist for the war, and eighteen thousand seamen, besides increasing the regular army by the addition of ten regiments. He now wrote to Congress: " It is recommended that you give the legal means for making this contest a short and a decisive one; that you place at the control of the Government, for the work, at least four hundred thousand men, and four hundred millions of dollars." The recommendation was a singular commentary on the prospect that had been held out of subduing the Confederate power by three months' levies, before the Congress should meet in the month of July to determine the disposition of the conquered States and the fate of the leaders. But Congress was generous; and, in excess of Mr. Lincoln's demand, voted him five hundred thousand men, to serve for a period not exceeding three years.

But the interest of the first Congress, under Mr. Lincoln's administra tion, is not confined to its military legislation. It is a period from which we may trace a spirit that essentially tended to revolutionize the political system and ideas of the North itself, and to erect on the ruins of the Constitution a despotic authority, whose consequences ran all through the war.

The first sessions of this Congress were signalized by a resolution refusing to consider any propositions but those looking to a continued and vigorous prosecution of the war, and confining all business to the military and naval operations of the Government; by a general approval of the acts done by the President without constitutional authority, including his suspension of the *habeas corpus;* and by the initiation of a barbarous policy of confiscation in a bill declaring free whatever slaves were em ployed in the service of "the rebellion," thus evidently containing the seed of that thick crop of Abolition legislation which was to ensue.

Mr. Lincoln had suspended the writ of *habeas corpus* without the consti tutional concurrence of Congress, and under a claim of authority to arrest without process of law all persons " dangerous to the public safety." This remarkable usurpation was tolerated by the country. Indeed, it obtained many ingenious defences in Northern newspapers. It was declared that the privilege of *habeas corpus* was really in the interest of no one but *quasi* criminals; and that what had been esteemed for centuries as the

Eng^d by B.B.Hall, N.Y.

Engraved expressly for the Lost Cause by E. A. Pollard.

bulwark of personal liberty, was really a matter of no great concern to the general public. An apologist for Mr. Lincoln wrote : " In such times the people generally are willing, and are often compelled, to give up for a season a portion of their freedom to preserve the rest ; and fortunately, again, it is that portion of the people, for the most part, who like to live on the margin of disobedience to the laws, whose freedom is most in danger. The rest are rarely in want of a *habeas corpus*."

This astounding and atrocious doctrine had already been put in violent practice in certain parts of the North. We have already referred to the military arrest of the municipal officers of Baltimore. It was but the beginning of a reign of terrour. There is place here for the following remarkable document, under the authority of which were arrested many leading members of the Legislature of Maryland :

[CONFIDENTIAL.]

"HEADQUARTERS ARMY OF THE POTOMAC,
"WASHINGTON, Sept. 12, 1861.

" GENERAL : After full consultation with the President, Secretaries of State, War, &c., it has been decided to effect the operation proposed for the 17th. Arrangements have been made to have a Government steamer at Annapolis to receive the prisoners and carry them to their destination.

" Some four or five of the chief men in the affair are to be arrested to-day. When they meet on the 17th, you will please have everything prepared to arrest the whole party, and be sure that none escape.

" It is understood that you arrange with General Dix and Governor Seward the *nodus operandi*. It has been intimated to me that the meeting might take place on the 14th ; please be prepared. I would be glad to have you advise me frequently of your arrangements in regard to this very important matter.

" If it is successfully carried out, it will go far toward breaking the backbone of the rebellion. It would probably be well to have a special train quietly prepared to take prisoners to Annapolis.

" I leave this exceedingly important affair to your tact and discretion—and have but one thing to impress upon you—the absolute necessity of secrecy and success. With the highest regard, I am, my dear General, your sincere friend,

" GEORGE B. McCLELLAN,
"Major-General U. S. A."

But the policy of arrests did not end with this singular violation of the freedom of a legislative body. Other citizens were taken. Military arrests were made in the dead hour of night. The most honourable and virtuous citizens were dragged from their beds, and confined in forts. Searches and seizures, the most rigorous and unwarrantable, were made without pretext of justification. Hopeless imprisonment was inflicted without accusation, without inquiry or investigation, and without the prospect of a trial. When, in the House of Representatives, at Washington, Mr. Vallandigham of Ohio moved a series of resolutions condemning these acts of despotic authority and intolerable espionage, including the seizure of despatches in the telegraph offices, they were unceremoniously laid on the table.

There was an evident disposition of the Northern people to surrender their constitutional liberties to any government that would gratify their political passions. A true account of the despotism of these times indicates, indeed, what little love of liberty there was in the North, and its low stage of sentimentalism on this subject; for wherever it has been observed in history that a nation has been willing to surrender liberty in an attempt at territorial ascendancy, it has always been the evidence of a coarse and materialistic character that serves well the ambitious designs of Despotism, and prefers a false greatness to the humbler realities of honour and happiness. In remarkable contrast to this tendency of the Northern people to submit to a subtraction of their liberties, and even to applaud it, while they imagined that their greed of resentment and lust of territory were to be satisfied, were the declarations and spirit of the new government erected in the South. There the body of civil liberties was undiminished and untouched. The muniments of constitutional law were not disturbed. In the midst of a war "waged not to destroy, but to preserve existing institutions," the South was recurring to the past rather than running into new and rash experiments, and exhibiting a spirit of Conservatism that the world had seldom observed in so vast a commotion.

In his message of July, 1861, Mr. Lincoln had referred to an attempt meditated by States at a position of "neutrality" in the war. On this subject he wrote, with more than usual acuteness:

"In the Border States, so called—in fact, the Middle States—there are those who favor a policy which they call 'armed neutrality;' that is, an arming of these States to prevent the Union forces passing one way, or the Disunion the other, over their soil. This would be disunion completed. Figuratively speaking, it would be building an impassable wall along the line of separation—and yet, not quite an impassable one; for, under the guise of neutrality, it would tie the hands of the Union men, and freely pass supplies from among them to the insurrectionists, which it could not do as an open enemy. At a stroke, it would take all the trouble off the hands of Secession, except only what proceeds from the external blockade. It would do for the Disunionists that which, of all things, they most desire—feed them well, and give them disunion without a struggle of their own. It recognizes no fidelity to the Constitution, no obligation to maintain the Union; and, while very many who favored it are, doubtless, loyal citizens, it is, nevertheless, very injurious in effect."

This passage of Mr. Lincoln's message naturally introduces us to the remarkable part taken by the State of Kentucky at the period of hostilities and in the opening scenes of the war. Her Legislature had passed a resolution, to the effect that the State should remain neutral in the contest pending, and would not permit the troops of either party to pass over or occupy her soil for belligerent purposes.

In assuming the part of a neutral, the attitude of Kentucky fell far below the hopes of the Confederate States; but even that plea was to be used to disguise designs which meditated nothing short of an eventual and open declaration of common cause with the Northern States. An election ensued for members of her Legislature in the month of August. In this canvass the intriguers of the Federal Government were at work; the war had fully opened; paper money in abundance was beginning to circulate; rich contracts for mules, hemp, and lumber, were scattered with lavish but discriminating hand, among the Union men of Kentucky; and when the election came, a large majority of men were returned who had professed before the people their fidelity to the neutral faith, but who, in reality, were prepared to throw the whole power of the State, as far as they could wield it, in favor of Lincoln and his war against the South.

After the returns of this election were made, it soon became evident that the Federals intended to occupy Kentucky, and to use her roads and mountains for marching invading columns upon the Confederate States. It became necessary to anticipate them. Brigadier-General Zollicoffer, of Tennessee, on the 14th of September, occupied the mountain passes at Cumberland, and the three long mountains in Harlan and Knox Counties, Kentucky, through which an invading column of Federals had been threatening for weeks to march from Hoskins' Cross-roads. And on the 3d of September Gen. Leonidas Polk advanced with part of his forces, and took possession of Hickman, Chalk Banks, and the town of Columbus, in Kentucky.

The position of the Legislature of Kentucky, and Gov. Magoffin, that Gen. Polk's occupation of Columbus was an act of invasion of their State, and violated its neutrality, was absurd. The enemy had chosen to make his battle-ground there, and to erect there the signs of armed contest; and the Confederates had, of course, the right to confront him on any line of operations he indicated. The Federal Government had disregarded the neutrality of Kentucky, and Mr. Lincoln had hooted at it; her representatives in the Congress of the United States had voted supplies of men and money to carry on the war against the Confederate States; Federal camps and depots of armies had been established in Kentucky; military companies had been organized within her territory; and at a rendezvous in Garrard County, known as Camp Dick Robinson, several thousand troops, among whom men from Tennessee, Ohio, Indiana, and Illinois, were mustered with Kentuckians into the service of the United States, were prepared not only to put down revolt at home, but to carry out the designs of the Washington Government for the subjugation of the South.

Nor was this all. The Federal forces were preparing to take possession of Columbus and Paducah, regarding them as important positions; and when Gen. Polk anticipated them in occupying the former place, it was only when the enemy had constructed a military work on the Missouri shore, immediately opposite, and commanding Columbus, and evidently intended to cover the landing of troops for the seizure of the town. Federal cannon had already been turned upon Columbus, and many of the inhabitants had fled in terrour from the indications of approaching hostilities.

In no sense did the Confederates intend to conquer or coerce Kentucky. But it was well understood that the people of that State had been deceived into a mistaken security, were unarmed, and in danger of being subjugated by the Federal forces, while a majority of them, if perfectly free to indicate their choice, would, it was thought, have espoused the cause of the Confederacy. Proclamation was made, on the part of the Confederates, of the desire to respect the neutrality of Kentucky, and the intention to abide by the wishes of her people, as soon as they were free to express them.

But Gen. Polk went even further than this. He offered to accede to the demand of Gov. Magoffin for the withdrawal of the Confederate troops from Kentucky, on condition that the State would agree that the troops of the Federal Government be withdrawn simultaneously, with a guaranty (which he would give reciprocally for the Confederate Government) that the Federal troops should not be allowed to enter or occupy any part of Kentucky in the future. This proposition was derided by the Federal partisans in Kentucky, and—as every proposition of equivalents in the war —was ridiculed in the Northern newspapers as a piece of "rebel" impertinence.

It was not long before the period of "policy" was past in Kentucky, and Federal agents were making daily arrests of all persons suspected of entertaining designs or sentiments hostile to the government at Washington. Many members of the State Legislature, true to the South, had vacated their offices and left their homes. What remained of this body enacted a law of pains and penalties, denouncing death, imprisonment, forfeitures and fines, against all who should oppose the Federal Government.

Among those Kentuckians who, fortunately for themselves and for the cause which they afterwards served, escaped arrest, and came within the Confederate lines, were John C. Breckinridge, late Vice-President of the United States, Col. G. W. Johnson, a prominent citizen, Thomas B. Monroe, Sr., for about thirty years District Judge of the United States, Humphrey Marshall, ex-member of Congress, and a distinguished officer in the Mexican war, and Capt. John Morgan, afterwards the "Marion" of Kentucky, and one of the most famous cavalry commanders in the West. Messrs. Breckinridge and Marshall proceeded to Richmond, and were appointed Brigadier-Generals in the Confederate service.

On assuming his new position, Gen. Breckinridge published an address to the people of Kentucky, some passages of which are of historical interest, as a description of the times, from a pen which, for many years, had been able and conspicuous in every cause of truth. He wrote:

"The Federal Government—the creature—has set itself above the creator. The atrocious doctrine is announced by the President, and acted upon, that the States derive their power from the Federal Government, and may be suppressed on any pretence of military necessity. Everywhere the civil has given way to the military power. The fortresses of the country are filled with victims seized without warrant of law, and ignorant of the cause of their imprisonment. The legislators of States and other public officers are seized while in the discharge of their official duties, taken beyond the limits of their respective States, and imprisoned in the forts of the Federal Government. A subservient Congress ratifies the usurpations of the President, and proceeds to complete the destruction of the Constitution. History will declare that the annals of legislation do not contain laws so infamous as those enacted at the last session. They sweep away every vestige of public and personal liberty, while they confiscate the property of a nation containing ten millions of people. The great mass of the Northern people seem anxious to sunder every safeguard of freedom; they eagerly offer to the Government what no European monarch would dare to demand. The President and his Generals are unable to pick up the liberties of the people as rapidly as they are thrown at their feet. General Anderson, the military dictator of Kentucky, announces, in one of his proclamations, that he will arrest no one who does not act, write, or speak in opposition to Mr. Lincoln's Government. It would have completed the idea if he had added, or *think* in opposition to it. Look at the condition of our State under the rule of our new protectors. They have suppressed the freedom of speech and of the press. They seize people by military force on mere suspicion, and impose on them oaths unknown to the laws. Other citizens they imprison without warrant, and carry them out of the State, so that the writ of *habeas corpus* cannot reach them. Every day foreign armed bands are making seizures among the people. Hundreds of citizens, old and young, venerable magistrates, whose lives have been distinguished by the love of the people, have been compelled to fly from their homes and families, to escape imprisonment and exile at the hands of Northern and German soldiers under the orders of Mr. Lincoln and his military subordinates."

The early military movements in Kentucky are to be considered as taking place along a line running through the interiour of the State, extending from Columbus in the West to Prestonburg and Pikeville in the mountains on the Virginia frontier.

From his strong position at Cumberland Mountain, Gen. Zollicoffer prepared for cautious advances upon the enemy. On the 19th of September, a portion of his command advanced to Barboursville, and dispersed a camp of fifteen hundred Federals. Gen. Zollicoffer continued to advance, and early in October reached the town of London in Laurel County, breaking up the enemy's camps in that region.

Meanwhile, Brigadier-General Buckner, with a force of Kentucky volunteers, advanced from the borders, and on the 18th of September entered the town of Bowling Green, in Warren County, eleven miles south of Green River, and immediately on the line of approach to Louisville. He issued a proclamation to the people of Kentucky, stating that their Legislature had been faithless to their will; that instead of enforcing neutrality, they had sought to make the State a fortress in which the armed forces of the United States might securely prepare to subjugate alike the people of Kentucky and of the Southern States. He declared that the Confederate troops occupied Bowling Green as a defensive position, and that he renewed the pledge previously given by their commanders, to retire as soon as the Federal forces would in like manner withdraw.

But the first serious collision of arms in Kentucky was to occur in the neighbourhood of the waters of the Ohio and the Tennessee; and to that end of the line of operations we must now take the attention of the reader.

THE BATTLE OF BELMONT.

Gen. Polk had for some time been strengthening his position at Columbus, and had also occupied Belmont, a small village on the Missouri shore, so as to command both banks of the stream.

With a view of surprising the small Confederate force on the west bank, Gen. U. S. Grant collected a fleet of large river steamboats, and embarking at night, steamed down the river unobserved. Within a few miles of Columbus and Belmont the river makes a sudden bend, and behind this bend Grant disembarked his forces, and began to advance towards Belmont, through the woods. When the morning of the 7th of November broke, the action commenced; the first intimation of the enemy's presence being a succession of rapid volleys. The troops were soon under arms, but the sudden surprise precluded all idea of a regular line or plan of battle.

It appears that when the enemy was reported landing troops a few miles above, the garrison in Belmont consisted of only two regiments. Gen. Pillow, with four regiments, immediately crossed, and assumed command. He had scarcely done so, when Grant's advance opened fire, and the fight soon became fierce and obstinate. The enemy made a desperate attempt to turn the left wing of the Confederates, but was defeated by the destructive fire of Beltzhoover's battery. This wing was severely taxed, as was also the right. Finding that they stood firm and unbroken, and, anxious for decisive action before reinforcements could reach Pillow, Grant repeatedly hurled his strongest force at the Confederate centre, which was in the open field.

The centre evidently faltered under these heavy and repeated attacks. Pillow ordered a charge, and the first line of the enemy was driven upon their reserves. But ammunition now began to fail, and word came that the wings could not maintain their position if the centre gave in, as there was every reason to fear it would do. Again a charge was ordered, which proved no less successful than the first. It was now found that the only battery of the Confederates had not a cartridge remaining, and most of the troops were similarly circumstanced; there was no alternative but to fall back until reinforcements should arrive from Columbus.

In moving back to the river bank, the Confederate line was more or less broken and disorganized; and the enemy appeared to be master of the field. He was already in full possession of the Confederate camps, and was burning them. But at the critical moment three regiments, which had crossed the river from Columbus, were ordered to move up the river bank, through the woods, and get in the enemy's rear. The enemy had seen the boats crossing with reinforcements, and played on them with a heavy battery; but the guns at Columbus replied, and in a few moments the enemy's pieces were silenced. Finding that Polk himself was crossing, and landing troops far up the river on his line of retreat, Grant immediately began to fall back, but had not proceeded far when he encountered Louisianians, Mississippians, Tennesseans, and others, formed on his flanks, subjecting him to loss every moment, while the guns at Columbus continued rapidly firing across the river, and from the high position of the works, telling with deadly effect. Under these circumstances resistance was hopeless, and Grant reluctantly ordered a retreat; but while conducting it, he was subjected to a terrific cross-fire from the Confederates, while Polk in person was pushing the rear vigorously, capturing prisoners and arms every yard of the road. The confusion, noise, and excitement were terrible, the Federals rapidly retreating to their boats, and the advance columns of their pursuers pouring deadly volleys into them. A defeat was suddenly and almost miraculously converted into a glorious triumph of Confederate arms.

In this obstinate conflict, in which the Confederates fought by detachments, and always against superiour numbers, it was officially stated that their loss in killed, wounded, and missing, was 632, while that of the enemy was claimed to have been treble in extent. He had been driven under a devouring fire, and even after he had reached the river, his crowded transports were assailed with the fire of thousands of deadly rifles. In Northern newspapers, Belmont was put down as "another Union victory." The style and effrontery of the falsehood was characteristic. The first part of the day, when Grant pushed the Confederates to the river, was glowingly described; but the subsequent flank movement which converted his early success into a defeat and a rout, and was, indeed, *the* event of the day, was dismissed in the briefest and most indifferent terms. Grant wrote: " The rebels *followed* in the rear to our place of debarkation." Such was the method of Northern misrepresentation. It is remarkable that, by ingenious suppression, or by the rouged falsehood of official reports, the North claimed, after Manassas, every event of the war as a Federal victory, unless where some political animosity brought out the details, or some personal rivalry extorted the truth.

With the Confederate victory of Belmont, we leave for the present the story of military operations in the West. We shall soon recur to that theatre, to find there some of the largest and most important events of the war. We shall discover that the enemy, in fact, conceived a new plan of invasion of the South, through Kentucky and Tennessee, by means of amphibious expeditions, composed of gunboats and land forces; and that a war which the Southern people supposed lingered on the Potomac, was suddenly transferred and opened with imposing scenes on the western waters.

CHAPTER XI.

IN the beginning of the war, General Winfield Scott had been entitled in Northern newspapers "the Greatest Captain of the Age." After the disaster of Manassas the same newspapers derided him as an imbecile; and in the meanest humiliation General Scott publicly announced himself an "old coward" for having yielded to popular clamour in fighting the battle, and thus sought by the most infamous confession the mercy of men prompt to insult his fallen fortunes.

The fickle course of popular applause in the North was to exalt a new

idol, and to designate a new victim.   The clamour was for young commanders.   Gen. George B. McClellan had been lifted into a sudden
popularity by the indifferent affair of Rich Mountain.   He was a graduate
of West Point; had been one of the Military Commission sent to the
Crimea; and just before the war had been employing his genius as superintendent of a railroad.   He was now to take command of the Federal
forces on the line of the Potomac, and to find himself suddenly exalted in
the newspapers to comparisons with Alexander, Cæsar, Hannibal and
Napoleon the Great.

The volatile, superficial and theatrically-inclined mind of the North is,
perhaps, in nothing more strikingly displayed than in its demonstrations
towards its public men.   Yankee fame has come to be one of the curiosi-
ties of the world.   Scott was " the Greatest Captain of the Age."   But
McClellan was " the Young Napoleon."   The name of the new hero appeared on placards, on banners, and in newspaper headings.   Reporters
stretched their ears to catch the least word he uttered; artists of illustrated journals dogged his steps; his eyes, hair, mouth, teeth, voice, manner and apparel were carefully described in newspaper articles.   Every
store of flattery and praise was exhausted upon a man who found himself
famous by nothing more than the caprice of the multitude.*

For months after the battle of Manassas an almost unbroken quiet extended along the line of the Potomac.   McClellan had tolerated the advance of the Confederate lines to Munson's Hill, within a few miles of
Alexandria; and every attempt to draw him out into a general engagement proved unavailing.   Northern politicians complained of his inactivity;

---

* There has been a curious Yankee affectation in the war.   It is to discover in the infancy or
early childhood of all their heroes something indicative of their future greatness, or of the designs
of Providence towards them.   Thus their famous cavalry commanders rode wild horses as soon as
they could sit astraddle; and their greatest commander in the latter periods of the war—Ulysses
S. Grant—when an infant in arms desired a pistol to be fired by his ear, and exclaimed, *frick
again !*—thus giving a very early indication of his warlike disposition.   The following, told of
McClellan in a Washington newspaper, during the days of his popularity, is characteristic :—

" THE INFANT NAPOLEON.—An incident which occurred in the city of Philadelphia in the winter
of 1826-7, is particularly worthy of record in our present crisis, inasmuch as it relates to the early
history of one who fills a position commanding the attention and admiration of the world, and particularly of our own country.   I will premise by saying I was in Philadelphia in the winter
spoken of, attending medical lectures under a distinguished surgeon, then a professor in one of the
institutions of the city.   A son was born to our professor, and the event scarcely transpired before
the father announced it to his delighted pupils.   Scales were instantly brought from a neighboring
grocer.   Into one dish he placed the babe, into the other all the weights.   The beam was raised,
but the child moved not !   The father, emptying his pockets, threw in his watch, coin, keys, knives
and lancets, but to no purpose—the little hero could not be moved.   He conquered every thing !
*And at last, while adding more and more weight, the cord supporting the beam gave way, and broke
rather than the giant infant would yield !*   The father was Dr. McClellan, and the son—General
McClellan ! our young commander on the Potomac.   The country will see a prophetic charm in
this incident."

the Confederates were immensely reassured by it; but there is reason to suppose that McClellan's splendid army, that was constantly entertaining attention with parades and reviews, was performing a well-designed part, and that the gorgeous pageant on the Potomac was intended as a veil to immense military preparations going on in other directions.

The Confederate advance having failed to bring on a general battle, although it was almost daily invited by heavy skirmishing, and it being impossible without a chain of strong fortifications to hold the advanced line of Mason's and Munson's hills, or even the interiour one of Fairfax Court-house and its flanks, it was decided by Gens. Johnston and Beauregard, on the 15th of October, to withdraw the army to Centreville. At the dead of night it was put in motion, and in perfect silence, without the beat of a drum or the note of a bugle, the men marched out of their forsaken entrenchments, and took the road to Centreville.

THE BATTLE OF LEESBURG.

The apparent retreat of the Confederates to Centreville encouraged McClellan to make an advance on the extreme left wing of their force. This enterprise brought on a conflict among the most sanguinary of the war, in view of the numbers engaged. The design of the Federal commander was to occupy the country covering the northern belt of Fairfax and Loudon counties; and while a column moved towards Dranesville, he ordered Gen. Stone, comanding on the line of the Potomac, nearly opposite to Leesburg, to throw across the river a sufficient force to co-operate with the lower movement.

The Confederate force in and around Leesburg was about two thousand men. It was a brigade composed of three Mississippi regiments and the 8th Virginia, comanded by Gen. Evans, whose name had been conspicuous on the field of Manassas. Before day broke on the 20th of October, the men were drawn up in line of battle, and Evans addressed them thus: "Gentlemen, the enemy are approaching by the Dranesville road, sixteen thousand strong, with twenty pieces of artillery. They want to cut off our retreat. Reinforcements can't arrive in time if they were sent. We must *fight*." The little army was at once put in motion across Goose Creek and along the Dranesville road, anticipating a desperate engagement with the Federal column reported to be moving in that direction under the command of Gen. McCall. A few hours after sunrise a Federal courier was captured proceeding on his way with despatches from McCall to Stone. His papers betrayed sufficient to reveal that it was designed to draw the Confederates from Leesburg along the Dranesville road, while Stone crossed the river and occupied the town.

Gen. Stone commenced the passage of the river on the 20th of October. A force of five companies of Massachusetts troops, commanded by Col. Devins, effected a crossing at Edwards' Ferry, and, a few hours thereafter, Col. Baker, who took command of all the Federal forces on the Virginia side, having been ordered by Stone to push the Confederates from Leesburg and hold the place, crossed the river at Conrad's Ferry, a little south of Harrison's Island, and on the direct road to Leesburg. Gen. Stone had ordered seven thousand five hundred men to co-operate in the movement. Baker's brigade, including the advanced companies under Devins, was two thousand three hundred strong, and he was rapidly reinforced until nearly the entire number designated by Stone had been thrown across the river.

Meanwhile Gen. Evans, who had taken a position at Goose Creek, awaited the approach of the enemy. The Federals had crossed the Potomac at different points, at Edwards' Ferry which was just above the mouth of Goose Creek, and at Conrad's Ferry, where a steep bank (Ball's Bluff) hung over the water. Finding that no advance from Edwards' Ferry was attempted, Gen. Evans ordered the 17th and 18th Mississippi regiments to move rapidly to the support of the 8th Virginia and some Mississippi companies, which held the approaches to Leesburg, and had already become hotly engaged with the main body of the enemy advancing from Ball's Bluff.

"If the enemy won't come to us we must go to them," exclaimed Evans, as he put the two Mississippi regiments in motion, which began a race of two miles to turn the tide of battle. The Federals who had occupied Ball's Bluff had advanced towards the wooded plain between the river and Leesburg, and held a semicircular line of battle, supported by four howitzers. Evans' order was, "to make the business short." As the fire of musketry became hot and general—for the Confederates had no opportunity to use their artillery—the Federals gave way, and fell back towards the bluff. Col. Baker urged his men to rally, and brought his disordered lines to a momentary stand. Gen. Evans, seizing the critical moment, ordered a charge. Virginians and Mississippians together rushed forward, making a resistless onset upon the Federal lines. A private sprang to the front, and advancing within eight feet of Col. Baker, fired five chambers of his revolver at him, piercing his head at the first shot, and striking him with nearly every ball. He fell dead. His terrified command gave way in utter rout, and fled towards the river. A portion, numbering several hundred men, attempted to make good their retreat by a flank movement to Edwards' Ferry, and were taken prisoners. But the bulk of the fugitives madly ran to the very verge of Ball's Bluff; and now ensued a scene of unutterable horrour, as these men were driven over the bluff on to the bayonets of their friends, thirty feet below.

Such slaughter, such havoc, such mangling of living men was scarcely ever seen before. A whole army was retreating, tumbling, rolling, leaping down the steep heights. Hundreds plunged into the rapid current; many were shot in the act of swimming; and others were drowned in the water, choked with the wounded and dead. Large flats had been used to bring over reinforcements. They now attempted to return with the wounded; but such was the consternation among the troops that large numbers rushed on board, trampling upon the bleeding men until they all sank together, amid frightful screams. There were men in that agonized mass of fugitives who had never seen the field of battle. They had been sent over while the contest was in progress; they had climbed the mud of the bluff, expecting to find before them a scene of victory. But before them glared a victorious and vengeful foe; and behind them rolled the deep river. All was consternation and dismay. A thousand men ran up and down the banks. Two Massachusetts companies had the presence of mind to display a white flag and surrender. Others rushed wildly into the stream; and the shrieks of the wounded and drowning mingled with the shouts of the victors and the rattle of musketry.

The results of the terrible disaster of Leesburg were studiously suppressed by the Washington authorities. Indeed, they had the hardihood to claim an advantage; representing that the movement towards Leesburg was merely a "reconnoissance," and was, in the main, "gallant" and "successful." But the Federal Congress happened to be in session at the time; and the opposition party brought out the stark and horrible truth of the affair. It was ascertained that the Federal loss was not less than 500 killed and drowned, 800 wounded, and about the same number of prisoners, making a total exceeding two thousand. The loss of the Confederates was only one hundred and fifty-three in killed and wounded. Evans' little command had defeated an army, probably three times its strength, and had inflicted upon it a loss greater in number than the whole Confederate force engaged.

After the lesson administered at Leesburg, McClellan for some months attempted nothing but some foraging expeditions; but he was constantly busy with the organization and *morale* of his army; and the material which was raw at Manassas was rapidly improving in discipline, stanchness and soldierly qualities. On the 20th of December occurred an affair, which was more creditable to the Federals than any that had yet taken place in the region of the Potomac, and constituted McClellan's first success since the engagement of Rich Mountain.

On the day named Gen. J. E. B. Stuart with a large foraging force, consisting of about twenty-five hundred men, fell in with the enemy near Dranesville. The Federals were in superiour force; Gen. Ord's brigade, which was also marching to the same neighbourhood for forage, being thirty-five hundred strong, while two other brigades were in supporting distance. A rocket, shot up by the enemy, gave to the Confederates the first intimation of their presence. To give his wagon-train time to retreat in safety, Gen. Stuart prepared for battle. He was exposed to a very severe cannonade from the enemy; and finding his men contending at serious disadvantage with an enemy greatly outnumbering them, and almost concealed in ambush, he, after a desultory engagement, drew off his forces, and fell back two miles. The enemy did not pursue. The Confederate loss in killed and wounded was about two hundred.

The affair of Dranesville was the last conflict of arms of any note that occurred near the Potomac in the first winter of the war. But within this period, we must remark an expedition, conducted by "Stonewall" Jackson, which was a most extraordinary enterprise, and was attended by such hardships and sufferings as made it a story of terrible interest and fearful romance.

In September, Jackson had been made a Major-General, and in the early part of October he was assigned to the command of the Confederate forces in and around Winchester. About this time the famous Col. Turner Ashby, with his own regiment and other cavalry detachments, making a total of some twelve hundred horse, was watching the river-front from Harper's Ferry to Romney. In December the enemy were strongly posted at Romney and Bath southwards; and Banks, with his whole army being north of the Potomac, it was evident that some great movement was in contemplation, which prudence demanded should be watched by a strong force.

A large part of Gen. Loring's command, after a march of two hundred and sixty miles, joined Gen. Jackson at Winchester. He was now at the head of about nine thousand men; and on the first day of January, 1862, with a portion of his force he marched from Winchester.

It was the object of Jackson to surprise the Federals stationed at Bath, otherwise known as Berkeley Springs. Amid the snow, sleet, rain and ice of the most severe days of the winter he commenced his march. He had to travel over fifty miles of the roughest country in the world, and he was obliged to take unfrequented roads to keep his movement secret. Penetrating the mountains on roads winding along their sides, and through their rugged defiles, exposed to sleet and hail in mid-winter, and enduring the bitterest cold, the march was one of almost indescribable suffering and horrour. The men were without tents. The roads were covered with ice two inches thick, and glazed over by the sleet, so that neither man nor horse could keep his feet except by great care. Horses had their knees and muzzles terribly injured and streaming with blood. Occasionally, horsemen, infantry and wagons would slip over an embankment; and men crippled, or filled with bruises and pains, laid down by the wayside to die, or staggered on in the terrible march. Many were bootless, hatless, and ragged. They were not allowed to kindle fires, being within a few miles of the enemy's posts ; and their most comfortable sleep was under stick arbours packed with snow.

Amid the sharp distresses of this march the command struggled on with patient courage, and almost superhuman spirit. On arriving at Bath, they found the Federals had retreated to the Potomac, and had waded the river on one of the coldest days of winter.

Having rested two or three days in Bath, Jackson made daily demonstrations at the river to induce the belief that his command was the advance of a large force about to cross into Maryland. The demonstration succeeded even beyond his expectations. The Federal troops in and around Romney amounted to eleven thousand men, under command of Gen. Shields. This officer felt so certain that Jackson was bent on crossing the Potomac, that, though forty miles above, he transferred his whole command to the north bank to dispute the supposed passage. As soon as Jackson was informed of this, he marched up the south bank to Romney, surprised and captured many of the enemy, and destroyed what he could not carry away of Shields' immense stores, amounting to some half a million of dollars. Leaving a small force in Romney, Jackson returned with his army to Winchester. The success of his expedition was complete ; but it had been terribly purchased, for hundreds of his brave men had sunk under the exposure of the march, or were long on the sick-list from its effects.

With this movement closed the campaign of the winter in Virginia. The armies of Johnston and Beauregard, at Centreville and Manassas, of Huger, at Norfolk, of Magruder on the Peninsula, of Jackson at Winchester, and the bodies of troops from Evansport to Acquia on the Potomac, in the Alleghany Mountains and around Richmond, rested for a season in their winter quarters ; and fields of Virginia soon to run red with blood, were now covered with mantles of snow and ice.

NAVAL OPERATIONS IN 1861.

The Federals had one immense and peculiar advantage in the war ; and they were prompt to use it. The superiourity which a large navy gave them may be estimated when we reflect that the sea-coast of the Confederacy stretched in a continuous line of eighteen hundred miles ; that along this were scattered sea-ports, many of them without the protection of the feeblest battery ; and that the Mississippi, with its tributaries was an inland sea, which gave access to the enemy almost as freely as the Gulf of Mexico.

At the opening of the war, President Lincoln found under his com
mand a navy of ninety ships of war, carrying eighteen hundred and nine
guns. In little more than a year from that time the Federal navy embraced three hundred and eighty-six ships and steamers, carrying three
thousand and twenty-seven guns. Keels were laid not only in the Eastern
ship-yards, but on the Mississippi and Ohio Rivers; iron armour was prepared; mortar ketches were built; the founderies and shops worked day
and night upon engines, plates, and guns.

While this wonderful energy was being displayed by the North in
preparations to operate against our sea-coast, and by fleets of gunboats on
the Upper Mississippi and its tributaries, to drive our armies out of Kentucky and Tennessee, the Confederate Government showed a singular
apathy with respect to any work of defence. The Confederate Congress
had made large appropriations for the construction of gunboats on the
Mississippi waters; there was the best navy-yard on the continent opposite Norfolk; there were valuable armouries with their machinery at Richmond; and although the Confederate Government was very far from
competing with the naval resources of the enemy, yet there is no doubt,
with the means and appliances at hand, it might have created a considerable fleet. In no respect was the improvidence of this Government more
forcibly illustrated than in the administration of its naval affairs; or its
unfortunate choice of ministers more signally displayed than in the selection
as Secretary of the Navy of Mr. Mallory of Florida, a notoriously weak
man, who was slow and blundering in his office, and a butt in Congress
for his ignorance of the river geography of the country.

The consequences of the defenceless and exposed condition of the Confederate sea-coast were soon to be realized; and many intelligent men
already took it as a foregone conclusion, that in the progress of the war the
Confederacy would lose not only all her sea-ports, but every fort and battery to which the floating guns of the enemy could get access.

In the year 1861, two naval expeditions were sent down the Carolina
coast; and their results gave serious indications of what was to be expected from this arm of the enemy's service on the slight fortifications of
our ocean frontier. The first of these expeditions was designed against
Hatteras Inlet. To reduce two extemporized works there, mounting altogether fifteen guns, the enemy, with his usual prodigality of preparation
and care to ensure victory, sent an enormous sea armament, carrying one
hundred heavy guns, and a naval and military force numbering not less
than three thousand men. The fleet was under the command of Commodore Stringham, while Maj.-Gen. Butler, of Massachusetts, commanded the
force intended to operate on land. On the 26th of August the expedition
sailed from Fortress Monroe, arriving off Hatteras on the 28th. Three
hundred and fifteen men, with a twelve-pound rifled gun, and twelve-

pound howitzer, were landed safely, but in attempting to land more, two gunboats were swamped in the surf. In the mean time the fleet opened a tremendous bombardment upon one of the Confederate works, Fort Clark. The ships, secure in their distance, and formidable by their long range guns, kept up a terrific fire, which rained nine and eleven inch shells upon the fort, at the rate of seven in a minute, shattering to pieces the wooden structures exposed, killing and wounding a few of the men, and cutting down the flag-staff from which floated the Confederate ensign. Finding the work untenable, it was decided by Commodore Barron, the Confederate officer in command, to retire to Fort Hatteras.

At half-past eight o'clock the next morning, the Federal fleet steamed in from the ocean, and approaching within a mile and a quarter of Fort Hatteras, renewed the bombardment. The unequal combat continued for some hours. Assaulted by nearly a hundred heavy cannon, the fort was unable to reach effectively with its feeble thirty-two pounders, the ships which lay at a safe distance, pouring from their ten-inch rifle pivot guns a storm of shells upon the bomb-proofs and batteries. About noon, the fort surrendered. The loss of the Confederates was ten killed, thirteen wounded, and six hundred and sixty-five prisoners. The Federals had five men wounded.

But the Federals were to obtain a much more important success at a point on the coast further south. In the latter part of October a great fleet of war-ships and transports began to arrive at Old Point, and in a few days they were ready for their departure. So formidable an armament had never before assembled in the waters of America. The naval force was under the command of Capt. Dupont, flag-officer of the South Atlantic Blockading Squadron; it consisted of fifteen war-steamers; the land force was embarked in thirty steam vessels and six sailing ships, and was under the command of Gen. T. W. Sherman. The whole force fell very little below twenty-five thousand men.

On the 3d of November the fleet was descried approaching the southern coast of South Carolina; and then for the first time it became apparent that the point they sought was Port Royal harbour. To defend the harbour and approaches to Beaufort, the Confederates had erected two sand forts—one at Hilton Head, called Fort Walker, and the other at Bay Point, called Fort Beauregard. The first had sixteen guns mounted, most of them thirty-two pounders. Fort Beauregard mounted eight guns, none of the heaviest calibre. The garrisons and forces in the vicinity, numbering about three thousand men, were under the command of Gen. Drayton.

Having carefully reconnoitred the position and strength of the forts, a bombardment was opened on Fort Walker in the morning of the 7th of November. The fleet steamed forward, delivering its broadsides with ceaseless violence, then turning in a sharp elliptic, it steamed back in the same order, so as to fire the other broadside at Fort Walker, and load in time to open on Fort Beauregard on getting within range. This manœuvre doubtless disturbed the aim of the artillerists in the forts; they fired wildly and with but little effect. The dense masses of smoke which the wind drove clear of the ships, and packed against the land batteries, obstructed their aim, and afforded only occasional views of the enemy through the lifting cloud. After sustaining a bombardment of about four hours, the forts surrendered. The condition of Fort Walker, at this time, according to the official report of Gen. Drayton, was "all but three of the guns on the water front disabled, and only five hundred pounds of powder in the magazine." The garrisons and the men outside the forts retreated across the plain separating them from the woods. The Federal loss in the engagement was eight killed and twenty-three wounded. The Confederates lost about one hundred in killed and wounded, all their cannon, a number of small arms, and all the stores collected in and around the forts.

The capture of Port Royal was an important Federal success. It gave to the enemy a point for his squadrons to find shelter, and a convenient naval depot. It gave him also a foothold in the region of the Sea-Islands cotton, and afforded him a remarkable theatre for his anti-slavery experiments. The Beaufort district, commanded now by the enemy's position, was one of the richest and most thickly settled of the State. It contained about fifteen hundred square miles, and produced, annually, fifty millions of pounds of rice, and fourteen thousand bales of cotton, and held a population of nearly forty thousand, of whom more than thirty thousand were slaves.

In the month of November, 1861, there was to occur a naval exploit of the enemy, of little prowess, but of such importance that it was to draw off public attention from the largest operations of the war, and fix it unanimously upon the issues of a single incident.

THE "TRENT" AFFAIR.

On the 8th of November, Capt. Wilkes, of the United States steam sloop-of-war San Jacinto, overhauled the English mail steamer Trent in the Bahama Channel, and demanded the surrender of the Confederate emissaries, Messrs. Mason and Slidell, who were passengers on board that vessel, and were proceeding with their secretaries on a mission representing the interests of the Confederacy at the courts of England and France. The San Jacinto had fired a shot across the bows of the mail steamer to bring her to, and as she did not stop for that, had fired a shell which burst close by her. The unarmed vessel was boarded by a party of marines under command of Lieut. Fairfax, who demanded the persons of the commissioners and their secretaries; and on their claiming the protection of the British flag, and refusing to leave it unless by actual physical force, hands were laid on Mr. Mason, Lieut. Fairfax and another officer taking him by the collar of the coat on each side, and, the three other gentlemen following, the whole party was thus transferred from the decks of the Trent. As this scene was taking place, Commander Williams, of the British Navy, who was in charge of the English mails on board the Trent, said: "In this ship I am the representative of Her Majesty's Government, and I call upon the officers of the ship and passengers generally, to mark my words, when in the name of the British Government, and in distinct language, I denounce this as an illegal act, an act in violation of international law; an act indeed of wanton piracy, which, had we the means of defence, you would not dare to attempt."

The news of this remarkable outrage was received in England with a storm of popular indignation. The very day it reached Liverpool, a public meeting was held, earnestly calling upon the Government to assert the dignity of the British flag, and demand prompt reparation for the outrage. This appeal went up from all classes and parties of the people. The British Government exhibited a determined sentiment and a serious concern in the matter. The Earl of Derby, who had been consulted by the Government, approved the resentful demand which it proposed to make upon the United States, and suggested that ship-owners should instruct the captains of outward-bound vessels to signalize any English vessels, that war with America was probable. The Liverpool underwriters approved the suggestion. The British Government made actual preparations for war. Reinforcements were sent to Canada, together with munitions of war for the few fortifications England possessed in that colony.

Meanwhile the North was revelling in what it supposed the cheap glory of the Trent affair, and making an exhibition of vanity and insolence concerning it, curious even among the usual exaggerations of that people. The act of Capt. Wilkes was not only approved by the Federal Secretary of the Navy; it was extravagantly applauded by him. He accumulated words of praise, and declared that it had been marked by "intelligence, ability, decision, and firmness." The man who had made himself a hero in a proceeding in which he encountered no peril, received the public and official thanks of the Congress sitting at Washington. The Northern press and people appeared to be almost insane over the wonderful exploit. The city of New York offered Capt. Wilkes the hospitality of the city. Boston gave him a festival. Gov. Andrew of Massachusetts declared that the act of taking four unarmed men from an unarmed vessel was "one of the most illustrious services that had rendered the war memorable," and exulted in the idea that Capt. Wilkes had "fired his shot across the bows of the ship that bore the English lion at its head," forgetting that the ship bore no guns to reply to a courage so adventurous. The New York *Times* wrote in this strain : " There is no drawback to our jubilation. The universal Yankee nation is getting decidedly awake. As for Capt. Wilkes and his command, let the handsome thing be done. Consecrate another Fourth of July to him ; load him down with services of plate, and swords of the cunningest and costliest art. Let us encourage the happy inspiration that achieved such a victory."

But while the " universal Yankee nation " was thus astir, and in a rage of vanity, the South watched the progress of the Trent question with a keen and eager anxiety. It was naturally supposed, looking at the determination of England on the one side and the unbounded enthusiasm in the Northern States in maintaining their side of the question, that war would ensue between the parties. It was already imagined in the South that such a war would break the naval power of the North, distract her means, and easily confer independence on the Southern Confederacy. There were orators in Richmond who already declared that the key of the blockade had been lost in the trough of the Atlantic. If the North stood to the issue, the prospect was clear. Gov. Letcher of Virginia addressed a public meeting in Virginia, and, in characteristic language, declared that he prayed nightly that in this matter, " Lincoln's backbone might not give way.' The one condition of war between England and the North, was that the latter would keep its position, and sustain the high tone with which it had avowed the act of Capt. Wilkes.

But this condition was to fail suddenly, signally ; and the whole world was to be amused by a diplomatic collapse, such as is scarcely to be found in the records of modern times. When the arrest of Messrs. Mason and Slidell was first made known at Washington, Secretary Seward had written to the Federal minister in London, advising him to decline any explanations, and suggesting that the grounds taken by the British Government should first be made known, and the argument commence with it. But the British Government entered into no discussion ; it disdained the argument of any law question in the matter ; and with singular dignity made the naked and imperative demand for the surrender of the commissioners and their secretaries. Mr. Seward wrote back a letter, which must ever remain a curiosity in diplomacy. He volunteered the argument for the surrender of the parties ; he promised that they should be " cheerfully " liberated ; he declared that he did it in accordance with " the most cherished principles " of American statesmanship ; but in the close of this remarkable letter he could not resist the last resort of demagogueism in mentioning the captured commissioners, who had for weeks been paraded as equal to the fruits of a victory in the field, as persons of no importance, and saying : " *If* the safety of this Union required the detention of the captured persons, it would be the right and duty of this Government to detain them." If there was anything wanting to complete the shame of this collapse, it was the shallow show of alacrity at concession, and the attempt to substitute a sense of justice for what all men of common dis-cernment knew was the alarm of cowardice.

The concession of Mr. Seward was a blow to the hopes of the Southern people. The contemplation of the spectacle of their enemy's humiliation in it was but little compensation for their disappointment of a European complication in the war.* Indeed, the conclusion of the Trent affair gave a sharp check to the long cherished imagination of the interference of England in the war, at least to the extent of her disputing the blockade, which had begun to tell on the war-power and general condition of the Confederacy. The Trent correspondence was followed by declarations, on the Government side in the British Parliament, too plain to be mistaken. In the early part of February, 1862, Earl Russell had declared that the blockade of the American ports had been effective from the 15th of August, in the face of the facts that the despatches of Mr. Bunch, the English consul at Charleston, said that it was not so ; and that authentic accounts and letters of merchants showed that any ships, leaving for the South, could be insured by a premium of seven and a half to fifteen per cent. But in the House of Commons, Mr. Gregory disputed the minister's state-ment, mentioned the evidence we have referred to, and asserted that Eng-land's non-observation of the Treaty of Paris was a deception for the Confederate States, and an ambuscade for the interests of commerce through-out the world.

* The Richmond *Examiner* had the following to say of the attitude of the enemy in the matter : " Never, since the humiliation of the Doge and Senate of Genoa before the footstool of Louis XIV., has any nation consented to a degradation so deep. If Lincoln and Seward intended to give them up at a menace, why, their people will ask, did they ever capture the ambassadours ? Why the ex-ultant hurrah over the event, that went up from nineteen millions of throats ? Why the glorification of Wilkes ? Why the cowardly insults to two unarmed gentlemen, their close imprisonment, and the bloodthirsty movements of Congress in their regard ? But, most of all, why did the Government of Lincoln indulge a full Cabinet with an unanimous resolution that, under no circumstances, should the United States surrender Messrs. Slidell and Mason ? Why did they encourage the popular senti-ment to a similar position ? The United States Government and people swore the great oath to stand on the ground they had taken ; the American eagle was brought out ; he screeched his loudest screech of defiance—then

'Dropt like a craven cock his conquered wing'

at the first growl of the lion. This is the attitude of the enemy."

CHAPTER XII.

THE year 1862 is a remarkable one in the history of the war. It opened with a fearful train of disasters to the Confederacy that brought it almost to the brink of despair, and then was suddenly illuminated by successes that placed it on the highest pinnacle of hope, and put it even in instant expectation of its independence.

In the latter part of 1861, while the Confederacy was but little active, the North was sending into camp, from her great population, regiments numbered by hundreds; was drilling her men, heaping up ammunition and provisions, building gunboats for the western rivers, and war-ships for the coast, casting mortars and moulding cannon. She was preparing, with the opening of the next campaign, to strike those heavy blows in Tennessee and Louisiana under which the Confederate States reeled and staggered almost to fainting, and from which they recovered by a series of successes in Virginia, the most important of the war, and the most brilliant in the martial annals of any people.

We enter first upon the story of disaster. Despite the victory of Belmont, the Confederate situation in Kentucky was one of extreme weakness. Gen. Albert Sydney Johnston had assumed command of the Confederate forces in the Western department. He had occupied Bowling Green in Kentucky, an admirably selected position, with Green River along his front, and railway communication to Nashville and the whole South. Had he simply to contend with an enemy advancing from Louisville, he would have had but little to fear; but Grant had command of the Cumberland and Tennessee rivers, and while he might thus advance with his gunboats and transports upon Nashville, Buell, the other Federal commander, was prepared to attack in front.

BATTLE OF FISHING CREEK.

Having failed, as we have seen, at Columbus, the next movement of the enemy in Kentucky was to be made against the Confederate right at Mill Springs, on the upper waters of the Cumberland. Brig.-Gen. Zollicoffer had been reinforced and superseded by Maj.-Gen. Crittenden, and a small but gallant army had been collected for the defense of the mountains. The position of the Confederates was advanced across the Cumberland to Camp Beech Grove; and the camp was fortified with earth-works.

The Federal army in Eastern Kentucky occupied Somerset and Columbia, towns to the north of, but in the vicinity of the upper part of the Cumberland River. Two strong columns of the enemy were thus advancing upon Gen. Crittenden; and he formed the determination to fall upon the nearest column, that under Thomas advancing from Columbia, before the arrival of the troops under General Schoepf from Somerset.

But there were other reasons which determined Crittenden with his small army of about four thousand men to risk a battle against Thomas' column, which consisted of two brigades of infantry, and was greatly his superiour in artillery. His troops had been in an almost starving condition for some time. For several weeks bare existence in the camp was very precarious, from want of provisions and forage. Regiments frequently subsisted on one third rations, and this very frequently of bread alone. Wayne County, which was alone productive in this region of Kentucky, had been exhausted, and the neighbouring counties of Tennessee could furnish nothing to the support of the army. The condition of the roads and the poverty of the intervening section rendered it impossible to transport from Knoxville, a distance of one hundred and thirty miles. The enemy from Columbia commanded the Cumberland River, and only one boat was enabled to come up with supplies from Nashville. With the channel of communication closed, the position became untenable without attack. Only corn could be obtained for the horses and mules, and this in such small quantities that often cavalry companies were sent out on unshod horses which had eaten nothing for two days.

On the afternoon of the 18th of January a council of war was called. The position of the enemy was unchanged; Fishing Creek, a tributary of the Cumberland, was swollen by recent rains; the force of the enemy at Somerset was cut off by this stream, and could not be expected to join Thomas' column moving from Columbia, until the freshet had subsided. It was unanimously agreed to attack Thomas, before the Somerset brigade could unite with him.

The march began at midnight. The first column, commanded by Gen. Zollicoffer, consisted of four regiments of infantry and four guns; the second, under Gen. Carroll, in support, of three regiments and two guns, the reserve of one regiment and two battalions of cavalry. The Confederates were poorly supplied with artillery; but happily the undulating and wooded surface of the country presented but little opportunity for the use of that arm.

As the morning of the 19th January broke, the firing of the enemy's pickets made a brisk prelude to the contest, and by eight o'clock the battle opened with great fury. Zollicoffer's brigade pushed ahead, and drove the Federals some distance through the woods, and were endeavouring to force their way to the summit of a hill which fully commanded the whole field. He was ascending the hill when the heaviest firing told where the battle raged. He sent for reinforcements, and the brigade of Gen. Carroll was ordered up. When, in another moment, it was announced that he was killed, a sudden gloom pervaded the field and depressed the army. He had fallen on the crest of the hill—the stronghold of the enemy, which he had almost driven them from, and which once gained, the day was ours. The enemy in front of him in the woods, after a few moments' cessation of firing and some movements, was taken by him to be a regiment of his own command, and he rode up to give them a command, when he was shot down, pierced by several balls.*

The fall of this gallant leader, and a movement of the enemy to flank the Confederates, completed their disorder. Gen. Crittenden attempted to rally the troops by the most conspicuous displays of personal daring, in which he seemed to court death, as he reined up his horse again and again abreast of the enemy's fire, and exhorted his men to stand their ground. But the tide of retreat had set in, and all that could be done was to steady the men as they moved back to their entrenchments at Camp Beech Grove. The Confederates left upon the field about three hundred killed and wounded, and lost about a hundred prisoners. But this was not the measure of the disaster.

The enemy did not attempt an energetic pursuit. He followed the retreating Confederates as far as their entrenchments, in front of which he halted for the night. The Confederates, unprovided with rations and the necessary supplies to enable them to hold their entrenched position, and fearing lest they should be cut off, retreated across the Cumberland River during the night. The crossing was effected by the aid of a small steamer, which had made its way with supplies for the army from Nashville some days previous. Time permitted, however, only the transportation of the men ; and Gen. Crittenden effected his retreat after having lost all his baggage, camp equipage, wagons, horses, and artillery.

The battle of Fishing Creek was not remarkable for lists of killed and wounded ; but it was undoubtedly the most serious disaster that had yet befallen the Confederate arms. It practically surrendered to the enemy the whole of Eastern Kentucky. The right of the defensive line of the Confederates was now broken, and the value of their position greatly impaired. On the other part of their line—that through Western Kentucky, where the rivers and railroads passed which afforded an entrance into Tennessee, and so to the heart of the Southern States—an inadequate force under Gen. Albert Sydney Johnston was extended from Bowling Green on the right to Columbus on the left, presenting to the enemy advantages of attack which he could not fail to perceive.

---

* The dead body of Zollicoffer was brutally insulted by the enemy. The Cincinnati *Commercial* contained the following sentiment expressed on behalf of what was styled in the usual Yankee magniloquence and virtuous phrase " a conquering army, battling for the right : "

" The corpse lay by the side of the road along which we all passed, and all had a fair view of what was once Zollicoffer. I saw the lifeless body as it lay in a fence-corner by the side of the road, but Zollicoffer himself is now in hell. Hell is a fitting abode for all such arch-traitors. May all the other chief conspirators in this rebellion soon share Zollicoffer's fate—shot dead through the instrumentality of an avenging God—their spirits sent straightway to hell, and their lifeless bodies lie in a fence-corner, their faces spattered with mud, and their garments divided up, and even the hair of their head cut off and pulled out by an unsympathizing soldiery of a conquering army, battling for the right."

Never was there such a popular delusion in the Confederacy as that with respect to the strength of Johnston's army. The Richmond newspapers could not "see why Johnston did not muster his forces, advance farther into Kentucky, capture Louisville, push across the Ohio, sack Cincinnati, and carry the war into Africa." But at the time these pleasing anticipations of an advance movement were indulged, Johnston actually did not have more than twenty-five thousand men. The utter inadequacy of his force, and the exposure of his flanks and rear, were well known to the proper Confederate authorities. But the Richmond Government appeared to hope for results without the legitimate means for acquiring them ; to look for relief from vague and undefined sources ; and to await, with dull expectation, what was next to happen. There is nothing more remarkable in the history of the war than the false impressions of the people of the South as to the extent of our forces at the principal strategic point in Kentucky, and the long and apathetic toleration by the Government in Richmond of a prospect that promised nothing but eventual disaster.

Shorly after the disaster at Fishing Creek, Gen. Beauregard had been sent from the Potomac to Gen. Johnston's lines in Kentucky. At a conference between the two generals, Beauregard expressed his surprise at the smallness of Gen. Johnston's forces, and was impressed with the danger of his position. Buell was in front ; the right flank was threatened by a large Federal force under Thomas ; while the Cumberland River offered an opportunity to an attack in the rear, and held the key to Nashville.

A large force of Federals had been collected at Paducah, at the mouth of the Tennessee River, with a view to offensive operations on the water. This river penetrated Tennessee and Alabama, and was navigable for steamers for two or three hundred miles. There was nothing to resist the enemy's advance up the stream but a weak and imperfectly constructed fort. The Cumberland was a still more important river, and the avenue to Nashville ; but nothing stood in the way of the enemy save Fort Donelson, and from that point the Federal gunboats could reach Nashville in six or eight hours, and strike a vital blow at the whole system of Confederate defences north of the capital of Tennessee.

Gen. U. S. Grant commenced his ascent of the Tennessee River early in February, 1862, with a mixed force of gunboats and infantry columns, the latter making parallel movements along the banks. On the 4th of February the expedition arrived at Fort Henry, on the east bank of the river, and near the lines of Kentucky and Tennessee. The fort was obviously untenable, being so absurdly located, that it was enfiladed from three or four points on the opposite shore, while other points on the eastern bank of the river commanded it at easy cannon range. But there were more than twenty-five hundred Confederate troops in the vicinity, under the command of Gen. Tilghman; and to cover the retreat of these, it became necessary to hold the fort to the last moment, and to sacrifice the small garrison for the larger number.

Gen. Grant was moving up the east bank of the river from his landing three miles below, with a force of twelve thousand men; whilst Gen. Smith, with six thousand men, was moving up the west bank to take a position within four or five hundred yards, which would enable him to enfilade the entire works. The only chance for Gen. Tilghman was to delay the enemy every moment possible, and retire his command, now outside the main work, to Fort Donelson. To this end it was necessary to fight the *eleven* guns of Fort Henry against an armament of fifty-four guns, and an enemy nearly twenty thousand strong, as long as possible.

Gen. Tilghman nobly devoted himself to the fate of the garrison, instead of joining the main body of troops retiring towards Fort Donelson, the safety of whom depended upon a protracted defence of the fort. He engaged the enemy for two hours and ten minutes; disabled one of his gunboats, and inflicted upon him a loss of seventy-three in killed and wounded; and surrendered only when the enemy was breaching the fort directly in front of his guns. The brave Confederate commander and the small garrison of forty were taken prisoners, after having sustained a loss of about twenty killed and wounded.

The fall of Fort Henry was an unimportant event, of itself; but it was the signal for the direction of the most anxious attention to Fort Donelson on the Cumberland.

BATTLE OF FORT DONELSON.

Grant approached Fort Donelson, with immense columns of infantry, and with his powerful fleet of gunboats under command of Commodore Foote. Gen. Johnston had devoted the larger part of his army to the defence of this important post. He had determined to fight for Nashville at Donelson; and he had given the best part of his army to do it, retaining only to cover his front about eleven thousand effective men. Gen. Buckner had repaired to Fort Donelson with a command embracing most of the troops who had composed the central army of Kentucky. On the 10th of February, Gen. Pillow arrived with a body of Tennessee troops. On the 13th, Gen. Floyd arrived with his brigade of Virginians, and as senior brigadier took command of the whole Confederate force assembled at Donelson.

The site of the fortification commanded a stretch of the river for more than two miles. The armament of the batteries consisted of eight 32-pounders, three 32-pound carronades, one 8-inch columbiad, and one 32-

pounder rifled gun.   A line of entrenchments about two miles in extent was occupied by the troops.

As the sun rose on the 13th of February, the cannonade from one of the enemy's gunboats announced the opening of the conflict, which was destined to continue for several days and nights.   At eleven o'clock the enemy's infantry moved forward upon the entrenchments, along the whole line.   They were met by a scorching fire, and were repeatedly driven back.   The day closed with the disastrous repulse of the enemy from the trenches at every point of assault.   They withdrew their infantry, but kept up an incessant fire of artillery and sharpshooters, by which the Confederates were harassed, and deprived of rest and refreshment.

It was expected that the next day the enemy would renew his attack upon the entrenchments.   The morning passed without any indications of such an onset.   The smoke of a large number of gunboats and steamboats on the river was observed a short distance below, and information at the same time was received within the Confederate lines of the arrival of reinforcements to the enemy, who was already reported to be more than twenty thousand strong.

At half-past two o'clock the Federal fleet drew near the fort. It consisted of six boats, carrying forty-six guns.   Five of these iron-plated batteries approached in line of battle, *en echelon*.   They kept up a constant fire for about an hour and a half.   Once the boats got within a few hundred yards of the fort.   When they reached the point of the nearest approach, the fire on both sides was tremendous.   That of the Confederate batteries was too destructive to be borne.   Fifty-seven shots struck the flag-ship, and more than a hundred in all, plunged upon the decks of the assaulting fleet.   Every boat was disabled, except one, which kept beyond the range of fire.   With great difficulty, the shattered iron-clads were withdrawn from the storm of shot hailed from the fort.   Fifty-four men were killed and wounded on the boats, while in the batteries not one man was killed or seriously hurt, and no injury was done to the works.

The incidents of two days had been altogether in favour of the Confederates.   Their casualties were small ; but their sufferings had been extreme. The conflict had commenced on one of the coldest days of winter ; the thermometer was twenty degrees below the freezing point ; and while the troops watched on their arms in the trenches, it sleeted and snowed. Many of the men had their feet and hands frozen.   Their clothes were stiff from frozen water.   In the engagement in the trenches, many of the wounded who could neither walk nor crawl had been left in the narrow space between the two armies ; and as no flag of truce was allowed, under which they might have been brought off, they lay there in the pitiless weather, calling in vain for help.   Many thus died who otherwise might have been saved, and those of the wounded who were recovered alive, not until the last act of the battle's tragedy had been closed, were blue with cold, and covered with frost and snow.

Reinforcements were now continually reaching the enemy. Transports were arriving nearly every hour, from which dark streams of men could be seen pouring along the roads, and completing the investment of the lines around the fort. Indeed, it might have been evident from the first, that the whole available force of the Federals on the western waters could and would be concentrated at Fort Donelson, if it was deemed necessary to reduce it. It was fair to infer that while the enemy kept up a constant menace of attack, his object was merely to gain time to pass a column above the works, both on the right and left banks, and thus to cut the Confederate communications and prevent the possibility of egress.

On the night of the 14th, Gen. Floyd called a council of the officers of divisions and brigades. It was unanimously determined that but one course was left by which a rational hope could be entertained of saving the garrison, and that was to dislodge the enemy from his position on our left, and thus to pass the troops into the open country lying southward, towards Nashville.

The plan of attack was that Gen. Pillow, aided by Brigadier-General Bushrod R. Johnson, with three brigades, should advance to the assault of the enemy on the right, while Gen. Buckner, with his force, chiefly of Kentucky and Tennessee troops, should advance upon the left and centre of the enemy along the Wynn's Ferry road, which led from the river and village of Dover, and was the only practicable route to Nashville. When Gen. Pillow moved out of his position next morning, he found the enemy prepared to receive him in advance of his encampment. For nearly two hours the battle raged fiercely on this part of the line, with very little change in the position of the adverse forces.

As the morning advanced, a brigade of Mississippians and Tennesseans was thrown forward, and advanced up a hollow, firing terrible volleys into the enemy's right flank. This heroic band of troops, less than fifteen hundred in number, marched up the hill, loading and firing as they moved, gaining inch by inch, on an enemy at least four times their number. For one long hour this point was hotly contested by the enemy. At last, unable to bear the hot assault, the Federals gave way, and fell back slowly to the left, retiring towards the Wynn's Ferry road.

Gen. Buckner's advance on the centre and left of the enemy was retarded by various causes, and it was nearly nine o'clock before this part of the Confederate forces became fairly engaged with the enemy. A portion of his artillery opened upon the flank and left rear of the enemy's infantry, who were being pressed back by Gen. Pillow's division.

As the enemy's line of retreat was along the Wynn's Ferry road, Gen. Buckner now organized an attack further to his right, up a deep valley, in rear of the position occupied by the enemy's batteries. The advance of his infantry column was covered by artillery. The movement, combined with the brisk fire of three batteries, induced a rapid retreat of the enemy, who abandoned a section of his artillery. At the same time that Buckner's infantry was thus penetrating the line of the enemy's retreat, Forrest, with a portion of his cavalry, charged upon their right, while Pillow's division was pressing their extreme right about half a mile further to the left.

It now appeared that the crisis of the battle was past. Victory, or such success as they had sought, seemed to be within the grasp of the Confederates. The Wynn's Ferry road was now not only open, but cleared of the enemy entirely on one side, and for a mile and a half on the other. Of this posture of affairs, Gen. Buckner, in his official report, writes : " I awaited the arrival of my artillery and reserves, either to continue the pursuit of the enemy, or to defend the position I now held, in order that the army might pass out on the road, which was now completely covered by the position occupied by my division. But Gen. Pillow had prevented my artillery from leaving the entrenchments, and also sent me reiterated orders to return to my entrenchments on the extreme right. I was in the act of returning to the lines, when I met Gen. Floyd, who seemed surprised at the order. At his request to know my opinion of the movement, I replied that nothing had occurred to change my views of the necessity of the evacuation of the post, that the road was open, that the first part of our purpose was fully accomplished, and I thought we should at once avail ourselves of the existing opportunity to regain our communications. These seemed to be his own views ; for he directed me to halt my troops and remain in position until he should have conversed with Gen. Pillow, who was now within the entrenchments. After that consultation, he sent me an order to retire within the lines, and to repair as rapidly as possible to my former position on the extreme right, which was in danger of attack."

It was long a source of keen regret among those few people in the Confederacy who knew the real history of the Fort Donelson battle, that their army did not attempt a retreat at the precise period of opportunity. But a few moments of that superabundant caution, which hesitates to seize the crisis, and insists upon reconnoitring an advantage, are often fatal upon a field of battle. It was thought by those superiour to Gen. Buckner in command, that it would be hazardous to attempt a retreat while the enemy, though defeated, was near at hand with fresh troops.

The hesitation was fatal. The effect of the violent attack of the Confederates on the enemy's right, followed up by Gen. Buckner's advance on his centre, had been to roll over his immense masses towards the right of the Confederate works, immediately in front of their river batteries. The advantage was instantly appreciated. The enemy drove back the Confederates, advanced on the trenches on the extreme right of Gen. Buckner's command, getting possession, after a stubborn conflict of two hours, of the most important and commanding position of the battle-field, being in the rear of our river batteries, and, advancing with fresh forces towards our left, drove back our troops from the ground that had been won in the severe and terrible conflict of the early part of the day.

After nine hours of combat, the enemy held the field; he had changed the fortune of the day by a quick and opportune movement; and he now held the Confederates in circumstances of desperation. Of the results of the day, Gen. Floyd reported: "We had fought the battle to open our way for our army, and to relieve us from an investment which would necessarily reduce us and the position we occupied by famine. We had accomplished our object, but it occupied the whole day, and before we could prepare to leave, after taking in the wounded and the dead, the enemy had thrown around us again, in the night, an immense force of fresh troops, and reoccupied his original position in the line of investment, thus again cutting off our retreat. We had only about 13,000 troops, all told. Of these we had lost a large proportion in the three battles. The command had been in the trenches night and day for five days, exposed to snow, sleet, mud, and ice and water, without shelter, without adequate covering, and without sleep."

The field of battle was thickly strewn with dead and wounded. The loss of the Confederates was estimated at fifteen hundred. That of the enemy Gen. Floyd conjectures, in his official report, to have been at least five thousand.

Ghastly spectacles were abundant, as the eye ranged over this scene of mortal strife; for the ground was in many places red with frozen blood, and the snow which lay under the pine thickets was marked with crimson streams. There were two miles of dead strewn thickly, mingled with fire-arms, artillery, dead horses, and the paraphernalia of the battle-field. Many of the bodies were fearfully mangled, and the ponderous artillery wheels had crushed limbs and skulls. The dead were promiscuously mingled, sometimes grappling in the fierce death-throe, sometimes facing each other as they gave and received the fatal shot and thrust, sometimes huddled in grotesque shapes, and again heaped in piles which lay six or seven feet deep.

"I could imagine," says an eye-witness of the field of carnage, "nothing more terrible than the silent indications of agony that marked the features of the pale corpses which lay at every step. Though dead and rigid in every muscle, they still writhed, and seemed to turn to catch the passing breeze for a cooling breath. Staring eyes, gaping mouths, clenched hands, and strangely contracted limbs, seemingly drawn into the smallest compass, as if by a mighty effort to rend asunder some irresistible bond which held them down to the torture of which they died. One sat against a tree, and, with mouth and eyes wide open, looked up into the sky, as if to catch a glance at its fleeting spirit. Another clutched the branch of an overhanging tree, and hung half-suspended, as if in the death-pang he had raised himself partly from the ground ; the other had grasped his faithful musket, and the compression of his mouth told of the determination which would have been fatal to a foe, had life ebbed a minute later. A third clung with both hands to a bayonet which was buried in the ground. Great numbers lay in heaps, just as the fire of the artillery mowed them down, mangling their forms into an almost undistinguishable mass."

Late in the night of the 15th of February, another conference of general officers was called. It was, indeed, a memorable one. Gen. Pillow appears to have favoured a proposition for a desperate onset upon the right of the enemy's forces, with the prospect of thus extricating a considerable proportion of the command. Gen. Buckner remarked, that it would cost the command three-fourths its present numbers to cut its way out, and it was wrong to sacrifice three-fourths to save one-fourth ; that no officer had a right to cause such a sacrifice. The alternative of the proposition was a surrender of the position and command. Gen. Floyd declared that he would not surrender himself a prisoner, and proposed to escape with such portion of his command as was possible on two small steamers, which had arrived from Nashville during the night. Gen. Pillow remarked that he thought there were no two persons in the Confederacy whom the "Yankees" would prefer to capture than himself and Gen. Floyd, and asked the latter's opinion as to the propriety of his accompanying him. To this inquiry Gen. Floyd replied that it was a question for every man to decide for himself. Gen. Pillow then addressed the inquiry to Gen. Buckner, to which Gen. Buckner remarked that he could only reply as Gen. Floyd had done ; that it was a question for every officer to decide for himself, and that in his own case he regarded it as his duty to remain with his men and share their fate, whatever it might be.

It was then arranged that the command should be passed. Gen. Buckner asked, "Am I to consider the command as turned over to me ?" Gen. Floyd replied, "Certainly, I turn over the command." Gen. Pillow replied quickly, "I pass it. I will not surrender." Gen. Buckner then called for pen, ink, paper, and a bugler, and prepared to open communication with the Federal commander.

A number of men had fallen in battle ; some of the sick and wounded had been removed ; and detachments of troops had escaped under Floyd, Pillow, and Forrest ; leaving the number surrendered by Gen. Buckner to the enemy less than nine thousand men. Gen. Grant had demanded "Unconditional Surrender"—words, which the Northern populace afterwards attached to his name as a peculiar title to glory ; and Gen.

Buckner replied: "The distribution of the forces under my command, incident to an unexpected change of commanders, and the overwhelming force under your command, compel me, notwithstanding the brilliant success of the Confederate arms yesterday, to accept the ungenerous and unchivalrous terms which you propose."

The fall of Fort Donelson was the heaviest blow that had yet fallen on the Confederacy. It opened the whole of West Tennessee to Federal occupation, and it developed the crisis which had long existed in the West. Gen. A. S. Johnston had previously ordered the evacuation of Bowling Green; and the movement was executed while the battle was being fought at Donelson. Gen. Johnston awaited the result of the battle opposite Nashville. At dawn of the 16th of February he received the news of a defeat. Orders were at once issued to push the army forward across the river as soon as possible. The city papers or extras of that morning published despatches announcing a "glorious victory." The city was wild with joy. About the time the people were assembling at the churches, it was announced by later extras that "Donelson had fallen." The revulsion was great. Governor Harris had been informed of the fact early in the morning, and had proceeded to Gen. Johnston's head-quarters to advise with him as to the best course to adopt under the altered circumstances. The General said that Nashville was utterly indefensible; that the army would pass right through the city; that any attempt to defend it with the means at his command would result in disaster to the army, and the destruction of the city; that the first and highest duty of the governor was to the public trusts in his hands, and he thought, to discharge them properly, he should at once remove the archives and public records to some safer place, and call the Legislature together elsewhere than at Nashville. Gen. Johnston retreated with his army towards Murfreesboro', leaving behind him a scene of panic and dismay.

The confusion at Nashville did not reach its height until a humane attempt was made to distribute among the poor a portion of the public stores which could not be removed. The lowest passions seemed to have been aroused in a large mass of men and women, and the city appeared as if it was in the hands of a mob. A detachment of Forrest's cavalry endeavoured to enforce order. Houses were closed, carriages and wagons were concealed, to prevent the mob from taking possession of them. Horses were being seized everywhere. After every other means failed, Forrest charged the mob, before he could get it so dispersed as to get wagons to the doors of the departments, to load up the stores for transportation. The loss of public stores by depredations was not less than a million of dollars. "In my judgment," said Col. Forrest, "if the quartermaster and commissary had remained at their posts, and worked diligently with the means at their command, the government stores might all have been saved between the time of the fall of Fort Donelson and the arrival of the enemy in Nashville."

We shall complete this chapter by a brief account of a defeat of Confederate arms that preceded by several days the fall of Fort Donelson, and took place on a widely separated theatre of the war. The thread of Confederate disaster takes us here from the tributaries of the Mississippi to the low and melancholy sea-line of North Carolina.

CAPTURE OF ROANOKE ISLAND BY THE ENEMY.

About the middle of January, 1862, Gen. Burnside entered Pamlico Sound at the head of an expedition, consisting of more than sixty vessels of all kinds, twenty-six of them gunboats, and with at least fifteen thousand men. It readily became apparent that Roanoke Island was the first object of his attack. This important island lies in the broad inlet between Pamlico and Currituck Sounds, and about midway between the main land and the narrow strip of bank which dykes out the ocean. It was of great moment to the South to defend it, for its possession by the enemy would unlock to them Albemarle and Currituck Sounds, open to them eight rivers, give them access to the country chiefly supplying provisions to Norfolk, and enable them to menace that city, and the four canals and two railroads running through the country by which it was surrounded.

Gen. Henry A. Wise, who had been ordered to the command of the department embracing Roanoke Island, declared that it should be defended at the expense of twenty thousand men, and many millions of dollars. But to his estimate of the importance of the position he found that the Richmond authorities had a deaf ear. On the 7th of January, 1862, Gen. Wise assumed command, and made an examination of the defences. He found them inadequate, in his opinion, to resist even the force then at Hatteras, and as the Burnside expedition began already to point to the North Carolina coast, he called urgently for reinforcements. He addressed a letter to Mr. Benjamin, the Confederate Secretary of War, and followed it by a personal interview, in which he strenuously insisted that more troops should be sent to the island. He urged that a large part of Gen. Huger's command, at Norfolk, might be safely detached, and used for the defence of Roanoke. He argued that the fifteen thousand men under Huger were idle, and were only kept at Norfolk in view of a possible attack, and that they would much more advantageously defend the city, by guarding the approaches through the Sound, than by remaining inactive. He explained that Roanoke Island guarded more than four-fifths of all Norfolk's supplies of corn, pork and forage, and that its capture by the enemy would cut the command of Gen. Huger off from all its most efficient transportation. But Mr. Benjamin would not adopt these views, and would not disturb Gen. Huger; he told Wise sullenly that there were no men to spare to reinforce him; and at last he brought the conferences and protestations of the General to an abrupt termination by a peremptory military order, dated the 22d of January, requiring him to proceed immediately to Roanoke Island.

The defences of the island consisted of seven small gunboats and six land batteries, not casemated, and wholly inefficient. After manning the forts, there were scarcely more than eight hundred effective men. In the sickness of Gen. Wise, who was confined to his bed at Nag's Head, the immediate command devolved upon Col. Shaw, the senior officer present.

In the morning of the 7th of February the enemy made an attack, with twenty-two heavy steamers, upon the little Confederate squadron under the command of Commodore Lynch, and upon Fort Bartow, the most southern of the defences on the west side of the island. The action commenced at two miles distance, the Confederate gunboats retiring slowly with the intention of drawing the enemy under the guns of the batteries. Soon the air was filled with heavy reports, and the sea was disturbed in every direction by fragments of shell. Explosions of shell rang through the air; and occasionally a large one hundred and twenty-four pounder thundered across the waves, and sent its ponderous shot in the midst of the flotilla. At times, the battery would be enveloped in the sand and dust thrown up by shot and shell. The scene of this bombardment, which lasted continuously from ten in the morning until half-past five in the afternoon, was a singular and picturesque one. The melancholy shore-line which bound it, was an unbroken one of dark cypresses and pines. On the water were the enemy's vessels rapidly pouring out shot and shell at the line of Confederate gunboats or at the batteries. Still further on, just gleaming through the sunlight, was the forest of masts and the white sails of the transports, kept far in the rear out of the reach of danger.

Our casualties on the gunboats were only one man killed and three wounded. But the engagement had been disastrous. The Curlew, our largest steamer, was sunk, and the Forrest, one of the propellers, disabled. Commodore Lynch writes, in his official report, that at the close of the action he had " not a pound of powder or a loaded shell remaining." This singular deficiency of ammunition and the disasters he had already sustained, determined the policy of retreat, and under cover of the night, the squadron was drawn off to Elizabeth City.

Gen. Burnside gave orders that a landing should be made on the island the next morning. It was accomplished under cover of the gunboats, about the centre of the western shore. At nine o'clock the enemy advanced through a country swampy and covered with forest. About the centre of the island an entrenchment had been thrown up, covered on the flanks by marshy ground ; and here the Confederates took position to dispute the enemy's advance. But the marshes were found to be practicable. The Federals advanced with flanking columns debouching to the right and left. Their overwhelming numbers literally crowded upon and crushed our battery of three field-pieces on the left,* while at the same time the enemy passed through the cypress swamp, which Col. Shaw thought impracticable, and turned the right flank. The order was given to spike the guns in the battery, and retreat to the northern end of the island. The Confederates were followed up to the shore, slowly and cautiously, by the enemy. Some effected their escape in boats, which were quickly towed away by a steamer ; but the bulk of the command was captured, including two boats conveying the wounded, which were compelled to return by the enemy's fire.

The capture of the island was immediately followed by the pursuit of the Confederate gunboats. A squadron, consisting of fourteen gunboats, was detached for that purpose, and, on the 10th of February, found the remaining Confederate vessels drawn up in line in the narrow channel which leads up to Elizabeth City. After a brief and desultory engagement, the crews of the Confederate gunboats, after setting fire to the vessels, abandoned them, and fled for the shore. Thus was the disaster of Roanoke Island complete. The Confederates had lost in all the actions but twenty-three killed and fifty-eight wounded. But the disaster in other respects was great. The enemy had taken six forts, forty guns, nearly two thousand prisoners, and upwards of three thousand small arms ; secured the water avenue of Roanoke River, navigable for one hundred and twenty miles ; got possession of the granary and larder of Norfolk, and threatened the back-door of that city.

The disaster of Roanoke Island dates the period when public censure towards the Richmond Government appeared to have first awakened. Heretofore the administration of that Government had gone on almost

---

* In this action was killed Capt. O. Jennings Wise, of the " Richmond Blues," a son of Gen. Wise, a young man of brilliant promise, prominently connected with the Richmond press before the war, and known throughout the State for his talents, chivalric bearing, and modesty of behaviour. A correspondent furnishes the following particulars of the death of this brilliant young officer :

"About ten o'clock Capt. Wise found his battalion exposed to the galling fire of a regiment ; turning to Capt. Coles, he said : ' This fire is very hot ; tell Col. Anderson we must fall back or be reinforced.' Capt. Coles turned to pass the order, and was shot through the heart, dying instantly. Capt. Wise was wounded, first in the arm and next through the lungs, which latter wound brought him to the ground. He was borne to the hospital in charge of Surgeon Coles, and received two additional wounds while being borne from the field. That evening Surgeon Coles put him into a boat to send him to Nag's Head, but the enemy fired upon it, and he was obliged to return. The enemy seemed to regret this, and treated him very kindly, taking him out of the boat on a mattress, and starting back to the hospital. The next day, about eleven o'clock A. M., he calmly and in his perfect senses, without suffering, softly passed away. A Federal officer, standing by him and witnessing his death, said, ' *There is a brave man !* ' "

without inquiry, the people presuming on the wisdom of their rulers, and having but little curiosity to penetrate the details of their business, or to violate that singular official reserve which was thrown around the military condition of the Confederacy from the first gun of the war down to the final catastrophe. But such a disaster as that referred to, in which improvidence stared out, and in which an army had been put, as it were, in a mash-trap—in a condition in which it could neither hope for success nor extricate itself from a besetting peril—provoked public inquiry, and demanded an investigation.*

A committee was accordingly ordered in the Confederate Congress to report upon the affair of Roanoke Island. It declared that the Secretary of War, Mr. J. P. Benjamin, was responsible for an important defeat of our arms, which might have been safely avoided by him; that he had paid no practical attention to the appeals of Gen. Wise; and that he had, by plain acts of omission, permitted that general and an inconsiderable force to remain to meet at least fifteen thousand men, well armed and equipped. No defence to this charge was ever attempted by Secretary Benjamin or his friends; and the unanimous conclusion of the committee, charging one of President Davis' Cabinet with a matter of the gravest offence known to the laws and the interests of the country, was allowed to remain on the public record without commentary or consequence.

* The Richmond *Enquirer* had the following commentary on the Roanoke Island affair. It contains a picture of Confederate improvidence, which was to be repeated at many stages of the war, and to put our scantiness and shiftlessness in frightful contrast with the active zeal and munificent preparations of the enemy:

" On the island no preparations whatever had been made. Col. Shaw's regiment, Col. Jordan's, and three companies of Col. Marten's regiment, had been on the island for months. These regiments numbered, all present, one thousand nine hundred and fourteen. Of these, about one thousand seven hundred were soldiers. There were four hundred and fifty absent and sick, leaving one thousand two hundred and fifty for all duty. From these, five batteries had to be manned, leaving, on the morning of the eighth, only eight hundred and three North Carolina infantry reported for duty. These had not been paid, or clothed, or fed, or drilled. The island had no implements for the labour on the works, no teams but two pair of broken-down mules, and no horses for field-artillery. There were but three pieces of field-artillery—one twenty-four pounder, one eighteen pounder, and one brass howitzer—the mules drew the latter, and the men the heavier pieces through the sand. There was only twelve-pounder ammunition for any of the large pieces. The forts, built on the island before Gen. Wise was assigned to the command, were all in the wrong places—at the north end of the island—leaving all the landings on the south end uncovered by a single battery. No breastworks had been made, and there were no tools to make any—the marshes at the south end of the island had no defensive works upon them. But one steam-tug and two barges were provided, and there were no means of retreat either by tugs or ferry. Thus it will be seen there were provided no means of defence, and still less of escape, though timely notice and a providential warning of twenty-five days had been given."

CHAPTER XIII.

EXCITEMENT ABOUT IRON VESSELS.—DISCUSSION IN THE NEWSPAPERS.—ADDITION OF IRON-CLADS TO THE FEDERAL NAVY.—WHAT M'CLELLAN THOUGHT OF THE VIRGINIA.—CAPTURE OF NEWBERN, &C.—OBJECTS OF BURNSIDE'S EXPEDITION.—BRANCH'S COMMAND AT NEW-BERN.—THE CONFEDERATE WORKS ON THE NEUSE RIVER.—RETREAT OF BRANCH.—FED-ERAL OCCUPATION OF NEWBERN.—CAPTURE OF FORT MACON.—THE ENTIRE COAST OF NORTH CAROLINA IN THE POSSESSION OF THE ENEMY.—THE SEA-COAST AN UNIMPORTANT PART OF THE CONFEDERATE DEFENCES.

THE series of disasters that befel the Confederates in the early months of 1862, may be distinctly and sufficiently traced to human causes. Instead of being ascribed to the mysterious dispensations of Providence, they are more properly named as the results of human mismanagement. The first important defeat of the Federal arms on the plains of Manassas was the initial point with the North of an enlarged scheme of war, and it was now simply giving proof of its "Anaconda Plan," and realizing the natural result of those immense preparations it had made by sea and land, to confound its adversary.

The rebukes which were now being administered to the vaingloriousness of the South were neither few nor light. The Confederates had been worsted in almost every engagement that had occurred since the fall of 1861. There had come disaster after disaster, culminating in the fall of Donelson, the occupation of Nashville, the breaking of our centre, the falling back on all sides, the realization of invasion, the imminence of perils which no one dared to name.

No one who lived in Richmond during the war can ever forget these gloomy, miserable days. In the midst of them was to occur the ceremony of the inauguration of the Permanent Government of the Confederate States. It was only a difference of name between two governments, one called Provisional and the other Permanent; for Mr. Davis had been unanimously elected President, and there was no change either of the organic law or of the *personnel* of the Administration. But the ceremony of the second inauguration of President Davis was one of deep interest to the public; for it was supposed that he might use the occasion to develop a new policy and to reanimate the people. The 22d of February, the day appointed for the inauguration, was memorable for its gloom in Richmond. Rain fell in torrents, and the heavens seemed to be hung with sable. Yet a dense crowd collected, braving the rain-storm in their eager interest to hear the President's speech from the steps of the Capitol. " It was then," said a Richmond paper, " that all eyes were turned to our Chief; that we hung upon his lips, hushing the beating of our heavy hearts that we might catch the word of fire we longed to hear—that syllable of sympathy of which a nation in distress stands so in need. One sentence then of defiance and of cheer—something bold, and warm, and human—had sent a thrill of lightning through the land, and set it ablaze with the fresh and quench-

less flame of renewed and never-ending fight. That sentence never came.
The people were left to themselves."

The Confederate President offered but little of counsel or encouragement to his distressed countrymen. He declared that the magnified proportions of the war had occasioned serious disasters, and that the effort
was impossible to protect the whole of the territory of the Confederate
States, sea-board and inland. To the popular complaint of inefficiency in
the departments of the Government, he replied that they had done all
which human power and foresight enabled them to accomplish. He lifted
up, in conclusion, a piteous, beautiful, appropriate prayer for the favour of
Divine providence.

But it is not to be supposed that the people of the Confederacy, although so little cheered or sustained by their rulers, despaired of the war.
There were causes, which were rekindling the fiercest flames of war apart
from official inspiration at Richmond. The successes of the enemy had
but made him more hateful, and strengthened the South in the determination to have done with him forever. They found new causes of animosity;
the war had been brought home to their bosoms; they had obtained practical lessons of the enemy's atrocity and his insolent design; and they
came to the aid of their Government with new power and a generosity that
was quite willing to forget all its short-comings in the past.

One great cause of animated resolution on the part of the Confederate
States was the development at Washington of the design upon slavery,
now advanced to a point where there could no longer be a doubt of the
revengeful and radical nature of the war. The steps by which the Federal
Government had reached this point were in a crooked path, and attended
by marks of perfidy. It had indeed given to the world on this subject an
astounding record of bad faith, calculated to overwhelm the moral sense
of the reader as he compares its different parts and approaches its grand
conclusion of self-contradiction the most defiant, and deception the most
shameless.

Never had there been such an emphatic protest of a political design as
that given by Mr. Lincoln on taking the reins of government, declaring
that there was no possible intention, no imaginable occasion, no actual desire to interfere with the subject of negro slavery in the States. Mr.
Seward, who had been constituted Secretary of State, and who had been
Mr. Lincoln's mouth-piece in Congress before the inauguration, had declared there: "Experience in public affairs has confirmed my opinion that
domestic slavery existing in any State is *wisely* left by the Constitution of
the United States, exclusively to the care, management, and disposition of
that State; and *if it were in my power I would not alter the Constitution
in that respect.*" Words could scarcely be more distinct and emphatic;
but Mr. Lincoln, in his inauguration address, had seen fit to add to them,

and, quoting from a former speech, announced to the country : " I have no purpose, directly or indirectly, to interfere with the institution of slavery in the States where it exists. I believe I have no lawful right to do so, and *I have no inclination to do so.*"

This assurance was again repeated after the commencement of hosti'i-ties, as if there was the most anxious purpose to obtain the ear of the Southern people on the subject, and to impress the world with the just and moderate designs of the war. In his letter of April, 1861, to the Federal minister at Paris, intended as a diplomatic circular for the courts of Europe, and an authoritative exposition of the objects and spirit of the war on the Northern side, Mr. Seward, by direction of the President, wrote : " The condition of slavery in the several States will remain just the same, *whether it succeeds* or fails. The rights of the States, and the condition of every human being in them, will remain subject to exactly the same laws and form of administration, whether the revolution shall succeed or whether it shall fail. Their constitutions and laws and customs, habits and institutions in either case will remain the same. It is hardly necessary to add to this incontestable statement the further fact that the new President, as well as the citizens through whose suffrages he has come into the administration, has always repudiated al. designs whatever, and wherever imputed to him and them, of *disturbing the system of slavery as it is existing under the Constitution and laws.* The case, however, would not be fully presented were I to omit to say that any such effort on his part would be *unconstitutional,* and all his acts in that direction would be prevented by the judicial authority, even though they were assented to by Congress and the people."

The first acts of the Federal authority in the active prosecution of the war, touching the institution of slavery, were busily conformed to these assurances. They even afforded an extravagant testimony of their sincerity. Fugitive slaves were not only arrested within the Federal military lines and returned to slavery, but were taken in the streets of Washington and returned, by judicial process, to their masters. On the 26th of May, 1861, Gen. McClellan issued an address to the people of Western Virginia, assuring them that not only would the Federal troops abstain from all interference with their slaves, but that they would crush any attempt at servile insurrection. Gen. McDowell issued an order forbidding fugitive slaves from coming into, or being harboured within his lines. When on the 31st of August, 1861, Gen. Fremont, in Missouri, issued an order declaring the negro slaves within his military department to be free men, it was instantly repudiated and nullified at Washington. At a later period, Gen. Hunter, commanding the Department of the South, issued an order putting the States of Georgia, South Carolina, and Florida under martial law, and declaring that, as slavery and martial law were incompatible, 'he

slaves in those States were forever free. Mr. Lincoln set aside this declaration, and made it an occasion of rebuke to the pragmatical commander,
who had thus attempted to extend to political objects the police regulations
of armies and camps.

It is remarkable how this affectation of non-interference with slavery
was laid aside by successive measures of the Federal Government, until at
last it discovered its real purpose of the entire excision of slavery, and
Mr. Lincoln fell into the arms of the extreme Abolition party, and adopted
the doctrine that the opportunity was to be taken in the prosecution of
hostilities to crush out slavery as the main cause of difference, and thus
assure the fruit of a permanent peace. The first official display of anti-
slavery sentiment in the war was in the extra session of Congress in July,
1861. Mr. Lovejoy, of Illinois, proposed a resolution, which was adopted,
declaring that it was no part of the duty of Federal soldiers to capture and
return fugitive slaves. This measure was apparently reasonable; but it
was significant of a badly-disguised sentiment, the consequences of which
were soon to be developed. Next to Lovejoy's resolution was that part of
the Confiscation Act, which specially provided that any owner of a slave,
or any person having a legal claim to his services, who should require or
permit such slave to take up arms against, or be in any way employed in
military or naval service against the United States, should thereby forfeit
all claim to him, any law of a State or of the United States to the contrary
notwithstanding.

The advance of the anti-slavery sentiment was now to be rapid and
decisive. In the Thirty-seventh Federal Congress, which met at Washington in December, 1861, it accomplished three measures, which put the Government of Mr. Lincoln on the verge of committal to the entire doctrine of
Abolitionists, and plainly informed the Southern people of the real *animus*
of the war.

Naval and military officers were prohibited, by an additional article
of war, under penalty of dismissal from the service, from employing the
forces under their command for the purpose of returning fugitive slaves.

In accordance with the recommendation of the President, a joint resolution was passed, declaring that the United States ought to co-operate
with any State which may adopt the gradual abolition of slavery, by
giving pecuniary aid to such State.

The third step was the forcible abolition of slavery in the District of
Columbia. By this act all persons held to service or labour within the
District, by reason of African descent, were freed from all claim for such
service or labour; and no involuntary servitude, except for crime, and
after due conviction, should hereafter exist in the District.

It is not within the design of this chapter or within the period of time
which it traverses, to follow further the record of the Washington Govern-

ment on the subject of slavery. The crowning act of deception was reserved for another time. But the record had already progressed far enough to assure the people of the South that the only safety for their domestic institutions was in a separate and independent political existence; that Northern faith was only a thing of convenience; that in the war the Con federates contended for no mere abstractions, but had at stake all their substantial rights and nearly every element of individual happiness.

There was a good deal of curious commentary in Southern newspapers how, step by step, the war of the North had changed its objects. But in a broad historical sense the explanation is obvious. History has shown that in all great civil commotions it is the most violent party, the party whose aim is most clearly defined, that gradually obtains the upper hand. It was thus that the Abolition party in the North gradually ascended, through four years of commotion and contest, and finally obtained the entire control of the war, and dictated its consequences.

We have referred to that public sentiment in the Southern Confederacy which about the time of the foundation of its Permanent Government came forward with fresh support of the war, and a new resolution for its prosecution. Happily, although this sentiment found but little encouragement on the part of President Davis, and was neither directed nor employed by him, it secured a medium of forcible expression and a channel of effective action through the new Confederate Congress summoned at Richmond. The measures of this Congress constitute the most critical and interesting pages of the Confederate annals. It is perhaps not saying too much to declare that the vigour of this body saved the Confederacy, rallied the strength of the country, and put on a hopeful footing a war which was languishing and almost in the last stages of neglect.

The Congress which preceded it—what is known as the Provisional Congress—was perhaps the weakest body that had ever been summoned in a historical crisis. It was the creature of State conventions; it was elected at a time when most of the ambition and virtue of the country were seeking the honours of the tented field; it was composed of third-rate professional politicians, who had no resources beyond the emoluments of office, who were in a constant intrigue for patronage, and who had no higher legislative training than that of a back-door communication with the Executive. The measures of this Congress must ever remain a stock for ridicule, or the theme of severer criticism. All its legislative ingenuity appears to have been to make feeble echoes to the Federal Congress at Washington. The latter authorized an army of half a million of men. The Provisional Congress at Richmond replied by increasing its army on paper to four hundred thousand men, but doing nothing whatever to collect such a force, and still relying on the wretched shift of twelve months' volunteers and raw militia. The Congress at Washington passed a sweeping confiscation law. That at Richmond replied by a " sequestration " act, which, by corrupt amendments allowing the Confederate " heirs " of alien enemies to rescue and protect the property, was converted into a broad farce. It was announced with flourishes; it was said that it would sweep into the Confederate treasury three hundred millions of dollars. Two years after the passage of this law its actual results were summed up by the Treasurer of the Confederate States as less than two millions of dollars!

A short while before the expiration of its official life the Provisional Congress passed a law, the effect of which was almost to disband our armies in the field, and put the Confederacy at the mercy of the enemy. Never was there such a silly and visionary measure of demagogueism applied to the stern exigencies and severe demands of a state of war. The purpose was to persuade the twelve months' volunteers to re-enlist; and to do this Congress passed a law granting to those who pledged themselves to re-enlist for the term of the war a sixty days' furlough. This extraordinary measure was inspired by the military genius of President Davis, and was directly recommended by him. It depleted our armies in the face of the enemy; it filled our military commanders with consternation; it carried alarm, confusion, and demoralization everywhere. Our army near the line of the Potomac, under the effect of this ill-timed and ill-judged law, was melting like snow. The streets of Richmond were almost daily filled with long processions of furloughed soldiers moving from the railroad depots on their way home. Gen. Beauregard had taken the alarm before he left the Army of the Potomac, and had exhorted the men to stand by their colours. Gen. Johnston had published a general order on the subject, and said as much as he could say on this subject of the exodus without discovering to the enemy the fearful decrease of his numbers, and inviting an attack upon the thin military line that now formed the only defence of Richmond.

Such was the condition of affairs when the Congress of 1862 took up the thread of Confederate legislation. It at once broke it, and commenced a series of measures of startling vigour. Its most important act was the Conscription law of the 16th of April, 1862, from which properly dates the military system of the Confederacy. Previous to this the Confederacy had had nothing that deserved the title of a military system, and had relied on mere popular enthusiasm to conduct the war. When the suggestion was first made in the newspapers of Richmond of the harsh and unpopular measure of conscription, other journals, notoriously in the interest of the Administration, denounced it on the singular demagogical plea that it conveyed a reflection upon the patriotism of the country. Even in his inaugural address in February, President Davis had avoided the unpopularity of a conscription law, and had passed over the difficult question with the general phrase that troops must be enlisted for long terms instead of short ones, for which they had hitherto taken the field. But it was no time to hesitate for popularity, and to entertain the prejudices of the ignorant, when the entire fortunes of the country were at stake. The Conscription law was barely in time to save the Confederacy. At another period, the Confederate Secretary of War stated that thirty days after the passage of this law, the terms of one hundred and forty-eight regiments would have expired, and left us at the mercy of an enemy which had every guaranty of success that numbers, discipline, complete organization, and perfect equipment could effect.

The law of the 16th of April withdrew every non-exempt citizen, between the ages of eighteen and thirty-five years, from State control, and placed him absolutely at the disposal of the President during the war. It annulled all contracts made with volunteers for short terms, holding them in service for two years additional, should the war continue so long. All twelve months' recruits below eighteen and over thirty-five years, who would otherwise have been exempted by this law, were to be retained in service for ninety days after their term expired. In every State one or more camps of instruction, for the reception and training of conscripts, was established ; and to each State an officer, styled a commandant of conscripts, was appointed, charged with the supervision of the enrollment and instruction of the new levies. The conscription law, besides its great value for recruiting service, gave solidity to the military system of the Confederacy, and centralized the organization of the army. Its efficiency in these respects was assisted by the appointment of lieutenant-generals, some commanding separate departments, and others heading army corps under a general in the field. The policy of organizing the brigades with troops and generals from the several States was pursued, as opportunities offered, without detriment to the public service.

Accompanying this great military reform in the Confederacy, there were other measures which gave evidence of awakened attention to the exigencies of the war. Laws were passed to ensure the destruction of all cotton and tobacco likely to come into possession of the enemy. The authorities were authorized to destroy these great staples of Southern production to keep it from the enemy ; and owners destroying them for the same purpose were to be indemnified upon proof of the value and the circumstances of destruction. A bill was passed for partisan service, intended as a premium for adventure in the war, authorizing the formation of bands of rangers, who were to have a designated share of all captures from the enemy.*

These and like measures indicated a new scale of operation in the war,

* It was an affectation of the enemy, in subsequent periods of the war, to entitle this portion of the Confederate forces " guerillas," and to apply this term generally to whatever bodies of Confeder-

and a new spirit in the conduct of hostilities. They were to show results in a few months. The campaign of 1862 covered the whole of a huge territory, and could only be decided by movements involving great expenditure of troops and time; while the bitter exhibitions of the North had envenomed the war, aroused the spirit of retaliation, and swelled the sanguinary tide of conflict.

We have seen that the Permanent Government of the Confederate States was inaugurated at a dark period of its fortunes. The military history closely following this event is not a little curious. It may be characterized as an alternation of light and shade; across the tract of disaster there being sudden and fitful gleams of light, such as the undaunted courage of our troops and the variable accidents of war might give in such circumstances of misgovernment as were adverse or embarrassing to a grand scale of successes. Of these, and of the reverses mingled with them, we shall proceed to treat in the resumption of the military part of our narrative; reaching, at last, through this alternation of victory and defeat, the point of that grand effulgence of our arms, that made the year 1862 the most memorable in Confederate annals.

THE TRANS-MISSISSIPPI.—BATTLE OF ELK HORN.

We left Gen. Price at the close of the Missouri campaign proper, halting his weary column at Springfield. While recruiting and drilling his men, Price watched for the first movements of the enemy, and early in January, 1862, the Federals began to advance. Price had taken up a strong position and fortified it, expecting that McCulloch would move forward to his assistance; but that commander did not stir, or make the slightest diversion in his favour; so that, finding the enemy closing in upon him rapidly, he withdrew from Springfield, and was obliged to cut his way through towards Boston Mountain, where McCulloch was reported to be. This he successfully accomplished, with some desultory fighting. Meanwhile Maj.-Gen. Earl Van Dorn had been appointed by President Davis to take command in the Trans-Mississippi Department, and had arrived

ate cavalry were particularly troublesome. The following resolution, in relation to partisan service, was adopted by the Virginia Legislature, May 17, 1862:

" Whereas, this General Assembly places a high estimate upon the value of the ranger or partisan service in prosecuting the present war to a successful issue, and regards it as perfectly legitimate; and it being understood that a Federal commander on the northern border of Virginia has intimated his purpose, if such service is not discontinued, to lay waste by fire the portion of our territory at present under his power,

" *Resolved, by the General Assembly,* That in its opinion, the policy of employing such rangers and partisans ought to be carried out energetically, both by the authorities of this State and of the Confederate States, without the slightest regard to such threats."

at Pocahontas, Arkansas. He resolved to go in person to take command of the combined forces of Price and McCulloch, and reached their headquarters on the 3d of March.

Van Dorn soon ascertained that the enemy were strongly posted on rising ground at a place called Sugar Creek, about sixty miles distant, having a force of some twenty-five thousand men, under Curtis and Sturgis. It was also reported that they did not intend to advance until the arrival of heavy reinforcements, which were rapidly moving up. Although not twenty thousand strong, Van Dorn resolved to attack them, and sending word to Albert Pike to hurry forward with his brigade of Indians, moved out of camp on the 4th of March, with Price and McCulloch's forces, his intention being to surround the enemy's advance, some eight thousand strong, under Sigel, at Bentonville.

Sigel, however, made a skilful retreat, and effected a junction with Sturgis and Curtis. On the 7th of March, both armies were in full view of each other. Early in the morning, Van Dorn had made every disposition for attack, and the advance began. The enemy were strongly posted on high ground, as usual, their front being covered with a heavy body of skirmishers and artillery, but they gave way as the Confederates advanced in like order upon them, and fell back upon the main body. Price's forces constituted our left and centre, while McCulloch was on the right.

To prevent the junction of reinforcements, known to be on the way, Van Dorn's attack was made from the north and west, his columns almost surrounding the foe. The fight was long and obstinate. About two o'clock, Gen. Van Dorn sent a dispatch to Gen. McCulloch, who was attacking the enemy's left, proposing to him to hold his position, while Price's left advance might be thrown forward over the whole line, and easily end the battle. Before the dispatch was penned, Gen. McCulloch had fallen; and the victorious advance of his division upon the strong position of the enemy's front was checked by the fall of himself and Gen. McIntosh, the second in command, in the heat of the battle, and in the full tide of success.

Curtis and Sturgis, perceiving the confusion on the Confederate right, rallied their commands, and presented a formidable front; the skilful Sigel covering the retreat in a slow and masterly manner. At one time during the day the enemy was thought to have been thoroughly beaten; but he now retired in excellent order to other positions some miles to the rear. The Confederates encamped for the night nearly a mile beyond the point where the enemy had made his last stand, Gen. Van Dorn establishing his headquarters at the Elk Horn tavern.

The success of the day had not been a decided one. The want of discipline in the various commands was painfully apparent to Van Dorn. The camps of the enemy had been taken with many prisoners, stores, cannon,

etc. ; and the men were so excited with their success that it was impossible to form them into line for exigencies. Van Dorn, indeed, surmised
that reinforcements had reached the enemy in great number, and felt himself too weak to accept another engagement on the morrow, should the enemy force one upon him. He therefore ordered the sick far to the rear,
and, destroying so much of the booty as could not be transported, began
to prepare for a retreat. At an early hour in the morning, he had made
every disposition for falling back to a strong position some seven miles to
the rear, at which point his supplies of ammunition had halted. Covering
this movement with a well-displayed disposition of force, the enemy were
received with valor, and their advance checked. Sharp fighting ensued,
but the enemy made but feeble efforts to move forward, satisfied to occupy the field after the second day's fight, while the Confederates retreated
many miles from it.

Gen. Van Dorn officially stated the Confederate loss in killed and
wounded to be about six hundred, while that of the enemy was conjectured to be more than seven hundred killed, and at least an equal number wounded. Gen. Curtis, in his official report, gives no statement of his
loss, and simply remarks that it was heavy. But the battle of Elk Horn
had an importance beyond the measure of its casualties. It may be said to
have decided for the present the question of Confederate rule in Missouri.
Thereafter, for a considerable time, the Trans-Mississippi was to be a blank
in the history of the war ; and the forces of Van Dorn and Price were to
be summoned from what was supposed to be their special and immediate
enterprise to a distant arena of conflict.

While this battle was being fought on the distant and obscure theatre
of the Trans-Mississippi, a scene was occurring not many miles from the
Confederate capital, the most remarkable in the war. On the 8th of March,
1862, the Confederates obtained their first important victory on the water
—an element where they had been supposed least able to compete with
the enemy.

NAVAL FIGHT IN HAMPTON ROADS.—THE VIRGINIA AND THE MONITOR.

We have heretofore referred to the limited naval resources of the Confederates, and the feeble administration which employed and directed
them. Naval enterprise in the Confederacy had been mainly occupied
with the privateer service, from which the most extravagant results had
been expected ; although so far it may be said that the only benefit which
we derived from issuing letters of marque was the acknowledgment by the
Federal government that the Confederates were actual belligerents, and

that prisoners made from them on the sea as well as on the land were to be considered as prisoners of war.

In the early summer of 1861 the Navy Department at Richmond had designed an iron-clad war vessel, which for the long period of eight months was in course of construction at the Gosport navy yard. A plan originated with Lieut. Brooke to convert the hull of the frigate Merrimac, which vessel had been scuttled and sunk by the Federals on their abandonment of Norfolk at the opening of the war, into a shot-proof steam battery, constructed with inclined iron-plated sides and submerged ends. The plates to protect her sides were prepared at the Tredegar Iron Works at Richmond; and their inclination and thickness, and form, were determined by actual experiment. The eaves of the casemates as well as the ends of vessels were submerged, and a ram was added as a weapon of offence.

This novel naval structure carried ten guns, eight broadside, one at the bow, and one at the stern. The other vessels of the Confederate squadron in the James river, under command of Captain Buchanan, were the Patrick Henry, six guns; the Jamestown, two guns; the Raleigh, the Beaufort and the Teazer, each of one gun. At the time of which we write a considerable naval force of the enemy had been collected in Hampton Roads, off Fortress Monroe. The fleet consisted of the Cumberland, of 24 guns; the Congress, 50 guns; the St. Lawrence, 50 guns; the steam-frigates Minnesota and Roanoke, 40 guns; and was under the command of Captain Marston, of the Roanoke. The Cumberland and the Congress lay off Newport News, about three hundred yards from the shore; the Congress about two hundred yards south of the Cumberland; whilst the remainder of the fleet were anchored off Fortress Monroe, about nine miles east of Newport News. With the force of twenty guns, Capt. Buchanan proposed to engage this formidable fleet, besides the enemy's batteries at Newport News, and several small steamers, armed with heavy rifled guns. Everything had to be trusted to the experiment of the Virginia. It was an enterprise sufficient to try the nerves of any commander to make the first trial of the offensive and defensive powers of a single vessel in the presence of an enemy with such an armament, when the slightest flaw would have proved fatal.

About eleven o'clock in the morning of the 8th of March the Virginia cast loose from her moorings at the Gosport navy yard, and made her way down Hampton Roads. On her approach being signalled, orders were immediately issued by Capt. Marston of the Roanoke for his own vessel, the Minnesota, and the St. Lawrence to get under weigh. The Cumberland and Congress had previously perceived "the great Secesh curiosity," and had beat to quarters, and prepared for action. The Virginia came slowly on, not making more than five knots per hour, and accompanied by the Raleigh and Beaufort. The pivot guns of the Cumberland opened on her at about a mile's distance.   There was no reply ; the vessel moved tran quilly on; hundreds of spectators at the wharves on both sides of the river watching her progress, and the crews of the enemy's frigates awaiting with derisive curiosity the singular iron roof bearing down upon them.   As she passed the Congress at three hundred yards she received a harmless broad-side.   " The balls bounced upon her mailed sides like india rubber."   Re-turning the broadside, and in the midst of a heavy fire from the shore batteries, the Virginia made straight for the Cumberland, which had been swung across the channel, to bring her full broadside to bear upon the ap-proaching enemy.   It was a crisis wrapped in fire and smoke.   Broadside after broadside of the Cumberland blazed out of her eleven nine-inch Dahlgrens.   The Virginia kept straight on, without returning a shot or showing a single man.   Minutes seemed hours.   Then there was a dull, heavy blow, and the iron-armed prow of the Virginia had struck the Cum-berland near the bow, and below the water line.   The frigate was driven back upon her anchors with great force ; a ragged hole had been opened into her in which a man might have passed ; the sound of the rush of water into her told that she was doomed.   Still her crew manned her guns, and were prepared to give an example of courage among the most memorable and brilliant of naval warfare.   The Virginia had backed, and was now sweeping the decks of the Cumberland with broadside after broadside in merciless succession.   But there was no sign of surrender on the part of the gallant enemy.   As the ship canted over, just ready to sink, she still kept up her useless fire.   Her last gun was fired just above the water, and as the brave gunner attempted to scramble out from the open port-hole, the water rushing swept him back, and he went down in the sinking vessel.   The Cumberland went down in fifty-four foot water, her pennant still flying from the mast-head above the waves that had engulphed her.   Some of the crew succeeded in swimming to land, others were saved by small boats from the shore ; but more than one hundred men went down into the watery grave that closed over the gallant ship.

Having sunk her first antagonist, the Virginia next turned her atten-tion to the Congress, which was left to fight the battle alone, as neither the Minnesota, which had grounded about one mile and a half from New-port News, the Roanoke, nor the St. Lawrence could approach near enough, from want of sufficient depth of water, to render material assis-tance.   Having witnessed the fate of the Cumberland, the commander of the Congress had hoisted sail, and with the help of a tug-boat had run the frigate ashore in water too shoal to permit the Virginia to run her down.   But the iron-clad, taking a position about two hundred yards from her, raked her fore and aft with shell, while the other small vessels of the Confederate squadron joined in the fire.   Every shell burst inside the frigate.   The effect was awful.   Blood and brains spurted in the air, and human bodies were cut in twain, or mangled in the most horrible manner. Arms, legs and heads were scattered in every direction, while here and there in the agonies of death might be found poor wretches, with their breasts torn completely out.

The Congress was fast aground, and could only bring two of her guns to bear on the Virginia. In a few moments her colours were hauled down, and a white flag hoisted at the gaff and half-mast, and another at the main. The little gunboat Beaufort was run alongside, with instructions from Capt. Buchanan to take possession of the Congress, secure the officers as prisoners, allow the crew to land, and burn the ship. The Congress was within rifle-shot from the shore, and as the Beaufort came alongside the prize, the enemy on the shore, having brought a Parrott gun down to the beach, opened upon the Confederate vessel a perfidious fire. The frigate had two white flags flying at the time. Lieut. Minor was severely wounded, and several of the crew of the Beaufort. But there were other additions to this treachery, for when the Beaufort had first come alongside of the Congress, Lieut. Parker, commanding the gunboat, had received the flag of the ship, and her surrender from Lieut. Prendergast, with the side-arms of the other officers. After having delivered themselves as prisoners of war on board the Beaufort, the officers were allowed, at their own request, to return to the Congress to assist in removing the wounded. They never returned, though they had pledged their honour to do so, and in witness of that pledge had left their swords with Lieut. Alexander, on board the Beaufort.

In the fire from the shore, Capt. Buchanan had received a severe wound in the thigh. He ordered the Congress to be destroyed by hot-shot and incendiary shell, her officers and crew having treacherously escaped to the shore; and finding himself disabled by his wound, transferred the command of the Virginia to Lieut. Catesby Jones, with orders to fight her as long as the men could stand to their guns. But there were now only two hours of daylight left. The Virginia bore down upon the stranded Minnesota. The Roanoke, after grounding, had gone down the Roads. The St. Lawrence, in tow of a steamer, had approached the Minnesota. She too grounded, and after receiving a single shell, and returning a harmless broadside, was dragged off, and steered down towards Fortress Monroe. The shoalness of the channel prevented the near approach of the Virginia to her third antagonist; but she continued to fire upon the Minnesota, until the pilots declared that it was no longer safe to remain in that position.

At 7 P. M., the Virginia hauled off, and returned to Norfolk, reserving for another day the completion of her work. She had already in a single half-day achieved one of the most remarkable triumphs ever made on the water. She had destroyed two powerful vessels, carrying three times her number of men, and full six times her weight of armament; she had engaged two other great vessels; and she had only been prevented from destroying them, because she could not come to close quarters with them. The Cumberland went into action with 376 men. When the survivors were mustered there were only 255. She lost 121 in killed and drowned. The crew of the Congress were 434 officers and men; of these, 298 got to shore, 26 of them being wounded, 10 mortally; there were in all 120 killed and missing; about 20 of these were made prisoners, leaving a roll of killed and drowned of 100 men. Besides these, 3 were killed on the Minnesota, and 16 wounded; an absolute loss of fully 250 officers and men. On the Virginia there were but two killed and eight wounded. On the other Confederate vessels four were killed and a few more wounded.

Early in the bright morning of Sunday, the 9th of March, the Virginia rounded the point of land at the mouth of the Elizabeth river. She approached the Minnesota. But lying near the vessel which was still stranded and supposed to be doomed, was a curious object, which some of the crew of the Virginia straining their eyes compared to a prodigious " cheese-box on a plank." It was *another iron-clad*—the enemy's experiment in naval architecture, which had come just in time to match the Confederate curiosity in floating batteries.

The new actor on the scene which had come in such a dramatic coincidence was a defensive structure, the invention of John Ericsson. He had named the invention the Monitor, in order to " admonish the South of the fate of the rebellion, Great Britain of her fading naval supremacy, and the English government of the folly of spending millions in fixed fortifications for defence." She was different in appearance from any vessel that had previously been used in war. Her deck, unprotected by any bulwark, rose about two feet above the water, whilst from it projected a turret about nine feet high, and a small box-looking place at the stern, used as a pilot-house. In the turret she carried her sole armament—two eleven-inch 168-pounder Dahlgren guns.

The two strange combatants approached each other; when within about one hundred yards' distance the Monitor opened fire. The contest continued for the space of two hours, the distance between the two vessels varying from half a mile to close quarters, in which they were almost side to side, belching out their fire, the heavy thugs on the iron sides of each being the only effect of the terrific cannonade. The strange-looking battery, with its black, revolving cupola, was more easily turned than the Virginia, and had the greater speed. The great length and draft of the Virginia rendered it exceedingly difficult to work her. Once in changing her position she got aground, but succeeded in getting afloat again, and turning rapidly upon the Monitor steamed directly at her, hoping with her terrible armed prow to end the contest. But the blow was not fairly given, and merely scraped the iron plates of her antagonist.

About noon the Monitor, probably rather in consequence of an injury that had almost blinded the sight of her commander than of any serious damage to the vessel, ran into shoal water and declined the further prosecution of the contest. The captain of the Minnesota then supposed that his hour was come, and prepared to destroy rather than surrender his vessel. But it had been found impossible by the Virginia to get nearer the Minnesota than she had the day before, and supposing that her guns had already disabled the frigate, she retired slowly from the scene of contest and returned to Norfolk.

The results of this day were indecisive, although there can be no doubt of the retreat of the Monitor; but each vessel had given proofs of invulnerability, which left their claims to advantage in the contest undecided. The injuries of the Virginia in the two days' fight were immaterial. Two of her guns had the muzzles shot off, the anchor and the flagstaffs were shot away, the smoke-jack and steam-pipes were riddled, the prow was twisted, and the armour somewhat damaged; but, with the exception of the injury done to her ram, she had suffered none other but what might be repaired in a few hours.

With reference to this wonderful contest in Hampton Roads the newspapers announced the conclusion that wooden ships were to be of no farther use in naval warfare, and that the great navies which France and Great Britain had built at such an immense cost were practically annihilated. Whatever haste there might be in this conclusion, the Government at Washington showed its early appreciation of the lesson in Hampton Roads. Almost immediately on the result of the action becoming known, a bill was introduced into the Senate to authorize the Secretary of the Navy to construct various iron vessels, both for coast and harbour defences, and also for offensive operations against the enemy's forts. The two combatants—the Virginia and the Monitor—which had given a sensation to the whole world, and turned the attention of every European government that had a strip of sea-coast to defend to the experiment of iron-clads, were never again engaged in contest. The first continued by her presence at Norfolk to guard the entry into James River, and was thought of such importance with respect to the Peninsular approach to Richmond that Gen. McClellan, who, as we shall see some months later, turned his design on Richmond in this direction, named as one of the preliminary conditions of the new campaign that this vessel should be "neutralized." She was to be "neutralized" in a way little expected by the Confederate public.

We may find in the close of this chapter an apppropriate place for a summary account of some other naval events belonging to this period of time in our narrative.

CAPTURE OF NEWBERN, &C.

The objects of Gen. Burnside's expedition were not accomplished with the capture of Roanoke Island. These objects, as stated in a memorandum furnished by Gen. McClellan, who directed the expedition as part of a general campaign for 1862, were an assault on Newbern, and, if possible, the destruction of the southern line of railroad through Goldsboro', and the Wilmington and Weldon railroad. The town of Beaufort, defended by Fort Macon, was next to be attacked, and the port opened, whilst operations against Wilmington were pointed to as the eventual objects of the expedition. On March 12th, the expedition started from Hatteras Inlet for its new object of attack. The troops were disembarked the next day eighteen miles below Newbern, and at daylight of the 14th advanced upon the Confederate works four miles below the town. These consisted of a line of detached forts of low relief. The entire Confederate force, under command of Gen. Branch, did not exceed five thousand men—a great part of them militia—and had to contend against an enemy outnumbering them at least three to one.

Fort Thompson was the most formidable fortification on the river, and mounted thirteen heavy guns. An attempt was made to storm the work, which was repulsed, and four Massachusetts companies which entered the fort from the railway track were driven out over the parapet. Another attempt was made, with increased numbers; and perceiving the enemy's gunboats moving up the river, and fearing that he would be surrounded, Gen. Branch ordered a retreat. It was commenced in good order, but finally became a rout. The guns of Fort Ellis were thrown down the embankment, Fort Lane was blown up, and the Confederates fled across the railway bridge over the Neuse. The bridge was fired by a raft laden with cotton and spirits of turpentine before the retreating column had passed over, and about five hundred prisoners were taken by the enemy. These, about fifty pieces of cannon, two small steamers, and large quantities of arms and ammunition, were the immediate fruits of the enemy's victory, at a cost estimated in Burnside's report as 91 killed and 466 wounded. The Confederate loss in killed and wounded was about one hundred and fifty.

Shortly after the enemy's occupation of Newbern, the town of Washington, situated at the mouth of Tar River, fell into their hands; the batteries for its defence having been dismantled, and the entrenchments abandoned by the small Confederate force that had been stationed there.

On the 25th of April, Fort Macon, which commanded the entrance of Beaufort harbour, was bombarded by three of the enemy's steamers, and three siege batteries on the shore. There were not more than five Confederate companies in the fort, and after sustaining a fire of ten hours they surrendered.

The reduction of this fort gave the Federal navy a port of entry, and a harbour fitted for vessels of heavy draught. So far the Burnside expedition had been a train of success. The Confederate position at Norfolk had been flanked; complete possession had been gained of Albemarle and Pamlico Sound; and now, by the fall of Fort Macon, the enemy had the entire coast of North Carolina. These blows on our coast disheartened the Confederacy, but, after all, they were of but little real value, and of scarcely any appreciable weight in the war. Burnside did not dare to pursue his enterprise into the interiour, and to follow out the programme of moving on the Weldon railroad. The vital points of the Confederacy were far in the interiour, and as we had but few war vessels our ports and harbours were of but little importance to us for naval purposes, and were really but picket posts in our system of defence.

CHAPTER XIV.

SINCE falling back to Murfreesboro', Gen. Johnston had managed, by combining Crittenden's division and the fugitives from Donelson, to collect an army of seventeen thousand men. His object was now to co-operate with Gen. Beauregard for the defence of the Valley of the Mississippi, on a line of operations south of Nashville. The line extending from Columbus, by way of Forts Henry and Donelson, had been lost. The disaster had involved the surrender of Kentucky, and a large portion of Tennessee to the enemy; and it had become necessary to re-organize a new line of defence south of Nashville, the object of which would be to protect the railroad system of the Southwest, and to ensure the defence of Memphis and the Mississippi.

CAPTURE OF ISLAND NO. 10 BY THE ENEMY.

Another concern was to put the Mississippi River in a state of complete defence; and on abandoning Columbus, it was decided to take a strong position about forty-five miles below it at Island No. 10. Gen. Polk, with the greater part of the garrison, retired towards Jackson, Tennessee, and Gen. McCown, with the remainder, was ordered to occupy and hold Island 10 and Madrid Bend.

When Gen. McCown arrived at the Island, he found it nearly destitute of defences. He reached there about the 24th of February, with Col. Kennedy's 21st Louisiana Regiment. At that time there were no batteries on the Island, and only two, partially armed and in bad working order, on the Tennessee shore. Col. Kennedy was ordered to commence fortifying the position immediately. The only fortification at New Madrid, was Fort Thompson, a small earth-work under the command of Col. E. W. Gantt. Gen. McCown immediately laid off, and ordered the construction of Fort Bankhead, at the mouth of Bayou St. John, which makes into the Mississippi just above New Madrid. Between the 25th of February and the 1st of March he was followed by a detachment of the forces from Columbus. The whole force at the two points—Island 10 and New Madrid—consisted of about fourteen regiments, some of them greatly reduced. This force was about equally divided between the two points.

On the first of March the enemy's cavalry appeared before New Madrid, and it was definitely ascertained that Gen. Pope was moving on that place, with a large force. He was not long in making his appearance. The Mississippi River was open to the gunboats of the enemy, down to Island 10, and the Confederate works there, for want of time, had not been completed. To hold both places, the Confederates had not more than five thousand effective men, and five or six wooden gunboats, under Commodore Hollins.

Despite the unfavourable prospect, Gen. McCown commenced an energetic course of operations. At New Madrid, Fort Bankhead was finished and strengthened, as was Fort Thompson by an abattis in front. Batteries and magazines were put in course of erection, and guns mounted daily at the Island. Such arrangements for securing stores and taking care of the sick, as the circumstances permitted, were promptly made.

Heavy skirmishing commenced at New Madrid about the first of March, and continued daily up to the 13th. The enemy had brought across with him a large train of artillery, including a number of 32-pounders, with which he made frequent attacks on the forts. These attacks were handsomely met; our gunboats participating in the conflict. The enemy established himself on the river below New Madrid, at Point Pleasant and other places, for the purpose of annoying our transports, and cutting off communication between New Madrid and Memphis.

During these thirteen days Gen. McCown was most active in his movements—passing from one point to the other, as he deemed his presence necessary—superintending the erection of batteries at the Island, and directing operations at New Madrid. Up to the 12th of March, the lines of the enemy had been gradually approaching our works at the latter place. The skirmishing and artillery conflicts had been continual and severe.

At midnight on the 12th, the enemy opened a fierce bombardment. The scene was terribly grand. A large number of the enemy's batteries were in full play, and were fiercely replied to, by all the guns from our forts and boats. The darkness, the hoarse voice of the wind, the rush of the waters, the roar and flash of the guns from the shore and from the river, made a scene exceeding all description. This bombardment continued but a short time, and soon the echoes of the last gun had died upon the waves; and the winds, and the sullen tones of the Mississippi were the only sounds that disturbed the silence of the night.

About daylight on the morning of the 13th the enemy again opened with their 24-pounders and an 8-inch howitzer. The principal point of attack was Fort Thompson, under the command of acting Brig.-Gen. E. W. Gantt, of Arkansas. This officer conducted the defence with skill and spirit, replying to the enemy so effectually as to dismount several of his guns.

The firing continued at intervals during the afternoon, but entirely ceased about sunset. The result of these bombardments determined Gen. McCown upon the evacuation of New Madrid. Our wooden gunboats had suffered severely under the enemy's fire; the garrison of New Madrid was small; and Pope's batteries were in a position which prevented reinforcements from being brought up the river.

On the night of the 13th March there was a heavy storm of rain and thunder, and under cover of the darkness the Confederate garrison evacuated New Madrid, and sought shelter either with that of Island 10, or in the works on the left bank. Thus Pope obtained possession of New Madrid, was able to isolate Island 10 from the Lower Mississippi, and eagerly expected the surrender of the other defences.

The evacuation was accomplished without any very serious loss. In the midst of a furious rain, and in the face of a powerful army of the enemy, it was hardly possible to have everything brought off. Gen. Gantt laboured assiduously to save whatever he could, at Fort Thompson, and was himself among the last who embarked. Our greatest loss was in heavy guns. These it was found impossible to get away; but they were spiked, and otherwise disabled. Some three or four transports were ordered to each fort, to take off the troops and munitions. Gen. Walker's brigade, from Fort Bankhead, was landed at the foot of the highlands about four miles below the Island; Gen. Gantt's from Fort Thompson, at Tiptonville.

But although the Confederates had surrendered New Madrid so easily, they had no idea of giving up Island 10. We have already stated that when Gen. McCown reached the Island the position was nearly destitute of defences. Now there were five fine batteries erected on the Island, and well armed, and an equal number on the Tennessee shore—mounting in all nearly sixty guns. Magazines had been provided, the ammunition assorted and arranged, and everything put in readiness for action.

From the Island to New Madrid by the river, it is about twelve miles —from New Madrid to Tiptonville about sixteen, and from Tiptonville across to the Island by land, about four miles. There was a river shore of twenty-seven miles, between the last two places, though they were in fact but a short distance apart. This shore had to be closely watched, for the enemy held possession of the Missouri side, from New Madrid to a point below Tiptonville. The brigades of Gantt and Walker were placed along the river, to guard it, with instructions to concentrate and drive the enemy back, if he should anywhere attempt a crossing.

On the morning of the 17th the enemy's fleet commenced shelling the Island at long range, to which the Confederates paid but little attention. About ten o'clock, however, they came within range, and opened on Rucker's battery. This battery was on the Tennessee shore, about a mile above the Island. It was located before Gen. McCown took command at the Bend, on rather low ground, but at an excellent point for commanding the river. The Mississippi was very high, and this battery was separated from the others by a wide slough. The platform was covered with water, and the magazine unsafe from dampness. The attack was made by five iron-clad gunboats (three of them lashed together about the centre of the stream, and one lying near either shore) together with the whole mortar fleet. The conflict was terrific. For nine long hours, shot and shell fell in, over and around the battery, in horrible profusion—tearing up its parapet, and sending death through the company engaged in its defence. The men worked their pieces standing half-leg deep in mud and water. The company was small and the labour great. In the afternoon, Capt. Rucker, finding his men exhausted by fatigue, asked for reinforcements, which were sent to him. For this purpose no detail was made, as a sufficient number of volunteers were found to supply his wants, and marched into the very jaws of death to the relief of their exhausted comrades. In the mean time, from fort and river, the conflict was still kept up with unabated fury. It seemed more than could be hoped from mortal courage and endurance, that the battery should be worked against such terrible odds. But it was, and at last, about night-fall, the enemy was compelled to withdraw, with some of his boats for the time disabled. Rucker had the last shot at him, as he retired up the river. The battery mounted five guns. Only two of them were in a condition to be worked, at the close of the fight.

Gen. McCown, under orders from Gen. Beauregard, left the Bend for Fort Pillow, on the night of the 17th of March, with six regiments of infantry, Bankhead's light battery, and a part of Stuart's, embarking at Tiptonville, and reaching the former place on the morning of the 18th. This movement was accomplished with such secrecy, that few, even of the officers remaining at the Bend, were aware of it until it was accomplished.

On the afternoon of the 19th, Gen. McCown was ordered to send from Fort Pillow three regiments, to report to Gen. Bragg, leave the remainder at that post, and return himself and re-assume command at Island 10, which he immediately did. Upon returning to the Island, he found the enemy engaged in cutting a canal across the Bend, on the Missouri side, from a point three miles above the Island to Bayou St. John, for the purpose of communicating with New Madrid without having to run our batteries. From this time up to the 30th, the enemy continued to shell at long range, but without effect. Gen. McCown, in the mean time, made a full reconnoissance of the Bend. In his despatches he expressed confidence in his ability to repel the enemy's boats, if they should attack his batteries, but strongly intimated his doubts as to his being able to stop them if they attempted to run by. He was also busily engaged in building flatboats and collecting canoes on Reetford Lake, ostensibly with the view of bringing over reinforcements, but actually for the purpose of securing his retreat, should the enemy force a crossing in numbers sufficient to overwhelm his command, now reduced to less than two thousand effective men.

On the 1st of April, Gen. McCown was relieved, and Gen. Mackall assigned to the defence of the Island. In the mean time the enemy had busily progressed in his herculean enterprise of digging a canal twelve miles long, across the peninsula formed by the winding of the river. This work was fatal to the defence of the Island, for it enabled the enemy to take it in its rear. On the night of the 6th of April, Gen. Mackall moved the infantry and a battery to the Tennessee shore, to protect the landing from anticipated attacks. The artillerists remained on the Island. The enemy's gunboats had succeeded in passing the Island in a heavy fog; he had effected a landing above and below the Island in large force; and the surrender of the position had become a military necessity.

But never was an evacuation so wretchedly managed. None of the means of retreat prepared by Gen. McCown were used; everything was abandoned; six hundred men were left to their fate on the Island; and the force transferred to the mainland was surrendered, except the few stragglers who escaped through the cane-brakes.

The enemy captured Mackall himself, two brigadier-generals, six colonels, several thousand stand of arms, two thousand rank and file, seventy pieces of siege artillery, thirty pieces of field artillery, fifty-six thousand solid shot, six steam transports, two gunboats, and one floating battery carrying sixteen heavy guns. The Southern people had expected a critical engagement at Island No. 10, but its capture was neatly accomplished without it; and, in the loss of men, cannon, ammunition, and supplies, the event was doubly deplorable to them, and afforded to the North such visible fruits of victory as had seldom been the result of a single enterprise. The credit of the success was claimed for the naval force under the command of Commodore Foote. The Federal Secretary of the Navy had reason to declare that "the triumph was not the less appreciated because it was protracted, and finally bloodless." The Confederates had been compelled to abandon what had been fondly entitled "the Little Gibraltar" of the Mississippi, and had experienced a loss in heavy artillery which was nigh irreparable.

Meanwhile, Gen. Beauregard was preparing to strike a decisive blow on the mainland, and the movements of the enemy on the Tennessee River were preparing the situation for one of the grandest battles that had yet been fought in any quarter of the war.

THE BATTLE OF SHILOH.

In the early part of March, Gen. Beauregard, convinced of the enemy's design to cut off his communications in West Tennessee with the eastern and southern States, by operating from the Tennessee River, determined to concentrate all his available forces at and around Corinth. By the first of April, Gen. Johnston's entire force, which had taken up the line of march from Murfreesboro', had effected a junction with Beauregard, and the united forces, which had also been increased by several regiments from Louisiana, two divisions of Gen. Polk's command from Columbus, and a fine corps of troops from Mobile and Pensacola, were concentrated along the Mobile and Ohio railroad, from Bethel to Corinth, and on the Memphis and Charleston railroad from Corinth to Iuka. The effective total of this force was slightly over forty thousand men.*

It was determined with this force, which justified the offensive, to strike a sudden blow at the enemy, in position under Gen. Grant, on the west bank of the Tennessee River, at Pittsburg, and in the direction of Savannah, before he was reinforced by the army under Gen. Buell, then known to be advancing for that purpose, by rapid marches from Nashville. The great object was to anticipate the junction of the enemy's armies, then near at hand; and on the night of the 2d of April, it was decided that the attack should be attempted at once, incomplete and imperfect as were the preparations of the Confederates for such a grave and momentous adventure. The army had been brought suddenly together, and there had been many difficulties in the way of an effective organization.

The enemy was in position about a mile in advance of Shiloh church— a rude, log chapel, from which the battle that was to ensue took its name —with the right resting on Owl Creek and his left on Lick Creek. The army collected here was composed of the flower of the Federal troops, being principally Western men, from the States of Illinois, Indiana, Wisconsin, and Iowa.

It was expected by Gen. Beauregard that he would be able to reach the enemy's lines in time to attack him on the 5th of April. The men, however, for the most part, were unused to marching, the roads narrow, and traversing a densely-wooded country, which became almost impassable after a severe rain-storm on the 4th, which drenched the troops in bivouac; hence the Confederate forces did not reach the intersection of the road from Pittsburg and Hamburg, in the immediate vicinity of the enemy, until late in the evening of the 5th; and it was then decided that the attack should be made on the next morning, at the earliest hour practicable.

The Confederate plan of battle was in three lines—the first and second extending from Owl Creek on the left to Lick Creek on the right, a distance of about three miles, supported by the third and the reserve. The first line, under Major-Gen. Hardee, was constituted of his corps, augmented on his right by Gladden's brigade, of Major-Gen. Bragg's corps. The second line, composed of the other troops of Bragg's corps, followed

---

* It was composed as follows:

First Army Corps, Major-Gen. L. Polk,	9,136
Second Army Corps, Gen. B. Bragg,	13,589
Third Army Corps, Major-Gen. W. J. Hardee,	6,789
Reserve, Brig.-Gen. John C. Breckinridge,	6,439
Total infantry and artillery,	35,953
Cavalry, Brig.-Gen. F. Gardner,	4,382
Grand Total,	40,335

the first at the distance of five hundred yards, in the same order as the first. The army corps under Gen. Polk followed the second line at the distance of about eight hundred yards, in lines of brigades, deployed with their batteries in rear of each brigade, moving by the Pittsburg road, the left wing supported by cavalry. The reserve, under Brig.-Gen. Breckinridge, following closely on the third line, in the same order, its right wing supported by cavalry.

In the early dawn of Sunday, the 6th of April, the magnificent array was moving forward for deadly conflict, passing easily through the thin ranks of the tall forest trees, which afforded open views on every side. But the enemy scarcely gave time to discuss the question of attack, for soon after dawn he commenced a rapid musketry fire on the Confederate pickets. The order was immediately given by the commanding General, and the Confederate lines advanced. Such was the ardour of the second line of troops, that it was with great difficulty they could be restrained from closing up and mingling with the first line. Within less than a mile, the enemy was encountered in force at the encampments of his advanced positions, but the first line of Confederates brushed him away, leaving the rear nothing to do but to press on in pursuit. In about one mile more, he was encountered in strong force along almost the entire line. His batteries were posted on eminences, with strong infantry supports. Finding the first line was now unequal to the work before it, being weakened by extension, and necessarily broken by the nature of the ground, Gen. Bragg ordered his whole force to move up steadily and promptly to its support.

From this time the battle raged with but little intermission. By half-past ten o'clock the Confederates had already captured three large encampments, and three batteries of artillery. Their right flank, according to the order of battle, had pressed forward ardently, under the immediate direction of Gen. Johnston, and swept all before it. Batteries, encampments, storehouses, munitions in rich profusion, were captured; and the enemy was falling back rapidly at every point. His left, however, was his strongest ground and position, and was disputed with obstinacy.

Mile after mile the Confederates rushed on, sweeping the camps of the enemy before them. Gen. Johnston was in advance, before the troops of Breckinridge and Bowen. He had addressed them in a few brief words, and given the order to "Charge!" when, at two o'clock, a minie-ball pierced the calf of his right leg. He supposed it to be a flesh wound, and paid no attention to it; but the fact was that the ball had cut an artery, and as the doomed commander rode onward to victory, he was bleeding to death. Becoming faint from loss of blood, he turned to Gov. Harris, one of his volunteer aides, and remarked, "I fear I am mortally wounded." The next moment he reeled in his saddle and fainted. Gov. Harris received the falling commander in his arms, and bore him a short

distance from the field, into a ravine. Stimulants were speedily administered, but in vain. One of his staff, in a passion of grief, threw his arms
around the beloved commander, and called aloud, to see if he would
respond. But no sign or reply came, and in a moment or two more, he
breathed his last.

Information of the fall of Gen. Johnston was not communicated to the
army. It was still pressing on in its career of victory ; and but little
doubt remained of the fortunes of the day. As the descending sun warned
the Confederates to press their advantage, the command ran along the line,
" Forward ! let every order be forward ! " Fairly in motion, they now
swept all before them. Neither battery nor battalion could withstand
their onslaught. Passing through camp after camp, rich in military spoils
of every kind, the enemy was driven headlong from every position, and
thrown in confused masses upon the river bank, behind his heavy artillery,
and under cover of his gunboats at the landing. He was crowded in
unorganized masses on the river bank, vainly striving to cross.

And now it might be supposed that a victory was to be accomplished
such as had not before illustrated the fortunes of the Confederacy. The
reserve line of the Federals was entirely gone. Their whole army was
crowded into a circuit of half to two-thirds of a mile around the landing.
They had been falling back all day. The next repulse would have put
them into the river, and there were not transports enough to cross a single
division before the Confederates would be upon them.

It is true that the broken fragments of Grant's army were covered by a
battery of heavy guns well served, and two gunboats, which poured a
heavy fire upon the supposed position of the Confederates, for they were
entirely hid by the forest. But this fire, though terrific in sound, and producing some consternation at first, did no damage, as the shells all passed
over, and exploded far beyond the Confederate position.

At last, the order was given to move forward at all points, and sweep
the enemy from the field. The sun was about disappearing, so that little
time was left to finish the glorious work of the day. The movement commenced with every prospect of success. But just at this time the astounding order was received from Gen. Beauregard to withdraw the forces
beyond the enemy's fire ! The action ceased.* The different commands,
mixed and scattered, bivouacked at points most convenient to their posi-

---

* Of this abrupt termination to the business of the day, and the condition of the enemy at the
time, a Confederate officer writes :

" From some cause I could never ascertain, a halt was sounded, and when the remnants of the
enemy's divisions had *stacked arms on the river's edge, preparatory to their surrender*, no one
stirred to finish the business by a *coup de main*. It was evidently ' drown or surrender ' with
them, and they had prepared for the latter, until, seeing our inactivity, their gunboats opened furiously, and, save a short cannonade, all subsided into quietness along our lines."

tions, and beyond the range of the enemy's guns. All firing, except a half-hour shot from the gunboats, ceased, and the night was passed in quiet.

Of this extraordinary abandonment of a great victory—for it can scarcely be put in milder phrase—Gen. Beauregard gives, in his official report of the action, only this explanation : " Darkness was close at hand ; officers and men were exhausted by a combat of over twelve hours without food, and jaded by the march of the preceding day through mud and water." But the true explanation is, that Gen. Beauregard was persuaded that delays had been encountered by Gen. Buell in his march from Columbia, and that his main force, therefore, could not reach the field of battle in time to save Gen. Grant's shattered fugitive forces from capture or destruction on the following day.

But in this calculation he made the great errour of his military life. When pursuit was called off, Buell's advance was already on the other side of the Tennessee. A body of cavalry was on its banks ; it was the advance of the long-expected Federal reinforcements ; an army of twenty-five thousand men was rapidly advancing to the opposite banks of the river to restore Grant's fortune, and to make him, next day, master of the situation. Alas ! the story of Shiloh was to be that not only of another lost opportunity for the South, but one of a reversion of fortune, in which a splendid victory changed into something very like a defeat !

As night fell, a new misfortune was to overtake Gen. Beauregard. His forces exhibited a want of discipline and a disorder which he seems to have been unable to control ; and with the exception of a few thousand disciplined troops held firmly in hand by Gen. Bragg, the whole army degenerated into bands of roving plunderers, intoxicated with victory, and scattered in a shameful hunt for the rich spoils of the battle-field. All during the night thousands were out in quest of plunder ; hundreds were intoxicated with wines and liquors found ; and while scenes of disorder and shouts of revelry arose around the large fires which had been kindled, and mingled with the groans of the wounded, Buell's forces were steadily crossing the river, and forming line of battle for the morrow.

About an hour after sunrise the action again commenced, and soon the battle raged with fury. The shattered regiments and brigades collected by Grant gave ground before our men, and for a moment it was thought that victory would crown our efforts a second time. On the left, however, and nearest to the point of arrival of his reinforcements, the enemy drove forward line after line of his fresh troops. In some places the Confederates repulsed them by unexampled feats of valor ; but sheer exhaustion was hourly telling upon the men, and it soon became evident that numbers and strength would ultimately prevail. By noon Gen. Beauregard had necessarily disposed of the last of his reserves, and shortly thereafter he determined to withdraw from the unequal conflict, securing such of the results of the victory of the day before as was then practicable.

As evidence of the condition of Beauregard's army, he had not been able to bring into the action of the second day more than twenty thousand men. In the first day's battle the Confederates engaged the divisions of Gen. Prentiss, Sherman, Hurlburt, McClernand and Smith, of 9,000 men each, or at least 45,000 men. This force was reinforced during the night by the divisions of Gens. Nelson, McCook, Crittenden, and Thomas, of Buell's army, some 25,000 strong, including all arms; also Gen. L. Wallace's division of Gen. Grant's army, making at least 33,000 fresh troops, which, added to the remnant of Gen. Grant's forces, amounting to 20,000, made an aggregate force of at least 53,000 men arrayed against the Confederates on the second day.

Against such an overwhelming force it was vain to contend. At 1 P. M. Gen. Beauregard ordered a retreat. Gen. Breckinridge was left with his command as a rear guard, to hold the ground the Confederates had occupied the night preceding the first battle, just in front of the intersection of the Pittsburg and Hamburg roads, about four miles from the former place, while the rest of the army passed in the rear, in excellent order. The fact that the enemy attempted no pursuit indicated his condition. He had been too sorely chastised to pursue; and Gen. Beauregard was left at leisure to retire to Corinth, in pursuance of his original design to make that the strategic point of his campaign.

The battle of Shiloh, properly extending through eighteen hours, was memorable for an extent of carnage up to this time unparalleled in the war. The Confederate loss, in the two days, in the killed outright, was 1,728, wounded 8,012, missing 957; making an aggregate of casualties 10,699. Of the loss of the enemy, Gen. Beauregard wrote: "Their casualties cannot have fallen many short of twenty thousand in killed, wounded, prisoners, and missing."

Gen. Beauregard was unwilling to admit that the experience of the second day had eclipsed the brilliant victory which he so unfortunately left unfinished on the banks of the Tennessee. He declared that he had left the field on the second day " only after eight hours' successive battle with a superiour army of fresh troops, whom he had repulsed in every attack upon his lines, so repulsed and crippled, indeed, as to leave it unable to take the field for the campaign for which it was collected and equipped at such enormous expense, and with such profusion of all the appliances of war." On the other hand, the North inscribed Shiloh as its most brilliant victory. An order of the War Department at Washington required that at meridian of the Sunday following the battle, at the head of every regiment in the armies of the United States there should be offered by its chaplain a prayer, giving " thanks to the Lord of Hosts for the recent manifestation of His power in the overthrow of the rebels and traitors."

But whatever may be the correct estimation of the battle of Shiloh, there was one event of it which was a most serious loss to the Confederacy, and an occasion of popular sorrow in every part of it. This was the death of Gen. Albert Sydney Johnston, the man especially trusted with the Confederate fortunes in the West, esteemed by his Government as the military genius of his country, and so gifted by nature with dignity, and with power over men, that it was said he was born to command. This illustrious commander had already figured in many historical scenes, and up to the period of his death had led one of the most eventful and romantic military lives on the continent. He had served in the Black Hawk war. In the Texan war of independence, he entered her army as a private soldier Subsequently he was made senior brigadier-general of the Texan army and was appointed to succeed Gen. Felix Houston in the chief command. This led to a duel between them, in which Johnston was wounded. In 1838, he was chosen Secretary of War of the new Republic under President Lamar; and the following year he organized an expedition against the Cherokee Indians. He subsequently settled on a plantation in Texas, and for several years remained there, leading the quiet life of a planter.

When the Mexican war broke out, he, once more, in 1846, and at the request of Gen. Taylor, resumed his profession of arms, and sought the battle-field. He arrived in Mexico shortly after the battles of Resaca and Palo-Alto, and was elected colonel of the first Texas regiment. After that regiment was discharged, he was appointed aide and inspector-general to Gen. Butler; and in that capacity he was at the famous battle of Monterey, and, during the fight, his horse was three times shot under him.

After the Mexican war, he obtained the appointment of paymaster of the regular army, with the rank of major. When the army was increased by four new regiments, Jefferson Davis, then Secretary of War, gave him command of the Second Cavalry, with his headquarters at San Antonio, Texas. In the latter part of 1857, he was appointed by President Buchanan to the command of the Utah expedition, sent to quell the Mormons. In the spring of 1858, he crossed the plains, and arrived at Salt Lake City, where, in consequence of his services, he was brevetted brigadier-general, and full commander of the military district of Utah. He was subsequently sent to California, and assumed command of the Department of the Pacific. There the commencement of the war found him; and on learning of the secession of his adopted State, Texas, he resigned his position in the United States army, and at once prepared to remove South, to espouse the cause of the Confederacy.

The Federal authorities had taken measures to arrest him, or, at least, to intercept his passage by sea. But he eluded their vigilance by taking the overland route. With three or four companions, increased afterwards to one hundred, on mules, he proceeded by way of Arizona, passed through Texas, and arrived at New Orleans in safety. This was in August, 1861, and, immediately proceeding to Richmond, he was assigned to the command of the Department of the Mississippi.

In the early part of the western campaign, Gen. Johnston had fallen under the censure of the newspapers. It has been said that this censure preyed upon his mind ; but if it did, he thought very nobly of it, for in a private letter, dated after the retreat from Bowling Green, and the fall of Fort Donelson, he wrote : " The test of merit, in my profession, with the people, is success. It is a hard rule, but I think it right." But a few days before the battle in which he fell, he expressed a resolution to redeem his losses at no distant day.

No more beautiful tribute could have been paid to the memory of the departed hero, than that made by Jefferson Davis himself ; and no more choice and touching language ever came from the polished pen of the Confederate President, than on this occasion. He announced the death in a special message to Congress. He said : " Without doing injustice to the living, it may safely be said that our loss is irreparable. Among the shining hosts of the great and good who now cluster around the banner of our country, there exists no purer spirit, no more heroic soul, than that of the illustrious man whose death I join you in lamenting. In his death he has illustrated the character for which, through life, he was conspicuous— that of singleness of purpose and devotion to duty with his whole energies. Bent on obtaining the victory which he deemed essential to his country's cause, he rode on to the accomplishment of his object, forgetful of self, while his very life-blood was fast ebbing away. His last breath cheered his comrades on to victory. The last sound he heard was their shout of victory. His last thought was his country, and long and deeply will his country mourn his loss."

The remains were carried to New Orleans. They were laid in state in the mayor's parlour, and the public admitted. The evidences of the public sorrow were most touching. Flowers, the testimonies of tender affection, encircled his coffin simply, but beautifully. And, attended by all the marks of unaffected grief, with gentle hands and weeping eyes moving softly around him, the great commander, with his sheathed sword still by his side, was borne to his final and eternal rest.

CHAPTER XV.

THE Confederate public had been disposed to find some consolation
for the disaster at Island No. 10 in the brilliant, though unfruitful story
of Shiloh. It was considered, too, that the river below Fort Pillow was
safe; and that while the army at Corinth covered Memphis, and held the
enemy in check on land, the rich and productive valley of the Lower
Mississippi was yet secure to the Confederacy.

But in the midst of these pleasing calculations and comparative re-assur-
ance, a great disaster was to occur where it was least expected, which was

THE LOST CAUSE.

to astound the people of the South, to involve the practical loss of another mass of rich territory, and to alarm the hopes of men in all parts of the world for the success of the Confederates. This unexpected event was the fall of New Orleans.

With respect to this disaster, we have to develop a long train of the secret history of the Confederate Administration—a history replete with evidences of mismanagement and shiftlessness that will be almost incredible to the world accustomed to read of the administration of governments in time of war, and to expect, at least, an average of intelligence in the conduct of public affairs.

THE FALL OF NEW ORLEANS.

New Orleans had been so long threatened with attack, that popular opinion in the Confederacy was disposed to take it as impregnable. For months the Federal fleet cruised about the Gulf with evident indecision, until people in New Orleans began to smile, and say : "They would think twice before attempting a rehearsal of the scenes of 1812." It was declared, on the authority of newspapers, that the city was inpregnable ; the forts, Jackson and St. Philip, sixty or seventy miles below the city, were considered but as the outer line of defences ; the shores of the river were lined with batteries ; and in the harbour were reported to be twelve gunboats, and certain iron-clad naval structures which, it was asserted, were superiour to the famous "Virginia," and would deal with a Federal fleet as hawks might with a flock of pigeons.

But penetrating this popular conceit and confidence, and going to official records for proofs, we shall discover that the facts were that New Orleans was in a shamefully defenceless condition ; that the Richmond authorities had persisted in the strange errour that the attack on the city was to come from above ; that they had consequently stripped it almost entirely of troops, and neglected the armament of its interiour line of defence ; and that the naval structures, which the authorities had declared would be fully able to protect the city under any circumstances, were, by the most wretched and culpable mismanagement, neglected, delayed, and finally found in a condition in which they were not of the slightest avail.

Gen. Mansfield Lovell assumed command of the defences of New Orleans late in October, 1861. The city at that time had been "drained of arms, ammunition, medical stores, clothing and supplies, which had been sent to other points," and the defences were in a thoroughly incomplete condition. The troops raised in Louisiana had been principally sent to Virginia and Pensacola, and those that remained were necessarily inadequate to the end desired, and required organization.

Several vessels were in course of construction by the Navy Department, but according to the express orders of President Davis "the fleet maintained at the port of New Orleans and vicinity formed no part of the command of Gen. Lovell." The first step taken by that officer was to secure ammunition, of which there was less than twenty pounds per gun ; the second was to complete the " raft between Forts Jackson and St. Philip, so as to make a complete obstruction under the fire of those works." On the 8th November, Gen. Lovell wrote to the Department that he had increased the armament of Forts Pike and Macomb, and thought he would be able to make a complete obstruction of the raft, so that if the enemy's ships should be stopped, they would be hammered to pieces. This obstruction was calculated to delay a " fleet under the close fire of more than one hundred heavy guns." Measures were also taken to obstruct the passage at Forts Pike and Macomb, and the river above the city, the commanding General " feeling satisfied that ships under steam can pass forts in an open channel."

On the 5th December, 1861, a statement was made to the War Department of the existing condition of affairs, in which it was shown that the city was defended by two lines of works, for which Gen. Lovell had 8,000 men, besides the militia of the city. Two powder mills were in running order, and the announcement was made that with a " sufficiency of this material, he should consider himself in a position to hold New Orleans for an indefinite length of time." The city was then strong enough to withstand any attack likely to be made, and Gen. Lovell stated that the enemy, who were at that time landing troops at Ship Island in large numbers, " could not take New Orleans by a land attack with any force they could bring to bear."

In the beginning of January the attention of the Department was directed to the necessity of giving to the commanding General the control of at least so much of the Navy Department as would enable him, by means of light-draught armed vessels, to protect the navigable streams along the coast ; Gen. Lovell adding, that " the blame of want of protection will rest upon me in any event, and I should, therefore, have some power to say what should be done." No answer to this request was made.

The Secretary of War, about this time, furnished Gen. Lovell with the plan and details of the river defence fleet, under Montgomery, for " service in the upper Mississippi," which was to be prepared at New Orleans, by Capts. Montgomery and Townsend, and the General was directed " merely to exercise such general supervision as to check any profligate expenditure."

On the 13th January, Gen. Lovell wrote, that " considering New Orleans to be in condition to resist an attack, I am turning my attention to the coast of Mississippi." The obstructions in the river at this time were complete, and the forts well manned.

On the 8th of February, the Secretary of War wrote as follows: "The President desires that, as soon as possible, on receipt of this letter, you despatch 5,000 men to Columbus to reinforce that point, sorely threatened by largely superiour forces. New Orleans is to be defended from above, by defeating the enemy at Columbus." Gen. Lovell replied: "I regret the necessity of sending away my only force at this particular juncture, and feel sure that it will create a great panic here, but will do my best to restore confidence by a show of strength."

On the 27th February, Gen. Lovell notified the Secretary of War that he had sent "eight regiments and two batteries from his department, besides five hundred shot guns," and added: "People are beginning to complain that I have stripped the department so completely; but I have called upon Gov. Moore for 10,000 volunteers and militia for State service. Raw troops with double-barrelled shot guns are amply sufficient to hold our entrenchments against such troops as the enemy can send to attack them."

In the same letter he adverted to the fact that he had "furnished Gens. Johnston and Polk large supplies." In his letter of March 6th he stated:

"This Department is being completely drained of everything. We have filled requisitions for arms, men and munitions, until *New Orleans is about defenceless*. In return we get nothing. Mobile and Pensacola, even Galveston, are defended by ten-inch columbiads, while this city has nothing above an eight-inch, and but few of them. The fortified line about the city is complete, but I have taken ten of the guns for the navy, and sixteen for the vessels that we are fitting up for the river expedition. My reliance to defend these lines will be with militia with double-barrelled guns and 32-pound carronades. If now you take the powder from me, we shall be in no condition to resist. The only thing to provide is a sufficiency of powder, to enable us to resist a prolonged attack of ships and mortar boats upon two points, Forts Pike and Macomb, and Forts Jackson and St. Philip. If the first are passed, we still have a land defence to make; if the last, a fleet can proceed at once to the city."

On the 9th, Gen. Lovell again wrote, after enumerating the troops sent away:

"You will thus perceive that this Department has been completely stripped of every organized body of troops. Persons are found here who assert that I am sending away all troops so that the city may fall an easy prey to the enemy. All requisitions for ammunition have been filled, until I have none left, except what is in the hands of troops. Neither have I funds placed at my disposal to create supplies in place of those sent off. If the enemy intends an attack here, he will make it soon, and I hope no further calls will be made until we are placed in a defensible condition."

While this correspondence was going on between Gen. Lovell and the War Department, we shall see what had become of the naval structures in the harbour, that were calculated, as the Richmond authorities claimed, to allay all the fears of Gen. Lovell, and to assure, in any circumstances, the safety of New Orleans. Mr. Benjamin, the Secretary of War, had written to Gen. Lovell: "From the recent experiment of the Virginia, and what I hear of the steamers of New Orleans, I feel confident that if even one of them can be got ready before you are attacked, she will disperse and destroy *any* fleet the enemy can gather in the river, above or below. The naval officers say that TIFT's steamer is far superiour to the Virginia."

In the report of Mr. Mallory, Secretary of the Navy, made to the Confederate Congress on the 27th of February, 1862, he had made the following statement: "There are now being constructed at New Orleans two large and formidable iron-plated steamships, of about fourteen hundred tons each, designed for the carrying of twenty of the heaviest guns. One of these, the Louisiana, has been launched, and is nearly completed, and the other, it is believed, will be completed in six weeks."

With reference to the construction of these vessels we may place here the testimony of Gov. Moore of Louisiana, taken before a secret committee of the Confederate Congress, not only for its interest to the immediate subject, but for its curious explanation of the way the affairs of the Confederacy were managed. The following are extracts from his testimony:

" My first active interposition, of which any record is kept, was on the 26th of February, 1862. Several weeks prior to that date I had been aware that the work on the ram Mississippi was not being prosecuted with the vigour and energy that our danger seemed to me to require. Many merchants and business men of New Orleans, and particularly the Committee of Public Safety, had spoken to me of the slow progress of the work, but I had refrained from any interference, except verbal expressions of my dissatisfaction to the Commanding General, (Lovell) who in turn assured me he had nothing to do with the work. At length the excuse was given for this torturing want of vigour, that the work could not proceed faster for want of funds. The Navy Department had not paid its obligations, and, in consequence, had lost credit. I therefore telegraphed the Treasury Department as follows:

"NEW ORLEANS, February 26th, 1862.

" C. G. MEMMINGER, *Secretary Treasury, Richmond:*

" The Navy Department here owes nearly a million. Its credit is stopped. If you wish, I will place two millions of dollars on account of the war tax, to the credit of the Government, so that the debts can be paid, and the works continued.

" [Signed] THOMAS O. MOORE, *Governor.*"

*   *   *   *   *   *   *

" One of the causes of the delay in completing the Mississippi was the insufficient number of hands employed. I had long been sensible of this, but there was no officer of the Government who seemed to feel authorized to interpose. I learned in April the excuse given was, that they could not be obtained, and I instantly addressed a letter to the ship-builders, of which the following is an extract. Its date is April 15th. 'The great importance of having at once completed the steam-ram Mississippi, induces me to call on you to render Mr. Tift, the builder, all the assistance that can be advantageously employed for that purpose. It may be that the ship, completed and fitted in fifteen days, as we hope will be done, may be worth to us as much, and perhaps more, than fifty thousand soldiers, as it is believed that she could clear the river of the whole United States navy.' A large addition of workmen was instantly made, the ship-builders furnishing as many men as the Tifts were willing to receive.

"Another cause of the delay was a failure of the Tifts to comprehend the fact that the city was in danger. I did not know, until after the city had fallen, that even if the wood-work had been completed, the means were not at hand to put her in fighting condition. I was subsequently informed that at the time the city fell, the plates for the ram were being manufactured in Atlanta, and her guns were scattered along the railroad from Weldon to Jackson, which latter place they did not reach until weeks afterward."

In the month of April, 1862, the condition of the defences of New Orleans was as follows: As against a land attack by any force the enemy could probably bring, the interiour line of fortifications, as adopted and completed by Major-Gen. Lovell, was a sufficient defence of the city, but his ability to hold that line against such an attack was greatly impaired by the withdrawal from him, by superiour authority, of nearly all his effective troops. The exteriour line was well devised, and rendered as strong as the means of his command allowed. But the iron-clad gunboats, Louisiana and Mississippi, were not ready for service. In this extremity it was indispensably necessary to obstruct the navigation of the Mississippi River between Forts Jackson and St. Philip; and to do this, a raft was completed under Gen. Lovell's direction. It consisted of a line of eleven dismasted schooners, extending from bank to bank, strongly moored, and connected by six heavy chains.

The Federal fleet which threatened New Orleans, consisted of forty-six sail, carrying two hundred and eighty-six guns and twenty-one mortars; the whole under the command of Flag-officer Farragut. The raft constructed by Gen. Lovell was placed about a mile below Forts Jackson and St. Philip. Unfortunately, a chasm was rent in it by a severe storm; and on the 16th of April, the enemy slowly steamed up the stream in strong force, and prepared to attack the forts.

Still there was no alarm in New Orleans, as it was popularly supposed that the enemy only intended a bombardment of the forts, and would accomplish but little in such an enterprise. Festivity prevailed in the city. Balls, parties, theatres, operas, and the like were the incidents of every twenty-four hours. Thousands flocked down the river, and on the levees viewed the bombardment with evident pleasure, for it was soon ascertained that the enemy's fire was inaccurate, and that few, if any, of their eleven-inch shell ever touched the forts. At night, the greatest vigilance was maintained, to inform commanders of the enemy's movements. On the 23d of April, the terrific bombardment had continued a whole week; the enemy had thrown over twenty-five thousand shells; and Gen. Duncan reported that two of his guns in Fort Jackson were dismounted; half a dozen killed and wounded was the total loss, and the works were as sound as ever.

The evening of the 23d of April closed without unusual incident. Our defences were thought to be impassable, and strong hopes were entertained that Farragut would soon give up the conflict as fruitless and abortive. Towards three o'clock on the morning of the 24th, the enemy's vessels were descried creeping up the river in full force, and as they steamed abreast of the forts were received with deafening roars from our artillery. The conflict became furious. Through a storm of fire the ships passed on, Farragut leading in the Hartford. They had not proceeded far when they encountered the Confederate fleet, consisting of seventeen vessels in all, only about eight of which were armed. The Confederate gunboats carried, some of them, two guns, and others only one. Nevertheless, they fought with desperation against the enemy's overwhelming force, until they were all driven on shore and scuttled or burned by their commanders. The Louisiana was unmanageable, and could only use two of her nine guns; so when it was perceived that nothing could prevent the enemy from breaking our line, she was run ashore, and blown up, although the enemy's broadsides had not injured her in the least. The Governor Moore, another of our boats, commanded by the brave Capt. Kennon, acted nobly among the enemy's twelve heavy sloops-of-war and gunboats, and fired its last cartridge at point-blank range, but was also run ashore and blown up, to prevent capture.

The scene of confusion that ensued in New Orleans, when the people, on the morning of the 24th of April, awoke to the news that the enemy's fleet had passed the forts, and were actually approaching the city, defies all description. People were amazed, and could scarcely realize the awful fact, and ran hither and thither in speechless astonishment. Very soon the flames seen issuing from shipyards in Algiers and other places, convinced them that the news was authentic, and that Government officers were then busily engaged destroying everything that was likely to be of value to the enemy. The unfinished Mississippi and other vessels were scuttled or fired, ammunition destroyed, and shot sunk in the river. The people, on their part, proceeded to the various cotton-presses, rolled out thousands of bales, and applied the torch; countless cotton ships were also sunk or fired, and steamboats by the dozen similarly destroyed. The roar of cannon sounded in the distance; the heat of the sun, and conflagrations in every direction, made the atmosphere oppressively hot, while dense columns of smoke darkened the air. It was a scene of terrible grandeur. The baleful glare of the conflagration struggled in rivalry with the sunlight; masses of smoke ascended grandly to the sky; great ships and steamers, wrapped in fire, floated down the river, threatening the Federal vessels with destruction by their fiery contact. And in this scene of dire and sublime destruction, there were perpetually tolled the alarm-bells of the city.

Having narrowly escaped capture in the naval engagement, Gen. Lovell rode rapidly by the Levee road, and arrived in town about two o'clock in the afternoon. Crowds gathered round him while he related the events of the engagement below, bearing testimony to the heroism of our little navy of indifferent vessels, and seeming bewildered at the unexpected calamity which had befallen him. He considered it advisable for his small force to retire without the limits of the city to avert a bombardment, and this idea was fully endorsed by the City Council. Accordingly, late in the day, his whole force, of not more than twenty-eight hundred effective men, departed by rail some fifteen miles above the city, with orders to keep within easy call in case of emergency.

The evacuation of the city by Gen. Lovell's troops was the signal for a new consternation, and another era of disorder in the city. Uproar and confusion continued throughout the day and all night, while now and then heavy guns could be heard down the river, as if the enemy was cautiously approaching, and firing at suspicious objects. Crowds of the poor were enjoying a rich harvest by the wholesale destruction of property, and scores of them could be seen with baskets, and bags, and drays, carrying off whatever plunder fell in their way. A low, murmuring voice filled the air—it was the conversation of assembled thousands. Some were for burning the city, rather than permit it to fall into the hands of the enemy; but the opinion prevailed that such foolish excesses should be at once put in check, and that the city, being entirely at the mercy of the foe, nothing should be done to provoke a bombardment.

On the morning of the 25th of April, Farragut's advance was observed steaming up towards the city. When abreast of the Chalmette batteries on both sides of the city, he was saluted with volleys from the earthworks, but, being uninjured, ran past and cast anchor at intervals before the city, with ports open, and every preparation made for a bombardment. Farragut then opened communication with the Mayor, and demanded the surrender of the city, together with Lovell's forces; but the latter were away, the city had been left under the exclusive jurisdiction of Mayor Monroe, and he avoided a formal surrender, declaring that if the enemy desired the removal of objectionable flags floating over the public buildings of New Orleans, he must do it by his own force.

The correspondence touching the surrender of the city was protracted until the 28th of April. There was a purpose in this. The confidence of the people had, in a measure, rallied; there were yet glimpses of hope. As long as Forts St. Philip, Jackson, and the Chalmette batteries remained intact, it was thought that something might be done to save the city. The enemy's fleet had no forces with which to occupy it; his transports were unable to get up the river, as long as the forts held out. The enemy's land forces, under Gen. Butler, were at Ship Island and Mississippi City. Had he attempted to march overland upon New Orleans, the levees would have been cut, and his men drowned in the swamps.

But the last hope was to be extinguished. While Farragut and Mayor Monroe were exchanging angry letters of great length, the overwhelming news reached New Orleans, that Forts St. Philip and Jackson had surrendered to the enemy. The surrender was made in consequence of a mutiny of the garrisons. On examining his guns in Fort Jackson, Gen. Duncan found many spiked, several dismounted, and not less than three hundred men clamoring around him for a surrender. Remonstrances, threats, and entreaties were alike useless. In vain Gen. Duncan declared to the men that it would be an eternal shame to give up the works, provisioned as they were, and scarcely touched by the enemy. In vain he vowed that the forts were impregnable. In vain he promised that he would blow up all Butler's transports in a trice, if his men would only stand by him. The soulless creatures who disgraced the Confederate uniform had no reply to these arguments and appeals. Nothing would satisfy them but surrender. Ragged, dusty, powder-blackened, and exhausted, Duncan reached New Orleans, to tell the story of the great misfortune; and as he narrated it on the levee he wept, and the hundreds who listened to him were silent with amazement and shame.

Farragut, being informed of the surrender of the forts, was now anxious to expedite the full and formal surrender of the city, before the arrival of Butler with his transports. The correspondence with the Mayor had continued through several days. On the 28th of April, Farragut addressed his ultimatum to that officer, complaining of the continued display of the *State* flag of Louisiana on the City Hall, and concluding with a threat of the bombardment of the city, by notifying him to remove the women and children from its limits within forty-eight hours. The flag was not removed, and the threat was not fulfilled. On the 1st of May, Farragut reluctantly consented to send his own forces to take down the flag.

About noon, he sent on shore a party of two hundred marines with two brass howitzers, who marched through the streets and formed before the City Hall. The officer in command ascended to the dome of the building, and took down the objectionable State banner—the sign of all State rights. The act was done in profound silence; there were no idle utterances of curiosity; indignation was impotent, and men with compressed lips and darkened brows witnessed the first ceremony of their humiliation, and saw erected above them the emblem of tyrannical oppression. A speechless crowd of many thousands thronged the streets; a line of bayonets glistened within the square; the marines stood statue-like; the very air was oppressive with stillness; and so, in dead silence, the Stars and Stripes were hoisted over New Orleans, and the city passed forever from the rule and power of the Confederates.

Thus, after an engagement the casualties of which might be counted by hundreds, fell New Orleans, with its population of one hundred and seventy thousand souls—the commercial capital of the South, and the largest *exporting* city in the world. It was a terrible disaster to the Confederacy. The fall of Donelson broke our centre in the West. The fall of New Orleans yet more sorely punished the vanity of the Confederates; annihilated their power in Louisiana; broke up their routes to Texas and the Gulf; closed their access to the richest grain and cattle country in the South; gave to the enemy a new base of operations; and, more than anything else, staggered the confidence of Europe in the fortunes of the Confederacy.* And yet these disasters were very far from deciding the war.

---

* The following document, put in our possession, discusses the evacuation of New Orleans in a military point of view, in a very intelligible style that will interest the general reader, and completes in all respects the story of the disaster:

Major-General Lovell's reasons for evacuating New Orleans.

"I determined to evacuate the city, when the enemy succeeded in passing the forts, for the following reasons: The principal and almost entire concentration of strength in guns, men, and ships, had been made at that point. It had been selected as the spot where the battle for the defence of New Orleans, against a fleet coming up the river, should be fought, and everything available for the defence below, both ashore and afloat, had been collected there, except the twelve guns on the river at the lower interior line, which had been put there to flank that line. The obstructions had been placed there, and, until swept away, had been a complete bar to the passage of a hostile fleet, and the Naval and River Defence officers had brought to bear at that point all their available strength; and although New Orleans was still in condition to resist any attack by land, yet when, after six days and nights of incessant conflict, the forts were passed, and all our defences afloat were either burnt or sunk, I knew that there was no material obstacle to prevent the fleet from proceeding at once to the city, and that all the guns, forts, and men on the other ten or twelve water approaches would go for nought.

"The twelve guns in the open earthworks at the lower line had but twenty rounds of powder each (the remainder having been given to the Louisiana), and could offer no serious resistance to a fleet which had already passed more than one hundred guns in masonry works, better manned, and amply supplied with powder.

"The city was surrounded by swamps, and there was but one outlet by land, viz., through the narrow neck between the river and Lake Pontchartrain. At Kenner, on the Mississippi, ten miles above the city, the firm ground between the river and swamp which borders the lake is narrowed to about three quarters of a mile, through which passes the Jackson Railroad. The river at this time was full to the tops of the levees, and a single one of their large ships of war, by anchoring at this point, would have commanded with her broadsides (at point-blank range) the only land exit from

THE FALL OF NEW ORLEANS.

A train of Confederate victories was to follow them, and the attention of the world was now to be fixed upon the campaign in Virginia.

New Orleans, sweeping with her guns (which would have been higher than the surface of the country) every foot of ground between the river and the lake.

"The obstructions placed across the Rigolets at Fort Pike had been swept away in a storm shortly before by some vessels which had broken adrift, and there was an open channel fully as wide as the Mississippi River into Lake Pontchartrain, which could easily be passed by the enemy at night. Such a movement, in connection with the placing of one or more ships at Kenner, would have completely surrounded New Orleans, cutting off all communications by land or water with the interiour. My efforts to accumulate provisions enough in the city to feed the population had proved abortive, and an examination made a few days previous to the evacuation, had satisfied me that there were not in the city provisions enough to sustain the population for more than eighteen days. Taking it for granted that the enemy would occupy Kenner, as, indeed, he did in a few days, we should have been starved into a surrender in less than three weeks, for when the hostile fleet anchored in front of the city, we were entirely cut off from Texas and Red River—our main sources of supply.

"I had more than three months' rations available for my troops (less than three thousand men), but this would have answered but a few days for more than one hundred and fifty thousand persons. Some of the steamers at the levee had been destroyed, and a number had fled up the river, so that the Jackson Railroad was the only means of transportation for removing the women, children, and non-combatants from the city, which removal it would have required months to accomplish. In the vicinity of New Orleans, and for many miles above, there was nothing but swamps filled with water, in which the families could take refuge, and, moreover, a great portion of the male protectors of these families were absent with our armies in Tennessee and Virginia, and, of course, could not superintend their removal. The plan, therefore, of removing the non-combatants, and remaining with the troops, was entirely impracticable. Thirteen of the enemy's ships were anchored abreast of the city with their guns looking down the streets, which they could have swept to the swamps in rear of the houses, or set on fire at a number of points, and had I continued to occupy it with troops, they would have been justified by the laws of war in opening fire after due notice to the women and children to withdraw from danger. I knew that they had not, and could not have for several days, any land forces to take possession, and having determined, for the reasons above stated, to evacuate the city, I thought it best to remove the troops at once and speedily, and thus convert New Orleans from a military position into that of an ungarrisoned city. By so doing, I should deprive the enemy of all pretext for a wanton and useless sacrifice of life and property, and as they were unable to occupy it, I would have a number of days for the undisturbed removal of the vast amount of public property which was on hand at that time. My troops, however, were placed at Camp Moore, only four hours' run from the city by rail, and I could have reoccupied it at any time for several days after the evacuation, if it had been deemed advisable. Had I regarded the outside popular clamor that would ensue, I should have subjected the people of New Orleans to a bombardment; but I did not think myself justified for such a purpose in spilling the blood of women and children, when I knew that in two or three weeks at farthest, want of food for the inhabitants would compel me to evacuate the city, or, if that had been then impossible, to surrender.

"I spoke to the Mayor, several members of the City Council, and many prominent citizens, on the subject, and while none seemed unwilling to undergo any danger, if by so doing they could arrive at favourable results, yet all, without exception, under the circumstances, approved of and advised the withdrawal of the troops.

"In determining upon the evacuation, I necessarily, as soon as the enemy's fleet had passed the forts, regarded the position the same as if both their army and navy were present before the city, making due allowance simply for the time it would take them to transport their army up; inasmuch as their ships, having passed Forts Jackson and St. Philip, they could at once place themselves in open and uninterrupted communication with their army at points from six to twenty miles above the forts, through various small water communications from the Gulf, made more available

But before passing to those memorable fields, we may glance at a sequel of the surrender of New Orleans, which, indeed, is among the most

by the extraordinary height of the river, and which, while we were in possession of the latter, I had
easily and without risk defended with launches and a part of the River Defence fleet. I had also
stationed Skymanski's Regiment at Quarantine for the same object. These, however, were all destroyed or captured by the enemy's fleet, after they got possession of the river between the forts
and the city.

"There was a further and very important reason for the course which I pursued. I knew that
if I remained in New Orleans, we should in all probability lose in a short time troops, guns, and
supplies of all kinds, and the enemy would then be in full possession of the river as far as Memphis,
which eventually fell also into their hands. By withdrawing my command, however, I would be
enabled to fortify, arm, and garrison Vicksburg, a strong and defensible position. On the 17th of
April I had written to Gen. Beauregard, recommending the fortification of Vicksburg, and asking
him for an engineer officer; and two days after the evacuation I advised the adjutant-general at
Richmond, Gen. Cooper, that I should occupy that place and Jackson. I sent thither a number of
heavy guns and quantities of ammunition, with the artillerists from the various forts near New Orleans, and sent Gen. Smith, with a brigade of infantry, to take command of the whole. The officers,
troops, and guns which held Vicksburg last summer, were almost entirely the same which I withdrew from New Orleans, rather than remain and submit to an inevitable surrender.

"Results have fully proved the wisdom of the military policy pursued by me in collecting all the
means in Department No. One and taking a new and stronger position on the Mississippi River.

"The evacuation of New Orleans and its occupation by the enemy, would necessarily be followed
sooner or later by the abandonment of the several forts and small works on the exterior line, which
were erected principally to defend the approaches to that city, and after its evacuation could no
longer serve any useful purpose, as the position of the enemy (in the river abreast the city) gave him
control of the Opelousas Railroad, thus enabling him to get in rear of the works at Barrataria Bay,
Grand Caillou, Bayou Lafourche, and Berwick Bay, by which he could cut off and capture all the
garrison, with small arms, ammunition, and stores, all of which were greatly needed at that time. I
directed them to be abandoned at once. The officers in command were ordered to report with their
troops and all transportable supplies at Camp Moore or Vicksburg. Some of them complied with
the order, but a portion of the garrison, after marching part of the way, refused to go further, and,
in spite of their officer, disbanded, and went to New Orleans.

"Forts Jackson and St. Philip surrendered in consequence of a mutiny among the men on the
28th of April. Forts Pike and Macomb were abandoned without my orders. When I returned to
the city from the lower forts on the 24th, I directed Col. Fuller, who was in command of the works
on the lakes, which comprised Forts Pike and Macomb, to have everything ready to abandon those
forts, in case I should so order it. Supposing that the enemy would occupy Kenner, and thus deprive me of the use of the Jackson Railroad, it was my intention to remove the troops, supplies, etc.,
across Lake Pontchartrain to Pass Manchac and Madisonville, holding the entrance to that lake by
the fort as long as possible. The enemy, however, did not interfere with the railroad at Kenner,
and the greater part of the men and public property were removed by rail. I went to Camp Moore
on the night of the 25th to arrange matters there, and on the morning of the 27th I received information that Col. Fuller had arrived at Covington, La., with the garrison of Forts Pike and Macomb.
This was the first knowledge I had of the abandonment of those works. I immediately directed
them to be reoccupied, and sent a letter to Capt. Poindexter of the navy, in command of the ships
on the lake, requesting his coöperation in this movement. Col. Fuller replied on the 28th that the
forts had been dismantled, the guns spiked, and the carriages destroyed, and that it was impossible
to reoccupy them. I was officially informed of the surrender of Forts Jackson and St. Philip on the
morning of the 29th, and deemed it, therefore, useless to make any further attempt to reoccupy
Forts Pike and Macomb. The cisterns in the two last-named works only held water enough to
serve the garrison a short time, and had to be supplied by steamers from a distance. They could

remarkable records of the war.   Any story of New Orleans is incomplete without the hero, Benjamin F. Butler.   This man, who was to reap the fruits of the victory of the Federal fleet, and enact the part of military ruler in New Orleans, was an example of that reputation so easily made in the North by brazen assertions, sensational dispatches, and coarse abuse of rebels.   Gen. Butler had been a small lawyer in Massachusetts ; his first experiment in politics was that of a Northern man with Southern principles ; he was a delegate to the Charleston Convention of 1860, and he was accustomed to relate with singular satisfaction the circumstance that he had voted in that body, more than forty times, for Jefferson Davis as the nominee for President of the United States !   When the war broke out, he was a ready convert to the popular doctrine in his State, and went in advance of it in his expressions of ferocity towards the people of the South.   He had already made himself infamous in Baltimore by his war upon non-combatants ; by browbeating quiet citizens ; by examining courts in which the severity of the military judge was curiously mingled with the peculiar skill and disreputable adroitness of the pettifogger ; and by his quick and apt invention of various instruments of moral torture.   The appearance of the man was extraordinary and revolting.   He had small, muddy, cruel eyes ; one of them was curtained by a drooping lid ; and there was a smothered glower in them indicative of ill-contained and violent passion.   The other of his features were almost covered up in enormous chops, with little webs of red veins in them ; and the whole expression of his face was that of a lecherous coarseness and a cunning ferocity.

Such was the tyrant of New Orleans.   He inaugurated his rule in the subdued city by the following order, directed against the women of New Orleans, which at once made his name infamous in all the Christian and civilized countries of the world, and obtained for him in the South the popular and persistent title of the " Beast : "

"HEADQUARTERS, DEPARTMENT OF GULF, NEW ORLEANS, *May* 15.

" As officers and soldiers of the United States have been subject to repeated insults from women calling themselves ladies, of New Orleans, in return for the most scrupulous non-interference and courtesy on our part, it is ordered hereafter, when any female shall by mere gesture or movement insult, or show contempt for any officers or soldiers of the United States, she shall be regarded and held liable to be treated as a woman about town plying her avocation.   By command of Maj.-Gen. BUTLER.

" GEO. C. STRONG, A. A. G."

The infamous " woman-order " was the prelude to a rule in New Orleans that excited the horrour and disgust of the civilized world.   The

not have held out for any great length of time for this reason, and I deemed it best to save their garrisons (composed of well-drilled artillerists) for the works at Vicksburg, where they have ever since rendered such good service.   But it was not intended to abandon them so soon, nor, indeed, 'till I had transferred all the public property from New Orleans."

newspapers which declined to publish an edict so disreputable were threatened with suppression; * and Mayor Monroe and some of the city authorities who ventured to protest against it, were arrested, shipped down to Fort Jackson, and for many months kept in confinement there. Then followed a series of acts of cruelty, despotism and indecency. Citizens accused of contumacious disloyalty, were confined at hard labour, with balls and chains attached to their limbs. Men, whose only offence was selling medicines to sick Confederate soldiers, were arrested and imprisoned. A physician who, as a joke, exhibited a skeleton in his window as that of a Yankee soldier, was sentenced to be confined at Ship Island for two years, at hard labour. A lady, the wife of a former member of Congress of the United States, who happened to laugh as the funeral train of a Yankee officer passed her door, received this sentence: " It is, therefore, ordered that she be not ' regarded and treated as a common woman,' of whom no officer or soldier is bound to take notice, but as an uncommon, bad, and dangerous woman, stirring up strife, and inciting to riot, and that, therefore, she be confined at Ship Island, in the State of Mississippi, within proper limits there, till further orders." The distinction of sex seems only to

---

* The following appeared in a Southern newspaper during the days of Butler's rule in New Orleans:

" Considering the character of the infamous order issued, with reference to the ladies of New Orleans, the following will be thought a well-designed act of retributive justice. Preparations were making for a dress-parade, and a number of officers had congregated in front of the St. Charles, Butler's headquarters. A handsome carriage was driven in front of the hotel, accompanied by servants in livery, with every sign of wealth and taste in the owner of the equipage. The occupant, dressed in the latest fashion and sparkling with jewelry, drew from her pocket her gold card-case, and taking therefrom her card, sent it up to Butler's rooms. The next day himself and lady called at the residence indicated on the card—a fine mansion in a fashionable part of the city—where a couple of hours were agreeably spent in conversation, followed by the introduction of wine and cake, when the highly-delighted visitors took their departure. Butler did not appreciate the fact that he had been made the victim of a successful " sell," until he learned shortly afterwards that he had been paying his respects to the proprietress of one of the most celebrated *bagnios* in the State, who is at this time ' *considered a woman of the town, plying her vocation as such.* ' "

As a matter of justice—or as a specimen of ingenious quibbling, as the reader may decide—we should not omit Gen. Butler's explanation and attempted justification of his " woman-order." The author of these pages, in the painful character of a prisoner of war, had, once, occasion to meet Gen. Butler, and to have some conversation with him, in the course of which Gen. B. volunteered a long defence of his rule in New Orleans. He declared that as to the " woman-order," when Lord Palmerston denounced it in the British Parliament, he might, if he had turned to the Ordinances of London, have found that it had been borrowed from that ancient and respectable authority. The " Ladies " of New Orleans, he said, did not interfere with his troops; it was the *demi-monde* that troubled him. One of this class had spat in an officer's face. Another had placed herself vis-a-vis to an officer in the street, exclaiming, " La, here is a Yankee; don't he look like a monkey !" It became necessary to adopt an order that " would execute itself," and have these women treated as street-walkers. " How do you treat a street-walker ? " said Gen. Butler; " you don't hug and kiss her in the street !" The General explained that he meant only that these women were to be treated with those signs of contempt and contumely usually bestowed upon street-walkers, so as to make them ashamed of themselves; and it was thus the order " executed itself."

have been recognized by Butler as a cowardly opportunity for advantage. In his office, in the St. Charles Hotel, the inscription was placed in plain sight: " *There is no difference between a he and a she adder in their venom.*" His officers were allowed to indulge their rapacity and lust at will; they seized houses of respectable citizens, and made them the shops of infamous female characters; they appropriated the contents of wine-rooms; they plundered the wardrobes of ladies and gentlemen; they sent away from the city the clothing of whole families; they " confiscated " pianos, libraries, and whatever articles of luxury and ornament pleased their fancy, and sent them as presents and *souvenirs* to their friends at home. It was the era of plunder and ill-gotten gains. Fines were collected at pleasure. Recusants were threatened with ball and chain. A trade was opened in provisions for cotton, and Butler's own brother was made banker and broker of the corrupt operations, buying confiscated property, trading provisions and even military stores for cotton, and amassing out of the distress of an almost starving people fortunes of princely amount and villainous history. No wonder that the principal of these outrages lived in perpetual alarm for the safety of his life. It was said that he wore secret armour. He certainly was never for a moment without an armed guard. Sentinels walked in five paces of him; and when he sat in his office, several pistols lay beside him, and a chair allotted to the visitor was chained to the wall while a pistol capped but *unloaded* was placed, as if carelessly, within reach, as a cunning decoy to the supposed assassin.*

A shocking incident of Butler's despotism in New Orleans was the execution of William B. Mumford, a citizen of the Confederate States, charged with the singular crime of having taken the Federal flag from the United States Mint, which was done before the city had surrendered, and was, in any circumstances, but an act of war. He was condemned to death for an insult to the enemy's ensign. It was scarcely to be believed that on such a charge a human life would be taken, deliberately and in cold blood. Butler was inexorable. The wife and children of the condemned man piteously plead for his life. Butler's answer was cruel and taunting. A number of citizens joined in a petition for mercy. Butler answered that

---

* We are indebted to James Parton, a Northern biographer of Butler, for mention of this ingenious device. Parton thus describes the arrangements of his hero's office, while transacting business:

"The office was a large room, furnished with little more than a long table and a few chairs. In one corner, behind the table, sat, unobserved, a short-hand reporter, who, at a signal from the General, would take down the examination of an applicant or an informer. The General began business by placing his pistol upon the table, within easy reach. After the detection of two or three plots to assassinate him, one of the aides caused a little shelf to be made under the table for the pistol, while another pistol, *unloaded*, lay upon the table, which any gentleman, disposed to attempt the game of assassination, was at liberty to snatch."

some vicious men in New Orleans had sent him defiant letters about Mumford's fate; that an issue had been raised, that it was " to be decided whether he was to govern in New Orleans or not "—and he decided it by keeping the word he had first pronounced, and sending Mumford to the gallows.

The condemned man was one of humble station in life, and was said to have been of dissipated habits. But he was faultlessly brave. On the gallows the suggestion was made to him that he might yet save his life by a humiliating and piteous confession. He replied to the officer who thus tempted him : " Go away." He turned to the crowd, and said, with a distinct and steady voice : " I consider that the manner of my death will be no disgrace to my wife and children ; my country will honour them." More than a thousand spectators stood around the gallows ; they could not believe that the last act of the tragedy was really to be performed ; they looked on in astonished and profound silence.

Before the era of Butler in New Orleans, the Confederates had had a large and instructive experience of the ferocity of their enemies, and their disregard of all the rules of war and customs of civilization. At Manassas and Pensacola the Federals had repeatedly and deliberately fired upon hospitals. In the naval battle in Hampton Roads, they had hung out a white flag, and then opened a perfidious fire upon our seamen. At Newbern they had attempted to shell a town containing several thousand women and children, before either demanding a surrender, or giving the citizens notice of their intentions. They had broken faith on every occasion of expediency ; they had disregarded flags of truces ; they had stolen private property ; they had burned houses, and desecrated churches ; they had stripped widows and orphans of death's legacies by a barbarous law of confiscation ; they had overthrown municipalities and State Governments ; they had imprisoned citizens, without warrant and regardless of age or sex ; and they had set at defiance the plainest laws of civilized warfare.

Butler's government in New Orleans, and his " ingenious " war upon the helplessness of men and virtue of women was another step in atrocity. The Louisiana soldiers in Virginia went into battle, shouting : " Remember Butler ! " It was declared that the display of Federal authority in the conquered city of New Orleans was sufficient to make the soldiers of the South devote anew whatever they had of life and labour and blood to the cause of the safety and honour of their country. And yet it was but the opening chapter of cruelty and horrours, exaggerated at each step of the war, until Humanity was to stand aghast at the black volume of misery and ruin.

CHAPTER XVI.

In the first part of the year 1862, the Federal Government, with plans fully matured, had under arms about six hundred thousand men ; more than one-third of whom were operating in the direction of Richmond. What Gen. McClellan himself said of the vast and brilliant army with which he designed to capture the Confederate capital was not extravagant. It was, indeed, " magnificent in material, admirable in dscipline and instruction, excellently equipped and armed." On March 1, 1862, the number of Federal troops in and about Washington had increased to 193,142, fit for duty, with a grand aggregate of 221,987.

Such was the heavy and perilous force of the enemy that, in the spring of 1862, hung on the northern frontier of Virginia. Let us see what was in front of it on the Confederate line of defence. Gen. Joseph E. Johnston had in the camps of Centreville and Manassas *less than thirty thousand men.* These figures are from an official source. " Stonewall " Jackson had been detached with eleven skeleton regiments to amuse the enemy in the Shenandoah Valley, passing rapidly between Banks and Shields, and giving them the idea that he meditated a formidable movement. Such was the force that in North Virginia stood in McClellan's path, and deterred him from a blow that at that time might have been fatal to the Southern Confederacy.

It had been the idea of the Washington authorities to despatch the Confederacy by a combined movement in the winter. The order of President Lincoln for a general movement of the land and naval forces against the Confederate positions on the 22d of February (Washington's birthday), directed that McClellan's army should advance for the immediate object of seizing and occupying a point upon the railroad southwest of Manassas Junction. But McClellan urged a different line of operations on the Lower Rappahannock, obtained delay, and did not advance.

In the mean time, Gen. Johnston had not been an idle spectator of the immense and overwhelming preparations of the enemy in his front. As a commander he was sagacious, quick to apprehend, and had that peculiar military reticence in connection with a sage manner and decisive action, that obtained the confidence of his men instead of exciting criticism, or alarming their suspicions. In the first winter months of 1862, he had determined to change his line on the Potomac. All idea of offensive operations on it had long ago been abandoned. It had become necessary in Gen. Johnston's opinion that the main body of the Confederate forces in Virginia should be in supporting distance of the Army of the Peninsula, so that, in the event of either being driven back, they might combine for final resistance before Richmond.

During winter, Johnston had been quietly transporting his immense stores towards the Rappahannock, removing every cannon that could be spared, and filling the empty embrasures with hollow logs painted black, which even at a few yards' distance much resembled thirty-two and sixty-four pounders. Never were preparations for a retreat so quietly and skilfully made. So perfectly were all things arranged that all stores, baggage, sick, material, and guns were removed far to the rear, before Johnston's own men realized the possibility of a retreat. It was only as the different brigades fell into line, and the main army defiled southward through Fauquier County that the men discovered the movement to be a general and not a partial one.

On the 8th of March, the Government at Washington issued a peremptory order to McClellan to move for the new base of operations he designed on the Chesapeake Bay, and to capture the Confederate batteries on the Potomac. The change in the situation which Johnston's skilful retreat had effected was not known in Washington. On the 9th of March McClellan's army was in motion. All Washington was in expectation; it was known that the second "On-to-Richmond" had commenced, and that the second grand army was about to pass its grand climacteric. At night Fairfax Court-House was reached, and the grand army encamped within a radius of two miles. At a late hour came the wonderful tidings that Manassas and Centreville had been evacuated! There was no enemy there. But there was a great conflagration in full flame, bridges and machine-shops just blown up, and other incendiary fires gleaming in the distance. Nothing was left in the famous Confederate position; it was desolate, though frowning in fortified grandeur. Thus had been accomplished in the face of the enemy the most successful and complete evacuation—the most secure and perfect retreat of which the history of the war furnishes an example. Johnston had safely escaped with his entire right and left wings; he had securely carried off every gun and all his provisions and munitions; and he had blown up or otherwise destroyed every bridge and culvert on turnpike and railroad along his route.*

When Johnston's army had crossed the Rappahannock, it was drawn up in line, and waited a week for the enemy; but McClellan refused the challenge, and moved down the stream near the sea-board. To contract

---

* In Gen. McClellan's official report of this period, he seeks to convey the impression to the reader that he was well aware of Johnston's evacuation, and only marched his troops to Manassas that they might gain " some experience on the march and bivouac preparatory to the campaign, and to get rid of the superfluous baggage and other impediments which accumulate round an army encamped for a long time in one locality." He continues : "A march to Manassas and back could produce no delay in embarking for the Lower Chesapeake, as the transports could not be ready for some time, and it afforded a good intermediate step between the quiet and comparative comfort of the camps round Washington and the rigours of active operations."

If Gen. McClellan had designed to have written something to be laughed at, he could not have better succeeded than in the sentences quoted above.

his left, Johnston fell back across the Rapidan, and increased the strength of the right against all flanking manœuvres. Large fleets of transports were gathered at the mouth of the Rappahannock, but few knew their object or destination. Johnston however divined it. He promptly took the idea that the Federals, while making a show of force along the Lower Rappahannock, would not attack ; their object being to transport their force with great celerity to the Peninsula, thinking to suprise Magruder at Yorktown, and seize Richmond before any troops could be marched to oppose them.

He was right. On March 13, a council of war was assembled at Fairfax Court-House, by McClellan. It agreed on the following resolution : "That the enemy, having retreated from Manassas to Gordonsville, behind the Rappahannock and the Rapidan, it is the opinion of Generals commanding army corps that the operations to be carried on will be best undertaken from Old Point Comfort between the York and James Rivers : provided, 1st, That the enemy's vessel Merrimac can be neutralized ; 2d, That the means of transportation sufficient for an immediate transfer of the force to its new base can be ready at Washington and Alexandria to move down the Potomac ; and, 3d, That a naval auxiliary force can be had to silence, or aid in silencing, the enemy's batteries on the York River ; 4th, That the force to be left to cover Washington shall be such as to give an entire feeling of security for its safety from menace."

While the scene of the most important contest in Virginia was thus being shifted, and Gen. Banks was transferring a heavy force from the Shenandoah Valley to take position at Centreville, in pursuance of McClellan's plan for the protection of Washington, a battle unimportant but bloody took place near Winchester.

BATTLE OF KERNSTOWN.

Gen. Shields had been left at Winchester by Banks with a division and some cavalry, and commanded, as he states in his official report, seven thousand men of all arms. Ascertaining that " Stonewall " Jackson was at New Market, he made a feint, pretended to retreat on the 20th of March, and at night placed his force in a secluded position, two miles from Winchester on the Martinsburg road. This movement, and the masked position of the enemy made an impression upon the inhabitants of Winchester that Shields' army had left, and that nothing remained but a few regiments to garrison the place. On the 22nd Ashby's cavalry drove in the enemy's pickets, and discovered only a brigade. The next day Jackson had moved his line near Kernstown, prepared to give battle and expecting to find only a small force of the enemy at the point of attack. He had less than twenty-five hundred men. It will amuse the Southern reader to find it stated in Gen. Shields' official report that Jackson had in the engagement of Kernstown eleven thousand men, and was, therefore, in superior force.

The engagement between these unequal forces commenced about four o'clock in the evening of the 23d of March, and terminated when night closed upon the scene of conflict. Jackson's left flank, commanded by Gen. Garnett, was finally turned, and forced back upon the centre, but only after a most desperate and bloody encounter. A long stone fence ran across an open field, which the enemy were endeavouring to reach. Federals and Confederates were both in motion for this natural breast-work, when the 24th Virginia, (Irish), ran rapidly forward, arrived at the fence first, and poured a volley into the enemy at ten paces distant. But the overwhelming numbers of the enemy soon swept over the fence, and drove the Confederate left into the woods, taking two guns and a number of prisoners.

During the night Gen. Jackson decided to fall back to Cedar Creek. The enemy pursued as far as Harrisonburg, but with little effect, as Ashby's famous cavalry, the terrour of the Federals, covered the retreat. In his official report Gen. Shields wrote that the retreat "became flight;" but in a private letter to a friend in Washington, he had previously written of the Confederates: "Such were their gallantry, and high state of discipline that at no time during the battle or pursuit did they give way to panic."

The Confederate loss in killed, wounded and prisoners is carefully estimated at 465. Gen. Shields stated his loss as 103 killed, and 441 wounded. It had been a fierce and frightful engagement; for Jackson had lost nearly twenty per cent. of his force in a very few hours of conflict. But the battle was without any general signification. It drew, however, upon Jackson a great deal of censure; "he was," says one of his officers, "cursed by every one;" and it must be confessed, in this instance at least, the great commander had been entrapped by the enemy.

But public attention in Richmond was speedily taken from an affair so small by daily announcements of fleets of transports arriving in Hampton Roads, and the vast extension of the long line of tents at Newport News. McClellan, having the advantage of water-carriage, had rapidly changed his line of operations, and was at the threshold of a new approach to Richmond, while the great bulk of the Confederate force was still in motion in the neighbourhood of the Rappahannock and the Rapidan.

It was a fearful crisis. The fate of Richmond hung upon the line held across the Peninsula, from Yorktown on the York River to Mulberry Island on James River, by Gen. Magruder with little more than ten thousand men. McClellan had three *corps d'armée* in the lines before Yorktown, and had in the field a force of nearly 90,000 infantry, 55 batteries of artillery (making a total of 330 field guns), and about 10,000 cavalry, besides a siege train of 103 guns. This estimate of his force did not include the garrison of Fortress Monroe of about 10,000 men, nor Franklin's division which arrived about the end of April. The commander of this force hesitated before a line of eleven thousand men. His hesitation again saved Richmond. He was again deceived as to the strength of the Confederates. With admirable adroitness Gen. Magruder extended his little force over a distance of several miles, placing a regiment in every gap open to observation, to give the appearance of numbers to the enemy. McClellan took to the spade, and commenced the operation of a regular siege against Yorktown. While he was constructing his parallels, Gen. Johnston moved down to reinforce the Confederate lines of the Peninsula, in time to save Magruder's little force from the pressure of enveloping armies.

McClellan had been deceived twice as to the force in his front. He was to be outwitted twice by the strategy of retreat. Gen. Johnston decided neither to stand a siege nor to deliver a battle at Yorktown. The enemy was in largely superiour force, besides his additional strength in gunboats, and the object was to force him to more equal terms. It was readily seen by Johnston that in falling back to defences already prepared nearer Richmond, and investing the line of the Chickahominy, he would obtain the opportunity of concentrating a large force in front of the capital, besides being unexposed to operations in his rear, which threatened him at Yorktown from McDowell's corps at Fredericksburg. It was the just and sagacious view of the situation, and again the great master of Confederate strategy was to teach the enemy a lesson in the art of war.

Johnston had obtained all the delay he desired in keeping the enemy before his lines ; and on the 4th day of May, when McClellan had nearly completed all his parallels, secured communications between the different batteries, and was almost ready to open fire on the town, the news came that the Confederate army had retired.

The whole Federal army was, at once, put in motion to pursue. The Confederate works were left intact, but excepting a few unwieldy columbiads, all ordnance had been carried off. The men made " dummies," and put them in the embrasures, besides stuffing old clothes to represent sentinels. The pursuing army toiled on through rain falling in torrents, over roads deep in mud, the men straggling, falling out and halting without orders, and artillery, cavalry, infantry and baggage intermingled in apparently inextricable confusion. The scene had much more the appearance of the retreat of a defeated army than the advance of a successful one.

BATTLE OF WILLIAMSBURG.

It may be well imagined that McClellan, sorely disappointed, and knowing very well that the people of the North, who were already clamouring for a change of commanders, would not be satisfied with the barren occupation of the deserted works of Yorktown, was anxious to snatch some sort of victory from the rear-guard of the Confederate retreat, which he might magnify in official dispatches and Northern newspapers.

On the morning of the 5th May, Gen. Hooker's division of Heintzelman's corps came up near Williamsburg with the Confederate rear-guard, commanded by Gen. Longstreet. The Federals were in a forest in front of Williamsburg; but as Hooker came into the open ground, he was vigorously attacked, driven back with the loss of five guns, and with difficulty held the belt of wood which sheltered and concealed his men from the Confederate fire. Other forces of the enemy were moved up, until Gen. Longstreet was engaging nine brigades of the Federal army. During the whole of the day, from sunrise to sunset, he held McClellan's army in check, drove the enemy from two redoubts he had occupied, and secured Johnston's retreat so effectually, that the next morning when the rear guard moved off, it did so as undisturbed as if the enemy were a thousand miles distant.

But Gen. Longstreet not only accomplished the important object of securing the retreat. He won a brilliant victory. Gen. McClellan himself confessed a loss of 456 killed, 1,400 wounded, and 372 missing, making a total of 2,228. And Longstreet carried off with him nine pieces of captured artillery. Yet so anxious was McClellan for the colour of victory that he dispatched to Washington news of a success, and represented as the process of " driving rebels to the wall," the leisurely retreat of Johnston to works around Richmond, prepared ten months ago under the prudent and skilful direction of Gen. Robert E. Lee, and already the amplest and strongest at any point in the Confederacy.

The fact was that McClellan's army had received a serious check at Williamsburg, which, if Gen. Longstreet had been able to take advantage of it, might have been converted into a disastrous defeat. McClellan had also planned a flank movement upon Johnston's retreat. This performance, too, proved a miserable failure, although the idea did credit to his genius.

The design was that Franklin should move to West Point, the head of the York River, and disembark a large force there to assail Johnston on the flank. On the 7th of May, Franklin attempted a landing under cover of his gunboats, at Barhamsville near West Point. The attempt was gallantly repulsed by Whiting's division of Texas troops. The fight was wild and confused. Franklin hurriedly fell back before an inferiour force, and did not halt until under the guns of his flotilla.

The incidents of Williamsburg and Barhamsville had been Confederate successes; and Johnston's movement to the line of the Chickahominy turned out a most brilliant piece of strategy. He had secured the safe retreat of his army, together with his baggage and supply train, and, although forced by the configuration of the land, and the superiourity of the enemy on the water, to abandon the peninsula of Yorktown, he had done so in a manner which illustrated his genius, and insured the safety and efficiency of his army.

EVACUATION OF NORFOLK—DESTRUCTION OF THE "VIRGINIA."

The retreat from Yorktown involved the surrender of Norfolk with all the advantages of its contiguous navy-yard and dock and the abandonment of the strong Confederate positions at Sewell's Point and Craney Island. Here was the old story of disaster consequent upon haste and imperfect preparations. The evacuation was badly managed by Gen. Huger; much property was abandoned, and the great dry-dock only partially blown up.*

But the evacuation was attended by an incident, which was a painful surprise to the Confederate people, an occasion of grief and rage, and a

---

* The circumstances of the evacuation of Norfolk were made the subject of an investigation in the Confederate Congress. Commodore Forrest testified as follows before the committee making the investigation:

"I understood that it was the intention of the Government to withdraw the troops under Gen. Huger, for the protection of Richmond, and that the navy-yard and public buildings were to be destroyed. Upon learning this, I had a conference with the Secretary of the Navy. I stated to him that I did not see any necessity for such a proceeding, and that if he would allow me to return, I could assure him that I would protect the yard and Norfolk from any attack that the enemy might make. He asked me particularly in what manner I could do it. I explained to him that I had eleven hundred employees at the navy-yard, good and true men, that they had been exercised at great guns and small arms weekly for several months, and that there were guns mounted in what is called Forrest entrenchments, in *lunette*—four in all, containing each three or four guns of forty-one hundred weight, 32-pounders, and that I did not apprehend anything disastrous from Burnside's force; that by placing the steamer Virginia in a proper position, I thought she might very well protect the harbour, and even if Gen. Huger's army was taken away, I thought the citizens would all turn out to man the batteries. To this he replied, they would starve us out. I informed him that they could not very well do that for some time to come, that we had four hundred barrels of pork, and four hundred barrels of beef stowed in the yard; that the forage there had been collected for three months for the cattle. To this he replied, that it had been determined upon as a military necessity, and must be carried out.

"Mr. Foote. What was the value of the navy-yard? What do you conjecture the amount of the injury to be which we suffered from the destruction of the navy-yard?

"Commodore Forrest. There is a printed schedule taken by a commissioner appointed by the Governour of the State of Virginia, which could be had from the Secretary of State of the Commonwealth. In that schedule it mentions the value of the public property to be $6,500,000, or thereabouts."

topic of violent comment in the Richmond newspapers. The famous iron-clad Virginia, popularly said to be worth fifty thousand troops in the field, was destroyed by the orders of Commodore Tatnall, her commander. "The iron diadem of the South," exclaimed the Richmond *Examiner*, "had been shattered by a wanton blow."

The Virginia had been unable to bring on a fight with the enemy's fleet. When McClellan was encamped before Yorktown, she appeared in Hampton Roads, when the whole Federal fleet declined the combat, and with the vaunted Monitor took shelter beneath the guns of Fortress Monroe. On this occasion the Virginia, in sight of the enemy's fleet, carried off three schooners lying in the Roads almost within range of the guns of the fleet, and yet there was no movement to engage her; and this spectacle, so galling to the *esprit du corps* of the Federal navy, was witnessed by the French and English ships-of-war lying off Norfolk.

After the enemy's occupation of Norfolk, both shores of the James River came into possession of the Federal troops, who were therefore enabled to cut off the Virginia from her necessary supplies. Commodore Tatnall resolved to take the vessel up the river above the lines occupied by the enemy. According to his statement, he had been assured by her pilots that if the ship was lightened they would take her with a draught of eighteen feet of water within forty miles of Richmond. The ship was being lightened; Commodore Tatnall had retired to bed, when another message was brought him that the ship had been so far lightened that her wooden hull below the plating was exposed, and that the pilots (whom Commodore Tatnall charged with cowardice and an unwillingness to engage in action) now declared that the westerly wind had so lowered the water in the river that it would be impossible to take the vessel above the Jamestown Flats, up to which point the shore on both sides was occupied by the enemy. The commander, aroused from his slumbers, and acquainted with the decision of the pilots, ordered the vessel to be destroyed. Her decks and roof were saturated with oil, her crew were disembarked in small boats, trains of powder were laid from each port-hole to different parts of the vessel, and these were lighted at a given signal. Simultaneously the ship was on fire in many parts, and after burning several hours the flames reached the magazine, about four o'clock in the morning of the 11th of May, when the Virginia was blown up with an explosion heard many miles distant. Not a fragment was ever afterwards found of the only naval structure that guarded the water approach to Richmond.

"The Virginia," reported Commander Tatnall, "no longer exists. I presume that a court of inquiry will be ordered to examine into all the circumstances, and I earnestly solicit it. Public opinion will never be put right without it." The court was ordered, and public opinion was "put right" by its decision that the destruction of the Virginia was unnecessary; that she might have been taken up the James to a point of safety, where she could still have barred the ascent of the river; and that then and there, if the worst ensued, was the time to decide upon the disposition to be made of the vessel.

NAVAL ENGAGEMENT AT DREWRY'S BLUFF.

The destruction of the Virginia left the James River open for the enemy's operations. The Galena, the Aroostook, the Monitor, Port Royal, and Naugatuck, steamed up the river on the 15th of May, under the command of Commodore Rodgers, and without opposition advanced within twelve miles of Richmond. Here was a half-finished fort at what was called Drewry's Bluff, mounting four guns. The river at this point was also obstructed by a double line of piles and sunken vessels, and the banks were lined with sharpshooters. It was a feeble barrier to Richmond; the protection of the river had been entrusted to the Virginia; and yet the fort proved a success, owing to the defect of the enemy's gunboats.

The Galena and Monitor approached within six hundred yards of the batteries, but the guns of the latter proved useless, as they could not be elevated sufficiently to reach the work constructed on the bluff. The armour of the Galena was badly injured, and this river monster lost thirty of her crew in killed and wounded. Notwithstanding, the engagement continued for upwards of four hours, when the gunboats were repulsed. The Confederate loss was five killed and seven wounded. This action was considered as proving that earthworks could not be reduced by gunboats, and decided the question for the enemy that the capture of Drewry's Bluff, and the water approach to Richmond were impracticable without the aid of a land force.

The possession of the James River below Drewry's Bluff was of but little present advantage to McClellan, as his base of supplies was on the Pamunkey, from which point there was rail communication to Richmond. He had advanced within sight of the spires of the Confederate capital. The investment of the line of the Chickahominy brought the two armies face to face within a few miles of Richmond, and opened one of the grandest scenes of the war, exhibiting the strength and splendour of the opposing hosts, and appealing to the eye with every variety of picturesque effect. For nearly a year an immense labour had been expended upon the fortifications of Richmond. Earthworks of magnitude arose on every side. They were constructed in different shapes, to suit the conformation of the ground; they swept all the roads, crowned every hillock, and mounds of red earth could be seen in striking contrast with the rich green of the landscape. Redoubts, rifle-pits, casemate batteries, horn works, and enfilading batteries were visible in great number, in and out of the woods, in all directions. Beyond, through the open and cultivated country in the neighbourhood of Richmond stretched the camp of the enemy. Wooded heights overlooked them, and the numerous tents of the army, the vast trains of wagons, the powerful park of artillery, together with the fleet of steamers and transports, presented a striking contrast to the usually quiet country.

The mere circumstance of McClellan's proximity to Richmond was, to the vulgar mind of the North, an indication of his success. The fact that his army had marched unopposed to within a few miles of the city excited the hopes of the ignorant masses. Rumour each day in New York announced the fall of Richmond. Nor was there any great feeling of security in the Confederate capital. There were alarm and excitement in the mixed and restless population of Richmond ; and the popular feeling found but little assurance in the visible tremour of the authorities. The Confederate Congress had adjourned in such haste as to show that the members were anxious to provide for their own personal safety. President Davis sent his family to North Carolina, and a part of the Government archives were packed ready for transportation. At the railroad depots were piles of baggage awaiting transportation, and the trains were crowded with women and children going to distant points in the country, and escaping from the alarm and distress in Richmond.

But the panic, like all excitements of this sort, was soon subdued on reflection, and shamed by the counsels of the brave and intelligent. The newspapers rebuked it in severe terms. The shop-windows were filled with caricatures of the fugitives. Much of the alarm was turned into ridicule. A meeting of citizens, assembled on the 15th of May, in the City Hall, were addressed by Gov. Letcher and Mayor Mayo, and applauded the sentiment that Richmond should be reduced to ashes before it should become a Yankee conquest.

The Legislature of Virginia acted with singular spirit, and led in the work of the restoration of public confidence. On the 14th of May it adopted the following resolution, which, indeed, deserves to be committed to history as an example of heroic fortitude and patriotic sacrifice :

" *Resolved*, by the General Assembly of Virginia, That the General Assembly hereby expresses its desire that the capital of the State be *defended to the last extremity*, if such defence is in accordance with the views of the President of the Confederate States, and that the President be assured that whatever destruction and loss of property of the State or individuals shall thereby result, will be cheerfully submitted to."

To this exhibition of the spirit of Virginia, President Davis responded in lively terms. He stated to a committee of the Legislature, which called upon him to ascertain his views, that he had never entertained the thought of withdrawing the army from Virginia and abandoning the State. But to some extent he spoiled the assurance by suggesting, in swollen words, that even if Richmond should fall, " the war could still be successfully maintained on Virginia soil *for twenty years.*"

The tardy battle for Richmond yet lingered. Public confidence and public courage rose each day of the delay. The eloquent press of Richmond was stirring the Southern heart. The Richmond *Despatch* wrote : " If there is blood to be shed, let it be shed here ; no soil of the Confederacy could drink it up more acceptably and none would hold it more gratefully. Wife, family, and friends are nothing. Leave them all for one glorious hour to be devoted to the Republic. Life, death, and wounds are nothing, if we only be saved from the fate of a captured capital and a humiliated Confederacy. Let the Government act ; let the people act. *There is time yet.*"

But while thus fluctuated the sentiment of Richmond there came an especial occasion to reanimate the cause of the Confederacy, to erect again the reputation of its arms, and to fill with gratitude and hope the hearts which had so long throbbed with anxiety in its besieged capital. That occasion was the splendid diversion of " Stonewall " Jackson in the Valley of Virginia. Public attention turned to the eccentric career of that commander to find a new hero, and an unexpected train of brilliant victories.

JACKSON'S CAMPAIGN IN THE VALLEY OF VIRGINIA.

When the principal scene of the war in Virginia was shifted from the lines of the Potomac, Gen. Jackson remained in the Shenandoah Valley. Ewell's division was sent to operate with him in that part of the State. The object of the combined force was to divert the army of McDowell at Fredericksburg from uniting with that of McClellan ; and beyond this design the authorities at Richmond had no expectations from Jackson's small command.

It was an idea originating with the adventurous commander himself to act on the aggressive, and to essay the extraordinary task of driving the Federal forces from the Valley, then there under the three commands of Banks, Fremont, and Shields.

In order to understand the disposition of all the opposing forces at this time west of the Blue Ridge, it will be necessary to make a brief and rapid *resumé* of operations and movements in that quarter for some weeks previous, so as to put before the reader a comprehensive scene and an intelligent situation.

The disposition of the enemy's forces west of the Blue Ridge was designed to co-operate with McDowell at Fredericksburg. They included the troops of Banks and Shields in the Shenandoah Valley, and those of Milroy, Blenker, and Fremont in Western Virginia. As soon as Jackson had been reinforced by Ewell's division, which crossed the Blue Ridge at McGackeysville, the commander proceeded in person to the position of Gen. Edward Johnson's little force, which was drawn up in a narrow valley, at a village called McDowell, with the heavy brigades of Milroy and Blenker in line of battle before them. The enemy was driven here after a brief engagement. Learning that his success at McDowell had so frightened Milroy and Blenker that they had called upon Fremont, who was a few marches behind, Jackson determined to deceive them and fall back. Moving at a fast rate down the Valley Pike, he proceeded to Newmarket, and was there joined by Ewell's force, which had been awaiting him at Swift Run Gap. The whole force now amounted to about fourteen thousand men ; and after a little rest, proceeded across the Shenandoah Mountains.

Let us see how now stood the forces of the enemy. When Shields, who had followed Jackson since the battle of Kernstown, found him strongly posted at McGackeysville, he declined to advance against him and, withdrawing his forces from between Woodstock and Harrisonburg, he regained the Valley, determined to push on towards McDowell at Fredericksburg. Banks had his force scattered up and down the Valley, the rear being at Front Royal. Blenker and Milroy were similarly bound through Western Virginia, but their defeat had diverted Fremont from his proper route, who immediately went to their assistance. Thinking, therefore, that Jackson was busily engaged in that distant quarter, and not likely to trouble them in the Valley again, Banks and Shields were commencing a movement towards Fredericksburg, unconscious of danger, when, on the morning of May 22d, Jackson and Ewell, with fourteen thousand men, were meditating an attack on their rear at Front Royal.

The rear-guard, consisting of the First Maryland Regiment, may be said to have been almost annihilated. Every man was killed, wounded, or captured, save fifteen ; nine hundred prisoners were taken on the retreat towards Strasburg ; and a vast quantity of the enemy's stores was destroyed. At the first shock of the action, Banks had his army in motion from Strasburg ; he feared that Jackson, moving from Front Royal on the converging road to Winchester, might cut him off from that supposed place of safety. His fears were nearly realized ; for at Middletown Jackson pierced his main column, took a number of prisoners, demoralized the retreat, and having driven a part of his rear towards Strasburg, turned on hot pursuit to Winchester.

On the 24th of May, Banks' army, in frantic retreat, entered the streets of Winchester. The citizens received them with shouts of derision. Many of the fugitives were on the run ; some shots were fired from the windows of houses; ordnance exploded; cavalry rode down stragglers; bands of plunderers hastily entered houses, bayonetted their occupants, and in one wild scene of unrestrained disorder, fury, and cowardice, Banks' army passed out of the ancient town, where the enemy had so long ruled in the insolence of power.

Banks' army had stood but a few moments before Winchester, and had broken under a distant fire of artillery. He had evidently no disposition to test the substance and strength of the foe by actual collision, and was only desirous to place the Potomac between himself and the danger of action. Never was there such a shameful retreat; such a deliberate abandonment by a commander of everything but the desire for safety. In forty-eight hours after he had got the first news of the attack on Front Royal, Banks was on the shore of the Potomac, having performed thirty-five miles of the distance on the last day of the retreat.

The fruits of Jackson's two days' operations were immense. Banks had escaped with the loss of all the material and paraphernalia that constitute an army. He had abandoned at Winchester all his commissary and ordnance stores. He had resigned that town and Front Royal to the undisputed possession of the Confederates. He had left in their hands four thousand prisoners, and stores amounting to millions of dollars. It was a rapid stroke and a splendid success which Jackson had made. Tidings of his victory were communicated to the Confederate army around Richmond in general orders. " The Federal army," wrote Gen. Johnston, " has been dispersed and ignominiously driven from the Valley of the Shenandoah, and those who have freed the loyal citizens of that district by their patriotic valour, have again earned, as they will receive, the thanks of a grateful country. In making this glorious announcement, on the eve of the memorable struggle about to ensue, the Commanding General does not deem it necessary to invoke the troops of this army to emulate the deeds of their noble comrades in the Valley." *

In falling back from Winchester, Gen. Jackson had to run the danger of being enveloped by the converging columns of Fremont and Shields. He succeeded ("through the blessing of an ever kind Providence ") in reaching Strasburg, before the two Federal armies could effect their contemplated junction in his rear. On the 5th of June he reached Harrisonburg, and, passing beyond that town, turned towards the east in the direction of Port Republic.

On the movement from Harrisonburg occurred the melancholy inci-

---

* We may imagine the historical value of Federal *official* documents on reading Gen. Banks' report of the events we have related. The drama from Strasburg to the Potomac is thus epitomized:

" My command had not suffered an attack and rout, but accomplished a premeditated march (!) of near sixty miles, in the face of the enemy (!), defeating his plans and giving him battle wherever he was found (! !)."

dent of the death of the famous cavalry commander of the Valley, Turner Ashby, whose name was connected with much of the romance of the war, and whose gentle enthusiastic courage, simple Christian faith, and royal passion for danger, constituted him one of the noblest and most beautiful types of modern chivalry. On the road from Harrisonburg to Port Republic, the 58th Virginia became engaged with the Pennsylvania Bucktails. Col. Johnson came up with the Maryland regiment, and by a dashing charge in flank drove the enemy off with heavy loss. Ashby was on the right of the 58th Virginia, and had just commanded a charge of bayonets upon the enemy, concealed in a piece of woods, when he fell dead not many yards from a fence where a concealed marksman had sped the fatal bullet. Gen. Jackson's tribute to the fallen officer, whose active and daring cavalry had so often co-operated with his arms, was an extraordinary one, considering the habitual measure of this great man's words. He wrote of Ashby: " As a partisan officer I never knew his superiour. His daring was proverbial ; his powers of endurance almost incredible ; his tone of character heroic, and his sagacity almost intuitive in divining the purposes and movements of the enemy."

BATTLES OF CROSS-KEYS AND PORT REPUBLIC.

On the 7th of June the main body of Gen. Jackson's command had reached the vicinity of Port Republic. The village is situated in the angle formed by the junction of the North and South Rivers, tributaries of the south fork of the Shenandoah. The larger portion of Jackson's command was encamped on the high ground north of the village, about a mile from the river. Gen. Ewell was some four miles distant, near the road leading from Harrisonburg to Port Republic. Gen. Fremont had arrived with his forces in the vicinity of Harrisonburg, and Gen. Shields was moving up the east side of the south fork of the Shenandoah, and was then some fifteen miles below Port Republic. Gen. Jackson's position was about equi-distant from both hostile armies. To prevent a junction of the two Federal armies, he had caused the bridge over the south fork of the Shenandoah at Conrad's store to be destroyed.

Fremont had seven brigades of infantry besides numerous cavalry. Ewell had three small brigades during the greater part of the action that was to ensue, and no cavalry at any time. His force was short of five thousand men. About ten o'clock the enemy felt along his front, posted his artillery, and, with two brigades, made an attack on Trimble's brigade on the right. Gen. Trimble repulsed this force, and, advancing, drove the enemy more than a mile, and remained on his flank ready to make the final attack. At a late hour of the afternoon, Gen. Ewell advanced both his wings, drove in the enemy's skirmishers, and, when night closed, was in possession of all the ground previously held by the enemy.

The victory—known as that of Cross-Keys—had been purchased by a small Confederate loss: 42 killed and 287 wounded. Gen. Ewell officially estimated the enemy's loss at 2,000. Gen. Fremont officially gives it at 625—exhibiting rather more than the usual difference between Federal and Confederate figures.

Meanwhile Gen. Jackson was preparing to give the final blow to Shields on the other side of the river; and on the morning after their victory, Ewell's forces were recalled to join in the attack at Port Republic. As day broke they commenced their march to the other field of battle seven miles distant.

The enemy had judiciously selected his position for defence. Upon a rising ground near the Lewis House, he had planted six guns, which commanded the road from Port Republic, and swept the plateau for a considerable distance in front. As Gen. Winder moved forward his brigade, a rapid and severe fire of shell was opened upon it. The artillery fire was well sustained by our batteries, which, however, proved unequal to that of the enemy. In the meantime, Winder, being now reinforced by a Louisiana regiment, seeing no mode of silencing the Federal battery, or escaping its destructive missiles but by a rapid charge, and the capture of it, advanced with great boldness for some distance, but encountered such a heavy fire of artillery and small arms as greatly to disorganize his command, which fell back in disorder. The enemy advanced across the field, and, by a heavy musketry fire, forced back our infantry supports, in consequence of which our guns had to retire.

It was just at this crisis, when the day seemed lost, that Ewell's forces appeared upon the scene. Two regiments—the 58th and 44th Virginia— rushed with a shout upon the enemy, took him in flank and drove him back, for the first time that day in disorder. Meanwhile Gen. Taylor was employed on the Federal left and rear, and, his attack diverting attention from the front, led to a concentration of the enemy's force upon him. Here the battle raged furiously. Although assailed by a superiour force in front and flank, with their guns in position within point blank range, the charge ordered by Taylor was gallantly made, and the enemy's battery, consisting of six guns, fell into our hands. Three times was this battery lost and won in the desperate and determined efforts to capture and recover it. At last, attacked in front and on flank, Taylor fell back to a skirt of woods. Winder, having rallied his command, moved to his support, and again opened upon the enemy, who were moving upon Taylor's left flank, apparently to surround him in the wood. The final attack was made. Taylor, with the reinforcement, pushed forward; he was assisted by the well-directed fire of our artillery; the enemy fell back; a few moments more, and he was in precipitate retreat. Four hundred and fifty prisoners were taken in the pursuit, and what remained of the enemy's artillery.

While the forces of Shields were in full retreat, Fremont appeared on the opposite bank of the south fork of the Shenandoah, with his army, and opened his artillery with but little effect. The next day withdrawing his forces, he retreated down the Valley. The battle of Port Republic closed the campaign of the Valley. It had been fiercely contested by the enemy, and the Confederate loss was quite one thousand in killed and wounded. But the termination of the campaign found Jackson crowned with an almost marvellous success. In little more than two weeks, he had defeated three Federal armies; swept the Valley of Virginia of hostile forces; thrilled Washington with alarm; and thwarted whatever plan the enemy might have entertained, in other circumstances, of environing Richmond by large converging armies.

On the 12th of June Jackson encamped near Weyer's Cave. Here the pious commander paused, to hold divine service in his army in commemoration of his victories. He was to be here but a few days before receiving orders to move towards Richmond, and to join in the impending contest for the capital.

CHAPTER XVII.

THE tardiness of McClellan afforded opportunity to the Confederates to recruit their forces, to realize the results of the conscription law, and to assemble before Richmond the largest army they were ever able to put on a single field in any time of the war. The enemy had had the start in the preparation of many months. He delayed the advance upon Richmond, hesitating which line to adopt, when an advance upon either of the proposed lines could hardly have failed of success. A month was lost before the advance was begun. Another month was occupied in the siege of Yorktown, where McClellan was held in check by eleven thousand men. Three weeks more were taken up in the cautious advance across the Peninsula. Thus three full months were lost by the Federal army before it was fairly in the neighbourhood of Richmond, and every day of these months was employed by the Confederates in enlarging their resources of defence.

Having reached the Chickahominy, McClellan threw a portion of his army across the river, and, having thus established his left, proceeded to pivot upon it, and to extend his right by the right bank of the Pamunkey, so as to get to the north of Richmond. While conducting this manœuvre and delaying an attack, the Confederate army was rapidly receiving reinforcements, and drawing troops from distant points to make a decisive battle. Huger's army, from Norfolk, united with Johnston before Richmond; forces, under Branch, in North Carolina, were rapidly brought forward by rail; and even as far as Charleston, troops were withdrawn to match Johnston's numbers as far as possible with those of the enemy. And in this instance the match of numbers was probably closer than ever before or afterwards in the great conflicts of the war. With Jackson's command in the Valley which it was intended to put on the Richmond lines at the proper moment, the force defending the Confederate capital may be estimated at about ninety thousand men; and McClellan's, considering his losses on the Peninsula, could scarcely be more than one hundred and twenty or thirty thousand men.

In the last days of May the position of the two armies around Richmond is described by the Chickahominy. This stream, tracing through heavy forests and swamps east of Richmond from a north-westerly to a south-easterly direction, formed the respective fronts of the two armies— the Confederates occupying the western, the Federals the eastern banks. The line occupied by the enemy was nearly a right line from north-west to south-east. His forces were stretched from a short distance above New Bridge, where his right rested, to Bottom's Bridge, which constituted his left. The line was about ten miles long. Across it ran five roads in the following order, from west to east: the Brook turnpike; the Mechanicsville turnpike, (Mechanicsville being a village on the north side of the Chickahominy); the Nine Mile road; York River railroad; the Williamsburg road; the Charles City road; and the Darbytown road.

Before the 30th of May, Gen. Johnston had ascertained that McClellan had thrown his left forward to a point within six miles of Richmond, a mile in front of a point locally designated the "Seven Pines," where Casey's division was posted. Couch's division was encamped in his rear, his right resting in front of Fair Oaks station, about six miles due east of Richmond. Gen. Keyes commanded both divisions. In front there was a heavy forest, and a screen of dense undergrowth. A terrific thunder storm had taken place on the night of the 29th of May, and floods of rain spirting in broad jets, had so swollen the Chickahominy in Keyes' rear, that Johnston indulged the prospect of having to deal with no other troops than those of this corps. In these circumstances, on the morning of the 30th May, he moved out to annihilate the enemy's left.

BATTLE OF SEVEN PINES.

Gen. Johnston's plan of battle was to embrace an attack at three points Gen. D. H. Hill, supported by the division of Gen. Longstreet, (who had the direction of operations on the right,) was to advance by the Williamsburg road, to attack the enemy in front; Gen. Huger, with his division, was to move down the Charles City road, in order to atack in flank the troops who might be engaged with Hill and Longstreet; Gen. Smith was to march to the junction of the New Bridge road and the Nine Mile road, to be in readiness either to fall on Keyes's right flank, or to cover Longstreet's left.

The greater part of the day was lost in vain expectation of Huger's movement—the most important part of the design, as it was to take the enemy's flank and insure his destruction. The movement was disappointed, as Huger could not cross the swollen stream in his front. At a late hour in the afternoon Longstreet determined to move upon the enemy with his own and Hill's division, and accomplish whatever results were possible in the far-spent day. Gen. Johnston remained with Smith on the left, to observe the field.

Through the thick woods, on marshy ground, in water in many places two feet deep, Longstreet's regiments moved on, brushing off occasionally a cloud of skirmishers that disputed their passage. As they came upon the enemy's works, a sheet of fire blazed in their faces. It was sharp, rapid work. Some of the regiments crept through the low brushwood in front of the redoubt, and, at a given signal from the flanking parties, made a rush for the guns, cleared them, and, entering pell-mell into the earthwork, bayonetted all who opposed them. Line after line of the enemy's works was carried; the victorious career of the Confederates swept through his successive camps and entrenchments; and as night fell he had been driven about two miles, and had left a track of retreat through swamp and water red with carnage.

On the left, where Johnston commanded in person, the enemy held his position until dark; Smith's division, with a portion of Whiting's, failing to dislodge him. On this part of the field Gen. Johnston was disabled by a severe wound in the shoulder.

The work of carnage in a few hours of daylight had been terrible The Confederate loss was more than four thousand. That of the enemy was stated in Northern journals to have exceeded ten thousand. McClellan officially states it at 5,739. The visible fruits of our victory were ten pieces of cannon, six thousand stand of arms, one garrison flag, four stand of regimental colors, a large number of tents, besides much camp equipage and stores.

On the following day, June 1, the enemy, having thrown across the Chickahominy two additional divisions, under command of Gen. Sumner, attacked the brigade of Gen. Pickett, which was supported by that of Gen. Pryor. The attack was vigorously repelled by these two brigades, the brunt of the fight falling on General Pickett. This was the last demonstration made by the enemy. This action, really of no consequence, was magnified in McClellan's dispatches as "the Battle of Fair Oaks," thus giving to the Northern public a new and most undue "sensation" to counteract the defeat of the previous important day.

It must be admitted that the Confederate public was but little affected by the victory of Seven Pines. It was a splendid feat of arms; but it accomplished no important results, and the ground which it gained was unimportant, and was speedily abandoned. Had Huger obeyed orders, Johnston might have demolished the enemy; as it was, McClellan's left was routed and demoralized, and we had gained nothing more substantial than a brilliant battle, when it had been intended to have embraced an attack at three points, and probably all along the line, if the enemy had accepted it.

The disabling wound, which Gen. Johnston had received, was the occasion of an important change of military commands. The Confederate Congress had some time ago passed a bill creating the office of commanding general, who should take charge of the military movements of the war. This measure was one of great significance, as the early attempt in the Confederacy to abolish the bipartite character of the Executive office, and to supply *two* agents for the management of the war.

The merits of the proposed reform were long a theme of discussion in the Confederacy. The President in his Executive capacity was the servant of Congress, and, therefore, could have nothing of the dictator in his action; but as "*Imperator*," or commander-in-chief of the army and navy, he might be almost despotic in the exercise of his powers. The army regulations would be his "Constitution;" but with the power to fill courts-martial with his creatures, his authority would be limited very much by his own will, and all appeals from their decisions would be from him the *Imperator* to him the civil magistrate. The theory of such a power was evidently on the verge of despotism. Abolish the *habeas corpus*, and the President, with his full bipartite powers, would be an autocrat, if he had the tact to be so without raising the anger of the people until he estab-

lished himself on firm grounds. Experience in the old Union had sufficiently taught the Confederates what little safety to public liberty was
to be expected from the representatives of the people, when Executive
patronage was brought to bear ; and indicated the additional lesson that
even where the Executive officer had not sufficient ability to be dangerous, he might become the tool of a proscriptive and tyrannical party.

After the first battle of Manassas, a certain adviser of President Davis,
who had some experience of the Congress at Montgomery, and knew the
numerous efforts to shape the action of the government in favour of local
interests, drew his attention to the bipartite nature of his office, and urged
him to assume more of the *Imperator*, as the best and speediest manner
of concentrating our forces for decisive action. From a conscientious
regard to the advisory power of Congress, President Davis then declined
to do this. How could he, as the executive officer of Congress, do it ?
Were not the two offices in one person clearly antagonistic ? The consequence was, that before the end of the first year of the war it was manifest
that a clear head and a vigorous will were wanting in the administration
of military matters. The conclusion came to be almost unanimous in the
public mind that the civil and military affairs of the Confederacy could
not be conducted by one head, and should be separated into two distinct
offices. It was argued that this plan involved the least danger to public
liberty ; that the civil and military powers being, each, in the control of
one clear head and strong hand, would probably be most effectually exercised in the accomplishment of our independence, and that the two heads
would not be as likely to unite for any end injurious to the public liberty
as a Cabinet of weak, plastic characters, put in place and held in hand by
one man.

In consequence of these views, a plan was matured by several leading
Confederate politicians, having for its object the division of the Executive
powers between a civil ruler, who should carry out the designs of Congress
and watch over the liberties of the people and the safety of the Constitution, and a military leader, *Imperator*, or commander-in-chief, who should
be entrusted with the conduct of the war, and look to Congress and the
Executive for the means to carry out his plan.

The scheme was this : Gen. R. E. Lee was to be commander-in-chief
and have the army of the Potomac ; Johnston to be entrusted with the
war in the Valley of the Mississippi East ; Price in Missouri ; Kirby
Smith in Louisiana and Texas ; Bragg in the South ; Beauregard in the
South-east, while Jackson, Longstreet, Hill, Whiting, and the other promising officers were to carry out their views. The commanders of divisions, above named, were to constitute a board of advisers to Congress, and
each to be entrusted with discretionary powers in his own district.

President Davis was probably aware of the details of this early plot against his power. He vetoed the bill creating the office of commanding general. But being personally well affected towards Lee, he took occasion of Johnston's disability to put the first not only in command of the field before Richmond, but to appoint him to the nominal office of commanding general, the order providing that he should "act under direction of the President." It was the successful career of the Confederacy from this date that for a time put out of mind the design upon the military autocracy of President Davis; but we shall hereafter see how this design was renewed, in what portentous circumstances it afterwards appeared, and how it assumed the tone and air of an almost revolutionary demand.

Gen. Lee assumed his new and important command with characteristic simplicity. He was naturally quiet, thoughtful and polite; and he was one of those rare men whose modesty became more conspicuous at each ascending stage of power and responsibility. A stranger would scarcely have recognized in the quiet gentleman who in a plain grey suit, without any insignia of rank, rode each day about the lines of Richmond, scarcely attracting observation, the man whose genius and resources commanded the unbounded confidence and hope of the Confederate people.

THE SEVEN DAYS' BATTLES AROUND RICHMOND.

Gen. Lee's plan of operations around Richmond was soon formed. It was very simple and comprehensive; and is at once understood on a general survey of the positions of the opposing armies. McClellan's base of supplies was near the head of York River. His left was established south of the Chickahominy, between White Oak Swamp and New Bridge, defended by a line of strong works. His right wing lay north of the Chickahominy, extending beyond Mechanicsville, the approaches from the south side being strongly defended by entrenchments. Lee's army was around Richmond; the divisions of Huger and Magruder, supported by those of Longstreet and D. H. Hill, in front of the enemy's left, and that of A. P. Hill extending fom Magruder's left beyond Meadow Bridge.

The intention of the enemy seemed to be to attack Richmond by regular approaches. The strength of his left wing rendered a direct assault injudicious, if not impracticable. It was therefore determined by Gen. Lee to construct defensive lines so as to enable a part of his army to defend the city, and leave the other part free to cross the Chickahominy, and operate on the north bank. By sweeping down the river on that side, and threatening his communications with York river, it was thought that the enemy would be compelled to retreat or give battle out of his entrenchments.

We have already noticed the operations of Gen. Jackson's command, including Ewell's division, in the Shenandoah Valley, and seen how successful they were in diverting the army of McDowell at Fredericksburg from uniting with that of McClellan. It was now important to summon the force to the defence of Richmond, and to do so with secrecy and dispatch. To mask his withdrawal from the Valley at the proper time, Jackson, after the defeat of Fremont and Shields, was reinforced by Whiting's division, composed of Hood's Texas brigade, and his own, under Colonel Law, from Richmond, and that of Lawton from the South. The deception succeeded even beyond expectation; and there is reason to suppose that McClellan remained in profound ignorance of Jackson's movement until his apparition on the lines of Richmond.

According to Lee's general order of battle, Gen. Jackson was to march from Ashland on the 25th of June, in the direction of Slash Church, encamping for the night west of the Central railroad, and to advance at three, A. M., on the 26th, and turn Beaver Dam. A. P. Hill was to cross the Chickahominy at Meadow Bridge, when Jackson's advance beyond that point should be known, and move directly upon Mechanicsville. As soon as the Mechanicsville bridge should be uncovered, Longstreet and D. H. Hill were to cross, the latter to proceed to the support of Jackson, and the former to that of A. P. Hill. The four commands were directed to sweep down the north side of the Chickahominy towards the York River railroad, Jackson on the left and in advance, Longstreet nearest the river and in the rear. Huger and Magruder were ordered to hold their positions against any assault of the enemy, to observe his movements, and follow him closely should he retreat.

Battles of Mechanicsville and Beaver Dam.

A. P. Hill did not commence his movement until three o'clock in the afternoon, when he crossed the river and advanced upon Mechanicsville. This place had been strongly fortified by Fitz-John Porter, whose services as an engineer and artillerist were highly valued by McClellan. As the Confederates advanced on Porter's works, artillery on both sides opened with a terrific roar. A deafening cannonade of half an hour disturbed the last hours of evening. The flash of guns, and long lines of musketry fire could be seen in bright relief against the blue and cloudless sky. As night drew on, a grander scene was presented to the eye. Barns, houses and stacks of hay and straw were in a blaze; and by their light our men were plainly visible rushing across the open spaces through infernal showers of grape. A few moments more and the Federal guns were silent; a loud noise of many voices was heard; and then a long, wild, piercing yell, and the place was ours.

The enemy was now forced to take refuge in his works on the left bank of Beaver Dam creek, about a mile distant. The position was one of extraordinary strength ; the banks of the creek in front were high and almost perpendicular ; the approach to it was over open fields ; there were no bridges, and the difficulty of crossing the stream had been increased by felling the woods on its banks. It was thought that the only possible method in which the position could be attacked was to cross the creek and swamp higher up ; and it was expected that Jackson would pass Beaver Dam above, and turn the enemy's right.

In the meantime Longstreet and D. H. Hill crossed the Mechanicsville bridge as soon as it was uncovered, and could be repaired. It was late before they reached the north bank of the Chickahominy. D. H. Hill's leading brigade under Ripley advanced to the support of the troops engaged, and at a late hour united with Pender's brigade of A. P. Hill's division in an effort to turn the enemy's left. In the excitement and darkness, Ripley advanced his line through the open fields, and had reached the road and swamp in front, when suddenly the enemy opened with grape, at seventy yards, and mowed down whole files of our men. The word to " charge ; " ran from wing to wing, and our men running down the bank to the road beneath, were stopped by the impassable swamp and abattis ; to the right, up the rising road, cannon also blazed in their faces, and well-posted infantry poured in showers of small shot. Retreat was the only alternative, and under cover of the darkness, it was effected with little additional loss. The fire was continued until about nine o'clock in the night, when the engagement ceased ; and thus closed the first day of the battles around Richmond.

In the morning of the 27th June Jackson's arrival on the enemy's left was still looked for. In expectation of it the battle was renewed at dawn. The fight continued with animation for about two hours. As the sun brilliantly rose over the tree-tops, illumining the field, the line of fight with its stream of fire ; bursting of caissons, shouts, yells ; the centre occupied by the strong redoubt ; crowds of combatants rushing in the charge ; soldiers reeling, bleeding, shouting, powder-blackened and fainting, madly firing random shots, and sinking from fatigue, formed a scene that was at once soul-stirring, sublime and horrible. But while this terrible and critical action was going on, Jackson was rapidly approaching to decide it. He had at last succeeded in crossing Beaver Dam creek above the enemy's position ; and the Federals no sooner perceived it than they abandoned their entrenchments, and retired rapidly down the river.

No time was now to be lost. Gen. Lee readily perceived that McClellan had endeavoured to force Porter into an energetic resistance thus far, to gain time to protect his centre on the north bank, situated in the neighbourhood of Gaines' Mills, near the river. As soon as the bridges over Beaver Dam could be repaired the several columns resumed their march. Longstreet and A. P. Hill moved along the edge of the Chickahominy on the rignt ; while Jackson, with whom D. H. Hill had united, was still far to the left, threatening the enemy's right rear as he gradually converged towards the river.

The position which McClellan had taken at Gaines' Mills was evidently intended for a decisive field. Here was to occur the heavy and obstinate battle for Richmond. The enemy occupied a range of hills, with his left on a wooded bluff, which rose abruptly from a deep ravine. The ravine was filled with sharpshooters, to whom its banks gave protection. A second line of infantry was stationed on the side of a hill, behind a breast work of trees, above the first. A third occupied the crest, strengthened with rifle trenches, and crowned with artillery. The approach to this position was over an open plain, about a quarter of a mile wide, commanded by this triple line of fire, and swept by the heavy batteries south of the Chickahominy. In front of his centre and right, the ground was generally open, bounded on the side of our approach by a wood, with dense and tangled undergrowth, and traversed by a sluggish stream which converted the soil into a deep morass.

Gen. Lee, having taken up his headquarters at a house on Hogan's plantation, awaited quietly the moment when his word of command would join the most important battle of the war. It was past noon. The columns of Hill and Longstreet halted in the open ground to await the arrival of Jackson's right at New Cold Harbour. Gen. Lee, quiet and serious, sat alone in the rear portico of Hogan's house. A crowd of military dignitaries were gathered in council upon the front door-steps and on the grassy sward. A low and eager conversation was kept up among them, while the great commander sat alone in thoughtful attitude, his fine, calm, open countenance serious in its expression, but without any line or shadow upon it of weak anxiety or irresolution. Presently a courier dashes up, and delivers a paper to Gen. Lee. As the commander mounts his horse it is understood that Jackson is at hand, and that the time for action has come.

Battle of Gaines' Mills.

Pressing on towards the York River railroad, A. P. Hill, who was in advance, reached the vicinity of New Cold Harbour about two o'clock, where he encountered the enemy. He soon became hotly engaged. The arrival of Jackson on our left was momentarily expected, and it was supposed that his approach would cause the extension of the enemy's line in that direction. Under this impression, Longstreet was held back until this movement should commence. The principal part of the Federal army was now on the north side of the Chickahominy. Hill's single division met this large force with impetuous courage. They drove the enemy back and assailed him in his strong position on the ridge. The battle raged fiercely, and with varying fortune, more than two hours. Three regiments pierced the enemy's line, and forced their way to the crest of the hill on his left, but were compelled to fall back before overwhelming numbers. The superior force of the enemy, assisted by the fire of his batteries, south of the Chickahominy, which played incessantly on our columns as they pressed through the difficulties that obstructed their way, caused them to recoil. Though most of the men had never been under fire until the day before, they were rallied, and in turn, repelled the advance of the enemy. Some brigades were broken, others stubbornly maintained their positions, but it became apparent that the enemy was gradually gaining ground.

Jackson had not yet arrived. It was a critical time. An urgent message was sent by Gen. Lee to Longstreet to make a diversion in favour of the attacking columns. The three brigades under Wilcox were at once ordered forward against the enemy's left flank with this view. Pickett's brigade making a diversion on the left of these brigades, developed the strong position and force of the enemy in Gen. Longstreet's front; and the latter found that he must drive him by direct assault, or abandon the idea of making the diversion. He at once determined to change the feint into an attack, and orders for a general advance were issued. Gen. R. H. Anderson's brigade was divided—part supporting Pickett's in the direct assault, and the other portions guarding the right flank of the brigades under Wilcox.

At this moment Jackson arrived; and the air was now rent with shouts as the combined commands prepared for the final charge of the day. Jackson's right division, that of Whiting, took position on the left of Longstreet. The opportune arrival of this division occupied the entire field. The gallant command of Confederates was now moved forward in the face of three lines of infantry fire, supported by batteries from both sides of the Chickahominy.

With fierce grandeur the charge swept on. On the right the troops pressed steadily forward, unchecked by the terrible fire from the triple lines of infantry on the hill, and the cannon on both sides of the river, which burst upon them as they emerged on the plain. The thousand continuous volleys of musketry seemed mingled into the grand roar of a great cataract, while the louder and deeper discharges of artillery bounded forth over the hills and down the valley, with a volume that seemed to shake the earth. The canopy of smoke was so thick that the sun was gloomily red in the heavens, while the clouds of dust in the rear, caused by the commotion of advancing and retreating squadrons of cavalry, was stifling and blinding. The dead and wounded marked the way of the intrepid advance; Whiting's brave Texans leading, closely followed by their no less daring comrades. The enemy were driven from the ravine to the first line of breastworks, over which our impetuous columns dashed up to the entrenchments on the crest. These were quickly stormed, fourteen pieces of artillery captured, and the enemy driven into the field beyond. Fresh troops came to his support, and he endeavoured repeatedly to rally, but in vain. He was forced back with great slaughter. The retreating columns soon became mingled into one black mass of troops. Night put an end to pursuit, and fell upon the scene of a great Confederate victory. Long lines of dead and wounded marked each stand made by the enemy in his stubborn resistance, and the field over which he retreated was strewn with the slain.*

On the morning of the 28th, it was ascertained that none of the enemy remained in our front north of the Chickahominy. As he might yet intend to give battle to preserve his communications, some cavalry, supported by Ewell's division, was ordered to seize the York River Railroad, and Gen. Stuart, with his main body, to coöperate. When the cavalry reached Dispatch Station, the enemy retreated to the south bank of the river, and burned the railroad bridge. Ewell, coming up shortly afterwards, destroyed a portion of the track. During the forenoon, columns of dust, south of the Chickahominy, showed that the Federal army was in motion. The abandonment of the railroad, and destruction of the bridge, proved that no further attempt would be made to hold that line. But from the position it occupied, the roads which led towards James River, would also enable it to reach the lower bridges over the Chickahominy, and retreat down the Peninsula. In the latter event, it was necessary that our troops should continue on the north bank of the river, and until the intention or Gen. McClellan was discovered, it was deemed injudicious to change their disposition.

* A Texan soldier writes of this charge : " A splendid battery of thirteen guns, manned by regulars, was just beyond, belching forth destruction, and it seemed almost like certain death to venture upon the brow of the hill ; but these were Texans. The most extraordinary fact about it was, that this terrible battle was being fought without any directions from officers on our side. We had lost all our field officers before we got to the first battery—the lieutenant-colonel mortally wounded, since dead ; the major badly wounded, since dead ; and many of the line officers killed or wounded. When I got to the top of that hill, I was almost completely exhausted, but as I got a breath, there I was, able and ready to go on when the word was given. The men had been firing from the brow of the hill, and had shot down many of the artillerymen, and so many of their horses that they could not get their guns away. They stood to their guns well, only running when they could do nothing else. We pushed forward, and placed our colours upon the battery, but as the enemy were still firing upon us, we commenced firing in return. Pretty soon a strong force opened fire upon our left, and changing our front in that direction, we poured in a heavy fire, which soon brought them to taw, as the greater part of two regiments threw down their arms, and ran to us, bringing their colours. Having delivered them over to another brigade, we pressed on in front, and drove the last Yankee from the field. As night was coming on, we were halted, and drawn up in line of battle. It was, indeed, a sad sight to look at the old regiment, a mere squad of noble men, gathered around their tattered colours. I could not realize that this little band of fifty or sixty men was the Fourth Texas. But it was even so. Out of five hundred and thirty men who went into the fight, there were two hundred and fifty-six killed, wounded, or missing : while many were completely broken down, and nearly every one was struck or grazed. We staid here all night without interruption, being heavily rein forced during the night."

During the afternoon and night of the 28th, the signs of a general movement were apparent, and no indications of his approach to the lower bridges of the Chickahominy having been discovered by the pickets in observation at those points, it became manifest that Gen. McClellan was retreating to the James River.

It had been the part of Magruder and Huger to watch the enemy, and to cut off or press his retreat. The battle of Gaines' Mills had forced McClellan from his original strongholds on the north side of the Chickahominy, and, with his communications cut off on the Pamunkey River, and encountered by the force on the south side of the Chickahominy, it was supposed that he would be unable to extricate himself from his position without a capitulation. But the enemy had been imperfectly watched at a conjuncture the most critical of the contest; a great and almost irreparable errour had been committed; and McClellan had succeeded in massing his entire force, and taking up a line of retreat by which he hoped to reach the cover of his gunboats on the James.

Early in the morning of the 29th, the pickets at Magruder's and Huger's front were attacked in force, but instead of giving ground, drove the enemy down the roads and through the woods, into and past their breastworks, and found them deserted. Far from profiting by this discovery, and commencing the pursuit, these Generals allowed the foe to pass across their front, instead of piercing his line of retreat by advancing down the Nine Mile road, the railroad, and the Williamsburg road, which would have cut these forces of the enemy into so many fragments.

The works abandoned by McClellan consisted of long lines of casemated batteries, and were found to be formidable and elaborate. An immense destruction of stores had been accomplished here. The neighboring fields and woods were covered with every description of clothing and camp equipage. There was every indication that the enemy had left his encampment in haste and disorder. In one place there were four tiers of barrels, fifty yards square, in a blaze, scores of barrels being all strewn around, which had contained ground coffee, sugar, rice, molasses, salt, tea, crackers, flour meal, etc., the heads of the barrels being broken and their contents strewn on the ground.

Battle of Savage Station.

Early on the 29th, Longstreet and A. P. Hill were ordered to recross the Chickahominy at New Bridge, and move by the Darbytown to the Long Bridge road. As soon as the retreat of the enemy was discovered, Gens. Huger and Magruder were ordered in pursuit, the former by the Charles City road, so as to take the Federal army in flank, and the latter by the Williamsburg road, to attack its rear. Jackson was directed to cross at Grapevine Bridge and move down the south side of the Chickahominy.

Magruder reached the vicinity of Savage Station about noon, where he came upon the rear guard of the retreating army.

McClellan's advance column had already been swallowed in the maw of the dreary forest. It swept onward fast and furious. Pioneer bands rushed along in front, clearing and repairing the single road; reconnoissance officers were seeking new routes for a haven of rest and safety. The Confederates were in the rear, pressing on with fearful power; and there was yet an expectation that Jackson's flank movement might cut off the retreat. Moments seemed hours. Back and forth dashed hot riders. Caravans of wagons, artillery, horsemen, soldiers, camp-followers, pressed through the narrow road, and at intervals swept onward like an avalanche The trace of agony was on the face of the commander, and the soldiers who carried muskets in their hands could perceive it. Presently the dull boom of a cannon and its echoing shell fell grimly upon the ear, and an ominous roar behind told the enemy that his rear was attacked.

Magruder had struck the enemy's rear; but Jackson had been delayed. The first, under the false impression that the enemy was advancing upon him, sent for reinforcements. Two brigades of Huger's division were ordered to his support, but subsequently withdrawn, it being apparent that the force in Magruder's front was covering the retreat of the main body. Jackson's route led to the flank and rear of Savage Station, but he was delayed by the necessity of reconstructing Grapevine Bridge. Late in the afternoon Magruder attacked the enemy with one of his divisions and two regiments of another. A severe action ensued, and was terminated by night. Owing to the lateness of the hour and the small force employed, the result was not decisive, and the enemy continued his retreat, under cover of darkness, leaving several hundred prisoners, with his dead and wounded, in our hands. The time gained in Magruder's action enabled the retreating column to cross White Oak Swamp without interruption, and destroy the bridge.

Jackson reached Savage Station early on the 30th. He was directed to pursue the enemy on the road he had taken, and Magruder to follow Longstreet by the Darbytown road. As Jackson advanced, his progress was arrested at White Oak Swamp. The enemy occupied the opposite side, and obstinately resisted the reconstruction of the bridge. Longstreet and A. P. Hill, continuing their advance on the 30th, soon came upon the enemy, strongly posted across the Long Bridge road, about a mile from its intersection with the Charles City road. Huger's route led to the right of the position, Jackson's to the rear, and the arrival of their commands was awaited, to begin the attack. On the 29th, Gen. Holmes had crossed from the south side of the James, with part of his division. On the 30th, reinforced by Gen. Wise with a detachment of his brigade, he moved down the river road, and came upon the line of the retreating army near Malvern Hill

Perceiving indications of confusion, Gen. Holmes was ordered to open upon the column with artillery. He soon discovered that a number of batteries, advantageously posted, supported by an infantry force superiour to his own, and assisted by the fire of the gunboats in James River, guarded this part of the line. Magruder, who had reached the Darbytown road, was ordered to reinforce Holmes, but, being at a greater distance than had been supposed, he did not reach the position of the latter in time for an attack. Huger reported that his progress was obstructed; but about 4 P. M., firing was heard in the direction of the Charles City road, which was supposed to indicate his approach. Longstreet immediately opened with one of his batteries, to give notice of his presence. This brought on the engagement; but Huger not coming up, and Jackson having been unable to force the passage of White Oak Swamp, Longstreet and Hill were without the expected support.

Battle of Frazier's Farm.

The superiority of numbers and advantages of position were on the side of the enemy. He occupied the open high lands constituting " Frazier's Farm," five miles northeast of Darbytown. The place was good for defence; the woods right and left of it swarmed with skirmishers; the ascending grade of the road was swept by cannon, while all attempts to flank the enemy's left would meet with broadsides from the gunboats at Curl's Neck, in the James River, two and a half miles distant.

The Confederates pressed forward under an incessant storm of lead; sixteen pieces of artillery belching forth shell, canister, and grape upon them, while they had but one battery on their side, which could not be got into position. The battle raged furiously until nine o'clock in the night. By that time, the enemy had been driven with great slaughter from every position but one, which he maintained until he was able to withdraw under cover of darkness. At the close of the struggle nearly the entire field remained in our possession, covered with the enemy's dead and wounded.

After the engagement, Magruder was recalled, to relieve the troops of Longstreet and Hill. The command of the latter was, indeed, prostrated by almost superhuman exertions. It had won the battle of Mechanicsville, fought five hours at Gaines' Mills, marched over a terrible road and circuitous route of forty miles, and had now borne the chief part in another of the series of engagements that had tracked the lines of Richmond with fire and destruction.

Battle of Malvern Hill.

Early on the 1st of July, Jackson reached the battle-field of the previous day, having succeeded in crossing White Oak Swamp, where he captured a part of the enemy's artillery and a number of prisoners. He was directed to continue the pursuit down the Willis Church road, and soon found the enemy occupying a high range, extending obliquely across the road, in front of Malvern Hill. On this position, of great natural strength, he had concentrated his powerful artillery, supported by masses of infantry, partially protected by earthworks. Immediately in his front the ground was open, varying in width from a quarter to half a mile, and sloping gradually from the crest, was completely swept by the fire of his infantry and artillery. To reach this open ground, our troops had to advance through a broken and thickly-wooded country, traversed, nearly throughout its whole extent, by a swamp passable at but few places, and difficult at those. The whole of it was within range of the batteries on the heights, and the gunboats in the river, under whose incessant fire our movements had to be executed. Jackson formed his line with Whiting's division on his left, and D. H. Hill's on the right, one of Ewell's brigades occupying the interval. The rest of Ewell's, and Jackson's own division were held in reserve. Magruder was directed to take position on Jackson's right, but before his arrival two of Huger's brigades came up and were placed next to Hill. Magruder subsequently formed on the right of these brigades, which, with a third of Huger's, were placed under his command. Longstreet and A. P. Hill were held in reserve, and took no part in the engagement.

The position taken by McClellan enabled him to turn at bay, with his rear protected by the James, and flanks partially covered by gunboats. From the magnificent bluff might be seen the Federal gunboats cruising in the river. The hill was crowned with numerous artillery. Owing to the obstacles presented by the woods and swamp, the Confederates had been unable to bring up sufficient artillery to oppose successfully the extraordinary force of that arm employed by the enemy.

The Confederate line of attack was not formed until a late hour in the afternoon. A general advance was to be made at a given signal. On the left, D. H. Hill pressed forward across the open field, and engaged the enemy gallantly, breaking and driving back his first line; but a simultaneous advance of the other troops not taking place, he found himself unable to maintain the ground he had gained against the overwhelming numbers and numerous batteries of the enemy. Jackson sent to his support his own division and that part of Ewell's which was in reserve, but owing to the increasing darkness and intricacy of the forest and swamp, they did not arrive in time to render the desired assistance. Hill was therefore compelled to abandon part of the ground he had gained, after suffering severe loss.

On the right, a more terrible and dramatic action was to occur. It was past four o'clock, and if anything was to be attempted, the work must be quick and desperate. An order had been dispatched by Gen. Magruder to bring up from all the batteries thirty rifle pieces, if possible, with which he hoped to shatter the enemy's infantry. It was soon evident that the artillery could not get up in time. Magruder determined to trust to the impetuous valour of his troops, and with fifteen thousand infantry to storm the hill at Crew's house. There was a run of more than six hundred yards up a rising ground, an unbroken flat beyond of several hundred yards, one hundred pieces of cannon behind breastworks, and heavy masses of infantry in support! The brigades advanced bravely across the open field, raked by the fire of the cannon, and the musketry of large bodies of infantry. Some were broken and gave way; others approached close to the guns, driving back the infantry, compelling the advanced batteries to retire to escape capture, and mingling their dead with those of the enemy. To add to the horrors of the scene, and the immense slaughter in front of the batteries, the gunboats increased the rapidity of their broadsides, and the immense missiles coursed through the air with great noise, tearing off the tree-tops, and bursting with loud explosions.

Towards sunset the concussion of artillery was terrific; the hill was clothed in sheets of flame; shells raced athwart the horizon; the blaze of the setting sun could scarcely be discovered through the canopy of smoke which floated from the surface of the plains and rivers. Piles of dead lay thick close to the enemy's batteries, and the baleful fires of death yet blazed among the trees, where our shattered columns had sought an imperfect cover behind the slight curtain of the forest.

It was now dark, and little could be done. The attack on Malvern Hill had failed for want of concert among the attacking columns. The assaults of the Confederates were too weak to break the Federal line, and, after struggling gallantly, sustaining and inflicting great loss, they were compelled successively to retire.

But the action of Malvern Hill was to be the last important incident of the drama of Richmond, and another day was to complete and reveal to the world McClellan's grand catastrophe. As night fell, the enemy silently retreated from Malvern Hill. In the morning of the 2d July it was discovered that McClellan had again retired, and was in full retreat, and Lee instantly recommenced the advance, although it rained in floods. But the Federals seemed to have vanished once more in the densely-timbered swamp. The outposts saw no signs of them, and most of the day was lost before it was ascertained whither McClellan had fled. Towards night it was discovered he had conducted his whole force by a narrow road through a thick swampy wood, several miles in extent, and was safe under his gunboats at Harrison's Landing.

McClellan had managed his retreat with skill. He had at last obtained a position on the river, our advance to which could be made but by one road, and that narrow, and swept with numerous artillery. He immediately began to fortify his position, which was flanked on each side by a creek, the approach to his front being commanded by the heavy guns of his shipping in addition to those mounted in his entrenchments. He had reached at last a safe cover for his shattered columns; but after a series of defeats that had demoralized his command, inflicted upon him a loss of not less than twenty thousand in killed and wounded, and was fatal to his designs upon Richmond. The immediate fruits of the Confederate success were the relief of Richmond from a state of siege; the rout of the great army which had so long menaced its safety; more than ten thousand prisoners, including officers of high rank; the capture or destruction of stores of the value of millions, and the acquisition of thirty-five thousand stand of small arms, and fifty-two pieces of superiour artillery.

It is true that this success, great as it was, fell below public expectation in Richmond, which had looked for the capitulation or annihilation of McClellan's entire forces, after they had been driven from the north side of the Chickahominy. Of this disappointment, Gen. Lee writes: "Under ordinary circumstances, the Federal army should have been destroyed. Its escape was due to causes already stated. Prominent among these was the want of correct and timely information. This fact, attributable chiefly to the character of the country, enabled Gen. McClellan skillfully to conceal his retreat, and to add much to the obstructions with which nature had beset the way of our pursuing columns. But regret that more was not accomplished, gives way to gratitude to the Sovereign Ruler of the Universe for the results achieved."

The expression of pious thanks was fervently repeated by Jackson. He wrote, in his official report: "Undying gratitude is due to God for this great victory—by which despondency increased in the North, hope brightened in the South, and the capital of Virginia and of the Confederacy was saved."

It was indeed a glorious success. A week before, and an invading army, superiour to the Confederates in numbers, and in the material of war, closely beleaguered their capital, and vauntingly proclaimed its speedy conquest. Now the remains of that confident and threatening host lay on the banks of James River, anxious only to recruit from the effects of disastrous defeats; and Richmond, erect and exultant, was secure in the protection of an army whose fresh victory had been obtained over a force that had had every resource that could be summoned to its assistance, every possible addition of numbers within the reach of the Federal Government, and every material condition of success to insure for it the great prize of the capital of the Confederacy.

CHAPTER XVIII.

EFFECT OF M'CLELLAN'S DEFEAT IN THE NORTH.—ORGANIZATION OF ANOTHER FEDERAL ARMY UNDER GEN. POPE.—POLITICAL SIGNIFICANCE OF POPE'S APPOINTMENT.—NEW MEASURES OF VIOLENCE IN THE WAR.—M'CLELLAN'S IDEAS OF THE CONDUCT OF THE WAR.—HIS "HARRISON-BAR LETTER."—DIVISIONS OF SENTIMENT IN THE NORTH AS TO THE CHARACTER AND MEASURES OF THE WAR.—POSITION OF THE DEMOCRATIC PARTY.—THE RADICALS IN CONGRESS.—THEIR ANTI-SLAVERY DESIGN.—THEIR THEORY OF REVENGE UPON THE SOUTH.—CARDINAL ERROUR OF THIS POLITICAL SCHOOL.—DECLARATION OF WENDELL PHILLIPS.—SYSTEM OF SPOLIATION AND DISFRANCHISEMENT IN THE SOUTH.—GEN. POPE'S ADDRESS TO HIS ARMY IN VIRGINIA.—HIS WAR UPON NON-COMBATANTS.—LEGALIZATION OF PLUNDER.—IRRUPTION OF THE NORTHERN SPOILSMEN INTO VIRGINIA.—POPE'S MILITARY LINES.—GEN. LEE BETWEEN TWO FORCES.—HE SENDS JACKSON AGAINST POPE.—HE THREATENS M'CLELLAN'S COMMUNICATIONS.—BATTLE OF CEDAR RUN.—BANKS AGAIN DECEIVED BY JACKSON.—A RAPID AND SEVERE ENGAGEMENT.—GEN. LEE MOVES OUT TO THE LINES OF THE RAPPAHANNOCK.—ADVENTUROUS MOVEMENT OF JACKSON TO REACH POPE'S REAR.—HIS PERILOUS POSITION.—HE IS APPARENTLY IN THE JAWS OF DESTRUCTION.—THE AFFAIR OF MANASSAS AND BRISTOE STATION.—THE SECOND BATTLE OF MANASSAS.—LONGSTREET'S MARCH TO REINFORCE JACKSON.—HIS PASSAGE OF THOROUGHFARE GAP.—HIS TIMELY AND CRITICAL ARRIVAL ON THE FIELD OF BATTLE.—A CLOSE CONTEST.—FIGHTING AT TEN PACES.—THE BATTLE OF THE FIRST DAY NOT DECISIVE.—DISPOSITION OF THE TWO ARMIES FOR THE GREAT CONTEST OF THE SECOND DAY.—JACKSON AT CLOSE QUARTERS.—HE DRIVES THE ENEMY.—THE WHOLE CONFEDERATE LINE OF BATTLE ADVANCING.—A SUBLIME SPECTACLE.—SCENES ON THE BANKS OF BULL RUN.—POPE RETREATS TO CENTREVILLE AND THENCE TOWARDS WASHINGTON.—JACKSON STRIKES HIM AGAIN.—ENGAGEMENT AT OX HILL.—POPE'S IMMENSE LOSSES.—HIS ABSURD CLAIM OF VICTORY.—LUDICROUS CORRESPONDENCE BETWEEN POPE AND HALLECK.—RAPID AND BRILLIANT CHANGE IN THE FORTUNES OF THE CONFEDERACY.—THE WAR TRANSFERRED FROM THE INTERIOUR TO THE FRONTIER.—ALARM IN THE NORTH.—POPULARITY IN THE CONFEDERACY OF AN OFFENSIVE WAR.—A TRUE STATEMENT OF GEN. LEE'S DESIGNS IN CROSSING THE UPPER POTOMAC AND INVADING MARYLAND.—WHY HE DID NOT MOVE UPON WASHINGTON AND ALEXANDRIA.—HIS PROCLAMATION AT FREDERICK.—WEAK RESPONSE OF THE MARYLANDERS.—EXPLANATION OF THIS.—CAPTURE OF HARPER'S FERRY, &c. —HOW JACKSON INVESTED IT.—M'CLELLAN AT THE HEAD OF THE FEDERAL ARMY.—HIS INACTIVITY.—HE BECOMES ACQUAINTED WITH LEE'S PLANS BY A CURIOUS ACCIDENT.—HE PRESSES FORWARD TO RELIEVE HARPER'S FERRY.—FIGHT IN BOONESBORO' GAP.—GEN. LEE RETIRES TO SHARPSBURG.—MEANWHILE JACKSON COMPLETES THE REDUCTION OF HARPER'S FERRY.—BATTLE OF SHARPSBURG.—COMPARATIVE STRENGTH OF THE TWO ARMIES.—FLUC-

TUATION OF THE TIDE OF BATTLE ON THE CONFEDERATE LEFT.—REPULSE OF THE ENEMY.
—THE CONFEDERATE CENTRE IS BROKEN AND RECOVERS.—THE ENEMY GETS POSSESSION
OF THE BRIDGE OVER THE ANTIETAM.—THE DAY CLOSES WITH THE ENEMY REPULSED AT
ALL POINTS, AND A VICTORY FOR THE CONFEDERATES.—WHY GEN. LEE DID NOT RENEW
THE BATTLE THE NEXT DAY.—WHY HE RETREATED.—M'CLELLAN'S CLAIM OF VICTORY.—
HOW IT WAS AN AFTERTHOUGHT.—LEE'S ARMY RECRUITING IN VIRGINIA.

THE news of the retreat of the great Federal army under the command
of McClellan from before Richmond to the James River, caused great
excitement throughout the North.   The details of the repulse fell upon the
community with disheartening effect, and produced such a shock as had
not been felt since the commencement of the war.   A fierce clamour was
raised against the unfortunate commander ; and the occasion of the organization and direction of another Federal army against Richmond under
Maj.-Gen. Pope, who had actually crossed the Rappahannock, as if to seize
Gordonsville, and move thence upon the Confederate capital, was busily
used to throw McClellan into the shade, to disparage his career, and to
break down whatever public confidence might yet be disposed to linger in
his name.   Divisions and recriminations between these two grand wings of
the Federal forces in Virginia were early developed.   Several of McClellan's generals of division asked relief from duty under him, regarding him
as inefficient and incompetent, and had been assigned to Pope's army.
The friends of McClellan were not slow to retaliate that Pope was an up-
start and braggart, who by trickery and partisan politics, had become chief
favourite of the Washington Cabinet, and a military impostor, convenient
only as a tool in the hands of the Radical party, who mistook brutality in
the war for vigour, and were for increasing the horrours of hostilities by
emancipating and arming the slaves, legalizing plunder, and making the
invaded country of the South the prey of white brigands and "loyal"
negroes.

The appointment of this man to the command of the Federal forces
gathered on the Rappahannock was significant of the design of the Washington Administration to introduce new measures of violence in the contest, and to re-enter upon the campaign in Virginia with a new trial of
warfare.   The desperate fortunes of the war were now to be prosecuted
with a remarkable exasperation.   Pope was a violent Abolitionist, a furious
politician ; his campaigns in the West had been remarkable only for the
bluster of official despatches, big falsehoods in big print, and a memorable
career of cruelty in Southeastern Missouri.   He had suddenly risen into
favour at Washington.   McDowell, a moderate Democrat, having no sympathy with the Anti-Slavery school of politics—who some months before
had been stationed at Fredericksburg, and was promised chief command
of the movement thence upon Richmond when joined by Banks, Shields,
and Fremont, but whose hopes had been destroyed by the rapid marches

and victories of " Stonewall " Jackson—was humiliated to find his plans and chief command entrusted to an incompetent man, and himself put in an obscure and subordinate position under Pope.

Whatever question there may have been of the military capacity of McClellan, it is certain that there were political reasons at Washington for putting him out of the way. He was a Democrat; his constant interpretation of the war had been that it was a contest for the restoration of the Union, not a war of vengeance, and should not be diverted or degraded from what he esteemed a noble and laudable object, by revengeful designs upon the population of the South and a recourse to savage outrage. He had already obtained certain respect from the people of the South by a studious regard for the rights of private property within the lines of his military command, and his honourable disposition to direct war and deal its penalties against bodies of armed men rather than against the general population of the country without regard to age, sex, and other conditions, appealing to humanity and protected under the civilized code of war. The distressed commander, under the weight of a great defeat, yet had power of mind to write, a few days after his retreat to James River, a letter to President Lincoln, at Washington, which, apart from his military career, must ever remain a monument of honour to his name. The text of this letter deserves to be carefully studied as the exposition of the doctrines of a party in the North, that was for limiting the objects of the war to its original declarations, and conducting it on humane and honourable principles :

" HEADQUARTERS ARMY OF THE POTOMAC,
"CAMP NEAR HARRISON'S LANDING, VA., *July 7*, 1862.

" MR. PRESIDENT : You have been fully informed that the rebel army is in the front, with the purpose of overwhelming us by attacking our positions or reducing us by blocking our river communications. I cannot but regard our condition as critical, and I earnestly desire, in view of possible contingencies, to lay before your excellency, for your private consideration, my general views concerning the existing state of the rebellion, although they do not strictly relate to the situation of this army, or strictly come within the scope of my official duties. These views amount to convictions, and are deeply impressed upon my mind and heart. Our cause must never be abandoned; it is the cause of free institutions and self-government. The Constitution and the Union must be preserved, whatever may be the cost in time, treasure, and blood. If secession is successful, other dissolutions are clearly to be seen in the future. Let neither military disaster, political faction, nor foreign war, shake your settled purpose to enforce the equal operation of the laws of the United States upon the people of every State.

" The time has come when the Government must determine upon a civil and military policy, covering the whole ground of our national trouble.

" The responsibility of determining, declaring, and supporting such civil and military policy, and of directing the whole course of national affairs in regard to the rebellion, must now be assumed and exercised by you, or our cause will be lost. The Constitution gives you power, even for the present terrible exigency.

"This rebellion has assumed the character of a war; as such it should be regarded, and it should be conducted upon the highest principles known to Christian civilization. It should not be a war looking to the subjugation of the people of any State, in any event. It should not be at all a war upon population, but against armed forces and political organizations. Neither confiscation of property, political executions of persons, territorial organizations of States, or forcible abolition of slavery, should be contemplated for a moment.

"In prosecuting the war, all private property and unarmed persons should be strictly protected, subject only to the necessity of military operations; all private property taken for military use should be paid or receipted for; pillage and waste should be treated as high crimes; all unnecessary trespass sternly prohibited, and offensive demeanour by the military towards citizens promptly rebuked. Military arrests should not be tolerated, except in places where active hostilities exist; and oaths, not required by enactments, constitutionally made, should be neither demanded nor received.

"Military government should be confined to the preservation of public order and the protection of political right. Military power should not be allowed to interfere with the relations of servitude, either by supporting or impairing the authority of the master, except for repressing disorders, as in other cases. Slaves, contraband under the act of Congress, seeking military protection, should receive it. The right of the Government to appropriate permanently to its own service slave labour should be asserted, and the right of the owner to compensation therefor should be recognized. This principle might be extended, upon grounds of military necessity and security, to all the slaves of a particular State, thus working manumission in such State; and in Missouri, perhaps in Western Virginia also, and possibly even in Maryland, the expediency of such a measure is only a question of time. A system of policy thus constitutional, and pervaded by the influences of Christianity and freedom, would receive the support of almost all truly loyal men, would deeply impress the rebel masses and all foreign nations, and it might be humbly hoped that it would commend itself to the favour of the Almighty.

"Unless the principles governing the future conduct of our struggle shall be made known and approved, the effort to obtain requisite forces will be almost hopeless. A declaration of radical views, especially upon slavery, will rapidly disintegrate our present armies. The policy of the Government must be supported by concentration of military power. The national forces should not be dispersed in expeditions, posts of occupation, and numerous armies, but should be mainly collected into masses, and brought to bear upon the armies of the Confederate States. Those armies thoroughly defeated, the political structure which they support would soon cease to exist.

"In carrying out any system of policy which you may form, you will require a commander-in-chief of the army, one who possesses your confidence, understands your views, and who is competent to execute your orders, by directing the military forces of the nation to the accomplishment of the objects by you proposed. I do not ask that place for myself. I am willing to serve you in such position as you may assign me, and I will do so as faithfully as ever subordinate served superior.

"I may be on the brink of eternity; and as I hope forgiveness from my Maker, I have written this letter with sincerity towards you and from love for my country.

"Very respectfully, your obedient servant,
"GEORGE B. McCLELLAN,
"Major-General Commanding.

"His Excellency A. LINCOLN, *President.*"

The letter of McClellan was significant of a remarkable division of sentiment in the North on the conduct of the war. That division was apparent in the Federal Congress, and marked by sharp lines of party conflict. The best portion of the Democratic party recognized the true proportions and character of the war; were for according all belligerent rights to the Confederates; and strenuously insisted that its objects should be limited to the restoration of the Union. They claimed that the war for the Union had been cheated of its due effect by the intrusion of sectional rancour and the injudicious or unfaithful acts of agents of the Government. They resisted the inauguration, now attempted at Washington, of a system of spoliation and disfranchisement in the invaded country of the South; they declared that such a system would rob the cause of its sanctity, and render success more difficult of attainment.

The Radical party, on the other hand, which controlled a majority of votes in Congress, were for extending the contest to the extinction of slavery, and punishing the "rebels" with every conceivable means that the quick imagination of hate and revenge could suggest. They could not realize the fact that the contest had risen to the dignity of war. Their great mistake was that they habitually underrated the extent and strength of "the rebellion," just as they had formerly underrated and contemned the grievances of the South and their hold on the Southern mind. They refused to apply even Vattel's test of a civil war, viz.: "that a considerable body of insurgents had risen against the sovereign;" they repudiated all its appurtenances of a humane code of warfare, the exchange of prisoners, etc.; and the consequences of such a theory were constantly recurring difficulties about belligerent rights on sea and land, and inhumanities which would sicken the heart of a savage. In fact, this party cared nothing for the success of the war unless it could be used for purposes of revenge upon the Southern people, and embrace a design upon their institution of slavery. Wendell Phillips, a famous Radical orator in the North, had not hesitated to declare that he would deplore a victory of McClellan, because "the sore would be salved over," and it would only be the victory of a slave Union; and that he thanked Beauregard for marshalling his army before Washington, because it had conferred upon Congress the constitutional power to abolish slavery.

The appointment of John Pope to what was now the most important command in Virginia was a triumph of the Radical party at Washington, and dated that system of spoliation and disfranchisement in the Southern States, now to be distinctly announced in forms of authority and in the text of official orders. Pope assumed his new command in the following address, which long amused the world as a curiosity in military literature and the braggart flourish of a man, whom the Richmond *Examiner* described as "a compound of Bobadil and Munchausen:"

"*To the Officers and Soldiers of the Army of Virginia:*

"By special assignment of the President of the United States, I have assumed command of this army. I have spent two weeks in learning your whereabouts, your condition, and your wants; in preparing you for active operations, and in placing you in positions from which you can act promptly and to the purpose. I have come to you from the West, where we have always seen the backs of our enemies—from an army whose business it has been to seek the adversary, and to beat him when found, whose policy has been attack and not defence. In but one instance has the enemy been able to place our Western armies in a defensive attitude. I presume that I have been called here to pursue the same system, and to lead you against the enemy. It is my purpose to do so, and that speedily. I am sure you long for an opportunity to win the distinction you are capable of achieving—that opportunity I shall endeavour to give you. Meantime I desire you to dismiss from your minds certain phrases which I am sorry to find much in vogue amongst you. I hear constantly of taking strong positions and holding them—of lines of retreat, and of bases of supplies. Let us discard such ideas. The strongest position a soldier should desire to occupy is one from which he can most easily advance against the enemy. Let us study the probable lines of retreat of our opponents, and leave our own to take care of themselves. Let us look before us and not behind. Success and glory are in the advance. Disaster and shame lurk in the rear. Let us act on this understanding, and it is safe to predict that your banners shall be inscribed with many a glorious deed, and that your names will be dear to your countrymen forever.

"JOHN POPE."

He followed this characteristic production with a series of general orders, making war upon the non-combatant population within his lines. He ordered the arrest of citizens, and on their refusing to take an "oath of allegiance," they were to be driven from their homes, and if they returned anywhere within his lines they should be "considered spies, and subjected to the extreme rigour of military law!"

By a general order of the Federal Government, the military commanders of that Government, within the States of Virginia, South Carolina, Georgia, Florida, Alabama, Mississippi, Louisiana, Texas, and Arkansas, were directed to seize and use any property, real or personal, belonging to the inhabitants of this Confederacy which might be necessary or convenient for their several commands, and no provision was made for any compensation to the owners of private property thus seized and appropriated by the military commanders of the enemy.

Pope went further than this authority, for he threw open all the country he occupied or controlled to unlimited spoliation by his soldiers. They were given to understand that they were free to enter upon a campaign of robbery and murder against unarmed citizens and peaceful tillers of the soil. The country was ravaged as by a horde of barbarians. Houses were robbed; cattle were shot dead in the fields; clothing and jewelry were stolen; and nothing was spared in this new irruption of the Northern spoilsmen. A Northern journal, more candid and honourable than its cotemporaries, referring to the depravity of Pope's troops in Virginia, said:

" The new usage which has been instituted in regard to protection of rebel property, and the purpose of the Government to subsist the army as far as practicable upon the enemy's country, has produced a decided revolution in the feelings and practices of the soldiery. Unless these innovations are guarded by far more stringent safeguards against irregular and unauthorized plundering, we shall have let loose upon the country, at the close of the war, a torrent of unbridled and unscrupulous robbers. Rapid strides towards villainy have been made during the last few weeks ; men, who at home would have shuddered at the suggestion of touching another's property, now appropriate remorselessly whatever comes within their reach. Thieving, they imagine, has now become an authorized practice."

The military movements in Virginia were now of surpassing interest. Pope was across the Rappahannock, with a strong advance guard south of Culpepper Court-House, and near Gordonsville. The enemy also appeared in force at Fredericksburg, and threatened the railroad from Gordonsville to Richmond, apparently for the purpose of co-operating with the movement of Pope.

From early indications Gen. Lee was inclined to believe that McClellan would not again operate on the Peninsula, but had concluded to transport most of his forces to the Rappahannock, and form a junction with Pope. But it was necessary to be very careful in making any movement between the two forces, and to await, as far as possible, the full development of the enemy's designs. To meet the advance of Pope, and restrain, as far as possible, the atrocities which he threatened to perpetrate upon defenceless citizens, Gen. Jackson, with his own and Ewell's division, was ordered to proceed towards Gordonsville, on the 13th of July. Upon reaching that vicinity, he ascertained that the force under Gen. Pope was superiour to his own, but the uncertainty that then surrounded the designs of McClellan, rendered it inexpedient to reinforce him from the army at Richmond. He was directed to observe the enemy's movements closely, and to avail himself of any opportunity to attack that might arise.

McClellan, who was still at Westover, on James River, continuing to manifest no intention of resuming active operations, and Gen. Pope's advance having reached the Rapidan, Gen. A. P. Hill, with his division, was ordered, on the 27th of July, to join Gen. Jackson. At the same time, in order to keep McClellan stationary, or, if possible, to cause him to withdraw, Gen. D. H. Hill, commanding south of James River, was directed to threaten his communications, by seizing favourable positions below Westover, from which to attack the transports in the river. That officer selected Coggin's Point, opposite Westover. On the night of the 31st of July, Gen. French, accompanied by Brig.-Gen. Pendleton, chief of artillery, placed forty-three guns in position within range of the enemy's shipping in the river, and of the camps on the north side, upon both of which fire was opened, causing consternation, and inflicting serious damage. The guns were withdrawn before daybreak, with the loss of one killed and two wounded by the gunboats and batteries of the enemy. This attack caused Gen. McClellan to send a strong force to the south bank of the river, which entrenched itself on Coggin's Point.

While the main body of Gen. Lee's army awaited the development of McClellan's intentions, Gen. Jackson, reinforced by A. P. Hill, determined to assume the offensive against Pope, whose army, still superiour in numbers, lay north of the Rapidan.

Only a portion of Gen. Pope's army was at Culpepper Court-House. The forces of Banks and Sigel, and one of the divisions of McDowell's corps, had been concentrated there; Banks' corps being pushed forward five miles south of the town. Gen. Jackson, who was anxious to meet his old acquaintance of the Shenandoah Valley, resolved to attack this portion of the Federal army, before the arrival of the remainder; and on the 7th August moved from Gordonsville for that purpose.

BATTLE OF CEDAR RUN.

On the 9th, Jackson's command arrived within eight miles of Culpepper Court-House, when the enemy was found near Cedar Run, a short distance northwest of Slaughter's Mountain. Early's brigade, of Ewell's division, was thrown forward on the road to Culpepper Court-House. The remaining two brigades, those of Trimble and Hays, diverging to the right, took position on the western slope of Slaughter's Mountain. Jackson's own division, under Brig.-Gen. Winder, was placed on the left of the road. The battle opened with a fierce fire of artillery, which continued for about two hours, during which Gen. Winder, while directing the movements of his batteries, was killed.

It was now above five o'clock in the evening, and there had scarcely been any demonstration beyond that of artillery. Gen. Banks, about this time, sent word to Pope, who was at Culpepper Court-House, seven miles away from the field, that the enemy had made no considerable demonstration upon him, and that he hardly expected a battle that afternoon. But the obtuse Federal commander, despite his lesson in the Shenandoah Valley, was again to be deceived by his wily and vigorous adversary. Banks' courier had but just started, when an advance of the Federal infantry uncovered, what had been unknown to their commander, the flanking force of Confederates on the slopes of the mountain. The infantry fight soon extended to the left and centre. Early became warmly engaged with the enemy on his right and front. He had previously called for reinforcements. As Gen. Hill had arrived with his division, one of his brigades,

Gen. Thomas', was sent to Early, and joined him in time to render efficient service. Whilst the attack upon Early was in progress, the main body of the Federal infantry moved down from the wood, through the corn and wheat-fields, and fell with great vigour upon our extreme left, and, by the force of superior numbers, bearing down all opposition, turned it, and poured a destructive fire into its rear. At this critical moment, Branch's brigade, of Hill's division, with Winder's brigade further to the left, met the Federal forces, flushed with their temporary triumph, and drove them back with terrible slaughter, through the woods. The fight was still maintained with obstinacy, between the enemy and the two brigades just named, when, reinforcements coming up, a general charge was made, which drove the enemy across the field into the opposite woods, strewing the narrow valley with his dead. At every point of their line the Federals fell back. It had been one of the most rapid and severe engagements of the war. The attack of Banks had failed; his centre and left were irreparably broken; and night alone saved him from the severe penalty of pursuit.

The next day, Gen. Jackson remained in position, and, becoming satisfied that Banks had been reinforced, proceeded to bury the dead, and collect the arms from the battle-field, and at night returned to the vicinity of Gordonsville. The official report of his loss was 223 killed and 1,060 wounded. It was closely estimated that the enemy's loss was at least two thousand, including four hundred prisoners in our hands.

Shortly after the victory at Cedar Run, it became apparent to Gen. Lee that Pope's army was being largely increased. The corps of Maj.-Gen. Burnside, from North Carolina, which had reached Fredericksburg, was reported to have moved up the Rappahannock, a few days after the battle, to unite with Gen. Pope, and a part of Gen. McClellan's army was believed to have left Westover for the same purpose. In this condition of affairs it was promptly decided by Gen. Lee, that the most effectual way to relieve Richmond from any danger of attack, would be to reinforce Gen. Jackson, and advance upon Pope. On the 13th August, Maj.-Gen. Longstreet, with his division, and two brigades, under Gen. Hood, were ordered to proceed to Gordonsville. At the same time, Gen. Stuart was directed to move with the main body of his cavalry to that point, leaving a sufficient force to observe the enemy still remaining in Fredericksburg, and to guard the railroad. Gen. R. H. Anderson was also directed to leave his position on James River, and follow Longstreet. On the 16th, the troops began to move from the vicinity of Gordonsville towards the Rapidan, on the north side of which, extending along the Orange and Alexandria Railroad, in the direction of Culpepper Court-House, the Federal army lay in great force.

It was intended that Longstreet and Jackson should cross the Rapidan,

an.1 attack the enemy's left flank; but Pope taking the alarm, nastily retreated beyond the Rappahannock.   While Gen. Lee was making demonstrations at various points of the river, Jackson's forces, some twenty-five
thousand strong, left the main body on the 25th August, and proceeded
towards the head-waters of the Rappahannock.   He was encumbered with
no baggage, and moved with great rapidity.   Crossing the river about
four miles above Waterloo, he pushed rapidly towards Salem, and, turning
the head of his column, proceeded eastward parallel with the Manassas
Gap Railroad, until he reached the village of Gainesville.   The design of
this rapid and adventurous movement of Jackson was, to move around the
enemy's right, so as to strike the Orange and Alexandria Railroad.   Longstreet, in the mean time, was to divert his attention by threatening him in
front, and follow Jackson as soon as the latter should be sufficiently
advanced.

On the 26th August, Gen. Jackson was between the large army of Pope
and the Federal capital.   It was a situation of extreme peril.   He was in
the rear of an enemy much more powerful than himself, far from all supports, liable to be attacked by superiour numbers from Washington, on
the one hand, and in danger of annihilation if Pope should face about and
co-operate with a force moving in that direction.   The enemy was being
heavily reinforced.   The corps of Heintzelman and Porter, probably twenty
thousand strong, joined Pope on the 26th and 27th of August, at Warrenton Junction.   Another portion of McClellan's army, transported from
Westover, consisting of the corps of Franklin and Sumner, were at Alexandria, intending to reinforce Pope's lines; making altogether an array
of force and a situation in which the Federal Government had reason to
expect a certain and splendid victory.   It seemed indeed that Jackson had
marched into the jaws of destruction, and had thrust into Pope's hands the
opportunity of an easy and brilliant conquest.

But Jackson's designs upon Pope's stores at Bristoe and Manassas
Station as well as upon his communications with Washington, were an important part of his expedition, were effectively carried out, and were
accomplished before Pope could realize that such a force was in his rear,
and that the demonstration upon his depots of supplies was not a mere
guerilla foray.   The amount of stores captured by Jackson was large.   At
Manassas, eight pieces of artillery were taken, and more than three hundred prisoners.   Here there was a vast accumulation of supplies: fifty
thousand pounds of bacon, one thousand barrels of corn-beef, two thousand barrels of salt pork, two thousand barrels of flour, quartermasters'
ordnance, and sutlers' stores, deposited in buildings, and filling two trains
of cars.   Having appropriated all that his army could use, Gen. Jackson
ordered the remainder of these stores to be destroyed, to avoid recapture
by the enemy.

On the 27th August, a considerable force of the enemy under Brig.-Gen. Taylor, approached from the direction of Alexandria, and pushed forward boldly towards Manassas Junction. After a sharp engagement, the enemy was routed and driven back, leaving his killed and wounded on the field, Gen. Taylor himself being mortally wounded during the pursuit. In the afternoon, the enemy advanced upon Gen. Ewell at Bristoe, from the direction of Warrenton Junction. They were attacked by three regiments and the batteries of Ewell's division, and two columns, of not less than a brigade each, were broken and repulsed. Their places were soon supplied by fresh troops; and it was apparent the Federal commander had now become aware of the situation of affairs, and had turned upon Gen. Jackson with his whole force. Gen. Ewell, upon perceiving the strength of the enemy, withdrew his command, part of which was at the time engaged, and rejoined Gen. Jackson at Manassas Junction, having first destroyed the railroad bridge over Broad Run. The enemy halted at Bristoe.

THE SECOND BATTLE OF MANASSAS.

It being evident that the design of Pope was to fall upon Jackson, and annihilate him in his isolated position, that alert Confederate commander rapidly withdrew from Manassas, and took a position west of the turnpike road from Warrenton to Alexandria, where he could more rapidly unite with the approaching column of Longstreet.

Taliaferro's division moved, during the night, by the road to Sudley, and crossing the turnpike near Groveton, halted on the west side, where it was joined by the divisions of Hill and Ewell. Perceiving during the afternoon of the 28th, that the enemy, approaching from the direction of Warrenton, was moving down the turnpike towards Alexandria, thus exposing his left flank, Gen. Jackson advanced to attack him. A fierce and sanguinary conflict ensued, which continued until about nine o'clock in the night, when the enemy slowly fell back, and left us in possession of the field.

The next morning, the 29th, the enemy had taken a position to interpose his army between Gen. Jackson and Alexandria, and about ten o'clock, opened with artillery upon the right of Jackson's line. The troops of the latter were disposed in the rear of Groveton, along the line of the unfinished branch of the Manassas Gap Railroad, and extended from a point a short distance west of the turnpike towards Sudley Mill—Jackson's division, under Brig.-Gen. Starke, being on the right, Ewell's, under Gen. Lawton, in the centre, and A. P. Hill on the left. The Federal army was evidently concentrating upon Jackson, with the design of overwhelming him before the arrival of Longstreet.

The latter officer was already approaching the critical field of battle on a rapid march. The preceding day he had reached Thoroughfare Gap— a wild, rude opening through the Bull Run Mountains, varying in width from one hundred to two hundred yards. The enemy held a strong position on the opposite gorge, and had succeeded in getting his sharpshooters in position on the mountain. Brig.-Gen. D. R. Jones advanced two of his brigades rapidly, and soon drove the enemy from his position on the mountain. Brig.-Gen. Hood, with his own and Gen. Whiting's brigade, was ordered, by a footpath over the mountain, to turn the enemy's right, and Brig.-Gen. Wilcox with his own and Brig.-Gen. Featherstone's and Pryor's brigades, was ordered through Hopewell Gap, three miles to our left, to turn the right and attack the enemy in rear. The movement was so successful that the enemy, after a brief resistance, retreated during the night.

Early the next morning, Longstreet's columns were united, and the advance to join Gen. Jackson was resumed. The noise of battle was heard before Longstreet reached Gainesville. The march was quickened. The excitement of battle seemed to give new life and strength to his jaded men. On a rapid march he entered the turnpike near Gainesville, moving down towards Groveton, the head of his column coming upon the field in rear of the enemy's left, which had already opened with artillery upon Jackson's right, as previously described. Longstreet took position on the right of Jackson, Hood's two brigades, supported by Evans, being deployed across the turnpike, and at right angles to it.

The timely appearance of Longstreet gave a new aspect to the field; and the enemy, discovering his movements, showed a disposition to withdraw his left from the attack. He changed his front, so as to meet the advance of Hood and Evans. However, about two o'clock in the afternoon, another effort was directed against Jackson, this time against his left, occupied by the division of Gen. A. P. Hill. The attack was received by his troops with great steadiness. The enemy was repeatedly repulsed, but again pressed the attack with fresh troops. Once he succeeded in penetrating an interval between Gen. Gregg's brigade on the extreme left, and that of Gen. Thomas, but was quickly driven back with great slaughter. The contest was close and obstinate, the combatants sometimes delivering their fire at ten paces. At last Early's brigade was ordered up, and drove the enemy back with heavy loss. While this action was taking place on Jackson's left, Gen. Longstreet ordered Hood and Evans to advance, but before the order could be obeyed, Hood was himself attacked, and his command at once became warmly engaged. Reinforced by Wilcox's and Kemper's brigades, Hood pressed forward; and after a severe contest, the enemy was repulsed, fell back, and was closely followed by our troops, who continued to advance until about nine o'clock in the night, when the action ceased.

The action of this day was not a general or decisive one. The enemy appears to have had no settled plan of attack, and to have experimented on the strength of our lines. But whatever the significance of the action, success was plainly with the Confederates; they had driven the enemy, advanced their positions, and were now prepared for a renewal of the engagement on the scene of the first great battle of the war.

The decisive contest was yet to take place; although Pope, quick to boast, and unscrupulous in his official dispatches, had already telegraphed to Washington that he had won a great victory, and was master of the field. As the morning of the 30th broke, the Confederates were under arms; the pickets of the two armies were within a few hundred yards of each other; and cannonading along the lines betokened the approaching contest. The troops of Jackson and Longstreet maintained their positions of the previous day. Fitzhugh Lee, with three regiments of his cavalry, was posted on Jackson's left, and R. H. Anderson's division, which arrived during the forenoon, was held in reserve near the turnpike. The line of battle stretched for a distance of about five miles from Sudley Springs on the left to the Warrenton road, and thence in an oblique direction towards the southwest. The disposition of the enemy's forces was, Gen. Heintzelman on the extreme right, and Gen. McDowell on the extreme left, while the army corps of Gen. Fitz-John Porter and Sigel, and Reno's division of Gen. Burnside's army, were placed in the centre.

For a good part of the day, the action was fought principally with artillery. But about three o'clock in the afternoon, the enemy having massed his troops in front of Gen. Jackson, advanced against his position in strong force. His front line pushed forward until engaged at close quarters by Jackson's troops, when its progress was checked, and a fierce and bloody struggle ensued. A second and third line, of great strength, moved up to support the first, but in doing so, came within easy range of a position a little in advance of Longstreet's left. He immediately ordered up two batteries, and two others being thrown forward about the same time by Col. S. D. Lee, under their well-directed and destructive fire the supporting lines were broken, and fell back in confusion. Their repeated efforts to rally were unavailing, and Jackson's troops being thus relieved from the pressure of overwhelming numbers, began to press steadily forward, driving the enemy before them. He retreated in confusion, suffering severely from our artillery, which advanced as he retired. Gen. Longstreet, anticipating the order for a general advance, now threw his whole command against the Federal centre and left. Hood's two brigades, followed by Evans, led the attack. R. H. Anderson's division came gallantly to the support of Hood, while the three brigades under Wilcox moved forward on his left, and those of Kemper on his right. D. R. Jones advanced on the extreme right, and the whole line swept steadily on.

The magnificent array swept the enemy before them, pausing only to drive them from each successive position. It was the most sublime spectacle that was ever witnessed on a battle-field. As far as the eye could range, a line of bayonets glittered in the sun. Now it could be observed passing through open fields. Again it would disappear in the woods. A brief pause would ensue, followed by the clatter of artillery riding to the front, and the awful roar of the guns. Then a shout would proclaim that the enemy was again in retreat, and the advance swept on, its bayonets catching now and then the light of the sun, while sheets of artillery fire blazed through clouds of smoke and dust. The ground which the men traversed was in many places red with blood. In wood and field, across creeks and brooks, the roar of battle continued, and long lines of smoke curling over tree-tops wafted away on the evening breeze. Lines of ambulances and stretchers followed the grand advance as it swept on in its deliberate work of destruction, leaving scenes of carnage in its rear. Groans and death-cries arose on every hand, mingling with the distant roar and rush of battle. Still the advance was relentless. As the masses of fugitives were driven across Bull Run, many were literally dragged and crushed under the water, the crowds of frenzied men pressing and trampling upon each other in the stream. The wounded and dying of both armies lined the banks. Some, in the endeavour to drink, had tumbled in, and from weakness unable to extricate themselves, had been drowned; others in the water clung to branches, and thus sustained themselves for a little while, and then were seen to let go their hold and disappear. The meadows were trodden down, wet and bloody. Hundreds of bodies had been ridden over and crushed by artillery or cavalry. In front was the brilliant spectacle of a valourous army in steady, relentless pursuit: in the rear was the ground, torn, scarred, bloody, piled with heaps of dead and dying, as monuments of war's horrours.

The pursuit continued until 10 P. M. The enemy escaped to the strong position of Centreville, about four miles beyond Bull Run, where his flight was arrested by the appearance of the corps of Franklin and Sumner, nineteen thousand strong. The next day Gen. Jackson was directed to proceed by Sudley's Ford to the Little River turnpike, to turn the enemy's right, and intercept his retreat to Washington. Jackson's progress was retarded by the inclemency of the weather and the fatigue of his troops, who, in addition to their arduous marches, had fought three severe engagements in as many days. He reached Little River turnpike in the evening, and the next day, September 1st, advanced by that road towards Fairfax Court House. The enemy, in the meantime, was falling back rapidly towards Washington, and had thrown out a strong force to Germantown, on the Little River turnpike, to cover his line of retreat from Centreville. The advance of Jackson's column encountered the enemy at Ox Hill, near Germantown, about 5 P. M. Line of battle was at once formed, and two brigades of A. P. Hill's division, those of Branch and Field, were thrown forward to attack the enemy, and ascertain his strength and position. A cold and drenching rain-storm drove in the faces of our troops as they advanced and gallantly engaged the enemy. They were subsequently supported by the brigades of Gregg, Thomas, and Pender; also of Hill's division, which, with part of Ewell's, became engaged. The conflict was maintained by the enemy until dark, when he retreated, having lost two general officers, one of whom, Major-Gen. Kearney, was left dead on the field.* Longstreet's command arrived after the action was over, and the next morning it was found that the enemy had conducted his retreat so rapidly, that the attempt to intercept him was abandoned. The proximity of the fortifications around Alexandria and Washington rendered further pursuit useless; and the Confederates rested near Chantilly, the enemy being followed only by the cavalry, who continued to harass him until he reached the shelter of his entrenchments.

In the series of engagements on the plains of Manassas, more' than seven thousand prisoners were taken, in addition to about two thousand wounded left in our hands. Thirty pieces of artillery, upwards of twenty thousand of small arms, numerous colours, and a large amount of stores, besides those taken by Gen. Jackson at Manassas Junction, were captured. Pope confessed to a loss of eight thousand killed and wounded in the battle of the 29th; and it may be safely concluded that in the series of engagements, his total loss was not less than twenty-five thousand.

He had sustained a most decisive defeat. It was a dark hour for the Northern people. Elated by Pope's false dispatches from the field, they had been counting on a splendid victory, and few were prepared to hear of the retreat and total demoralization of the army in three days. Now the war was transferred from the gates of Richmond to those of Washington. It was in vain that the Government in the latter city attempted to misrepresent the situation, and to support Pope's ludicrous claim that he was a victor. Such a claim was actually made by Pope even after he had been driven to Centreville; and the correspondence on that occasion between him and Halleck might be taken as a burlesque on Yankee official dispatches, if the originals did not exist in Washington. On the night of the 30th of August, Pope, at Centreville, had dispatched to Halleck, at Washington: " *The enemy is badly whipped*, and we shall do well enough. *Do not be uneasy.* We will hold our own here. We have delayed the

---

* Gen. Kearney met his death in a singular manner. He was out reconnoitering, when he suddenly came upon a Georgia regiment. Perceiving danger, he shouted, "Don't fire—I'm a friend!" but instantly wheeled his horse round, and, lying flat down upon the animal, had escaped many bullets, when one struck him at the bottom of the spine, and, ranging upwards, killed him almost instantly.

enemy as long as possible without losing the army. We have damaged him heavily, and *I think the army entitled to the gratitude of the coun-try.*" And Halleck replied : " My dear General, you have done nobly." But the Northern public was in no humour to join in the congratulation, or to be amused by such stuff in official dispatches. A terrible situation was before their eyes. The Confederates had won the crowning victory of the campaign in Virginia ; they would certainly attempt a new adven-ture ; and so greatly had they risen in the opinion of their enemies, that no project was thought too extravagant, or enterprise too daring, for the troops of Lee and Jackson.

The change in the fortunes of the Confederacy had been rapid, deci-sive, and brilliant. The armies of Gens. McClellan and Pope had now been brought back to the point from which they set out on the campaigns of the spring and summer. The objects of those campaigns had been frus-trated, and the designs of the enemy on the coast of North Carolina, and in Western Virginia, thwarted by the withdrawal of the main body of his forces from those regions. Northeastern Virginia was freed from the pres-ence of Federal soldiers up to the entrenchments of Washington, and as Lee's army marched towards Leesburg, information was received that the troops which had occupied Winchester had retired to Harper's Ferry and Martinsburg.

The war was thus transferred from the interiour to the frontier ; the supplies of rich and productive districts were made accessible to our armies ; our forces were advancing upon the lines of the Potomac with increased numbers, improved organization, and the prestige of victory ; and the Northern public, which, a little more than two months ago, was expecting the fall of Richmond and the surrender of the Confederate cause, now trembled for Pennsylvania and Ohio, and contemplated the probabili-ty of the Confederate occupation of Washington city.

A large majority of the Southern people had long been in favour of transferring the war to the enemy's country at the earliest practicable moment. Their own experiences of the rigour of the war made them naturally anxious to visit its hardships and penalties upon the Northern people in their own homes ; it was declared that it was necessary to give the enemy some other realization of the war than that of an immense money job, in which many profited ; and military science was adduced to explain that the offensive was the proper character to give to every war, and that the ulterior design to take it should be the end of all the actions of the belligerents.

On the 3d September, Gen. Lee's army moved towards Leesburg, and it was soon understood that he designed crossing the Upper Potomac, and transferring hostilities to the soil of Maryland. But in this first experi-ment of Confederate invasion, it must be remarked that Gen. Lee's designs and expectations were much more moderate than those commonly enter tained by the Confederate public. He did not desire to permit the season for active operations to pass without endeavouring to inflict further injury upon the enemy; and as the works around Washington and Alexandria were too strong to be attacked, it was decided to find a new field of opera-tions across the Potomac, somewhere between the Blue Ridge and the Federal capital.

When Lee crossed the Potomac, his army still continued to be divided into three commands—viz., the corps of Gen. Jackson, consisting of the divisions of Gens. A. P. Hill, Ewell, and his own division; and that of Gen. Longstreet, composed of the divisions of Gens. McLaws, Walker, Anderson, and Hood; and a division under Gen. D. H. Hill, which usually acted independently of either of the generals commanding corps. The cavalry, under Gen. Stuart, continued to cover the advance of the army. The scene of operations selected was the country between Washington and the range of hills bearing the name of South Mountain, and forming a continuation of the chain of the Blue Ridge on the northern side of the Potomac.

On the 5th September the army crossed the fords of the Potomac, and on the 6th Jackson's corps entered Frederick City (Maryland), situated on the right bank of the Monocacy River, a tributary of the Potomac. The divisions of Longstreet and D. H. Hill followed Jackson's corps across the Potomac, and the line of the Monocacy River was for a short time occu-pied by the Confederate forces.

At Frederick, Gen. Lee issued the following proclamation to the peo-ple of Maryland, to explain the reasons that had induced him to enter their territory, and to reassure their supposed preference for the Confed-erate cause:

"HEADQUARTERS ARMY OF NORTHERN VIRGINIA,
"Near FREDERICK, Monday, Sept. 8th, 1862.

"To THE PEOPLE OF MARYLAND:

"It is right that you should know the purpose that has brought the army under my command within the limits of your State, so far as that purpose concerns yourselves. The people of the Confederate States have long watched with the deepest sympathy the wrongs and outrages that have been inflicted upon the citizens of a commonwealth allied to the States of the South by the strongest social, political, and commercial ties, and re-duced to the condition of a conquered province. Under the pretence of supporting the Constitution, but in violation of its most valuable provisions, your citizens have been arrested and imprisoned, upon no charge, and contrary to all the forms of law. A faith-ful and manly protest against this outrage, made by an illustrious Marylander, to whom, in better days, no citizen appealed for right in vain, was treated with contempt and scorn. The Government of your chief city has been usurped by armed strangers; your Legislature has been dissolved by the unlawful arrest of its members; freedom of speech and of the press has been suppressed; words have been declared offences by an arbitrary decree of the Federal Executive, and citizens ordered to be tried by military commission for what they may dare to speak.

"Believing that the people of Maryland possess a spirit too lofty to submit to such a Government, the people of the South have long wished to aid you in throwing off this foreign yoke, to enable you again to enjoy the inalienable rights of freemen, and restore the independence and sovereignty of your State. In obedience to this wish, our army has come among you, and is prepared to assist you with the power of its arms in regaining the rights of which you have been so unjustly despoiled. This, citizens of Maryland, is our mission, so far as you are concerned. No restraint upon your free will is intended; no intimidation will be allowed within the limits of this army, at least. Marylanders shall once more enjoy their ancient freedom of thought and speech. We know no enemies among you, and will protect all of you, in every opinion. It is for you to decide your destiny, freely, and without constraint. This army will respect your choice, whatever it may be; and while the Southern people will rejoice to welcome you to your natural position among them, they will only welcome you when you come in of your own free will.

"R. E. LEE, *General Commanding.*"

The response of the people of Maryland to this appeal was not what Gen. Lee had been led to expect; it was equivocal, timid, inconsiderable. Instead of the twenty or thirty thousand recruits which he had believed he would obtain on the soil of Maryland, he found the people there content to gaze with wonder on his ragged and poorly-equipped army, but with little disposition to join its ranks. It is true that he had penetrated that part of the State which was not well affected towards the South, but in close neighbourhood and sympathy with Pennsylvania; and that whatever Southern sympathy there might be in Eastern Maryland, and in the noble city of Baltimore, it could scarcely reach him when it was held back at the point of the bayonet, and suppressed in the shadow of Federal forts. Frederick City, indeed, was not without some display of welcome. But expressions of confidence and joy appeared to have been lost in the one prevailing sentiment of wonder that the ragged men, stained with rain, and dust, and dirt, so devoid of all the pomp of war, so unlike what they had been accustomed to see of soldiers, could be the army which had defeated in so many engagements the apparently splendid troops of the North, and which had been heralded by imagination as a shining host, bearing aloft the emblem of victory, and kindling in the breast of the spectator the passion for glory.*

---

* The correspondent of a Northern journal thus writes of the appearance of the famous Jackson and the troops he led into Maryland:

"Old Stonewall was the observed of all observers. He was dressed in the coarsest kind of homespun, seedy and dirty at that; wore an old hat which any Northern beggar would consider an insult to have offered him; and in his general appearance was in no respect to be distinguished from the mongrel, bare-footed crew who followed his fortunes. I had heard much of the decayed appearance of the rebel soldiers, but such a looking crowd! Ireland in her worst straits could present no parallel; and yet they glory in their shame!"

CAPTURE OF HARPER'S FERRY, ETC.

It had been supposed by Gen. Lee that the advance upon Frederick would lead to the evacuation of Martinsburg and Harper's Ferry, thus opening the line of communication through the valley. This not having occurred, it became necessary to dislodge the enemy from those positions, before concentrating the army west of the mountains. To accomplish this with the least delay, Gen. Jackson was directed to proceed with his command to Martinsburg, and, after driving the enemy from that place, to move down the south side of the Potomac upon Harper's Ferry.

On the 14th of September Gen. Jackson had succeeded in investing Harper's Ferry, with its garrison of nearly thirteen thousand men, on three sides. A division of Longstreet's corps, under McLaws, had been sent to attack and shut it up on the Maryland side, and now occupied the fertile tract of country which is enclosed by the continuation of the Maryland Heights and the South Mountain spur of the Blue Ridge. The two ranges run nearly parallel for a little distance from the river, with an intervening space of about two miles in breadth, but the South Mountain branches off in the neighbourhood of Boonsboro', forming what is called the " Pleasant Valley."

But at this time occurred a most critical movement on the part of the enemy, originating in one of those little accidents which sometimes disconcerts the schemes of the greatest commanders. After the defeat of Pope, McClellan had again been placed at the head of the Federal armies in and around Washington. He was evidently at a loss to understand Lee's movements ; he remained inactive for several valuable days ; and he was restrained by President Lincoln's fears, who was anxious lest Gen. Lee, having, by a feint of advance into Maryland, drawn the army from Washington, should turn around and capture the city by a *coup de main*. But accident, at last, revealed to him, not only the precise nature of Lee's plans, but the exact disposition of his forces.

Of the curiosity displayed towards Jackson, a Confederate officer, who shared the campaign in Maryland, gives the following amusing account :

" Crowds were continually hanging round his headquarters, and peeping through the windows, as if anxious to catch him at his " incantations." Others, again, actually thought that he was continually praying, and imagined that angelic spirits were his companions and counsellors ; and it was not until the great man had mounted his old horse, and frequently aired himself in the streets, that many began to think him less than supernatural. His shabby attire and unpretending deportment quite disappointed the many who expected to see a great display of gold lace and feathers ; and when he ordered his guards to clear his quarters of idle crowds, many went away muttering, ' Oh! he's no great shakes after all ! ' "

A copy of the order directing the movement of the army from Frederick had been sent to D. H. Hill; and this vain and petulant officer, in a
moment of passion, had thrown the paper on the ground. It was picked
up by a Federal soldier, and McClellan thus strangely became possessed
of the exact detail of his adversary's plan of operations.

His first thought was to relieve Harper's Ferry. He immediately
began to push forward rapidly, and on the afternoon of the 13th was
reported approaching the pass in South Mountain on the Boonesboro' and
Frederick road. By penetrating the mountains at this point, he would
reach the rear of McLaws, and be enabled to relieve the garrison at Harper's Ferry. To prevent this, Gen. D. H. Hill was directed to guard the
Boonesboro' Gap, and Longstreet ordered to march from Hagerstown to his
support.

The small command of Gen. Hill repelled the repeated assaults of the
Federal army, and held it in check for five hours. Several attacks on the
centre were gallantly repulsed by Colquitt's brigade, and Rodes, on the
left, maintained his position against heavy odds with the utmost tenacity.
Longstreet, leaving one brigade at Hagerstown, had hurried to the assistance of Hill, and reached the scene of action between three and four, P. M.
His troops, much exhausted by a long, rapid march and the heat of the
day, were disposed on both sides of the turnpike. The battle continued
with great animation until night. On the south of the turnpike, the enemy was driven back some distance, and his attack on the centre repulsed
with loss. His great superiourity of numbers enabled him to extend beyond
both of the Confederate flanks. By this means he succeeded in reaching
the summit of the mountain, beyond our left, and pressing heavily from
that direction, gradually forced our troops back, after an obstinate resistance. Darkness put an end to the contest. The effort to force the passage of the mountains had failed, but it was manifest that, without reinforcements, we could not hazard a renewal of the engagement, as the
enemy could easily turn either flank. Information was also received that
another large body of Federal troops had, during the afternoon, forced
their way through Crampton's Gap, only five miles in rear of McLaws.
Under these circumstances, it was determined by Gen. Lee to retire to
Sharpsburg, where he would be upon the flank and rear of the enemy,
should he move against McLaws, and where he could more readily unite
with the rest of the army.

The resistance that had been offered to the enemy at Boonesboro',
secured sufficient time to enable Gen. Jackson to complete the reduction
of Harper's Ferry. On the afternoon of the 14th, when he found that the
troops of Walker and McLaws were in position to coöperate in the attack
he ordered Gen. A. P. Hill to turn the enemy's left flank, and enter Harper's Ferry. Gen. A. P. Hill observing a hill on the enemy's extreme left

occupied by infantry without artillery, and protected only by abattis of felled timber, directed Gen. Pender with his own brigade, and those of Archer and Col. Brockenbrough, to seize the crest, which was done with slight resistance. At the same time he ordered Gens. Branch and Gregg to march along the Shenandoah, and taking advantage of the ravines intersecting its steep banks, to establish themselves on the plain to the left and rear of the enemy's works. This was accomplished during the night. Under the direction of Col. Crutchfield, Gen. Jackson's chief of artillery, ten guns, belonging to Ewell's division, were posted on the east side of the Shenandoah, so as to enfilade the enemy's entrenchments on Bolivar Heights, and take his nearest and most formidable works in reverse. Gen. McLaws, in the meantime, made his preparations to prevent the force which had penetrated at Crampton's Gap from coming to the relief of the garrison.

The attack on the garrison began at dawn. A rapid and vigorous fire was opened from the batteries of Gen. Jackson and those on Maryland and Loudoun Heights. In about two hours the garrison surrendered. Seventy-three pieces of artillery, about thirteen thousand small arms, and a large quantity of military stores, fell into our hands.

Leaving Gen. A. P. Hill to receive the surrender of the Federal troops, and secure the captured property, Gen. Jackson, with his two other divisions, set out at once for Sharpsburg, ordering Gens. McLaws and Walker to follow without delay. Gen. Jackson arrived early on the 16th, and Gen. Walker came up in the afternoon. The progress of McLaws was slow, and he did not reach the battle-field at Sharpsburg, until some time after the engagement of the 17th began.

BATTLE OF SHARPSBURG.

Gen. Lee was now prepared to deliver battle, and to meet the mighty Federal host with about forty thousand men. McClellan's force was certainly not less than ninety thousand men. We have placed here the own official estimate of each commander of the strength of his respective army, as the justest exhibition of the disproportion of the forces joined in the battle of Sharpsburg.

The commands of Longstreet and D. H. Hill occupied a position along the range of hills between the town and the Antietam, nearly parallel to the course of that stream; Longstreet on the right of the road to Boonesboro', and Hill on the left. The extreme left was held by Jackson, his right resting upon the Hagerstown road, and his left extending towards the Potomac.

As the sun of the 17th September rose, the batteries on either side opened fire. The heaviest fire of the enemy's artillery was directed against oui left, and, under cover of it, a large force of infantry attacked Gen. Jackson. This heroic commander held the strongest part of a line which extended over four miles. The advance of the enemy was met by his troops with the utmost resolution, and for several hours the conflict raged with great fury and alternate success. Hood's two brigades were moved to the support of Jackson. The enemy's lines were broken and forced back; but fresh numbers advanced to their support, and the Federals began to gain ground. The desperate resistance they encountered, however, delayed their progress until the troops of Gen. McLaws arrived, and those of Gen. Walker could be brought from the right. With these timely reinforcements the tide changed; the Confederates again advanced, and the enemy were driven back in confusion, closely followed by our troops, beyond the position occupied at the beginning of the engagement. The enemy renewed the assault on our left several times, but was repulsed with loss. He finally ceased to advance his infantry, and for several hours kept up a furious fire from his numerous batteries, under which our troops held their position with great coolness and courage.

The attack on our left was speedily followed by one in heavy force on the centre. This was met by part of Walker's division, and the brigades of G. B. Anderson and Rodes, of D. H. Hill's command, assisted by a few pieces of artillery. The enemy was repulsed, and retired behind the crest of a hill, from which they kept up a desultory fire.

Gen. R. H. Anderson's division came to Hill's support, and formed in rear of his line. At this time, by a mistake of orders, Gen. Rodes' brigade was withdrawn from its position. The enemy immediately pressed through the gap thus created, and G. B. Anderson's brigade was broken, and retired. The heavy masses of the enemy again moved forward, being opposed only by four pieces of artillery, supported by a few hundreds of men, belonging to different brigades. The firm front presented by this small force, and the well directed fire of the artillery, under Captain Miller, of the Washington Artillery, and Captain Boyce's South Carolina battery, checked the progress of the enemy, and in about an hour and a half he retired.

While the attack on the centre and left was in progress, the enemy made repeated efforts to force the passage of the bridge over the Antietam, opposite the right wing of Gen. Longstreet, commanded by Brig.-Gen. D. R. Jones. This bridge was defended by Gen. Toombs with two regiments of his brigade. Gen. Toombs' small command repulsed five different assaults, made by a greatly superiour force, and maintained its position with distinguished gallantry.

In the afternoon, the enemy began to extend his line, as if to cross the Antietam below the bridge, and at four, P. M., Toombs' regiments retired from the position they had so bravely held. The enemy immediately crossed the bridge in large numbers, and advanced against Gen. Jones, who held the crest with less than two thousand men. After a determined and brave resistance, he was forced to give way, and the enemy gained the summit.

Gen. A. P. Hill had arrived from Harper's Ferry, having left that place at half-past seven, A. M. He was now ordered to reinforce Gen. Jones. Hill's batteries were thrown forward, and united their fire with those of Gen. Jones. The progress of the enemy was immediately arrested, and his line began to waver. At this moment Gen. Jones ordered Toombs to charge the flank, while Archer, supported by Branch and Gregg, moved upon the front of the Federal line. The enemy made a brief resistance, then broke, and retreated in confusion towards the Antietam, pursued by the troops of Hill and Jones, until he reached the protection of the batteries on the opposite side of the river.

It was now nearly dark, and the enemy had massed a number of batteries to sweep the approaches to the Antietam, on the opposite side of which the corps of Gen. Porter, which had not been engaged, now appeared, to dispute our advance. Our troops were much exhausted, and greatly reduced in numbers by fatigue and the casualties of battle. Under these circumstances, it was deemed injudicious to push our advantage further, in the face of fresh troops of the enemy much exceeding the number of our own. They were accordingly recalled.

This repulse of the enemy ended the engagement. The sum of the day's work was, that every effort of the enemy to dislodge us from our position had been defeated with severe loss. The conflict had been protracted and sanguinary. The spoils of the victory were not great. A few prisoners and guns were taken. As for our loss, it had indeed been heavy, amounting to not less than two thousand killed and six thousand wounded; including among the former, two general officers, Gens. Branch and Starke. The Federals, having been the assailants, their loss was yet more severe, reaching the terrible aggregate of twelve thousand dead or disabled men. Their sacrifice of officers had been serious. Gens. Mansfield and Reno were killed, and twelve other Generals were among the wounded.

Gen. Lee had especial reasons for not renewing the battle the next day. The arduous service in which his troops had been engaged, their great privations of rest and food, and the long marches, without shoes, over mountain roads, had greatly reduced their ranks before the action began; and they had been seriously diminished in the terrible action they had just fought. Although too weak to assume the offensive, Gen. Lee awaited without apprehension a renewal of the attack. The day passed without any demonstration on the part of the enemy, who, from the reports received, was expecting the arrival of reinforcements. As Gen. Lee could not look for a material increase of strength, and the enemy's numbers could be largely and rapidly augmented, it was not thought to be prudent to wait until he should be ready again to offer battle. During the night of the 18th September, his army was accordingly withdrawn to the south side of the Potomac, crossing near Shepherdstown without loss or molestation.

It is curious to observe by what successive steps the North constructed the pretence of a victory at Sharpsburg. McClellan never claimed a victory until assured of Lee's retreat into Virginia. On the 19th, he telegraphed to Washington : " I do not know if the enemy is falling back to an interiour position, or recrossing the river. We may safely claim the victory as ours." He did not assert this until more than thirty hours had elapsed subsequent to the engagement at Sharpsburg ! Some few hours after the above telegram, he consoled the authorities at Washington by saying : " Our victory is complete ! The enemy is driven back into Virginia. Maryland and Pennsylvania are now safe ! "

If McClellan was under the impression that he had won a victory, he showed but little disposition to improve it, or to gather its fruits. He attempted no pursuit ; and when, some days later, a force he had thrown across the Potomac was dislodged by an attack of A. P. Hill's division, he wrote to Washington asking for reinforcements ; and on the 27th September renewed the application, stating his purpose to be to hold the army where it was, and to attack Lee, *should he attempt to recross into Maryland*. Meanwhile the Confederate army moved leisurely towards Martinsburg, and remained in the vicinity of Bunker Hill and Winchester, to recruit after a campaign which has few parallels in history for active operation and brilliant results.

CHAPTER XIX.

THE WESTERN THEATRE OF THE WAR.—VALLEY OF THE MISSISSIPPI.—EVACUATION OF CORINTH.—IMPORTANT OBJECTS OF THE MOVEMENT.—ITS SUCCESS.—THE HALLECK-POPE DISPATCH.—AN ENORMOUS FALSEHOOD.—GEN. BEAUREGARD'S COMMENTS ON IT.—CAPTURE OF MEMPHIS.—AN UNEQUAL FIGHT ON THE RIVER.—BOMBARDMENT OF VICKSBURG.— GREAT IMPORTANCE OF THIS POINT.—PREPARATIONS FOR ITS DEFENCE BY VAN DORN.— THE IRON-CLAD ARKANSAS.—SHE RUNS THE GAUNTLET OF THE ENEMY'S FLEET.—THRILL-ING SCENE OF THE ADVENTURE.—FAILURE OF THE FIRST ATTEMPT OF THE ENEMY UPON VICKSBURG.—ENGAGEMENT AT BATON ROUGE.—SUCCESS OF BRECKINRIDGE'S ATTACK.— HE WAITS FOR THE IRON-CLAD ARKANSAS.—SHE BECOMES UNMANAGEABLE AND IS FIRED BY HER CREW.—WITHDRAWAL OF BRECKINRIDGE FROM BATON ROUGE.—CONFEDERATE OCCUPATION OF PORT HUDSON.—THE KENTUCKY CAMPAIGN.—GEN. BRAGG IN COMMAND OF THE CONFEDERATE ARMY IN THE WEST.—HOW GEN. BEAUREGARD WAS RETIRED.— BRAGG'S PLAN OF OPERATIONS AGAINST KENTUCKY.—MORGAN'S RAID.—DISPOSITION OF THE FEDERAL FORCES WEST OF THE ALLEGHANY MOUNTAINS.—CO-OPERATION OF KIRBY SMITH WITH BRAGG'S COLUMN.—BATTLE OF RICHMOND.—KIRBY SMITH IN A POSITION TO THREATEN BOTH CINCINNATI AND LOUISVILLE.—BRAGG'S MOVEMENT TO INTERCEPT BUELL.—THE LATTER CONCENTRATING AT BOWLING GREEN.—GREAT SUCCESS OF BRAGG'S MOVEMENT SO FAR—HIS BOASTFUL DISPATCH TO RICHMOND.—HIS POLITICAL OBJECT IN INVADING KENTUCKY.—HIS PROCLAMATION AT GLASGOW.—SURRENDER OF THE FEDERAL GARRISON AT MUMFORDSVILLE.—BRAGG'S WHOLE ARMY BETWEEN NASH-VILLE AND LOUISVILLE.—HIS SPLENDID OPPORTUNITY.—HE DOES NOT USE IT.—HE PERMITS BUELL TO PASS TO LOUISVILLE WITHOUT A BATTLE.—HIS WEAK EXCUSE FOR A FATAL ERROUR.—THE FEDERALS NOW ABLE TO RESUME THE OFFENSIVE IN KENTUCKY. —BRAGG'S UNCERTAIN MOVEMENTS.—HIS DISARRANGED PLAN OF BATTLE.—GEN. POLK'S DISOBEDIENCE OF ORDERS.—BATTLE OF PERRYVILLE.—BRAGG'S UNFORTUNATE DISTRIBU-TION OF FORCES.—MISAPPREHENSION OF KIRBY SMITH.—WITHERS' DIVISION NOT IN THE FIGHT.—THE ENEMY DRIVEN.—ARRIVAL OF ANOTHER OF HIS CORPS UPON THE FIELD.—BRAGG RETIRES UPON BRYANTSVILLE.—HE DETERMINES TO EVACUATE KENTUCKY. —RETREAT THROUGH CUMBERLAND GAP.—DISAPPOINTMENT AT RICHMOND.—ERROURS OF THE KENTUCKY CAMPAIGN.—HOW FAR IT WAS A CONFEDERATE SUCCESS.—ITS LARGE CAPTURES.—NORTH ALABAMA AND MIDDLE TENNESSEE REDEEMED.—BRAGG IN FRONT OF NASHVILLE.—OPERATIONS IN THE SOUTHWEST.—BATTLE OF CORINTH.—MOVEMENTS OF VAN DORN AND PRICE.—THE AFFAIR OF IUKA.—VAN DORN'S REASONS FOR ATTACK-ING CORINTH.—GALLANT AND IMPETUOUS CHARGE OF PRICE'S TROOPS.—THE SECOND DAY'S FIGHT.—MISMANAGEMENT OF THE ATTACK ON THE ENEMY'S WORKS.—TERRIBLE

SLAUGHTER AT COLLEGE HILL.—THE CONFEDERATES REPULSED.—AFFAIR ON THE HATCHIE
RIVER.—VAN DORN'S RETREAT.—REVIEW OF THE SUMMER AND AUTUMN CAMPAIGNS OF
1862.—GLORY OF THE CONFEDERATE ARMS.—REFLECTION OF THE LONDON TIMES ON THE
" NEW NATIONALITY."

WHILE the events we have related in the two preceding chapters were
taking place in Virginia and on its borders, an important campaign was
occurring in the country west of the Alleghany Mountains, and in the
valley of the Mississippi River; and while Lee entered Maryland, Bragg
invaded Kentucky, threatening the line of the Ohio, thus in every direction
bringing the front of the war to the enemy's own territory. But before
reaching that period wherein the Confederate arms in the West were
carried to the frontier, as by a parallel movement with the operations in
Virginia, it is necessary to recount a number of preceding events in the
Western theatres of the war, in which the lights of victory and shadows
of defeat were strangely mingled.

EVACUATION OF CORINTH.

At the last point of our narrative of operations in the West, Gen.
Beauregard was holding Corinth; an important strategic position, protecting his communications by the two railroads intersecting there. The
trans-Mississippi campaign being considered closed for some time, Price
and Van Dorn, with a division of Missourians and some Arkansas troops,
had crossed the Mississippi and joined Beauregard, with a view of operating on the east bank of the river. It was soon ascertained that the
immense forces of Grant and Buell, combined under command of Halleck,
were slowly advancing. The movement of the enemy threatened Beauregard's left, along the Mobile and Ohio railroad, while he had already
pushed along the Memphis and Charleston road, camping about three
miles from Corinth. To foil the design of the enemy; to protect his
most important line of Southern communication; to obtain a better
position to fortify; and to secure the health of his troops, Gen. Beauregard decided to evacuate Corinth. The objects of the movement were
all important. Our main railroad communication with Richmond via
Chattanooga, was in the enemy's possession, and the only line of communication we now had with the Confederate capital was the devious
one, by way of Mobile, Alabama, and Georgia. Corinth was indefensible. It was a wretched site for a camp, utterly destitute of water,
good or bad, and what little could be obtained, was scooped up from the
sand, or from pools fed by occasional rains.

The evacuation was commenced on the 30th of May. Remaining in rear of the Tuscumbia and its affluents, some six miles from Corinth, long enough to collect stragglers, Gen. Beauregard resumed his march, concentrating his main forces at Baldwin. On the 7th of June he left Baldwin, it offering no advantages of a defensive character, and assembled the main body of his forces at Tupelo. The position selected was an excellent one to protect the south branches of the Mobile and New Orleans railroads. The movement of Gen. Beauregard was a surprise to the enemy, and a decided success. His effective force did not exceed forty-seven thousand men of all arms, and he had skilfully avoided attack from an enemy superiour in numbers. By holding Corinth, he had gained time, and held the enemy in check without a battle; and by retreating when he did, he out-generaled Halleck, rendered him powerless to move, and saved Mississippi from the inroad of a large army, which would have followed him into the interiour at an earlier season of the year, but was now unable to do so, from weakened forces and the great heats.*

Gen. Halleck attempted to break the news of his discomfiture by a flaming official despatch to Washington, in which he was assisted by Gen. John Pope, then acting under him, to one of the most monstrous falsehoods of the war. This false despatch is so characteristic of the Federal method in dealing with the facts of the war, that it may be copied here for a general lesson to the reader:

* The correspondent of a Northern journal thus betrays the disappointment of the enemy, and he damage to his expectations and plans in Beauregard's evacuation of Corinth:

"I went all over the tented field of the enemy—all over the fortifications—all over the town— talked with the frank druggist and the sturdy Irishman that had worked upon the railroad. And so do I write what I saw in grief, mortification, chagrin, and shame. I said yesterday: 'I'll write no more; others may; I can't. Patriotism will not let me write what I have seen, and can swear to.' When I write such words as I am sometimes compelled to, if I write at all, I am afraid lest, in exposing military imbecility, I shall wound and damage our beautiful commonwealth, that struggles so tremendously for existence and perpetuity.

"But I do religiously believe that it is best now for the commonwealth to hear and heed what is bitter, undisputed fact—the Confederate strategy since the battle of Shiloh has been as successful as it has been superiour. Taking the enemy's stand-point, and writing when and where I do, I cannot possibly imagine how it could have been more eminent for perfection and success. Taking our stand-point—the stand-point of the Union's hopes and Halleck's fame—I cannot possibly imagine how it could have been more mortifyingly disastrous. If the attack at Shiloh was a surprise to Gen. Grant, the evacuation of Corinth was no less a surprise to Gen. Halleck. If the one ruined Grant, the other has laid out in pallid death the military name and fame of Major-Gen. Halleck.

"The druggist says he was two weeks getting away. But aside from such testimony, could the army of Beauregard be removed so cleanly, and completely, and noiselessly, during a night, or day and night, or two days and two nights? Did it require the tremendous concussion of the magazine explosion to get into our ears—what we could not get into our eyes—the evacuation? Why, that was the last act of the mortifying drama. On Friday morning we went in. The prisoners that we captured amounted to about four hundred. Four hundred! Even the beggarly picket regiments and light artillery that fought us so boldly, got away. Those that we caught declare that they were kept in ignorance of the movements at Corinth, and were as much surprised at the evacuation as ourselves. Corinth has been searched in vain for a spiked or disabled gun. Shame on us, what a clean piece of evacuation it was."

"Headquarters, June 4, 1862.

" Gen. Pope, with forty thousand men, is thirty miles south of Corinth, pushing the enemy hard. He already reports ten thousand prisoners and deserters from the enemy, and fifteen thousand stand of arms captured.

" Thousands of the enemy are throwing away their arms. A farmer said, that when Beauregard learned that Col. Elliot had cut the railroad on his line of retreat, he became frantic, and told his men to save themselves the best way they could.

" We have captured nine locomotives and a number of cars. One of the former is already prepared, and is running to-day. Several more will be in running order in two or three days. The result is all I could possibly desire.

" H. W. HALLECK, *Major-General Commanding.*"

Gen. Beauregard's comments on the above, published in the *Mobile Register*, were to the following effect :

"Headquarters, Western Department, June 17th.

" GENTLEMEN: My attention has just been called to the dispatch of Major-Gen. Halleck, commanding the enemy's forces, which, coming from such a source, is most remarkable in one respect—that it contains as many misrepresentations as lines.

" Gen. Pope did not ' push hard ' upon me with forty thousand men thirty miles from Corinth on the 4th inst., for my troops occupied a defensive line in the rear of ' Twenty Mile Creek,' less than twenty-five miles from Corinth, until the 8th inst., when the want of good water induced me to retire at my leisure to a better position. Moreover, if Gen. Pope had attempted, at any time during the retreat from Corinth, to push hard upon me, I would have given him such a lesson as would have checked his ardour ; but he was careful to advance only after my troops had retired from each successive position.

" The retreat was conducted with great order and precision, doing much credit to the officers and men under my orders, and must be looked upon, in every respect, by the country, as equivalent to a brilliant victory.

" Gen. Pope must certainly have dreamed of taking ten thousand prisoners and fifteen thousand stand of arms ; for we positively never lost them. About one or two hundred stragglers would probably cover all the prisoners he took, and about five hundred damaged muskets is all the arms he got. These belonged to a convalescent camp, four miles south of Corinth, evacuated during the night, and were overlooked on account of the darkness. The actual number of prisoners taken during the retreat was about equal on both sides, and they were but few.

" Major-Gen. Halleck must be a very credulous man, indeed, to believe the absurd story of ' that farmer.' He ought to know that the burning of two or more cars on a railroad is not sufficient to make ' Beauregard frantic ' and ridiculous, especially when I expected to hear every moment of the capture of the marauding party, whose departure from Farmington had been communicated to me the day before, and I had given, in consequence, all necessary orders ; but a part of my forces passed Booneville an hour before the arrival of Colonel Elliot's command, and the other part arrived just in time to drive it away and liberate the convalescents captured ; unfortunately, however, not in time to save four of the sick, who were barbarously consumed in the station-house. Let Col. Elliot's name descend to infamy as the author of such a revolting deed. Gen. Halleck did not capture nine locomotives. It was only by the accidental destruction of a bridge, before some trains had passed, that he got seven engines in a damaged condition, the cars having been burned by my orders.

" It is, in fact, easy to see how little the enemy respect truth and justice when speaking of their military operations, especially when, through inability or over-confidence, they meet with deserved failure.

"If the result be all he desired, it can be said that Major-Gen. Halleck is easily satisfied; it remains to be seen whether his Government and people will be of the like opinion.

" I attest that all we lost at Corinth and during the retreat would not amount to one day's expense of his army.   G. T. BEAUREGARD."

CAPTURE OF MEMPHIS.

A few days after Gen. Beauregard's movement from Corinth, the city of Memphis having been abandoned by the Confederate garrison departing to another scene of action, was easily captured by the large Federal fleet in the Mississippi River. The capture was made on the 6th of June. The evacuation of Forts Pillow and Randolph had taken place two days before. In the river near Memphis was a small fleet of Confederate boats. It consisted of the General Van Dorn, (flag-ship,) General Price, General Bragg, Jeff. Thompson, General Lovell, General Beauregard, Sumter, and Little Rebel, all under the command of Com. Montgomery. Each of these boats carried an armament of two guns, with the exception of the Jeff. Thompson, which had four.

The Federal gunboats consisted of the following: the gunboat Benton, (flag-ship of Com. Davis,) mounting fourteen guns; gunboat St. Louis, thirteen guns; gunboat Mound City, thirteen guns; gunboat Louisville, thirteen guns; gunboat Cairo, thirteen guns; gunboat Carondelet, thirteen guns; three mortar-boats, and twenty rams and transports. This overwhelming force advanced, with several of their rams in front, their iron-clad gunboats in the centre, two and three abreast, and their mortar-boats and transports bringing up their rear.

The unequal fight lasted but a few hours. The Jeff. Thompson, Beauregard, Sumter, and Bragg were respectively disabled, run ashore, or set on fire, their crews meanwhile escaping to the woods. The Jeff. Thompson was blown up, the Beauregard sunk near the shore, her upper-works remaining above the surface. The Sumter and Bragg were the only boats that could be brought off, and these were subsequently anchored in front of the city, with the odious flag of the invaders flying at their mast-heads. The Confederate loss did not exceed fifty in killed and wounded, and one hundred prisoners. On the boats captured and destroyed, there was but a small quantity of stores and munitions, and everything in the city of value to the government had been removed. Beyond the mere fact of obtaining possession of the position, the victory of the enemy was a barren one.

BOMBARDMENT OF VICKSBURG.

But the enemy was now to attempt a much more important step towards opening the navigation of the Mississippi River—a result persistently demanded by the Northwestern States as the price of their contributions to the war, and their support of the Administration at Washington.

The Confederates had been prompt to perceive the great importance of Vicksburg; and on the fall of New Orleans, Gen. Lovell had ordered a detail of his force to garrison the place and construct works for its defence. It was the most important point in the Valley of the Mississippi. Thousands of men, supplies, and *matériel* were continually crossing the river—much of our provisions for the armies in the East and West being derived from Texas, parts of Louisiana, and Arkansas. Could the Federals obtain possession of Vicksburg, all the agricultural products of the Northern and Western States would pass down unmolested to the Gulf; the enemy would gain free access to the whole river front, supply themselves abundantly with cotton, sugar, molasses, and other products, disjoin the east and west Mississippi States, and, having the Confederacy fairly on its flanks, could operate with impunity upon numberless points, divide our forces, and open a new prospect of subjugation.

When in the summer of 1862, Gen. Earl Van Dorn was assigned to the defence of Vicksburg, he found the city besieged by a powerful fleet of war vessels, and an army. Many of the citizens retired to the interiour, while the Confederate troops marched in, and pitched their tents in the valleys and on the hills adjacent in convenient position to support batteries and strike assailants. Breckinridge's division occupied the city. Additional guns were brought up from Mobile, from Richmond, from Columbus and elsewhere, and put in battery, preparatory for a grand trial of artillery with the enemy's fleet.

The attacking force of the enemy was at first confined to Porter's mortar fleet, and Farragut's gunboats, with their attendant array in transports, which had ascended the river from New Orleans. The evacuation of Fort Pillow, and the fall of Memphis, opened the new danger of a combination between the upper and lower fleets of the enemy. The junction was effected early in July, and thus a force of more than forty gunboats, mortar-boats, rams and transports lay in menace before the city. On the 12th of July it opened fire.

While the enemy had been completing his preparations for the bombardment of Vicksburg, the Confederates had been engaged in a well-masked enterprise, and Com. Lynch having improvised a ship-yard near

Yazoo City, had been hard at work, night and day, fitting out a ram, called the Arkansas. At the mouth of the Yazoo River, a raft had been built, to afford some sort of protection to the fleet of river passenger and freight boats, that had escaped from New Orleans, and were now concealed in this river, and to put bounds to the enemy's curiosity. One of these vessels was razeed by Com. Lynch, and the construction of the ungainly Arkansas begun. Four large guns were placed aboard; and on the 15th of July, Gen. Van Dorn issued an order to prepare her for immediate and active service, it being intended to use her as part of his force for the relief of Vicksburg.

In the early morning of this day, this rough ungainly vessel, which it was anticipated might compete with the deeds of the famous Virginia in Hampton Roads, passed through the raft of the Yazoo, and commenced the fearful gauntlet of the enemy's vessels drawn up in parallel lines to receive her when passing the channel of the Mississippi River. Frigates, rams, gunboats—all were ready to annihilate that iron-clad mass of timber slowly floating towards them. Presently an iron-clad left her position, and boldly steaming up between the lines of dark hulls, opened fire at a considerable distance. The Arkansas was silent, and nothing was seen but a rush of steam as the monster slowly entered the channel. Once her bow gun was fired, smashing the boiler and machinery of one of the enemy's vessels. A few moments more, and a terrific fire from both of the enemy's squadrons was poured upon the strange vessel, which appeared now as a mass of sparks floating between parallel lines of curling smoke. On the bluff were a thousand breathless spectators of the fearful scene. The Arkansas moved on. Fighting at long range, the Federal fleet slowly followed, and the nearer she approached the bluff, the quicker the Arkansas fought. At last finding her safe under the Confederate batteries, the enemy gave up the chase, and amid cheers from the excited spectators on the bluff and a salvo of artillery, the Arkansas slowly turned the point and was moored before Vicksburg!

With the failure to destroy or take the Arkansas, the siege of Vicksburg practically ended. The attack on the batteries soon ceased, and the enemy, baffled and enraged by an unexpected, determined and persistent defence, vented his wrath in impotent and barbarian effort to destroy the city. On the 27th of July, both fleets disappeared, foiled in their struggle to reduce the place. The casualties on our side, during the entire siege, were twenty-two killed and wounded. Not a gun was dismounted, and but two were temporarily disabled.

ENGAGEMENT AT BATON ROUGE.

Satisfied of the enemy's disappearance from Vicksburg, Gen. Van

Dorn resolved to strike a blow before he had time to organize and mature
a new scheme of assault. The Federals held Baton Rouge, the capital of
Louisiana, forty miles below the mouth of Red River, with a land force of
about three thousand five hundred men, in conjunction with four or five
gunboats, and some transports. It was a matter of great necessity to us
that the navigation of Red River should be opened as high as Vicksburg
Supplies, much needed, existed there, difficult to be obtained from any
other quarter, and strong military reasons demanded that we should hold
the Mississippi at two points, to facilitate communications and co-operation
between Van Dorn's district and the trans-Mississippi department. The
capture of Baton Rouge, and the forces of the enemy at that point, would
open the Mississippi, secure the navigation of Red River, then in a state
of blockade, and might make practicable the recapture of New Orleans.

To secure these objects, orders were given to Gen. Breckinridge to
move upon Baton Rouge with a force of five thousand men, picked from
the troops at Vicksburg, and there was added to his command the effective
force of Gen. Ruggles, then at Camp Moore, making a total force of six
thousand men. To ensure the success of the plan, the Arkansas was ordered to co-operate with the land force by a simultaneous attack from the
river. All damages sustained by the Arkansas from the fleets of the
enemy had been repaired, and when she left the wharf at Vicksburg for
Baton Rouge, she was deemed to be as formidable, in attack or defence, as
when she defied a fleet of forty vessels of war, many of them iron-clads.

By epidemic disease the land force under Gen. Breckinridge was reduced to less than three thousand effective men, within the period of ten
days after he reached Camp Moore. Advised, however, by telegram every
hour of the progress of the Arkansas towards Baton Rouge, and counting
on her co-operation, Breckinridge, on the morning of the 5th August, determined to attack the enemy with his whole effective force, then reduced
o about two thousand five hundred men. The attack was gallantly made ;
and the enemy, driven from all his positions, was forced to seek protection
under the cover of his gunboats.

Breckinridge had listened in vain for the guns of the Arkansas. She
never reached the scene of contest. After arriving within a short distance
of Baton Rouge, in ample time for joint action at the appointed hour of
attack, she had suddenly become unmanageable, from a failure in her
machinery, which all the efforts of her engineers could not repair. Lieut.
Stevens, her commander, moored her to the shore ; and on the cautious
approach of the enemy, he landed her crew, cut her from her moorings,
fired her with his own hands, and turned her adrift down the river. With
every gun shotted, the Confederate flag floating from her prow, and not a
man on board, the Arkansas bore down upon the enemy. It was a strange
spectacle, this vessel, abandoned by commander and crew, and dedicated

to sacrifice, yet fighting a battle like a thing of life. Her guns were discharged as the flames reached them, and when her last shot was fired, the explosion of her magazine ended the brief career of the Arkansas.

Unable, without the co-operation of this vessel, to penetrate the cover of the enemy's gunboats, Gen. Breckinridge withdrew his troops at ten o'clock in the morning. He had fought a brilliant action, but was unable to pursue his victory further. Our casualties amounted to four hundred and sixty-seven. The force of the enemy brought into action was not less than forty-five hundred men. We had eleven pieces of field artillery. They brought to bear on us not less than eighteen pieces, exclusive of the guns of the fleet. In one respect the contrast between the opposing forces was very strking. The Federal troops were well clothed, and their encampments showed the presence of every comfort and even luxury. Our men had little transportation, indifferent food, and no shelter. Half of them had no coats, and hundreds of them were without either shoes or socks; yet no troops ever behaved with greater gallantry, and even reckless audacity.

Advised of the result of Gen. Breckinridge's expedition, Gen. Van Dorn immediately ordered the occupation of Port Hudson, a point selected for its eligibility of defence, and for its capacity for offensive annoyance of the enemy, established batteries, manned them with experienced gunners, and guarded them by an adequate supporting force, holding Baton Rouge, in the meanwhile, in menace. The effect of these operations was the evacuation of Baton Rouge by the enemy, and his disappearance from the Mississippi between the capital of Louisiana and Vicksburg. The results sought by the movement against Baton Rouge were thus, to a great extent, obtained. The Confederates held two points of the Mississippi—more than two hundred miles of distance intervening—unmolested by the enemy, and closed to him. The navigation of the Mississippi River, from the mouth of Red River to Vicksburg, was opened to our commerce, giving us also the important advantage of water connection, by the latter river, with the most important portion of the trans-Mississippi region, from which indispensable supplies were drawn.

THE KENTUCKY CAMPAIGN.

But while the Confederate situation on the Mississippi River was thus satisfactory, Gen. Bragg, who now commanded the whole Confederate army of the West, in place of Gen. Beauregard, was preparing for an important campaign, the object of which was to relieve Western Tennessee and Alabama from the presence of the enemy by an advance against Kentucky, with possibly the ultimate object of capturing and holding Louisville on the Ohio, and occupying permanently the eastern portion of the State.

In the lull of operations incident to the position of his army at Tupelo, after the successful evacuation of Corinth, Gen. Beauregard had sought to recuperate his health by a short respite from duty. He turned over the command to Gen. Bragg, with instructions looking to the preparation of the army for the field at once on his return, which he anticipated would be in three weeks. But no sooner had President Davis heard of this step, than he telegraphed Gen. Bragg to assume permanent command—taking the opportunity to inflict upon Gen. Beauregard a mark of his displeasure, and in fact to encourage the curious report in Richmond that he had become insane, and was no longer fitted for a command.

Gen. Bragg's expedition was preceded by extended raids of Morgan and Forrest into Kentucky and Tennessee. The former, who had at first attracted attention as a captain of irregular cavalry, and was now a brigadier-general in the Confederate service, in the month of July, with a force numbering less than two entire regiments of cavalry, penetrated the State of Kentucky, passed through seventeen towns, destroyed millions of dollars worth of United States property, and returned to Tennessee with a loss in all his engagements of not more than ninety men in killed, wounded, and missing.

The campaign of Gen. Bragg was to take place amid intricate and formidable combinations of the enemy. In the country west of the Alleghany the Federal Government had prepared an extensive programme of operations. In the south, Gen. Butler occupied New Orleans, whilst Admirals Farragut and Porter guarded the Lower Mississippi, and bombarded Vicksburg. Commanding the Army of Tennessee, in the neighbourhood of Corinth, with his advance as far south as Holly Springs and his right at Memphis, was Gen. Grant, with Gens. Sherman, Rosecrans, and McClernand under his command. Further east was the Federal Gen. Mitchell, between Corinth and Chattanooga, opposed to a small force under Gen. Adams; whilst threatening Eastern Tennessee, was Buell's army, and occupying Cumberland Gap, was Gen. Morgan.

Early in August four divisions of Bragg's command were concentrated near Chattanooga, and awaited the arrival of the artillery, cavalry, and baggage train, which necessarily moved across the country by land. A conference was held here with Gen. Kirby Smith, commanding the Department of East Tennessee ; and it was soon determined that all his force should be used to operate upon the enemy's left at Cumberland Gap, and he was requested to confer with Brig.-Gen. Humphrey Marshall, commanding in Southwestern Virginia, with whom he was already in correspondence, to secure his co-operation also in the movement.

After returning to Knoxville, Gen. Smith asked for further assistance :

and two fine brigades, under Brig.-Gen. P. R. Cleburne and Col. Preston Smith were sent to him, in addition to the division which had gone from Tupelo. The remainder of Bragg's immediate command, the Army of the Mississippi, divided between Maj.-Gen. Polk and Hardee, made every preparation, and awaited only its baggage train and artillery to cross the Tennessee River, and enter upon its arduous and perilous campaign over the mountains dividing East and Middle Tennessee.

The movement of the artillery and wagons across the mountain region of North Alabama having been successfully accomplished, late in August, Bragg commenced crossing the river at Chattanooga, with very limited means. The enemy, with a largely superiour force, occupied the lines of the railroads from Decatur to Bridgeport, Alabama, from Decatur to Nashville, and from Nashville to Stevenson, with large detached commands at McMinnville and Cumberland Gap. Having crossed the river at Chattanooga, the column took up its line of march on the 28th August, over Waldron's Ridge and the Cumberland Mountain for Middle Tennessee. Gen. Kirby Smith had already successfully passed through Northeastern Tennessee, and gained the rear of Cumberland Gap, held by the enemy in strong force well fortified.

Leaving a sufficient force to hold the enemy in observation, his dislodgment being considered impracticable, Smith moved, as authorized, with the remainder of his command, on Lexington, Kentucky. This rich country, full of supplies so necessary to us, was represented to be occupied by a force which could make but feeble resistance. Hurrying forward by forced marches through a wild and mountainous country, the Confederates appeared in front of the town of Richmond on the 29th of August.

BATTLE OF RICHMOND.

Gen. Cleburne's division, which was in advance, came upon the enemy's advance about six miles from Richmond, early in the day, and drove it from the field, before the remainder of the column was brought into action.

Falling back about three miles and a half, and receiving reinforcements, the enemy again made a stand, and were again driven from the field in confusion. Gen. Smith did not pursue rapidly, and the enemy formed his line of battle in the outskirts of Richmond, his forces having swelled to the number of ten thousand men, Gen. Nelson commanding.

The enemy's centre and left was here attacked by Preston Smith's division, while Churchill, with a brigade, moved to the left. Under the combined attack, the Federals were utterly routed, and retreated in terrible confusion. A detachment of Confederate cavalry came in upon their flank, and scattered them in all directions, capturing all their artillery and trains. Not a regiment escaped in order. In the last engagement we took prisoners from thirteen regiments. Our loss, killed and wounded, was about four hundred; that of the enemy over one thousand, and his prisoners about five thousand. The immediate fruits of the victory were nine pieces of artillery, some ten thousand small arms, and large quantities of supplies.

Pushing forward from Richmond, the Confederate force entered Lexington on the 2d September, and Frankfort on the 17th, and was thus in a position to threaten either Cincinnati, about eighty miles, or Louisville, about fifty miles distant.

The movement of Kirby Smith made it necessary for Gen. Bragg to intercept Gen. Buell, now rapidly moving towards Nashville, or to move towards the right, so as to secure a junction with Smith when necessary. On reaching Middle Tennessee, it was found that the enemy's main force, by use of railroads and good turnpikes, had concentrated in Nashville, and was strongly fortified. With a heavy demonstration against this position, Bragg's force was thrown rapidly to Glasgow, reaching that point the 13th of September, before any portion of the enemy passed Bowling Green. As soon as the movement was discovered, the enemy moved in haste by rail and turnpike, but reached Bowling Green only in time to find the Confederates had seized and now held both roads near Cave City.

So far the Confederate movements in Kentucky were a decided success, and promised the most important results. The enemy's communications were severed, and his forces separated, whilst our own connections were secured. Without firing a gun, we had also compelled the evacuation of all Northern Alabama and Middle Tennessee, south of the Cumberland. On the 12th September, Bragg sent a fulsome despatch to Richmond, greatly exciting the hopes of the Government there. He telegraphed: "My advance will be in Glasgow to-day, and I shall be with them to-morrow; my whole force will be there on the 14th. We shall then be between Buell and Kirby Smith, for which I have been struggling. The troops are in good tone and condition, somewhat footsore and tired, but cheerful. They have submitted most heroically to privations and hardships, and have maintained their reputation for discipline. Our greatest want has been breadstuffs, but we shall be in a plentiful country at Glasgow and beyond. With arms we can, not only *clear* Tennessee and Kentucky, but I confidently trust, *hold them both*. Gen. Buell, with the larger portion of his army, is concentrating at Bowling Green. From Glasgow we can examine him and decide on the future."

Gen. Bragg had a political object in invading Kentucky, which was to afford a rallying point for what he believed to be the Secession sentiment of the State. From his headquarters at Glasgow he issued a proclamation, informing the people of Kentucky that he had come with the Confederate army of the West to offer them an opportunity to free themselves from the tyranny of a despotic ruler. They came not as conquerours or despoilers, but to restore to them the liberties of which they had been deprived by a cruel and relentless foe ; to guaranty to all the sanctity of their homes and altars, to punish with a rod of iron the despoilers of their peace, and to avenge the cowardly insults to their women.

On the 17th September, the Federal garrison at Mumfordsville surrendered to Gen. Bragg's advanced divisions. Hardee's wing moved by Cave City, direct upon Mumfordsville, and Polk, by another road, crossed the river some miles to the right, and gained the enemy's rear in the afternoon of the 16th. An immediate demand for the surrender of the garrison was made, and the next morning an unconditional surrender was obtained. We secured 4,267 prisoners, 10 pieces of artillery, 5,000 small arms, and a proportional quantity of ammunition, horses, mules, and military stores.

Bragg's whole army was now on the road between Nashville and Louisville—the road by which Buell would be forced to march if he sought to interpose his army between the Confederates and the Ohio. It was apparently an excellent opportunity of striking not only a military but a political blow against the Federal cause in Kentucky. Bragg might press on, and, in conjunction with Kirby Smith, capture Louisville, or he might, with equal forces, meet Buell in the field, and force him back to Nashville. He adopted neither course. After the success of Mumfordsville, he suffered Buell and his wagon trains to pass between him and the Ohio River, almost within sight of his lines, while he marched away to Bardstown, and thence to Frankfort. Thus Buell entered Louisville, and Gen. Morgan, who had, by Kirby Smith's advance, been cut off with his detachment at Cumberland Gap, effected his retreat to Cincinnati ; the first road between Nashville and Louisville having been left open by Bragg's march to Frankfort from the west, the second between Cumberland Gap and Nashville by Kirby Smith's march to the same point from the east, the great opportunity of the Kentucky campaign was lost, and the Federals were able to resume the offensive in that State.

The remarkable failure of Gen. Bragg to deliver battle at Mumfordsville was the subject of much censure and criticism, which never obtained any reply from him but a weak and insufficient explanation in his official report. He there alleged that his movement towards Bardstown was to procure subsistence ; that his army was reduced to three days' rations, and that " a serious engagement would not fail, whatever its results, to materially cripple him."

Gen. Polk, left at Bardstown in command, was directed by Gen. Bragg, if pressed by a force too large to justify his giving battle, to fall back in the direction of the new depot, near Bryantsville, in front of which it was proposed to concentrate for action. Arriving in Lexington on the 1st

October, Gen. Bragg met the Provisional Governor of the State, who had previously been invited to accompany him, and arranged for his installation at the Capitol on the 4th. The available forces of Kirby Smith, just returned to Lexington, were ordered immediately to Frankfort. Learning of a heavy movement of the enemy from Louisville, Gen. Bragg ordered Polk, " to move from Bardstown with his whole available force, by way of Bloomfield towards Frankfort, to strike the enemy in flank and rear," and informed him that Smith would attack in front.

The plan of battle, however, was disarranged, as Polk, after a council of his officers, decided not to risk the attack, but to move as originally instructed by Bragg towards Harrodsburg. Proceeding rapidly to that point himelf, Gen. Bragg was met there by Polk on the 6th of October, with the head of the column which had marched from Bardstown on the 3d. It was now determined to concentrate all the forces in front of Lexington, and to make a battle there. But before this order was put in full operation, information was received that the enemy, in limited force, was pressing upon Gen. Hardee at Perryville ; that he was nowhere concentrated against us, but was moving by separate columns ; his right near Lebanon, a corps in front of Perryville, and his left, two entire corps, extending by way of Macksville to Frankfort, a line of at least sixty miles.

Written orders were given to Gen. Polk to move Cheatham's division, now at Harrodsburg, back to Perryville, and to proceed to that point himself, " attack the enemy immediately, rout him, and then move rapidly to join Maj.-Gen. Smith," as before ordered ; and it was added, " No time should be lost in this movement." Meanwhile, during the same day, Gen. Bragg had received repeated and urgent applications from Gen. Smith (near Frankfort) by express, representing the enemy to be in strong force in his immediate front, and earnestly asking for reinforcements. Accordingly, Withers' division had been detached and sent to him, and was far on the way thither at the time when the movement to Perryville was ordered.

BATTLE OF PERRYVILLE.

It thus happened that by misapprehension, Bragg had made an unfortunate distribution of his forces, and deceived as to the real strength of the enemy in the vicinity of Perryville, was forced to give battle there at serious disadvantage. Polk arrived at Perryville with Cheatham's division before midnight of the 7th, and the troops were placed by Gen. Hardee in the line of battle previously established. Our forces now in this position consisted of three divisions of infantry, about 14,500—and two small brigades of cavalry, about 1,500 strong.

It was past noon of the 8th October when the action commenced. It was fought by our troops with a gallantry and persistent determination to conquer, which the enemy could not resist ; and though he was largely more than two to our one, he was driven from the field with terrible loss. Night closed the operation just as a third corps of the enemy threw the head of its columns against our left flank. We had entire possession of the battle-field, with thousands of the enemy's killed and wounded, several batteries of artillery, and six hundred prisoners.

In the progress of the engagement, we had advanced so far as to expose our left flank to the third corps under McCook, just arrived from the direction of Lebanon. Gen. Bragg, therefore, caused our line, which rested upon the field till midnight, to fall back to its original position.

Assured that the enemy had concentrated his three corps against him, and finding that his loss had already been quite heavy in the unequal contest against the two corps under Crittenden and Gilbert, Gen. Bragg gave the order to fall back at daylight on Harrodsburg, and sent instructions to Smith to move his command to form a junction with him, at that place. Thence, on the 11th, the whole force was retired upon Bryantsville.

Gen. Bragg was now no longer able to attack and rout an enemy largely superiour in numbers ; and to evacuate Kentucky had become an imperative necessity. The season of autumnal rains was approaching ; the rough and uneven roads leading over the stupendous mountains of Eastern Tennessee and Kentucky, to and through Cumberland Gap, would then become utterly impassable to an army. Should Bragg remain till then, and meet with a reverse, his army would be lost. Accordingly all necessary arrangements were made, and the troops put in motion by two columns, under Polk and Smith, on the 13th October for Cumberland Gap. After a rapid march, with some privations in the absence of baggage trains, which had been sent ahead, the Confederate forces passed the Gap with immaterial loss from the 19th to the 24th of October.

This retreat of Bragg was certainly a sore disappointment to the hopes which his first movements in Kentucky had occasioned and his sensational despatches had unduly excited. His campaign was long a theme of violent criticism in the Confederacy. The detachment of Kirby Smith and the operation on different lines in Kentucky ; the loss of the opportunity at Mumfordsville ; and the failure to assemble all the Confederates in the field at Perryville, were pointed out as so many errours in the campaign. But the popular mind in criticising military operations is too prone to forget what is accomplished, while pointing out what might have been attempted. The Kentucky campaign was in a great measure a Confederate success. Though compelled to yield a portion of the valuable territory from which we had driven the enemy, the fruits of the campaign were large. With a force enabling us at no time to put more than forty thousand men, of all arms, and in all places in battle, we had redeemed North

Alabama and Middle Tennessee, and had recovered possession of Cumber-land Gap, the gateway to the heart of the Confederacy. We had killed, wounded, and captured no less than twenty-five thousand of the enemy; taken over thirty pieces of artillery, seventeen thousand small arms, some two million cartridges for the same; destroyed some hundreds of wagons, and brought off several hundred more, with their teams and harness complete; replaced our jaded cavalry horses by a fine mount; lived two months upon supplies wrested from the enemy's possession; secured material to clothe the army; and, finally, secured subsistence from the redeemed country to support not only Bragg's army, but also large forces in other parts of the Confederacy. In four weeks after passing Cumberland Gap, Bragg's army was found, with serried ranks, in front of the enemy at Nashville; better organized, better disciplined, better clothed and fed, in better health and tone, and in larger numbers than when it entered on the campaign, though it had made a march at least three times as long as that of the enemy in reaching the same point, and was moreover entirely self-sustained.

OPERATIONS IN THE SOUTHWEST.—BATTLE OF CORINTH.

When Gen. Bragg moved into Kentucky, he left to Van Dorn and Price the enemy in West Tennessee. These orders were however changed, and Price was directed to follow Rosecrans across the Tennessee River into Middle Tennessee, whither it was then supposed he had gone. To make a demonstration in favour of Price, Gen. Van Dorn marched his whole command on the 20th day of September to within seven miles of Bolivar, driving three brigades of the enemy back to that place, and forcing the return from Corinth of one division, which had been sent there to strengthen Grant's army.

Gen. Price, in obedience to his orders, marched in the direction of Iuka, to cross the Tennessee, but was not long in discovering that Rosecrans had not crossed that stream. This officer, in connection with Grant, attacked him on the 19th day of September, and compelled him to fall back towards Baldwin, on the Mobile and Ohio Railroad. On the 25th Van Dorn received a despatch, by courier, from Price, stating that he was at Baldwin, and was then ready to join with his forces in an attack on Corinth, as had been previously suggested. The forces met at Ripley, on the 28th September, according to agreement, and marched the next morning towards Pocahontas, which place was reached on the 1st October.

The disposition of the enemy's forces at this time was as follows: Sherman, at Memphis, with about six thousand men; Hurlburt, afterwards Ord, at Bolivar, with about eight thousand; Grant (headquarters at Jack son), with about three thousand; Rosecrans at Corinth, with about fifteen thousand, together with the following outposts, viz. : Rienzi, twenty-five hundred; Burnsville, Jacinto, and Iuka, about six thousand; at important bridges, and on garrison duty, about two or three thousand, making in the aggregate about forty-two thousand (42,000) men in West Tennessee. Memphis, Jackson, Bolivar, and Corinth were fortified, the works mounting siege guns, the outposts slightly fortified, having field pieces. Memphis, Bolivar, and Corinth are in the arc of a circle, the chord of which, from Memphis to Corinth, makes an angle with a due east line about fifteen degrees south. Bolivar is about equi-distant from Memphis and Corinth, somewhat nearer the latter, and is at the intersection of the Hatchie River and the Mississippi Central and Ohio Railroad.

It was a situation in which the enemy could scarcely determine at what point the Confederates would make their principal attack. In the event of operations being conducted against Bolivar, Rosecrans was prepared to fall on the Confederate right rear, whilst if Corinth should be attacked, a similar duty would devolve on the garrison of Bolivar.

Gen. Van Dorn determined to attempt Corinth. He had a reasonable hope of success. Field returns at Ripley showed his strength to be about twenty-two thousand men. Rosecrans at Corinth had about fifteen thousand, with about eight thousand additional men at outposts, from twelve to fifteen miles distant. He might surprise him, and carry the place before these troops could be brought in. Van Dorn therefore marched towards Pocahontas, threatening Bolivar, then turned suddenly across the Hatchie and Tuscumbia, and on the morning of the 3d October, attacked Corinth without hesitation, and did surprise that place before the outpost garrisons were called in.

Rosecrans' forces occupied a position outside the defences of the town, three divisions forming the first two lines, and one division slightly in rear as a reserve. He was anxious to retire slowly within the inner line of works, and gave orders to that effect; but Price's troops, flushed with the excitement of an attack, and anxious to wipe out the recollection of their repulse at Iuka, advanced rapidly, and pressed hard on the Federal centre, capturing two guns from Davies' division, and driving the Federals within their inner line of redoubts.

Gen. Van Dorn anticipated an easy success on the following morning, and telegraphed to Richmond the announcement of a great victory. It would seem that he was entirely unaware of the strength of the enemy's works at Corinth, and of the trial which yet remained for the courage and devotion of his troops.

The Confederate plan of battle for the next day was, that Price should open with a large battery of artillery, and then attack in force with his left, and that while thus engaged, Lovell's division should press forward, and attack with vigour on our right. Gen. Hebert, who commanded a division on the left, was to lead in the attack. Daylight came, and there was no attack on the left. Of this failure to execute his orders, Gen. Van Dorn says, in his official report: " A staff officer was sent to Hebert to inquire the cause. That officer could not be found. Another messenger was sent, and a third; and about seven o'clock Gen. Hebert came to my headquarters, and reported sick." Gen. Price then put Brig.-Gen. Green in command of the left wing; and it was eight o'clock before the proper dispositions for the attack at this point were made. In the mean time, the centre, held by Maury's division, became engaged with the enemy's sharp-shooters, and the battle was brought on, and extended along the whole centre and left wing. One brigade after another went gallantly into the action, and, pushing forward through direct and cross-fire, over every obstacle, reached Corinth, and planted their colours on the last stronghold of the enemy. A hand to hand contest was being enacted in the very yard of Gen. Rosecrans' headquarters, and in the streets of the town. The enemy was followed and driven from house to house with great slaughter. In the town were batteries in mask, supported by heavy reserves, behind which the retreating enemy took shelter, and which opened upon our troops a most destructive fire at short range. The heavy guns of College Hill—the enemy's most important work—were for a moment silenced, and all seemed about to be ended, when a heavy fire from fresh troops from Iuka, Burnsville, and Rienzi, that had succeeded in reaching Corinth in time, poured into our thinned ranks.

Our troops gave way. They were pushed down College Hill, and followed by the enemy through the woods and over the ground they had gained by such desperate courage. At the very time the day was lost, Lovell's division was advancing, and was on the point of assaulting the enemy's works, when he received orders to throw one of his brigades (Villepigues') rapidly to the centre, to cover the broken ranks thrown back from Corinth. The movement was well executed, and the enemy did not dare to press his success.

The next day it was determined by Van Dorn to fall back towards Ripley and Oxford, and thus again take position behind the lagoons and swamps of Mississippi. The movement was accomplished with but little molestation from the enemy, beyond an affair in crossing the Hatchie, in which Gen. Ord, who commanded the enemy's advance, was held in check and punished. The following was found to be our loss in the severest conflicts with the enemy, and on the march to and from Corinth, viz.: killed, 594; wounded, 2,162; prisoners and missing, 2,102. One piece of artillery was driven in the night by a mistake into the enemy's lines, and captured. Four pieces were taken at the Hatchie bridge, the horses being shot. Two pieces of artillery were captured from the enemy at Corinth by Gen. Lovell's division, one of which was brought off. Five pieces were also taken by Gen. Price's corps, two of which were brought off—thus resulting in a loss to us of only two pieces. The enemy's loss in killed and wounded, by his own account, was 2,127. We took over three hundred prisoners.

The retreat from Corinth was not a rout. But the engagement there was a serious disaster to the Confederates, and cost Van Dorn his command ; censured as he was for having carried his men against works, the strength of which he had underrated, and then having failed to make proper combinations in the attack. This event may be said to have closed for some time the campaign in the West. It had not completed all the expectations of the Southern public. It is true that the country between Nashville and Chattanooga was re-occupied by the Confederate forces ; but the decisive event of the campaign was the retreat from Kentucky, and as public expectation in the South had been disappointed when Lee retired across the Potomac, so did it experience a similar feeling when it was known that Bragg had retreated through the Cumberland Mountains.

These were the two turning-points of the autumn campaigns of 1862. Whatever the territorial results of these campaigns, their moral effect was great, and the position of the Confederates was now very different from what it had been in the early part of the year. The glory of their arms now attracted the attention of the world. They had carried their arms from Chattanooga to Louisville, and, although forced to retire, had proved that the subjugation of the West was a task which the enemy had only commenced. They had raised the siege of Richmond, threatened Washington, and beaten the enemy back in that quarter to what had been the threshold of the war. The London *Times* declared that the history of these campaigns comprised a list of military achievements almost without parallel, and added : " Whatever may be the fate of the new nationality, or its subsequent claims to the respect of mankind, it will assuredly begin its career with a reputation for genius and valour which the most famous nations may envy."

CHAPTER XX.

Eng.ᵈ by H.B.Hall, N.Y.

GENˡ R. E. LEE

Engraved expressly for the 'Lost Cause' by E. A. Pollard.

ABOUT the close of the year 1862, two heavy battles were fought on the two main theatres of the war, Virginia and Tennessee, and were the great topics of the period referred to.

OPERATIONS IN VIRGINIA.—BATTLE OF FREDERICKSBURG.

After Lee's retreat into Virginia, McClellan appeared to be concentrating in and near Harper's Ferry, but made no forward movement. On the 6th October President Lincoln had ordered an immediate advance, recommending that McClellan should take the interiour line between Washington and Lee's forces, and make an early battle. McClellan hesitated, and seemed disposed to spend time in complaints of inadequate supplies, and in incessant demands for reinforcements. Meanwhile, to ascertain the position and designs of the enemy, Gen. Lee ordered the famous cavalry commander Gen. Stuart to cross the Potomac above Williamsport, to reconnoitre the Federal positions, and, if practicable, to enter Pennsylvania, and do all in his power to impede and embarrass the military operations of the enemy. The order was executed with skill, address, and courage. Gen. Stuart, with twelve or fifteen hundred cavalry, passed through Maryland, occupied Chambersburg, and destroyed a large amount of public property, making the entire circuit of Gen. McClellan's army, and thwarting all the arrangements by which that commander had reported his capture certain.

About the last of October, the Federal army began to incline eastwardly from the mountains, moving in the direction of Warrenton. As soon as this intention developed itself, Longstreet's corps was moved across the Blue Ridge, and about the 3d of November, took position at Culpepper Court House, while Jackson advanced one of his divisions to the east side of the Blue Ridge. The enemy gradually concentrated about Warrenton, his cavalry being thrown forward beyond the Rappahannock, in the direction of Culpepper Court House, and occasionally skirmishing with our own, which was closely observing his movements.

Here McClellan's hesitation and timidity were very evident. Weeks wore on without any decided movement. The beautiful autumn weather had passed, without any demonstration of moment from the enemy, and now cold, bleak November whistled over the fields and mountains of Virginia. But on the 5th of November there was an unusual sensation and stir in the Federal camp, for on that day a messenger arrived at Warrenton, and delivered to McClellan an order to resign the command of the army to Gen. Burnside, and to report himself at Trenton in New Jersey. The order was unexpected. Whatever the military demerits of McClellan,

it was undoubtedly designed at Washington as a *coup d'etat*, with reference
to the fall elections of 1862, and influenced by the argument that a time
when the Administration party was incurring defeat in the elections, it
was dangerous to allow a political opponent to possess the confidence and
to hold the chief command of the main army.

Gen. Burnside found at his command a splendid army. It was now
divided into three grand divisions, each consisting of two corps, and commanded by Gens. Sumner, Hooker, and Franklin. It was at once proposed by Burnside to move from Warrenton to a new line of operations,
and to make a campaign on the Lower Rappahannock. His plan was to
march rapidly down the left bank of that river, to cross by means of pontoons at Fredericksburg, and to advance on Richmond by Hanover Court
House. For this plan of operations against the Confederate capital, the
advantages were claimed that it would avoid the necessity of the long lines
of communication which would have to be held in case of a movement
against Richmond by Gordonsville; that, in fact, the Federal army, after
arriving at Fredericksburg, would be at a point nearer to Richmond than
it would be even if it should take Gordonsville; and that it would all the
time be as near Washington as would be the Confederates, thus covering
that city and defeating the objection to the adoption of the line of the
Peninsular campaign.

On the 15th November, it was known by Gen. Lee that the enemy
was in motion towards the Orange and Alexandria Railroad, and one regiment of infantry, with a battery of light artillery, was sent to reinforce the
garrison at Fredericksburg. On the 17th, it was ascertained that Sumner's
corps had marched from Catlett's Station, in the direction of Falmouth,
and information was also received that, on the 15th, some Federal gunboats
and transports had entered Acquia Creek. This looked as if Fredericksburg was again to be occupied, and McLaws' and Ransom's divisions, accompanied by W. H. Lee's brigade of cavalry and Lane's battery, were
ordered to proceed to that city. To ascertain more fully the movements of
the enemy, Gen. Stuart was directed to cross the Rappahannock. On the
morning of the 18th, he forced a passage at Warrenton Springs, in the face
of a regiment of cavalry and three pieces of artillery, guarding the ford,
and reached Warrenton soon after the last of the enemy's column had left.
The information he obtained confirmed the impression that the whole Federal army, under Burnside, was moving towards Fredericksburg. On the
morning of the 19th, therefore, the remainder of Longstreet's corps was
put in motion for that point.

It arrived there before any large body of the enemy had appeared. It
is true that the Stafford Heights on the north bank of the river, were held
by a Federal detachment many days ere the approach of the Confederate
forces, but they had never attempted to cross over into the town. Picket

firing was now constant along the river. But there were many who yet believed that Burnside had no serious intention of attacking, regarding his demonstration at the river as a harmless display of force to divert attention from his real designs.

Such surmise was soon banished from the mind. On the 21st it became apparent that Gen. Burnside was concentrating his whole army on the north side of the Rappahannock. On the same day, Gen. Sumner summoned the corporate authorities of Fredericksburg to surrender the place, and threatened, in case of refusal, to bombard the city at nine o'clock, next morning. The weather had been tempestuous for two days, and a storm was raging at the time of the summons. It was impossible to prevent the execution of the threat to shell the city, as it was completely exposed to the batteries on Stafford Hills, which were beyond our reach. The city authorities were informed by Gen. Lee that while his forces would not use the place for military purposes, its occupation by the enemy would be resisted, and directions were given for the removal of the women and children as rapidly as possible.

The threatened bombardment did not take place. But the inhabitants were advised to leave the town in view of the imminence of a collision between the two armies, and almost the entire population, without a murmur abandoned their homes. The country around for miles was strewn with tents and rude shelters, where the women and children of the town had betaken themselves; and along the roads, in the rude blasts of winter, wandered many of the poor without aught of worldly property beyond some scanty packs of food and clothing borne on their backs.

Gen. Burnside now commenced his preparations to force the passage of the Rappahannock and advance upon Richmond. Lee's left wing, under Jackson, had not yet arrived, although it was rapidly pushing forward. On his arrival, the disposition of the Confederate forces was soon made. D. H. Hill's division was stationed near Port Royal, and the rest of Jackson's corps so disposed as to support Hill or Longstreet, as occasion might require. Our lines in the vicinity of Fredericksburg extended from the river about a mile and a half above, along the range of hills in the rear of the city to the Richmond Railroad. As these hills were commanded by the opposite heights, in possession of the enemy, earthworks were constructed upon their crests, at the most eligible positions for artillery.

On the Stafford Heights the enemy had an array of military force the most brilliant and magnificent of modern times. Burnside's total numerical strength was about one hundred and fifty thousand men. A more than ordinary powerful artillery was attached to the army, of which no less than one hundred and forty-three guns, overlooking the town of Fredericksburg, commanded the course of the river and the opposite bank. The Confederates numbered about eighty thousand men. They were drawn up along the heights in the rear of Fredericksburg, which, retiring in a semi-circle from the river, embrace within their arms a plain six miles in length, and from two to three in depth. It seemed as if nature had prepared here an arena for one of the grandest conflicts of arms that had yet been witnessed in the war. The landscape, stretching from the hills to the river, was like an amphitheatre; the intrenched Confederates holding an upper tier of seats, and the stage being the valley in which were placed the red-brick buildings of Fredericksburg. Outside of the town a few houses were scattered here and there over the scene, and the leafless woods added to the bleak aspect of the country. Small detachments of the Confederate forces were quartered in the deserted houses, from which rose few and feeble clouds of smoke; while on the banks of the river the active picket walked his post through piercing winds and sleet and rain.

Before dawn, on the 11th December, our signal guns announced that the enemy was in motion. About two, A. M., he commenced preparations to throw bridges over the Rappahannock, opposite Fredericksburg, and one about a mile and a quarter below, near the mouth of Deep Run. Two regiments of Barksdale's brigade, McLaws' division, the Seventeenth and Eighteenth Mississippi, guarded these points, the former, assisted by the Eighth Florida, of Anderson's division, being at the upper. The rest of the brigade, with the Third Georgia regiment, also of Anderson's division, was held in reserve in the city. From daybreak until four, P. M., the troops, sheltered behind the houses on the river bank, repelled the repeated efforts of the enemy to lay his bridges opposite the town, driving back his working parties, and their supports, with great slaughter.

At the lower point of the river near Deep Run there was no such protection. Here the enemy made a prodigious effort to lay his pontoons, and swarms of men could be seen moving to and fro with beams and boats. Our sharpshooters maintained an annoying fire, and for a moment the enemy retired. Then commenced a terrible cannonade, as more than a hundred guns were pointed at the city. Houses fell, timbers crashed, dust rose, flames ascended, while there poured out from the city a stream of unlucky citizens who had remained too long, or had screened themselves in hope of the enemy's speedy arrival. Unable to withstand the fire of the batteries and a superiour force of the enemy's infantry on the river banks, our troops were withdrawn; and soon loud cheers from the Federals announced that the bridge was completed. Burnside's advance into Fredericksburg was bravely resisted until dark. But Gen. Lee had accomplished the most important condition for a successful battle; he had gained the necessary time for the concentration of his forces.

It had been Burnside's hope, by rapidly crossing the river to take Lee at a serious disadvantage. He had discovered that a large portion of the Confederate force had been thrown down the river, and it was his design to separate, by a vigorous attack, the forces on the river below from the forces behind and on the crest in the rear of Fredericksburg. But in this prospect he was disappointed. He found Lee in compact lines prepared to receive him; and availing himself of the dense fogs on the river, he continued during the 12th December, to cross his men at and below Fredericksburg very much at his leisure, and without material interruption.

Our artillery could only be used with effect when the occasional clearing of the mist rendered the enemy's columns visible. His batteries on the Stafford Heights fired at intervals upon our position. Longstreet's corps constituted our left, with Anderson's division resting upon the river, Ransom's division supported the batteries on Marye's and Willis' Hills, at the foot of which Cobb's brigade, of McLaws' division, and the 24th North Carolina, of Ransom's brigade, were stationed, protected by a stone wall. The Washington Artillery, under Col. Walton, occupied the redoubts on the crest of Marye's Hill, and those on the heights to the right and left, were held by part of the reserve artillery, Col. E. P. Alexander's battalion, and the division batteries of Anderson, Ransom, and McLaws. A. P. Hill, of Jackson's corps, was posted between Longstreet's extreme right and Hamilton's Crossing, on the railroad. His front line, consisting of the brigades of Pender, Lane, and Archer, occupied the edge of a wood. Lieut.-Col. Walker, with fourteen pieces of artillery, was posted near the right, supported by two Virginia regiments. Early and Taliaferro's divisions composed Jackson's second line—D. H. Hill's division his reserve. Gen. Stuart, with two brigades of cavalry and his horse artillery, occupied the plain on Jackson's right, extending to Massaponax Creek.

On the morning of the 13th, the plain on which the Federal army lay, was still enveloped in fog, making it impossible to discern its operations. At an early hour the batteries on the heights of Stafford began to play upon Longstreet's position. In the intervals of the fire, noises from the valley and loud-toned commands told of marching and counter-marching in the fog and mists. The rattle of picket-firing on our right gave tokens of the impending battle. All was feverish expectation. A little past nine o'clock the sun lifted the foggy veil from the valley, and there stood the Federal array, right, left, and centre, just on the point of moving.

Dense masses appeared in front of A. P. Hill, stretching far up the river, in the direction of Fredericksburg. As they advanced, Maj. Pelham, of Stuart's horse artillery, who was stationed near the Port Royal road with one section, opened a rapid and well-directed enfilade fire, which arrested their progress. Four batteries immediately turned upon him, but he sustained their heavy fire with a courage that in half an hour made him one of the most famous names in the Confederacy. Thirty Federal cannon were striving in vain to silence him; and yet the young artillerist —only twenty-two years of age—was firm as a rock, his unyielding courage

and composure under the deadliest fire making him for a time a spectacle
for the whole field.

Meanwhile the enemy extended his left down the Port Royal road, and
his numerous batteries opened with vigour upon Jackson's line. Eliciting
no response, his infantry moved forward to seize the position occupied by
Lieut.-Col. Walker. The latter, reserving his fire until their line had approached within less than eight hundred yards, opened upon it with such
destructive effect as to cause it to waver, and soon to retreat in confusion.

About one, P. M., the main attack on the right began by a furious cannonade, under cover of which three compact lines of infantry advanced
against Hill's front. They were received as before by our batteries, by
whose fire they were momentarily checked, but soon recovering, they
pressed forward, until coming within range of our infantry, the contest became fierce and bloody. Here at one time the enemy broke the Confederate line, turning the left of Archer and the right of Lane. But reinforcements from Jackson's second line were rapidly brought forward, and restored the battle. After a severe contest, the enemy was routed, driven
from the woods; and although largely reinforced, he was driven back, and
pursued to the shelter of the railroad embankment. Here he was gallantly
charged by the brigades of Hoke and Atkinson, and driven across the plain
to his batteries. The repulse of the enemy on our right was now decisive,
and the attack was not renewed, although his batteries kept up active fire
at intervals, and sharpshooters skirmished along the front during the rest
of the afternoon.

While these events were transpiring on our right, the enemy, in formidable numbers, made repeated and desperate assaults on the left of our line.
Here was fixed the chief interest of the field. Fresh divisions had crossed
the river at Fredericksburg, and the mass of Burnside's army was now concentrated in front of Longstreet's strong position. Strong columns of attack were formed under the withering fire of the Confederate batteries to
attack Marye's and Willis' Hills towering immediately in their front. All
the batteries on the Stafford Heights directed their fire upon the positions
occupied by the Confederate artillery with a view to silence it, and cover
the movement of the infantry.

Our artillery did not reply to the furious cannonade. But as the
masses of the enemy came forward—one immediately in front and one on
each flank of Marye's Hill—the Washington artillery corps poured into
these dense lines of infantry a rapid and destructive fire. Still, the enemy,
notwithstanding the havoc caused by our batteries, pressed on with great
determination. His ranks were frequently broken; but at last his lines
had staggered within one hundred yards of the foot of the hill. At this
time our infantry suddenly rose and poured such rapid volleys into them,
that the advance was impeded by their own dead. As the columns halted

and staggered and swayed or broke, our men from breastworks and rifle-pits, and from every imaginable place, were pouring into their bleeding masses showers of small shot. It was too much for human endurance. Six different attacks, or rather frantic dashes, were directed against the almost impregnable position of the foe. It was an exhibition of courage that was worthy of a better cause and deserved a better direction. It was no longer a scientific battle, but a wholesale slaughter of human beings. In vain Sumner pushed forward French, Hancock, and Howard ; each division was repulsed with terrible loss ; the Irish brigade advanced impetuously, and almost perished within a short distance of the Confederate guns; all was in vain ; and Gen. Burnside, who, two miles across the river, sat upon the heights, glass in hand, saw the successive defeat of each assaulting column. When night closed in, the shattered masses of the enemy had disappeared in the town, leaving the field covered with dead and wounded.

Burnside was now at an appalling extremity. His shattered army was cowering beneath the houses of Fredericksburg, with a river in its rear, which, though threaded by pontoon bridges, would have been impassable under the pressure of attack. The thought in Richmond was that the time had at last come when the consequences of a great Confederate victory would be pursued, and its results completed ; and the public waited with impatience to hear that Gen. Lee had assumed the offensive, and despatched his crippled enemy on the banks of the river. The North trembled for the same result. One day might decide the fate of the large and yet magnificent remnants of Burnside's army ; they might be annihilated, or take the alternative of capitulation ; and the great event might put a new aspect on the war, which had so long lingered in the trail of wasted and unfruitful blood. Expectation was high in Richmond ; there was a keen impatience for the finishing blow. But in the midst of these feelings came the astounding news that two days had passed without any renewal of the battle on Gen. Lee's part, and that on the succeeding night Burnside had crossed the river without a single effort at interruption, and that a great Federal army, supposed to be in the jaws of destruction, was now quietly reorganizing in perfect security on the north bank of the river.

Various excuses have been made for Gen. Lee's omission to assume the offensive, and realize the proper result of his victory at Fredericksburg. These excuses have mostly originated in the generosity of friends and admirers. But the great commander himself, averse to all efforts of others to cover up any failure of his own, and insensible to the offers of misrepresentation made to him by flatterers, has nobly and candidly confessed his errour. In an official report he says : "The attack on the 13th had been so easily repulsed, and by so small a part of our army, that it was not supposed the enemy would limit his effort to one attempt, which, in view of the magnitude of his preparations, and the extent of his force, seemed to be comparatively insignificant. Believing, therefore, that he would attack us, it was not deemed expedient to lose the advantages of our position, and expose the troops to the fire of his inaccessible batteries beyond the river, by advancing against him. But we were necessarily ignorant of the extent to which he had suffered, and only became aware of it, when, on the morning of the 16th, it was discovered that he had availed himself of the darkness of night, and the prevalence of a violent storm of wind and rain, to recross the river."

The battle of Fredericksburg presented a disproportion of loss on the Federal and Confederate sides, such as no battle of the war had as yet exhibited. A great victory, measured by the list of casualties, had been obtained by the Confederates with a comparatively small loss. Gen. Burnside, in his official report, stated: " Our killed amounts to 1,152, our wounded to about 9,000, and our prisoners to about 700." A few days after he despatched: " On the authority of our medical director, the whole number of wounded is between six and seven thousand." Gen. Lee, in his official despatch, writes: " Our loss during the entire operations, since the movements of the enemy began, amounts to about eighteen hundred killed and wounded." Among the killed were two conspicuous names—Brig.-Gen. Maxcy Gregg of South Carolina, and Brig.-Gen. Thomas R. R. Cobb of Georgia—men, who, aside from military merit, had earned the reputation of statesmen, and had adorned the councils of the South by brilliant eloquence and chivalrous sentiment. " The country," wrote Gen. Lee, " consents to the sacrifice of such men as these, and the gallant soldiers who fell with them, only to secure the inestimable blessing they died to obtain." This sentiment was written when the cause of the Confederacy was above all earthly things in the minds of its people, and when the dying words of Gregg were commemorated like a phrase of antique heroism: " Tell the Governor of South Carolina I cheerfully yield my life for the independence of my State! "

OPERATIONS IN TENNESSEE.—BATTLE OF MURFREESBORO.

Our last notice of operations on the Western theatre of the war, left Gen. Bragg in front of Nashville. The bulk of his army had gone into camp at Murfreesboro, while the brigades of Forrest and Wagner, about five thousand effective cavalry, were absent, annoying Grant's rear in West Tennessee, and breaking the enemy's railroad communications in Northern Kentucky. The main Federal army now in Tennessee, under command of Gen. Rosecrans, maintained itself with some difficulty at Nashville and on the line of the Cumberland. It was only a portion of the enemy's forces which threatened the Confederacy from the West; for Grant was moving from West Tennessee into Mississippi, while a strong detached force under Sherman was organizing for a separate expedition down the Mississippi River against Vicksburg. The Confederate positions were the lines of the Tallahatchie River, the approaches by rail into Mississippi and the fortifications at Vicksburg. Such was the situation in the West at the close of the year 1862, when Bragg confronted Rosecrans, and prepared for an important battle, likely to decide the fate of Tennessee.

In the absence of Bragg's cavalry, Rosecrans determined to seize the opportunity for attack, and to advance from Nashville. He prepared to force the passage of Stone River north of Murfreesboro, and on the 26th December commenced to move his forces; McCook, with three divisions, forming the right column, Thomas the centre with two divisions, and Crittenden the left with three divisions. The total of this force has been officially stated by Rosecrans at about forty-seven thousand men; but Gen. Bragg declares that from papers captured from the enemy in the subsequent battle, it was discovered that his strength was nearly, if not quite seventy thousand men, while we had on the field on the morning of the battle, less than thirty-five thousand men, of which thirty thousand were infantry and artillery.

The Confederate army was collected in and around Murfreesboro; Polk's corps and three brigades of Breckinridge's division holding the town. The three cavalry brigades of Wheeler, Wharton, and Pegram, occupied the entire front of our infantry, and covered all approaches within ten miles of Nashville. It was thus impossible that any movement of the enemy could take place without due notice being received at the Confederate headquarters. When it was known that he was advancing, preparations were made to receive him; the detached portion of Hardee's corps at Eagleville was brought up; and on the 28th December our main force of infantry and artillery was concentrated in front of Murfreesboro, whilst the cavalry, supported by three brigades of infantry and three batteries of artillery, impeded the advance of the enemy by constant skirmishing and sudden, unexpected attacks.

The whole force of the enemy was concentrated on and near the direct road on the west of Stone River. Crittenden's corps formed the left of the line, Thomas the centre, of which Negley's division was drawn up in advance, and Rousseau's in reserve, and McCook's corps the right. The road and the river divided both armies into two wings. The ground was favourable to manœuvre—large open fields, densely wooded tracts of cedar and thinner ones of oak; the gentle swells of the land were scarcely increased by the banks of Stone River, which ran through the lines of both armies, was fordable at almost every point for infantry, and at short intervals practicable for artillery. The Confederate line of battle was about nine miles in length. Polk's corps, consisting of Withers' and Cheatham's divisions, formed our left wing. Hardee's corps, consisting of Breckinridge's and Cleburne's divisions, with McCown's division, held in reserve on his right flank, was formed on the east bank of the river, its left resting near the Nashville road, and its right extending towards the Lebanon pike.

On the night of the 30th December both armies bivouacked at a distance not greater in some places than five hundred yards, the camp-fires of the two being within distinct view. Both commanders prepared to attack the next day. Rosecrans drew up an elaborate plan of battle, and expressed uneasiness at McCook's position on the right. By seven o'clock in the morning of the 31st December, the troops were preparing for the battle.

But the enemy's attack had been anticipated. At the break of day on the cold and cloudy morning, Gen. Hardee gave the order to advance, and commenced the battle by a rapid and impetuous charge on McCook's position. The enemy here was taken completely by surprise; general and staff-officers were not mounted; artillery horses not hitched, and infantry not formed. One of McCook's divisions, after a sharp but fruitless contest, was—to use the words of Gen. Rosecrans himself—" crumbled to pieces." Hardee continued to push the enemy, pursuing his victorious career for miles, while captured artillery, flying battalions, and hosts of prisoners, attested the rout. The entire right wing of Rosecrans was being driven in the greatest disorder, and it appeared that the day was already decided. McCook's corps was driven for six miles towards the centre. For hours continued the rapid movement of the noise of battle towards the north, and, at last, the streams of fugitives and stragglers passing towards the Nashville road, and making their way in the greatest disorder through the cane-brakes, convinced Rosecrans, of what had been before reported to him, that McCook's corps was utterly routed. The Federal commander was remarkable for self-possession and *sang-froid*. As report of disaster after disaster came to him, he remarked : " We will soon rectify it." He was incorrectly told that McCook was killed " We cannot help it," he replied ; " men who fight must be killed. Never mind ; let us fight this battle." It was a crisis in which such cool words were remarkable. It was now near noon, and Rosecrans had his right wing broken ; he had already lost twenty-eight pieces of cannon, and not less than five thousand prisoners ; and it was in such circumstances that he was to prepare a new disposition of his forces, and impart a new inspiration to dispute what remained of the day.

A new line of battle was rapidly developed. Rousseau's division was hurried forward from the centre, and Crittenden was ordered to abandon all idea of an advance, and to march as quickly as possible two out of his three divisions to support the right wing. These movements were masked by immense cedar forests. The whole of the Federal right and centre was now drawn up nearly at right angles with the position it held in the morning. The right of the left wing held the angle of high ground between the rail and river. Here the enemy massed his artillery, and seemed to bid defiance to the hitherto victorious career of the Confederates.

Finding that the enemy had concentrated such a force on Hardee's front as to check his further progress, Gen. Bragg sent orders for Breckinridge's division to move from the right to reinforce Polk ; but there was a considerable delay in carrying out this order, owing to a threat of an advance on the Federal left, and a rumour of fresh forces appearing on the Lebanon pike. " These unfortunate misrepresentations," said Gen. Bragg, " on that part of the field which, with proper caution, could not have existed, withheld from active operations three fine brigades until the enemy had succeeded in checking our progress, had re-established his lines, and had collected many of his broken battalions."

Having settled the question that no movement was being made against our right, and none to be apprehended, Breckinridge was ordered to leave two brigades to support the battery on his side of Stone River—and with the remainder of the force to cross to the left, and report to Polk. By the time this could be accomplished it was too late to send this force to Hardee's support, who was unable to make further progress, and he was directed to maintain his position. Polk was directed with these reinforcements to throw all the force he could collect upon the enemy's extreme left, and thereby either carry that strong point which had so far resisted us so successfully—or failing in that, at least to draw off from Hardee's front the formidable opposition there concentrated. The three brigades of Jackson, Preston, and Adams were successively reported for their work.

Upon this flank, his strongest defensive position resting on the riverbank, the enemy had concentrated not less than twenty pieces of artillery, masked almost from view, but covering an open space in front of several hundred yards, supported right and left and rear by heavy masses of infantry. A terrible trial awaited the devoted men who were to attack this position. As they pressed up to the edge of the cedar forest, and swarmed out into the open field, it was a grand scene. Every feature of it was keenly cut and clearly defined. The day was one of surpassing beauty. The gray suits of the Confederates dotted the dark line of the cedars ; presently they could be seen to thicken in order of battle, with the bright glitter of their steel flashing in the heavy green of the thicket. As they passed into the open field, the hostile array imparted sublimity to the spectacle. Great masses of troops moved steadily forward, careless of the batteries, which tore open their ranks, and scattered them bleeding upon the soil. They marched through the destroying storm dauntlessly. Two attempts were made to carry the enemy's position. But each time the whole extent of their lines was engirdled with a belt of flame and smoke, and the ground strewn with their dead. For two hours the battle raged with horrible slaughter, and neither side receded until near five o'clock. Then the nearly exhausted armies suspended operations for the night, excepting the play of a few batteries.

It had been a desperate but undecided contest. The advantage was with the Confederates. They had driven the enemy's right almost upon his left, captured nearly one-third of his artillery, compelled him to change front under fire, and occupied that part of the field from which he had been driven in the morning. Rosecrans had shown a great power in handling troops, and had performed a manœuvre requiring high qualities of generalship; for he had successfully formed a new line in presence of an enemy and under his attacks.

The next day—1st January, 1863—Gen. Bragg telegraphed to Richmond: "God has granted us a happy New Year." The exultation of the despatch was extravagant, and was certainly not justified by what ensued. The first of January passed without any important event. Breckinridge had been transferred to the right of Stone River to resume the command of that position, now held by two of his brigades. It was soon reported that no change had occurred, except the withdrawal of the enemy from the advanced position occupied by his left flank. Finding, upon further examination, that this was the case, the right flank of Polk's corps was thrown forward to occupy the ground for which we had so obstinately contended the evening before. This shortened our lines considerably, and gave us possession of the centre of the battle-field, from which we gleaned the spoils and trophies throughout the day, and transferred them rapidly to the rear.

On the 2d January, Van Cleve's division of the enemy's forces was thrown across the river, and occupied the eminence from which Gen. Polk's line was commanded and enfiladed. The dislodgement of this force or the withdrawal of Polk's line was an evident necessity. The latter involved consequences not to be entertained. Orders were accordingly given for the concentration of the whole of Breckinridge's division in front of the position to be taken. An addition was made to his command of ten Napoleon guns, and the cavalry forces of Wharton and Pegram, about two thousand men, were ordered to join in the attack on his right. The instructions given to Breckinridge were to drive the enemy back, crown the hill, intrench his artillery, and hold the position.

The attack was made at 4 P. M. Van Cleve's division gave way, retired in confusion across the river, and was closely followed by the Confederates. The enemy however, had disposed his batteries on the hill on the west side of the river, and Negley's division was ordered up to meet the onset. The firing was terrific. In about half an hour the Confederates lost two thouand men. Breckinridge's command was driven back in considerable disorder; but the pursuit of the enemy was checked by Anderson's brigade of Mississippians, which was thrown forward from Polk's line, staggered the enemy, and saved all the guns not captured before its arrival.

Next day the rain fell in torrents. Each General anticipated an attack from his opponent, and neither appeared willing to commence a new battle. Meanwhile Bragg was deceived into the belief that the enemy was receiving reinforcements, and in view of the exhausted condition of his army, determined to withdraw from the unequal contest. In the night of the 3d January, the retreat was commenced without molestation from the enemy. The next day Rosecrans moved into Murfreesboro, and Bragg retired to Tullahoma, which, as a base of operations, and as a position of defence, offered great advantages.

The occupation of Murfreesboro afforded the North some pretence of claiming a victory. But the position was of little importance, and the works neither extensive nor strong. The actual results of the battle were in favour of the Confederates. Our loss exceeded ten thousand, nine thousand of whom were killed or wounded. As our offset to this loss, we had taken considerably over six thousand prisoners, and had captured over thirty pieces of cannon, sixty thousand stand of small arms, ambulances, mules, and horses, with a large amount of other valuable property, all of which was secured and appropriated to proper uses. Besides all this secured, we destroyed not less than eight hundred wagons, mostly laden with various articles, such as arms, ammunition, provisions, baggage, clothing, medicine, and hospital stores. We had lost only three pieces of artillery, all in Breckinridge's repulse. Rosecrans gave his loss in killed and wounded as 8,778. Of this estimate Gen. Bragg remarks: "One corps, commanded by Maj.-Gen. Thomas L. Crittenden, which was least exposed .n the engagement, report over five thousand killed and wounded. As the enemy had two other corps, and a separate division, third of a corps, and cavalry, his loss is safely estimated at three thousand killed and sixteen thousand wounded. Adding the six thousand two hundred and seventy-three prisoners, we have a total of twenty-five thousand two hundred and seventy-three."

The battle of Murfreesboro was the subject of much criticism in the Confederacy, and the occasion of various commentaries. Gen. Bragg was famous for his profuse censure of his officers, and his ascription of every failure in his campaigns to the fault of some subordinate officer. He never wrote an official report without such unpleasant and suspicious element of recrimination in it. He made the battle of Murfreesboro a text of censure of his subordinates; he declared that the remissness of Breckinridge, on the first day of action, checked Hardee's success, and made the victory incomplete. But he found in this terrible battle the occasion of a beautiful and memorable tribute to the private soldier of the Confederacy. He wrote: " To the private soldier a fair word of praise is due, and though it is so seldom given and so rarely expected, that it may be considered out of place, I cannot, in justice to myself, withhold the opinion ever entertained, and so often expressed during our struggle for independence. In the absence of instructions and discipline of our armies, and of the confidence which long associations produce between veterans, we have, in a great measure, to trust to the individuality and self-reliance of the private soldier. Without the incentive or the motive which controls the officer, who hopes to live in history, without the hope of reward, actuated only by a sense of duty and patriotism, he has in this great contest justly judged that the cause was his own, and gone into it with a determination to conquer or die, to be free or not to be at all. No encomium is too high, no honour too great for such a soldier. However much of credit and glory may be given, and probably justly given, to the leaders in the struggle, history will yet award the main honour, where it is due, to the private soldier, who, without hope of reward, and with no other incentive than a conscientiousness of rectitude, has encountered all the hardships, and has suffered all the privations. Well has it been said: The first monument our Confederacy raises, when our independence shall have been won, should be a lofty shaft, pure and spotless, bearing this inscription : ' *To the unknown and unrecorded dead.*' "

OPERATIONS IN THE TRANS-MISSISSIPPI.

In other quarters of the war less important than Virginia and Tennessee, the latter part of the year 1862 was without considerable interest. Since the commands of Price and Van Dorn had moved east of the Mississippi, the campaign in the extensive country west of that river had become feeble and irregular. It was marked, however, by one battle—that of Prairie Grove—the dimensions of which were large for that campaign, and the results of no little importance to the country of the Trans-Mississippi.

In the latter months of 1862, Maj.-Gen. T. C. Hindman was commanding what was known as the District of Arkansas. Lieut.-Gen. Holmes was commanding the Trans-Mississippi department, with his headquarters at Little Rock. Gen. Blunt, commanding about seven thousand Federal troops, had advanced from Springfield as far as Cane Hill, Arkansas, driving Gen. Marmaduke, who was commanding a small division of cavalry. Gen. Hindman, with about eight thousand Missouri, Texas, and Arkansas infantry and artillery, was at Van Buren. It was considered necessary to oppose the further advance of Blunt ; and accordingly, on the

1st December, Gen. Hindman put his whole force in motion to meet the enemy, and, if possible, drive him back, as a large supply of quartermaster and commissary stores had been collected at Van Buren.

Owing to delays occasioned by crossing the river and the bad condition of our transportation, the command did not reach the camp on Cove Creek until the evening of the 5th. The position was six miles from Cane Hill, the same where Gen. Price halted on his retreat from Springfield in the winter of 1861. When Gen. Hindman reached this place, he learned that Blunt was camped at Cane Hill, and that Gen. Herron, with five thousand men, was pushing on rapidly from Springfield to reinforce him. It was immediately determined by Hindman to meet this latter force, and, defeating it, to turn upon Blunt, and force him to surrender. He issued an extravagant address to his soldiers, and designated the enemy opposed to them as a combination of "Pin Indians, free negroes, Southern tories, Kansas Jayhawkers, and hired Dutch cut-throats." He declared that unless this ruthless force was defeated, the country would be ruined.

In order that Gen. Hindman's plan of operations might be effectual, it was necessary to engage Blunt's attention so as to prevent his falling back to Fayetteville, and forming a junction with Herron. For this purpose, early in the morning of the 6th December, a regiment of cavalry was sent to drive in the enemy's outposts nearest us. At sunrise, the 11th Missouri infantry were pushed forward as far as the cavalry had advanced, to deploy as if to invite attack. It only succeeded in developing a party of Indians, who declined attacking. In the evening, Hindman's whole force was moved up to the ground occupied by the 11th Missouri infantry, and a regiment of cavalry was ordered to drive in the skirmishers, and feel the main body. Some desultory fighting ensued, and continued until nightfall.

Hindman's whole command, resting on their arms, were ordered to move at two o'clock in the morning on the roads towards Fayetteville, to attack Herron's force approaching the field of battle. A regiment of cavalry was ordered to remain with one battery of light field pieces, and to commence shelling the enemy in front at daylight. The next morning, the command struck the Fayetteville and Cane Hill road, and surprised the advance-guard of Herron's force, capturing two hundred prisoners.

This success appears to have confused Gen. Hindman, and, instead of atacking Herron immediately and with vigour, he divided his force, sending Parsons' brigade in the direction of Cane Hill, as if expecting an attack from Blunt. Meanwhile, Blunt, anticipating a flank movement, had fallen back, and Hindman made a new disposition of his forces. But valuable time had been lost, and the attack was not made on Herron's force until half-past three o'clock in the afternoon. In our line of battle, the Arkansas troops were on the right flank, the First Missouri brigade forming the centre, the Second Missouri brigade the left, and the Texan troops the reserve. The action had scarcely commenced, when Gen. Blunt, who, having burned his stores and his train, had made a rapid movement, by an obscure road leading through a valley, reached the battle-field. The new force appeared upon the Confederate left. It was necessary for the First Missouri brigade to change its front from the east to the north, to meet the charge which the enemy was now preparing to make. Just as the evolution was completed, the combined forces of the enemy advanced to the charge. It was gallantly met by the two Missouri brigades. As night fell, the action was decided. The enemy was driven from the field; Blunt swinging around, uniting with Herron, and both retreating. The Federal forces fell back six miles.

The evidences of victory were with the Confederates. Their loss was about two hundred killed and five hundred wounded; that of the enemy, by his own accounts, exceeded a thousand. It appears, however, that Hindman, who had blundered during the day, although he had yet succeeded in driving the combined forces of Herron and Blunt, was so impressed with the fact they had formed a junction, that he determined to retreat during the night. The wheels of his artillery were muffled, and the Confederates actually retreated from a field of victory. Thus terminated the battle of Prairie Grove (as it was called by the Confederates); the importance of which was that it virtually decided the war north of the Arkansas River.

The country of the Trans-Mississippi suffered from peculiar causes in the war. A great part of it not only laboured under military incompetency; but singular disorders affected the whole population, and an enormous despotism cursed the land. Gen. Hindman, who had but a weak head in military matters, exhibited an iron hand in the management of other affairs, usurped all authority in the country he occupied, and exercised a tyrannical rule, that only finds a parallel in antique despotism. His conduct was made the subject of a special investigation in the Congress at Richmond. It was discovered that he had established within his military lines what he was pleased to call a " government *ad interim*." He superseded the entire civil authority; he deliberately amplified the conscription law by proclamation; he declared martial law throughout Arkansas and the northern portion of Texas; and he demanded, under the penalty of death, the services of all whom he had tyrannically embraced in his conscription lists. Crops were ravaged; cotton burned, or appropriated to unknown purposes; while straggling soldiers, belonging to distant commands, traversed the country, armed and lawless, robbing the people of their property under the pretence of " impressing " it for the Confederate service. To a great part of the country within the limits of his command Hindman extended no protection whatever. Hostile Indians began collecting on the border, and Federal emissaries were busy among the Cherokees and Creeks, inciting disaffection. Detachments of Federal cavalry penetrated, at will, into various parts of the upper half of Arkansas, plundering and burning houses, stealing horses and slaves, destroying farming utensils, murdering men loyal to the Confederacy, or carrying them into captivity, forcing the oath of allegiance on the timid, and disseminating disloyal sentiments among the ignorant.

Such a condition of affairs could not long be tolerated, although the statements of it were slow in reaching Richmond, and obtaining the just consideration of the Government there. The cruelties and disorders of Hindman—notoriously the favourite of President Davis—became at last so enormous in Arkansas, that it was unsafe that he should remain there longer, when he was brought across the Mississippi River, and assigned to some special duty. It was indeed remarkable that the people of the Trans-Mississippi, with such an experience of maltreatment, and in spite of a conviction that the concerns of this distant portion of the Confederacy were grossly neglected at Richmond, should yet have, even to the latest period of the war, faithfully kept and fondly cherished their attachment to the vital principle of our struggle and the common cause of our arms. It was an exhibition of devotion and of extraordinary virtue in the Confederate States west of the Mississippi River that should be omitted in no historic record of the war.

CHAPTER XXI.

THE beginning of the year 1862—when the heavy operations of the war on land were suspended by the rigour of winter—presents a convenient period for review of some political questions in the war.

The thread of Anti-Slavery legislation appeared for some time to have been broken with the decree of emancipation in the District of Columbia. President Lincoln evidently hesitated to identify his Administration further with the radical party in the war. A formidable opposition was gathering in the North with especial reference to the Anti-Slavery acts of the Government at Washington ; it was declared that these acts were diverting the war to the ends of fanaticism, and that the Government had deliberately violated the pledge contained in the resolution offered by Mr. Crittenden of Kentucky, and passed almost unanimously in the House of Representatives at the beginning of the civil conflict, to the effect that the war should not be waged in hostility to the institutions of any of the States. President Lincoln, as we have already seen, had been advised, in the summer of 1862, that McClellan disapproved of any infraction of the laws of civilized and Christian warfare; that he disapproved of arbitrary arrests in places where the insurrection did not prevail; that he did not contemplate any seizure of private property for the support of the army, or measures for punishing or desolating the region invaded; but that he earnestly desired that the war should be carried on as a duel between organized armies, and not against non-combatants; that the institutions of the States should be protected; that no proclamation of freedom, incensing a servile race to indiscriminate massacre of helpless whites, and inviting the destruction of unoffending blacks, should be permitted; in fine, that, wherever it was possible, the military should be subordinate to the civil authority, and the Constitution alone should be the guide and glory of heroic sacrifice.

It is remarkable that President Lincoln, in the summer of 1862, gave no distinct and decided evidence that this plan of action was obnoxious to him. His course at this time on the slavery question was rather disposed to conciliate both parties in the North; and he did nothing more than make a bungling experiment at compromise in proposing a scheme of compensated emancipation, which being excessively visionary and impracticable, soon passed out of the public mind. It was readily seen by men of all parties that this scheme would create a pecuniary burden which the Government would be utterly unable to carry along with the expenses of the war. At the rate of $300, it was calculated that the slaves in the insurgent States would be worth $1,049,508,000; and adding the cost of compensation to the Border States, at the same rate, the aggregate expense of emancipation would be $1,185,840,300. There was no disposition on the part of the tax-paying public to meet such liabilities in addition to the war debt; and the scheme of compensated emancipation never went further than a record of votes in Congress. That body passed a resolution that "the United States ought to co-operate with any State which may adopt gradual abolishment of slavery, giving to such State pecuniary aid, to be used by such State in its discretion, to compensate for the inconveniences, public and private, produced by such a change of system." In pursuance of this resolution, President Lincoln transmitted to Congress the draft of a bill upon the subject. The bill was referred to a committee, but no action was taken upon it, nor did any of the Border States respond to the President's invitation to take the initiative in his scheme, and try the virtue of the resolution adopted by Congress.

But although the scheme of compensated emancipation was visionary with regard to the objects it professed, it is quite possible that it may have served a secret purpose of Mr. Lincoln, and that it was really intended to test the sentiment of both sections of the country, and to prepare the way for the more vigorous treatment of the subject of slavery. The time was coming when he would have to decide between the conservative and radical elements of the North, and determine a question which was being pressed upon him by public sentiments which could not be compromised. On the 15th September, 1862, a memorial was presented to him by a deputation from Chicago, praying for the immediate issue of a proclamation of emancipation. Mr. Lincoln entertained the delegation with a long and rambling discourse. He was represented in the Northern newspapers to have made the following characteristic and interesting reply :

" The subject presented in the memorial is one upon which I have thought much for weeks past, and I may may even say for months. I am approached with the most opposite opinions and advice, and that by religious men, who are equally certain that they represent the Divine will. I am sure that either the one or the other class is mistaken in that belief, and perhaps in some respects both. I hope it will not be irreverent for me to say that if it is probable that God would reveal His will to others, on a point so connected with my duty, it might be supposed He would reveal it directly to me ; for, unless I am more deceived in myself than I often am, it is my earnest desire to know the will of Providence in this matter. And if I can learn what it is, I will do it ! These are not, however, the days of miracles ; and I suppose it will be granted that I am not to expect a direct revelation. I must study the plain physical facts of the case, ascertain what is possible, and learn what appears to be wise and right.

" The subject is difficult, and good men do not agree. For instance, the other day, four gentlemen of standing and intelligence from New York, called as a delegation on business connected with the war ; but before leaving, two of them earnestly besought me to proclaim general emancipation, upon which the other two at once attacked them. You know also that the last session of Congress had a decided majority of anti-slavery men, yet they could not unite on this policy. And the same is true of the religious people. Why, the rebel soldiers are praying with a great deal more earnestness, I fear, than our own troops, and expecting God to favour their side : for one of our soldiers, who had been taken prisoner, told Senator Wilson, a few days since, that he met nothing so discouraging as the evident sincerity of those he was among in their prayers. But we will talk over the merits of the case.

" What good would a proclamation of emancipation from me do, especially as we are now situated? I do not want to issue a document that the whole world will see must necessarily be inoperative, like the Pope's bull against the comet ! Would my word free the slaves, when I cannot even enforce the Constitution in the rebel States? Is there a single court, or magistrate, or individual that could be influenced by it there ? And what reason is there to think it would have any greater effect upon the slaves than the late law of Congress, which I approved, and which offers protection and freedom to the slaves of rebel masters who come within our lines ? Yet I cannot learn that that law has caused a single slave to come over to us. And suppose they could be induced by a proclamation of freedom from me to throw themselves upon us, what should we do with them ? How can we feed and care for such a multitude? Gen. Butler wrote me a few days since that he was issuing more rations to the slaves who have rushed to him than to all the white troops under his command. They eat, and that is all."

Such were the views entertained by Mr. Lincoln on the 15th day of September, 1862, on the subject of emancipation. The time of this conference was significant. The progress of the war was inauspicious; the Confederates had penetrated the North, and were actually threatening Washington; and at all such periods of wavering confidence in the war, the Northern Government was singularly prompt to incline towards the moderate party, and to hold up in its progress to radicalism. It was certainly no time to decide domestic institutions in the Confederacy when that belligerent was actually threatening the existence of the Government at Washington. But at this precise conjuncture of politics the battle of Sharpsburg was fought; the mask was dropped; and on the 22d September, 1862, President Lincoln issued a preliminary proclamation of emancipation, of which the following is the important portion:

"That on the first day of January, in the year of our Lord one thousand eight hundred and sixty-three, all persons held as slaves within any States or designated part of a State, the people whereof shall then be in rebellion against the United States, shall be then, thenceforward, and forever free; and the Executive Government of the United States, including the military and naval authority thereof, will recognize and maintain the freedom of such persons, and will do no act or acts to repress such persons, or any of them, in any efforts they may make for their actual freedom.

"That the Executive will, on the first day of January aforesaid, by proclamation, designate the States and parts of States, if any, in which the people thereof respectively shall then be in rebellion against the United States; and the fact that any State, or the people thereof, shall on that day be in good faith represented in the Congress of the United States, by members chosen thereto at elections wherein a majority of the qualified voters of such State shall have participated, shall, in the absence of strong countervailing testimony, be deemed conclusive evidence that such State, and the people thereof, are not then in rebellion against the United States."

This was followed by the proclamation of 1st January, 1863, designating the States in which emancipation should take immediate effect; the notice of one hundred days, counting from the preliminary proclamation, having expired.

Thus was consummated the triumph of the Abolition party of the North. Thus was, at last, avowed the war upon slavery, and thus deliberately planned the robbery of the Southern people to the extent of two thousand millions of dollars. It is true that this proclamation was for the time of no effect, and that when it was issued it was worth no more than the paper on which its bold iniquity was traced; nevertheless, it was the avowal of a principle, the declaration of a wish, the deliberate attempt of the Chief Magistrate of a nation to do that which was repugnant to civiliz-

ation and all morals. The misrepresentation of the emancipation proclamation, as a deed of philanthropy, was absurd enough. A candid world
found no difficulty in interpreting it as an act of malice towards the master
rather than one of mercy to the slave. A crime was attempted in the
name of liberty and humanity; and various hypocritical pretences were
used to cover up what was an unholy infatuation, a ruthless persecution,
a cruel and shameful device, adding severity and bitterness to a wicked
and reckless war.

The new measure was adopted in the name of a "*military necessity*."
Aside from its falsehood, the plea was one that dishonoured the North, and
placed it in shameful inconsistency. Again and again it had been proclaimed to the world, that "the rebellion was weak, and would be crushed
out in sixty days;" at other times, it was declared that "Union men
abounded in the South, and would welcome Federal troops as deliverers;
and yet now the invader was so hopeless of his task, that it was a "military
necessity" that he obtain help of slaves! If the proclamation had been
designed as a "military necessity," it was very clear that it should end
with the war, and be confined to the special mission for which it had been
invoked. The fact was that the real design was political, not military;
that emancipation was not the exigency of the war, but the permanent
triumph of fanaticism under a false pretence. We shall see at a future time
how beyond the point of this proclamation the Anti-Slavery legislation at
Washington was enlarged by the establishment of a Bureau of Freedmen's
Affairs, to determine all questions relating to persons of African descent,
and finally, by an amendment of the Constitution, the effect of which was
to entomb slavery forever, to erect emancipation into a constitutional reform, and thus exhibit and confirm what was its original design.

The effect of the emancipation proclamation on the Confederates was
decided. It secured a new lease of war, and animated the people of the
South to desperate exertion. In a message, communicated on the 12th
January, 1863, to the Congress at Richmond, President Davis said: "The
proclamation will have a salutary effect in calming the fears of those who
have constantly evinced the apprehension that this war might end by some
reconstruction of the old Union, or some renewal of close political relations
with the United States. These fears have never been shared by me, nor
have I been able to perceive on what basis they could rest. But the
proclamation affords the fullest guaranty of the impossibility of such a
result. It has established a state of things which can lead to but one of
three consequences—the extermination of the slaves, the exile of the whole
white population of the Confederacy, or absolute and total separation of
these States from the United States." The entire newspaper press of the
Confederacy echoed the sentiment of the President. It was declared that
the outrage of forcible emancipation would awaken a deeper resentment

than ever inflamed the people of the South before; that it had quenched the last sentiment of respect that lingered in their breasts for the United States Government; that it would unite them more resolutely than ever, and make it to the individual interest of every person in the bounds of the Confederacy to sustain and strengthen it with every dollar and every arm, and every prayer, and every energy of manly virtue and Christian encouragement.

The effect of the proclamation in the North was to strengthen the Opposition; and the preliminary announcement of emancipation in September, 1862, was undoubtedly a main element of success in the Democratic triumphs in the fall elections of that year. The gains of the Democratic party at this time were the subject of great concern to those in power at Washington. In the face of a majority of 107,000 against them in 1860, the Democrats had carried the State of New York. The metropolis of New York was carried by a Democratic majority of 31,000—a change of 48,000 votes in twelve months. Within the great States of New Jersey, New York, Pennsylvania, Ohio, Indiana, and Illinois, the results of the popular elections were a more or less emphatic avowal of opposition to the schemes of those who were using the power of the Government for narrow and sectional and despotic purposes. The significance of these elections was not only confined to the issue of emancipation. A large portion of the Northern people pronounced against the entire policy of Mr. Lincoln's Administration. They condemned that relic of the worst times of French tyranny, the *lettres de cachet;* they raised their voices against irresponsible arrests; they complained of the small measure of success in the war, and the disappointment of the hopes of the people in this regard; and while protesting against the edict of emancipation, they reminded Mr. Seward of his declaration, made on the 10th March, 1862, in a letter to Mr. Adams in London, that such a measure " would re-invigorate the declining insurrection in every part of the South."

On the 15th December, 1862, Mr. Cox, Democratic member from Ohio, in a speech in the House of Representatives, described the condition of the North, and exhibited a bill of particulars against Mr. Lincoln's Administration, which may be taken as a declaration of the principles and views of his party. He stated that the present cost of the war to the North was $1,000,000 per day, which was not being replaced; for all that was spent in war was, by the laws of economy, a loss to those who spend it, as a mere pecuniary transaction, and not counting ultimate and moral results. He declared that since Mr. Lincoln's Administration came into power there had been lost to the country, merely as a matter of business, not counting debt and taxes of a national or State character, at least three hundred millions in the destruction of property, interference with established business, increase in wages, spoliation of railroads, depots, produce, corn, wheat, flour, cotton, hay, crops, &c. He pointed out the fact that the Government had devised a system of taxation by tariff which imposed a burden on the West, to benefit manufacturing in New England, and paid indirectly sixty millions into the treasury and hundreds of millions into the pockets of capitalists, from the consumers, who were mostly farmers in the West. He complained of a system of internal taxation, costing for collection some four millions extra, which might have been saved, and levying in one year $150,000,000 as interest only on a great national debt, and with an army of newly-made office-holders, with exorbitant salaries. He stated that within six hundred and fifty-one days, a party had succeeded which proposed, by legislation and proclamation, to break down a labour system in eleven States, of four millions of negroes, whose industry had been productive hitherto, worth, on or before the 4th of March, 1861, an average of $500 apiece, being in all two thousand millions of dollars. He prophesied that when this capital was destroyed the objects of this pseudo-philanthropy would remain on hand, North and South, as a mass of dependent and improvident black beings, for whose care the tax would be almost equal to the war-tax, before their condition would again be fixed safely and prosperously. He concluded with the summary and startling statement that within these six hundred and fifty-one days the rights of personal liberty, freedom from arrest without process, freedom for press and speech, and the right of *habeas corpus* had been suspended and limited, and, at times, destroyed ; and in the place of resurrected and promised liberty to four million blacks, the North had the destruction of that liberty which the past eight hundred years had awarded to the Anglo-Saxon race.

The triumphs of the Democratic party had taken place in the most powerful and populous States of the North. The States in which the party gained in the fall elections of 1862 contained a majority of the Free State population ; had two-thirds of the wealth of the North ; and furnished a majority of the troops in the field against us. This important and imposing demonstration of public opinion in the North was interpreted by the Republican party as significant of a Democratic design of " reconstruction," in which the Southern States might be brought back into the Union with new constitutional guaranties. But this idea, if it was ever seriously entertained by the Democratic party of the North, found enough to discourage it in the manner in which the bare suggestion of it was cried down in all parts of the Confederacy, and by every organ of public opinion there. The Confederate press desperately and savagely denounced the idea of " reconstruction." The *Examiner* said of the Northern people : " They do not yet understand that we are resolute to be rid of them forever, and determined rather to die than to live with them in the same political community again." The *Dispatch* declared : " We warn the

Democrats and conservatives of the North to dismiss from their minds at once the miserable delusion that the South can ever consent to enter again, upon any terms, the old Union. If the North will allow us to write the Constitution ourselves, and give us every guaranty we would ask, we would sooner be under the Government of England or France than under a Union with men who have shown that they cannot keep good faith, and are the most barbarous and inhuman, as well as treacherous of mankind. . . . . But do not expect us to degrade ourselves and cast dishonour upon the graves of our kindred by ever returning to the embrace of those whose hands are dripping with the tears and blood of our people." The leaders and politicians of the Confederacy were not behind the press in denouncing the idea of any possible reunion with the North. Alexander H. Stephens, Vice-President of the Confederate States, made a speech in North Carolina, which in view of the sequel attached to this man, is a curious personal reminiscence of the war. He said: " As for reconstruction, such a thing was impossible—such an idea must not be tolerated for an instant. Reconstruction would not end the war, but would produce a more horrible war than that in which we are now engaged. The only terms on which we can obtain permanent peace is final and complete separation from the North. Rather than submit to anything short of that, let us resolve to die like men worthy of freedom."

It appeared indeed that the people of the South had fully made up their minds; that they were prepared to suffer all the calamities of the most protracted war; and that they would never, on any terms, politically affiliate with a people, who were guilty of an invasion of their soil, and whose atrocities in the war had caused the whole civilized world to shudder.

MILITARY OPERATIONS IN THE EARLY MONTHS OF 1863.

Before reaching the great campaign of 1863, dated with the fighting months of summer, we find certain minor operations of the war within the period of winter and early spring, of which we may coveniently give here a summary account. The heavy rains of winter and early spring prevented heavy movements on land, and this period in the history of the war we shall generally find occupied by attempts of the enemy on the seacoast or by amphibious expeditions on the inland waters of the Confederacy. The most important of the events referred to as preceding what may be indicated as the grand campaign of 1863, were the recapture of Galveston by the Confederates; renewed attempts of the enemy on Vicksburg, with some other enterprises on the waters of the Mississippi; and the repulse of the Federal fleet at Charleston. The narrative of these events is mostly a story of successes for the Confederates—the sum of which was considerable, and the effect a spirited preparation and an auspicious prospect for the larger issues of the year.

Gen. Magruder, who had been appointed to the command of the Con federate forces in Texas, found the harbours of this coast in the possession of the enemy from the Sabine River to Corpus Christi, and the line of the Rio Grande virtually abandoned. He resolved to regain the harbours, if possible, and to occupy the Valley of the Rio Grande in force. The first step of his enterprise contemplated the expulsion of the enemy's vessels from the harbour of Galveston, and the re-possession of that town. Having assembled all the moveable artillery that could be collected in the neighbourhood, he occupied in force the works erected opposite the island on which the town of Galveston stands, and commanding the railway bridge which connects it with the mainland. He also fitted up as gunboats two steamers, the Bayou City and the Neptune, making them shot-proof, by means of bulwarks of cotton bales. The enemy's fleet, then lying in the waters of Galveston, consisted of the Harriet Lane, carrying four heavy guns, and two 24-pounder howitzers, commanded by Capt. Wainwright; the Westfield, flag-ship of Commodore Renshaw; a large propeller, mounting eight heavy guns; the Owasco, a similar ship to the Westfield, mounting eight heavy guns; the Clifton, a steam propeller, four heavy guns; the Sachem, a steam propeller, four heavy guns; two armed transports; two large barques; and an armed schooner.

The enemy's land forces—a few hundred men—were stationed at the end of a long wharf, and were crowded into large buildings immediately under the guns of the steamships. The approaches landward to this position were impeded by two lines of strong barricades, and communication with the shore was destroyed by the removal of portions of the wharf in front of the barricades. It thus became necessary for storming parties to advance by wading through the water, and to mount on the end of the wharf by scaling ladders.

It was arranged by Gen. Magruder that the naval and military operations should be simultaneous, and should commence before daybreak on the 1st January, 1863. The co-operation of the cotton-boats with the land forces was extremely difficult to obtain—the distance the former had to run being thirty miles. The attack was opened a little past midnight by a shot from our land batteries. The moon had gone down, but the Federal ships were still visible by the light of the stars. Leading the centre assault, Gen. Magruder approached to within two squares of the wharves, where the enemy's land forces were stationed, and where he was within three hundred yards of the enemy's formidable fleet. While Magruder engaged the vessels with artillery, the storming party advanced to the assault; the men wading through the water, and bearing with them their scaling ladders with which they endeavoured to reach the end of the wharf on which the enemy was stationed. A severe conflict took place at this point, the Confederates being exposed to a fire of grape, canister, and shell, and at last being compelled to take the shelter of the buildings near the wharf.

As the morning advanced, our fire still continuing, the long-expected cotton-boats came dashing down the harbour, and engaged the Harriet Lane, which was the nearest of the enemy's ships, in gallant style, running into her, one on each side, and pouring on her deck a deadly fire of rifles and shot-guns. The gallant Capt. Wainwright fought his ship admirably. He succeeded in disabling the Neptune, and attempted to run down the Bayou City. The Confederate boat adroitly evaded the deadly stroke; although, as the vessels passed each other, she lost her larboard wheel-house in the shock. Again the Bayou City, while receiving several broadsides almost at the cannon's mouth, poured into the Harriet Lane a destructive fire of small arms. Turning once more, she drove her prow into the iron wheel of the Harriet Lane, thus locking the two vessels together. Followed by officers and men, Commodore Leon Smith leaped to the deck of the hostile ship, and after a moment of feeble resistance she was ours.

After the surrender, the Owasco passed along side, pouring into the Harriet Lane a broadside at close quarters; but she was soon forced to back out by the effect of our musketry. Commodore Smith then sent a flag to Commodore Renshaw, whose ship, the Westfield, had, in the mean time, been run aground, demanding the surrender of the whole fleet, and giving three hours time to consider. These propositions were accepted by the commanding officer, and all the enemy's vessels were immediately brought to anchor with white flags flying. Within an hour of the expiration of the period of truce, Gen. Magruder sent another flag to Commodore Renshaw, whose ship was among the most distant, claiming all his vessels immediately under our guns as prizes, and giving him further time to consider the demand for the surrender of the whole fleet. This message was borne by two Confederate officers. While they were on their way in a boat, to fulfil their mission, Commodore Renshaw blew up his ship, and was himself accidentally blown up with it. They boarded the ship of the next in command, who dropped down the bay, still having them on board, and carried them some distance towards the bar, while still flying the white flag at the mast-head. Meanwhile, the first period of truce having expired, the enemy's ships under our guns, discovering that the Confederate boats and their prize were too much damaged to pursue, and regardless of the white flags still flying at their mast-heads, gradually crept off. The small Federal force which held the wharf, perceiving that they were abandoned by the fleet, surrendered as prisoners.

The capture of Galveston was thus completed; besides which we had taken one fine steamship and two barques, run ashore the flag-ship of the commodore, and driven off two war steamers, breaking the blockade of the port, and temporarily reopening it to commerce.

We have already noticed some attempt of the enemy to open the Mississippi River, and to renew commercial communication between the Northwestern States and their natural port at New Orleans. The interest of the war in the West, after the battle of Murfreesboro', may be said to have culminated in Vicksburg, and the campaign in the State of Mississippi was chiefly important in so far as it affected the operations for the reduction of this town, which closed the course of the great river to the Federal fleets.

The second attempt against Vicksburg was to be made by Gen. Sherman, who in the latter part of December, 1862, with four divisions under his command, accompanied by several gunboats, commenced the descent of the Mississippi River. The expedition was a shameful failure. Sherman, having landed his forces, attempted to capture the town from the northwestern side, and during the last days of December, there was some desultory fighting, when the Federal commander, without making any concentrated attack on the Confederate position, abandoned the enterprise, and re-embarked his troops at Milliken's Bend. The weak and disgraceful issue of this expedition is chiefly remarkable for its connection with the name of a commander declared incompetent, at this period of the war, and yet destined to win the reputation of a hero from the fickle multitude of the North.

After Sherman's failure, Gen. Grant made the third attempt upon Vicksburg, endeavouring, by combined naval and military operations, to turn the rear of the line of defence. Several expeditions were planned in the spring months of 1863, to turn the defences of the town, by means of the vast network of rivers, such as the Tallahatchie, Yazoo Pass, and Sunflower, which connect the Mississippi River with the Yazoo. These expeditions terminated without success, and are chiefly memorable for devastations of the country, which, indeed, was the usual resource of the enemy whenever disappointed in the accomplishment of military results.

While Grant was thus operating against Vicksburg, an attempt was made by the lower Federal fleet, under Farragut, to pass the batteries at Port Hudson, so as to co-operate with Admiral Porter's fleet on the upper waters. On the night of the 14th March, the Hartford, Farragut's flagship, steamed slowly up the river, passing the first of the line of batteries, followed by the Richmond, Mississippi, Monongahela, Genesee, Albatross, Kineo, the iron-clad Essex, the gunboat Sachem, and a mortar flotilla of six schooners. The Confederate batteries were silent, waiting to bring the whole fleet under their guns before they went to work. Presently there was one grand, long, deafening roar, and the battle was commenced. A great fire had been lighted on the river's bank, near one of the most for-

midable works, to throw light across the stream and to illumine the enemy's vessels. The artillerists on shore had no difficulty in sighting their
guns. The sheets of flame that poured from the sides of the vessels at
each discharge, lit up nearly the whole stretch of river, placing each craft
in strong relief against the black sky. The fleet soon lost its orderly line
of battle. The Hartford was struck, but being a swift vessel, succeeded,
with her consort, the Albatross, in running past the batteries. The Richmond, and the vessels following her, turned round; but as the Mississippi
was executing this manœuvre, a shot tore off her rudder, and another went
crushing through the machinery. She drifted aground on the right bank
of the river. She was being rapidly torn to pieces by shot from the batteries, when her commander abandoned her. Lightened by the departure
of the crew, and influenced by the current, she floated off, stern foremost,
down the river, in a sheet of flame, exploding her magazine, and sinking
near Providence Island. The enterprise against Port Hudson had proved
a failure, and Gen. Banks, who was advancing from Baton Rouge to take
part in the anticipated siege, was content to march back again.

So far the Confederate strongholds on the Mississippi had bid defiance
to the foe, and months of costly preparation for their reduction had been
spent in vain. But after Sherman's repulse from Vicksburg some compensation was sought in an easier enterprise, and McClernand, who succeeded him in command, organized an expedition of two *corps d'armée*,
and a fleet of three iron-clads, and several gunboats, against Arkansas
Post, a village on the Arkansas River, about fifty miles from its mouth.
The position had been fortified by the Confederates, and was held by Gen.
Churchill with about thirty-three hundred effective men. On the 11th
January, a combined attack was arranged between Gen. McClernand and
Admiral Porter. Before the final assault was made, the garrison, finding
themselves unable to reply to the fire of the gunboats, and overwhelmed
by superiour numbers, hoisted a white flag, and surrendered. The importance of this capture by the enemy was, that he obtained a fortified
point guarding the navigation of the Arkansas River, and shutting out its
commerce from the Mississippi.

For some time the enemy had been making preparations for an attack
on Charleston from the sea. There was an especial desire in the North to
capture and punish this city, where the first movements of the war had
commenced, and it was fondly hoped that on the anniversary of the first
capture of Sumter there would be a change of flags, and the Federal ensign
would again float from its walls. To accomplish this pleasant event, a
large fleet, including many iron-clads built after the model of the Monitor,
had been assembled at Port Royal, under command of Admiral Dupont,
and about the first of April was ready for action at the mouth of Charleston Harbour. There were seven iron-clads of the Monitor pattern;

other descriptions of iron-clads were exemplified in the Keokuk and Iron sides, the latter being an armour-plated frigate, with an armament of eighteen 10, 11, and 15-inch guns. It was to be a trial between new forces of tremendous power. The defences at Charleston had been materially strengthened by Gen. Beauregard, who had been assigned to the coast service; and it was thought scarcely possible that any floating thing could breast unharmed the concentrated storm of heavy metal from the guns of Sumter, Moultrie, and Battery Bee, the three principal works in the throat of the harbour. A test was at last to be obtained of a long-mooted question, and iron-clads, which were claimed to be the most impenetrable vessels ever constructed, were to come within point-blank range of the most numerous and powerful batteries that had ever been used in a single engagement.

In the afternoon of the 7th April, the line of iron-clads, comprising seven Monitors, the Ironsides, and Keokuk, entered the channel, and passed Battery Bee, and along the front of Morris Island. No sound came from the batteries; not a man was seen on the decks of the iron-clads; the sea was smooth as glass, and thus calmly and majestically the whole line of vessels passed the outer batteries. At ten minutes after three, the fleet, having come within range, Fort Sumter opened its batteries, and, almost simultaneously, the white smoke could be seen puffing from the low sand-hills of Morris and Sullivan's Islands indicating that the batteries there had become engaged. Five of the iron-clads forming in line of battle in front of Fort Sumter, maintained a very rapid return fire, occasionally hurling their fifteen-inch shot and shell against Fort Moultrie and minor batteries, but all directing their chief efforts against the east face of Fort Sumter. The firing became terrific. The Ironsides, from her position, engaged Fort Moultrie; Battery Bee mingled the hoarse thunder of its guns in the universal din, and the whole expanse of the harbour entrance, from Sullivan's Island to Cummings' Point, became enveloped in the smoke and constant flashes of the conflict. The iron-clads kept constantly shifting their position; but, whichever way they went, their ports always turned towards the battlements of Sumter, pouring forth their terrible projectiles against the walls of that famous stronghold.

Presently the Keokuk pushed ahead of her companions, placed herself within less than nine hundred yards of the fort, and seemed to challenge it to combat. A circle of angry flashes radiated towards her from all sides; she had made herself the target of the most powerful guns the Confederates could command. In a few moments, she was disabled, and crept slowly out of fire. The remainder of the fleet, more or less severely injured, withdrew, and in thirty minutes from the time when the first gun opened, the action was over, and a victory obtained, which went far to impeach the once dreaded power of the iron-clads of the enemy. Admiral

Dupont, " convinced of the utter impracticability of taking the city of Charleston with the force under his command," retired to Port Royal, leaving the stranded, riddled wreck of the iron-clad Keokuk as evidence of his defeat. All his vessels had sustained serious injury. The Confederates, with but two death casualties, had driven off an iron-clad fleet, obtained a complete triumph, and destroyed the prestige of the description of vessel named after the Monitor, the first of its class.

CHAPTER XXII.

THE military situation in the spring months of 1863 may be described by a few general lines drawn through the country, and bounding the main theatres of the war. In Virginia either army was in view of the other from the heights overlooking the town of Fredericksburg, whilst the country between the Rappahannock and the Potomac was at various times visited by detachments of Stuart's daring cavalry. The army of Tennessee was tied to no special line of operations; it was embarrassed by no important point, such as Richmond requiring to be defended; it had thus greatly the advantage over the army of Virginia; and yet we have seen, and shall continue to see, that it was far inferiour in activity and enterprise to the latter, and that, while Gen. Lee was overthrowing every army that came against him, Bragg was idle, or constantly yielding up territory to a conquering foe. From March till June, in 1863, Gen. Bragg's forces remained idly stretching from Shelbyville to the right, while the Federals, holding a line from Franklin to Woodbury, again and again, afforded opportunities of attack on detached masses which the dull Confederate commander never used. West of the Alleghany Mountains the war had travelled steadily southward to Tennessee, Mississippi, and Arkansas. In Mississippi we held the line of the Tallahatchie and the town of Vicksburg, while Grant threatened the northern portion of the State, and McClernand menaced Vicksburg. West of the Mississippi the war had been pushed to the banks of the Arkansas River, the Federals held Van Buren, and Hindman's weak and shifting tactics opposed an uncertain front to further advance of the enemy in this distant territory.

The great campaign of 1863 was to open in Virginia. There were especial reasons at Washington for an early resumption of the campaign. The Democratic party was gaining strength, in the absence of any grand success in the war; and the term of service of many of the Federal soldiers in Virginia was so near expiration that it was thought advisable to try again the issue of battle at a period somewhat earlier in the year than the date of former operations against Richmond. A change of commanders, which had come to be the usual preliminary of the resumption of Federal campaigns, was not omitted.* Gen. Joe Hooker was raised from the

---

* Mr. Headley, a Northern authour, in his interesting work, "The Campaigns of Sherman and Grant," makes the following very just commentary on the Northern mania for a " change of commanders." Referring to the achievements of these two popular heroes of the war, he says :

"It is not to be supposed that they were the only two great generals the war had produced, or the only ones who were able to bring it to a successful issue. It is an errour to imagine, as many do, that the Government kept casting about for men fit to do the work these men did, and, after long searching, at length found them. Several were displaced, who would have, doubtless, succeeded in bringing us ultimate victory, had they been allowed a fair trial. The errour was in supposing that men, capable of controlling such vast armies, and carrying on a war of such magnitude and covering almost a continent in its scope, were to be found ready-made. They were not to leap forth, like Minerva from the head of Jupiter, completely panoplied and ready for the service to which they were determined. A war of such magnitude, and covering the territories that ours did, would have staggered the genius of Napoleon, or the skill of Wellington, even at the close of their long experience and training. To expect, therefore, that officers, who had never led ten thousand men to battle, were suddenly to become capable of wielding half a million, was absurd. Both the army and the leaders, as well as the nation, had to *grow* by experience to the vastness of the undertaking. A mighty military genius, capable at once of comprehending and controlling the condition of things, would have upset the government in six months. Trammelled, confined, and baffled by 'ignorance and unbelief,' it would have taken matters into its own hand. Besides, such prodigies do not appear every century. We were children in such a complicated and wide-sweeping struggle; and, like children, were compelled to learn to walk by many a stumble. Greene, next to Washington, was the greatest general our revolutionary war produced; yet, in almost his first essay, he lost Fort Washington, with its four thousand men, and seriously crippled his great leader. But Washington had the sagacity to discern his military ability beneath his failure, and still gave him his confidence. To a thinking man, that was evidently the only way for us to get a competent general—one capable of planning and carrying out a great campaign. Here was our vital errour. The Government kept throwing dice for able commanders. It is true that experience will not make a great man out of a naturally weak one ; but it is equally true that without it, a man of great natural military capacity will not be equal to vast responsibilities and

position of corps commander to that of general-in-chief, and appointed to take command of the *fifth* attempt against Richmond. He was an immense braggart. His popular designation was " Fighting Joe Hooker.' He had made himself famous in the newspapers by his fierce criticisms of McClellan's campaigns; had predicted certain capture of Richmond under his own leadership; and was just the man whose boastful confidence might kindle anew the hopes of the credulous people of the North.

THE BATTLE OF CHANCELLORSVILLE.

On the 27th of April Hooker began his grand movement over the Rappahannock. His great numerical force enabled him to divide his army, and yet to maintain his superiority at all points. His left wing, under Sedgwick, crossed at Fredericksburg, intending to attack and occupy the heights above the town, and seize the railway to Richmond. Meanwhile the stronger portion of his army crossed the river some miles above Fredericksburg, at the United States', Ely's, and Germania fords, and began to move toward Chancellorsville—the name of a place marked by a large house, formerly a tavern, and a few out-houses, about eleven miles above Fredericksburg, and about four miles south of the point of confluence of the Rapidan and the Rappahannock. On the 30th April, having got all his forces across the river, he issued a flaming address, announcing that " the operations of the last three days have determined that our enemy must ingloriously fly, or come out from behind their defences and give us battle on our own ground, where certain destruction awaits him." So confident was he of success that he declared that Lee's army was " the property of the Army of the Potomac." Indeed, his chief concern appears to have been to cut off Lee's retreat; and as his army crossed the river, the cavalry was to move around the Confederate position, one body under Averill, marching on Gordonsville, the other under Stoneman, interposing between Lee's army and Richmond, to cut the lines of rail and destroy his communications. The disposition of forces was such that the Northern newspapers declared that it was at once conclusive of the fate of Lee and of the Confederacy itself. Never

combinations. Our experience proved this; for both Grant and Sherman came very near sharing the fate of many that preceded them. Nothing but the President's friendship and tenacity saved the former after the battle of Pittsburgh Landing. His overthrow was determined on; while the latter was removed from the department of Kentucky, as a crazy man. Great by nature, they were fortunately kept where they could grow to the new and strange condition of things, and the magnitude of the struggle into which we had been thrown. If the process of changing commanders the moment they did not keep pace with the extravagant expectations of the country, and equally extravagant predictions of the Government, had been continued, we should have been floundering to this day amid chaos and uncertainty."

were such strains of exultation heard in New York and Washington since the first field of Manassas. The common conversation was that the Confederates were between two fires; that Hooker had them just where he wanted them; that they could not retreat; that they would be annihilated; that " the rebellion " was nearly at an end.

Gen. Lee was certainly now in the most trying situation of the war. He was out-numbered by an enemy, whose force, compared with his own, was—as we have the precise statement of Gen. Lee himself—as *ten to three ;* and he was threatened by two attacks, the inferiour of which—that of Sedgwick at Fredericksburg—was equal in numbers to his whole army. Despite desertions and the difficulties of the recruiting service, the strength of the Federal army operating in Northern Virginia had been kept up to about 150,000 men. Gen. Lee had less than 50,000 men. He had been compelled to detach nearly a third of the army with which he had fought at Fredericksburg to confront demonstrations of the enemy on the coasts of Virginia and North Carolina; and Longstreet had been sent to command the department which included Richmond and its vicinity, together with the State of North Carolina, placed under the immediate supervision of Gen. D. H. Hill.

There was nothing more remarkable about the great Confederate commander than his cheerful self-possession, his calm, antique courage in the most trying and terrible circumstances of life. There was no expression of uneasiness on his part; no sign of dismay in the calm, grand face; and the quiet and collected orders which he gave, alone indicated a movement almost unexampled in its daring to crush the enemy whose numbers had enveloped him. He watched the movement of Sedgwick at Fredericksburg, as well as the one higher up the river under Hooker, until he had penetrated the enemy's design, and seen the necessity of making a rapid division of his own forces to confront him on two different fields.

On the 29th of April, Gen. Lee drew back his army in the direction of Chancellorsville, leaving Early's division to guard Marye's Heights at Fredericksburg. At Chancellorsville he learned from Gen. Anderson, who, with two brigades—Posey's and Mahone's—had been guarding the upper fords of the river, that the main body of the Federal army was advancing from that direction, and threatened his left rear. A force nearly one hundred thousand strong was on what had formerly been the left rear of the Confederates and was now the front. Taking from the account the forces left at Fredericksburg, Lee was out-numbered nearly three to one. His army consisted of Jackson's three divisions and two of Longstreet's former corps—McLaw's and Anderson's. He had in his rear Sedgwick's force, which equalled in strength his whole army; and it appeared, indeed, that he would be crushed, or forced to retreat with both flanks exposed along the Richmond rail, which was already at the mercy of Stoneman's cavalry

On the 1st of May Hooker ordered an advance to be made from Chancellorsville in the direction of Fredericksburg. At the close of the day his army held the ground from the neighbourhood of Banks' Ford to Chancellorsville, and thence with the right thrown back, covered the road to Germania Ford. But while Gen. Lee kept the enemy amused this day by several attacks and feints, preparations were in progress for a flank march, in which the terrible Stonewall Jackson was to try again the success of his favourite movements.

The flank march of Jackson commenced at night; his corps consisting of three divisions, under A. P. Hill, Rodes, and Trimble. He was directed to move by a road behind the line-of-battle to the road that led to Germania Ford, where the extreme right of the Federal army—Howard's corps—rested. The route lay through the Wilderness, a district of country covered with scrubby oaks and a thick, tangled undergrowth. Availing himself of its cover, Jackson marched around the right flank of Hooker's army, without that general having any knowledge of the critical movement which was in progress almost within reach of his guns. Near sunset of the 2d of May, he was in position at Wilderness Church. The two divisions of McLaw and Anderson kept up a succession of feints on Hooker's front, while Jackson, with stealthy and alert movement, prepared to fall like a raging tiger upon his flank.

But few hours of day-light were left when Jackson commenced his attack. It was sudden and furious. Marching rapidly from the direction of Germania Ford, he fell suddenly on Howard's corps in the forest. The yell of his soldiers was the only signal of attack. The whole corps of the enemy was broken; it retreated in confusion and dismay; in vain Hooker interposed himself to check the flight; his right wing was being fiercely driven down upon Anderson's and McLaw's sturdy veterans, and the fate of his army hung in a balance.

Presently there was a halt in the pursuit. The enemy had succeeded in rallying some of his artillery near a stone wall directly in the line of the retreat. Then Jackson, in company with a number of his own and a part of A. P. Hill's staff, rode forward to reconnoitre, and proceeded beyond the front line of skirmishers. When he had finished his observations, he rode back in the twilight to rejoin his men, that he might order a fresh attack. A North Carolina regiment mistook the party, as they galloped through the foliage, for the enemy. Some one cried out " Cavalry," " charge ! " and immediately the regiment fired. Jackson fell, struck by three balls, two through the left arm, and another penetrating the palm of the right hand. He was placed on a litter; one of the bearers was shot down by the enemy's skirmishers; the General, falling, received a severe contusion of the side, and was for two hours nearly pulseless from the shock. For five minutes he lay actually within the line of the Federal skirmishers, and under a heavy fire of artillery. Some of his men becoming aware of his danger, rushed forward, and plucked, from the terrible fire of artillery, the prostrate form of their beloved commander. He was placed in an ambulance, and carried to the field hospital at Wilderness Run.

With Jackson's fall the impetus of the Confederate attack ceased. Gen. Stuart, who succeeded to the command, renewed the fight at nine o'clock, and continued it until the enemy's right had been doubled in on his centre in and around Chancellorsville. But the fiery energy of Jackson was wanting to carry forward the troops, and to make what was already a severe repulse of the enemy a terrible and irremediable disaster.

A messenger was despatched to Gen. Lee, with the intelligence of the wounding of his great lieutenant. He found the General on a bed of straw about four o'clock in the morning. He told him that Jackson was severely wounded, and that it had been his intention to press the enemy next day—Sunday—if he had not fallen. Gen. Lee quietly said, " These people shall be pressed to-day." The grand, simple commander never had any other name for the enemy than " these people." He rose from his bed of straw, partook of his simple fare of ham and cracker, sallied forth, and made such dispositions as rendered that Sabbath-day a blessed one for the Confederacy.

At day-break, on the 3d, the three divisions of Jackson's old corps advanced to the attack. Meanwhile Anderson's division was pushed forward by Gen. Lee to assault the strongly-entrenched position of the enemy in front of Chancellorsville. On one side the Federals were being forced back in the direction of Chancellorsville. On the other side Anderson's men pressed through the woods, over the fields, up the hills, into the very mouths of the enemy's guns, and forced him to take shelter behind a second line of entrenchments in rear of Chancellorsville. There were ladies at Hooker's headquarters, in the large house which gave the name to the battle-field. They were taken away by one of Hooker's staff, as the firing became hot. One of the ladies fainted. It was a forlorn sight to see that troupe passing through the Federal lines at such a time. Soon after they left, the house, which was a large and elegant structure, took fire, and burned to the ground. Hooker's headquarters were transferred to the rear, and his crippled army, surrounded on all sides, except toward the river, was anxious now only for retreat.

It was ten o'clock in the morning. The capture or destruction of Hooker's army now appeared certain. But just then news was received that Sedgwick, who had crossed the river at Fredericksburg, had taken Marye's Heights, which had been held by Barksdale's brigade, less than two thousand men, and six pieces of the Washington Artillery. The hill was flanked, and its brave defenders, who had held it against three assaults, were cut off from their supports, and compelled to surrender. Gen. Early, finding that Sedgwick had gained this position on his left, and was pressing forward his forces towards Chancellorsville, withdrew, and took up a position near Salem Church, about five miles from Fredericksburg, where he threw up some slight field-works.

The movement of Sedgwick made it necessary for Gen. Lee to arrest the pursuit of Hooker, and caused him to send back towards Fredericksburg the division of McLaw to support Early and check the enemy's advance. On the evening of the 3d, Sedgwick's advanced troops were driven back without difficulty. On the 4th the battle was renewed. The enemy was evidently attempting to establish communication with Hooker along the river road, and for this purpose had massed a heavy force against McLaw's left. A portion of Anderson's force was marched fifteen miles to his support; but Gen. Lee, who had come upon the field, having discovered the enemy's design, ordered Anderson to unite with Early, so as to attack that part of the enemy's line which he had weakened by his demonstration on McLaw, and thus threaten his communication with Fredericksburg. The combined attack was made just before sunset. Sedgwick's men hardly waited to receive it; they fled precipitately towards Banks' Ford; and during the night they recrossed the river in the condition of an utterly defeated and demoralized army.

Thus, on the night of the 4th of May ended the remarkable series of battles on the lines of the Rappahannock. There had been three distinct engagements: that of the Wilderness, where Jackson succeeded in turning the enemy's flank; that most properly called the battle of Chancellorsville, around which point the enemy centred and made his best fight; and that of Salem Church which closed with Sedgwick's rout and retreat across the river.

The enemy was now driven from every point around Fredericksburg, and it but remained to make short work of Hooker at United States Ford. That commander, cowed and hemmed in within his straitened lines by a few Confederate divisions, had scarcely fired a gun while Sedgwick's corps, a few miles off, was being overwhelmed and driven back in disgraceful confusion. He called a council of war, and determined to retreat. The night of the 5th afforded him the opportunity; there was a drenching storm of wind and rain; pontoons were laid; the several corps crossed the river; and the next morning the enemy's whole force was over the river, and on the march to its former camps at Falmouth.*

---

* It is curious to notice the hardy falsehoods of official dispatches. Although Hooker had sustained one of the worst defeats in the war, he issued the following rubbish in a *congratulatory address* (!) to his army:

"General Order, No. 49.

"The Major-General Commanding tenders to the army his congratulations on its achievements of the last seven days. If it has not accomplished all that was expected, the reasons are well-

The loss of the enemy was terrible. We had taken nearly eight thousand prisoners; Northern accounts stated Sedgwick's loss at five thousand; that of Hooker in killed and wounded was probably twice as large; and but little is risked in putting all his losses at twenty-five thousand men. Gen. Lee's loss was less than ten thousand. He had won one of the most remarkable victories on record; illustrated the highest quality of generalship, the self-possession and readiness of a great commander, and confirmed a reputation now the first in war. Indeed, this reputation had not properly commenced in the Seven Days Battles around Richmond; for it was only when Lee moved out to the lines of the Rappahannock that there commenced the display of his great tactical abilities. He had now fought the most difficult and brilliant battle of the war. Amid all the achievements and wonders of his future career, Chancellorsville must ever remain the master-piece of his military life.

Now and then there were developed in the South certain facts and figures concerning the war, officially verified, and so unlike the stories of the newspaper and the printed catchpenny, that the public mind was startled from former convictions, and put on a new train of inquiry. This was especially so with reference to the unequal match of force in the war. The Southern people had a general impression that they were largely outnumbered in the contest; that the North was greatly superiour in men, material, and all the apparatus of conquest. But their notions of this inequality were vague, and in no instance came up to the full measure of

known to the army. It is sufficient to say, that they were of a character not to be foreseen or prevented by human sagacity or resources.

"In withdrawing from the south bank of the Rappahannock before delivering a general battle to our adversaries, the army has given renewed evidence of its confidence in itself and its fidelity to the principles it represents.

"By fighting at a disadvantage, we would have been recreant to our trust, to ourselves, to our cause, and to our country. Professedly loyal and conscious of its strength, the Army of the Potomac will give or decline battle whenever its interests or honour may command it.

"By the celerity and secrecy of our movements, our advance and passage of the river was unäisputed, and on our withdrawal not a rebel dared to follow us. The events of the last week may well cause the heart of every officer and soldier of the army to swell with pride.

"We have added new laurels to our former renown. We have made long marches, crossed rivers, surprised the enemy in his entrenchments, and wherever we have fought we have inflicted heavier blows than those we have received.

"We have taken from the enemy 5,000 prisoners and fifteen colours, captured seven pieces of artillery, and placed *hors de combat* 18,000 of our foe's chosen troops.

"We have destroyed his depôts, filled with vast amounts of stores, damaged his communications, captured prisoners within the fortifications of his capital, and filled his country with fear and consternation.

"We have no other regret than that caused by the loss of our brave companions, and in this we are consoled by the conviction that they have fallen in the holiest cause ever submitted to the arbitration of battle.

"By command of Major-General HOOKER,

"S. WILLIAMS, Assistant-Adjt.-General."

the Northern advantage in this respect.   It was the policy of the Confederate Government to keep all military matters secret, and to give, even to our own people, exaggerated impressions of the strength of our forces in the field.   Our armies were always popularly accounted much larger than they really were, and a pleasant delusion was maintained, until some occa sion would bring out official figures, and shock the public with surprise Who would have supposed, until Beauregard's official figures were published, that the army of the First Manassas numbered less than thirty thousand men, and that five Confederate regiments on that field held in check, for two hours, a column of fifteen thousand Federal infantry? Who would have imagined, looking at the newspapers of the day, that Albert Sidney Johnston, who was popularly expected, in the first year of the war, to take Cincinnati, and to march to the Northern Lakes, never had more than twenty-odd thousand men to meet all the emergencies of the early campaign in Kentucky and Tennessee?   Who would have believed, unless on the official authority of the great Confederate Chieftain himself, that Gen. Lee whipped " *the finest army on the planet*," under Hooker, with less than one-third his force?   These are matters of official history, and stand in sharp contrast to the swollen narratives of the newspaper, and in singular relations to the Northern assertion of martial prowess in the war.

While the great victory of Chancellorsville was causing joy and congratulation throughout the Confederacy, Gen. Stonewall Jackson lay dying at a small farm-house, a few miles from where he had led his last and most famous attack.   No one had supposed that his wounds would prove mortal; it had already been announced from his physician that amputation had been decided upon, and he would probably very soon thereafter be in a condition to be removed to Richmond.   But while preparations were being made there to receive the distinguished sufferer, there came the appalling news that an attack of pneumonia had supervened, and that there were no hopes of his recovery.   He expired on Sunday, the eighth day of his suffering.   He had declared: "If I live it will be for the best—and if I die, it will be for the best; God knows and directs all things for the best."   His last moments were mostly occupied with lively expressions of that trust and confidence in God, which had marked his life for many years, and which he had carried into all the details of his wonderful career.   There were various reports of his last words.   They were not religious ones.   His last utterance in the delirium that preceded death was: "Tell Major Hawks to send forward provisions to the men.   Let us cross over the river and rest under the shade of the trees."   And thus passed over the dark river and into eternal rest, the spirit of the great man, whose exploits had been amongst the most brilliant in the military history of the world, and whose character must ever remain an interesting subject for the student of mankind.

CHARACTER OF " STONEWALL " JACKSON.

THERE was probably no more ambitious man in the Southern Confederacy than " Stonewall " Jackson. The vulgar mind thinks that it easily discovers those who are the ambitious men in a community. It readily designates as such those who aspire to office and public positions, who seek sensations, court notoriety in newspapers, and hold up their hands for the applause of the multitude. But ambition, in its true and noble sense, is very different from these coarse bids for popular favour. There is a class of apparently quiet minds which, choosing seclusion and mystery, and wearing an air of absence, or even misanthropy, moving in their daily walks with an appearance of profound unconcern, are yet living for history, and are daily and nightly consumed with the fires of ambition. It is this sort of ambition which cherishes and attempts ideals; which is founded on a deep and unconquerable self-esteem; and which is often haughtily and even grimly silent, from a consciousness of its own powers, or an ever present belief in its destiny.

Of such an order of ambition those who knew Gen. Jackson best declare that he was singularly possessed. He believed in his destiny, whatever religious name he chose to attach to that transcendental and ravishing sentiment; he was fond of repeating to his intimate friends that " mystery was the secret of success;" and because he went about his work with a silent and stern manner, that was no proof of the opinion of the populace, that he was simply a machine of conscientious motives, with no sentiment in his composition but that of duty.

It is not unfrequently the experience of truly great men, that they have to live through a period of utter misapprehension of their worth, and often of intense ridicule. Such was the painful experience of Gen. Jackson. At the Virginia Military School at Lexington, where he was a professor before the war, he was thought to be stupid and harmless, and he was often the butt of the academic wit of that institution. Col. Gillem, who taught tactics there, was taken to be the military genius of the place, and afterwards gave evidence of the correctness of this appreciation by actually losing, during the war, in the mountains of Northwestern Virginia the only regiment that he was ever trusted to command. At the battle of Manassas, despite the critical and splendid service which Jackson did there (for he stayed the retreat in the rear of the Robinson House, and in the subsequent charge pierced the enemy's centre), his stiff and odd figure drew upon him the squibs of all the newspaper correspondents on the field. His habit of twisting his head, and interpolating " Sir " in all his remarks was humorously described in the Charleston *Mercury*. At a later period of his military career, when he made his terrible wintry march in 1861–2, from Winchester to Bath and Romney, and became involved in differences with Gen. Loring, it was actually reported that he was insane. A colonel came to Richmond with the report that Jackson had gone mad; that his mania was that a familiar spirit had taken possession of a portion of his body; and that he was in the habit of walking by himself and holding audible conversations with a mysterious being.

It was about this time that Gen. Jackson came under the fitful cloud of President Davis' displeasure; and he was so much affected by the course of the Richmond authorities towards him in his affair with Loring, that, at one time, he determined to resign. The extreme sensibility of his nature, and his ardent *ambition*, were unmasked in the letters he wrote his wife, alluding to the then probable close of his military career, and submitting to what he supposed "the will of God" in this abrupt termination of his hopes. But it was not decreed by Providence that the Confederate cause should then lose the services of Jackson, and its chief ornament be plucked from it, and its great pillar of strength cast down through a paltry official embroilment in Richmond. By the earnest persuasions of Governor Letcher and others, Gen. Jackson was induced to withdraw his letter of resignation; and that sword which might have been dropped in an obscure quarrel was yet to carve out the most brilliant name in the war.

The fame of Jackson was first secured, and permanently erected in the popular heart, by his splendid and ever-memorable campaign in the valley of Virginia, in the spring of 1862. In that campaign, as we have seen, in the period of three weeks, he fought four battles; recovered Winchester; captured four thousand prisoners; secured several million dollars' worth of stores; chased Banks' army out of Virginia and across the Potomac, and accomplished a list of deeds that threw the splendour of sunlight over the fortunes of the Confederacy, and broke, at the critical moment, the heaviest shadows of defeat and misfortune that had so far befallen them. In the Seven Days Battles the name of Jackson again rose like a star. And yet it was to gather new effulgence, when the names of Second Manassas and the Wilderness were to be inscribed, alike on the banners of the Confederacy and the escutcheon of his own fame.

Jackson's intense religious character has naturally come in for a large share of public admiration and curiosity. To his merits as a commander, he added the virtues of an active, humble, consistent Christian, restraining profanity in his camp, welcoming army colporteurs, distributing tracts, and anxious to have every regiment in his army supplied with a chaplain. Prayer-meetings and "revivals" were common occurrences in his camp, and in these he was quite as active and conspicuous as in the storm and action of battle. It was said that he treated the itinerant preachers and

" circuit-riders " who flocked to his camp with much more distinction than any other visitors ; and the story is told how, on one occasion, when the horse driven by one of these itinerants balked at a hill, Jackson himself insisted upon leading and assisting the animal up the acclivity in the astonished sight of his whole army.

His nature was epicene. We but seldom see a combination of feminine tenderness with a really strong will ; but when we do, we see masked iron in the man, and discover the rarest and loftiest type of greatness. Such a combination was most sincere and striking in Jackson. An authentic anecdote is told of him, illustrating his extreme tenderness to whatever was weak or helpless. Stopping at the house of a friend, one wintry night, he showed much concern for a little delicate girl of the family, and counselled them to see that her bed was comfortable. After the family had retired, Jackson was seen to leave his chamber and approach the bedside of the little girl, where for some moments he busied himself tucking the bedclothes around her, and making the little creature as snug as possible.—The large, rough hand that did this gentle task, was the same that wielded the thunderbolt of battle, and that cleft like flaming lightning the hosts of the Wilderness.

Jackson's habits in the field were those of almost superhuman endurance. Neither heat nor cold appeared to make the slightest impression upon him. He cared nothing for good quarters and dainty fare. He often slept on the ground, wrapped in his blanket. His vigilance was marvellous ; he never seemed to sleep ; he let nothing pass without his personal scrutiny. His active determination and grim energy in the field, were scarcely to be expected from one who, in preceding years, had been a quiet professor in a college of youths. As for the rapidity of his marches, that was something portentous.*

---

* An officer on the staff of Jackson, at the time he was ordered to the Shenandoah Valley, writes as follows, in a pleasant private letter, of his experiences of the campaign, and of the peculiarities of the commander :

"When we were ordered up the Valley with old Jackson, it was considered to be a source of congratulation to all for going into active service ; but, believe me, I would have willingly gone back into winter-quarters again after a week's trial, for Jackson is the greatest marcher in the world. When we first moved up here, our orders were for a march to Charlestown ; next day we moved back to Winchester ; in a few days again back to Charlestown ; and thence, from one place to another, until at last I began to imagine that we were commanded by some peripatetic philosophical madman, whose forte was pedestrianism. With little or no baggage, we are a roving, hungry, hardy lot of fellows. ' Stonewall ' may be a very fine old gentleman, and an honest, good-tempered, industrious man, but I should admire him much more in a state of rest than continually seeing him moving in front. And such a dry old stick, too ! As for uniform, he has none—his wardrobe isn't worth a dollar ; and his horse is quite in keeping, being a poor, lean animal, of little spirit or activity. And don't he keep his aides moving about ! Thirty miles' ride at night through the mud is nothing of a job ; and if they don't come up to time, I'd as soon face the devil, for Jackson takes no excuses when duty is on hand. He is solemn and thoughtful, speaks but little, and always in a

The London *Times*, a journal whose judgments of men were taken in the cotemporary world almost as the sentences of history, frequently compared Jackson to Napoleon. "He was," said this great organ of European opinion, "one of the most consummate Generals that this cen tury has produced. * * * That mixture of daring and judgment, which is the mark of 'Heaven-born' Generals distinguished him beyond any man of his time. Although the young Confederacy has been illustrated by a number of eminent soldiers, yet the applause and devotion of his countrymen, confirmed by the judgment of European nations, have given the first place to Jackson. The military feats he accomplished moved the minds of the people with astonishment, which it is only given to the highest genius to produce. The blows he struck at the enemy were as terrible and decisive as those of Bonaparte himself."

There can be no doubt in history of the military genius of Jackson. There is a certain ignorant idea of genius as a thoughtless and careless disposition of mind, which gets its inspirations without trouble, and never descends to actual labour. Such was not the genius of Jackson; and such is not true genius. He was an active, laborious thinker; he wrestled with great thoughts; he had his silent calculations; but having once apprehended the true thought, and got to a point in his meditations, he acted with a rapidity, a decision, and a confidence, that scorned hesitation, refused longer to think, and took the appearance of impetuous inspiration.

Danger, in a certain sense, intoxicated him. But it did not produce that intoxication which confuses the mind, or makes it giddy with a crowd of images. It was that sort of intoxication which strings the nerve, stimulates the brain, concentrates the faculties, and gives a consciousness of power that is for the moment irresistible. In battle, he was not much in motion; but his eyes glowed; his face was blazoned with the fire of the conflict; his massive jaw stiffened; his voice rang out sharp and clear; every order and remark was as quick and pertinent as if it had been studied for hours. One could scarcely recognize in this figure of intense activity, all alive, with every faculty at play, the man who used to occupy himself with rambling soliloquies in the rear of his tent; who presented the appearance of an inanimate figure-head in his pew at the Presbyterian

calm, decided tone; and from what he says there is no appeal, for he seems to know every hole and corner of this valley as if he had made it, or, at least, as if it had been designed for his own use. He knows all the distances, all the roads, even the cow-paths through the woods, and goat-tracks along the hills. I have frequently seen him approach in the dead of night, and enter into conversations with sentinels, and ride off through the darkness. In my opinion, Jackson will assuredly make his mark in this war, for his untiring industry and eternal watchfulness *must* tell upon a numerous enemy unacquainted with the country, and incommoded by large baggage-trains."

church in Lexington; and who often got up out of his camp-bed at night to spend hours in silent prayer and meditation.

It may readily be imagined that the wonderful career of Jackson and his personal eccentricities drew upon him a crowd of apocryphal anecdotes in the newspapers. Some of them were very absurd. His person was as variously represented in newspaper paragraphs as if, instead of being familiar to thousands, he inhabited the dim outlines of another century. One journal described him as an absurdly ugly man with red hair; another gave his portrait as that of an immense brain, and features on which nature had stamped the patent of nobility. One newspaper correspondent declared that he always wore the brim of his cap on the middle of his nose. Another declared that he was an execrable rider, and looked like a loose jumping-jack on horseback.

There is a popular disposition to discover something curious or grotesque in great men. But there was really but little of this sort to be discovered in Jackson, and scarcely anything that could be pointed out as objects of vulgar curiosity. It is true his figure was queer and clumsy; but the features of his face were moulded in forms of simple grandeur; and its expression was as unaffected as that of Lee himself. He was not an ugly man. The vulgar might call him such; and the newspaper passion for caricature did so represent him. Nor did he have in face or figure those marks which the silly admiration of woman expects to find in military heroes. He did not wear long, greasy hair falling over his shoulders; he did not stand in dramatic attitudes; he did not keep his eyes unnaturally stretched; he did not thrust out his chest, as if anxious to impose himself upon public attention. His features were singularly simple and noble. A broad forehead, rising prominently over his eyes, and retreating at that easy angle which gives a certain majesty to the face, covered a massive brain; his nostrils were unusually large; his jaw heavy and well-set; and, although his features were coarse, they were combined in that expression of dignity and power which, to the intelligent and appreciative, even among women, is the greatest charm of the masculine face.

The death of Jackson cast a shadow on the fortunes of the Confederacy, that reached to the catastrophe of the war. It was not only a loss to his country; it was a calamity to the world: a subtraction from the living generation of genius: the extinction of a great light in the temples of Christianity. The proposition was eagerly made in the South to erect to his memory a stately monument. The State of Virginia sent an artist to Europe to execute his statue. Thousands followed him to the grave, and consecrated it with tributes of affection and the testimonies of devotion. Who, then, regarding this fervour of admiration and gratitude, could have supposed that the Southern mind could ever become so chilled in any change of events, or in any mutation of fortune, as to forget alike its debts of gratitude and its objects of pride in the glorious past; and that the time could ever come when the household effects of Stonewall Jackson would be sold under the hammer of an auctioneer, and the family of this man committed to the trials and chances of poverty!

CHAPTER XXIII.

VICKSBURG, THE SECOND PRIZE OF THE WAR.—GEN. GRANT.—WHAT HIS PERSISTENCY WAS
WORTH.—HIS NEW SCHEME OF ATTACK.—TWO PARTS OF THE ENTERPRISE.—PORTER'S
GUNBOATS RUN THE BATTERIES.—GRANT'S MARCH FROM MILLIKEN'S BEND.—BLINDNESS
OF GEN. PEMBERTON AT VICKSBURG.—ANTECEDENTS AND CHARACTER OF THIS COM-
MANDER.—HIS EXTREME INCOMPETENCY.—PRESIDENT DAVIS BLAMED.—HIS CAPRICE AND
OBSTINACY.—GRANT CROSSES THE MISSISSIPPI AND MOVES TOWARDS PORT GIBSON.—GEN.
JOHNSTON'S TELEGRAM TO PEMBERTON.—CRITICAL OPPORTUNITY OF THE CAMPAIGN.—
PEMBERTON REFUSES TO USE IT, AND DISREGARDS JOHNSTON'S DESPATCH.—BATTLE OF
PORT GIBSON.—EXTRAORDINARY VALOUR OF BOWEN'S COMMAND.—GRANT TURNS GRAND
GULF AND MOVES UPON JACKSON.—GEN. JOHNSTON'S ARRIVAL AT JACKSON.—SITUATION
AND STRENGTH OF THE CONFEDERATE FORCES.—EVACUATION OF JACKSON.—JOHNSTON
OFFERS A SECOND OPPORTUNITY OF ATTACK TO PEMBERTON.—THE LATTER DISOBEYS THE
ORDER AND COMMITS A FATAL ERROUR.—SHERMAN'S INCENDIARY RECORD IN JACKSON.—
HIS USE OF THE FIRE-BRAND.—GRANT FORCES BATTLE UPON PEMBERTON.—BATTLE OF
BAKER'S CREEK.—TREMENDOUS EXERTIONS OF STEVENSON'S DIVISION.—GEN. LORING
FAILS TO SUPPORT HIM, REMAINS INACTIVE, AND IS CUT OFF IN THE RETREAT.—PEMBER-
TON'S NEW POSITION UPON THE BIG BLACK.—ITS STRENGTH.—IT IS SHAMEFULLY ABAN-
DONED.—DISGRACEFUL RETREAT OF PEMBERTON'S ARMY.—THE FATE OF VICKSBURG VIR-
TUALLY DECIDED AT THE BIG BLACK.—GEN. JOHNSTON ORDERS THE EVACUATION OF
VICKSBURG.—PEMBERTON ENTRAPPED THERE.—SIEGE AND SURRENDER OF VICKSBURG.—
CONFIDENCE OF THE GARRISON RESTORED.—PROSPECT OF RELIEF FROM JOHNSTON.—HOW
IT WAS VISIONARY.—TWO ASSAULTS OF THE ENEMY REPULSED.—PAINFUL OPERATIONS OF
SIEGE.—SUFFERINGS OF THE GARRISON.—JOHNSTON HAS SOME HOPE OF EXTRICATING THE
GARRISON.—TAYLOR'S ATTACK AND REPULSE AT MILLIKEN'S BEND.—PEMBERTON'S DE-
SPATCH TO JOHNSTON.—THE REPLY: "SOMETHING MAY YET BE DONE TO SAVE VICKS-
BURG."—JOHNSTON PREPARES TO ATTACK ON 7TH JULY.—PEMBERTON SURRENDERS ON
FOURTH OF JULY.—HIS CONFERENCE WITH GRANT.—A TERRIBLE DAY'S WORK.—EXTENT
OF THE DISASTER TO THE CONFEDERATE CAUSE.—SURRENDER OF PORT HUDSON.—OTHER
EVENTS IN THE REGION OF THE MISSISSIPPI CONNECTED WITH THE FALL OF VICKSBURG.—
OPERATIONS IN THE TRANS-MISSISSIPPI.—BATTLE OF HELENA.—OBJECT OF GEN. HOLMES'
MOVEMENT ON HELENA.—AN EXTRAORDINARY MARCH.—AN EXTRAORDINARY COUNCIL OF
WAR.—GEN. PRICE PROTESTS AGAINST AN ATTACK.—HE IS ORDERED TO TAKE "GRAVE-
YARD" FORT.—HE SUCCEEDS.—THE OTHER ATTACKS FAIL.—DISASTROUS RETREAT OF GEN.
HOLMES.—THE CAMPAIGN IN LOWER LOUISIANA.—GEN. TAYLOR'S CAPTURE OF BRASHEAR
CITY AND ITS FORTS.—HIS OPERATIONS IN THE LAFOURCHE COUNTRY.—HIS SUCCESSES
NEUTRALIZED BY THE FALL OF VICKSBURG AND PORT HUDSON.—BANKS RETURNS TO NEW
ORLEANS AND THE ENEMY HOLDS THE ENTIRE LINE OF THE MISSISSIPPI.

THE object of the enemy's operations, second to Richmond, was distinctly the possession of Vicksburg and the opening of the whole length of the Mississippi River. Enormous efforts had been made to obtain these two great prizes. Five attempts upon Richmond had failed. Three attempts upon Vicksburg—that of Porter's fleet; that of Sherman's army; and that of Grant, which may be designated as an attempt to force a passage to the rear of the town, including the project of a canal across the isthmus and the enterprises known as the Yazoo Pass and Sunflower Expeditions—had accomplished nothing. Foiled again at Chancellorsville, in the great aim of the Virginia campaign, the enemy turned with renewed vigour upon the second object of the war, and public attention was immediately directed to the great campaign likely to decide the fate of the Mississippi Valley.

Gen. Grant had already obtained a great reputation for persistency—a slight title to merit, it may be remarked, when a commander has at his disposal abundant means, and at his back a government so generous and rich as never to call its officers into account for the loss of life and of treasure in any case of ultimate success. He now proposed to change his plan of operations against Vicksburg. He determined to invest the town, and having turned the defences on the Mississippi and Yazoo Rivers, to cut off the defenders from all communication with the east. One part of the enterprise was to run Porter's gunboats and a number of transports past the works at Vicksburg; while a land force, consisting of two corps, under Grant in person, should march from Milliken's Bend to Carthage, a distance of thirty-five miles, interrupted by marshes and streams. Both movements succeeded. On the 16th and 22d April, two fleets of gunboats and transports ran the batteries with insignificant disaster, and repeated the lesson that had been taught more than once in the war, that, unless where obstructions have been placed, steamers will run the gauntlet of almost any fire. By the last of April, Grant, having marched down the west bank of the river, and joined Porter's gunboats at Carthage, was ready to execute the next step in his scheme of attacking Vicksburg from the southeast.

His adventure was a complete surprise to Gen. Pemberton at Vicksburg. This commander, who had been appointed to what the Confederates designated as the department of Mississippi and East Louisiana, had been so blind as to suppose Grant's object was not Vicksburg, but Bragg's army in Tennessee, and as late as the middle of April, he had proposed to order troops to Tullahoma, under the delusion that Rosecrans would be reinforced from Grant's army. The mistake was characteristic of a commander who was in no way qualified for the great trust to which he had been exalted. The appointment of Gen. Pemberton to the defence of

Vicksburg was an unfortunate one; it was probably the most unpopular single act of President Davis, who was constantly startling the public by the most unexpected and grotesque selections for the most important posts of the public service. Pemberton had not yet fought a battle in the war. He was a Pennsylvanian by birth; he had been a major in the old United States service; and from this inconsiderable rank, without a single record of meritorious service in the Confederacy, he had been raised by a stroke of President Davis' pen to the position of a lieutenant-general, and put in command of a post second in importance to the Confederate capital. He had previously had some uneventful commands at Norfolk and at Charleston. He was removed thence in consequence of frequent protests; but in each instance with promotion, as if the President was determined to mark his contempt for a public opinion which did not appreciate his favourite, or hoped to inspire a dull brain by adding another star to his collar. He was sent to Vicksburg with a larger command and a more extensive field, to show eventually the accuracy of the public judgment as to his capacity even for subordinate positions. With armies so intelligent as those of the Confederacy, no man unfitted for command could long maintain their confidence and respect. He might intrench himself with all the forms and parade of the schools; but intelligent soldiers easily penetrated the thin disguise, and distinguished between the pretender and the man of ability. So it was at Vicksburg. Pemberton had already given there early evidence of his unfitness for command. While Grant was assiduously engaged under his eye, for months, in preparing the powerful armament which was to spend its force on the devoted fortress, his adversary took no notice of the warning. The water batteries, which might have been strengthened, were afterwards found to be so imperfect as to inflict but slight damage on the gunboats, and permit the run of all the transports of a large army with equal impunity. The fortifications of Grand Gulf, where Grant was now making his next demonstration, had been neglected, until the tardy attempt rendered the accumulation of guns and stores there an easy prey to the enemy. Vicksburg, with an abundant country around it, had only two months' instead of twelve months' provisions. How was Pemberton engaged? Immersed in official trifles, laboriously engaged in doing nothing, while the murmurs around him and the friction of events had developed personal characteristics which, with want of confidence of officers and men, rendered him highly unpopular. Of a captious and irritable nature, a narrow mind, the slave of the forms and fuss of the schools, Gen. Pemberton was one of those men whose idea of war began with a bureau of clothing and equipment, and ended with a field-day or dress-parade. Warning after warning was sounded; but President Davis turned a deaf ear to them, not, perhaps, that he cared especially for Pemberton, but because his own vanity was so exacting that even to question his infallibility of selection was an offence not to be condoned.

Gen. Grant, having effected a junction with the gunboats below Vicksburg, next determined to turn the works at Grand Gulf, which defended the mouth of the Big Black River, by landing at a point lower down the river. Accordingly he marched by its right flank, crossed opposite Bruinsburg, and on the 30th April landed on the left bank, and immediately pushed forward towards Port Gibson, a small town near the mouth of the Big Black River.

Gen. Pemberton, who appeared to have been at last aroused to a sense of the danger of his position, telegraphed the news of Grant's movement to Gen. Johnston, nominally commanding the Western armies, and then at Tullahoma with Bragg. He received orders to attack at once. Gen. Johnston despatched : " If Grant crosses the river, unite all your troops to beat him. Success will give back what was abandoned to win it." It was the critical opportunity of the campaign. Grant had landed with about 50,000 men. By drawing all his forces from different posts, leaving only enough in Vicksburg to answer Porter's chronic bombardment, Gen. Pemberton could have concentrated nearly 40,000 troops, and these, with the advantage of a difficult country, and with slight field-works, might at all events have delayed Grant until Vicksburg was provisioned, and Johnston had arrived with reinforcements. But we shall see that the bewildered commander, without the resolution to risk a decisive battle, committed the unpardonable errour of allowing his army to be cut up in detail by an enemy with massed forces.

BATTLE OF PORT GIBSON.

The only Confederate force which was to meet the enemy's advance towards Port Gibson was a division of troops under Gen. Bowen. This brave and devoted officer had been left with a few thousand men to confront an overwhelming force of the enemy, as Gen. Pemberton had insisted upon putting the Big Black River between the enemy and the bulk of his own forces, which he declared were necessary to cover Vicksburg. Gen. Bowen had fifty-five hundred men. He was opposed by the corps of Gen. McClernand, numbering probably twenty thousand men. An engagement ensued on the banks of a small stream, which crossed the road from Bruinsburg. The enemy, by the extraordinary valour and constancy of the small force of Confederates, was kept back for an entire day, until just before sunset Gen. Bowen was compelled to fall back, executing a retreat without confusion, and saving the bulk of his army.

The position of Grand Gulf turned, and the battle of Fort Gibson won,

Grant pushed his column direct towards Jackson. Gen. Johnston reached Jackson on the night of the 13th May. He received there a despatch from Gen. Pemberton, dated 12th May, asking for reinforcements, as the enemy, in large force, was moving from the Mississippi, south of the Big Black, apparently toward Edwards's Depot, "which will be the battle-field, if I can forward sufficient force, leaving troops enough to secure the safety of the place."

Before Johnston's arrival at Jackson, Grant, as we have seen, had beaten Gen. Bowen at Port Gibson, made good the landing of his army, occupied Grand Gulf, and was marching upon the Jackson and Vicks-burg Railroad.

On reaching Jackson, Gen. Johnston found there the brigades of Gregg and Walker, reported at six thousand; learned from Gregg that Maxcy's brigade was expected to arrive from Port Hudson the next day; that Gen. Pemberton's forces, except the garrison of Port Hudson (five thousand) and of Vicksburg, were at Edwards's Depot—the General's head-quarters at Bovina; that four divisions of the enemy, under Sherman, occupied Clinton, ten miles west of Jackson, between Edwards's Depot and ourselves. Gen. Johnston was aware that reinforcements were on their way from the East, and that the advance of those under Gen. Gist would probably arrive the next day, and with Maxcy's brigade, swell his force to about eleven thousand.

Upon this information he sent to Gen. Pemberton a despatch, inform-ing him of his arrival, and of the occupation of Clinton by a portion of Grant's army, urging the importance of re-establishing communications, and ordering him to come up, if practicable, on Sherman's rear at once, and adding: "To beat such a detachment would be of immense value. The troops here could co-operate. All the strength you can quickly assemble should be brought. Time is all-important."

On the 14th May, the enemy advanced by the Raymond and Clinton roads upon Jackson. Johnston did not propose to defend the town; he had no sufficient force to do so; he therefore ordered Gregg and Walker to fall back slowly, offering such resistance to the march of the Federal columns as to allow time to remove or destroy the stores accumulated in Jackson. This work accomplished, Gen. Johnston retreated by the Canton road, from which alone he could form a junction with Pemberton.

It will be perceived that Grant was now between the two Confederate armies; but he was superiour in numbers not only to each, but to both united. Johnston had proposed the brilliant hazard of crushing an im-portant detachment of the enemy at Clinton, and had urged the para-mount necessity of re-establishing communications between the two Con-federate forces. Pemberton appears to have been completely blind to these considerations. In disobedience of the orders of his superiour, and in opposition to the views of a majority of the council of war, composed of al. his generals present, before whom he placed the subject, he decided to make a movement by which the union with Johnston would be impossible. It was a fatal errour.   The irresolute commander had, at first, expected to fight at Edwards's Depot, being unwilling to separate himself further from Vicksburg.   When he received Johnston's order to march on Sherman's rear at Clinton, and when the council of war, called by him, approved the movement, he hesitated, did not move for twenty-eight hours, and invented a compromise, in which equally abandoning his own preconceived plan of battle, and disobeying the orders of Gen. Johnston, he moved, not to risk an attack on Sherman, but in another direction towards Raymond, flattering himself that he was about to cut the enemy's communications.

The delay and aberration of Pemberton left Jackson at the mercy of the enemy, and opened the way to Vicksburg.   On the 15th April Gen. Sherman's corps marched into Jackson.   The incendiary record of this famous officer commenced here ; the first of his long list of conflagrations and peculiar atrocities dates with the burning, the plunder, and sack of Jackson.   The little town of two main streets, with detached villas, inhabited by wealthy planters, was surrendered to a soldiery licensed to rob, burn, and destroy.   Private houses, the Catholic church, the hotel, the penitentiary, and a large cotton-factory were burned.   As Sherman's troops marched out, a volume of smoke rose over the devoted town, while here and there rolled up fiercely great masses of flame attesting the infernal work of the man who, not content, in the nineteenth century and in a civilized country, to fight with the sword, had taken a weapon from another age—in the fire-brand of the savage.

Meanwhile Grant, having ascertained Pemberton's movement, directed McClernand's and McPherson's corps to move by the Jackson and Vicksburg railroad, and by the road from Raymond to meet him.   Sherman had been ordered to evacuate Jackson and to take a similar direction. Pemberton's disposable force consisted of seventeen thousand five hundred men.   On the 16th May, while moving on the road to Raymond, a courier handed him a despatch from Gen. Johnston, stating that, as the attack on Sherman had failed, the only means by which a union could now be effected between the two forces, was that Pemberton should move directly to Clinton, whither Johnston had retired.   An order of counter-march was issued.   But already heavy skirmishing was going on in Pemberton's front ; he found it impossible to extricate himself for a reverse movement ; and his situation was such that he was compelled to give battle on the ground selected by the enemy.

BATTLE OF BAKER'S CREEK.

The Confederate line of battle was formed in a bend of what was known as Baker's Creek, across the Jackson and Vicksburg railroad. After a desultory fire, the battle commenced in earnest about noon; Hovey's division attacking the centre of Pemberton's line, held by Stevenson's division, while two other divisions of the enemy threatened to turn the Confederate left. To relieve the centre, Gen. Loring was ordered to attack with his own division and that of Bowen. Gen. Loring did not attack. The enemy remained steadily in his front, in heavy force, occupying a series of ridges, wooded, and commanding each other, and forming a very strong position.

Meanwhile Stevenson's sixty-five hundred troops bore the brunt of the battle, sustained the heavy and repeated attacks of the enemy, broke Hovey's line, and drove it in disorder. But there were three other divisions of Grant's army marching from Raymond, and about to come into action. The only reinforcements that came to Stevenson's overtasked troops, were two brigades of Bowen. Loring was inactive; he again disobeyed orders to move to the left, and remained engaged with the movements of the enemy in his front. Stevenson continued the unequal battle until the enemy's division from Raymond had arrived on the field, when the Confederate line at last gave way and broke in confusion from the field.

Gen. Loring states that he was making dispositions for an attack upon the enemy's right, by which he hoped to " overwhelm it and retrieve the day," when he received orders from Pemberton to retreat and bring up the rear. If such an attack was designed, it was too late; the day was already lost. The retreat of the Confederates was by the ford and bridge of Baker's Creek. As soon as the enemy realized that they were leaving the field, he moved forward in heavy force. The retreat was covered with great spirit. Brigadier-Gen. Tilghman, of Loring's command, having become separated from it, was left with less than fifteen hundred effective men to sustain the attack of six or eight thousand of the enemy, with a fine park of artillery. But he was advantageously posted; he not only kept the enemy in check, but repulsed him on several occasions, and thus kept open the only line of retreat left to the army. He was killed as he was serving with his own hands a twelve-pound howitzer. His bold stand saved a large portion of the army; but the retreating columns were not yet across the stream. A message was sent to Gen. Loring: " For God's sake, hold your position until sundown, and save the army." A few moments later, a despatch was received from Gen. Bowen, stating that the enemy had crossed the bridge and out-flanked him, that he had been compelled precipitately to fall back, and that Loring must do his best to save his division. Gen. Loring, having ascertained that it was impossible to attempt the passage of the Big Black at any point, determined to force the rear of the enemy between Raymond and Utica, and to make his retreat through the east and effect a junction with the forces of Gen. Johnston in the neighbourhood of Jackson. He succeeded in doing so with the loss of his artillery.

On the following day, 17th May, Pemberton's shattered and demoralized forces had taken up a position upon the east bank of the Big Black River. The position was a strong one in a bend of the river, sheltered by patches of wood, with marshes extending on either side towards the river. The works were provided with a sufficient quantity of artillery; they were manned by a considerable force; and the position might have been held against largely superiour numbers. But the events of the previous day had demoralized the troops; they abandoned their position at the first assault of a Federal brigade; they left in the enemy's possession eighteen pieces of artillery; they scattered in wild and tumultuous flight. "The retreat," says Gen. Pemberton himself, "became a matter of *sauve qui peut*." By nightfall the fugitive disordered troops were pouring into the streets of Vicksburg, and the citizens beheld with dismay the army that had gone out to fight for their safety, returning to them under the shame of defeat, and in the character of a wild and blasphemous mob.

The fate of Vicksburg may be said to have been virtually decided, when Pemberton was driven into it, and the lines of the enemy drawn around it. Gen. Johnston so regarded it. When he learned of the disaster at Baker's Creek, he despatched to Pemberton: "If Haynes's Bluff be untenable, Vicksburg is of no value and cannot be held. If, therefore, you are invested in Vicksburg, you must ultimately surrender. Under such circumstances, instead of losing both troops and place, you must, if possible, save the troops. If it is not too late, evacuate Vicksburg and its dependencies, and march to the northeast." Before the despatch was received Gen. Pemberton had fallen back to Vicksburg.

Of this unfortunate situation Gen. Johnston writes: "Had the battle of Baker's Creek not been fought, Gen. Pemberton's belief that Vicksburg was his base, rendered his ruin inevitable. He would still have been besieged, and therefore captured. The larger force he would have carried into the lines, would have added to and hastened the catastrophe. His disasters were due, not merely to his entangling himself with the advancing columns of a superiour and unobserved enemy, but to his evident determination to be besieged in Vicksburg, instead of manœuvring to prevent a siege."

SIEGE AND SURRENDER OF VICKSBURG

Gen. Pemberton had in Vicksburg eight thousand fresh troops, not demoralized by defeat. When he arrived in town from the battle-field at Big Black, a general feeling of distrust was expressed in his competency, and the place was regarded as lost. Every one expected Grant's army to march into Vicksburg that night, while there was no means of defence and no spirit in the troops. Gen. Pemberton set to work, reorganizing the army for the last desperate struggle. Gen. Baldwin went out to review the line of defences, and imagining that the first assault would be made on the left wing, he petitioned to be assigned to hold that position with his veteran troops, upon whose fidelity and courage he could depend. The army was placed in position on the lines, and placed in the ditches, with Gen. Baldwin on the left, and Gen. Lee on the right. The centre was held by Gens. Pemberton, Smith, and Forney. As these dispositions were made, the confidence of the troops was gradually restored; they saw the purpose of defence; and they were entertained with the prospect that their besieged condition would soon be relieved by Johnston's army.

But such prospect was not a little visionary. The truth of the situation was that Pemberton had trapped himself in Vicksburg, to surrender to famine what could not be won by assault. Gen. Johnston had come to the Mississippi Department with no army of his own, beyond a few troops, to take charge of Pemberton's, which he found broken to pieces, and the remnants sheltered in Vicksburg. To collect a new army by appeals to the Richmond authorities, the Governor of Mississippi, and other quarters, became his only resource. With all his efforts only twenty thousand men could be raised, many of them raw troops, without field-guns and proper equipment; while Grant had been reinforced to eighty thousand men, besides the co-operation of Porter's fleet. He had also entrenched himself on every side with a difficult river between himself and Johnston. For the latter to have dashed himself against the enemy in such circumstances, might have been esteemed an act of magnificent daring; but it would not have been war. If Pemberton, instead of crowding superserviceable troops in a fortress to consume its scant supplies, or become the victims of disease or war, had thrown sufficient garrison into Vicksburg, and kept at large twenty thousand men, he could have so reinforced Johnston as to have enabled him to act promptly before Grant had entrenched himself, and thus relieve Vicksburg from the purpose of his efforts, by giving him occupation outside. But none of these things were done. Johnston's resources were utterly inadequate to any good purpose; he could not collect a sufficient force to break the investment of Vicksburg; and the prospect even of making a diversion or opening communication with the garrison was uncertain and difficult.

Vicksburg was invested by the enemy on the eastern side: Sherman holding the right of the lines, McPherson the centre, and McClernand the left. A new base of supplies was established, leading from the Yazoo directly to the rear. Guns were planted in opposition to the long, fortified series of works of the Confederates.

On the 19th May, the division of Gen. Blair, and a brigade of Sherman's division assaulted what was thought to be a weak place in the Confederate line of defence. They were severely repulsed. On the 22d a more concerted attack was ordered by Gen. Grant, and the whole line was bombarded by cannon. At an early hour the left, under McClernand, gained a foot-hold at an angle of the works, but was dislodged; and the enemy withdrew from the attack, after having suffered a loss of some twenty-five hundred men disabled. The attempt to take Vicksburg by storm seems to have been abandoned after this; and it was determined to reduce the position by siege and parallel works.

And now commenced a terrible task. Fort was erected against fort, and trench dug against trench. The enemy's sappers constructed their corridors and passages and pits amid a blazing fire of hostile musketry, and the fiercest rays of the summer sun. The Confederates, confined to the narrow limits of the trenches, with their limbs cramped and swollen, never had, by day or by night, the slightest relief. They were exposed to burning suns, drenching rains, damp fogs, and heavy dews. The citizens, women, and children, prepared caves in the hill, where they took refuge during the almost incessant bombardment. Thus, through the months of May and June continued the weary siege. The spirits of the troops were in a measure kept up by news received from Johnston's army, by means of messengers who found a way through the swamps and thickets of the Yazoo.

Although Gen. Johnston was too weak to save Vicksburg, he entertained some hope of extricating the garrison. With this view Gen. Taylor, commanding in the Trans-Mississippi, was ordered to co-operate with Pemberton from the west bank of the Mississippi. But the movement miscarried; Taylor's attack on the Federal camp at Milliken's Bend was repulsed; and all hope of help from the West was ultimately abandoned.

On the 22d June a despatch was received from Pemberton by Gen. Johnston, suggesting that the latter should make to Grant "propositions to pass this army out, with all its arms and equipages," and renewing his (Pemberton's) hope of his being able, by force of arms, to act with Johnston, and expressing the opinion that he could hold out for fifteen days longer. Johnston was moved by the determined spirit of the despatch. He replied: *" Something may yet be done to save Vicksburg.* Postpone both of the modes suggested of merely extricating the garrison. Negotiations with Grant for the relief of the garrison, should they become necessary, must be made by you. It would be a confession of weakness on my part, which I ought not to make, to propose them. When it becomes necessary to make terms, they may be considered as made under my authority."

On the 29th June, field transportation and other supplies having been obtained, Johnston's army marched toward the Big Black, and on the evening of July 1st encamped between Brownsville and the river.

Reconnoissances, which occupied the second and third, convinced Gen. Johnston that the attack north of the railroad was impracticable. He determined, therefore, to make the examinations necessary for the attempt south of the railroad—thinking, from what was already known, that the chance for success was much better there, although the consequences of defeat might be more disastrous.

On the night of the 3d July a messenger was sent to Gen. Pemberton with information that an attempt to create a diversion would be made to enable him to cut his way out, and that Johnston hoped to attack the enemy about the 7th.

On the Fourth of July Pemberton surrendered Vicksburg. The explanation has been made in his behalf that he never received Johnston's despatches, encouraging the hope that both Vicksburg and the garrison might be saved; and Gen. Pemberton has declared that had he received these despatches: "I would have lived upon an ounce a day, and have continued to meet the assaults of all Grant's army, rather than have surrendered the city until Gen. Johnston had realized or relinquished that hope."

As it was, he determined to surrender Vicksburg on the anniversary of the Fourth of July for the very singular reason that it would gratify the enemy's " vanity " to enter the stronghold of the great river on that particular day, and that such a concession might procure better terms than at any other time. The preliminary note for terms was despatched on the 3d July. Correspondence on the subject continued during the day, and was not concluded until nine o'clock the next morning. Gen. Pemberton afterwards came out, and had a personal interview with Grant, in front of the Federal line, the two sitting for an hour and a half in close communion. A spectator says: " Grant was silent and smoking, while Pemberton, equally cool and careless in manner, was plucking straws and biting them as if in merest chit-chat."

It was a terrible day's work for such a display of *sang froid.* It was the loss of one of the largest armies which the Confederates had in the field; the decisive event of the Mississippi Valley; the virtual surrender of the great river; and the severance of the Southern Confederacy. The numbers which surrendered at the capitulation of Vicksburg were twenty-three thousand men, with three Major-Generals, and nine Brigadiers, upwards of ninety pieces of artillery, and about forty thousand small-arms. Weakness from fatigue, short rations, and heat, had left thousands of the troops decrepit. Six thousand of them were in the hospitals, and many of them were crawling about in what should be convalescent camps. Four thousand citizens and negroes, besides Pemberton's army, included all the souls within the walls of Vicksburg. When we consider that these people had for a month and a half been in daily terrour of their lives, never being able to sleep a night in their homes, but crawling into caves, unable to move except in the few peaceful intervals in the heat of the day, we may appreciate what a life of horrour was theirs.

The first result of the surrender of Vicksburg, was the fall of Port Hudson, and the consequent supremacy of the Federal arms along the entire length of the Mississippi. Gen. Banks had invested this place; he had made two assaults on the 27th May and on the 14th June; and he had been repulsed by Gen. Gardner, who held the place with about five thousand men. When the news was communicated to Gardner that Vicksburg had surrendered, knowing that all hope of relief was at an end, he determined that it was useless to prolong resistance, and on the 9th July surrendered himself and the garrison as prisoners of war.

These events on the Mississippi constituted a reverse, which the resources of the Confederacy, neither in men nor means, could endure without great strain. Across the river the train of disaster appears to have extended. The fall of the strongholds of the Mississippi resulted in the retreat of our army from Little Rock, and the surrender to the enemy of the important valley in which it was situated; while a campaign auspiciously begun in Lower Louisiana was abandoned in consequence of the release of Banks' forces from the siege of Port Hudson. To these events we must now take the reader so as to gather up the several threads of the narrative of the war in the West.

OPERATIONS IN THE TRANS-MISSISSIPPI—BATTLE OF HELENA.

In the month of May it was deemed advisable by Gen. E. Kirby Smith, then commanding the Trans-Mississippi Department, that a demonstration should be made on the west side of the river in order that Vicksburg might be relieved. He accordingly directed Gen. Holmes to put the troops in Arkansas in motion to operate against Helena, a place on the west side of the river eighty miles south of Memphis and three hundred miles north of Vicksburg. It was occupied by a garrison of four thousand Federal troops, with a gunboat in the river.

On the morning of May 31st most of the troops in Arkansas were put in motion for an advance. The weather was very wet, the creeks all full, and the ground covered with water. For the expedition Gen. Holmes had Price's Division of infantry, consisting of Parsons' Missouri Brigade numbering 1,000, and McRay's Arkansas Brigade of 400 ; Fagan's Brigade of Arkansas infantry, numbering 1,500 ; and Marmaduke's Division of Arkansas and Missouri cavalry, numbering 2,000 ; making a total of 4,900. These several commands formed a junction at Jacksonport, and on the morning of 22d June commenced their march in the direction of Helena. It was a toilsome and dangerous march—one of the most extraordinary recorded in the history of the war. The infantry were in water to their waists on two-thirds of the road. Heavy details of worn-out men were employed in dragging the wagons through difficult places. The mules would be unhitched, a long rope fastened to the wagon, and a hundred men pull it through. There was no pontoon train, and over the swollen streams bridges of floating logs would be constructed, which a loaded wagon would sink several feet under water. In making this terrible march, twelve days were consumed, and on the evening of the 3d July the jaded men had reached within four miles of Helena.

Precious time had been lost. A council of war was called, in which occurred a remarkable scene. Gen. Holmes explained the strength of the position to be attacked. Helena was surrounded by a range of rough, wooded hills, which shut it into the river, except a narrow bottom next the river, both above and below. The place was defended by three prominent forts, one protecting the approach by the north, one at the south, and the " Grave-Yard " fort, in the rear of the centre of the city.

Gen. Price was not in favour of an attack. He argued that the enemy was doubtless expecting them, and had concentrated as many troops as he deemed sufficient to defend the place, and that, if it had been necessary to call troops from Vicksburg for this purpose, the object of the expedition had already been accomplished, and the only action of the troops should be to operate so as to detain such reinforcements at Helena. He thought this might be done most effectually by surrounding the place, cutting off the enemy's supplies, both from the country and the river, and harassing him by picket-fighting. Even if Helena were taken, he thought it would be a dearly-bought victory ; it was untenable ; and if any of the garrison escaped, and doubtless they had transports in waiting, their expulsion would but strengthen the enemy at Vicksburg, thereby defeating the very object of the expedition.

Gen. Holmes wanted the *éclat* of victory. He replied with warmth : " Gen. Price, I intend to attack Helena immediately, and capture the place, if possible. This is my fight. If I succeed, I want the glory ; and if I fail, I am willing to bear the odium." Then turning to the other officers, he said : " At twelve o'clock, to-night, we move towards Helena." Gen. Marmaduke, with his command, was ordered to attack the northern fort; Gen. Fagan was to attack the southern fort; and Gen. Price was to assault and capture the centre fort—the attack to commence simultaneously at day-light.

About day-break the first gun fired was by the battalion of sharpshooters belonging to Parsons' brigade, who encountered an outpost of the enemy. Price moved in column of division, the 9th Missouri Infantry in advance. The hills were high, the ravines deep; but the men pressed forward in good order, the enemy shelling them at every step of the march. When the last ridge was reached, the command was halted, and the men rested and closed up, ready for the assault. They were now within two or three hundred yards of the fort. By this time the firing had commenced on the right and left, and it was known that Fagan and Marmaduke were at work. The command was given by Gen. Price to charge with fixed bayonets. The troops moved in gallant style, at the run, over and through fallen timber and roughly constructed abatis, up hills, and into gullies. They were never checked once, and were soon in possession of the fort.

Price's division had done the work assigned it. Heavy guns from the gunboat in the river now commenced playing upon the captured fort. The men sheltered themselves, as well as they could, and awaited further orders. Meanwhile Fagan had moved against the southern fort, and when within two hundred yards of it, had commenced a fire of small-arms, which provoked such a heavy response of artillery, that his men were compelled to fall back. Twice was the assault repeated, and with the same result. Marmaduke met with no better success. Gen. Holmes, seeing the failures of Fagan and Marmaduke, ordered two regiments of Parsons' brigade to attack the southern fort in the rear. The movement was attempted; but under the fire of the gunboat and the cross-fire of the other two forts, and that of the whole infantry force of the enemy, it was impossible to advance. Fagan and Marmaduke having withdrawn their forces, it became necessary to attempt the withdrawal of Price's division. With the whole force of the enemy concentrated upon this division, and separated as it was from any support, its retreat was one of mortal peril at every step. It was accomplished with heavy loss. The battle was lost; six hundred Confederates had been disabled, and about four hundred taken prisoners. Gen. Holmes the next morning commenced his march back to Little Rock. The white flag had been run up at Vicksburg; all hope of the connection of the Trans-Mississippi with the eastern portions of the Confederacy was at an end; and Gen. Holmes had made the first step of the retreat which, at last abandoning Little Rock, was to surrender to the enemy the most valuable portion of Arkansas.*

---

* An esteemed correspondent writes us these personal incidents of the Battle of Helena:

THE CAMPAIGN IN LOWER LOUISIANA.

Almost cotemporary with these disastrous events was a remarkable episode of success in the lower country of the Trans-Mississippi, which had, at one time, kindled in the South the hope of the recapture of New Orleans, but finally came to naught on account of insufficient forces.

In the latter part of June, Gen. "Dick" Taylor, who commanded in Lower Louisiana, organized an expedition upon Brashear City and its forts. Col. Majors, who commanded a brigade of cavalry on the Atchafalaya, was ordered to open communication by way of the lakes with Gens. Mouton and Green, who were to co-operate in front of the enemy's position. The junction having been made by Majors, after a successful campaign through the Lafourche country, a combined attack was made on Brashear City on the 22d June, and the forts taken at the point of the bayonet. Eighteen hundred prisoners were captured, nearly five million dollars worth of stores, and a position occupied that was the key to Louisiana and Texas.

It was thought that the capture of Brashear City might force the enemy to raise the siege of Port Hudson, and that Banks would be driven to the choice of abandoning his operations against this place or losing New Orleans. But these expectations failed; the second diversion to relieve Vicksburg and Port Hudson was too late; and Gen. Taylor, learning of the fall of these strongholds and the consequent release of Banks' forces,

"Gen. Holmes is a brave man, and was under the hottest fire. After the centre fort had been captured, and the heavy fire from the gunboat and the two other forts had been opened on it, Gen. Holmes was standing on the parapet, eagerly looking for Fagan, who was his favourite, to plant his colours on the fort he was attacking. While thus standing, Gen. Parsons, who was sheltering himself in the fort, bawled out: "Come down, General! you will be hit. Don't you hear the shot whistling around you?" "I have the advantage of you, Gen. Parsons, I am deaf, and cannot hear them."

"Another incident of the battle should be recorded as a just tribute to the memory of a brave man. At the battle of Prairie-Grove, Lt. Richard Spencer, of the 9th Missouri Infantry, was taken sick, and was unable to engage in the fight. While at Jacksonport en route for Helena, he was again taken sick. At Prairie-Grove his colonel had accused him of cowardice, and said that his sickness was a mere excuse to keep out of the fight. When the command left Jacksonport, the surgeon of the regiment advised Lieut. Spencer to remain in hospital, which he refused to do. On the march, the surgeon noticing that he was quite unwell, repeatedly urged him to ride in an ambulance, which he declined. Once on the march it became necessary to detail an officer to remain in charge of some baggage, and Spencer was detailed for the purpose. He refused to obey the order, and told his colonel that he had been accused of cowardice for not going into the former fight, and that now he was determined to go if he had to drag his body into action; that he had rather die than live under such an imputation. He was finally excused from remaining with the baggage. Scarcely able to walk, he marched to Helena, led his company into the fort, and was shot dead through the head."

was no longer able to hold the Lafourche country, and was compelled to abandon the territory he had won. The last serious effort on the line of the Mississippi was at an end; a great prize had passed in the hands of the enemy beyond redemption; and it was already said, by extravagant newspapers in Washington and New York, that the dawn of a conquered peace was breaking upon the country.

CHAPTER XXIV.

A SINGLE day before the fall of Vicksburg occurred, far away, what may be emphatically entitled *the most important battle of the war.* It was fought on the soil of Pennsylvania, on whose wheat-fields President Davis had declared, on the floor of the United States Senate in Washington, when war was first threatened, should be carried the contest for the rights of the South.

During the few weeks following the brilliant victory of Chancellorsville, never did affairs look so propitious for the Confederates. The safety of Vicksburg was not then seriously questioned ; Bragg confronted Rosecrans with a force strong enough to hold him at bay ; and the Confederates had the choice of two campaigns : either to reinforce Bragg from Lee's army, over a distance that might be accomplished in ten days, with two lines of railroad as far as Chattanooga, or to change the defensive attitude in Virginia, and make a second experiment of the invasion of the North. The alternative of these campaigns was suggested in Richmond. The latter was decided upon. It was thought advisable to clear Virginia of the Federal forces, and put the war back upon the frontier ; to relieve the Confederate commissariat ; to counterbalance the continual retreat of the armies of Tennessee and Mississippi by an advance into Northern territory, offer a counterpoise to the movements of the enemy in the West, and possibly relieve the pressure there on the Confederate armies. These reasons determined an offensive campaign of Lee's army.

Gen. Longstreet was recalled from North Carolina ; and the Army of Northern Virginia, preparatory to the campaign, was re-organized, and divided into three equal and distinct corps. To Gen. Longstreet was assigned the command of the first corps, consisting of the divisions of McLaw, Hood, and Pickett ; to Gen. Ewell, who had succeeded to the command of Jackson's old corps, were assigned the divisions of Early, Rodes, and Johnson ; and to Gen. A. P. Hill was the third corps given, consisting of the divisions of Anderson, Pender, and Heth. Each of these three corps numbered about 25,000 men, making the total strength of the army 75,000, irrespective of the cavalry.

On the plains near Culpepper were the preparations made for the grand campaign. It was the beautiful month of May. All was bustle and activity ; the freshness of the air and the glow of expectation animated the busy scene. Trains were hurried up filled with munitions of war ; new and splendid batteries of artillery were added to the army ; the troops, as far as possible, were newly equipped, and ordnance trains were filled to their utmost capacity. The cavalry, 15,000 strong, were reviewed at Brandy Station ; crowds of ladies attended the display ; and Gen. Stuart, the gallant commander, whose only weakness was military foppery and an inordinate desire of female admiration, rode along the lines on a horse almost covered with bouquets. Nearly a week was consumed in reviewing cavalry, infantry, and artillery. By the first of June all was in readiness, and the advance was ordered.

Gen. Ewell's corps, in the lead, pushed rapidly forward, and marched across the Blue Ridge Mountains, by way of Front Royal, into the Shenandoah Valley upon Winchester. Here he surprised Gen. Milroy, defeated him ; and it was with difficulty that the Federal general, with a few of his officers, escaped through the Confederate lines under cover of the night, and succeeded in crossing the Potomac at Harper's Ferry. Three thousand prisoners, thirty pieces of artillery, over one hundred wagons, and a great quantity of stores were captured in and near Winchester, and seven hundred men surrendered to Gen. Rodes at Martinsburg. With this auspicious opening of the campaign, Ewell promptly moved up to the Potomac, where he occupied all the fords.

Longstreet's corps had been directed to march on Culpepper, his right flank guarded by detachments of Stuart's cavalry, which watched the fords of the Rappahannock, while A. P. Hill's corps remained near Fredericksburg, to deceive the enemy by an appearance of strength. These movements were not entirely unobserved by Gen. Hooker. He had reason to suppose that some of the Confederate forces had been withdrawn from his front; and accordingly, on the 5th of June, a strong reconnoissance was sent across the river on Lee's right. But the skilful Confederate commander, who was now performing a great master-piece of strategy, succeeded in masking his real strength, and leading Hooker to suppose that his entire army was still in the neighbourhood of Fredericksburg. On the 7th June another reconnoissance was directed, and an expedition of cavalry, which had crossed the Rappahannock at Beverly's and Kelly's Fords, attacked Gen. Stuart at Brandy Station. This force of the enemy was routed by Stuart, and forced to recross the river, after having lost four hundred prisoners and three pieces of artillery. Although this later reconnoissance developed to a certain extent the direction of Gen. Lee's march, Hooker was too dull to comprehend its importance, and, never dreaming of any movement into the Northern territory beyond perhaps a raid for commissary purposes, contented himself with making a disposition of his forces to cover Washington, and taking up a strong position between Manassas and Centreville, so as to interpose his army between the Confederate forces and what he supposed to be the object of their campaign.

Lee marched rapidly forward in pursuance of his plans. He had played with the enemy so as to mislead him entirely. Hooker followed Lee to the passes of the Blue Ridge, but was so uncertain whether he meant to give battle there, or move up the Valley, that time was lost, and instead of bringing the point to an issue at once in Virginia, the Federal commander had to hastily cross the Potomac, and take position in Maryland. Lee crossed the Potomac in the vicinity of Shepherdstown, on the 24th of June. The corps of Ewell had preceded him two days before, and on the 23d had occupied Chambersburg. On the 27th of June the whole of Lee's army was at Chambersburg. An advance on Harrisburg had been contemplated; but the design was abandoned on the 29th, in consequence of the information that the Federal army was moving northwards, and so menacing the communication of the Confederate army with the Potomac. To check the enemy's advance, therefore, Gens. Longstreet, Hill, and Ewell were ordered to proceed to Gettysburg. Thus within twenty days the great Confederate commander had brought his entire army from Fred-

ericksburg, by the way of the Shenandoah Valley to Gettysburg in Pennsylvania, without obstruction, and executed a wonderful feat of strategy.
It is true that other commanders in the war had made longer marches and
accomplished more magnificent distances. But to estimate properly the
generalship of Lee, it must be remembered that when he set out on this
expedition, he was confronted by one of the largest and best appointed
armies the enemy ever had in the field; that Winchester, Martinsburg,
Harper's Ferry, and Berryville were garrisoned by hostile forces; that the
Federal cavalry were in splendid condition; and yet in the face of all these
facts, he had marched along the Rappahannock, over the passes of the
Blue Ridge, up the Shenandoah Valley, and across the fords of the Potomac into Pennsylvania, without his progress being arrested.

When the Confederate army obtained a footing on the soil of Pennsylvania, there were many people who supposed that as here there was no
friendly disposition of the invaded, no reputation of political sympathy, as
in Maryland, to interpose between them and the penalties of war, the
troops would be prompt to exact a severe retribution for the cruelties of
the enemy displayed in the desolated homes and fields of the South. But
no such thing occurred; no such expectation was answered. On the contrary, no sooner had Gen. Lee crossed the line than he announced that
private property would be respected, and proceeded, by general orders, to
restrain all excesses of his troops, and, in fact, to give to the invaded people of Pennsylvania a protection which even those of the South had not
always had against the impressments and other exactions of the war. No
house was entered without authority; no granary was pillaged; no property was taken without payment on the spot; and vast fields of grains
were actually picketed by Confederate guards, mounted on almost starved
horses.

So far as these orders of Gen. Lee maintained the discipline and morals
of his troops, prevented them from degenerating into ruffians, and declined
retaliation of this sort, they were generally sustained by the public opinion
of his countrymen, for exasperated as they were by what they had experienced of the enemy's barbarities in their own homes, the Southern
people were so proud of their reputation for chivalry, and plumed themselves so much on this account, that they were willing to sacrifice for it almost any other passion of the war. But there was an obvious distinction
in this matter, and the Richmond *Examiner* indicated it in a striking and
powerful censure of Gen. Lee's course. It was said that only a few persons
in the South recommended retaliation *in kind;* that it was not advised
that houses should be burned, or robbed, jewelry stolen, and women raped
in Pennsylvania, in exact imitation of the acts of Northern troops in Virginia and Mississippi; but that such guard on the discipline and honour
of Confederate soldiers was not inconsistent with a devastation of the

enemy's country, done with the deliberation of general orders, and by the army acting in line of battle; and that such retribution, while it could have brought no historical discredit on the Confederate arms, was due the suffering people of the South, was necessary to teach the enemy a lesson, and indicated a kind of operation which, removed from the enemy's own barbarity, would equally avoid that weak warfare which irritated instead of alarming an invaded people, and thus strengthened their forces and obtained recruits for them on their own soil. Gen. Lee appears never to have comprehended this argument. We shall see hereafter in what coin his civilities in Pennsylvania were paid back, and how, notwithstanding the constant exertions of the Confederates, for what President Davis termed the reputation of "Christian warriours," the ingenious falsehoods of an enemy, himself constantly in the commission of the worst atrocities, entitled them the worst of savages, and turned upon them the phrase of "*rebel barbarities.*" But surely one reflection here cannot escape the world. It is the extreme improbability of such "barbarity" on the part of a people who, in the third year of the war, exhibited this magnanimity in Pennsylvania, and even in the character of an invading army, declined to take advantage of some of the most ordinary penalties of war.

On the 28th of June, Gen. Hooker, at his own request, was relieved from the command of the Federal army, and Gen. Meade, whose antecedents were those of an efficient corps and division commander, was appointed to succeed him. A great alarm pervaded the North. The Governors of Ohio, Pennsylvania, New York, Maryland, and Western Virginia called out their militia forces. But these feverish displays were of little consequence. It was easily seen by the intelligent that the security of the North rested upon Meade's army, and on the strongly fortified lines of Washington, and that if this array was once broken, hastily levied militia could afford no protection against Lee's army, and that thus the war was about to culminate in a grand contest of regular arms. It was a sharp, fearful issue. Gen. Meade found himself in command of a splendid army of about one hundred and fifty thousand men. He comprehended the necessity of rapid and decisive action. Rapidly organizing his forces, he marched out to meet the Confederates. Making a disposition of his forces so as to cover both Washington and Baltimore at the same time, he moved forward cautiously until his advance reached Gettysburg. About one mile from the town, a line of entrenchments was thrown up on a range of hills, and a heavy force moved forward through and beyond the town to watch the movements of his adversary.

THE BATTLE OF GETTYSBURG.

The great battle opened on the 1st July. The enemy's advance, consisting of the Eleventh Corps, was met by Heth's division, and shortly thereafter Ewell hurled the main body of his corps on the Federal column. When within one mile of the town, the Confederates made a desperate charge. The Federal line was broken; the enemy was driven in terrible confusion; the streets of the small town soon became thronged with fugitives; and Ewell, sweeping all before him, charged through the town, strewing every step of his progress with the enemy's dead, and taking five thousand prisoners. The crowded masses of fugitives poured through the town in rout and confusion, ascending the slopes of a hill towards a cemetery that covered its apex.

It was not later than five o'clock in the evening, but the success was not followed up. As Ewell and Hill prepared for a fresh attack, they were halted by Gen. Lee, who deemed it advisable to abstain from pressing his advantage until the arrival of the remainder of his army. The unfortunate inaction of a single evening and night enabled Meade not only, on his part, to bring up all his forces, but to post them on an almost impregnable line, which the Confederates had permitted a routed detachment of a few thousand men to occupy and hold.

The failure of Gen. Lee to follow up the victory of the 1st, enabled the enemy to take at leisure, and in full force, one of the strongest positions in any action of the war, and to turn the tables of the battle-field completely upon the Confederates. On the night of the 1st July, Gen. Meade, in person, reached the scene of action, and concentrated his entire army on those critical heights of Gettysburg, that had bounded the action of the first day, designated by the proper name of Cemetery Ridge. This ridge, which was just opposite the town, extended in a westerly and southerly direction, gradually diminishing in elevation till it came to a very prominent ridge, called "Round Top," running east and west. The Confederates occupied an exteriour ridge, less elevated, distant from the lines occupied by the Federals from a mile to a mile and a half. On this sunken parallel was arranged the Confederate line of battle—Ewell's corps on the left, beginning at the town with Early's division, then Rodes' division; on the right of Rodes' division was the left of Hill's corps, commencing with Heth's, then Pender's and Anderson's divisions. On the right of Anderson's division was Longstreet's left, McLaw's division being next to Anderson's, and Hood on the extreme right of our line, which was opposite the eminence upon which the enemy's left rested.

There was long a persistent popular opinion in the South that Gen. Lee, having failed to improve the advantage of the first day, did wrong thereafter to fight at Gettysburg. But this charge must be discussed with care. Gen. Lee, himself, has explained how a battle was forced upon him. He says : " It had not been intended to fight a general battle at such distance from our base, unless attacked by the enemy ; but finding ourselves unexpectedly confronted by the Federal army, it became a matter of difficulty to withdraw through the mountains with our large trains. At the same time the country was unfavourable for collecting supplies, while in the presence of the enemy's main body, as he was enabled to restrain our foraging parties by occupying the passes of the mountains with regular and local troops. A battle thus became, in a measure, unavoidable. Encouraged by the successful issue of the first day, and in view of the valuable results which would ensue from the defeat of the army of Gen. Meade, it was thought advisable to renew the attack."

It is true that the position of the enemy was one of extraordinary strength. But the Army of Northern Virginia was in an extraordinary state of proficiency ; it was flushed with victory ; it had accomplished so many wonders in the past that it was supposed to be equal to anything short of a miracle ; and when, on the morning of the 2d, Gen. Lee reconnoitred the field, and scanned the heights which looked upon him through brows of brass and iron, he was noticed to rise in his stirrups, and mutter an expression of confidence. He decided to attack.

The action of the 2d July did not commence until about two o'clock in the afternoon. Under cover of a heavy fire from the Confederate batteries, Longstreet advanced against the Federal left, and Ewell, from Gettysburg and Rocky Creek, moved forward Johnson's, Rodes', and Early's divisions against the right, his guns keeping up a continuous fire on the slopes of Cemetery Hill. Whilst the two corps on the flanks advanced to the attack, Anderson's division received orders to be prepared to support Longstreet, and Pender and Heth to act as a reserve, to be employed as circumstances might require.

Longstreet, having placed himself at the head of Hood's and McLaw's divisions, attacked with great fury. The first part of the enemy's line he struck was Sickles' corps, which he hurled back with terrible loss on the heights in its rear. The Confederates delivered their fire at short musket range, then charged up the steep ascent with the peculiar yell of the Southern soldier. Meade, seeing that the real attack was against his left, hurried reinforcements rapidly from his centre. For two hours the battle raged with sublime fury, and on the semi-circle of Round Top trembled the fiery diadem of victory and all the issues of the day. The fire was fearful and incessant ; three hundred pieces of artillery belched forth death and destruction on every side ; the tumultuous chorus made the earth tremble ; and a dense pall of smoke fitly constituted a sulphurous canopy for scenes of infernal horrour. Longstreet, with hat in hand, seemed to court the death which avoided him. At one moment it was thought the day was won. Three brigades of Anderson's division moved up, had made a critical attack, and Wilcox and Wright almost gained the ridge; but reinforcements reached the Federals; and, unsupported by the remainder of Anderson's division, Longstreet's men failed to gain the summit of the hill, or to drive back the enemy from the heights of the Round Top.

On the Confederate left, Ewell's success had been better. He had moved forward to the assault of Cemetery Hill; Johnson's division forced its way across the broken ground near Rocky Creek, sustaining considerable loss from the fire poured down upon it from the higher ground; Early's division advanced to storm the ridge above Gettysburg, and Rodes on the right moved forward in support. But the attack was not simultaneous. Hayes' and Hoke's brigades of Early's division, succeeded in capturing the first line of breastworks, but were driven back by the weight of numbers. Johnson, however, gained important ground, and when night fell, still retained hold of the position he had seized on the right bank of Rocky Creek.

The summary of the second day's action was that the Confederates had obtained some advantage; that the Round Top had, at least, been temporarily in their possession, showing that it was not impregnable; that on the left, important positions had been taken; and so the result was such as to lead Gen. Lee to believe that he would ultimately be able to dislodge the enemy, and to decide the Confederate commander upon a last, supreme effort for decisive victory.

The morning of the 3d July wore away with but little incident of conflict. On the extreme left, where Johnson occupied the right bank of Rocky Creek, there was some desultory action; but Gen. Lee did not attempt to assist this part of the line, hoping to retrieve whatever might occur there by a vigorous movement against the centre of the enemy's position. Early in the morning he ascended the College cupola in Gettysburg to reconnoitre. Pickett's division of three brigades, numbering less than five thousand men, which had been left to guard the rear, reached the field of Gettysburg on the morning of the 3d. This body of Virginia troops was now to play a part the most important in the contest, and on this summer day to make a mark in history, to survive as long as the language of glorious deeds is read in this world.

About noon there was a deep calm in the warm air. Gen. Lee determined to mass his artillery in front of Hill's corps, and under cover of this tremendous fire to direct the assault on the enemy's centre. To this end more than one hundred pieces of artillery were placed in position. On the opposite side of the valley might be perceived the gradual concentration of the enemy in the woods, the preparations for the mighty contest that was at last to break the ominous silence with a sound of conflict such as was scarcely ever before heard on earth. It was a death-like silence. At 12. 30, P. M., the shrill sound of a Whitworth gun pierced the air. Instantly more than two hundred cannon belched forth their thunder at one time. It was absolutely appalling. An officer writes : " The air was hideous with most discordant noise. The very earth shook beneath our feet, and the hills and rocks seemed to reel like a drunken man. For one hour and a half this most terrific fire was continued, during which time the shrieking of shell, the crash of falling timber, the fragments of rocks flying through the air, shattered from the cliffs by solid shot, the heavy mutterings from the valley between the opposing armies, the splash of bursting shrapnell, and the fierce neighing of wounded artillery horses, made a picture terribly grand and sublime."

Into this scene of death moved out the Confederate column of assault. Pickett's division proceeded to descend the slope of hills and to move across the open ground. The front was thickly covered with skirmishers ; then followed Kemper's and Garnett's brigades, forming the first line, with Armistead in support. On the flanks were—Heth's division, commanded by Pettigrew, of Hill's corps, and Wilcox's brigade of McLaw's corps, the former on the left, the latter on the right of the Virginians. Pickett led the attack. The five thousand Virginians descended the hill with the precision and regularity of a parade. As they reached the Emmittsburg road, the Confederate guns, which had fired over their heads to cover the movement, ceased, and there stood exposed these devoted troops to the uninterrupted fire of the enemy's batteries, while the fringe of musketry fire along a stone wall marked the further boundary of death to which they marched. No halt, no waver. Through half a mile of shot and shell pressed on the devoted column. It was no sudden impetus of excitement that carried them through this terrible ordeal ; it was no thin storm of fire which a dash might penetrate and divide. In every inch of air was the wing of death. Against the breadth of each man's body reared the red crest of Destruction.

Steadily the Virginians press on. The name of Virginia was that day baptized in fire, and illuminated forever in the temple of History. There had been no such example of devotion in the war. Presently wild cries ring out ; the smoke-masked troops are in the enemy's works ; there is a hand-to-hand contest, and again and again the Confederate flag is lifted through the smoke over the shrinking columns of the enemy. Garnett is dead. Armistead is mortally wounded. Kemper is shot down. Every brigadier of the division is killed or wounded. But Pickett is unscathed in the storm ; his flashing sword has taken the key of the enemy's position, and points the path of the conflict through his broken columns ; the glad shout of victory is already heard ; and on the distant hill of observation, where a little group of breathless spectators had watched the scene, Long street turns to Gen. Lee to congratulate him that the day is won.

Vain! vain! Overlooking the field, Gen. Lee saw that the troops of Pettigrew's division had wavered. Another moment, and they had fallen back in confusion, exposing Pickett's division to attack both from front and flank. The courage of Virginians could do no more. Overwhelmed, almost destitute of officers, and nearly surrounded, the magnificent troops of Pickett gave way. Slowly and steadily they yielded ground, and, under the heavy fire which the artillery poured into their broken ranks, they retraced their steps across the fatal valley.

Gen. Lee was never known to betray on any battle-field a sign, either of exultation or disappointment. As he witnessed the last grand effort of his men, and saw it fail, he was seen for a moment to place his finger thoughtfully between his lips. Presently he rode quietly in front of the woods, rallying and encouraging the broken troops, uttering words of cheer and encouragement. To a foreign military officer of rank, who had come to witness the battle, he said very simply: "This has been a sad day for us, Colonel—a sad day; but we can't expect always to gain victories." There was no dramatic circumstance about him; no harangue; but nothing could be more affecting, nothing more sublime than to witness that when this plain gentleman rode through the throng of broken troops, saying such simple words as, "Never mind," "We'll talk of this afterwards," "Now we want all good men to rally," every fugitive paused, and badly wounded men took off their hats to cheer him! The Army of Northern Virginia never knew such a thing as panic. It never needed a harangue to stir its blood on a battle-field. It never had a dramatic accessory to its courage. Lee's presence alone was inspiration, order, recovery. An English colonel, who rode by the side of the great Confederate commander, remarks: "Gen. Lee and his officers were evidently fully impressed with a sense of the situation; yet there was much less noise, fuss, or confusion of orders, than at any ordinary field-day; the men, as they were rallied in the wood, were brought up in detachments, and lay down quiet and coolly in the positions assigned to them."

The enemy did not move from his works, and the new crisis for which Gen. Lee had so quietly prepared, did not come. Night fell over the third scene of bloodshed. The Confederate loss in this frightful series of engagements exceeded ten thousand men. Some of the details of this loss exhibit instances of desperate conflict which shock the heart. In Pickett's division, out of twenty-four regimental officers only two escaped unhurt. The Ninth Virginia went in two hundred and fifty strong, and came out with only thirty-eight men. In another part of the field the Eighth Georgia rivalled this ghastly record of glory. It went into battle with thirty-two officers, out of which twenty-four were killed or wounded. The Federal loss in the engagement proper of Gettysburg is not known. Gen. Meade acknowledged to the total loss during the campaign of 23,186 killed, wounded, and missing. Nearly half of these are to be found in the total of prisoners, including the captures at Winchester.

The morning of the 4th July dawned upon the two armies still confronting each other. They occupied precisely the same ground that each occupied on the first day's fight. No disposition was shown by either to attack the other. About twelve o'clock Lee made preparations to withdraw such of the wounded as could be transported in ambulances and wagons. These were placed in line, and, under a strong escort, sent back towards the Potomac. This consumed the afternoon and night of the 4th. On the morning of the 5th July the Confederate line of battle was drawn in, leaving a heavy skirmish line to confront the Federals. By midnight of the 5th, Lee's rear guard was well out from Gettysburg, and retiring in perfect order. There was no excitement, no panic. The entire wagon and supply trains, every piece of artillery, large herds of cattle and horses, and about seven thousand prisoners, were all brought off safely.

On reaching Hagerstown, Lee found that the recent rain had so swollen the Potomac that the army could not recross in safety. Line of battle was again formed, with the left resting upon Hagerstown, and the right upon the Potomac. Hastily constructed earthworks were thrown up, and every preparation was made to receive the Federals, who, it was reported, were rapidly advancing. Meade followed up the pursuit, but showed no disposition to attack. He was too badly crippled to offer battle. No disposition was evinced on either side to bring on an engagement. Lee continued in this position until the pontoons were constructed for the passage of his army over the river. He crossed over in face of the enemy, who had arrived on the 12th, and taken up position, " with no loss of material, except a few disabled wagons and two pieces of artillery." *

---

* The following official communication from Gen. Lee makes its own commentary on the unreliability of despatches of Federal generals :

"HEADQUARTERS ARMY NORTHERN VIRGINIA, 21st July, 1863.

" Gen. S. Cooper, Adjutant and Inspector-General C. S. A. Richmond, Va.:

" General—I have seen in Northern papers what purported to be an official despatch from Gen. Meade, stating that he had captured a brigade of infantry, two pieces of artillery, two caissons, and a large number of small arms, as this army retired to the south bank of the Potomac, on the 13th and 14th inst.

" This despatch has been copied into the Richmond papers, and as its official character may cause it to be believed, I desire to state that it is incorrect. The enemy did not capture any organized body of men on that occasion, but only stragglers and such as were left asleep on the road, exhausted by the fatigue and exposure of one of the most inclement nights I have ever known at this season of the year. It rained without cessation, rendering the road by which our troops marched to the bridge at Falling Waters very difficult to pass, and causing so much delay that the last of the troops did not cross the river at the bridge until 1 P. M., on the 14th. While the column was thus detained on the road, a number of men, worn down with fatigue, lay down in barns and by the road-

The pursuit of Lee was resumed by a flank movement of the Federal army, crossing the Potomac at Berlin, and moving down the Loudon Valley. The cavalry were pushed into several passes of the Blue Ridge Mountains, but despite all efforts of the Federal forces, Gen. Lee succeeded in once more establishing his men on the Rapidan, while the enemy took position on the Rappahannock, and thus terminated the campaign Meade, by the final battle of Gettysburg, had saved the North; but he had yet left unfulfilled the task which his countrymen had allotted to him, of cutting off and destroying the Army of Northern Virginia.

Gettysburg may be taken as the grand climacteric of the Southern Confederacy. It was the customary phrase of John M. Daniel, editor of the Richmond *Examiner*, that on the 3d July, on the heights of Gettysburg, the Confederates were "*within a stone's throw of peace.*" The expression is not extravagant, when we reflect what would have been the moral effect of defeating Meade's army, and uncovering New York, Philadelphia, and Washington; when, too, the fate of Vicksburg was not decided, and the vitals of the Confederacy were untouched.

It was in anticipation and in assurance of a victory so decisive that the Confederates had prepared their first distinct proposition of peace. The proper history of "peace negotiations" commences a few days before Gettysburg. When Lee crossed the Pennsylvania line, a mission was prepared in Richmond and entrusted to Vice-President Stephens, who was ordered to proceed to Washington with the following letter, intended to mask his real intentions. This letter, apart from its use as a decoy to the real diplomatic matter in hand, has a certain independent interest:

" RICHMOND, 2d *July*, 1863.

" *Hon. Alex. H. Stephens, Richmond, Va.* :

" SIR : Having accepted your patriotic offer to proceed as a military commissioner, under flag of truce, to Washington, you will herewith receive your letter of authority to the Commander-in-Chief of the Army and Navy of the United States.

" This letter is signed by me as Commander-in-Chief of the Confederate land and naval forces.

" You will perceive, from the terms of the letter, that it is so worded as to avoid any political difficulties in its reception. Intended exclusively as one of those communications between belligerents which public law recognizes as necessary and proper between

side, and though officers were sent back to arouse them, as the troops moved on, the darkness and rain prevented them from finding all, and many were in this way left behind. Two guns were left in the road. The horses that drew them became exhausted, and the officers went forward to procure others. When they returned, the rear of the column had passed the guns so far that it was deemed unsafe to send back for them, and they were thus lost. No arms, cannon, or prisoners were taken by the enemy in battle, but only such as were left behind under the circumstances I have described. The number of stragglers thus lost I am unable to state with accuracy, but it is greatly exaggerated in the despatch referred to.

"R. E. LEE, *General.*"

hostile forces, care has been taken to give no pretext for refusing to receive it on the ground that it would involve a tacit recognition of the independence of the Confederacy.

"Your mission is simply one of humanity, and has no political aspect.

"If objection is made to receiving your letter on the ground that it is not addressed to Abraham Lincoln as *President* instead of Commander-in-Chief, &c., then you will present the duplicate letter, which is addressed to him as President, and signed by me as President. To this letter objection may be made on the ground that I am not recognized to be President of the Confederacy. In this event, you will decline any further attempt to confer on the subject of your mission, as such conference is admissible only on a footing of perfect equality.

"My recent interviews with you have put you so fully in possession of my views that it is scarcely necessary to give you any detailed instructions, even were I at this moment well enough to attempt it.

"My whole purpose is, in one word, to place this war on the footing of such as are waged by civilized people in modern times, and to divest it of the savage character which has been impressed on it by our enemies, in spite of all our efforts and protests. War is full enough of unavoidable horrours, under all its aspects, to justify, and even to demand, of any Christian ruler who may be unhappily engaged in carrying it on, to seek to restrict its calamities, and to divest it of all unnecessary severities. You will endeavour to establish the cartel for the exchange of prisoners on such a basis as to avoid the constant difficulties and complaints which arise, and to prevent for the future what we deem the unfair conduct of our enemies, in evading the delivery of prisoners who fall into their hands, in retarding it by sending them on circuitous routes, and by detaining them sometimes for months in camps and prisons, and in persisting in taking captive non-combatants.

"Your attention is also called to the unheard-of conduct of Federal officers in driving from their homes entire communities of women and children, as well as of men, whom they find in districts occupied by their troops, for no other reason than because these unfortunates are faithful to the allegiance due to their States, and refuse to take an oath of fidelity to their enemies.

"The putting to death of unarmed prisoners has been a ground of just complaint in more than one instance, and the recent execution of officers of our army in Kentucky, for the sole cause that they were engaged in recruiting service in a State which is claimed as still one of the United States, but is also claimed by us as one of the Confederate States, must be repressed by retaliation if not unconditionally abandoned, because it would justify the like execution in every other State of the Confederacy, and the practice is barbarous, uselessly cruel, and can only lead to the slaughter of prisoners on both sides, a result too horrible to contemplate without making every effort to avoid it.

"On these and all kindred subjects you will consider your authority full and ample to make such arrangements as will temper the present cruel character of the contest, and full confidence is placed in your judgment, patriotism, and discretion that, while carrying out the objects of your mission, you will take care that the equal rights of the Confederacy be always preserved.

"Very respectfully,

"JEFFERSON DAVIS."

Mr. Stephens proceeded only as far as Fortress Monroe, where he was intercepted by a despatch peremptorily forbidding his access to the Federal capital. Whether the authorities there were aware or not of the real nature of his mission it is since ascertained that, apart from the written text which it bore, it was to sound the Washington Government on the question of peace. There could be no other proper conclusion, judging from the importance of the emissary, and the absurd futility of his going to Washington merely to protest against the enemy's cruelties in conducting the war.

The whole explanation of the affair is that Mr. Stephens was fully empowered in certain contingencies, to propose peace ; that President Davis had sent him on this extraordinary visit to Washington, anticipating a great victory of Lee's army in Pennsylvania ; that the real design of the mission was disconcerted by the fatal day of Gettysburg, which occurred when Mr. Stephens was near Fortress Monroe ; and that it was in the insolent moments of this Federal success that he was so sharply rebuffed by the Washington authorities. Considering the conjuncture of the occasion and the circumstances in which the President of the Southern Confederacy sought to signalize what he supposed would be a great victory of his arms, by a distinct and formal proposition of peace at Washington, it may be said that, notwithstanding the disappointment of the event, and the jeer of the enemy, Mr. Davis occupied a proud position in this matter, and one that merited the applause of the Christian world.

CHAPTER XXV.

GETTYSBURG and Vicksburg were twin victories for the Federals—twin disasters for the Confederates. They marked the line where the war turned, and the fortunes of the Southern Confederacy declined. The disaster of Vicksburg was a shock to the whole internal economy of the South; and this period of military disaster was coincident with a distress in material resources, in which some men already thought to discover signs of the fatal decay of the Confederacy. Money has been designated as "the sinews of war;" and when it is known that the Confederate currency declined a thousand per cent. on the news of these military disasters, it may well be comprehended what occasions of alarm and anxiety they were. The whole concern of the Confederate finances invites a studious consideration, which may well take place here at a period which affected so much their virtue and integrity. And the subject is so distinct that, without regard to any particular date of our narrative, we may extend our view of it through the whole period of the war.

THE FINANCIAL SYSTEM OF THE SOUTHERN CONFEDERACY.

The South was in a condition of complete isolation in the war. The laws of finance were less disturbed by extraneous influences than was ever the case in any country of equal extent, population and civilization before. The community consisted of several millions of people, occupying a large territory without a specie circulation, and compelled to establish a thoroughly artificial system of finance adapted to the condition of war. The case was anomalous. Very valuable lessons in finance might be learned from the history of the Confederate system, if space were allowed to trace its development, step by step, throughout its extraordinary career, and to mark the influence which it exerted upon the social condition, the public and private morals, and the fortunes of the Confederacy. It may be said generally that the result of the war was powerfully influenced by the condition of the Confederate finances, as much so as by any other cause.

It is the most striking peculiarity of modern wars that they are conducted chiefly by means of credit in the form of paper issues. The system was inaugurated by Great Britain; and its result is the mammoth debt of the British government. The revolutionary governments of France, as they succeeded each other in the various stages of transition between the autocracy of the Bourbons and the Empire, copied the British example, and created enormous debts which shared the fate of the ephemeral powers which incurred them. All the governments of Europe, with scarcely an exception, now labour under the burden of obligations incurred in expensive wars. In proportion with the facility of public credit, has been the magnitude of the scale on which modern wars have been conducted. And if in America the people have reason to boast of the stupendous magnitude of the armies which they brought into the field, and of the extent and costliness of their military operations, the marvellous exhibition will be found to have been due, not so much to the boundlessness of their resources, as to the lavish and reckless manner in which they employed a credit never before brought into requisition. Nor would it be over-stepping the bounds of truth to say, that the war spirit in either section was fed and stimulated, in a very great degree, by the profits which the heavy public expenditures brought to large classes of persons directly responsible for the war, and connected with its operations. This modern scheme of throwing the burden of debts incurred in war upon the shoulders of posterity has done more to stimulate costly and bloody conflicts between nations and peoples, than all the harmonizing influences of modern civilization and Christianity have done to restrain them. Until the system of credit is counterbalanced by some other scheme, by which the persons immediately connected with the public operations shall be impoverished rather than enriched by a state of war, we shall have no occasion to expect the Millennium.

The three most conspicuous examples of the abuse of credit for purposes of war, antecedent to those furnished by the two belligerents in the American conflict, were those of Great Britain, France, and Russia. The debt of the British government at the close of the Napoleonic wars, was eight hundred and eighty-five millions of pounds sterling. In March, 1863, after a lapse of nearly half a century, embracing the costly expenditures of the Crimean war, it had been reduced, by dint of resolute taxation, no lower than the amount of seven hundred and eighty million pounds sterling, or about thirty-nine hundred millions of dollars.

The amount of *Assignats* issued by the Revolutionary authorities of France, counting all the different series, reached the enormous amount of forty thousand millions of francs.* These were followed by a second species of paper money called *Mandates,* to the amount of twenty-four hundred millions of francs. The great bulk of both these forms of circulation, amounting in the aggregate to more than forty-two thousand millions of francs, or eighty-five hundred millions of dollars, proved a loss to their holders ; a circumstance which is thought to have been fortunate for France rather than otherwise, in proving the means of divesting her, at the same time with the burden itself, of the spurious authorities that had imposed it.

The British debt was contracted almost altogether in the form of bonds at long dates, upon the faith of which the Bank of England put forth a proportionate amount of its own notes of circulation. It is true that the Exchequer bills issued by government for temporary purposes, went directly into the hands of the public ; but they also soon found their way, for the most part, into the Bank of England ; and constituted, like the bonds, a basis of additional circulation. In this respect, it will be observed, the English and French systems were essentially different. In England the circulation was not identical with the debentures of government, but was issued through the agency of a banking company, which made of the government bonds a basis for the security of the circulation. In France, the government itself put forth its obligations in the form of a currency, declared it to be the medium of exchange by law, and denounced heavy penalties against the refusal to accept it as money. The comparative merits of the two systems were strikingly exemplified by the result. The French issues, as we have seen, went on augmenting in volume until they reached

* The statement seems incredible ; but it is made on the authority of the *American Encyclopedia.*

forty-two thousand millions of francs (in the aggregate of *Assignats* and *Mandates*), and continued to decline in value until the whole mass of circulation became utterly valueless. The volume of currency in England, on the other hand, never reached an unmanageable aggregate. The circulating notes of the Bank of England never aggregated quite thirty millions of pounds sterling, or one hundred and fifty millions of dollars Nor did the pound sterling, in proper form, ever experience a depreciation comparable with that which has generally attended the excessive issue of paper currency, during a state of war, in other countries; for the pound sterling note of England reached its maximum depreciation in 1814, when it sank to the value of £5 10s. to the ounce, or about 1.55 to the unit in gold. We shall see that in the United States, during the war, the greenback dollar sank to the value of 2.85 for one in gold; and that the Confederate paper dollar sank at the end, to the low value of 60 for one.

During the protracted wars which the Russian Empire prosecuted for a long series of years upon its Circassian frontier, a large employment of credit was found to be requisite. An expedient similar to that employed by Great Britain was resorted to, in the establishment of an institution called the *Bank of Assignats*. This establishment furnished the proper currency of the Empire for many years, and its circulation is believed never to have exceeded in periods of the most pressing military exigency more than eight hundred and thirty-six millions of roubles. A most remarkable circumstance connected with the history of this circulation is, that it underwent a most excessive appreciation, above gold in value, during the winter of Napoleon's Russian campaign, rising in value as the invader approached the heart of the country, and receding as he retired.

Unfortunately for themselves, neither of the two belligerents in America took any measures for establishing a proper relation between the efflux and reflux of the currency, during the gigantic war which we have under consideration. If a Bank of Exchequer had been established at the beginning, endowed with functions like those exercised by the Bank of England during the first two decades of the present century, having entire control of the circulation, and acting as the principal factor of the government in the negotiation of its bonds, the evils of a ruinously depreciated currency might have been avoided. As it was, each new demand of the government for money, instead of being supplied by the sale of bonds, and the receipt of a part of the circulation already outstanding, was met by a new and additional issue of notes; those previously issued still remaining, for the most part not needed and not employed, in the hands of the public. There was thus a perpetual efflux of notes of circulation; and no returning influx, to keep up an active demand for them and to sustain their value. The public credit was made the prey of a multitude of sharpers and brokers, who could all have been kept in due subordination by a great banking corporation, having a capital of hundreds of millions of dollars, able to " place " the public bonds as rapidly as funds were needed; and, by means of large discounts, establishing a steady reflux current of circulation back into its own coffers. It is one of the plainest maxims of finance that if a currency be issued in a continuous stream, without any measure being taken to establish a counter-current of the same circulation back into the source from which it issued, depreciation is inevitable. Where a circulation is put forth through the agency of a bank, it is done in the process of discounting the negotiable paper of punctual men of business; and the reflux is created by the return of the same amount of circulation into the bank in payment of the discounted paper when it falls due. Every piece of paper that is discounted, has its pay-day; and the reflux of currency corresponds with the efflux. The bank may fail; but this efflux is not relaxed by that fact alone; for the necessity of paying the negotiable paper which it held under discount, will absorb precisely the amount of circulation which was issued in the act of discounting it. A powerful bank of exchequer, however unnecessary or vicious a part of our Federal machinery it may be in periods of peace, is an admirable agency in time of war for regulating the heavy circulation which is always found to be one of the necessary attendants of a state of warfare.

Neither of the two belligerent governments in the American war took the proper pains, if they took any pains at all, to ensure a healthful reflux current into the Treasury of the circulation which they so profusely issued. The outgo of circulation was enormous and continuous; while there was no income at all, or if there was any, none sufficient to create any sensible demand for the currency, or to impart any stable value to it.

Let us see briefly, for purposes of illustration, what was the financial condition of the two belligerents at the close of the war. The aggregate debt incurred by the Federal government, in the progress of the war, has been officially stated, in frequent monthly bulletins from the Treasury Department, at about two thousand eight hundred millions of dollars. It is the generally received opinion in financial and official circles that the debt, when all audited and settled, will reach the round sum of three thousand millions of dollars. There was outstanding in the United States in the form of currency issued from the Federal Treasury, on the 31st of July, 1865, the aggregate sum of seven hundred and eleven millions of dollars; composed of five per cent. notes, six per cent. compound interest notes, greenbacks not bearing interest, and fractional currency. Up to that date, the circulation of the National Banks had reached one hundred and fifty seven millions, and the supposed amount of the notes of State banks still in circulation, was about eighty millions. The aggregate circulation in the Northern States, therefore, had reached, at the end of the war, the prodigious amount of about nine hundred and fifty millions of dollars. The circulation of the Bank of England, we have seen, did not exceed, at the end of the Napoleonic wars, one hundred and fifty millions of dollars, which is not one-sixth of the amount of the circulation which the war left in the North. The price of gold in New York, compared with greenbacks, for several months after the close of the war fluctuated near the point of one for one and forty-five hundredths; while the maximum depreciation of paper, during the war, was two and eighty-five hundredths. The maximum depreciation of the pound sterling note in England was one and fifty-five hundredths.

The total cost of the war to the Confederate government had reached at its close, according to the opinion of intelligent officers of the Treasury, about thirty-five hundred millions of dollars. Of this total about twenty-five hundred millions consisted of eight, seven, six, and four per cent. bonds of long dates; of Treasury notes outstanding of both the old and new issue; of unsettled accounts due from government, audited or in the process of being audited in the accounting departments; and of debt that had been cancelled in the form of the old currency, and income received in the form of taxes. The residue of the expenditure remained in the form of unpaid claims against Government in the hands of the people, for property purchased or impressed and damages sustained from the army. In fact, the cost of the war on the Confederate side, measured in Confederate currency, was nearly the same as that on the Federal side; for it is to be observed that the three thousand millions of dollars at which the Federal debt is generally estimated, embraces only the Federal debt proper; and does not embrace the expenditures made by States, cities, counties, and corporations generally. An intelligent authority classifies the war debt of the North as follows: Federal debt, three thousand millions; State debt one hundred and thirty-five millons; city debt, one hundred millions; and county debt five hundred millions; making a grand aggregate of about three thousand seven hundred and fifty millions of dollars. The municipal indebtedness of the South, incurred on account of the war, was very inconsiderable. The complete disorganization which attended the disastrous termination of the struggle renders it impossible to arrive at an exact knowledge as yet either of the Confederate debt or of the municipal debt; but the latter was comparatively so inconsiderable as to constitute scarcely an appreciable element in the grand total of the Confederate finances. The system of bounties was wholly unknown at the South; a patriotic public opinion and an energetic conscription sufficing to force every man of self-respect into the army, or into some branch of the public service. The bounty system, with its frauds and corruptions, was a feature of the war known only to the North.

We come now to speak more exclusively of the course of finance in the Southern States. Early in the winter of the first year of the war, and rather earlier than was supposed to be necessary, the banks of the Southern States suspended specie payments. The specie in their vaults at the time, as shown by their published reports, was about thirty millions of dollars in the total, and the paper circulation outstanding, in the form of bank notes, was about fifty millions. An estimate of the quantity of specie at the time in circulation among the people of the South must be conjectural; but the weight of intelligent opinion is in favour of the conclusion that this amount did not exceed twenty millions of dollars. Thus the war found the South in possession of only about fifty millions of coin, and with a paper circulation afloat of about the same amount. No reports were made to the Confederate authorities by the banks, of their accounts, and the foregoing data are derived from reports made shortly antecedent to the war. The specie in the hands of the people was of course immediately hoarded; and was afterwards employed to a great extent in contraband trade; that in the vaults of the banks remained for a long time unused; but afterwards was in part secreted, in part taken possession of by the Confederate Government, or turned over to its custody, and some of it captured. Yet much of it must have gone abroad through the blockade during the war, as the termination of the struggle revealed a very small portion of the thirty millions, at first held by the banks, as still in their possession.

The suspension of the banks early in the winter of 1861-'62 was not from any inability to protect their circulation. This latter had recently gone down very much in amount; and the banks were abundantly able to provide for it. The suspension was resorted to for the purpose of preventing the drain of specie which would have resulted from the large purchases of merchandise at the North which the prospect of a long embargo would have induced. The specie was saved; but it proved a curse rather than a blessing to the country. If by some talismanic power every dollar of it could have been transformed into iron coins like those of Lycurgus, the Confederacy would have been a gainer. It was extensively used in the smuggling trade throughout the war, and the goods brought in through its agency were sold at such enormous prices in Confederate currency as to contribute very powerfully to the discredit of that circulation among the people. True, the patriotic men and women of the country prided themselves in homespun; but far too many manifested a more eager desire for exotic fabrics than ever before.

The first financial measure of the Confederate Government was the issuing of the fifteen million loan, bearing eight per cent. interest, payable in specie, for which an export duty of one-eighth of a cent per pound on cotton was levied and pledged. The second financial measure was the negotiation of heavy loans from most of the banks in the form of discounts upon negotiable notes drawn by the Secretary of the Treasury. After these measures other loans in heavy amounts, upon bonds at long dates, were periodically made; and the baneful system was instituted of Treasury notes put out in the form of notes of circulation, in amounts ranging from the fractions of a dollar up to notes of five hundred dollars. If to these measures we add the cotton bonds, which were employed in England and Europe for the purchase of war material, and the cotton loan upon which they were based at home, we shall have mentioned all the leading measures of finance employed by the Confederacy.

The fifteen million loan was early disposed of at satisfactory rates. For a time the interest which had been stipulated to be paid in specie was actually discharged according to the terms of the contract; but before the close of the war the bondholders were either not paid at all or consented to arrangements less difficult to the Treasury than the payment of specie. This fifteen million loan in fact produced sore inconvenience to the Government during the later years of the war, and was the first subject with reference to which it was obliged to forfeit its faith to the holders of its paper.

The temporary loans negotiated from the banks were easily provided for. By the time that the loans matured, the Treasury was able to discharge them by means of the Treasury notes prepared for circulation. But it was found in the sequel that these accommodations cost the banks dearly. It has already been mentioned that at the outbreak of the war the circulation of the Southern banks was quite inconsiderable in amount. To meet the demand of the Government for loans, the banks very considerably increased their outstanding circulation; in fact, they doubled, and, in many instances, qradrupled it; a thing which was perfectly safe during a suspension of specie payments. Indeed, a large increase of circulation was found to be quite necessary, after the disappearance of specie and under the stimulus imparted by the war to all branches of trade. The fifty millions of currency found in circulation by the war was wholly inadequate to the active state of business superinduced by the war. The banks accomplished two objects by one measure. In granting a loan to the Secretary of the Treasury, they placed a large amount of funds in the hands of the Confederate Government; and they supplied, by the same act, the deficiency of currency which was so stringently felt by the people. But the act proved their ruin. The notes of circulation which they thus put forth, following that law of finance which makes a base currency drive out of circulation one less base, were hoarded. The bank notes, when lent by these institutions to the Government soon spread over the country. They were succeeded by similar paper issued in the form of currency by the Confederate Government. The Treasury notes were distrusted, and in proportion as they were distrusted, the notes of the banks were hoarded. The law of finance which has been adverted to had a quick and striking exemplification. The notes of the old familiar banks of the States were reserved and put away by the people, and did not emerge from their retreat until after the close of the war. They then began again to be seen in the hands of the people. But they had come forth from their hiding places too late. The banks had been ruined, and were found unable to pay any part of their debts except a percentage upon their circulation. The notes of the different institutions varied in market value according to the accidental circumstances which influenced the original amount of accommodations which they had granted in 1861 to the Confederate Secretary of the Treasury.

In the aggregate these accommodations had considerably exceeded the capital stock of the banks. The Confederate Treasury had paid off the accommodation notes due the banks with Treasury notes. The whole amount of private discounts due the banks from individuals were discharged by the agency of the same medium. Thus the whole capital stock and assets of the banks were soon transformed into Treasury notes; while the heavy amount of their own notes which they had lent to the Government, disappeared from circulation and went into private hoards, where they could not be reached. They had a heavy debt outstanding, which could not be discharged; and their whole available means consisted of a daily depreciating currency, which they were obliged to receive in payment of all dues to themselves. At the close of the war this currency turned into dead leaves, and they were left in the possession of no assets at all except the small amount of real estate occupied by their counting houses, and the small modicum of specie which they had been able to save from taxes, impressment, and robbery. Stockholders thus lost all their shares, and the value of assets in hand was sufficient to meet but a meagre percentage of the outstanding circulation, which the banks had imprudently put forth in originally granting such liberal loans to the Confederate Government.

With the negotiation of the fifteen million loan, and the exhaustion of the means of the banks, all regular financiering ceased with the Confederate Government. After that, money was manufactured by machinery to meet the wants of the Government, and paid out as rapidly as it was needed. Thus the volume of the circulation increased almost in equal ratio with the expenditures of the Government. Considerable loans in the form of bonds at long dates were authorized, and a good deal of success was obtained in disposing of the bonds. But these sales were exceedingly out of proportion to the magnitude of the expenditures; and the heavy margin of deficiency was boldly made up by the issue of Treasury notes. We might recite here in detail the various acts of Congress that were passed authorizing the different loans and directing the preparation and employ-ment of Treasury notes of circulation. But the recital would be tedious, dreary, and insipid. Suffice it to say that no measure whatever was taken to secure a reflux of the circulation to the source of issue, and thereby to restrict the volume of currency within manageable limits, and create a demand for it essential to the maintenance of its value.

The patriotism of the people, however, provided a partial demand for these notes. The growing redundance of currency produced high prices; and high prices produced large funds for investment in the hands of the wealthy classes. These made it a point of patriotism to invest their surplus capital in the securities of the Government. Legislatures authorized and the courts directed the funds held by fiduciaries to be invested in the eight and seven per cent. bonds of the Confederacy. Necessity also came in aid of patriotism to promote these investments. The great majority of capitalists knew not what better disposition to make of their Treasury notes than to convert them into Confederate bonds. The bonds drew interest; the notes drew none; except indeed those hundred dollar seven-thirty notes, which in fact were bonds. For a brief period after the first rise of prices consequent upon the inflation, real estate came briskly into market, and a great deal of it changed hands. But this species of investment soon terminated. Speculation in the necessaries of life and in the staples of the country was resorted to extensively by the class of men known as sharpers; but it was distasteful to respectable people and highly disreputable in public opinion. The consequence was, that the wealthy and respectable capitalists, who were men of public spirit and patriotic impulses, eschewed these questionable operations, and converted their treasury notes into interest-bearing bonds, drawn at long dates. Many, indeed, in an unbounded faith in the success of the Confederacy, purchased negroes; but the amount of this property available for purchase was very small in proportion to the vast capital accumulated in the hands of the people.

It so happened, therefore, that the very redundance of the currency produced in partial degree a remedy for its own cure. The very excess of circulation produced a necessity for its conversion into bonds. But the misfortune was, that the remedy, as long as it lasted, always came too late for the cure of the evil. It did not come into action until the depreciation of the currency had taken place. The reflux did not return by a natural flow, but resulted from a damming-up process. A competent agency should have been employed, which should have watched, directed, and controlled the movement from the beginning; an agency clothed with absolute power over the circulation, and endowed with a sufficient capital to ensure a ready sale at reasonable prices of the public bonds.

The progress of the depreciation of the Confederate money was at first gradual; but afterwards very rapid. In January, 1862, a dollar in gold was worth at the brokers' shops in Richmond one dollar twenty cents in currency. In July, 1862, it was still worth one dollar twenty cents. In January, 1863, it had fallen to three dollars ten cents. In midsummer, 1863, the value varied from twelve to twenty. It afterwards, as we shall see, fell much lower. It must be observed, however, that these brokers' rates, were invariably a long period in advance of the rates acted upon in the interiour. As late as the summer of 1862, Confederate money was taken at par in the settlement of all transactions originating before the war, and made the basis of the general transactions of the country at the old rate of prices. The brokers' rates were either unknown to the people or totally disregarded by them. Not until the volume of the currency had swollen beyond all reasonable proportion, did the people at large consent to fix a depreciated value upon this money. Even then they did so under compulsion. Remorseless speculators had succeeded in engrossing the entire stock of many of the comforts and prime necessities of life. These were held at exorbitant prices ; and in order to compass the means of purchasing them, the yeomanry of the country were obliged to rate their own property at higher prices in Confederate money than the old prices obtaining before the war. It is a well-known fact that the Richmond rates of Confederate money were, throughout the war, far below those which prevailed in the Confederacy at large ; and it is a general fact, that the rates of this money improved as the distance from Richmond increased. This fact was partly due to the circumstance, that Richmond was the great focus of Government disbursements, and was constantly flooded to excess with the currency ; partly to the circumstance, that it was the base from which all smuggling operations were carried on, at which of course gold for the smuggling trade was more in demand, and commanded the highest prices ; and thirdly, to the circumstance that it was the centre and resort of the speculating classes, and the principal depository of their wares, at which the final sales and last profits on the commodities bought up in the country for speculation, were realized. It may be remarked, without a material aberration from the truth, that after the first eighteen months of the war had elapsed, and the Confederate money had become very redundant, the business of the country, at a distance from Richmond, was done, for probably as long a period as twelve months, upon the basis of five for one in Confederate currency. After that period, the change of rate to fifteen or twenty for one was rather abrupt ; and upon the latter basis transactions proceeded for another twelve months ; after which the rate was very unsettled in the interiour.

Another observation must be made with reference to the brokers' prices of gold. A comparison of Confederate money with gold did not, during the war, afford a true criterion of the value of either commodity. Gold was unnaturally scarce and dear in the Confederacy. The old dollar's value, in property not affected by the condition of war, was not sufficient to purchase a dollar in gold. Real estate did not approximate the prices in gold which it had commanded before the war. Boarding at the best hotels could be procured for fifty cents a day in gold, which had cost two dollars and fifty cents before the war. A suit of clothing which before the war would have cost thirty dollars, could now be obtained for ten or fifteen in gold. In short, gold had greatly appreciated in the Confederacy, and the gold dollar no longer represented the old dollar's worth. The extraordinary demand for it produced by blockade running, and the smuggling trade, and the small supply of it which the war had found in the Confederacy, rendered still smaller by the process of hoarding, had imparted to it an extraordinary value. It had thus ceased to be a standard of value, and had become a very scarce commodity of commerce. The real value of Confederate money is not to be estimated by the quantity of gold which it commanded at the brokers' shops.

The case of gold was different at the North, from that which we have just described. There commerce was unaffected by a blockade; the usual supplies of gold continued to be received; no extraordinary demands of specie for exportation were experienced, and it remained, throughout the period of war, as accurate and reliable a standard of value as ever. The depreciation of Federal currency can therefore be measured with absolute certainty by comparing it with gold. In the Confederacy, however, the case was not the same. As we have seen, gold bore an abnormal value; and conclusions in regard to the depreciation of Confederate money founded merely upon its relation to gold, would be erroneous. The old dollar's worth, if it could be definitely ascertained, in such commodities as were not affected by the condition of war, would be the true standard of value. Until the final six or eight months of the Confederacy, the general transactions of the interiour country proceeded on a basis of value for Confederate money measured by the old dollar's worth, which was much higher than the values furnished by the brokers' quotations in Richmond.

It is interesting to observe the similarity of career which is presented in the cases of the money of the Southern Confederacy, and of the Congress of the first American Confederation. We have already stated the gradual depreciation of the one. The progress of the depreciation in the old Continental money, though somewhat more tardy, was in the same degree. In May, 1777, the Continental paper dollar was worth at the rate of two and two-thirds for one in specie. In December it was worth four for one. In March, 1778, it was worth five for one; in December, six for one. In February, 1779, it was worth ten for one; in June, twenty; in September, twenty-four; in December, thirty-nine. After the year 1779 it seemed to have no value. The total amount of this old Continental money that was issued, was two hundred millions of dollars; and it was worth to those who received it, at the period when paid out by the Government, only thirty-six and a half millions of dollars. A similar scaling of the money of the Confederate Treasury would reduce the cost of the war on the Southern side to less than a thousand millions of dollars. The difference between that sum and the nominal cost measures the aggregate depreciation of the money.

The principal cause of the depreciation of this money, in the last twelve months of the war, was the distrust of success entertained by the classes who controlled the value of the money. The principal causes of its deprecation in the antecedent period, were the excessive issues of it by Government, and the influence of speculation. It is probably useless to declaim against a vice so prejudicial as speculation to both the individual and general interests of a country circumstanced like the Confederacy. It is a display of the worst form of selfishness; a selfishness that feeds upon the privation, want, and necessity of fellow-citizens engaged in mortal struggle with a formidable public enemy; a selfishness that appropriates all that it can grasp, at a time when each individual should give up for the general good all that can be spared; a selfishness worse than that for which Ananias and Sapphira were struck down by the hand of God, inasmuch as it seeks not only to withhold what is one's own, but to engross also whatever else can be compassed by craft and greed. The best communities contain persons of this sordid temper; and the temptation to its indulgence in a country isolated and beleaguered by armies and blockading fleets, where the supplies of every article are limited, are too strong to be resisted by the class whose inclinations are set in that direction. The speculation commenced in such articles as cut nails, salt, and leather. There were but two nail factories in the Confederacy, and the stocks of these establishments were accessible and easily engrossed. Within the first six months of the war, the entire stock of cut nails in the Confederacy were in the hands of less than half a dozen speculators in Richmond; and the price was abruptly put up from four dollars to seven, and then to ten per keg. There was but one considerable saline in the Confederacy, and this was operated by a single firm, which ran up the price of this prime necessary of life, within two years, from the ante-war price of one cent per pound, to twenty-five cents per pound in specie or fifty cents in Treasury notes. Leather was one of those articles which, though tanned in very numerous establishments conducted on a small scale throughout the country, yet was everywhere found to be in smaller quantity than was needed by the people, and which might safely be bought up right and left wherever found. These are but examples of the subjects of the speculation and extortion that became rife throughout the Confederacy. The effect was greatly to augment and aggravate the burden of the war upon the people; but its most serious evil was in the depreciating influence it exerted upon the currency. The great mass of the people were desirous to receive this money at the normal rates; but finding themselves obliged to pay extortionate prices for commodities which they stood in need of purchasing, they were driven, against their will, to demand increased prices for the products and property which they sold. The fury and intensity of speculation forced tae people into reluctant acquiescence in the depreciation of the currency. But there is this consolatory observation to be made on the subject: namely, that the classes who devoted themselves assiduously to speculation, as a general rule, came out losers at the close of the war; while the masses of people who eschewed this disreputable avocation, generally saved a comfortable portion of their original means.

That the depreciation of the Confederate currency was partially superinduced by speculation and circumstances other than its mere redundancy, is sufficiently proved by the fact, that the grand total of circulation in the North reached the stupendous figure of nine hundred and fifty millions of dollars, while the depreciation of greenbacks, at the close of the war, was less than one and a half for one. It is plain, therefore, that depreciation is not the necessary result of mere redundancy, and may be prevented by provident and timely measures. The ability with which the Federal finances were conducted, especially in avoiding this depreciation, is one of the most remarkable incidents of the war.

If early and proper measures had been adopted, the Confederate currency would doubtless, likewise, have proved as manageable as any other branch of the Confederate finances. These measures should have looked to the provision of an adequate demand for the circulation that was issued in such profusion. This demand could have been abundantly established by means of taxation, of the sale of Government bonds of long dates, and by the intervention of a system of discounts through the instrumentality of a Bank of Exchequer. The circulation should not have been issued directly from the Treasury. It should have been placed under the absolute control of an issuing agency, which would have served as a regulator and balance-sheet in the movement, and preserved an equilibrium between the efflux and influx of the circulation. Taxation should have been imposed from the beginning, and executed promptly; not postponed several years, and then tardily put in force. The sales of bonds should have been conducted by a great and respectable banking institution, directed by eminent and reputable financiers; not entrusted to ignorant and irresponsible stock and exchange brokers. Such a financial institution could have established and maintained an influx of the circulation commensurate with the efflux. With this reflux in full flow, the volume of the currency might have been increased with impunity. And, if, besides, the circulation had been in the form of notes of the bank, rather than in that of notes of the Treasury; then, when the unfortunate end came, the debts due to the bank would still have given a partial value to this circulation; and prevented the total wreck of cash means which at last overtook the people of the South.

CHAPTER XXVI.

THE most remarkable military event of the midsummer of 1863 was the successful defence of Charleston against a most imposing demonstration of the enemy's power by land and by sea. We have seen how unsuccessful was the naval attack upon this city in April, 1863. It was not long, however, before another attempt was planned upon Fort Sumter and Charleston, the steps of which were the military occupation of Morris Island and the establishment of batteries on that island to assist in the reduction of Fort Sumter. The establishment of these batteries and the reduction of the Confederate works—Fort Wagner and Battery Gregg—was a matter of great engineering skill, and Gen. Q. A. Gillmore was selected to command the land forces of the enemy engaged in these operations. Morris Island was on the south side of the entrance to the harbour, about three and a half miles in length, low, narrow, and sandy, and separated from the mainland adjacent to it by soft, deep, and impracticable marshes. Its capture, although principally designed to open a way to the enemy's iron-clads, would also serve the purpose of making the blockade of Charleston harbour more thorough and complete, by allowing a portion or all of the blockading fleet to lie inside the bar. But the most important object, as we have indicated, was to secure a position whence it was hoped Fort Sumter might be demolished, and the co-operation of a heavy artillery fire extended to the fleet, when it was ready to move in, run by the batteries on James and Sullivan's Islands, and reach the city.

Gen. Gillmore assumed command on the 12th June, and at once proposed to commence a base of operations on Folly Island. This island, the south end of which controlled the waters of Stone Harbour and Inlet and the water approaches from James Island, had been occupied in force by the enemy since the 7th April. But Gen. Beauregard appears to have had no idea of what was going on there; he never made a reconnoisance of the enemy's outposts on the island; and he was bitterly accused in the Richmond *Sentinel*, the organ of President Davis' administration, for a want of vigilance, which had permitted the enemy, unknown to him, to construct a base of operations actually within speaking distance of his pickets. It is true that the enemy threw up earthworks and mounted heavy guns on Folly Island under a screen of thick undergrowth; but it is certainly to the last degree surprising that he should have succeeded in secretly placing in battery forty-seven pieces of artillery so near to the Confederate lines that a loud word might have revealed the work, and exposed moreover to a flank and reverse view from their tall observatories on James Island. Indeed there was a circumstance yet more curious. A blockade runner had been chased ashore just south of the entrance to Lighthouse Inlet, and it actually occurred that the vessel was wrecked by Confederate soldiers within pistol range of the enemy's battery on Folly Island, without their being in the least aware of such a grim neighbour.

This battery was ready to open fire on the 6th July. A plan of attack upon Morris Island was now deliberately formed, one part of which was a strong demonstration of Gen. Terry's division, some four thousand infantry, on James Island so as to draw off a portion of the Confederate force on Morris Island. While this demonstration was taking place, two thousand men of Gen. Strong's brigade were to embark in small boats in Folly River, effect a landing on Morris Island, and, at a given signal, attempt to carry Fort Wagner by assault. The batteries on the north end of Folly

Island were also ordered to be unmasked, by opening out the embrasures and cutting away the brushwood in front of them.

At daybreak of the 10th July, forty launches containing Strong's assaulting column crept up Folly River with muffled oar-locks; the iron-clad fleet crossed the bar, and took up its position in the main ship-channel off Morris Island; two hundred axemen suddenly sprung from behind the batteries on Folly Island, and felled the trees which hid them from view; embrasure after embrasure was laid bare; and at five o'clock the first gun was heard from the suddenly revealed battery, and the dense white smoke which rose above the tall pines marked the new line of conflict. Meanwhile the assaulting column had landed; the Confederate lines were drawn within eight hundred yards of Fort Wagner; and offensive operations were suspended for the day.

An assault on Fort Wagner was ordered at five o'clock the next morning. The Seventh Connecticut Regiment was to take the lead, followed by the Seventy-Sixth Pennsylvania and Ninth Maine. Gen. Strong, who led the assaulting column, gave a Cromwellian order: "Aim low, and put your trust in God!" The Connecticut soldiers took the double-quick, and with a cheer rushed for the works. Before they reached the outer works, they got a terrible fire from the Confederate rifles, and the fort opened with three 8-inch howitzers, heavily charged with grape and canister. The men went over the outer works with an extraordinary courage, that must be recorded to their honour, and were advancing to the crest of the parapet, when it was discovered that the regiments which were to support them had staggered back and lost their distance. The Connecticut regiment was left to effect its retreat through a sheet of fire. Nearly one half of them were killed or wounded. But the loss of the Confederates was quite as large. Gen. Beauregard estimated his losses in opposing the landing of the enemy at three hundred killed and wounded, including sixteen officers. The attack was undoubtedly a surprise to him, as he had persisted in the belief that the demonstration against Charleston would be made by the old route—James Island—and accordingly had almost stripped Morris Island of his artillerymen and infantry, to meet the advance of Terry.

But although the assault on Fort Wagner was repulsed, the remissness of Gen. Beauregard with respect to the battery on Folly Island was to cost dear enough. It compelled the evacuation of all the fortified positions of the Confederates on the south end of Morris Island; in fact, surrendered all the island except about one mile on the north end, which included Fort Wagner and Fort Gregg on Cumming's Point; and virtually made the reduction of these works but a question of time. It was very clear that the enemy, having once obtained a foothold on Morris Island, would eventually compel an evacuation by the operations of siege, and that it was impossible to defend forever a small island cut off from communication by an enormous fleet. It only remained for Gen. Beauregard to repair as far as possible the errour he had already committed, and to find some compensation for what had already occurred. And well did he do this secondary duty. Admitting the impracticability of defending Morris Island after the position of the enemy on it was fully established and covered by the iron-clads, Gen. Beauregard yet appreciated the opportunity of holding the island long enough to replace Sumter by interiour positions, and saw clearly that every day of defence by Wagner was vital to that of Charleston. For two months this policy was successful.

Gen. Gillmore was not content with his first essay to take Fort Wagner by storm. He held a conference with Admiral Dahlgren, commanding the fleet, and determined to attempt, with the combined fire of the land batteries and the gunboats, to dismount the principal guns of the work, and either drive the Confederates from it, or open the way to a successful assault. Batteries were accordingly established, and were ready to open fire on the 18th July, when the enemy's fleet, consisting of four Monitors, the Ironsides, a frigate, and four gunboats, some of which threw shell from mortars, closed in opposite Fort Wagner.

About noon the enemy's vessels commenced hurling their heaviest shot and shell around, upon, and within Fort Wagner, and, with intervals of but a very few minutes, continued this terrible fire, until one hour after the sun had gone down. Vast clouds of sand, mud, and timber were sent high up into the air. Forty-eight hours the Monitors and the Ironsides had kept up a continuous fire, and Fort Wagner had not surrendered. For eight hours, fifty-four guns from the land batteries had hurled their shot and shell within her walls, and still she flaunted the battle-flag of the Confederacy in the face of the enemy. Once during the day the flag was shot down. Immediately it was run up about ten feet above the parapet, a little cluster of men rallied around it, waved their hats, and then disappeared, and were not again seen during the day. There was no other sign of human life about the fort. It appeared as if the garrison was dead or conquered. " But," said a Federal officer, who watched the scene, " there were a few later developments that proved their opinion was the correct one who said this profound silence on the rebel side was significant, not of defeat and disaster, but of ultimate success in repulsing our assault ; that they were keeping themselves under cover until they could look into the eyes of our men, and send bullets through their heads, and would then swarm by thousands with every conceivable deadly missile in their hands, and drive us in confusion and with terrible slaughter back to our en trenchments."

Gillmore had selected the time of twilight for the storming party to move to the attack, in order that it might not be distinctly seen from the

James Island and Sullivan's Island batteries, and from Fort Sumter. But this time there was to be no surprise. As the bombardment relaxed, it was known at Fort Wagner that such a demonstration on the part of the enemy was not without its object; and every man was ordered by Gen. Taliaferro, who commanded the fort, to the parapet to prepare for the expected assault of the enemy.

At dusk the assaulting column was formed on the beach. A regiment of negro soldiers, the Fifty-fourth Massachusetts, was, for peculiar reasons, put in the extreme advance. There were eleven regiments in solid column As the head of it debouched from the first parallel, a tremendous fire from the barbette guns on Fort Sumter, from the batteries on Cumming's Point, and from all the guns on Fort Wagner, opened upon it. The guns from Wagner swept the beach, and those from Sumter and Cumming's Point enfiladed it on the left. Still the column staggered on within eighty yards of the fort. And now a compact and most destructive musketry fire was poured upon it from the parapet, along which gleamed a fringe of fire. In five minutes the first line of the enemy had been shot, bayoneted, or were in full retreat. The First Brigade, under the lead of Gen. Strong, failed to take the fort. The Second recoiled; and the few troops that had clambered to the parapet, now found the most desperate task to effect a retreat. It was a night black with tempest. Even if they surrendered, the shell of Sumter were thickly falling around them in the darkness, and, as prisoners, they could not be safe until victory, decisive and unquestioned, rested with one or the other belligerent. It was a retreat of untold horrours. Men rolled in the ditch, or dragged their bloody bodies through the sand-hills, on their hands and knees. About midnight there was silence at last; the battle was over; the ocean beach was crowded with the dead, the dying, and the wounded. The loss of the enemy was severe —fifteen hundred and fifty killed and wounded, according to his own statement, which must have been below the truth, as the Confederates buried six hundred of his dead left on the field. Their own loss was not more than one hundred in killed and wounded.

After this second successful defence of Fort Wagner the remainder of the month of July, and the early part of August, were employed by the enemy in erecting siege-works, and mounting heavy siege-guns, preparatory to the bombardment of Fort Sumter, as it was found that Fort Wagner did not interfere with the engineer corps at work. Meanwhile Gen. Beauregard and the Mayor of Charleston issued another urgent appeal to the landed proprietors and others to send in their negroes to work on the fortifications; and the Governor of the State made an even stronger appeal. There was, however, much indifference shown in promptly responding; and though an act of the Legislature had been passed involving a penalty on refusal, many of the planters preferred paying it to allowing their negroes to be so employed.

But to the desultory operations on Fort Wagner a remarkable episode was to take place. Gen. Gillmore flattered himself that he had discovered the precise point where to establish a battery from which he would be able to batter down the forts in the harbour and even the city of Charleston. It was said that he had at his disposal pieces whose range and effects surpassed all conception; and Northern newspapers were filled with the story of a new discovery called "the Greek Fire," which was to be poured upon Charleston, and consume "the cradle of secession." The prospect of what such devilish agents of destruction might accomplish was pleasing to many of the Northern people; it was announced that Gillmore was experimenting in liquid fire, that he had made a new style of bombs, and many other pyrotechnic inventions, and that he might soon be expected to "roll his fire-shells through the streets of Charleston."

The point whence such work was to be accomplished, and where Gillmore thought to discover the vitals of Charleston, was nearly midway between Morris and James Islands, seven thousand yards distant from the lower end of Charleston city. Here, on the marsh-mud—where a crab might crawl, but where a man would sink in a few minutes to the depth of twenty-five feet—there was prepared a plan of a battery for one 8-inch Parrott rifle (300-pounder). It was a singular achievement of labour and skill. The work had to be done under cover of darkness, and it was necessary to hide the pieces of wood during the day with grass and sea-weed. In the night-time piles were driven in the mud-shoal which separated the two islands; fifteen thousand bags of sand, about one hundred and ten pounds each, were brought in the vessels to make a *terre-plein* and a parapet. The work was executed in fourteen nights, from the 2d till the 18th of August. After breaking, by its great weight, several trucks, the monster gun was finally hauled up, and placed in position, and Charleston, four miles and a half away, little dreamed that the "*Swamp Angel*" *—

---

* The following effusion of a Northern writer gives an explanation of this name, in which blasphemy and devilish hate are united. The poetry reads like the exultation of a fiend.

The "Swamp Angel" hears the traitor boasting of security, and sends forth its dreadful warning that "nowhere in these United States are traitors safe from the avenging wrath of the Republic."

> "Flaunting, and boasting, and brisk, and gay,
> The streets of the city shine to-day.
> Forts without, our army within,
> To think of surrender were deadly sin;
> For the foe far over the wave abide,
> And no guns can reach o'er the flowing tide.
> They can't? Through the air, with a rush and a yell,
> Come the screech and the roar of the howling shell;
> And the populous city is still alive
> With the bees that are leaving the ancient hive;
> And the market-places are waste and bare,
> And the smoke hangs thick in the poisoned air;
> And the ruins alone shall remain to tell
> Where the hymn of destruction was sung by the shell."

as this new agent of destruction was called—was looking into her streets.

On the 21st August, Gen. Gillmore addressed to Gen. Beauregard a demand for the evacuation of Morris Island and Fort Sumter, and threatening, if not complied with, "in less than four hours, a fire would be opened on the city of Charleston, from batteries already established within easy and effective reach of the heart of the city."

The reply of Gen. Beauregard was memorable. He wrote, in a letter ad dressed to Gillmore : " It would appear, sir, that despairing of reducing these works, you now resort to the novel means of turning your guns against the old men, the women and children, and the hospitals of a sleeping city ; an act of inexcusable barbarity, from your own confessed point of view, inasmuch as you allege that the complete demolition of Fort Sumter within a few hours by your guns seems to you a matter of certainty ; and your omission to attach your signature to such a grave paper, must show the recklessness of the course upon which you have adventured, while the fact that you knowingly fixed a limit for receiving an answer to your demand, which made it almost beyond the possibility of receiving any reply within that time, and that you actually did open fire and threw a number of the most destructive missiles ever used in war into the midst of a city taken unawares, and filled with sleeping women and children, will give you a bad eminence in history—even in the history of this war."

If the enemy's execution had equalled his desire, there is no doubt that the city of Charleston would have been reduced to ruins and ashes ; women and children murdered indiscriminately ; and an outrage committed that would have shocked the sensibilities of the world. But happily Gen. Gillmore was not able to do what he threatened, and what that cowardly hate in the North, whose invocation against the South was, "Kill all the inhabitants," waited for him to accomplish. The attempted bombardment of Charleston was a failure. Some few missiles from the Federal batteries on Morris Island reached the city. Twelve 8-inch shells fell in the streets ; several flew in the direction of St. Michael's steeple ; but fortunately no one was injured. The " Swamp Angel " fired only a few shots. At the thirty-sixth discharge the piece burst, blowing out the entire breech in rear of the vent. No guns were placed in the Marsh Battery after this ; the " Greek Fire " proved a humbug ; and firing upon the city was not resumed until after all of Morris Island came into the enemy's possession.

The formidable strength of Fort Wagner, as developed in the unsuccessful assault of the 18th July, induced Gen. Gillmore to modify his plan of operations, and while pressing the siege of Fort Wagner by regular approaches, to turn his fire over the heads of both this work and Fort Gregg upon the walls of Sumter. It was thus determined to attempt the demolition of Fort Sumter from ground already in the enemy's possession, so that the iron-clad fleet could, with as little delay as possible, enter upon the ex ecution of their part of the joint programme. The early elimination of this famous fort from the conflict, considered simply as auxiliary to the reduction of Fort Wagner, was greatly to be desired, and elaborate arrangements were at once commenced to place the breaching guns in position.

On the 18th August, Gillmore opened heavily against the east face of Fort Sumter from his land batteries enfilading it. The cannonade was continued throughout the day, nine hundred and forty-three shots being fired. The effect was to batter the eastern face heavily, doing considerable damage, and to disable one ten-inch gun and a rifled forty-two pounder. On the 22d the enemy threw six hundred and four shots at the fort, disabling some of the barbette guns, demolishing the arches of the northwest face, and scaling the eastern face severely. The next day the fire from the enemy's land batteries was kept up on Sumter, disabling the only ten-inch columbiad that remained, and the three rifled forty-two-pounders in the northern salient of the second tier. The eastern face was badly scaled, and the parapet seriously injured.

On the 24th August Gen. Gillmore reported to Washington " the practical demolition of Fort Sumter as the result of our seven days' bombardment of that work." The assertion was insolent and absurd. Fort Sumter had, indeed, been severely injured ; but it was in one respect stronger than ever ; for the battering down of the upper walls had rendered the casemated base impregnable, and the immense volume of stone and debris which protected it, was not at all affected by the enemy's artillery. Although apparently a heap of ruins, it still afforded shelter to the Confederate heroes, who raised the standard of the South each time it was beaten down ; and it was still protected by the batteries of Fort Wagner, which the Federals had vainly endeavoured to carry by assault. Gen. Gillmore must, at all hazard, overcome this obstacle. He opened the trenches by means of the rolling sap, making work enough for a company of miners. Five parallels were established in succession, and two batteries were constructed, with *bandages*, under fire of James and Sullivan's Islands. From this moment Fort Wagner received more fire than she could return ; solid shot and shells fell right and left ; no living soul could remain upon the parapets ; everything was shattered in pieces ; the arches of the casemates commenced to crumble in, and to crush the defenders who had sought refuge there.

For two days and nights the fort had been subjected to the most terrific fire that any earthwork had undergone in all the annals of warfare. All the light mortars of the enemy were moved to the front, and placed in battery ; the rifled guns were trained upon the fort ; and powerful calcium lights aided the night work of the cannoniers and sharpshooters and blinded the Confederates. It was a scene of surpassing grandeur. The calcium lights turned night into day, and brought the minutest details of the fort into sharp relief. For forty-two consecutive hours, seventeen siege and coehorn mortars unceasingly dropped their shells into the work while thirteen heavy Parrott rifles—100, 200, and 300-pounders—pounded away at short though regular intervals. Peal on peal of artillery rolled over the waters; a semi-circle of the horizon was lit up; an autumnal moon hung in the misty sky; and ear and eye were alike appealed to with emotions of sublimity and grandeur. The shock of the rapid discharges trembled through the city, calling hundreds of citizens to the battery, wharves, steeples, and various look-outs, where, with an interest never felt before, they gazed on a contest that might decide the fate of Charleston itself.

On the night of the 6th September, Gen. Gillmore ordered an assault on Fort Wagner at the hour of low tide on the following morning. The assault was to be made in three columns. About midnight a deserter reported to him that the Confederates were evacuating the island. The work of evacuation had commenced at nine o'clock that night, and was already concluded. All the garrison had got off upon the Chicora, an iron-clad gunboat of the Confederates, and fourteen barges. Fort Gregg had been equally abandoned. Morris Island was thus the prize of the enemy, who now possessed themselves of Cumming's Point, from which they could plainly see Charleston at a distance of four miles.

The Northern public at once jumped to the conclusion that Gillmore had the key of Charleston, and had at last opened the gate to the Monitors and iron-clads, which, at leisure, might ascend the harbour. Gillmore himself insisted that he had done his part of the work; that " Fort Sumter was a shapeless and harmless mass of ruins; " and he indicated that it only remained for Admiral Dahlgren, with his fleet, to enter upon the scene, and accomplish the reduction of Charleston. But from this view the Federal admiral dissented; he indicated that Gen. Beauregard had accomplished a new object by his long retention of Morris Island; that, in fact, he had replaced Sumter by an interiour position, had obtained time to convert Fort Johnson from a forlorn old fort into a powerful earthwork, and had given another illustration of that new system of defence practised at Comorn and Sebastapol, where, instead of being any one key to a plan of fortification, there was the necessity of a siege for every battery, in which the besiegers were always exposed to the fire of others. He was unwilling, too, to risk the destructive defences and infernal machines with which the passes were blockaded. The Confederates had given out that by no possibility could one of the gunboats escape these, and Dahlgren's squadron of iron-clads and Monitors did not dare venture far up the harbour past Fort Ripley and within range of the immediate defences of the city.

Gillmore claimed that he had reduced Fort Sumter; but the Confed-

erate flag still floated over it.   It had been held through the siege and can
nonade by the First South Carolina Artillery, under Col. Alfred Rhett, until
its armament had been disabled; and the services of the artillerymen being
elsewhere required, Gen. Beauregard determined that it should be held by
infantry.   On the night of the 4th September, the Charleston Battalion,
under Maj. Blake, relieved the garrison; Maj. Stephen Elliot relieving
Col. Rhett in command of the post.   On the 7th of September, Admiral
Dahlgren, determined to test Gillmore's assertion that Sumter was a
" harmless mass of ruins," summoned the fort to surrender.   Gen. Beauregard telegraphed to Maj. Elliot to reply to Dahlgren that he could have
Fort Sumter when he took·it and held it, and that in the mean time such
demands were puerile and unbecoming.

In the evening of the 7th September, the iron-clads and Monitors approached Fort Sumter closer than usual, and opened a hot fire against it.
In the night of the 9th September thirty of the launches of the enemy attacked Fort Sumter.   Preparations had been made for the event.   At a
concerted signal, all the batteries bearing on Sumter assisted by one gunboat
and a ram, were thrown open.   The enemy was repulsed, leaving in our
hands one hundred and thirteen prisoners, including thirteen officers.
There were also taken four boats and three colours, and the original flag
of Fort Sumter, which Maj. Anderson was compelled to lower in 1861,
and which Dahlgren had hoped to replace.

After this repulse of the Federals in their last attack upon Fort Sumter, but little more was done during the year by the enemy, except
bombarding the forts and shelling Charleston at intervals during day and
night, until this became so customary that it no longer excited dismay or
was an occasion of alarm to even women and children.   The city was intact and safe; Gillmore had expended many thousand lives and thrown
shell enough to build several iron-clads to obtain a position that proved
worthless; Admiral Dahlgren feared the destruction of a fleet which had
cost so much sacrifice, and refused to ascend the harbour; and the demonstration upon Charleston degenerated into the desultory record of a fruitless bombardment.   The Northern public appeared to sicken of the experiment of Parrott guns and monster artillery, and read with disgust the daily
bulletins of how many hundred useless shots had been fired, and of how
much ammunition had been grandly expended in a great noise to little purpose.   " How many times," asked an indignant Philadelphia paper, " has
Fort Sumter been taken?   How many times has Charleston been burned?
How often have the people been on the eve of starvation and surrender?
How many times has the famous Greek Fire poured the rain of Sodom
and the flames of hell upon the secession city?   We cannot keep the count
—but those can who rang the bells and put out the flags, and invoked the
imprecations, and rejoiced at the story of conflagration and ruin."

CHAPTER XXVII.

THERE was no Confederate commander so remarkable for long foresight and for the most exact fulfilment of prophetic words as Gen. Joseph E. Johnston. He was more profound than Lee; his mind could range over larger fields; at all times of the war his cool, sedate judgments were so in opposition to the intoxicated senses of the Confederate people, that he was rather unpopular than otherwise, and rested his reputation on the apprecia-tive and intelligent, who steadily marked him as the military genius of the Confederacy.   It remained for the sequel to justify the reputation of this greatest military man in the Confederacy, who, cooler even than Lee him-self, without ardour, made up almost exclusively of intellect, saw more clearly than any other single person each approaching shadow of the war, and prophesied, with calm courage, against the madness of the Administra-tion at Richmond and the extravagant vanity of the people.

When the Vicksburg campaign was decided upon at Richmond, Gen. Johnston then warned the authorities there that they should make choice between Mississippi and Tennessee ; and in urging the retention of the latter State, he declared, with singular felicity of expression, that it was " the shield of the South."   In six weeks after the battle of Murfreesboro, our army in Tennessee was as strong as when it fought that battle, and, with ordinary generalship, might have driven Rosecrans from the State. But when Stevenson's division was sent to the lines of the Mississippi, Johnston saw the errour ; he sent to Richmond a protest against it, which he thought of such historical importance as to duplicate and to copy care-fully among his private memoranda ; and he then predicted that the Rich-mond Administration, in trying to hold the Mississippi River and Ten-nessee, would lose both, and that the enemy, once pressing the northern frontier of Georgia, would obtain a position that would eventually prove the critical one of the war.

With his forces reduced for the defence of Vicksburg, Gen. Bragg in-sisted upon regarding his army in Tennessee as one merely of observation. Rosecrans was in his front, and Burnside, who commanded what was called the Army of the Cumberland, was in a position, by an advance to-wards Knoxville, to threaten his rear.   In July, Gen. Bragg occupied a ridge extending from Bellbuckle towards Bradyville, very strong by na-ture on the right and made strong by fortifications on the left, in front of Shelbyville.   An injudicious disposition of forces left Hoover's Gap unde-fended by our army.   Rosecrans advanced upon Hoover's Gap.   Three brigades of Confederates moved rapidly up, and held them in the Gap over forty hours.   This position gained placed Rosecrans on Bragg's flank, who, to save his army, commenced a retreat, which was eventually con-tinued to Chattanooga.

EXPEDITION OF JOHN MORGAN.

As part of the general plan of action in the West, and an important contribution to the success of Gen. Bragg's retreat, we must notice here a remarkable expedition of the famous cavalier, Gen. John Morgan, the effect of which, although its immediate event was disaster, was to create an important diversion of Burnside's army, large detachments of which were drawn after Morgan into and through Kentucky, and to prevent that Federal commander from getting in rear of Bragg's army at the time it was menaced in front by Rosecrans, at Shelbyville.

In the latter part of the month of June the command of Gen. Morgan, consisting of detachments from two brigades, and numbering nearly three thousand men, approached the banks of the Cumberland. The passage of the river was weakly contested by three Ohio regiments, which had advanced from Somerset, Kentucky. Gen. Morgan was obliged to build a number of boats, and commenced crossing the river on the 1st July. By ten o'clock next morning his whole regiment was over the river; the advance proceeding to Columbia, where, after a brief engagement, the enemy was driven through the town.

Passing through Columbia, Gen. Morgan proceeded towards Green River Bridge, and attacked the enemy's stockade there with two regiments, sending the remainder of his force across at another ford. The place was judiciously chosen and skilfully defended; and the result was that the Confederates were repulsed with severe loss—about twenty-five killed and twenty wounded.

At sunrise on the 4th July, Gen. Morgan moved on Lebanon. The Federal commander here—Col. Hanson—made a desperate resistance; placing his forces in the depot and in various houses, and only surrendering after the Confederates had fired the buildings in which he was posted. About six hundred prisoners were taken here, and a sufficient quantity of guns to arm all of Morgan's men who were without them.

Rapid marches brought Morgan to Bradensburg on the 7th July; and the next day he crossed the Ohio, keeping in check two gunboats, and dispersing a force of militia posted with artillery on the Indiana shore. When the pursuing column of the enemy, which had increased now to seven regiments and two pieces of artillery, reached the banks of the river, it was to find the passenger boat on which Gen. Morgan had effected a crossing in flames, and to see far back on the opposite shore the rear-guard of his force rapidly disappearing in the distance.

On the 9th July Morgan marched on to Corydon, fighting near four thousand State militia, capturing three-fourths of them, and dispersing the remainder. He then moved without a halt through Salisbury and Palmyra to Salem, where he destroyed the railroad bridge and track and a vast amount of public stores. Then taking the road to Lexington, after riding all night, he reached that point at daylight, capturing a number of supplies, and destroying during the night the depot and track at Vienna, on the Jeffersonville and Indianapolis Railroad. Leaving Lexington, he passed on north to the Ohio and Mississippi Railroad near Vernon, where, finding Gen. Manson with a heavy force of infantry, he skirmished with him two hours as a feint, while the main command moved round the town to Dupont, where squads were sent out to cut the roads between Vernon and Seymour on the west, Vernon and Lawrenceburg on the east, Vernon and Madison on the south, and Vernon and Columbus on the north.

From Vernon Gen. Morgan proceeded to Versailles, capturing five hundred militia there and gathering on the road. From Versailles he moved without interruption across to Harrison, Ohio, destroying the track and burning small bridges on the Lawrenceburg and Indianapolis Railroad. At Harrison he burned a fine bridge. Leaving Harrison at dusk, he moved around Cincinnati, passing between that city and Hamilton, destroying the railroad, and a scout running the Federal pickets into the city, the whole command marched within seven miles of it. Daylight of the 14th found him eighteen miles east of Cincinnati.

The adventurous commander had now performed a wonderful circuit; he had traversed two enormous States, destroying property, probably to the extent of ten millions of dollars; he had cut an entire net of railroads; he had paroled nearly six thousand prisoners, and thrown several millions of people into frantic consternation. He had done his work, and the anxiety now was to escape. It was no easy matter. The country had been aroused, and it was reported that twenty-five thousand men were under arms to pursue or to intercept " the bloody invader."

After passing Cincinnati, the jaded command of Confederates proceeded towards Dennison, and making a feint there, struck out for the Ohio. Daily were they delayed by the annoying cry of " Axes to the front," a cry that warned them of bushwackers, ambuscades, and blockaded roads. It appeared that every hillside contained an enemy and every ravine a blockade. It was not until the evening of the 19th July, that the command, dispirited and worn down, reached the river at a ford above Pomroy.

At 4 p. m., two companies were thrown across the river, and were instantly opened upon by the enemy. A scout of three hundred men were sent down the river a half mile, who reported back that they had found a small force behind rifle-pits, and asked permission to charge. The rifle-pits were charged, and one hundred and fifty prisoners captured. A courier, arriving about the same time, reported that a gunboat had approached near our battery, and upon being fired upon had retired precipitately.

Gen. Morgan finding this report correct, and believing that he had sufficient time to cross the command, was using every exertion to accomplish the task, when simultaneously could be heard the discharge of artillery from down the river—a heavy, drumming sound of small arms in the rear and right; and soon from the banks of the river, came up three black columns of infantry, firing upon our men, who were in close column, preparing to cross. Seeing that the enemy had every advantage of position, an overwhelming force of infantry and cavalry, and that his men were becoming completely environed, the command was ordered by Gen. Morgan to move up the river double-quick. Three companies of dismounted men, and perhaps two hundred sick and wounded were left in the enemy's possession. The bulk of the command pressed rapidly to Belleville, about fourteen miles, on a running fight, and commenced fording, or rather swiming, at that point. Three hundred and thirty men had effected a crossing, when again the enemy's gunboats were upon them—one iron-clad and two transports. It was a terrible adventure now to cross the river; but even under the hot fire a party of officers, headed by Col. Adam R. Johnson, plunged into the stream, and commenced the struggle of life and death. Of the fearful scene which ensued, one of the party writes: " The Colonel's noble mare falters, strikes out again, and boldly makes the shore. Woodson follows. My poor mare, being too weak to carry me, turned over, and commenced going down; encumbered by clothing, sabre, and pistols, I made but poor progress in the turbid stream. An inherent love of life actuated me to continue swimming. Behind me I heard the piercing call of young Rogers for help; on my right, Capt. Helm was appealing to me for aid; and in the rear my friend, Capt. McClain, was sinking. Gradually the gunboat was nearing me. Should I be able to hold up until it came; and would I then be saved to again undergo the horrours of a Federal bastile? But I hear something behind me snorting! I feel it passing! Thank God! I am saved! A riderless horse dashes by; I grasp his tail; onward he bears me, and the shore is reached. Col. Johnson, on reaching the shore, seizes a ten-inch piece of board, jumps into a leaky skiff, and starts back to aid the drowning. He reaches Capt. Helm, but Capt. McClain and young Rogers are gone."

Gen. Morgan was not of the fortunate party that escaped across the river. With two hundred of his men he broke through the enemy's lines on the north side of the Ohio, and continued his flight in the direction of New Lisbon, with the design of reaching the river higher up. Forces were despatched to head him off, and the brave cavalier, who had so often given occasion of surprise and mystery to the enemy, was, at last, brought to bay at a point on the river where there was no escape, except by fighting his way through, or leaping from a lofty and almost perpendicular precipice. Here he surrendered himself and the remnant of his command.

Of the infamous treatment of this distinguished captive and his comrades, the following memorandum was made in the War Department at Richmond, signed by Lieut.-Col. Alston, as a personal witness: " They were carried to Cincinnati, and from thence he [Gen. Morgan] and twenty-eight of his officers were selected and carried to Columbus, Ohio, where they were shaved and their hair cut very close by a negro convict. They were then marched to the bath room, and scrubbed, and from there to their cells where they were locked up. The Federal papers published, with great delight, a minute account of the whole proceedings. Seven days afterwards, forty-two more of Gen. Morgan's officers were conveyed from Johnson's Island *to the penitentiary*, and subjected to the same indignities."

But these hardships and outrages did not break the spirit of these brave men. The very officer who made the memorandum quoted above, dared to write in his jail-journal this sentiment of defiance : " There are a hundred thousand men in the South who feel as I do, that they would rather an earthquake should swallow the whole country then yield to our oppressors—men who will retire to the mountains and live on acorns, and crawl on their bellies to shoot an invader wherever they can see one."

SURRENDER OF CUMBERLAND GAP.

In the month of September occurred the surrender of Cumberland Gap —a misfortune which President Davis declared " laid open Eastern Tennessee and Southwestern Virginia to hostile operations, and broke the line of communication between the seat of Government and Middle Tennessee " —and an event which some of the Richmond papers characterized as " one of the most disgraceful of the war." These serious charges demand a close investigation of the subject ; and it will be seen that Cumberland Gap is but another instance in which such charges, on a detail of facts, recoil upon the Richmond Administration itself.

About the last of August, 1863, the Federal forces under Gen. Burnside, entered Tennessee, and occupied Knoxville on the 2d September. A large part of these forces passed through the Cumberland Mountains from Kentucky into Tennessee at Big Creek Gap, forty miles south of Cumberland Gap, which latter position was held by Gen. Frazier for the Confederates. On the 21st August, Gen. Buckner, who was in command of the Confederate forces in East Tennessee, ordered Gen. Frazier to hold " the Gap," which was an important protection to that country and to Southwestern Virginia ; stating, moreover, that if the enemy broke through between this post and Big Creek Gap—the left and rear of Gen. Frazier—he (Buckner)would check them. This despatch left Gen. Frazier under the impression that he would be protected in his rear. But on the 30th August Gen. Buckner again despatched to Frazier to evacuate the Gap with all speed, to burn and destroy everything that could not be transported, and to report to Gen. S. Jones at Abingdon, Virginia, one hundred and twenty-five miles distant.

Gen. Frazier was not satisfied of the genuineness of this order; he suspected some trick of the enemy; he had been left under the recent and emphatic impression that East Tennessee was to be held; and he telegraphed in cipher to Gen. Buckner, stating that he had about forty days' rations, that he believed he could hold the position, and asking to be informed if his superiour insisted upon the order of evacuation. The order was countermanded within twenty-four hours, and Buckner's last instructions were to hold the Gap.

Knoxville had at this time been abandoned; and Gen. Buckner and his forces were at Loudon, about thirty miles southwest of Knoxville, at the crossing of the Holstein or Tennessee River. Gen. Frazier prepared for a vigorous defence of the Gap. It was not the "easily defensible pass" which President Davis declared it to be. There were three public roads uniting in it: the Virginia Road, leading eastward to Powell's Valley; the Kentucky Road, running through the Gap from Knoxville into Kentucky; and the Harlan Road, leading along the north side of the mountain. In consequence of the broken nature of the country, declivities, ravines, etc., the artillery commanded these roads very imperfectly. The Kentucky Road to the south at various points in its windings could be reached within range of the guns; but neither of the other roads could be commanded with artillery for a greater distance than about four hundred yards. Batteries were placed to defend these approaches. But the character of the ground permitted an enemy to approach in many directions over the spaces between the roads. The line of proper outward defences for the force in Gen. Frazier's command was about two miles in circuit, which comprised the various rifle-pits placed at irregular intervals, as the surface indicated proper points for their location on or near the summit of the mountain. An unfinished block-house in an isolated position, about a mile and a half from the Gap, was defended by one gun. This position had a limited command of the space around it, owing to the steep declivity and broken ground; but as it commanded the works of the Gap, it was important to prevent its occupation by the enemy. The rifle-pits and artillery epaulements were very incomplete, owing to the rocky nature of the ground, the want of tools, and blasting powder, and the small force of workmen that could be spared from other necessary duties. There were several approaches to the Gap by ravines and depressions through which an enemy could throw a large force under cover of darkness or heavy fog. The chief defences had been prepared to meet a force on the north side; and these were the reliance of Gen. Frazier when he expressed the opinion that he would be able to hold the position, as he anticipated an attack only from that direction.

Ten thousand men should have been assigned for the permanent defence of this position. The fact was that the force at Gen. Frazier's command amounted to seventeen hundred men, with one hundred rounds of ammunition. Of the situation, Gen. Frazier writes: "I will express the opinion arrived at, after a full knowledge of all the conditions, gained during a month, that an assaulting force, equal to the garrison could carry it *as easily as the open field*, if guided, or informed of its weak points, by disaffected persons in the vicinity—especially during the prevalence of fogs, which greatly demoralized the men, who were unaccustomed to service and had never been in action."

On the 4th September, Gen. Frazier was informed that the enemy was in possession of Knoxville, and had started a heavy force towards the Gap, and was running the cars to Morristown, within forty miles of his post. He was also informed that a large force, said to be sixteen regiments and two trains of artillery, were at Barboursville, Kentucky, *en route* for the Gap. Not believing that so large a force of the enemy would be sent against him from Knoxville until after successful engagement with Gen. Buckner, Gen. Frazier sent a cavalry regiment to meet the force said to be advancing from Knoxville, engage it, and uncover its strength. This force of cavalry, six hundred strong, was cut off, and compelled to retreat to Jonesville, thirty-six miles distant.

On the 7th September, Gen. Shackleford, who had approached the Gap from the south side, demanded its surrender. On the following day, Col. De Coucy, who had come up with a brigade on the Kentucky side, made the same demand on his part.

During the afternoon of the 8th September, Gen. Frazier assembled his regimental commanders, and had an informal conference with them. There was no council of war, and no votes were taken. There was a division of opinion as to the course to be pursued, but the officers separated on the final understanding to make a determined defence and with the expectation that Gen. Buckner would soon relieve the garrison.

On the 9th September reinforcements joined the enemy on the Tennessee side, and Gen. Frazier received a summons to surrender from Gen. Burnside himself. He had also received information about this time that the Confederate forces at Loudon Bridge had burned the bridge, and that Buckner had retreated towards Chattanooga. Gen. Burnside's presence at the Gap, so unexpected, was deemed by the garrison sufficient proof that he had nothing to fear from the Confederate forces further south, and that all hope of succour from Gen. Buckner was at an end. In the afternoon of the preceding day, Gen. Frazier had received a despatch from Gen. S. Jones, commanding at Abingdon, Virginia, to the effect that he should not give up the Gap without a stubborn resistance, and that he would send a force which he thought strong enough to relieve the garrison.

Of what ensued on the reception of this despatch, Gen. Frazier gives the following explanation: "I asked the courier if any troops had arrived at Abingdon, or if it was known there that Gen. Buckner had burned Loudon Bridge and retreated south, and also if they knew that Gen. Burnside had moved north with a large force. He replied, that there were no troops in Abingdon, but some were expected, and that they were ignorant of recent operations in Eastern Tennessee. I thus perceived that Gen. Jones was ignorant of my situation, and of the enemy's late movements, and knowing that the entire force under Gen. Jones could not cope successfully with Gen. Burnside, and that Gen. Lee could not reinforce him to any extent, as Gen. Meade was reported as pressing him, in East Virginia, I concluded, if Gen. Jones should attempt to relieve me, that the relieving force would be destroyed, and the occupation of the Virginia salt works follow, of course. The despatch of Gen. Jones referred to I destroyed, fearing it might fall into the hands of the enemy, show the weakness of Gen. Jones, and lead to an attack upon him to destroy these salt works. I thus perceived that my command could effect nothing by a temporary resistance, and that even could I hope to cut my way out, and attempt an escape up the valley, I should be thwarted in the attempt without artillery or cavalry, as the enemy had a formidable force of these arms, and could cut me up, or capture my forces in detail. I also reflected, that such a step, if partially successful, would draw the enemy towards Abingdon, and probably result in extending their operations to that place ; when a surrender of the Gap would probably satisfy his desire for conquest at that time."

About midday of the 9th September, Gen. Burnside sent in a second demand for surrender, stating that sufficient time for consultation had been allowed, and that he had a force large enough to carry the position by assault, and wished to spare the effusion of blood. After an attempt to make terms, Gen. Frazier surrendered unconditionally.

The occupation of Cumberland Gap gave Burnside an uninterrupted line of communication from Knoxville to Chattanooga, and opened the way to the consummation of the plan of the enemy, which was to move against Chattanooga on a double line of operations, and make there a new and formidable front directly against the heart of the Confederacy.

THE BATTLE OF CHICKAMAUGA.

Chattanooga is one of the great gate-ways through the mountains to the champaign country of Georgia and Alabama. It is situated at the mouth of the valley formed by Lookout Mountain and the Missionary Ridge. The first-named eminence is a vast palisade of rocks, rising twenty-four hundred feet above the level of the sea, in abrupt, rocky cliffs, from a steep, wooded base. East of Missionary Ridge is another valley, following the course of Chickamauga Creek, and having its head in McLemore's Cove.

Immediately after crossing the mountains to the Tennessee River, Rosecrans, who was moving with a force of effective infantry and artillery, amounting to fully seventy thousand men, threw a corps by way of Sequatchie Valley—a cañon or deep cut splitting the Cumberland range parallel—hoping to strike the rear of Gen. Buckner's command, whilst Burnside occupied him in front. Buckner, however, was directed by Gen. Bragg to withdraw to the Hiawassee; and the enemy then commenced a movement against the Confederate left and rear, showing plainly that he intended a flank march towards Rome.

To save the State of Georgia, Chattanooga had to be abandoned. Gen. Bragg, having now united with him the forces of Buckner, evacuated Chattanooga on the 7th September, and, after a severe march through the dust, which was ankle deep, took position from Lee and Gordon's Mill to Lafayette, on the road leading south from Chattanooga, and fronting the east slope of Lookout Mountain.

Gen. Bragg's effective force, exclusive of cavalry, was a little over thirty-five thousand men. But in view of the great conflict that was to ensue, Gen. Longstreet's corps was on the way from Virginia to reinforce him, and with this prospect it was determined to meet the enemy in front, whenever he should emerge from the mountain gorges. During the 9th September, it was ascertained that Rosecrans, supposing that Bragg was retreating, had pressed on his columns to intercept him, thus exposing himself in detail, and that a large force of Thomas' corps was moving up McLemore's Cove. Cheatham's division was moved rapidly forward to Lafayette in front; a portion of D. H. Hill's corps occupied Catlett's Gap in Pigeon Mountain (a spur of Lookout, about fifteen miles from Chattanooga), flanking the enemy on his right; while Gen. Hindman, in conjunction with Hill, was ordered to attack the enemy immediately in the Cove.

The attack was delayed; a day was lost, and with it the opportunity of crushing a column of the enemy; and when Hindman, with whom Gen. D. H. Hill had contumaciously refused to co-operate, and who had therefore to await the junction of Buckner's command, was at last ready to move, Thomas had discovered his errour, retreated to the mountain passes, and thus rescued the Federal centre from the exposed position in McLemore's Cove.

To understand the advance of Rosecrans' army, it would seem that Thomas' and McCook's corps crossed the Tennessee at Bridgeport, marching over Sand Mountain into Will's Valley, and thence down McLemore's Cove in the direction of Lafayette. Crittenden's corps had crossed above Chattanooga at Harrison's, and was moved in the direction of Ringgold.

A portion of Parke's corps of Burnside's army, and a brigade of his cavalry, came down from Knoxville to Loudon and Cleveland.

A council of war was held by Gen. Bragg at Lafayette, on the 15th, and it was resolved to advance towards Chattanooga, and attack the enemy wherever he could be found. By the 19th he had moved his army by divisions, and crossed it at several fords of the Chickamauga, and bridges north of Lee and Gordon's Mills. Longstreet had reached Ringgold in the afternoon of the same day. The reinforcements which he brought were five brigades of his corps, about five thousand effective infantry and no artillery. It was contemplated by Gen. Bragg to make a flank movement, and turn the enemy's left, so as to get his forces between him and Chattanooga, and thus cut off his retreat, believing that the main force of the enemy was at Lee and Gordon's Mills, and upon which he had intended to move. But he was anticipated; and as he was preparing for the movement the enemy commenced a counter-attack, Thomas' corps making a desperate effort to turn the right wing of the Confederates. The attack was gallantly met by Walker's division, whose troops broke through two lines, and captured two batteries. But the enemy was largely reinforced here, and hurrying forward his multiplied numbers to recover his lost ground, when Cheatham, who had been in reserve, moved forward with his veterans, and met the shock of battle. It was a terrible, doubtful, and long encounter. Our lines wavered before the desperate struggle of the enemy, and for three hours the fight was kept up with varied success.

It was near sunset when Cleburne—"the Stonewall Jackson of the West"—who commanded a division in Hill's corps, passed to the front over the bloody ground that had been so stubbornly contested by Cheatham, charging the enemy up to the very breastworks. A crashing fire of musketry from the enemy made Cleburne's men reel, when forward dashed his batteries, and opened a terrific fire on the enemy's works, while the division charged with such impetuosity that the enemy recoiled, and were driven half a mile from their line of battle.

That night the Confederate troops slept on the field surrounded by the dead. No cheerful fire dispelled the gloom, and profound silence brooded over the field of carnage.

The proper commanders were summoned by Gen. Bragg, and received specific information and instructions touching the disposition of the troops for the grand and decisive action of the next day. The whole force was divided for the next morning into two commands, and assigned to the two senior Lieut.-Generals, Longstreet and Polk: the former on the left, where all his own troops were stationed, the latter continuing his command of the right. Lieut.-Gen. Longstreet reached Gen. Bragg's headquarters about 11 P. M., and immediately received his instructions. After a few hours' rest, he moved at daylight to his line just in front of Bragg's position. Lieut.-Gen. Polk was ordered to assail the enemy on the extreme right at day-dawn on the 20th, and to take up the attack in succession rapidly to the left. The left wing was to await the attack by the right, take it up promptly when made, and the whole line was then to be pushed vigorously and persistently against the enemy throughout its extent.

At dawn, Gen. Bragg was in the saddle, surrounded by his staff, eagerly listening for the sound of Polk's guns. The sun rose, and was mounting the sky, and still there was no note of attack from the right wing. Bragg chafed with impatience, and at last despatched one of his staff-officers, Maj. Lee, to ascertain the cause of Polk's delay, and urge him to a prompt and speedy movement. Gen. Polk, notwithstanding his clerical antecedents, was noted for his fondness of military ostentation, and carried a train of staff officers whose numbers and superb dress were the occasions of singular remark. Maj. Lee found him seated at a comfortable breakfast, surrounded by brilliantly dressed officers, and delivered his message with military bluntness and brevity. Gen. Polk replied that he had ordered Hill to open the action, that he was waiting for him, and he added: "Do tell Gen. Bragg that my heart is overflowing with anxiety for the attack—overflowing with anxiety, sir." Maj. Lee returned to the commanding-general, and reported the reply literally. Bragg uttered a terrible exclamation, in which Polk, Hill, and all his generals were included. "Maj. Lee," he cried, "ride along the line, and order *every captain* to take his men instantly into action." In fifteen minutes the battle was joined; but three hours of valuable time had been lost, in which Rosecrans was desperately busy in strengthening his position.

It was 10 o'clock when the battle opened on the right wing of the Confederates, and the command "forward" ran down their ranks. Breckinridge moved forward with his division, but, after a severe contest, was pressed back. Had the reserve ordered forward to Breckinridge's support come up in time, the enemy's position might have been carried, and prevented the conflict of the afternoon. As it was, notwithstanding the partial repulse, several pieces of artillery were captured and a large number of prisoners.

At the same time each succeeding division to the left gradually became engaged with the enemy, extending to Longstreet's wing. Walker's division advanced to the relief of Breckinridge, and, after an engagement of half an hour, was also compelled to retire under the severe fire of the enemy. The gallant Tennesseans, under Cheatham, then advanced to the relief of Walker, but even they wavered and fell back under the terrible fire of the enemy. Cleburne's division, which had several times gallantly charged the enemy, had also been checked, and Stuart's division, occupying the centre and left of our line, detached from Buckner's corps, had recoiled before the enemy.

About three o'clock in the afternoon, Gen. Longstreet asked Gen Bragg for some of the troops of the right wing, but was informed by him that they had been beaten back so badly that they could be of no service. Longstreet had but one division that had not been engaged, and hesitated to venture to put it in, as the distress upon the Confederate right seemed to be almost as great as that of the enemy upon his right. He therefore concluded to hold Preston's division for the time, and urge on to renewed efforts the brave men who had already been engaged many hours. The enemy had obtained some heights near the Crawfish Spring Road, and strong ground upon which to rally. Here he gathered most of his broken forces, and reinforced them. After a long and bloody struggle, Johnson and Hindman gained the heights. Kershaw made a handsome attack upon the heights, simultaneously with Johnson and Hindman, but was not strong enough for the work. It was evident that with this position gained Longstreet would be complete master of the field. He therefore ordered Gen. Buckner to move Preston forward. Before this, however, Gen. Buckner had established a battery of twelve guns, raking down the enemy's line which opposed our right wing, and at the same time having fine play upon any force that might attempt to reinforce the hill that he was about to attack. Gen. Stewart, of his corps, was also ordered to move against any such force in flank. The combination was well-timed and arranged. Preston dashed gallantly at the hill. Stewart flanked a reinforcing column, and captured a large portion of it. At the same time, the fire of the battery struck such terrour into a heavy force close under it, that there were taken a large number of prisoners. Preston's assault, though not a complete success at the onset, taken in connection with the other operations, crippled the enemy so badly that his ranks were badly broken, and by a flank movement and another advance the heights were gained. These reinforcements were the enemy's last or reserve corps, and a part also of the line that had been opposing our right wing during the morning. The enemy broke up in great confusion along Longstreet's front, and, about the same time, the right wing made a gallant dash, and gained the line that had been held so long and obstinately against it. A simultaneous and continuous shout from the two wings announced our success complete. The enemy had fought every man that he had, and every one had been in turn beaten. The day had been certainly saved by Longstreet; but it is but justice to add that his masterly manœuvre was followed up, and completed by Gen. Polk, and that it was under their combined attack that the enemy at last gave up the field.

The enemy was totally routed from right, left, and centre, and was in full retreat to Chattanooga, night alone preventing further pursuit. Polk's wing captured twenty-eight pieces of artillery, and Longstreet's twenty-one, making forty-nine pieces of cannon, both wings taking nearly an equal number of prisoners, amounting to over eight thousand, with fifteen thousand stand of arms, and forty stands of regimental colours. The enemy's loss in killed, wounded, and prisoners, could not have been less than twenty thousand. Our own loss was heavy, and was computed by Gen. Bragg as "two-fifths of his army." The enemy was known to have had all his available force on the field, including his reserve, with a portion of Burnside's corps, numbering not less than eighty thousand, while our force was not fifty thousand. Nothing was more brilliant in all of Napoleon's Italian campaigns. Chickamauga was equally as desperate as the battle of Arcola; but it was productive of no decisive results, and we shall see that it was followed, as many another brilliant victory of the Confederates, by almost immediate consequences of disaster.

CHAPTER XXVIII.

THE morning after the battle of Chickamauga, Gen. Bragg stopped at
the bivouac of Longstreet, and asked his views as to future movements.
Gen. Longstreet suggested crossing the river above Chattanooga, so as
to make ourselves sufficiently felt on the enemy's rear, as to force his evacuation of Chattanooga—indeed, force him back upon Nashville, and, if we
should find our transportation inadequate for a continuance of this move-

ment, to follow up the railroad to Knoxville, destroy Burnside, and from there threaten the enemy's railroad communication in rear of Nashville.

The reasons which induced Gen. Bragg to decline this plan of campaign were detailed in a report to the War Department at Richmond, in which he wrote: "The suggestion of a movement by our right, immediately after the battle, to the north of the Tennessee, and thence upon Nashville, requires notice only because it will find a place on the files of the Department. Such a movement was utterly impossible for want of transportation. Nearly half our army consisted of reinforcements just before the battle, without a wagon or an artillery horse, and nearly, if not quite, a third of the artillery horses on the field had been lost. The railroad bridges, too, had been destroyed to a point south of Ringgold, and on all the road from Cleveland to Knoxville. To these insurmountable difficulties were added the entire absence of means to cross the river, except by fording at a few precarious points too deep for artillery, and the well-known danger of sudden rises, by which all communication would be cut off, a contingency which did actually happen a few days after the visionary scheme was proposed. But the most serious objection to the proposition was its entire want of military propriety. It abandoned to the enemy our entire line of communication, and laid open to him our depots of supplies, whilst it placed us with a greatly inferiour force beyond a difficult and, at times, impassable river, in a country affording no subsistence to men or animals. It also left open to the enemy, at a distance of only ten miles, our battle-field, with thousands of our wounded and his own and all the trophies and supplies we had won. All this was to be risked and given up for what? To gain the enemy's rear, and cut him off from his depot of supplies by the route over the mountains, when the very movement abandoned to his unmolested use the better and more practicable route of half the length on the south side of the river. . . . . Our supplies of all kinds were greatly reduced, the railroad having been constantly occupied in transporting troops, prisoners, and our wounded, and the bridges having been destroyed to a point two miles south of Ringgold. These supplies were ordered to be replenished, and as soon as it was seen that we could be subsisted, the army was moved forward to seize and hold the only communication the enemy had with his supplies in the rear. His important road, and the shortest by half to his depot at Bridgeport, lay along the south bank of the Tennessee. The holding of this all-important route was confided to Lieut.-Gen. Longstreet's command, and its possession forced the enemy to a road double the length, over two ranges of mountains, by wagon transportation. At the same time, our cavalry, in large force, was thrown across the river to operate on this long and difficult route. These dispositions, faithfully sustained, ensured the enemy's speedy evacuation of Chattanooga for want of food and forage. Possessed of the shortest road his depot and the one by which reinforcements must reach him, *we held him at our mercy, and his destruction was only a question of time.*"

This was a bold statement of Bragg; but it seemed that for once a least his swollen boasts were to be realized, and the enemy at Chattanooga starved into surrender. Starvation or retreat stared in the face of the Army of the Cumberland; its supplies had to be dragged for sixty miles across the country and over abominable roads; and even if it ventured on retreat, it would have to abandon its artillery and most of its *materiel*. At this critical period, Gen. Rosecrans was relieved, Gen. Thomas succeeding him; and a few days afterwards, Gen. Grant arrived, having been placed in command of a military division, composed of the departments of the Ohio, Cumberland, and Tennessee, in which were the armies of Gens. Burnside, Thomas, and Sherman.

It was the first task of Grant to relieve Thomas in Chattanooga. Reinforced by Hooker with two corps, it was decided that this force should cross the Tennessee River at Bridgeport, making a lodgment on the south side of it, three miles below where Lookout Mountain abuts on the river—this movement being intended to open navigation to the ferry, thus shortening land transportation, and securing certain supplies to the Federal army.

Four thousand men were detailed to execute this movement. Fifty pontoons, carrying twelve hundred men, were floated on the night of the 26th October down the river, passing three miles in front of Longstreet's pickets, without drawing their attention. The alarm was not given until the enemy attempted a landing at the ferry; and another body of three thousand Federals, who had marched down to a concealed camp opposite, being quickly ferried across, the Confederates were forced back and compelled to retreat to Lookout Mountain. In less than forty hours a whole corps of the enemy was across the river. A portion of this force halted in a position plainly visible from Lookout Mountain; and a night attack on the 29th October was planned upon it by Longstreet, who hoped by a surprise to frustrate the entire movement, and to capture the whole of Hooker's wagon train. The attack failed from insufficient force; it was made with only six Confederate regiments, and was withdrawn after three hours' fighting with considerable loss. Grant's lodgment on the south side of the Tennessee was now assured; he was in firm possession of the new lines of communication; he had attained all the results he had anticipated; and his relief of Chattanooga was now to be taken as an accomplished fact.

But although the Federal army near Chattanooga had now no fears of starvation or retreat, Grant hesitated to assume the offensive against the strong positions in his front. Gen. Sherman had been ordered from the region of the Mississippi with four divisions; but before his arrival, Grant obtained the astounding news that Longstreet, with eleven thousand infantry, had been detached from Bragg's front (although the Confederates were in momentary expectation of battle, already overmatched by numbers, and in the face of an enemy drawing reinforcements from every quarter), and that this veteran commander, with the best part of the army, had gone to Knoxville to attack Burnside, and with the visionary project of regaining East Tennessee, and perhaps through its gateways again penetrating Kentucky, and making the battle-ground of the Confederacy in this impossible country.

This extraordinary military movement was the work of President Davis, who seems, indeed, to have had a singular fondness for erratic campaigns. His visits to every battle-field of the Confederacy were ominous. He disturbed the plans of his generals; his military conceit led him into the wildest schemes; and so much did he fear that the public would not ascribe to him the hoped-for results of the visionary project, that his vanity invariably divulged it, and successes were foretold in public speeches with such boastful plainness, as to put the enemy on his guard and inform him of the general nature of the enterprise. On the 12th October President Davis visited the field of Chickamauga. He planned the expedition against Knoxville. He was in furious love with the extraordinary design, and in a public address to the army he could not resist the temptation of announcing that "the green fields of Tennessee would shortly again be theirs."

The announcement of this enterprise alone remained to determine Grant to attack. Burnside was instructed to lure Longstreet to Knoxville, and retire within his fortifications, where he could stand a protracted siege. Lookout Mountain had been evacuated by the Confederates, and Bragg had moved his troops up to the top of Missionary Ridge.

THE BATTLE OF MISSIONARY RIDGE.

On the 25th November, the enemy prepared for the grand assault, Sherman's force having come up, and occupied the northern extremity of Missionary Ridge. Hooker had scaled the rugged height of Lookout Mountain, and the Federal forces maintained an unbroken line, with open communications, from the north end of this dizzy eminence, through Cheat Valley, to the north end of Missionary Ridge. There were more than eighty thousand veteran troops in this formidable line. The Confederate army, numbering not half so many, had yet a position that should have decided the day. They held the crest of the ridge, from McFarlan's Gap almost to the mouth of the Chickamauga; the position was four to six hundred feet in elevation; and it had been strengthened by breastworks wherever the ascent was easy. The position was such that the enemy was exposed to an artillery fire while in the plain, and to the infantry fire when he attempted the ascent of the hill or mountain.

The right wing of the Confederates was held by Hardee, with the divisions of Cleburne, Walker, Cheatham, and Stevenson. Breckinridge commanded on the left his old division, Stewart's, and part of Buckner's and Hindman's. The enemy's first assault was made upon Hardee, who repulsed it with great slaughter. The attack was made here by Sherman, and his bleeding columns staggered on the hill. A second attack on the Confederate left wing was ordered at noon, and repulsed. It was late in the afternoon, when, with an audacity wholly unexpected, Grant ordered a general advance of his lines to the crest of Missionary Ridge. As the Federal columns moved up at a rapid rate, in face of the batteries, whose ill-directed and purposeless fire did not serve to check them, a brigade in the Confederate centre gave way, and in a few moments, what had been a regular and vigorous battle, became a disgraceful panic and an unmitigated rout. Never was a victory plucked so easily from a position so strong. Availing himself of the first gap in the Confederate line, the enemy turned upon their flanks, and poured into them a terrible enfilading fire, that scattered them in confusion. The day was shamefully lost. Gen. Bragg attempted to rally the broken troops; he advanced into the fire, and exclaimed, "Here is your commander," and was answered with the derisive shouts of an absurd catch-phrase in the army, "Here's your mule."

An army notoriously lacking confidence in their commander; made weak and suspicious by the detachment from it of Longstreet's veteran divisions; and utterly demoralized by one of Bragg's freaks of organization before the battle, in shuffling over all the commands, and putting the men under new officers, abandoned positions of great strength; broke into a disorderly retreat from a line which might easily have been held against twice their numbers; and gave to the Confederacy what President Davis unwillingly pronounced "the mortification of the first defeat that had resulted from misconduct by the troops."

The consequence of this disaster was that Gen. Bragg left in the hands of the enemy all of his strong positions on Lookout Mountain, Chattanooga Valley, and Missionary Ridge, and finally retired with his whole army to a position some twenty or thirty miles to the rear. His army was put in motion on the road to Ringgold, and thence to Dalton. Grant claimed as the fruits of his victory seven thousand prisoners, and forty-seven pieces of artillery.

LONGSTREET'S EXPEDITION AGAINST KNOXVILLE.

We have seen that in the beginning of November Longstreet had been despatched by Bragg up the valley towards Knoxville, where Burnside was operating. A part of the army of the latter lay at Loudon, where Longstreet first struck and drove the enemy, capturing at Lenoir Station a train of eighty-five wagons, many of them loaded with valuable medical stores. At Bean Station he captured thirty wagons, a quantity of forage, and some horses ; and in the Clinch Valley, forty other wagons, laden with sugar and coffee. Burnside continued to fall back upon Knoxville, but was overtaken at Campbell's Station on the 16th of November. Here he was severely pressed by Longstreet, who hoped to break the retreat into a rout. A running fight of two miles ensued, and Burnside reached Knoxville at daylight the next morning ; Longstreet advancing, and laying regular siege to the place.

But while he was investing the place, news came of the great disaster at Missionary Ridge, and Longstreet, well understanding that Grant would now detach a column to relieve Knoxville, saw the necessity of quick work, and determined to risk an assault upon the place. On a hill near the Kingston road was a work, called Fort Sanders, which commanded the approaches to the town. It was a very strong work, and in front of it were felled trees, with the tops turning in all directions, and making an almost impassable mass of brush and timber. A space around the fort was cleared, and the ditch in front was about ten feet deep, with the parapet nearly twenty feet high.

In the morning of the 29th November, the assaulting column, consisting of three brigades of McLaw's division, moved up the slope, and was met by a heavy artillery fire, which fearfullly mowed down the advancing soldiers. Still onward they pushed, struggling through the network of fallen timber and other devices laid down to impede them. But, the intricate passage by which they had to mount, was too difficult for them easily to master. The foremost parties stumbled and fell over each other in confusion ; at the same time the enemy's fire poured fiercer and fiercer on their heads. The embrasures of the fort, and the whole line of the parapet blazed forth at once. Nevertheless, this did not effectually stop the advance. Pushing on over every obstacle, they soon reached within pistol-shot of the fort ; then, suddenly, the enemy's guns launched forth from every quarter, and the Confederate line was shattered. Some, however, managed to spring into the ditch, and clamber up the glacis, planting their flag almost side by side with the Federal colours. They were not supported, however, by the rest of the charging column ; and the attack was withdrawn after a loss of some seven hundred in killed, wounded, and prisoners.

The assault having failed, and news of Sherman's approach from Chattanooga reaching him, Longstreet had no other alternative than to raise the siege, and occupy a new line of operations. He retreated towards Rutledge up the valley, pursued by the combined forces of Burnside and Sherman. On the 13th December, he reached Bean Station, where, being hard pressed by the enemy, he turned and attacked his advance, driving him back to Russellville. Having shaken off the enemy here, Longstreet proceeded to take a position in Northeastern Tennessee, establishing his headquarters at Rogersville. He had hoped to find his railroad communications with Virginia open; but at this time Averill's raid had cut the railroad, compelling Longstreet to fall back upon his own resources, and completely isolating him in a wild and difficult country. The weather was bitterly cold; the mountains were covered with snow; more than half of the men were barefooted; and the cavalry was engaged in daily skirmishes with the enemy, while gleaning supplies east of a line drawn from Cumberland Gap to Cleveland. In February, 1864, the lines of communication with Virginia were repaired; but it was not until the rigour of winter broke that the hardy soldiers under Longstreet united again with Gen. Lee in Virginia, and were on the old ground about Gordonsville.

OPERATIONS IN VIRGINIA IN THE FALL OF 1863.

While such was the train of disaster that followed the brilliant but ill-starred victory of Chickamauga, the record of the operations of the Army of Northern Virginia was comparatively slight, and afforded but little compensation with reference to the general fortunes of the war. From July until October, Gen. Lee quietly rested on the Rapidan, without any incident beyond a grand review of his army. Longstreet had been detached from him; Meade had lost two corps under Hooker, which had been sent to balance the Confederate reinforcement on the Tennessee lines; and the two armies, thus diminished, continued to watch each other, until the public, North and South, became anxious and clamorous for fresh struggles and a new excitement.

That excitement was suddenly given. In October, Gen. Lee prepared to put into execution a campaign, which promised the most brilliant results, as its ultimate object appears to have been to flank Meade, and get between the enemy and Washington. The movement commenced on the 9th October, when Gen. Lee with a portion of his command crossed the river, and by circuitous and concealed roads contrived to get up near Culpepper without notice of the enemy. A cavalry division and a detachment of infantry under Gen. Fitzhugh Lee remained to hold the lines south of the Rapidan and to make a show of force there to deceive the enemy; while Gen. Stuart advanced with Hampton's division to protect from observation the flank of the army then moving towards Madison Court-House.

On the 11th the bulk of the Confederate army was at Culpepper; the command of Gen. Fitzhugh Lee, uniting with that of Stuart, quickly followed; and Lee had now so manœuvred that he had actually turned Meade's flank. But unfortunately for the success of the movement, the Federal commander had taken timely alarm; he had crossed the Rappahannock, and was rapidly retreating along the line of railroad running to Alexandria.

On the 12th, Lee arrived on the Rappahannock, at Warrenton Springs, after a skirmish with the Federal cavalry at Jeffersonton. That night, Gen. Stuart pushed on to Warrenton. He had guarded the flank of the army, driven off the enemy's forces everywhere, and performed invaluable service. The next day the army pushed on, the cavalry now in advance. Meade's army was at this time across the Rappahannock, and believed to have halted at Warrenton Junction, and between that point and Catlett's Station. Two thousand cavalry were sent down from Warrenton to reconnoitre in the direction of Catlett's. On arriving near the latter place, they found the enemy were moving heavy columns of infantry along the railroad towards Manassas; and they thereupon immediately turned to retrace their steps toward Warrenton; but on reaching a road which crossed their route, leading from Warrenton Junction to Manassas, they found that the enemy were also moving infantry in large masses along this road. They were thus completely hemmed in. Nothing remained but to "lay low," in camp parlance, within a distance of the enemy where every word of command could be distinctly heard.

The body of Confederate cavalry was concealed in a thicket of pines. The accidental discharge of a fire-arm, the neighing of a horse, the rattling of an artillery chain, would have discovered them to the enemy. The night was passed in fearful suspense. Stuart gave his officers and men to understand that surrender was not to be thought of, but that the enemy was to be fought to the last. A council of war having been called, it was resolved, as the best thing that could be done under the circumstances, to desert the nine pieces of horse artillery, and for the cavalry in six columns to endeavour to cut their way through the enemy. But after some reflection, Stuart resolved not to do this. At daybreak the rear-guard of the enemy were seen in camp cooking their breakfasts, not a quarter of a mile distant. Gen. Stuart had sent several scouts on foot through the enemy's lines to announce his situation to Gen. Lee. He ordered them to put on infantry knapsacks, and, shouldering muskets, to advance in the darkness to the road, fall into the enemy's column, and, crossing it, to make their way to Warrenton, and say to Gen. Lee that he was surrounded, and he "must send some of his people to help him out." Three of the scouts reached Warrenton in safety.

The last division of the enemy halted and bivouacked opposite Stuart and within one hundred and fifty yards of his position—so close that he could hear the Federal cavalrymen pouring out oats to feed their horses. During the night two of Meade's staff straggled into his lines, and were taken prisoners. At daylight next morning, Stuart was informed by the cracking of skirmishers' muskets, that Lee had received his message, and was sending " some of his people " to help him. As Lee's advancing columns attracted the enemy's attention, Stuart, from the rear, opened on them with grape and canister. The enemy was much disordered by the cannonade from so unexpected a quarter, and, taking advantage of the confusion, Stuart limbered up his guns, and, with cavalry and artillery, dashed through the hostile ranks, and rejoined Gen. Lee. The enemy suffered a loss of one hundred and eighty killed in this affair.

Lee's whole army was reunited at Warrenton, and a halt was made to supply the troops with provisions. On the 14th, he again pushed on in two columns, and, by different roads towards Bristoe Station, where the rear-guard of Meade, under Gen. Warren, was attacked by the advance of Gen. Hill. As Hill's corps approached the station, what appeared to be a small portion of the enemy was discovered behind a long embankment of the railroad, and two brigades of Heth's division were ordered to dislodge them. A severe action ensued, in which Hill was repulsed, with three or four hundred killed and wounded, and the loss of five pieces of artillery.

Before the main body of Lee's army could get up the action was over , Meade had retreated across Broad Run ; and the next morning was reported to be fortifying beyond Bull Run. The enemy had thus been forced back to the old battle-fields around Centreville and Manassas. Gen. Lee deemed it unwise to continue the pursuit further, as the entrenchments around Washington and Alexandria rendered it impossible to turn Meade's position ; and the country affording no subsistence to the Confederate army, while the enemy, on the other hand, was at the door of his magazines, it returned to the line of the Rappahannock.

The flank movement had failed in what it had designed ; but it was accompanied with a considerable success in the Valley district ; the sum of its incidents was in favour of the Confederates, and its visible fruits were large. Gen. Imboden, who commanded in the Shenandoah Valley, had been left to guard the mountain passes, while the flank movement and advance of Lee was in progress. He not only performed this service, but on the 18th October, pressed on to Charlestown, took the town with four hundred and thirty-four prisoners, and brought off a large amount of captured property.

The entire movement of October cost the Confederates about one thousand men. Its fruits were two thousand four hundred and thirty-six prisoners, including forty-one commissioned officers. The railroad was destroyed from Manassas to Rappahannock Station; and Gen. Lee having placed his troops again in position, on both sides of the railway, upon the line of the Rappahannock, Ewell on the right, Hill upon the left, and the cavalry protecting each flank, quietly awaited the time when Meade, repairing the railroad, should again advance and confront him.

On the 6th November the enemy came in force upon Lee's army at Rappahannock Station and Kelly's Ford. Near the latter place the enemy crossed the river; and Gen. Rodes, who had fallen back before superiour numbers, was reinforced by Johnson's division. To meet the demonstration at the bridge near which Ewell's corps was stationed, Early's division was put in motion, and the two brigades of Hoke and Hayes were passed to the other side, to hold the north bank, and watch the enemy's front. It was believed that these troops would be able to maintain their position if attacked, the nature of the position being such that the enemy could not attack with a front more extended than their own; and that even if they were compelled to withdraw, they might do so safely under cover of the guns on the banks of the river.

The night was excessively dark; a high wind effectually prevented the movements of the enemy being heard; and taking advantage of these circumstances, two entire Federal corps advanced to overwhelm the small force of Confederates exposed on the north side of the river. The first line of the enemy was broken and shattered; but the second and third lines continued to advance, overwhelming Hayes, and, by a movement towards the left, enclosing Hoke's brigade in a manner that rendered escape impossible. Owing, it is said, to an opposite wind, no information was obtained of the attack on the south side of the river, until too late for the artillery stationed there to aid in repelling it. The darkness of the night and the fear of injuring our own men, who were surrounded by and commingled with the enemy, prevented Gen. Early from using artillery; and the unlucky commander witnessed the loss of the greater portion of two of his brigades, without, as he declared, the possibility of an effort to extricate them. Many of our men effected their escape in the confusion; some by swimming the river, and others by making their way to the bridge, passing over under a shower of balls. But not less than two thousand prisoners were left in the hands of the enemy, and was the cost to us of this unfortunate surprise.

On the 27th November, another incident, but without general significance, occurred on the line of the Rappahannock. On that day Meade again advanced upon the Confederates at Germania Ford, his immediate object being to get in the rear of Johnson's division, which was posted in the advance about a mile and a half from the river. In the action thus brought on, the enemy was punished and repulsed with a loss of several hundred in killed and wounded. The next day, Meade withdrew from the front, and re-occupied his position about Brandy Station on the Orange and Alexandria Railroad. This virtually ended the campaign for the year 1863.

In other parts of Virginia there were operations about the close of the year, which must be very briefly and generally referred to, as they belong to a very minor theatre of the war. That theatre lay between Gen. Lee's lines in Virginia and East Tennessee in the district commanded by the active and eccentric Gen. Sam Jones, and almost constantly disturbed by incursions and raids of the enemy. Here the great annoyance was from the famous Federal raider Averill, who, after a various and unequal career, succeeded in December, 1863, in striking the Virginia and Tennessee Railroad at Salem, and badly severing what was at that time the most important line of communication in the Confederacy.

Gen. Lee finding no prospect of Longstreet's arrival or other reinforcement from the West, retired to the old line of the Rapidan. The Federal forces went into winter-quarters on the line of the Rappahannock about the 6th December; the Confederate army did the same on the Rapidan; and the curtain of winter dropped on the great scenes of the war in Virginia.

CHAPTER XXIX.

THE Federal successes of 1863 produced a well-defined effect upon political parties in the North, and the elections there of this year were in remarkable contrast to those of 1862. It is significant of the little virtue of all the political organizations of the North during the time of the war that opposition to the administration at Washington was checked at every success of its arms, and declined in exact proportion as its military power ascended. The weak instinct of politicians readily took to the stronger side; and although there was a large party in the Confederacy that looked for a certain co-operation of the Democratic party in the North, it was readily understood by the intelligent that that co-operation was only to be obtained by making the Confederate side the stronger, by increasing the prospects of its success by victories in the field—in short, that the only hope of peace for the South was in the vigour of her resistance and the pressure of the enemy's necessities. This estimate of the Democratic alliance in the North was plainly enough stated in the Richmond journals and put in very blunt English. In anticipation of the elections of 1863, the Richmond *Enquirer* said : " It is nothing to us which of their factions may devour their ' spoils ; ' just as little does it signify to us whether they recover or do not recover that constitutional liberty which they so wantonly threw away in the mad pursuit of Southern conquest and plunder. But it is of the utmost importance to us to aid in stimulating disaffection among Yankees against their own government, and in demoralizing and disintegrating society in that God-abandoned country. We can do this only in one way—namely, by thrashing their armies and carrying the war to their own firesides. Then, indeed, conscientious constitutional principles will hold sway ; peace platforms will look attractive ; arbitrary arrests will become odious, and *habeas corpus* be quoted at a premium. This is the only way we can help them. In this sense and to this extent, those Democrats are truly our allies, and we shall endeavour to do our duty by them."

The Democratic party in the North went into the fall elections of 1863 on the issue of a general opposition to the Lincoln Administration ; at the same time promising a vigorous " constitutional " prosecution of the war. The result was a triumph of the Administration from Minnesota to Maine ; the Democrats were everywhere defeated ; and the significance of this defeat was that opposition to the authorities at Washington had been subdued either by the strong hand of lawless power or by the appliance of selfish arguments, that they had no longer anything to fear, and that the overthrow of free government in the North was complete. President Lincoln wrote that " the crisis was past." The elections of 1863 had given him, as it were, a *carte blanche* for his government. Certainly no more striking illustration could be given of this fact than the arrest and exile of Mr. Vallandigham, who was probably the most talented and prominent representative of the so-called " peace party " in the North, and had stood as Democratic candidate for Governor of Ohio. This single act of the Washington Administration is sufficient illustration of the license it had now assumed in the insolent and giddy moments of military success, and the lengths to which it now dared to go in defying the Constitution, and involving the liberties of its own people with the designs of the war.*

---

* The following correspondence, with reference to the case of Mr. Vallandigham, discusses the whole subject of *Military Arrests*, and covers a topic in the war so large and important, that a full copy of it is afforded for the reference of the reader :

" *To His Excellency the President of the United States*.

" The undersigned, officers of a public meeting held at the city of Albany on the sixteenth day of May, instant, herewith transmit to your Excellency a copy of the resolutions adopted at the said

It is true that the outrage upon Mr. Vallandigham, and, through him, upon the whole body of American liberties, was the occasion of some forcible

meeting, and respectfully request your earnest consideration of them. They deem it proper on their personal responsibility to state that the meeting was one of the most respectable as to numbers and character, and one of the most earnest in the support of the Union ever held in this city.

"Yours, with great regard,

"ERASTUS CORNING, President.

"RESOLUTIONS.

"*Resolved*, That the Democrats of New York point to their uniform course of action during the two years of civil war through which we have passed, to the alacrity which they have evinced in filling the ranks of the army, to their contributions and sacrifices, as the evidence of their patriotism and devotion to the cause of our imperilled country. Never in the history of civil wars has a government been sustained with such ample resources of means and men as the people have voluntarily placed in the hands of the Administration.

"*Resolved*, That as Democrats we are determined to maintain this patriotic attitude, and, despite of adverse and disheartening circumstances, to devote all our energies to sustain the cause of the Union, to secure peace through victory, and to bring back the restoration of all the States under the safeguards of the Constitution.

"*Resolved*, That while we will not consent to be misapprehended upon these points, we are determined not to be misunderstood in regard to others not less essential. We demand that the Administration shall be true to the Constitution; shall recognize and maintain the rights of the States and the liberties of the citizen; shall everywhere, outside of the lines of necessary military occupation and the scenes of insurrection, exert all its powers to maintain the supremacy of the civil over military law.

"*Resolved*, That in view of these principles we denounce the recent assumption of a military commander to seize and try a citizen of Ohio, Clement L. Vallandigham, for no other reason than words addressed to a public meeting, in criticism of the course of the Administration, and in condemnation of the military orders of that General.

"*Resolved*, That this assumption of power by a military tribunal, if successfully asserted, not only abrogates the right of the people to assemble and discuss the affairs of government, the liberty of speech and of the press, the right of trial by jury, the law of evidence, and the privilege of habeas corpus, but it strikes a fatal blow at the supremacy of law, and the authority of the State and federal constitutions.

"*Resolved*, That the Constitution of the United States—the supreme law of the land—has defined the crime of treason against the United States to consist 'only in levying war against them, or adhering to their enemies, giving them aid and comfort;' and has provided that 'no person shall be convicted of treason, unless on the testimony of two witnesses to the same overt act, or on confession in open court.' And it further provides that 'no person shall be held to answer for a capital or otherwise infamous crime, unless on a presentment or indictment of a grand jury, except in cases arising in the land and naval forces, or in the militia, when in actual service in time of war or public danger;' and further, that 'in all criminal prosecutions, the accused shall enjoy the right of a speedy and public trial by an impartial jury of the State and district wherein the crime was committed.'

"*Resolved*, That these safeguards of the rights of the citizen against the pretensions of arbitrary power were intended more especially for his protection in times of civil commotion. They were secured substantially to the English people, after years of protracted civil war, and were adopted into our Constitution at the close of the Revolution. They have stood the test of seventy-six years of trial, under our republican system, under circumstances which show that, while they constitute the foundation of all free government, they are the elements of the enduring stability of the republic.

"*Resolved*, That, in adopting the language of Daniel Webster, we declare, 'it is the ancient and undoubted prerogative of this people to canvass public measures and the merits of public men.' It

expressions of public indignation. A Democratic meeting in New Jersey resolved "that in the illegal seizure and banishment of the Hon. C. L.

is a 'home-bred right,' a fireside privilege. It has been enjoyed in every house, cottage, and cabin in the nation. It is as undoubted as the right of breathing the air or walking on the earth. Belonging to private life as a right, it belongs to public life as a duty, and it is the last duty which those whose representatives we are shall find us to abandon. Aiming at all times to be courteous and temperate in its use, except when the right itself is questioned, we shall place ourselves on the extreme boundary of our own right, and bid defiance to any arm that would move us from our ground. 'This high constitutional privilege we shall defend and exercise in all places—in time of peace, in time of war, and at all times. Living, we shall assert it; and should we leave no other inheritance to our children, by the blessing of God we will leave them the inheritance of free principles and the example of a manly, independent, and constitutional defence of them.'

"*Resolved*, That in the election of Governor Seymour, the people of this State, by an emphatic majority, declared their condemnation of the system of arbitrary arrests and their determination to stand by the Constitution. That the revival of this lawless system can have but one result—to divide and distract the North, and destroy its confidence in the purposes of the Administration. That we deprecate it as an element of confusion at home, of weakness to our armies in the field, and as calculated to lower the estimate of American character and magnify the apparent peril of our cause abroad. And that, regarding the blow struck at a citizen of Ohio as aimed at the rights of every citizen of the North, we denounce it as against the spirit of our laws and Constitution, and most earnestly call upon the President of the United States to reverse the action of the military tribunal which has passed a 'cruel and unusual punishment' upon the party arrested, prohibited in terms by the Constitution, and to restore him to the liberty of which he has been deprived.

"*Resolved*, That the President, Vice-Presidents, and Secretary of this meeting be requested to transmit a copy of these resolutions to his Excellency the President of the United States, with the assurance of this meeting of their hearty and earnest desire to support the Government in every constitutional and lawful measure to suppress the existing rebellion.

"PRESIDENT LINCOLN'S REPLY.

"EXECUTIVE MANSION, WASHINGTON, June 12, 1863.

"*Hon. Erastus Corning and others:*

"GENTLEMEN: Your letter of May 19th, inclosing the resolutions of a public meeting held at Albany, New York, on the 16th of the same month, was received several days ago.

"The resolutions, as I understand them, are resolvable into two propositions—first, the expression of a purpose to sustain the cause of the Union, to secure peace through victory, and to support the Administration in every constitutional and lawful measure to suppress the rebellion; and secondly, a declaration of censure upon the Administration for supposed unconstitutional action, such as the making of military arrests. And from the two propositions a third is deduced, which is, that the gentlemen composing the meeting are resolved on doing their part to maintain our common Government and country, despite the folly or wickedness, as they may conceive, of any Administration. This position is eminently patriotic, and as such, I thank the meeting and congratulate the nation for it. My own purpose is the same; so that the meeting and myself have a common object, and can have no difference, except in the choice of means or measures for effecting that object.

"And here I ought to close this paper, and would close it, if there were no apprehension that more injurious consequences than any merely personal to myself might follow the censures systematically cast upon me for doing what, in my view of duty, I could not forbear. The resolutions promise to support me in every constitutional and lawful measure to suppress the rebellion; and I have not knowingly employed, nor shall knowingly employ, any other. But the meeting, by their resolutions, assert and argue that certain military arrests, and proceedings following them, for which I am ultimately responsible are unconstitutional. I think they are not. The resolutions quote from the

Vallandigham, the laws of the country have been outraged, the name of
the United States disgraced, and the rights of every citizen menaced, and

Constitution the definition of treason, and also the limiting safeguards and guarantees therein provided for the citizen on trial for treason, and on his being held to answer for capital or otherwise infamous crimes, and, in criminal prosecutions, his right to a speedy and public trial by an impartial jury. They proceed to resolve ' that these safeguards of the rights of the citizens against the pretensions of arbitrary power were intended more *especially* for his protection in times of civil commotion.' And, apparently to demonstrate the proposition, the resolutions proceed : ' They were secured substantially to the English people *after* years of protracted civil war, and were adopted into our Constitution at the close of the Revolution.' Would not the demonstration have been better, if it could have been truly said that these safeguards had been adopted and applied during the civil wars and during our Revolution, instead of after the one and at the close of the other ? I, too, am devotedly for them after civil war, and before civil war, and at all times, ' except when, in cases of rebellion or invasion, the public safety may require' their suspension. The resolutions proceed to tell us that these safeguards ' have stood the test of seventy-six years of trial, under our republican system, under circumstances which show that while they constitute the foundation of all free government, they are the elements of the enduring stability of the republic.' No one denies that they have so stood the test up to the beginning of the present rebellion, if we accept a certain occurrence at New Orleans ; nor does any one question that they will stand the same test much longer after the rebellion closes. But these provisions of the Constitution have no application to the case we have in hand, because the arrests complained of were not made for treason—that is, not for the treason defined in the Constitution, and upon the conviction of which the punishment is death ; nor were the proceedings following, in any constitutional or legal sense, ' criminal prosecutions.' The arrests were made on totally different grounds, and the proceedings following accorded with the grounds of the arrests. Let us consider the real case with which we are dealing, and apply to it the parts of the Constitution plainly made for such cases.

" Prior to my installation here it had been inculcated that any State had a lawful right to secede from the Union, and that it would be expedient to exercise the right whenever the devotees of the doctrine should fail to elect a President to their own liking. I was elected contrary to their liking; and accordingly, so far as it was legally possible, they had taken seven States out of the Union, had seized many of the United States forts, and had fired upon the United States flag, all before I was inaugurated, and, of course, before I had done any official act whatever. The rebellion thus begun soon ran into the present civil war ; and, in certain respects, it begun on very unequal terms between the parties. The insurgents had been preparing for it more than thirty years, while the Government had taken no steps to resist them. The former had carefully considered all the means which could be turned to their account. It undoubtedly was a well-pondered reliance with them that in their own unrestricted efforts to destroy Union, Constitution, and law, all together, the Government would, in great degree, be restrained by the same Constitution and law from arresting their progress. Their sympathizers pervaded all departments of the Government and nearly all communities of the people. From this material, under cover of ' liberty of speech,' ' liberty of the press,' and *habeas corpus*, they hoped to keep on foot amongst us a most efficient corps of spies, informers, suppliers, and aiders and abettors of their cause in a thousand ways. They knew that in times such as they were inaugurating, by the Constitution itself, the *habeas corpus* might be suspended ; but they also knew they had friends who would make a question as to who was to suspend it ; meanwhile their spies and others might remain at large to help on their cause. Or if, as has happened, the executive should suspend the writ, without ruinous waste of time, instances of arresting innocent persons might occur, as are always likely to occur in such cases ; and then a clamor could be raised in regard to this, which might be, at least, of some service to the insurgent cause. It needed no very keen perception to discover this part of the enemy's programme so soon as by open hostilities their machinery was fairly put in motion. Yet, thoroughly imbued with a reverence for the guaranteed rights of individuals, I was slow to adopt the strong measures which by degrees I have been forced to regard as being within the exceptions of the Constitution and as indispensable to the public safety. Nothing is better

that it is now the duty of a law-respecting people to demand of the Administration that it at once and forever desist from such deeds of des-

known to history than that courts of justice are utterly incompetent to such cases. Civil courts are organized chiefly for trials of individuals, or, at most, a few individuals acting in concert; and this in quiet times, and on charges of crimes well defined in the law. Even in times of peace, bands of horse-thieves and robbers frequently grow too numerous and powerful for the ordinary courts of justice. But what comparison in numbers have such bands ever borne to the insurgent sympathizers even in many of the loyal States? Again, a jury too frequently has at least one member more ready to hang the panel than to hang the traitor. And yet, again, he who dissuades one man from volunteering, or induces one soldier to desert, weakens the Union cause as much as he who kills a Union soldier in battle. Yet this dissuasion or inducement may be so conducted as to be no defined crime of which any civil court would take cognizance.

"Ours is a case of rebellion—so called by the resolutions before me—in fact, a clear, flagrant, and gigantic case of rebellion; and the provision of the Constitution that 'the privilege of the writ of *habeas corpus* shall not be suspended unless when, in cases of rebellion or invasion, the public safety may require it,' is the provision which specially applies to our present case. This provision plainly attests the understanding of those who made the Constitution, that ordinary courts of justice are inadequate to 'cases of rebellion'—attests their purpose that, in such cases, men may be held in custody whom the courts, acting on ordinary rules, would discharge. *Habeas corpus* does not discharge men who are proved to be guilty of defined crime; and its suspension is allowed by the Constitution on purpose that men may be arrested and held who cannot be proved to be guilty of defined crime, 'when, in cases of rebellion or invasion, the public safety may require it.' This is precisely our present case—a case of rebellion, wherein the public safety does require the suspension. Indeed, arrests by process of courts, and arrests in cases of rebellion, do not proceed together altogether upon the same basis. The former is directed at the small percentage of ordinary and continuous perpetration of crime, while the latter is directed at sudden and extensive uprisings against the government, which, at most, will succeed or fail in no great length of time. In the latter case, arrests are made, not so much for what has been done as for what probably would be done. The latter is more for the preventive and less for the vindictive than the former. In such cases the purposes of men are much more easily understood than in cases of ordinary crime. The man who stands by and says nothing when the peril of his government is discussed cannot be misunderstood. If not hindered, he is sure to help the enemy; much more, if he talks ambiguously—talks for his country with 'buts,' and 'ifs,' and 'ands.' Of how little value the constitutional provisions I have quoted will be rendered, if arrests shall never be made until defined crimes shall have been committed, may be illustrated by a few notable examples. General John C. Breckinridge, General Robert E. Lee, General Joseph E. Johnston, General John B. Magruder, General William B. Preston, General Simon B. Buckner, and Commodore Franklin Buchanan, now occupying the very highest places in the rebel war service, were all within the power of the government since the rebellion began, and were nearly as well known to be traitors then as now. Unquestionably, if we had seized and held them, the insurgent cause would be much weaker. But no one of them had then committed any crime defined in the law. Every one of them, if arrested, would have been discharged on *habeas corpus*, were the writ allowed to operate. In view of these and similar cases, I think the time not unlikely to come when I shall be blamed for having made too few arrests rather than too many.

"By the third resolution, the meeting indicate their opinion that military arrests may be constitutional in localities where rebellion actually exists, but that such arrests are unconstitutional in localities where rebellion or insurrection does not actually exist. They insist that such arrests shall not be made 'outside of the lines of necessary military occupation and the scenes of insurrection.' Inasmuch, however, as the Constitution itself makes no such distinction, I am unable to believe that there is any such constitutional distinction. I concede that the class of arrests complained of can be constitutional only when, in cases of rebellion or invasion, the public safety may require them; and I insist that in such cases they are constitutional wherever the public safety does require them,

potism and crime." To a meeting in Philadelphia, Mr. Fernando Wood wrote: "Do not let us forget that those who perpetrate such outrages as

as well in places to which they may prevent the rebellion extending as in those where it may be already prevailing; as well where they may restrain mischievous interference with the raising and supplying of armies to suppress the rebellion, as where the rebellion may actually be; as well where they may restrain the enticing men out of the army, as where they would prevent mutiny in the army; equally constitutional at all places where they will conduce to the public safety, as against the dangers of rebellion or invasion. Take the particular case mentioned by the meeting. It is asserted, in substance, that Mr. Vallandigham was, by a military commander, seized and tried 'for no other reason than words addressed to a public meeting, in criticism of the course of the Administration, and in condemnation of the military orders of the general.' Now, if there be no mistake about this—if this assertion is the truth and the whole truth—if there was no other reason for the arrest, then I concede that the arrest was wrong. But the arrest, as I understand, was made for a very different reason. Mr. Vallandigham avows his hostility to the war on the part of the Union; and his arrest was made because he was labouring, with some effect, to prevent the raising of troops, to encourage desertions from the army, and to leave the rebellion without an adequate military force to suppress it. He was not arrested because he was damaging the political prospects of the Administration, or the personal interests of the commanding general, but because he was damaging the army, upon the existence and vigour of which the life of the nation depends. He was warring upon the military, and this gave the military constitutional jurisdiction to lay hands upon him. If Mr. Vallandigham was not damaging the power of the country, then his arrest was made on mistake of fact, which I would be glad to correct on reasonably satisfactory evidence.

"I understand the meeting, whose resolutions I am now considering, to be in favour of suppressing the rebellion by military force—by armies. Long experience has shown that armies cannot be maintained unless desertion shall be punished by the severe penalty of death. The case requires, and the law and the Constitution sanction, this punishment. Must I shoot a simple-minded soldier boy who deserts, while I must not touch a hair of a wily agitator who induces him to desert? This is none the less injurious when effected by getting a father or brother or friend into a public meeting, and there working upon his feelings till he is persuaded to write the soldier boy that he is fighting in a bad cause, for a wicked administration of a contemptible government, too weak to arrest and punish him if he shall desert. I think that in such a case to silence the agitator and save the boy is not only constitutional, but withal a great mercy.

"If I be wrong on this question of constitutional power, my errour lies in believing that certain proceedings are constitutional when, in cases of rebellion or invasion, the public safety requires them, which would not be constitutional when, in absence of rebellion or invasion, the public safety does not require them. In other words, that the Constitution is not in its application in all respects the same, in cases of rebellion or invasion involving the public safety, as it is in times of profound peace and public security. The Constitution itself makes the distinction; and I can no more be persuaded that the government can constitutionally take no strong measures in time of rebellion, because it can be shown that the same could not be lawfully taken in time of peace, than I can be persuaded that a particular drug is not good medicine for a sick man, because it can be shown not to be good food for a well one. Nor am I able to appreciate the danger apprehended by the meeting that the American people will, by means of military arrests during the rebellion, lose the right of public discussion, the liberty of speech and the press, law of evidence, trial by jury and *habeas corpus*, throughout the indefinite peaceful future, which I trust lies before them, any more than I am able to believe that a man could contract so strong an appetite for emetics during temporary illness as to persist in feeding upon them during the remainder of his healthful life.

"In giving the resolutions that earnest consideration which you request of me, I cannot overlook the fact that the meeting speak as 'democrats.' Nor can I, with full respect for their known intelligence, and the fairly presumed deliberation with which they prepared their resolutions, be permitted to suppose that this occurred by accident, or in any way other than that they preferred to designate themselves 'democrats' rather than 'American citizens.' In this time of national peril I the arrest and banishment of Mr. Vallandigham do so as necessary war measures. Let us, therefore, strike at the cause and declare for peace and

would have preferred to meet you upon a level one step higher than any party platform, because I am sure that, from such more elevated position, we could do better battle for the country we all love than we possibly can from those lower ones where, from the force of habit, the prejudices of the past and selfish hopes of the future, we are sure to expend much of our ingenuity and strength in finding fault with and aiming blows at each other. But since you have denied me this, I will yet be thankful, for the country's sake, that not all democrats have done so. He on whose discretionary judgment Mr. Vallandigham was arrested and tried is a democrat, having no old party affinity with me ; and the judge who rejected the constitutional view expressed in these resolutions, by refusing to discharge Mr. Vallandigham on *habeas corpus*, is a democrat of better days than these, having received his judicial mantle at the hands of President Jackson. And still more, of all those democrats who are nobly exposing their lives and shedding their blood on the battle-field, I have learned that many approve the course taken with Mr. Vallandigham, while I have not heard of a single one condemning it. I cannot assert that there are none such. And the name of President Jackson recalls an instance of pertinent history. After the battle of New Orleans, and while the fact that the treaty of peace had been concluded was well known in the city, but before official knowledge of it had arrived, General Jackson still maintained martial or military law. Now that it could be said the war was over, the clamor against martial law, which had existed from the first, grew more furious. Among other things a Mr. Louaillier published a denunciatory newspaper article. Gen. Jackson arrested him. A lawyer by the name of Morel procured the United States Judge Hall to order a writ of *habeas corpus* to relieve Mr. Louaillier. Gen. Jackson arrested both the lawyer and the judge. A Mr. Hollander ventured to say of some part of the matter that ' it was a dirty trick.' Gen. Jackson arrested him. When the officer undertook to serve the writ of *habeas corpus*, Gen. Jackson took it from him, and sent him away with a copy. Holding the judge in custody a few days, the General sent him beyond the limits of his encampment, and set him at liberty, with an order to remain till the ratification of peace should be regularly announced, or until the British should have left the Southern coast. A day or two more elapsed, the ratification of the treaty of peace was regularly announced, and the judge and others were fully liberated. A few days more, and the judge called Gen. Jackson into court and fined him a thousand dollars for having arrested him and the others named. The General paid the fine, and there the matter rested for nearly thirty years, when Congress refunded principal and interest. The late Senator Douglas, then in the House of Representatives, took a leading part in the debates, in which the constitutional question was much discussed. I am not prepared to say whom the journals would show to have voted for the measure.

" It may be remarked, first, that we had the same Constitution then as now ; secondly, that we then had a case of invasion, and now we have a case of rebellion ; and thirdly, that the permanent right of the people to public discussion, the liberty of speech and the press, the trial by jury, the law of evidence, and the *habeas corpus*, suffered no detriment whatever by that conduct of Gen. Jackson, or its subsequent approval by the American Congress.

" And yet, let me say that, in my own discretion, I do not know whether I would have ordered the arrest of Mr. Vallandigham. While I cannot shift the responsibility from myself, I hold that, as a general rule, the commander in the field is the better judge of the necessity in any particular case. Of course, I must practise a general directory and revisory power in the matter.

" One of the resolutions expresses the opinion of the meeting that arbitrary arrests will have the effect to divide and distract those who should be united in suppressing the rebellion, and I am specifically called on to discharge Mr. Vallandigham. I regard this as, at least, a fair appeal to me on the expediency of exercising a constitutional power which I think exists. In response to such appeal I have to say, it gave me pain when I learned that Mr. Vallandigham had been arrested— that is, I was pained that there should have seemed to be a necessity for arresting him—and that it will afford me great pleasure to discharge him so soon as I can, by any means, believe the public safety will not suffer by it. I further say that, as the war progresses, it appears to me, opinion and

against the war." But these protests were within narrow limits; they effected nothing; they were absolutely worthless. The savage wit of

action, which were in great confusion at first, take shape and fall into more regular channels, so that the necessity for strong dealing with them gradually decreases. I have every reason to desire that it should cease altogether, and far from the least is my regard for the opinions and wishes of those who, like the meeting at Albany, declare their purpose to sustain the Government in every constitutional and lawful measure to suppress the rebellion. Still I must continue to do so much as may seem to be required by the public safety.   A. LINCOLN."

REPLY OF THE ALBANY DEMOCRACY.

" *To His Excellency Abraham Lincoln, President of the United States* :

" SIR : Your answer, which has appeared in the public prints, to the resolutions adopted at a recent meeting in the city of Albany affirming the personal rights and liberties of the citizens of this country, has been referred to the undersigned, the committee who prepared and reported those resolutions. The subject will now receive from us some further attention, which your answer seems to justify, if not to invite. We hope not to appear wanting in the respect due to your high position if we reply with a freedom and earnestness suggested by the infinite gravity and importance of the questions upon which you have thought proper to take issue at the bar of public opinion.

" You seem to be aware that the Constitution of the United States, which you have sworn to protect and defend, contains the following guarantees, to which we again ask your attention : First. Congress shall make no law abridging the freedom of speech or of the press. Second. The right of the people to be secure in their persons against unreasonable seizures shall not be violated, and no warrant shall issue but upon probable cause supported by oath. Third. No person, except soldiers and mariners in the service of the Government, shall be held to answer for a capital or infamous crime, unless on presentment or indictment of a grand jury, nor shall any person be deprived of life, liberty, or property without due process of law. Fourth. In all criminal prosecutions the accused shall enjoy the right of a speedy and public trial by an impartial jury of the State or district in which the crime shall have been committed, and to be confronted with the witnesses against him.

" You are also, no doubt, aware that on the adoption of the Constitution these invaluable provisions were proposed by the jealous caution of the States, and were inserted as amendments for a perpetual assurance of liberty against the encroachments of power. From your earliest reading of history, you also know that the great principles of liberty and law which underlie these provisions were derived to us from the British Constitution. In that country they were secured by *magna charta* more than six hundred years ago, and they have been confirmed by many and repeated statutes of the realm. A single palpable violation of them in England would not only arouse the public indignation, but would endanger the throne itself. For a persistent disregard of them, Charles the First was dethroned and beheaded by his rebellious subjects.

" The fact has already passed into history that the sacred rights and immunities which were designed to be protected by these constitutional guarantees have not been preserved to the people during your administration. In violation of the first of them, the freedom of the press has been denied. In repeated instances newspapers have been suppressed in the loyal States because they criticised, as constitutionally they might, those fatal errours of policy which have characterized the conduct of public affairs since your advent to power. In violation of the second of them, hundreds, and we believe thousands, of men have been seized and immured in prisons and bastiles, not only without warrant upon probable cause, but without any warrant, and for no other cause than a constitutional exercise of the freedom of speech. In violation of all these guarantees, a distinguished citizen of a peaceful and loyal State has been torn from his home at midnight by a band of soldiers, acting under the order of one of your generals, tried before a military commission, without judge or jury, convicted and sentenced without even the suggestion of any offence known to the Constitution

John Mitchel in Richmond had this reply in one of its journals : " This would sound very well if the said ' declaring for peace ' could have any

or laws of this country. For all these acts you avow yourself ultimately responsible. In the special case of Mr. Vallandigham, the injustice commenced by your subordinate was consummated by a sentence of exile from his home pronounced by you. That great wrong, more than any other which preceded it, asserts the principles of a supreme despotism.

" These repeated and continued invasions of constitutional liberty and private right have occa·sioned profound anxiety in the public mind. The apprehension and alarm which they are calculated to produce have been greatly enhanced by your attempt to justify them. Because in that attempt you assume to yourself a rightful authority possessed by no constitutional monarch on earth. We accept the declaration that you prefer to exercise this authority with a moderation not hitherto exhibited. But, believing as we do that your forbearance is not the tenure by which liberty is enjoyed in this country, we propose to challenge the grounds on which your claims of supreme power are based. While yielding to you, as a constitutional magistrate, the deference to which you are entitled, we cannot accord to you the despotic power you claim, however indulgent and gracious you may promise to be in wielding it.

" We have carefully considered the grounds on which your pretensions to more than legal authority are claimed to rest ; and if we do not misinterpret the misty and cloudy forms of expression in which those pretensions are set forth, your meaning is, that while the rights of the citizen are protected by the Constitution in time of peace, they are suspended or lost in time of war, when invasion or rebellion exists. You do not, like many others in whose minds reason and the love of regulated liberty seem to be overthrown by the excitements of the hour, attempt to base this conclusion upon a supposed military necessity existing outside of and transcending the Constitution, a military necessity behind which the Constitution itself disappears in a total eclipse. We do not find this gigantic and monstrous heresy put forth in your plea for absolute power, but we do find another equally subversive of liberty and law, and quite as certainly tending to the establishment of despotism. You claim to have found, not outside but within the Constitution, a principle or germ of arbitrary power, which in time of war expands at once into an absolute sovereignty, wielded by one man, so that liberty perishes, or is dependent on his will, his discretion, or his caprice. This extraordinary doctrine you claim to derive wholly from that clause of the Constitution which, in case of invasion or rebellion, permits the writ of *habeas corpus* to be suspended. Upon this ground your whole argument is based.

" You must permit us to say to you, with all due respect, but with the earnestness demanded by the occasion, that the American people will never acquiesce in this doctrine. In their opinion the guarantees of the Constitution which secure to them freedom of speech and of the press, immunity from arrest for offences unknown to the laws of the land, and the right of trial by jury before the tribunals provided by those laws, instead of military commissions and drum-head courts-martial, are living and vital principles in peace and in war, at all times and under all circumstances. No sophistry or argument can shake this conviction, nor will the people require its confirmation by logical sequences and deductions. It is a conviction deeply interwoven with the instincts, the habits, and the education of our countrymen. The right to form opinions upon public measures and men, and to declare those opinions by speech or writing, with the utmost latitude of expression, the right of personal liberty, unless forfeited according to established laws and for offences previously defined by law, the right when accused of crime to be tried where law is administered, and punishment is pronounced only when the crime is legally ascertained ; all these are rights instantly perceived without argument or proof. No refinement of logic can unsettle them in the minds of freemen ; no power can annihilate them ; and no force at the command of any chief magistrate can compel their surrender.

" So far as it is possible for us to understand, from your language, the mental process which has led you to the alarming conclusions indicated by your communication, it is this : The *habeas corpus* is a remedial writ, issued by courts and magistrates to inquire into the cause of any imprisonment or restraint of liberty, on the return of which and upon due examination the person imprisoned is

effect whatever in bringing about peace.   If a man in falling from a tower could arrest his fall by declaring against it, then the declarations of Demo-

discharged if the restraint is unlawful, or admitted to bail if he appears to have been lawfully arrested, and is held to answer a criminal accusation.   Inasmuch as this process may be suspended in time of war, you seem to think that every remedy for a false and unlawful imprisonment is abrogated ; and from this postulate you reach, at a single bound, the conclusion that there is no liberty under the Constitution which does not depend on the gracious indulgence of the Executive only. This great heresy once established, and by this mode of induction there springs at once into existence a brood of crimes or offences undefined by any rule, and hitherto unknown to the laws of this country ; and this is followed by indiscriminate arrests, midnight seizures, military commissions, unheard-of modes of trial and punishment, and all the machinery of terror and despotism.   Your language does not permit us to doubt as to your essential meaning, for you tell us, that ' arrests are made not so much for what has been done, as for what probably would be done.'   And, again : ' The man who stands by and says nothing when the peril of his government is discussed, cannot be misunderstood.   If not hindered (of course by arrest) he is sure to help the enemy, and much more if he talks ambiguously, talks for his country with "buts" and "ifs" and "ands." '   You also tell us that the arrests complained of have not been made ' for the treason defined in the Constitution,' nor ' for any capital or otherwise infamous crimes, nor were the proceedings following in any constitutional or legal sense criminal prosecutions."   The very ground, then, of your justification is, that the victims of arbitrary arrest were obedient to every law, were guiltless of any known and defined offence, and therefore were without the protection of the Constitution.   The suspension of the writ of *habeas corpus*, instead of being intended to prevent the enlargement of arrested criminals until a legal trial and conviction can be had, is designed, according to your doctrine, to subject innocent men to your supreme will and pleasure.   Silence itself is punishable, according to this extraordinary theory, and still more so the expression of opinions, however loyal, if attended with criticism upon the policy of the government.   We must respectfully refuse our assent to this theory of constitutional law.   We think that men may be rightfully silent if they so choose, while clamorous and needy patriots proclaim the praises of those who wield power ; and as to the ' buts,' the ' ifs,' and the ' ands,' these are Saxon words and belong to the vocabulary of freemen.

"We have already said that the intuition of a free people instantly rejects these dangerous and unheard-of doctrines.   It is not our purpose to enter upon an elaborate and extended refutation of them.   We submit to you, however, one or two considerations, in the hope that you will review the subject with the earnest attention which its supreme importance demands.   We say, then, we are not aware that the writ of *habeas corpus* is now suspended in any of the peaceful and loyal States of the Union.   An act of Congress approved by you on the third of March, 1863, authorized the President to suspend it during the present rebellion.   That the suspension is a legislative and not an executive act, has been held in every judicial decision ever made in this country, and we think it cannot be delegated to any other branch of the government.   But passing over that consideration, you have not exercised the power which Congress attempted to confer upon you, and the writ is not suspended in any part of the country where the civil laws are in force.   Now, inasmuch as your doctrine of the arbitrary arrest and imprisonment of innocent men, in admitted violation of express constitutional guarantees, is wholly derived from a suspension of the *habeas corpus*, the first step to be taken in the ascent to absolute power, ought to be to make it known to the people that the writ is in fact suspended, to the end that they may know what is their condition.   You have not yet exercised this power, and therefore, according to your own constitutional thesis, your conclusion falls to the ground.   It is one of the provisions of the Constitution, and of the very highest value, that no *ex post facto* law shall be passed, the meaning of which is, that no act which is not against the law when committed can be made criminal by subsequent legislation.   But your claim is, that when the writ of *habeas corpus* is suspended, you may lawfully imprison and punish for the crimes of silence, of speech, and opinion.   But as these are not offences against the known and established law of the land, the constitutional principle to which we now refer plainly requires that you should, before taking cognizance of such offences, make known the rule of action, in order that the people

crats against the war might be of some avail. As it is, they resemble that emphatic pronouncement of Mr. Washington Hunt: 'Let it be proclaimed

may be advised in due season, so as not to become liable to its penalties. Let us turn your attention to the most glaring and indefensible of all the assaults upon constitutional liberty, which have marked the history of your administration. No one has ever pretended that the writ of *habeas corpus* was suspended in the State of Ohio, where the arrest of a citizen at midnight, already referred to, was made, and he placed before a court-martial for trial and sentence, upon charges and specifications which admitted his innocence according to the existing laws of this country. Upon your own doctrine, then, can you hesitate to redress that monstrous wrong?

"But, sir, we cannot acquiesce in your dogmas that arrests and imprisonment, without warrant or criminal accusation, in their nature lawless and arbitrary, opposed to the very letter of constitutional guarantees, can become in any sense rightful, by reason of a suspension of the writ of *habeas corpus*. We deny that the suspension of a single and peculiar remedy for such wrongs brings into existence new and unknown classes of offences, or new causes for depriving men of their liberty. It is one of the most material purposes of that writ to enlarge upon bail persons who, upon probable cause, are duly and illegally charged with some known crime, and a suspension of the writ was never asked for in England or in this country, except to prevent such enlargement when the supposed offence was against the safety of the government. In the year 1807, at the time of Burr's alleged conspiracy, a bill was passed in the Senate of the United States, suspending the writ of *habeas corpus* for a limited time in all cases where persons were charged on oath with treason, or other high crime or misdemeanor, endangering the peace or safety of the government. But your doctrine undisguisedly is, that a suspension of this writ justifies arrests without warrant, without oath, and even without suspicion of treason or other crime. Your doctrine denies the freedom of speech and of the press. It invades the sacred domain of opinion and discussion. It denounces the 'ifs' and the 'buts' of the English language, and even the refuge of silence is insecure.

"We repeat, a suspension of the writ of *habeas corpus* merely dispenses with a single and peculiar remedy against an unlawful imprisonment; but if that remedy had never existed, the right to liberty would be the same, and every invasion of that right would be condemned not only by the Constitution, but by principles of far greater antiquity than the writ itself. Our common law is not at all indebted to this writ for its action of false imprisonment, and the action would remain to the citizen, if the writ were abolished forever. Again, every man, when his life or liberty is threatened without the warrant of law, may lawfully resist, and if necessary in self-defence, may take the life of the aggressor. Moreover, the people of this country may demand the impeachment of the President himself for the exercise of arbitrary power. And when all these remedies shall prove inadequate for the protection of free institutions, there remains, in the last resort, the supreme right of revolution. You once announced this right with a latitude of expression which may well be considered dangerous in the present crisis of our national history. You said: 'Any people, anywhere, being inclined and having the power, have the right to rise up and shake off the existing government, and form a new one that suits them better. Nor is this right confined to cases where the people of an existing government may choose to exercise it. Any portion of such people that can may revolutionize and make their own of so much of their territory as they inhabit. More than this, a majority of any portion of such people may revolutionize, putting down a minority intermingled with or near about them, who may oppose their movements.' (Vol. 19, *Congressional Globe*, p. 94.) Such were your opinions, and you had a constitutional right to declare them. If a citizen now should utter sentiments far less dangerous in their tendency, your nearest military commander would consign him to a dungeon or to the tender mercies of a court-martial, and you would approve the proceeding.

"In our deliberate judgment the Constitution is not open to the new interpretation suggested by your communication now before us. We think every part of that instrument is harmonious and consistent. The possible suspension of the writ of *habeas corpus* is consistent with freedom of speech and of the press. The suspension of that remedial process may prevent the enlargement of the accused traitor or conspirator until he shall be legally tried and convicted or acquitted; but in

upon the house-tops that no citizen of New York shall be arrested without process of law.' There is no use in bawling from the house-tops what

this we find no justification for arrest and imprisonment without warrant, without cause, without the accusation or suspicion of crime. It seems to us, moreover, too plain for argument, that the sacred right of trial by jury, and in courts where the law of the land is the rule of decision is a right which is never dormant, never suspended, in peaceful and loyal communities and States. Will you, Mr. President, maintain, that because the writ of *habeas corpus* may be in suspense, you can substitute soldiers and bayonets for the peaceful operation of the laws; military commissions, and inquisitorial modes of trial for the courts and juries prescribed by the Constitution itself? And if you cannot maintain this, then let us ask where is the justification for the monstrous proceeding in the case of a citizen of Ohio, to which we have called your attention? We know that a recreant judge, whose name has already descended to merited contempt, found the apology on the outside of the supreme and fundamental law of the Constitution. But this is not the foundation on which your superstructure of power is built. We have mentioned the act of the last Congress professing to authorize a suspension of the writ of *habeas corpus*. This act now demands your special attention, because if we are not greatly in error, its terms and plain intention are directly opposed to all the arguments and conclusions of your communication. That act, besides providing that the *habeas corpus* may be suspended, expressly commanded that the names of all persons theretofore or thereafter arrested by authority of the President, or his cabinet ministers, being citizens of States in which the administration of the laws has continued unimpaired, shall be returned to the courts of the United States for the districts in which such persons reside, or in which their supposed offences were committed; and such return being made, if the next grand jury attending the courts does not indict the alleged offenders, then the judges are commanded to issue an order for their immediate discharge from imprisonment. Now, we cannot help asking whether you have overlooked this law, which most assuredly you are bound to observe, or whether it be your intention to disregard it? Its meaning certainly cannot be mistaken. By it the national Legislature has said that the President may suspend the accustomed writ of *habeas corpus*, but at the same time it has commanded that all arrests under his authority shall be promptly made known to the courts of justice, and that the accused parties shall be liberated, unless presented by a grand jury according to the Constitution, and tried by a jury in the ancient and accustomed mode. The President may possibly, so far as Congress can give the right, arrest without legal cause or warrant. We certainly deny that Congress can confer this right, because it is forbidden by the higher law of the Constitution. But, waiving that consideration, this statute, by its very terms, promptly removes the proceeding in every case into the courts where the safeguards of liberty are observed, and where the persons detained are to be discharged, unless indicted for criminal offences against the established and ascertained laws of the country.

"Upon what foundation, then, permit us to ask, do you rest the pretension that men who are not accused of crime may be seized and imprisoned, or banished at the will and pleasure of the President or any of his subordinates in civil and military positions? Where is the warrant for invading the freedom of speech and of the press? Where the justification for placing the citizen on trial without the presentment of a grand jury and before military commissions? There is no power in this country which can dispense with its laws. The President is as much bound by them as the humblest individual. We pray you to bear in mind, in order that you may duly estimate the feeling of the people on this subject, that for the crime of dispensing with the laws and statutes of Great Britain, our ancestors brought one monarch to the scaffold, and expelled another from his throne.

"This power, which you have erected in theory, is of vast and illimitable proportions. If we may trust you to exercise it mercifully and leniently, your successor, whether immediate or more remote, may wield it with the energy of a Cæsar or Napoleon, and with the will of a despot and a tyrant. It is a power without boundary or limit, because it proceeds upon a total suspension of all the constitutional and legal safeguards which protect the rights of a citizen. It is a power not inaptly described in the language of one of your secretaries. Said Mr. Seward to the British minis-

everybody knows to be nonsense. * * * Demand, quotha? The starling that Mr. Sterne saw in the cage said only 'I can't get out.' It

ter in Washington : ' I can touch a bell on my right hand and order the arrest of a citizen of Ohio. I can touch the bell again and order the imprisonment of a citizen of New York, and no power on earth but that of the President can release them. Can the Queen of England, in her dominions, do as much ?' This is the very language of a perfect despotism, and we learn from you with profound emotion that this is no idle boast. It is a despotism unlimited in principle, because the same arbitrary and unrestrained will or discretion which can place men under illegal restraint, or banish them, can apply the rack or the thumbscrew, can put to torture or to death. Not thus have the people of this country hither understood their Constitution. No argument can commend to their judgment such interpretations of the great charter of their liberties. Quick as the lightning's flash, the intuitive sense of freemen perceives the sophistry and rejects the conclusion.

"Some other matters, which your Excellency has presented, demand our notice.

"In justification of your course as to Mr. Vallandigham, you have referred to the arrest of Judge Hall at New Orleans, by order of Gen. Jackson ; but that case differs widely from the case of Mr. Vallandigham. New Orleans was then, as you truly state, under ' martial or military law.' This was not so in Ohio, where Mr. Vallandigham was arrested. The administration of the civil law had not been disturbed in that commonwealth. The courts were open, and justice was dispensed with its accustomed promptitude. In the case of Judge Hall, Gen. Jackson in a few days sent him outside the line of his encampments, and set him at liberty ; but you have undertaken to banish Mr. Vallandigham from his home. You seem also to have forgotten that Gen. Jackson submitted implicitly to the judgment of the court which imposed the fine upon him : that he promptly paid it ; that he enjoined his friends to assent, ' as he most freely did, to the decision which had just been pronounced against him.'

"More than this, you overlook the fact that the then administration (in the language of a well-known author) ' mildly but decidedly rebuked the proceedings of General Jackson," and that the President viewed the subject with ' surprise and solicitude.' Unlike President Madison, you in a case much more unwarranted, approve the proceedings of your subordinate officer, and in addition justify your course by a carefully considered argument in its support.

"It is true that after some thirty years, Congress, in consideration of the devoted and patriotic services of Gen. Jackson, refunded the amount of the fine he had paid ! But the long delay in doing this, proved how reluctant the American people were to do anything which could be considered as in any way approving the disregard shown to the majesty of the law, even by one who so eminently enjoyed their confidence and regard.

"One subject more, and we shall conclude. You express your regret that our meeting spoke ' as Democrats ;' and you say that ' in this time of national peril you would have preferred to meet us upon a level one step higher than any party platform.' You thus compel us to allude to matters which we should have preferred to pass by. But we cannot omit to notice your criticism, as it casts, at least, an implied reproach upon our motives and our proceedings. We beg to remind you that when the hour of our country's peril had come, when it was evident that a most gigantic effort was to be made to subvert our institutions and to overthrow the government, when it was vitally important that party feelings should be laid aside, and that all should be called upon to unite most cordially and vigorously to maintain the Union ; at the time you were sworn into office as President of the United States, when you should have urged your fellow-citizens in the most emphatic manner to overlook all past differences and to rally in defence of their country and its institutions when you should have enjoined respect for the laws and the Constitution, so clearly disregarded by the South, you chose, for the first time, under like circumstances, in the history of our country, to set up a party platform, called the ' Chicago platform,' as your creed ; to advance it beyond the Constitution, and to speak disparagingly of that great conservative tribunal of our country, so highly respected by all thinking men who have inquired into our institutions—THE SUPREME COURT OF THE UNITED STATES.

"Your administration has been true to the principles you then laid down. Notwithstanding

would have been more 'manly' to scream—'I demand to get out; I proclaim on the house-tops that I will get out.'"

While thus "the strong government" at Washington had grasped the liberties of the country, it promised a fresh infusion of vigour in the war. It increased its army; it exhibited, as its strength on the water, a navy of nearly six hundred vessels, seventy-five of which were iron-clads or armoured steamers; and it made preparations for the prosecution of hostilities which were alarming enough by the side of the now rapidly decreasing resources of the Southern Confederacy. The Congress which assembled at Richmond in the winter of 1863, was immediately and anxiously occupied with the decrease of our armies, and the yet more alarming diminution of our subsistence. These two concerns engaged all the resources and ingenuity of its legislation. It was said that the war had become a question of men and of food.

The conscription law had disappointed expectation. When the first measure was passed, limited to the ages of eighteen and thirty-five, it was estimated that even that partial call would yield eight hundred thousand men. A very simple arithmetical process will disclose this number. The free population of the several States of the Confederacy not wholly occupied by the enemy was at the time of the passage of the first act of

the fact that several hundred thousand Democrats in the loyal States cheerfully responded to the call of their country, filled the ranks of its armies, and by 'their strong hands and willing arms' aided to maintain your Excellency and the officers of government in the possession of our national capital; notwithstanding the fact that the great body of the Democrats of the country have in the most patriotic spirit given their best efforts, their treasure, their brothers and their sons, to sustain the government and to put down the rebellion, you, choosing to overlook all this, have made your appointments to civil office, from your cabinet officers and foreign ministers down to the persons of lowest official grade among the tens of thousands engaged in collecting the revenues of the country, exclusively from your political associates.

"Under such circumstances, virtually proscribed by your administration, and while most of the leading journals which supported it approved the sentence pronounced against Mr. Vallandigham, it was our true course—our honest course to meet as 'Democrats,' that neither your Excellency nor the country might mistake our antecedents or our position.

"In closing this communication, we desire to reaffirm our determination, and we doubt not that of every one who attended the meeting which adopted the resolutions we have discussed, expressed in one of those resolutions, to devote 'all our energies to sustain the cause of the Union.'

"Permit us, then, in this spirit, to ask your Excellency to reëxamine the grave subjects we have considered, to the end that on your retirement from the high position you occupy, you may leave behind you no doctrines and no further precedents of despotic power to prevent you and your posterity from enjoying that constitutional liberty which is the inheritance of us all, and to the end, also, that history may speak of your administration with indulgence if it cannot with approval.

"We are, sir, with great respect, yours very truly,

"JOHN V. L. PRUYN,

"Chairman of Committee.

"ALBANY, June 30, 1863."

conscription (1862) as follows, giving only fractions of the population for those States partially overrun by the enemy :

Alabama,	529,164
Arkansas,	324,323
Florida,	78,686
Georgia,	595,097
Louisiana,	376,913
Mississippi,	354,699
North Carolina,	661,586
A fourth of Missouri,	264,588
South Carolina,	301,271
Two thirds of Tennessee,	556,042
Texas,	420,651
Half of Virginia,	552,591
Total,	5,015,618

This being the aggregate population, what proportion of it were males between the ages of eighteen and thirty-five ? By the census of 1850, the population of the United States was twenty-three millions one hundred and ninety-one thousand eight hundred and seventy-six. Of this total, seven millions forty-seven thousand nine hundred and forty-five were given as between the ages in question. Half this number would give three millions five hundred and twenty-three thousand nine hundred and seventy-two as the males between those ages ; which number is fifteen per cent. of the aggregate population. This ratio applied to the white population of the Confederacy, as stated above, would give as the number that should have been produced by the first act of conscription seven hundred and fifty-two thousand three hundred and forty-two men. If we should add to this number the volunteers from that population of the States of Kentucky, Maryland, and portions of Virginia and Missouri not embraced in the basis of estimate, and the volunteers offering from ages not embraced in the prescribed figures, the aggregate soldiery of the Confederacy would reach the number of eight hundred thousand.

The conscription law of the Confederacy had since been extended to the age of forty-five ; and in 1863 it was further extended, by the repeal of the clause allowing substitutions, which it was declared would add more than seventy thousand men to the army. And yet about this time the rolls of the Adjutant-General's office in Richmond showed little more than four hundred thousand men under arms ; and of these, Mr. Seddon, the Confederate Secretary of War, declared that, owing to desertions and other causes, " not more than a half, never two-thirds of the soldiers were in the ranks." When we contemplate the actual result to which the conscription was thus reduced, we may imagine how harsh had become the war, and how averse the people of the South to the demands of its necessities. Indeed, the Confederate Government had committed a great oversight in failing to enlist troops for the whole period of the war, when it first commenced; for, as is usual at the beginning of all political revolutions, great unanimity and patriotic zeal prevailed among the people throughout the country, which rendered that measure both feasible and easy. But lost opportunities seldom return. This important measure, so easy at the outset of the war, was quite impossible in its advanced stages, as the ardour of the people was cooled or abated by the hardships and vicissitudes inseparable from a state of hostility.

The most striking of these hardships was the want of food, the actual pang of starvation in the army. Provisions were very scarce all through the country, so much so as to excite fears of a famine. Poverty and its attendant necessities befell those who had never dreamed of want. Many families who had been reared in affluence and luxury, were in need of the common necessaries of life. Young, delicate ladies often had to perform menial offices, such as cooking and washing for their families, having lost their servants by the war, or having been driven by other necessities to the last resources of economy. In the army the suffering was more vital; and had it not been for the scanty additions of provisions and clothing, which the love of relatives and friends occasionally sent them, many of the troops would have been compelled to disband, or would have perished in their camps. As it was, desertions were rapidly taking place, as the rigour of winter came on. It required all the popularity of Gen. Lee, and the exercise of every available faculty of his mind, to keep even his veteran army in Virginia together. A tithe-tax was instituted by the Confederate Congress, by which it was hoped to furnish supplies to the armies; but this and all kindred measures on the subject of subsistence were so badly executed, that the results invariably disappointed the calculation.

Indeed, the subject of the Confederate commissariat was so closely connected with the general fortunes of the war; it did so much to determine its conclusion; it exhibits so many characteristic instances of mal-administration in Richmond, that a distinct consideration of it here, up to the time we are now discussing, is not out of place, and will prepare the reader for much that is to follow in the general history of the war.

HISTORY OF THE CONFEDERATE COMMISSARIAT.

In January, 1862, a report was made to the Confederate Congress in Richmond, on the general administration of the Bureau of Subsistence, particularly with reference to certain contracts for obtaining supplies, which had been unfavourably reported to the public and to Congress. In that report, the following occurs : " In the packing season of 1860–'61 upward of three million head of hogs were packed at the various porkeries of the United States, besides those packed by farmers at home, of which less than twenty thousand were packed at regular establishments south of the lines of our armies. Of this whole number, experts estimate that the product of about one million two hundred thousand hogs was imported in the early part of the last year from beyond our present lines into what is now the Southern Confederacy. This was accomplished, and to the extent of a bountiful supply by the action of the State authorities in some cases, by the enterprise of private parties, and by this department, through agencies of its own. Of this number it is estimated that about three hundred thousand hogs, or their bacon equivalent, have been consumed by our State and Confederate armies since the commencement of hostilities. Tennessee then became the main reliance for the future use of the army, which, together with the accessible portions of Kentucky, had been so ravaged by hog cholera and injured by short corn crops for three years preceding the year just closed, that the number slaughtered at the porkeries within her limits had deviated from two hundred thousand head to less than twenty thousand. It was into this field, just recovering from these disasters, and almost the sole resource of the army, and the planters and inhabitants of cities, that this department had to enter as a purchaser, dubious of a sufficiency, but assured of a heavy and active competition."

Shortly after the date of this report, the successive captures of Forts Henry and Donelson caused the loss of a considerable portion of the supplies referred to. The subsequent campaign lost us Kentucky and much of Tennessee, and left the Confederacy comparatively bare of meat.

In this early prospect of distress a number of propositions were made to the Confederate Government by responsible and energetic parties, to exchange through the enemy's lines meat for cotton. But to this favourable exchange President Davis was opposed ; he was actually weak enough to suppose that if a little cotton was kept from the enemy, the North would be unable to pay the January interest of 1863 ; and he was among those stupid financiers who were for confining cotton, as if there were magical salvation in it, and hoarding this inert wealth of the South.

In the fall of 1862, a party properly vouched for proposed, for an equivalent in cotton, to deliver thirty thousand hogsheads of bacon through the lines. It was alleged that there was enough cotton to feed and clothe our army, in a section tributary to Memphis, which city was then, and had been for some time previous, in the secure possession of the enemy ; that such cotton must otherwise probably be destroyed to prevent its falling into the hands of the enemy ; but that the owners, as a general rule, though willing to let the government have their crops, were averse, if not stubbornly opposed to having them destroyed.

This proposition was submitted to President Davis. It was endorsed in the bureau of subsistence : " The alternative is thus presented of violating our policy of withholding cotton from the enemy or risking the starvation of our armies ; " and it was suggested that the Commissary General be authorized to contract for bacon and salt, limiting the amount of purchase to what was absolutely necessary to feed the army and supply it with blankets and shoes, showing that no law forbade this traffic ; that the precedents of other wars justified it ; and advising that the Commissary General should, under such circumstances, upon his own statement of the necessity, be allowed to make the contract, which, this officer added, nothing less than the danger of sacrificing our armies would induce " him to acquiesce in." Upon that letter the President endorsed as follows :

" SECRETARY OF WAR—Is there any necessity for immediate action ? Is there satisfactory evidence that the present opportunity is the last which will be offered ? Have you noted the scheme of the enemy for the payment of their next accruing interest on their public debt ? You will not fail to perceive the effect of postponing the proposed action until January 1, 1863, if it be necessary at any time to depart from the well-defined policy of our government in relation to cotton.

                                                            " JEFF. DAVIS.
" OCTOBER 31, 1862."

President Davis was assured that the consequences of the refusal of this policy of exchange would be most serious. Col. Northrop, the Commissary General, informed him that present efforts, even if successful, would not produce cured bacon for the next year. The departments of the east had been exhausted, while the increasing number of refugees, driven from their homes by the enemy's arms, added to the consumers. The results hoped for from Tennessee were not probably equal to the demands of the troops on the west of the mountains and in Tennessee. A statement was made in the bureau of subsistence, that the supply of hogs for 1862 would be about one hundred thousand short of the supply for the preceding year, and that the supply of beef was well nigh exhausted. This statement was communicated to President Davis, with the following endorsement by Mr. Randolph, then Secretary of War : " Unless the deficiency be made up by purchases beyond the limits of the Confederacy, I apprehend serious consequences."

President Davis refused to see the necessity so plainly indicated to him. He still lingered in the conceit of an early termination of the war, and in spite of the plainest figures he persisted in the belief that the requisite amount of supplies for the army might still be procured from sources within the Confederate States. How far he was mistaken in this, will be shown by the following reply to one of his calls for information about the close of the year 1862 :

" It will be observed that the President, through Gen. Smith, calls for information on three points, and to these exclusively is the answer addressed.

" *First*—Every source within the Confederate lines from which supplies could have been obtained last year or this has been fully explored. All such have either been exhausted or found inadequate. If in any small portion of the Confederacy supplies have not been aimed at, it was because it was known that such portion would not afford enough for the current domestic supply of that particular area. It has been erroneously supposed that Southern Georgia and Alabama, and certain portions of Florida, would afford large amounts of stock, but they have not done it. They have not even fully fed those posts which from geographical position would naturally draw from them, and they cannot do as much in the future as they have done in the past.

" This appears abundantly from facts within my knowledge and from testimony in this office.

" *Second*—To state more fully the reasons for immediate action it is necessary to recapitulate :

" The report states a clear deficit of bacon of 8,116,194 pounds, or twenty-five per cent. ; a clear deficit in salt beef of 36,000 beeves, at an average of five hundred pounds —making 18,000,000, or ninety per cent. per bullock. Whole value of the above, in rations, 22,516,194. Total deficit per cent., 43.

" This calculation is upon the basis of the forces this year in camp and field. Further : it does not include immense supplies purchased from private hands, which cannot be had at all for this winter, because the stock to create them is not in the Confederate lines, and the salt cannot be had if the stock could. Besides, large local supplies have been completely exhausted, as in Loudon and Fauquier and other districts. And even the above estimated subsistence is not at all secure. The hogs, though bargained for, have not all been driven to places of safety. The salt to cure them has not all been secured, and what has been engaged has not all been delivered, and must take its chances for transportation over long distances, upon uncertain roads discordantly connected. It is not safe, then, to rely on these estimates. Added to that, the winter is at hand; the rises of the rivers all impending; invasion on a large scale is imminent; the supplies which had been hoped for from the enemy's lines are not to be expected.

" The supplies now offered are ample, and are tendered at lower rates in cotton, even at the extreme bid, than they can be bought at for Confederate currency in our own lines. If not availed of now they most probably never will be, for lack of power and opportunity.

" And, finally, both Mobile and Charleston are pressing for large supplies out of resources which must be held for the armies of Virginia, or the border States will be lost ; while the same reserves, and the accumulations I have been endeavouring to make in Tennessee, are demanded by the armies of General Bragg.

" *Third*—As to the relative advantages of procuring supplies from Memphis and from the vicinity of New Orleans, the proposition to make such purchases is not a new idea. They were made at the commencement of the war to an extent which is little known. In an elaborate report on the operations of this Bureau, made by Major Ruffin, under my order and superintendence, and submitted to Congress in January last, it is stated : Experts estimate that the product of about 1,200,000 hogs was imported in the early part of last year (1861), from beyond our present lines into what is now the Southern Confederacy. This was accomplished by the action of State authorities ; in some cases by the enterprise of private parties, and by this department, through agencies of its own. Of this number it is estimated that about 300,000 hogs, in their bacon equivalent, have been consumed by our State and Confederate armies since the commencement of hostilities. This was for a period of eight months, and shows a requirement of 450,000 hogs per annum. For a considerable part of that period the army was a mere fraction of the magnitude which it has since reached. Those who think that the stimulus of high prices, under the apprehension of a great scarcity, has so increased our supply of meat as to enable us to dispense with this large balance, forget that the counties most capable of such development are precisely those which have suffered most from the war. Elsewhere it must have been a new enterprise, such as could not be expected to succeed when the best men were in the army.

"Therefore I urge that supplies be engaged both from Memphis and from the vicinity of New Orleans, and for these additional reasons: It may be safely estimated that the army will consume and waste the product of not less than five hundred thousand hogs, of which we calculate to receive only about one third from our Confederate limits. I will not be prudent to rely upon obtaining the amount needed from one single source of supply; it will be well to divide the risk. Moreover, other articles are needed nearly as much as meat. The salt works in Louisiana are not to be depended on; the supply to be obtained from Saltville, in Virginia, is limited. The wants of citizens, daily becoming more urgent and alarming, will absorb all of that, if permitted, and the drafts of the Government upon the same fund will cause ruinous prices and great destitution.

"One reliable party in New Orleans offers to supply one hundred thousand sacks of salt, or more than is called for by the rapidly expiring contract at Saltville. Other articles—such as coffee and flour—are also offered from New Orleans. The supply of flour from that quarter will enable the soldiers from the Southwest to use that in part as a bread ration instead of corn meal, which must otherwise be their sole reliance for bread The reserve of coffee for the sick is being rapidly consumed. No other prospect of getting more presents itself, but the necessity of a sufficiency is important. The success of the enterprise is doubtful; but the opportunity afforded by the venality of the enemy ought not to be lost. If we thereby obtain the use of the Mississippi from Memphis to New Orleans, until such time as the whole or a large part of the needed supplies shall have been obtained, it will be a great benefit.

"Its effect upon the *morale* of the enemy, and the political results of such a policy, however important in themselves, are questions which, as they have not entered into my calculations, I do not discuss. My action proceeds entirely from a sense of the absolute necessity of these supplies to feed the army, and to subdue the want which has already manifested itself both in Gen. Lee's army and the Army of the West, under the privations to which they have been subjected.   Respectfully,

"L. B. NORTHROP."

No official reply was ever received to this communication. Indeed about this time President Davis left Richmond on a visit to Mississippi, and in a speech before the Legislature of that State pronounced the solemn opinion that the war would soon come to an end. For this reason and "on political principles" the policy of using cotton to get supplies through the lines, and taking advantage of the wide-spread venality of the enemy was negatived. The arguments against this trade were specious and trifling. It was said that the Federal finances were in such a condition that if they could not obtain cotton, upon which to draw bills wherewith to pay their then accruing January interest, their credit would explode, and the war would speedily cease from the bankrupting of our assailants. Hence they wanted cotton. It was also asserted that they did not want cotton, but only sought, under cover of a contract for supply, to find out the channels of navigable streams, to ascertain the location and condition of certain defences, and otherwise to spy out the land. A third argument was that the trade on the part of the government would demoralize the people among whom it might be conducted; and the newspapers added that to trade through New Orleans and let cotton clear from that port "would make Europe think we had caved, who thereupon would decline to recognize us or to intervene." Such were the fancies and punctilios which persuaded the Confederate Government to persist in a line of policy, the steady and inevitable tendency of which was to bring its armies to the verge of starvation.

The project of getting supplies through the enemy's lines thus discouraged, it was necessary for the Commissary General to cast about for a new resource; and in 1863 the experiment was first attempted of obtaining supplies, especially meat and coffee, from foreign ports through the blockade. A scheme of contract was prepared on the basis of an association of individual enterprise with government capital, which, it was thought, if properly arranged, would combine the power and money of the one with the energy and skill of the other. Especially in a business as hazardous as blockade running would such an association, it was thought, be an advantage as securing to the individuals the insurance of many ventures, and to the government the vigilance and intelligence of private parties. It was contemplated that the private parties should sell the cotton and purchase the return cargo, charging two and a half per cent. commission on each transaction; and that the government should purchase the cotton on this side at a commission of two and a half per cent., with a reserved right to the government to all the private freight room, when claimed at an agreed rate per ton; which was two-thirds less than had been previously demanded by other blockade runners, and paid by the government.

Here again was the story of gross mismanagement and slip-shod administration on the part of the Confederate authorities. Great quantities of meat were left to rot at Nassau and Bermuda; payments were not promptly made; and the new resource that had promised such grand results dwindled into insignificant numbers. Contracts for supplies, payable in cotton, in our Atlantic ports, were made with several parties; but in no instance with success. Either the amount involved was too small to tempt the venality of those who could control or purchase an evasion of the blockade, or the engagement to deliver meat alone was found to be too small an inducement to those engaged in blockade running.

In consequence of these failures, and of the refusal to be allowed to pur chase on the Mississippi, the army, especially in Virginia, was put upon short rations. First, they were reduced to one half pound of meat per day —which, if it could have been kept up at that, would have been sufficient —then to one-third of a pound—though this allowance was not agreed to or adhered to by several of the Generals commanding—and then to one quarter of a pound. Upon this last allowance the Army of Northern Virginia wintered.

The policy of running the blockade, so far as the government was interested in it for subsistence, was the occasion of odious monopolies, violations of contract, misunderstandings, &c., and proved of little advan tage to the government, and of questionable profit to private parties. What was known as the Crenshaw or Collie line of steamers did not start until the spring of 1864, and then under unfavourable auspices. One steamer was lost on the coast of Ireland, in coming out ; another upon her second trip ; but two others, both very superiour steamers, were put upon the line, one or both of which had been paid for by large advances made by Crenshaw & Co., and were running successfully. Under their contract the government was obliged to furnish the whole cargo of cotton for each vessel, but, having failed to do so, and the private parties having been required, against the terms of the contract, to supply their own cotton to the vessel at market rates—a demand which was acceded to rather than raise the issue—it was determined to take other parties into the contract. This was rendered necessary by the inability of the government to trans port the cotton, and by the inability of the private parties to supplement the government deficiencies in that particular. The government was ac cordingly induced by the private parties to sell one-fourth of its three-fourths interest in the steamers to the Supply Importing Company, composed of various railroad companies and others interested in railroads in the South. This—though the terms of the contract were changed, and the parties be came, as was contended by the government, mere carriers, whereby the subsistence department lost the benefit of the arrangement it had proposed —at once obviated the difficulties about transporting cotton ; and, as this new contract provided for twelve steamers, it was hoped that some good results might be at last reached. But just as this business had got well under way, the government decided upon taking the Atalanta, the best of the steamers referred to above, for a cruiser. It was urged, in opposition to this, that the tested speed and capacity of this vessel had induced the private parties interested to enter into large contracts for vessels in Eng land, and to assume heavy obligations to pay for the government interest in them ; that there were large quantities of subsistence stores at the Isl ands, purchased by Crenshaw & Co. for the commissariat, which were much needed by the army, and might spoil if permitted to remain. But the government insisted upon taking the ship. Other vessels were built, and paid for by the credit of the private parties, and by receipts of cotton from those successively put on the line; and the enterprise went on, but with results far below the necessities of the country.

During the whole period of the efforts to put the question of meat supply from abroad upon what the bureau of subsistence deemed a proper footing, the meat in the limits of the Confederacy was being constantly reduced in amount, though under constantly increasing efforts to get it for the army.

The well-known effects of a depreciating currency in causing supplies to be hoarded, rendered it necessary to impress them. This mode was legalized by acts of Congress, which failed, however, to enforce it by any penalty, and rendered it nugatory in many instances by requiring that in all cases the impressment should be accompanied by a proffer of the money. In some States the feeling against it had rendered it almost inoperative, and the judiciary, gubernatorial or legislative action of several had practically nullified the law. As a substitute, to last until the currency could have been amended, it might have answered; but experience showed that, as a permanent system, it would be resisted and evaded to such an extent as to render it of little avail in drawing out a sufficiency, when to furnish it even for the army was to produce privation at home. Under the rapid depreciation of our currency, which was now thought by many to have reached a point of hopeless bankruptcy, and when the prices under the schedule fixed by the Commissioners of Appraisement in the various States were merely nominal, it was regarded by the people as an unjust and tyrannical tax, to be resisted to the point of compelling its abandonment as a mode of supply.

It will thus be seen, on a general survey of the whole subsistence policy of the Confederate government—its practical rejection of trade with the enemy, its feeble and mismanaged efforts in running the blockade, and the small yield of impressments—that there could be but one result and that a constant diminution of supplies to the point of starvation. It was a policy of blunders; it lacked some steady and deliberate system; and it finally, as we shall see, in the close of the year 1864, got to that point where the whole system of Confederate defence was bound to break down by *the want of subsistence, even without a catastrophe of arms!*

It is astonishing what silly devices were hit upon in Richmond to meet the coming necessity, and how the empirical remedies of shallow brains aggravated the disorder. One of these so-called remedies proved one of the vilest curses that was ever fastened upon the Confederacy. On the 6th November, 1863, an order was issued by the Secretary of War, that no supplies held by a party for his own consumption, or that of his employés or slaves, should be impressed, and that "no officer should at any time, unless specially ordered so to do by a general Commanding, in a case of exigency, impress supplies which were on their way to market for sale on arrival."

The construction given to that order filled the land with purchasers—private individuals, railroad companies, manufacturers of all kinds, corporations of every class, relief associations of cities, towns and counties, were personally or by their agents in the market buying a year's supply, unlimited as to price, and protected from impressment. Speculators, whose purchases were generally *in transitu*, found themselves protected, and the government playing into their hands. The sudden influx of purchasers into the market stimulated the cupidity of producers and holders of the necessaries of life, and induced them to withhold their supplies, under the expectation of higher prices, and actually raised the prices of all the prime articles fully one hundred per cent. within a single month. The purchasing officers of the government could not buy; nor was it reasonable to expect parties to sell to the government at schedule price, when double that price was offered at their doors by others. They could not impress, for holders had, with great promptness, contracted for all their supplies to parties who paid them higher prices, and thus it naturally and surely happened that the regular supplies of the government were cut off. The whole land was infected by speculators pampered by Mr. Seddon, the Secretary of War; and the soldier, who was without shelter fighting our battles, found himself discriminated against in favour of the private citizen—who, with a roof above him, could better stand a short allowance of food,—and put at the mercy of the most heartless and hateful speculators, who had no conception of the war beyond that of dollars and cents.

It has been remarked that the shiftlessness of the people of the South, their want of commercial tact or of *business knowledge*, so to speak, however it might have been doubted before, was fully proved in the war, and that this cause, as much as anything else, contributed to the ruin and prostration of the Confederacy. The unbusiness-like mind of the South was well illustrated in its commissariat; and the mismanagement of this bureau confirms the truth of the general observation. It is curious, indeed, how this observation extends to all the affairs of the Confederacy. There was a stock of childish expedients in times of grave distress in the Confederacy, at which the world was rather disposed to laugh, despite the necessities they indicated. When iron became scarce, an association of ladies was formed to advertise an appeal all through the Confederacy for broken pots and pans with which to build an armoured steamer. When the Confederate finances declined, it was proposed by a foolish woman of Mobile, who had probably never heard of the law of supply and demand, that all of her sex in the Confederacy should be shorn, and each head of hair bringing a certain price in the European markets, to realize thus many millions of dollars; and the proposition was seriously entertained in the newspapers. But what shall be said of the government that actually and officially, in the course of a system of finance to meet necessities counted by thousands of millions of dollars, made appeals to the people to donate silver plate and jewelry, and published monthly lists of contributions of rings, sugar-pots and spoons! These curious lists may still be found in the files of the Richmond newspapers. Such vagaries are subjects of grave consideration by the historian. They illustrate the general character of make-shifts in the war. He who seeks to solve the problem of the downfall of the Southern Confederacy, must take largely into consideration the absence of any intelligent and steady system in the conduct of public affairs; the little circles that bounded the Richmond Administration; the deplorable want of the commercial or business faculty in the Southern mind.

CHAPTER XXX.

ALTHOUGH the Northern public was gratified in contemplating the sum of Federal victories in the year 1863, it had yet to see in the early months of 1864 a remarkable train of Confederate successes, which, in the aggregate, did much to re-animate the Confederates, and to subdue expectation at Washington. These successes were principally a decisive victory in Florida; the defeat of Sherman's expedition in the Southwest; and a triumphant issue in the most important campaign that had yet taken place west of the Mississippi River.

GEN. P. G. T. BEAUREGARD.

LEIUT. GEN. RICHD S. EWELL.

LEIUT. GEN. J. LONGSTREET.

LEIUT. GEN. S. JACKSON.

LEIUT. GEN. A. P. HILL.

MAJ. GEN. J. E. B. STEWART.

GEN. A. S. JOHNSTON.

Engd by H. B. Hall, N. Y.

Engraved expressly for the Lost Cause by E. A. Pollard.

BATTLE OF OCEAN POND.

The operations against Charleston having been virtually abandoned, it was decided at Washington to use the surplus troops in an attempt upon Florida. A command of six or seven thousand men, including two regiments of negroes, was organized under Gen. Seymour, left Charleston harbour in eighteen transports, and in the month of February ascended the St. Mary's River. The enemy was allowed to land, as the small Confederate force under Gen. Finnegan was unequal for anything like a battle, and was awaiting reinforcements despatched by Gen. Beauregard, in whose military department the State of Florida was included. Colquitt's brigade arrived in time to unite with Finnegan and hold the position at Oulustre not far from Ocean Pond, an inland lake, where it was proposed to cover the capital of the State and defend the road from Lake City to Tallahassee. The joint Confederate force did not number more than five thousand men.

On the 20th February, this little force was advanced several miles to meet the enemy. A severe battle opened in the afternoon; for two hours the enemy was steadily pushed back; until at last about sunset, a simultaneous attack of the Twenty-Seventh and Sixth Georgia Regiments on the enemy's centre and flank broke his whole line into confusion. Five pieces of artillery were taken, two thousand small arms, and five hundred prisoners. The enemy left upon the field three hundred and fifty dead, and abandoned all of his severely wounded. The action was decisive, as it resulted in the expulsion of the enemy from Florida, and the preservation of this State to the Confederacy.

SHERMAN'S EXPEDITION IN THE SOUTHWEST.

Another notable event about this time was Sherman's expedition into Central Mississippi, in which, with an army of about thirty thousand men, he proposed to sever his communications behind him, and to strike off into the heart of the country. It was his first experiment of " the movable column," but unlike that in the later months of 1864, it had opposing military forces to encounter, and came to the most wretched grief.

The conceit of the Federal commander was to operate upon what was called a " strategic triangle "—to move from Vicksburg to Mobile, by the way of Selma; a heavy column of cavalry to start from Memphis, move rapidly across Mississippi and Alabama, come upon the flank of Gen. Polk's army, and harass his retreat while Sherman rushed upon him in front; and thus by the possession of Mobile and Selma to obtain two important water-bases—the one on the Mississippi at Vicksburg, the other at

Mobile on the Gulf, and to establish his army firmly in the triangle formed by the Alabama and Tombigbee Rivers, and the railroad leading from Selma to Demopolis and Meridian. The immediate objects of the movement were to cut off Mobile from Johnston, who lay in front of Grant on the lines in North Georgia, to break up Polk's army, and then to turn down on Mobile, and co-operate with Farragut's fleet, which was at that time thundering at the gates of this city.

On the 3d February, Sherman left Vicksburg with about thirty thousand infantry, pushed east, and crossed the entire State of Mississippi to Meridian. A few days later the cavalry column, eight thousand strong, under command of Gens. Smith and Grierson, started from Corinth and Holly Springs, and passed, with the usual incidents of pillage and destruction, through one of the richest districts of the Confederacy. The junction of this cavalry force with Sherman at Meridian was the critical point of his plan, and it was thought would enable him to advance upon Demopolis and Selma.

Gen. Polk's little army having been reinforced by two or three brigades from the Mobile garrison for the purpose of checking the enemy far enough to save his accumulated stores and supplies, was yet in no condition to give battle, being but half of Sherman's numbers; and, therefore, evacuated Meridian, and retired to Demopolis. Meanwhile Gen. Forrest, with not more than twenty-five hundred cavalry, had been detached to watch the movements of Smith's and Grierson's commands, and was left to confront eight thousand of the best-equipped cavalry that the enemy had ever put in the field. But the great cavalry chief of the West showed no hesitation. He struck the enemy on the broad prairies near West Point; and at Okalona, on the 21st February, he had a more important action, and put the enemy in shameful retreat back to Memphis.

This action of Forrest was decisive of the campaign; it broke down Sherman's means of subsisting his infantry; and it illustrated on what slight conditions depend the defeat or success of an enterprise which leaves a well-defined base to penetrate the interiour of a country. Sherman in his first experiment of "the movable column" obtained only the cheap triumphs of the ruffian and plunderer. He was compelled to make a hasty retreat over one hundred and fifty miles of a country he had ravaged and exhausted; he accomplished not a single military result; he demoralized a fine army; and of the cavalry which was to co-operate with him, this master of billingsgate in the army declared "half went to h—ll, and half to Memphis."

THE RED RIVER EXPEDITION.

Gen. Banks, the Federal commander, had remained for some months idle and ostentatious in New Orleans, with just as much of the State of

Louisiana in the Union as was covered by his pickets. But he hoped to signalize the year 1864 by a remarkable expedition, which was to proceed up Red River as far as Shreveport, thence across the country into the central region of Texas, thereby destroying the Confederate lines on Red River, and their supplies, which were then drawn principally from that portion of Texas.

He proposed to move on this expedition with a land force, and a squadron of gunboats and transports—the former numbering about forty thousand men. Maj.-Gen. "Dick" Taylor was at this time commanding the Confederate forces operating along the west bank of the Mississippi River. Gen. Kirby Smith was commanding the Trans-Mississippi Department, with headquarters at Shreveport. Gen. Price was temporarily commanding the district of Arkansas, with headquarters in the field, in the neighbourhood of Camden. The Confederate force in Arkansas numbered about eight thousand effective men. That of the Federals was conjectured to be about fifteen thousand men, the greater part of which, under Gen. Steele, held Little Rock. Gen. Taylor had about ten thousand men, Louisiana and Texas troops.

About the middle of March, Gen. Banks commenced his advance up Red River; and about two weeks later, Gen. Steele commenced advancing from Little Rock, in the direction of Shreveport, intending to unite with Banks at that point, and to assist in capturing the place. Gen. Taylor made some desultory attempts to oppose or check the advance of the enemy, but he was gradually forced back by overwhelming numbers, retreating as slowly as possible in order to give his reinforcements time to reach him before he fell back to Shreveport. Gen. Smith had ordered two brigades of Missouri infantry and two brigades of Arkansas infantry, which had been operating in Arkansas, to go to Taylor's relief; and he also hurried up some cavalry from Texas.

BATTLE OF MANSFIELD.

Red River is a very narrow and tortuous stream, and at the time of the expedition was quite low. At Alexandria, one hundred and sixty miles below Shreveport, are the "Falls," which obstruct the channel and prevent navigation in low water. On the road from Shreveport to Alexandria, forty miles from the former place, is Mansfield, a little village of about five hundred inhabitants. Twenty miles from Mansfield, on the same road, is the village of Pleasant Hill. Twenty miles further on is Blair's Landing on Red River. Still further on, forty miles above Alexandria, on Old River, which in high water communicates with Red River, we come to Natchitoches, the oldest town on Red River, the scene of the last con

ference between the agents of Aaron Burr and Gen. Hamilton in reference
to the expedition of the former to conquer the Spanish and unfriendly
powers in Louisiana and Mexico.

Gen. Smith had determined to make a stand at a point between Mansfield and Shreveport, where he calculated on having his army concentrated,
expecting by the superiour valour of his men to defeat the enemy's large
force, but if not, to fall back on Shreveport, and fight from fortifications.
On the morning of April 8th, Gen. Taylor, with his command now augmented to fifteen thousand, had reached within two miles of Mansfield, and
had halted, determined to have an affair with the enemy. The Arkansas
and Missouri infantry organized into two divisions, the Missourians under
Gen. Parsons and the Arkansians under Gen. Tappan, and both under
Gen. Churchill, were at Keachi, a village twenty miles from Mansfield.
Churchill was under orders to march his command until he formed a junction with Taylor. Accordingly, his command, on the 8th of April, marched
from Keachi to Mansfield, a distance of twenty miles, and reached their
camp after dark.

Gen. Banks was marching his army by brigades, with intervals of from
one to three miles, each brigade with its train—a favourite plan of marching with the Federal troops.   The place selected by Gen. Taylor for
engagement was calculated to give great advantage to the party attacked.
He expected that as soon as Banks' forces came up they would attack him,
as they had been doing for the past twenty days.

The ground selected was a large plantation three-quarters of a mile in
width, and three or four miles in length. The Mansfield and Alexandria
road ran across it. The ground traversed by the road was higher than on
either side, forming a ridge. Gen. Taylor, in falling back, crossed the
clearing, and halted his command on the west side, in the timber. The
advance-guard of Gen. Banks discovering that the Confederates had halted,
also halted. It appeared as if each party desired the other to attack, and
several hours were passed in inactivity. About four o'clock in the afternoon, Gen. Taylor, becoming impatient, and desiring to camp, determined
to drive back the advance-guard of the enemy. For this purpose he sent
forward a battalion of skirmishers, which the enemy perceiving when
about half way across the field, sent a regiment of cavalry to cut it off.
Gen. Taylor, to save his skirmishers, sent a regiment to their relief; the
enemy immediately developed an entire brigade; the Louisiana Brigade
was ordered to charge, and thus in a few moments a general action was
provoked.

The Louisiana troops moved gallantly forward, at a rapid run, making
across the clearing half-a-mile, under a terrible fire of the enemy's artillery
and small arms. There was no pause until they struck the enemy, broke
the line of his first brigade, and captured nearly the whole of it. A sec-

ond line of the enemy shared the same fate. In this line one of the Federal regiments called for " quarter," and ceased firing, when Gen. Mouton rode up to receive their surrender. Several shots were fired at him, and he fell dead, his body pierced by four balls. Incensed at this atrocious act of cowardice and treachery, the Louisiana troops poured into the regiment that had called for quarter volley after volley of musketry, shattering it, and killing or wounding nearly every man in it. It was nearly dark when the battle ceased. The enemy was driven back ; both wings of his army were flanked ; he lost eight hundred killed and wounded, several thousand prisoners, one hundred and fifty wagons, eighteen pieces of artillery, and five or six thousand stand of small arms.

At two o'clock next morning, Churchill's corps, which had not been in the engagement of the night before, was ordered forward, and put in the advance in pursuit of the enemy, who was soon discovered to be in full retreat. A detachment of cavalry in advance, acting as skirmishers, were constantly picking up stragglers. A thousand men were captured in this way during the day. The scene of the disorderly retreat was decidedly picturesque. The Zouaves, in their wide trousers, loose jackets, and skull caps, all red, torn, dirty, and with lapdogs frequently in their arms, which they had stolen as they had come up, presented a singular spectacle, as they were marched to the rear in squads of fives, tens, or fifties, generally by a Texas cavalry-man, accoutred in ragged pants, a wide hat, and big spurs, armed with a long Enfield rifle, and riding a Spanish mule or a mustang pony. On the road from the battle-field to within a few miles of Pleasant Hill, the Confederates were never out of sight of a deserted wagon, some burned and some left standing, ambulances, caissons, boxes of ammunition, boxes of crackers, packages of medicines, dead Federals, dead horses, and broken and abandoned guns. Some of the wagons were loaded with *cradles*, intended for cutting the wheat crop of Texas, and many of them had in them various articles which had been stolen from citizens in the march.

BATTLE OF PLEASANT HILL.

As the Confederates advanced within three miles of Pleasant Hill, it was reported that the enemy had made a stand there. The troops in advance were halted to rest them, and to give time to the rear to close up. A council of war was called by Gen. Taylor, who thought that the enemy would again retreat as soon as our force developed itself.

Pleasant Hill, as before stated, is a small village through which runs the main road to Alexandria. To the southwest of the village was a large clearing traversed by three deep gullies. On the southeast corner stood what was known as the College Building.

From the point where the Confederates halted a road makes a detour from the main road and comes into a clearing back of the village, at the southwest corner. Just before entering the clearing, a road branches off from this and makes a still greater detour to the south, and comes into the clearing back of the college. Gen. Taylor, supposing that the enemy had formed across the main road, directed Walker's division of Texas troops, the cavalry in reserve, and also the Louisiana infantry in supporting distance to advance along the road, attack, and drive him. Churchill with his corps was ordered to take the road which has been described as leading around the village, and thereby strike the enemy in the flank. Gen. Taylor was not aware that this road came in at the southwest corner, but thought it came in at the southeast corner near the College, and hence failed to caution Churchill against coming in too soon. The army advanced as directed, and Churchill, provided with a guide, moved forward. When he came to where the other road led off to the right, the guide insisted that Gen. Taylor intended the troops to take it, and come in by the College. Gen. Churchill replied that Gen. Taylor had not spoken of turning off that road, and as the main road led forward he determined to continue on it. The guide, knowing the country well, understood Gen. Taylor's plan, although the commander had blundered in describing it. Churchill advanced until he reached the edge of the clearing, then marched to the left, forming his line parallel with the main road, but three-quarters of a mile from it. The Federals had formed a line across the road in the thick timber, and had thrown up logs and rails several feet high to protect them. They had also formed two lines, on the left flank of this first line, and at right angles to it, and parallel to the road, in two gullies running through the clearing, with their left resting on the edge of timber. Their reserve line was formed beyond the village, the right flank resting on the main road and the left extended to the vicinity of the College. A battery was planted at the west end of the village in the road, and another planted on the rising ground near the College. The enemy's forces were thus admirably posted to repel an attack and to take advantage of any success they might obtain. They kept their positions well covered by heavy bodies of sharpshooters, and the Confederates had to advance in line of battle in full force to discover their position.

Gen. Walker had advanced along the road, but had met with so much resistance from skirmishers as to induce Gen. Churchill to believe that he had discovered the enemy, and was really in his rear. He therefore ordered an advance at double-quick in the direction of the firing. Meanwhile Walker, having driven in the skirmishers, discovered the enemy in large force concealed in the underbrush, and ordered a charge. But the brush was almost impenetrable, and the enemy was in a cover from which he could not be easily driven. In front of his position for one hundred yards the small trees were cut off as by an even scythe about four feet high, by the incessant volleys of the enemy's fire. Churchill, coming up soon, struck the first line of the enemy posted in the gully. The vigour of the attack was remarkable; the troops ran over the first line of the enemy, never pausing to take prisoners, and merely shouting to the affrighted Federals to get to the rear. In a few moments a second line of the enemy was pushed back, and Churchill was soon up where Walker was attacking. By the combined assault the enemy was driven from his position, and fell back to the gullies in the field.

Walker's and Churchill's men were now intermixed and in some confusion. Col. Burns, commanding the 2d Brigade of Missouri infantry, succeeded in getting his brigade in order, and, supported by the other commands, moved by the right flank until he came into position to charge the enemy in their new position. In a few moments the Federals were driven back through the village. The 11th Missouri infantry captured a battery which had been planted in the road. In charging the enemy, our forces came full against the village, and Burns' brigade, being in advance in the flank movement, were consequently ̣n the extreme right, and reached beyond the main part of the village. Just as they had driven the enemy through the village, the line of his reserves, which, by its position, was immediately on our right flank, commenced firing, and advancing the left, which had rested near the College. The Confederates were thus suddenly exposed to a flanking and rear fire. They were scattered from the last charge, and fell into disorder.

About two hundred of the Missouri brigade were taken prisoners. A confusion and panic ensued, which it soon became impossible to arrest. The retreat on the part of Churchill's corps was converted into a rout, with no enemy pursuing. Gen. Parsons passed the fugitive troops on a fleet horse, shouting: " The enemy are on you ; meet me at Mansfield." Some of the officers led the men in their flight. One officer came galloping by the Field Infirmary, crying out : " Get away from here ; the enemy have planted a battery on the hill, and will commence firing in a minute." The enemy had no battery in less than a mile, and the officer was so badly frightened that he had mistaken two of our pieces, which a panic-stricken lieutenant had deserted, for a Federal battery. But there were instances of gallantry even in this retreat. Col. Burns attempted long to rally his brigade, and failing, *followed* it from the field as calmly as if he were returning from drill. Col. Moore, commanding the 10th Missouri infantry, was the last to leave the field. On foot he had collected about fifty men, and was sharpshooting the enemy as long as he attempted to follow. Through the efforts of Cols. Burns and Moore, principally, the troops were halted and organized about two miles from the village. Part of Walker's command remained on the ground taken from the enemy, as also some

cavalry and a regiment of Arkansas infantry. Instead of showing any inclination to pursue or even attempting to take the ground he had lost, the
enemy commenced falling back immediately, leaving his dead and wounded
on the field. As night fell, Gen. Smith arrived upon the field, ordered
Churchill's corps back to Arkansas to the relief of Gen. Price, and directed
Gen. Taylor to follow up the enemy.

The Confederate loss in the battle of Pleasant Hill was two hundred
killed, five hundred wounded, and about two hundred and fifty prisoners.
The Federal loss was killed three hundred, wounded eight hundred, prisoners two thousand. In about a week thereafter our prisoners were returned, in partial payment of a deficiency on a former exchange. The
Federal prisoners were sent to Tyler, Texas.

The morning following the battle, Gen. Green, with his Texas cavalry,
was put in advance in pursuit of the enemy. The gunboat squadron was
retreating down the river. The cavalry fired upon it at Blair's Landing,
and Gen. Green was killed by the fragment of a shell. The enemy was
vigorously annoyed all the way to Alexandria; and there he was compelled to make a stand, to gain time to get his boats over the rapids, as the
river had fallen so much as to make it impossible to float them over. Gen.
Taylor's force had been weakened too much to attack and drive the enemy
from his fortifications; and "Yankee ingenuity" triumphed over the
"Falls" by the construction of a tree-dam six hundred feet across the river.
The boats were floated off, and the land forces passed on by the light of
the burning town, which they fired as they left. It was the last act of
atrocity in a career of unparalleled cowardice and crime. Along the line
of Banks' march but few sugar-houses, cotton gins, or even dwelling-
houses were left standing. It was said that his troops marched on their
retreat "with a torch in their right hand, plunder in their left, and their
arms on their backs."

Gen. Banks, instead of winning laurels, and harvesting the wheat-fields
of Texas, returned to New Orleans ruined in military reputation, with the
loss of eight thousand killed and wounded, six thousand prisoners, thirty-
five pieces of artillery, twelve hundred wagons, one gunboat, and three
transports and about twenty thousand stand of small arms. Most of the
captured wagons belonged to Steele, who, after various skirmishes in
Arkansas, had returned to Little Rock with two wagons out of a train
of near eight hundred, and after having lost all of his artillery. Thus ended
the expedition to capture Shreveport and overrun Texas; and thus dissolved the vision of Banks' splendid empire west of the Mississippi, now
practically reduced to the tenure of New Orleans, the banks of the river,
and a strip of sea-coast.

We have seen that three notable expeditions of the enemy, in the early
part of 1864—that against Florida, that against Mississippi and Alabama,

and that against Texas,—had resulted in extreme disaster. They were followed by some expeditions and episodes on the Confederate side, which must be briefly mentioned here, as their results, although successful, threw but little weight into the scales of the war. Such was the expedition by which Forrest, in the month of April, spread terrour along the banks of the Mississippi, stormed Fort Pillow,* and cut a swath across the State of Kentucky. Such, too, was the expedition of Hoke, which captured in North Carolina the strong position of Plymouth, that protected the whole Roanoke Valley, taking in the place sixteen hundred prisoners and twenty-five pieces of artillery. The latter success was thought, indeed, to be of permanent value, as it left the enemy only two places, Washington and Newbern, on the coast of North Carolina; but the force that had moved to Plymouth had to be recalled to the great campaign about to take place in Virginia, and the line of operations it had drawn was soon obliterated from the general map of the war.

In a general history there is but little space for detached events. We have briefly treated those which preceded the large and active campaigns of 1864. But we must make an exception to this rule in case of an expedition of Federal cavalry, directed against Richmond, in the month of March, which, although a very small incident in military view, is to be taken among the most interesting events of the war, as containing one of the most distinct and deliberate evidences of the enemy's atrocity that had yet been given to a shocked and surprised world.

THE RAID OF ULRIC DAHLGREN.

About the close of February, an expedition of Federal cavalry was organized to move towards Richmond, in which Col. Ulric Dahlgren—a son of the Federal admiral who had operated so ineffectually against Charleston—

---

* In the capture of Fort Pillow the list of casualties embraced five hundred out of a garrison of seven hundred; and the enemy entitled the affair "The Fort Pillow Massacre," and Northern newspapers and Congressional committees circulated absurd stories about negro troops being buried alive. The explanation of the unusual proportion of carnage is simple. After the Confederates got into the fort, the Federal flag was not hauled down; there was no surrender; relying upon his gunboats in the river, the enemy evidently expected to annihilate Forrest's forces after they had entered the works; and so the fighting went on to the last extremity. Some of the negro troops, in their cowardice, feigned death, falling to the ground, and were either pricked up by the bayonet, or rolled into the trenches to excite their alarm—to which circumstance is reduced the whole story of "burying negroes alive." Forrest was a hard fighter; he had an immense brain; but he knew but little about grammar and dictionaries. In describing the alarm and bewilderment in Fort Pillow to a superiour officer—who, by the way, has frequently expressed the opinion that Forrest, notwithstanding his defects in literary education, stood second only to Stonewall Jackson as the most remarkable man of the war,—Forrest said: "General, the d—d Yankees kept firing *horizontally* right up into the air."

was second in command.   One branch of the expedition under Gen. Custer was to create a diversion and distract attention in the direction of Charlottesville ; the other was to divide at Beaver Dam, one part of it under Gen. Kilpatrick to move down on the north side of Richmond, the other, commanded by Dahlgren, to cross the James River at some point in Goochland County, make an attack upon the south of the capital, which was supposed to be undefended, release the Federal prisoners there, fire " the hateful city," and murder in cold blood the President and his principal officers !   Such was the fiendish plot of the enemy, the chief part of which was to be enacted by a young man some twenty-odd years old, whose education, social pretensions, and soft manners would scarcely have given one the idea of an enterprise which compassed all the revenge, villainy, and cowardice of the most savage warfare.

The parts of Custer and Kilpatrick were very weakly carried out.   The first reached the vicinity of Charlottesville, and finding Stuart's horse artillery there, retreated at a rapid pace, and fell back to his infantry supports at Madison Court-House.   The second, moving down on the Brook turnpike, came, on the 1st March, near the outer line of the Richmond fortifications, and without once getting within range of the artillery, took up a line of march down the Peninsula.   Meanwhile, Dahlgren, not venturing to cross the high water of the James River, abandoned his enterprise on the south side of Richmond, and, unapprised of the ludicrous cowardice and retreat of Kilpatrick, proposed, by moving down the Westham plank-road, which skirted the river, to effect a junction with him, with a view to further operations or to the security of his retreat.

On the night of the 1st March, Dahlgren pursued his way towards Richmond, with seven or eight hundred horsemen.   The night was very dark ; there was nothing on the road but a force of local soldiery, composed of a battalion of artisans in the Richmond Armory and a battalion of department clerks ; this thin force of unskilled soldiers was all that stood between Dahlgren and the revenge he had plotted to pour in blood and fire upon the devoted capital of the Confederacy.   But it was sufficient. The valorous cavalry that came on with shouts of " Charge the d—d mlitia," broke at the first fire ; and a single fire of musketry, that killed eleven of his men, sufficed to scatter in shameful flight Dahlgren's picked command of " braves."

After this dastardly event, Dahlgren, anxious now only for his retreat, divided what of his force he could collect, so as to increase his chances of escape.   The force under his immediate command moved down the south bank of the Pamunkey, and in the afternoon of the next day crossed the Mattapony at Ayletts in King and Queen County.   As the ferry-boat at this place had been taken up and hid, Lieut. Pollard, who had posted from Richmond to chase the raiders, supposing they would not attempt to cross here, and wishing to dispute the passage of the river wherever it might be attempted, went, with a few men of " Lee's Rangers," farther up the river to Dunkirk, where it was thought the enemy would endeavour to cross. But the raiders, having found an old flat-boat at Ayletts, succeeded in crossing here, swimming their horses. Lieut. Pollard, now finding that the enemy had succeeded in crossing the river below him, immediately left Dunkirk, and went in pursuit, with the intention of hanging on his rear, and harassing him as much as possible with his handful of men.

The rear-guard of the enemy was overtaken a short distance above Bruington Church, and driven down the road on their main body. The party under Lieut. Pollard, numbering now about twenty, advanced, and a desultory fire was kept up for a mile or two. Pollard's party was afterwards joined by some "Home-Guards," under Capt. R. H. Bagby, and the whole force now probably numbered thirty men.

The enemy, having reached the forks of the road near the point where "Butler's Tavern" once stood, took the right fork. Here Lieut. Pollard asked the advice and information of persons who were familiar with the roads and country, and it was decided to ambush the enemy at a point about a mile and a half below Stevensville. The enemy numbered about one hundred and had forty negroes with him. A feint was made by sending a few men in pursuit of the fugitives, while the main force hastened down the left fork of the road leading to Stevensville. The place of ambush was reached about dark.

In the mean time Pollard's force had been increased by a detachment from the 24th Virginia Cavalry, Capt. McGruder commanding, and now numbered about seventy or eighty men. These were also joined by Capt. Fox, of the 5th Virginia Cavalry, with a few men, and he, being the ranking officer, assumed command of the whole force, which was ranged along the road in ambush.

Scouts were sent out to ascertain the whereabouts of the enemy, who, it was found, had reached a point about a mile distant, on what was called the "River Road," where they were in bivouac. A consultation was held among the Confederate officers, and it was at one time decided to attack the enemy, but the final decision was to await his approach.

Some of the officers thought that the raiders would remain in bivouac only long enough to feed their horses, while others thought that they would not advance before morning, or, at least, before the rise of the moon about 2 or 3 A. M. Those who held the latter opinion went to neighbouring houses for the purpose of securing a little rest. Among these was Lieut. Pollard, who was, consequently, not present when the enemy came up.

The enemy advanced about 11 o'clock at night, Col. Dahlgren leading his men. He saw a few men in the road, and ordered them to surrender He was answered by a fire from a few guns. The fire was returned by a few shots from the enemy's front. There was no " desperate fight ; " there was no " cutting the way out," nothing of the sort. A few guns were fired on each side, resulting in the killing of Col. Dahlgren—possibly by his own men—and the wounding of two or three privates. Thrown into confusion by the slight fire, and panic-stricken, the raiders fled down the road they had just come up, and endeavoured to escape through a field immediately in front of the concealed position of the Confederates. They were baffled in this by a creek which ran from the place of ambush into the Mattapony. Near this creek they camped during the remainder of the night, and, having been deserted completely by their officers, surrendered the next morning, probably eighty soldiers and thirty negroes—others being picked up during the day.

The great interest of the affair remained to be disclosed. There were discovered on the dead body of Dahlgren a written address to his men, and other documents, revealing to the startled sensibilities of the people of Richmond the horrours which they had narrowly escaped. The Confederates had here documentary evidence of the atrocious spirit of the enemy, which it was important to exhibit to the world ; for whatever had been the constant assertion on this subject, the persistent denials of Northern prints, their audacious recrimination, and the stereotypes of Federal hypocrisy about " Union," " cause of humanity," " hopes of the world," etc., had heretofore imposed upon the credulous, and put a certain garb of virtue on the most iniquitous designs. But here at last the enemy had, by a document plainer and more significant than any published to the world from the bureaux of Washington, revealed the stark and deformed genius of the war.

On the person of Dahlgren there was discovered the following address to the officers and men of the command, written on a sheet of paper having in printed letters on the upper corner, " Headquarters Third Division, Cavalry Corps, ——, 1864 : "

" *Officers and men :*

" You have been selected from brigades and regiments as a picked command to attempt a desperate undertaking, which, if successful, will write your names on the hearts of your countrymen in letters that can never be erased, and will cause the prayers of our fellow-soldiers, now confined in loathsome prisons, to follow you and yours wherever you may go.

" We hope to release the prisoners from Belle Island first, and having seen them fairly started, we will cross the James River into Richmond, destroying the bridges after us, and exhorting the released prisoners to *destroy and burn the hateful city, and do not allow the rebel leader Davis, and his traitorous crew to escape.* The prisoners must render great assistance, as you cannot leave your ranks too far, or become too much scattered, or you will be lost.

" Do not allow any personal gain to lead you off, which would only bring you to an ignominious death at the hands of citizens. Keep well together, and obey orders strictly, and all will be well, but on no account scatter too far; for in union there is strength.

" With strict obedience to orders, and fearlessness in the execution, you will be sure to succeed.

" We will join the main force on the other side of the city, or perhaps meet them inside.

" Many of you may fall; but if there is any man here not willing to sacrifice his life in such a great and glorious undertaking, or who does not feel capable of meeting the enemy in such a desperate fight as will follow, let him step out, and he may go hence to the arms of his sweetheart, and read of the braves who swept through the city of Richmond.

" We want no man who cannot feel sure of success in such a holy cause.

" We will have a desperate fight; but stand up to it when it does come, and all will be well.

" Ask the blessing of the Almighty, and do not fear the enemy.

" U. DAHLGREN,

" *Colonel Commanding.*"

It might be supposed that the Richmond authorities would have attempted some substantial retaliation, in view of these murderous and incendiary disclosures, and would have treated those of Dahlgren's raiders who had been captured as the felons they really were. But President Davis was weak and melodramatic on the subject of retaliation; a distinct victim had never yet been exacted for innumerable murders and massacres committed by the enemy; a single act of substantial retaliation had never been done by the Confederate Administration; and now the utterly absurd and puerile notice in Richmond of the Dahlgren raid was to bury the body of its leader in a concealed grave, and to put several tons of powder under the Libby Prison to intimidate its inmates. Such stupid melodrama is almost incredible in the head of a great government, and merely gave occasion to the enemy to exclaim about " rebel barbarities," and to surround with romance a deed of villainy from which the public, without such appeals to their interest and sympathy, would have turned with aversion. Indeed so far did the misrepresentation and hypocrisy of the North go on this subject, that the authenticity of the papers found on Dahlgren was denied, and with that singular disposition of Northern newspapers to interpret as heroism, and entitle as fame, the worst villainies of the war, and its most ruthless and comprehensive works of destruction, the name of Ulric Dahlgren was written as " the young hero of the North," who had been " assassinated " on the path to glory.

The authenticity of " the Dahlgren Papers "—the most important only of which we have copied above—is probably no longer a question with the intelligent. But to put it beyond all dispute, we annex here detailed statement of the circumstances of the discovery of these papers, obtained from the living witness under whose eye they first came:

STATEMENT OF EDWARD W. HALBACH IN RELATION TO "THE DAHLGREN PAPERS."

"In the summer of 1863, I, Edward W. Halbach, was living at Stevensville, in King and Queen County, Virginia. I had already been exempted from military service on account of the condition of my health, and was now exempt as a schoolmaster having the requisite number of pupils. But feeling it my duty to do what I could to encounter the raids of the enemy, I determined to form a company of my pupils between the ages of thirteen and seventeen years. My commission and papers prove that the company was formed, and accepted by the President for "Local Defence." A member of this company, thirteen years of age at the time, captured the notorious "Dahlgren Papers." The name of this boy is William Littlepage.

"Littlepage and myself were at Stevensville when the rangers passed that place on their way to the appointed place of ambush. Being determined to participate in the affair, we set off on foot, having no horses to ride, and reached the rendezvous a little after dark. The Yankees came up in a few hours, and were fired on. Immediately after this fire, and while it was still doubtful whether the enemy would summon up courage enough to advance again, in a word, before any one else ventured to do so, Littlepage ran out into the road, and, finding a "dead Yankee" there, proceeded to search his pockets to see, as he said, if he might not be fortunate enough to find a watch. The little fellow wanted to own a watch, and, as the Yankees had robbed me, his teacher, of a gold watch a short time before, I suppose he concluded that there would be no harm in his taking a watch from a "dead Yankee;" but his teacher always discouraged any feeeling of this kind in his pupils. Littlepage failed to secure the prize by not looking in the overcoat pockets, and the watch (for there was really one) was found afterwards by Lieut. Hart. But in searching the pockets of the inner garments, Littlepage *did find* a segar-case, a memorandum-box, etc.

"When the Yankees had been driven back and thrown into a panic by the suddenness of our fire and the darkness of the night, a Confederate lieutenant, whom, the enemy had captured at Frederick Hall, embraced the opportunity presented to make his escape, and actually succeeded in getting over to our side.

"We could, by this time, hear the enemy galloping rapidly over the field, and arrangements were soon made to prevent their possible escape. Our force determined to go down the road towards King and Queen Court-House, and barricade it.

"But, as before mentioned, myself and the only member of my company had with me, were on foot, and unable to keep up with the horsemen. It was therefore decided that the prisoners whom we had captured should be left in my charge. In the confusion, however, all the prisoners had been carried off by others, save the one claiming to be a Confederate officer, which he afterwards proved to be—and a gallant one at that. But, under the circumstances, I felt compelled to treat him as an enemy, until time should prove him a friend.

"Wishing to find a place of safety, and feeling that it would be hazardous for so small a party to take any of the public roads (for we knew not how many more Yankees there were, nor in what direction they might come), I decided to go into the woods a short distance, and there spend the night. My party consisted of myself, Littlepage, the "lieutenant," and several other gentlemen of King and Queen County. We walked into the woods about a quarter of a mile, and sat down.

"Up to this time, we had not even an intimation of the name and rank of the officer commanding the enemy. In fact, we felt no curiosity to know. All we cared for was to punish as severely as possible the raiders with whom we were contending. We knew that *one* man was killed, but knew not who he was. We were just getting our places for the night, and wrapping up with blankets, garments, etc., such as we had, for the ground was freezing, and we dared not make a fire, when Littlepage pulled out a segar-case, and said: 'Mr. Halbach, will you have a segar?' 'No,' said I; 'but where did you get segars these hard times?' He replied that he had got them out of the pocket of the Yankee who had been killed, and that he had also taken from the same man a memorandum-book and some papers. 'Well,' said I, 'William, you must give me the papers, and you may keep the segar-case.'

"Littlepage then remarked that the dead Yankee had a wooden leg. Here the Lieutenant, greatly agitated, exclaimed: 'How do you know he has a wooden leg?'

"'I know he has,' replied Littlepage, 'because I caught hold of it, and tried to pull it off.'

"'There!' replied the Lieutenant, 'you have killed Col. Dahlgren, who was in command of the enemy. His men were devoted to him, and I would advise you all to take care of yourselves now, for if the Yankees catch you with anything belonging to him, they will certainly hang us all to the nearest tree.'

"Of course it was impossible for us to learn the contents of the papers, without making a light to read them by, or waiting till the next morning. We did the latter; and, as soon as day broke, the papers were read, and found to contain *every line and every word* as afterwards copied into the Richmond newspapers. Dahlgren's name was signed to one or more of the papers, and also written on the inside of the front cover of his memorandum-book. Here the date of purchase, I suppose, was added. The book had been written with a degree of haste clearly indicated by the frequent interlineations and corrections, but the orders referred to had also been re-written on a separate sheet of paper; and, as thus copied, were published to the world. Some of the papers were found loose in Dahlgren's pockets, others were between the leaves of the memorandum-book.

"The papers thus brought to light were preserved by myself in the continual presence of witnesses of unquestionable veracity, until about two o'clock in the afternoon of the day after their capture; at which time myself and party met Lieut. Pollard, who, up to this time, knew nothing in the world of the existence of the Dahlgren Papers. At his request, I let him read the papers; after doing which he requested me to let him carry them to Richmond. At first, I refused, for I thought that I knew what to do with them quite as well as any one else. But I was finally induced, by my friends, against my will, to surrender the papers to Lieut. Pollard, mainly in consideration of the fact that they would reach Richmond much sooner through him than through a semi-weekly mail. The papers which were thus handed over to the Confederate Government—I state it again—*were correctly copied by the Richmond newspapers*.

A thousand and one falsehoods have been told about this affair—by our own men as well as by the Yankees. Some of our own men were actuated by motives of selfishness and ambition to claim each one for himself the whole credit of the affair; when, in fact, the credit belongs to no particular individual, but, collectively, to the whole of our party. We were a strange medley of regulars, raw troops, old farmers, preachers, schoolboys, etc. But I believe that all present did their duty, only to find that all the credit was afterwards claimed, with a considerable degree of success among the ignorant, by those who were not present.

"The credit of the command of our party belongs alone to Capt. Fox, than whom there was no more chivalric spirit in either army. In making this statement, I am actuated only by a desire to do justice to the memory of one who was too unassuming to sound his own trumpet. I am also told, by soldiers, that Lieut. Pollard deserves a considerable degree of credit, for the part he played in following and harassing the enemy up to the time they took the right fork of the road near Butler's Tavern.

"You are, of course, aware of the fact that the enemy has always denied the authenticity of the Dahlgren Papers, and declared them to be *forgeries*. To prove the utter absurdity and falsehood of such a charge, I submit the following :

"1. The papers were taken by Littlepage from the person of a man whose name he had never heard. It was a dark night, and the captor, with the aid of the noon-day sun, could not write at all. I afterwards taught him to write a little in my school.

"The question occurs : Can a boy who cannot write at all, write such papers, and sign to them an unknown name? If they had been forged by any one else, would they have been placed in the hands of a child? Could any one else have forged an unknown and unheard of name?

"2. The papers were handed to me immediately after their capture, in the presence of gentlemen of undoubted integrity and veracity, before whom I can prove that the papers not only were not, but could not have been, altered or interpolated by myself. These gentlemen were with me every moment of the time between my receiving the papers and my delivering them to Lieut. Pollard.

"3. If Lieut. Pollard had made any alterations in the papers, these would have been detected by every one who read the papers before they were given to him, and afterwards read them in the newpapers. But all agree that they were correctly copied. In short, human testimony cannot establish any fact more fully than the fact that Col. Ulric Dahlgren was the author of the "Dahlgren Papers."

"With regard to the part taken by myself in this affair, I lay no claim to any credit. I do not write this version of the affair to gain notoriety. I have made it a rule not to mention my own name, except in cases where I found that false impressions were being made upon the public mind. You know very well that my being Littlepage's captain entitled me to claim the capture of the papers for *myself*. But this I have never done. And, even when called upon by Gen. Fitz. Lee to give my affidavit to the authenticity of the papers, I wrote him word that Littlepage was the captor of them. In his letter to Lieut. Pollard, which was forwarded to me, he asked : 'Who is Capt. Halbach?' I replied, for myself, that I was nothing more than the humble captain of a company of school-boys, and that if I deserved any credit, it was only so much as he might choose to give me for preserving the papers, when advised to destroy them, to avoid being captured with them in my possession, which, I was told, would result in the hanging of our little party.

"I have never given the information herein contained before, because I had hoped that it would be given to the public by others, and I give it now, because I regard it as a duty to do so. My own course, after the killing of Dahlgren, was as follows : I joined those who agreed to bury him decently in a coffin, and in compliance with a promise made to a scout by the name of Hogan, I prepared a neat little head-board with my own hands, to mark his grave. This was not put up, because the messenger from Mr. Davis for the body of Dahlgren arrived while we were taking it out of the ground where it had been hastily buried."

CHAPTER XXXI.

OPENING OF THE GREAT SPRING CAMPAIGN OF 1864.—EXPLANATION OF RENEWED CONFIDENCE IN RICHMOND.—PROSPECT FOR THE CONFEDERATES IN THE PRESIDENTIAL CONTEST OF 1864.— A NEW THEORY OF PEACE.—VALUE OF ENDURANCE.—THE MISSION OF MESSRS. HOLCOMBE, CLAY AND THOMPSON.—THEY LEAVE WILMINGTON WHEN THE CAMPAIGN ON THE RAPIDAN OPENS.—U. S. GRANT APPOINTED LIEUTENANT-GENERAL OF THE FEDERAL ARMIES.—CHARACTER OF GRANT.—COMPARED WITH BUELL.—GEN. GRANT'S LOW AND GROSS CONCEPTION OF WAR.—THE FEDERAL GOVERNMENT PREPARES AN ARMY ORGANIZATION OF ONE MILLION OF MEN.—DISTRIBUTION OF THE FEDERAL FORCES IN VIRGINIA.—STRENGTH OF THE ARMY OF THE POTOMAC.—POSITION AND NUMBERS OF GEN. LEE.—HIS GREAT ANXIETY.— APPEAL OF CONFEDERATE WOMEN.—THE BATTLES OF THE WILDERNESS.—GRANT CROSSES THE RAPIDAN.—LEE SPRINGS UPON HIS FLANK.—ATTACK OF EWELL AND HILL.—THE CONFEDERATE LINE BROKEN.—GORDON'S SPLENDID CHARGE.—GALLANT CONDUCT OF PEGRAM'S AND HAYS' DIVISIONS.—NIGHT ATTACK OF THE ENEMY.—THE SECOND DAY'S BATTLE.— HILL'S CORPS BROKEN.—LONGSTREET COMES UP AND TURNS THE FORTUNES OF THE DAY.— HE IS SHOT DOWN BY HIS OWN MEN.—GEN. LEE OFFERS TO LEAD A CHARGE.—TOUCHING REMONSTRANCES OF THE MEN.—THE CONFEDERATE ATTACK WITHDRAWN.—RESULTS OF THE DAY.—GORDON'S NIGHT ATTACK.—GRANT'S WHOLE ARMY ON THE VERGE OF ROUT.— HIS IMMENSE LOSSES.—MOVEMENTS OF THE TWO ARMIES TO SPOTTSYLVANIA COURT-HOUSE —MASTERLY PERFORMANCE OF LEE.—A MELANCHOLY EPISODE TO THE CAMPAIGN.— SHERIDAN'S EXPEDITION.—DEATH OF GEN. STUART.—BATTLES OF SPOTTSYLVANIA COURT-HOUSE.—COMBAT OF ANDERSON'S CORPS.—THE FIGHTING ON THE 10TH MAY.—THE BATTLE ON THE 12TH.—A SALIENT OF THE CONFEDERATE LINE TAKEN.—GREAT SLAUGHTER OF THE ENEMY.—GRANT CONFESSES A FAILURE, AND WAITS SIX DAYS FOR REINFORCEMENTS.—OPERATIONS ON THE SOUTH SIDE OF RICHMOND.—GRANT'S INSTRUCTIONS TO BUTLER.—SIGEL'S COLUMN IN WESTERN VIRGINIA, ANOTHER PART OF THE COMBINATION.— BUTLER'S BOASTFUL DESPATCH.—HE DARES "THE WHOLE OF LEE'S ARMY."—HE IS DEFEATED BY BEAUREGARD, AND HIS ARMY "BOTTLED UP."—OPERATIONS IN THE KANAWHA AND SHENANDOAH VALLEYS.—SIGNAL DEFEAT OF SIGEL.—GRANT'S COMBINATION BROKEN DOWN.—HE MOVES TO THE NORTH ANNA RIVER.—IS FOILED AGAIN BY LEE.—HE CROSSES THE PAMUNKEY RIVER.—"THE PENINSULA" MADE THE BATTLE-GROUND AGAIN.—THE SUM OF GLORY ACHIEVED BY LEE'S ARMY.—STATEMENT AS TO LEE'S REINFORCEMENTS.— THE FEDERAL HOST HELD AT BAY BY AN ARMY OF FIFTY THOUSAND MEN.—GASEOUS NONSENSE IN NEW YORK ABOUT GRANT'S GENERALSHIP.—HIS OPERATIONS IN MAY ABSURD AND CONTEMPTIBLE FAILURES.

IT is remarkable that at the opening of the great spring campaign of 1864, there should have simultaneously prevailed at Washington the opinion that the operations of the year would certainly restore the Union, and at Richmond the opinion that the coming campaign was more likely to accomplish the independence of the Southern Confederacy than any preceding one of the war. These opinions were probably equally sincere and intelligent. Some special explanation must be found for a conflict of judgment so sharp and decided. The North trusted to its acumulation of men and material to make the fourth year of the war the triumphant one for its cause. The South, to a certain extent, had been encouraged by the series of successes we have remarked in the first months of this year ; but this animation is not sufficient to account for the large measure of expectation and confidence with which she entered upon the dominant campaign of 1864. There was a special occasion of hope and reassurance.

Despite the little benefit, beyond verbal assistance, which the Confederate cause had derived from the Democratic party in the North, and despite the losses of that party in the elections of 1863, it was observed, in the spring of 1864, that it was beginning to raise a peace platform for the next Presidential election. That critical election was the point of a new prospect for the South. It was evident that there was a serious impatience in the North at the prolongation of the war ; and it was probable that if the South could maintain the *status quo* through another campaign, and put before the North the prospect of another and indefinite term of hostilities, the present rulers at Washington would be discredited, the Democratic party get into power, and the Northern public be persuaded to accept as the conclusion of the war some favourable treaty, league, or other terms short of an actual restoration of the Union. It was said, with reason, in Richmond, that such was Northern impatience that the question of the war had simply become one of *endurance* on the part of the South ; that even without positive victories in the field, and merely by securing *negative results* in the ensuing campaign, the Democratic party would be able to overthrow the Administration at Washington, and to open negotiations with Richmond as between government and government.

How seriously this argument was entertained in Richmond, may be understood from the fact that, simultaneously with the opening of the campaign in Virginia, President Davis prepared a mission to open communication with the Democratic party in the North, and to conduct in pace with the military campaign whatever political negotiation might be practicable in the North. The commissioners entrusted with this intrigue were Messrs. Thompson, of Mississippi, Holcombe, of Virginia, and Clay, of Alabama ; and they were to proceed to a convenient place on the Northern frontier, and use whatever political opportunities the military events of the war might develop. They ran the blockade at Wilmington on the night of the day that the first gun on the Rapidan opened the momentous campaign of 1864.

The bloody drama of the war was to recommence on the banks of this stream, where Gen. Lee's army had been stationed during the winter. On the Federal side a new and important actor was to appear on the scene. Gen. Ulysses S. Grant, who had had a long run of success in the West, had been appointed lieutenant-general and commander-in-chief of all the Federal forces, and was now to answer the expectation of his admirers by a campaign in Virginia and the repetition of the enterprise upon the Confederate capital. The Richmond journals complimented him as a " man of far more energy and ability than any that had yet commanded the Army of the Potomac," but " his performances would bear no comparison whatever to those of Gen. Lee."

The new Federal commander in Virginia was one of the most remarkable accidents of the war. That a man without any marked ability, certainly without genius, without fortune, without influence, should attain the position of leader of all the Federal armies, and stand the most conspicuous person on that side of the war, is a phenomenon which would be inexplicable among any other people than the sensational and coarse mobs of admiration in the North. Gen. Grant's name was coupled with success ; and this circumstance alone, without regard to merit of personal agency, without reference to any display of mental quality in the event, was sufficient to fix him in the admiration of the Northern public. It mattered not that Grant had illustrated no genius ; it mattered not that he had smothered Fort Donelson by numbers ; it mattered not that he had succeeded at Vicksburg through the glaring incompetency of a Confederate commander, and by the weight of eighty thousand men against twenty odd thousand ; the North was prepared to worship him, without distinguishing between accident and achievement, and to entitle him the hero of the war.

It is a curious commentary on the justice of popular judgment, that while Grant was thus elevated to power and fame, the man who rescued him at Perryville and again at Shiloh, and whose heroism and genius had saved there the consequences of his stupidity, should be languishing in obscurity. This man was Gen. Buell. It was he who had contributed most to Grant's success, and whose masterly manœuvres had done more to reclaim the Mississippi Valley for the Federals than any other commander, and who now had been sacrificed to the spirit of political intrigue. At a time when popular passion clamoured for the desolation of the South, Gen. Buell persisted, with a firmness rarer and more admirable even than he exhibited in the crisis of battle, in conducting the war on the principles of humanity ; and by this noble moderation he incurred the displeasure of the faction that controlled the Government at Washington. The Radicals waged a war of extermination ; but he proposed, with the sagacity of a statesman, to conciliate the good will of the South, while he overcame its resistance by an exertion of physical force. His system was too refined for the comprehension, and too liberal for the vindictive temper of the dominant party, and he was forced to relinquish the command of the superb army he had organized, and to resign a commission which he might have illustrated by splendid achievements.

It is some consolation to reflect that the verdict of history is neither the sensation of a mob nor the fiat of a political faction. Gen. Grant will have his proper place surely and exactly assigned in the ultimate records of merit in the war. No one will deny this man credit for many good qualities of heart and great propriety of behaviour. He had that coarse, heavy obstinacy, which is as often observed in the Western backwoodsman as in a higher range of character. But he contained no spark of military genius; his idea of war was to the last degree rude—no strategy, the mere application of the *vis inertiæ ;* he had none of that quick perception on the field of action which decides it by sudden strokes; he had no conception of battle beyond the momentum of numbers. Such was the man who marshalled all the material resources of the North to conquer the little army and overcome the consummate skill of Gen. Lee. He, who was declared the military genius of the North, had such a low idea of the contest, such little appreciation of the higher aims and intellectual exercises of war that he proposed to decide it by a mere competition in the sacrifice of human life. His plan of operations, as he himself described it, was " to hammer continuously against the armed force of the enemy and his resources, until by mere attrition, if in no other way, there should be nothing left to him but an equal submission with the loyal section of our common country to the Constitution and laws of the land."

At Washington, the arrangements for the spring campaign of 1864 were made, on the part of the government, to put forth its strength. In all the bureaus of the War Department supplies were provided on a scale of great magnitude, to meet any exigency that could be foreseen. The estimates were based upon an army organization of one million of men. The States were called upon to strengthen the armies by volunteers; new drafts were ordered and put in execution throughout all the Northern States; vast supplies of arms, ammunition, clothing, subsistence, medical stores and forage were provided and distributed in depots to meet the wants of the troops wherever they might operate; horses, mules, wagons, railroad iron, locomotives and cars, bridge timber, telegraph cable and wire, and every material for transportation and communication of great armies under all conditions were supplied. Congress, with unstinting hand, voted large appropriations for recruiting, paying and supplying the troops.

Gen. Grant assumed command as Lieutenant-General of the armies of the United States on the 17th day of March, 1864. The distribution of the Federal armies operating in Virginia was as follows : The Army of the Potomac, commanded by Major-General Meade, had its headquarters on the north side of the Rapidan. The Ninth Corps, under Major-General Burnside, was, at the opening of the campaign, a distinct organization, but on the 24th day of May, 1864, it was incorporated into the Army of the Potomac. The Army of the James was commanded by Major-Gen. Butler, whose headquarters were at Fortress Monroe. The headquarters of the Army of the Shenandoah, commanded by Major-Gen. Sigel, were at Winchester.

The available strength of the enemy's force on the line of the Rapidan, including the Ninth Corps, was 141,166 men. Besides there were in what was known as the Department of Washington and the Middle Department 47,751 men, available as reinforcements to the Army of the Potomac; making therefore a total of about 180,000 men, as the force which Gen. Lee had to meet with *less than forty thousand muskets !*

The Confederate army on the Rapidan, at the beginning of the campaign, consisted of two divisions of Longstreet's corps, Ewell's corps, A. P. Hill's corps, three divisions of cavalry, and the artillery. Ewell's corps did not exceed fourteen thousand muskets at the beginning of the campaign. On the 8th of May, the effective strength of Hill's corps was less than thirteen thousand muskets, and it could not have exceeded eighteen thousand in the beginning of the month. Longstreet's corps was the weakest of the three when all the divisions were present, and the two with him had just returned from an arduous and exhausting winter campaign in East Tennessee. His effective strength could not have exceeded eight thousand muskets. Gen. Lee's whole effective infantry, therefore, did not exceed forty thousand muskets, if it reached that number. The cavalry divisions were weak, neither of them exceeding the strength of a good brigade. The artillery was in proportion to the other arms, and was far exceeded by Grant's, not only in the number of men and guns, but in weight of metal, and especially in the quality of the ammunition. Gen. Lee's whole effective strength at the opening of the campaign was not over fifty thousand men of all arms. There were no means of recruiting the ranks of his army, and no reinforcements were received until the 23d of May.

The Confederate public was but little aware of this terrible disparity of force; but Gen. Lee was greatly affected by it as he contemplated the thin line which stood between the insolent host of the enemy and the Capital of the Confederacy. In April he issued a general order directing to be observed " a day of fasting, humiliation, and prayer." All military duties, unless absolutely necessary, were to be suspended, and the chaplains were desired to hold divine service in their regiments and brigades. Officers and men were " requested " to attend. This passed, the final preparations were made for the deadly struggle that, it was evident, would soon commence. " For your stricken country's sake, and ours," said the

" wives, daughters, sisters, and friends " of the Confederate soldiers in a published address to them, " be true to yourselves and our glorious cause. Never turn your back on the flag, nor desert the ranks of honour, or the post of danger. You are constantly present to our minds. The women of the South bestow all their respect and affection on the heroes who defend them."

THE BATTLES OF THE WILDERNESS.

Gen. Lee was not idle in adopting all precautionary measures to meet the enemy. He strongly intrenched his lines, dug rifle-pits at the fords of the Rapidan, and kept a good force on the Gordonsville road so as to hold the communication open to Richmond by that route, while by the way of Fredericksburg he destroyed the bridges and rails in order to prevent, or make more difficult, the enemy's advance in that direction.

The works occupied by Lee's army on the Rapidan extended on the right three miles below Raccoon ford. Ewell's corps and Hill's lay behind those defences, and stretched out on each side of Orange Court-House, along a line of twenty miles. Longstreet occupied the country around Gordonsville, thirteen miles southwest of the position on the Rapidan.

Grant, having declined to assail Lee's front, determined to turn it by a movement on the Confederate right. On Tuesday night, May 3d, the Federal army broke up its encampment in the county of Culpepper, and at dawn of next morning crossed the Rapidan at the old fords—Ely's and Germania—and in much the same line that Meade attempted in the previous November, and where Lee had caused Hooker to retreat a year before. The Second corps, commanded by Gen. Hancock, in front, crossed at Ely's ford, the Fifth corps, under Warren, took the Germania ford, while the Sixth, Sedgwick's, followed immediately upon it.

As soon as Gen. Lee ascertained that Grant had certainly cut loose from his base at Culpepper Court House, and was moving rapidly past his right, he put his own army in motion, sending Ewell's corps down the turnpike and A. P. Hill's down the plank road, and ordering Longstreet, who had arrived at Gordonsville, to move his corps down on the right of Ewell's line of march, so as to strike the head of the enemy's column.

The advance of Ewell's corps—Edward Johnson's division—arrived within three miles of Wilderness Run in the evening, and encamped. Rodes lay in his rear ; and Early was next at Locust Grove, all ready to strike at Grant's advance the next morning. At about six o'clock in the morning of the 6th May the enemy was discovered by the skirmishers thrown out, and Johnson immediately pressed forward to gain a hill where he proceeded to form his troops in line of battle.

The enemy advanced in such order as was practicable in a tangled forest. The Fifth corps, accompanied by two pieces of artillery, that came thundering along the turnpike, assailed the Confederate line at the intersection of the road. Receiving, as it advanced, a terrible fusilade without any sign of wavering, the rear rank pressing forward those of the front, the attacking masses delivered from a forest of rifles a fast and furious fire upon Johnson's line. Closing in upon it with great spirit in front, and threatening to envelop it on its right, they succeeded, after a brief struggle, in forcing back part of the brigade of Gen. J. M. Jones that had been formed across the turnpike. Jones strove, in desperation, to rally his broken troops, but with no avail; and, as the brave general was imploring his men to stop their flight, a ball struck him, and he fell from his saddle a bleeding corpse.

The decisive moment of the battle was now at hand. Stewart moved from his position in the line of battle to close the gap left in it by the brigade of Jones. As the Federal masses poured through, his men rushed forward with a cheer; and, driving them back by the impetus of their charge, captured their guns. At the same time Ewell ordered Daniels' and Gordon's brigades of Rodes' division to form on the right and charge. Gordon, holding command of the movement, crushed through the enemy's first lines and captured as he went forward a whole regiment, men, officers, and colors. Driving on furiously he struck back the Federal front in confusion upon its supports; and scattering both like leaves before a storm, forced them off the field in utter rout for a mile and a half.

Soon after the onslaught upon the Confederate front, the Sixth corps of the Federal army advanced upon its left flank. The attack here was repulsed by Pegram's and Hay's division. The furious onslaught of Hay's men did not expend itself until they had forced the enemy to retreat in confusion for nearly a mile. In advance of all others on that face of the attack, these splendid troops, having left nearly one-third of their number on the field, fell back with Pegram's gallant men to the general line of battle.

Skirmishing continued outside the lines. Immediately before the close of the evening, the skirmishers of Pegram, on Johnson's left, came running in, and soon afterwards his sharpshooters sprang back from their rifle-pits in his immediate front. A column, three lines deep, moved upon him from the depths of the forest, and, firing heavily as they came on, pressed towards his works furiously. His stanch Virginians, however, met the attack resolutely, and, covered partially by their works, hurled volley after volley in withering blasts, breast high, into its serried ranks.

But the work of carnage was not yet sufficient for Grant. In five lines a column renewed the attack after nightfall; but did so without other result than to increase terribly the hundreds of men that, dead or dying outside the Confederate works, lay weltering in their gore. Pegram fell in this last attack severely wounded. The repulse which he guided as he fell, closed the work of war for the day on the left, and witnessed the Confederates still in possession of their improved position and advanced lines.

The results of the day were that the enemy had been beaten back as often as he advanced, with heavy loss, including two thousand prisoners and four guns. Longstreet not having arrived, owing to the greater distance he had to march, Gen. Lee refrained from pressing his advantage, and slept upon the battle-field. His own loss was comparatively slight, his troops understanding how to take advantage of the rough country and entangled woods in which they fought. Longstreet reached a point ten miles from the battle-field by the middle of the afternoon, but, owing to the peculiar condition of the atmosphere, and the density of the forest, he was unable to hear the report of Hill's and Ewell's guns, and was ignorant that the two armies had been engaged until midnight, when he received an order from Gen. Lee to cross over to the plank road to the aid of Hill.

It was two o'clock in the morning of the 6th when Longstreet aroused his sleeping men from their bivouac, and marched on to the field of battle. Hill's troops were aware of his approach, and that he was to take their place on the line, and, having been marching and fighting all the previous day, and sleeping but little that night, they got ready to retire as the head of Longstreet's corps reached the ground. Unfortunately, Grant renewed the attack just at this time, threw Heth's and Wilcox's divisions of Hill's corps into confusion, and pushed them back upon Longstreet's column, which had not yet deployed into line.

The disordered ranks surged already within one hundred and fifty yards of the position of Gen. Lee. But at this moment three regiments of Kershaw's division came into line, and this Spartan band held the enemy in check until the remainder of the division and finally Longstreet's entire corps could be brought up. Then ensued a furious and bloody combat all along Longstreet's front. His veteran corps, which had made the circuit of half the Confederacy within the last twelve months, never fought better or more successfully. Grant had taken advantage of the disorder among Hill's troops, and hurled heavy masses upon the point, hoping to turn the Confederate right wing, and throw himself between Lee and Richmond. He would have succeeded but for Longstreet's timely arrival.

At 11 o'clock Longstreet was ordered, with some select brigades, to pass to the right and attack the enemy in flank. The order was promptly executed. Falling suddenly upon Grant's left, he drove the enemy in confusion, bending his line back upon itself, and gaining the plank road a mile in advance of the scene of the recent conflict.

The fortunes of the day were evidently turned. Gen. Longstreet now moved forward with his staff to take his place at the head of the advance; and was received as he passed along the moving mass with shouts of applause. As he galloped forward, Gen. Jenkins spurred to his side to grasp his hand, with the pleasure of an old friend,—for Longstreet had but newly arrived from several months' campaign in Eastern Tennessee. But, hardly had the mutual congratulations passed each other's lips, when a deadly volley from Mahone's brigade, concealed in bushes along the road —mistaking Longstreet, Jenkins, and the rest, for a party of the flying foe —poured into them, at short range. Jenkins fell instantly from his horse a lifeless corpse, while Longstreet received a ball that entered his throat and passed out through his right shoulder. Bleeding profusely, he was helped from his horse so prostrated that fears were entertained of his immediate death. Placed on a litter, the wounded General was removed from the field; but feeble though he was from loss of blood, he did not fail to lift his hat from time to time as he passed down the column, in acknowledgment of its cheers of applause and sympathy.

The fall of Longstreet was an untimely event, and the delay it occasioned gave opportunity to the enemy to reform his line. The field was well contested on both sides; but at one time the aspect of affairs was so alarming that Gen. Lee had, as Fields' division came under fire, placed himself at the head of Gregg's brigade of Texans. With that devotion which constituted the great charm of his character, he ordered them to follow him in a charge upon a line of the enemy, sweeping down upon his front. The response was not shouts. A grim and ragged soldier of the line raised his voice in determined remonstrance. He was immediately followed by the rank and file of the whole brigade in positive refusal to advance until their beloved commander had gone to his proper position of safety. Yielding to this touching solicitude, Gen. Lee withdrew, while the brave Texans fulfilled the promise by which they had urged his withdrawal, and, breasting a storm of bullets, drove the enemy on their front back to his entrenchments. What was the exposure of the devoted commander during the day, may be judged from the circumstances of the explosion of a shell under his own horse, the killing of the horse of his Adjutant-Gen., Lieut.-Col. Taylor, and the wounding of another officer attached to his person, Lieut.-Col. Marshall,—events which caused great and most affectionate anxiety in the army, and determined the troops to watch more carefully over a life in which they considered were bound up the fortunes of their country.

So far the enemy had been driven back on the Confederate right, and was firmly held in check; while on the left, Ewell, battling severely, and defeating an attempt of the enemy to outflank him, held his own, and joined his line of battle with that which had been restored on the right wing. During the afternoon Brig.-Gen. Wofford, of Anderson's corps, was permitted, at his own request, to move upon the rear of the Federal left wing. He got possession of their camps, destroyed and brought off a good deal of material, and created great consternation among the teamsters and quartermasters. About twilight Brig.-Gen. Gordon, of Ewell's corps, attacked the enemy's left, captured Gen. Seymour and a large portion of his brigade, and excited a panic which put Grant's whole army on the verge of irretrievable rout. Brigade after brigade fled from the Federal works, and, attempting, one after another, to wheel around into line in order to check the advance, was borne back under the rapidity of Gordon's movement. The woods in front were alive with masses of men, struggling to escape with life. Gordon swept all before him for a distance of two miles. But the forest through which he advanced was so dense with undergrowth, that by the nightfall he had become separated from his supports. He paused before he had completed a movement that came near completely routing the entire Federal right. The enterprise, notwithstanding its incompleteness, was crowned with brilliant success. The Confederate loss in that service numbered, in killed and wounded, but twenty-seven, while on the enemy's side Gens. Shaler and Seymour, with the greater part of their commands, were taken prisoners, and the entire Sixth corps of the Army of the Potomac had been broken up in panic.

In these two days of terrible battle in the Wilderness the Confederate wounded, by the official reports of the surgeons, were estimated at six thousand, and their killed at less than one thousand. The wounds were comparatively slight, owing to the protection afforded by the trees and the absence of artillery, which could not be used in consequence of the dense and almost unbroken forest. The loss of the enemy was out of all proportion to what it had inflicted: 269 officers and 3,019 men killed; 1,017 officers and 18,261 men wounded, and 177 officers and 6,667 men missing—making an aggregate of 27,310.

On the 7th May, both armies moved their position—Grant's to take an interiour road towards Richmond by the Spottsylvania Court-house, and Lee's, back, apparently, towards Orange Court-house, but in reality to reach Spottsylvania before the enemy. The advance of Lee arrived first and took up a good position, the main army quickly following. The situation which the Northern newspapers interpreted as " the retreat of Lee " bore in every respect the evidences of his generalship and success. He had succeeded in throwing his entire army right across the path by which Grant must march if he would get " on to Richmond."—He had not only repulsed all his assaults at the Wilderness, but held him there until he could throw his own army in front of him. It was a masterly performance, and made it necessary for Grant to deliver battle there or make another effort to turn the Confederate position.

To this movement there was an episode, which is chiefly remarkable for the fall in it of Gen. J. E. B. Stuart, the brilliant commander of the Confederate cavalry in Virginia. An expedition of Federal cavalry, commanded by Gen. Sheridan, was directed to make a bold dash around Lee's flank towards Richmond. It passed around the right flank of the Confederates to the North Anna River; committed some damage at Beaver Dam; moved thence to the South Anna and Ashland Station, where the railroad was destroyed; and finally found its way to the James River, where it joined the forces of Butler. On the 10th May, a portion of Sheridan's command, under Custer and Merrill, were encountered by a body of Stuart's cavalry near Ashland, at a place called Yellow Tavern, on the road to Richmond. An engagement took place here. In a desperate charge, at the head of a column, Gen. Stuart fell, terribly wounded. He was immediately taken to Richmond, and every effort made to save his valuable life; but in vain. He died the next day.*

* From some memoirs of Gen. Stuart, collected from his staff officers, we extract some incidents indicative of the character of the man, designated as the "Prince Rupert of the Confederate Army:"

"One of the marked traits of this *preux chevalier* was his indifference to danger, which impressed every one. It would be difficult to imagine a coolness more supreme. It was not that he seemed to defy peril—he appeared unconscious of it. At the battle of Oxhill, in September, 1862, he advanced a piece of artillery down the road to Fairfax Court-house, and suddenly found himself in the presence of a buzzing hornet's nest of Federal sharp-shooters, who rose from the tall weeds a few score yards distant, and poured a deadly fire into the cannoniers. Stuart was at the gun directing the firing, and sat on his horse, full front to the fire, with so perfect an air of unconsciousness that it was hard to believe that he realized his danger. When a staff officer said, 'This fire is rather peculiar, General,' Stuart seemed to wake up, as it were, to whistling bullets, and said, indifferently, 'It is getting rather warm.' He met his death in this way, and the only matter for astonishment is that he was not killed long before. He was constantly on the most advanced line of skirmishers, cheering them on, the most conspicuous mark to the enemy. He used to laugh when he was warned against such exposure of himself, and said that he was not afraid of any ball 'aimed at him;' but I know that he never expected to get through the war. He deeply deplored its existence, and said, one day, 'I would lay down my right hand and have it cut off at the wrist to end it.' But he was conscientious in his espousal of the Southern cause, and was ready to die for it.

"The habitual temper of his mind toward his adversaries was cool and soldierly. Federal prisoners were treated by him with uniform courtesy, and often left his headquarters declaring that they would never forget the kindness they had experienced. I remember an appeal once made to him by a prisoner, which amused everybody. One of his escort spoke roughly to the prisoner, when the latter, seeing the General, exclaimed: 'Gen. Stuart, I did not come here to be blackguarded,' at which Stuart laughed good-humouredly, and reprimanded the person who had addressed the prisoner.

"At Verdiersville, in August, 1862, Stuart stopped at a deserted house on the roadside, and lay down with his staff and escort, without videttes, pickets, or other precaution. The consequence was that he was aroused by the tramp of Federal cavalry close on him, and had just time to throw himself, hatless, on his unbridled horse, leap the fence and fly. He left his hat, coat, and gloves, which his adversaries carried off in triumph; but at Catlett's soon after retorted by capturing General Pope's coat and hat, which was a fair offset.

"The gay, humorous, and high spirits of the man, did not wholly desert him even on the most serious occasions. Nothing was more common than to hear him humming a song during an engage-

BATTLES OF SPOTTSYLVANIA COURT-HOUSE.

As Lee's advance—consisting of Longstreet's corps under Anderson—reached Spottsylvania Court-house, on the 9th May, the men had been

ment, and I was reading the other day somewhere a soldier's description of a fight in Culpepper, and what an electric effect was produced upon the infantry by the appearance of Stuart riding in front of them, singing gaily and cheering them on. At Chancellorsville, when Jackson fell, he was called to command the corps, and led the assault in person on the next morning. An eye witness says that he could not get rid of the idea that Henry of Navarre had come back, except that Stuart's 'plume' was black! Everywhere, like Navarre, he was in front, and the men 'followed the feather.' At the risk, however, of spoiling this romantic picture, and passing from the sublime to what some persons may call the ridiculous, an additional fact may be stated, namely: That Gen. Stuart, attacking with Jackson's veteran corps, and carrying line after line of works, moved at the head of his men, singing 'Old Joe Hooker, will you come out of the wilderness.'

"There was nothing notable in Stuart's habits except his abstinence from all stimulants, coffee excepted. At his broad, paper-covered desk, in the long winter evenings, he busied himself not with 'official' work only. A favourite amusement with him was the composition of parodies in verse, some of them exceedingly good. He was not a great reader. He was fonder of society, of telling stories, jesting, and whiling away time with his staff. No boy could be merrier than Stuart, at such moments, and he dearly loved a practical joke.

"No analysis of military movements or discussion of military endowments is here intended; but it is almost impossible to separate Stuart, the man, from Stuart, the soldier. He was ready for a 'fight or a frolic,' and gifted by nature with an enormous animal physique, which enabled him to defy fatigue, whether produced by marching night and day, or dancing until dawn. Ambitious, fond of glory, and sensitive to blame or praise, he was yet endowed with a bold and independent spirit which enabled him to defy all enemies. He was warm-hearted, and never did man love friends more dearly. Stuart always seemed to be a perfect embodiment of the traits generally attributed to the English cavaliers. There was in him a rollicking love of frolic, a gallantry towards ladies, a fondness for bright colors, brilliant spectacles, and gay adventure, which made him resemble strongly the class of men who followed the fortunes of Charles the I., and at Naseby died rather than retreat or surrender. Stuart's nerve was of stern stuff, and under all that laughter there was a soul that no peril could touch. That bright blue eye looked into the very face of death without a quiver of the lid, and dared the worst. A man more absolutely indifferent to danger, I believe, never lived; and, like some chevalier of olden days, he rode to battle with his lady's glove upon his helm, humming a song, and determined to conquer or fall."

The following account of Gen. Stuart's last moments was published in the Richmond newspapers:

"About noon, President Davis visited his bedside and spent some time with the dying chief. In reply to the question put by the President, 'General, how do you feel?' he replied, 'Easy, but willing to die, if God and my country think I have fulfilled my destiny, and done my duty.'

"During the day, occasional delirium attacked him, and, in his moments of mental wandering, his faculties were busy with the past. His campaigns on the Peninsula, his raid into Pennsylvania, his doings on the Rapidan, and his several engagements, were subjects that quickly chased themselves through his brain. Fresh orders were given as if still on the battlefield and injunctions to his couriers to 'make haste.' Then he would wander to his wife and children, one of whom, his eldest boy, had died a year previous, while fighting on the Rappahannock, and in relation to whom he had said, when receiving a telegram that the boy was dying, 'I must leave my child in the hands of God; my country needs me here; I cannot come.' Then his mind would again carry him on to the battlefield; and so it continued throughout the day. Occasionally his intellect was clear, and he

marching rapidly, and for two miles had double-quicked it, and consequently were much jaded. But they were ready for work, tired as they were. Kershaw's division led the corps, and was the first to reach the ground. Two brigades were sent against a cavalry force of the enemy holding the Court-house, and two others were placed behind a thin rail fence and some frail obstructions which had been thrown across the road

was then calm and resigned, though at times suffering the most acute agony. He would even, with his own hand, apply the ice that was intended to relieve the pain of his wound.

"As evening wore on, mortification set in rapidly. In answer to his inquiry, he was told that death was fast approaching. He then said, 'I am resigned, if it be God's will, but I would like to see my wife. But, God's will be done.' Several times he roused up, and asked if she had come. Unfortunately, she was in the country at the time, and did not arrive until too late.

"As the last moments approached, the dying man, with a mind perfectly clear and possessed, then made a disposition of his effects. To Mrs. Gen. R. E. Lee, he directed that the golden spurs be given as a dying memento of his love and esteem for her husband. To his staff officers he gave his horses ; and other mementoes he disposed of in a similar manner. To his young son he left his sword. He then turned to the Rev. Dr. Peterkin, of the Episcopal Church, of which he was a strict member, and asked him to sing the hymn commencing :

'Rock of ages cleft for me,
Let me hide myself in thee.'

"In this he joined with all the strength of voice his failing powers permitted. He then prayed with the minister and friends around him ; and, with the words, 'I am going fast now. I am resigned ; God's will be done,' yielded his fleeting spirit to Him who gave it.

"The funeral of this much lamented and brave general took place on the 13th, at five o'clock, from St. James's Church, corner of Marshall and Fifth streets.

"At the appointed hour the cortege appeared in front of the church, and the metallic coffin, containing the remains of the noble soldier, whose now silent voice had so often startled the enemy with his stirring battle-cry, was carried down the centre-aisle, and placed before the altar. Wreaths and a cross of evergreens, interwoven with delicate lilies of the valley, laurel, and other flowers of purest white, decked the coffin.

"The pall-bearers were Gen. Bragg, Maj.-Gen. McCown, Gen. Chilton, Brig.-Gen. Lawton, Commodore Forrest, Capt. Lee, of the navy, and Gen. George W. Randolph, formerly Secretary of War.

"The scene was sad and impressive. President Davis sat near the front, with a look of grief upon his careworn face ; his cabinet officers were gathered around, while on either side were the Senators and Representatives of the Confederate Congress. Scattered through the church were a number of generals and other officers of less rank, among the former Gen. Ransom, commanding the Department of Richmond. Hundreds of sad faces witnessed the scene ; but the brave Fitz Hugh Lee and other war-wearied and war-worn men, whom the dead Stuart had so often led where the red battle was fiercest, and who would have given their lives for his, were away in the fight, doubtless striking with a double courage as they thought of their fallen general.

"The short service was read by Rev. Dr. Peterkin, a funeral anthem sung, and the remains were carried out and placed in the hearse, which proceeded to Hollywood Cemetery, followed by a long train of carriages.

"No military escort accompanied the procession, but the hero was laid in his last resting-place on the hillside, while the earth trembled with the roar of artillery and the noise of the deadly strife of armies—the one bent upon desecrating and devastating his native land, and the other, proudly and defiantly standing in the path and invoking the blessing of Heaven upon their cause, to fight in better cheer for the memory of such as Stonewall Jackson and J. E. B. Stuart."

by which a force of Federal infantry was advancing. The latter fell into the errour of supposing that the force behind the fence was dismounted cavalry, and rushed forward with the utmost confidence. The Confederates reserved their fire until their foes got within a few paces, and then, taking deliberate aim, gave them a volley which covered the ground with their slain. The combat was short and sharp; some of the Federals got to the fence, and actually used the bayonet; but in less than half an hour they were driven rapidly back, leaving five hundred dead and mortally wounded, and two hundred prisoners in the hands of the victorious Confederates.

On the 10th May, the struggle was renewed at an early hour, Warren's corps being the one most hotly engaged against the Confederates, though all were fighting heavily. About half-past 5 P. M. two divisions of Hancock's Second corps crossed the Po River, and advanced against Lee's left, making a strong show of giving battle there. Lee, supposing the enemy was massing forces at that point, moved his troops during the night and next day to that quarter, but, in the morning of the 12th, it was found that Hancock was again in the centre, and vigorously assaulting Johnson's division.

This division held a salient of the Confederate line; and as the enemy, taking the forces within in flank, rushed over the angle, they were quickly in possession of the work, capturing most of Johnson's men along with their commander, and taking twenty pieces of artillery. Charge after charge was made by the Confederates to regain what ground they had lost. It was a conflict of sublime fury and terrible carnage. The dead and wounded lay piled over each other, "the latter often underneath the former." What remained of Ewell's corps held the enemy in check with a courage that nothing could subdue. Gen. Hill moved down from the right, joined Ewell, and threw his divisions into the struggle; Longstreet came on from the extreme left of the Confederate line; it was a dead-lock of slaughter, in which neither side gained ground, and the intervening spaces were piled with the slain. At the close of the day the enemy held about three hundred yards of the Confederate works; he had taken twenty-five pieces of artillery and about two thousand men in Johnson's division; he had inflicted a loss of about six or seven thousand; but his own loss was stated at eighteen thousand men, and at this cost he had purchased what the Northern newspapers called a "brilliant victory," but of which Gen. Grant had been candid enough to state: "The advantage gained did not prove decisive."

Thus, without decisive results—certainly without any appreciable advantage on the Northern side—had been fought a series of battles such as had never been compressed into so many days in the history of man, and such as had never before been exhibited by a single army, contending against an adversary more than three times its numbers. In those days Lee's army made its surpassing record of heroism. Grant was not shamed. The Moloch of the North had not yet been sated. The great military genius that was to resolve generalship into the fierce and brutal consumption of human life, who had taken the field with triple Lee's numbers, found it necessary, after the first series of conflicts to call for reinforcements, and that before his adversary had received one additional musket for his own thinned ranks. From the 13th to the 18th May, Grant consumed the time in manœuvring and awaiting the arrival of reinforcements from Washington. He attempted to compose the anxiety of the authorities there by a display of resolution. He telegraphed to President Lincoln : " I propose to fight it out on this line if it takes all summer."

OPERATIONS ON THE SOUTH SIDE OF RICHMOND.

While Grant was engaged on the Rapidan, there were other movemens in progress which were parts of his combination, and which belong to the great military drama in Virginia.

The column of Butler—what was known as the Army of the James— was the most important correspondent of his movement, intended to operate against Richmond on the south side. In advance of the movements on the Rapidan, the following letter of instructions was addressed to Gen. Butler, explaining the part of the campaign against Richmond assigned to him :

"FORT MONROE, VA., *April* 2, 1864.

" *General :* In the spring campaign, which it is desirable shall commence at as early a day as practicable, it is proposed to have co-operative action of all the armies in the field, as far as this object can be accomplished.

" It will not be possible to unite our armies into two or three large ones to act as so many units, owing to the absolute necessity of holding on to the territory already taken from the enemy. But, generally speaking, concentration can be practically effected by armies moving to the interiour of the enemy's country from the territory they have to guard. By such movements they interpose themselves between the enemy and the country to be guarded, thereby reducing the number necessary to guard important points, or at least occupy the attention of a part of the enemy's force, if no greater object is gained. Lee's army and Richmond being the greater objects towards which our attention must be directed in the next campaign, it is desirable to unite all the force we can against them. The necessity of covering Washington with the Army of the Potomac and of covering your Department with your army makes it impossible to unite these forces at the beginning of any move. I propose, therefore, what comes nearest this of anything that seems practicable. The Army of the Potomac will act from its present base, Lee's army being the objective point. You will collect all the forces from your command that can be spared from garrison duty, I should say not less than twenty thousand effective men—to operate on the south side of James River, Richmond being your objective point. To the force you already have will be added about ten thousand men from South Carolina, under Maj.-Gen. Gillmore, who will command them in person. Maj.-Gen. W. F. Smith is ordered to report to you, to command the troops sent into the field from your own Department.

" Gen. Gillmore will be ordered to report to you at Fortress Monroe, with all the troops on transports, by the 18th instant, or as soon thereafter as practicable. Should you not receive notice by that time to move, you will make such disposition of them and your other forces as you may deem best calculated to deceive the enemy as to the real move to be made.

" When you are notified to move, take City Point with as much force as possible. Fortify, or rather entrench, at once, and concentrate all your troops for the field there as rapidly as you can. From City Point directions cannot be given at this time for your further movements.

" The fact that has already been stated—that is, that Richmond is to be your objective point, and that there is to be co-operation between your force and the Army of the Potomac—must be your guide. This indicates the necessity of your holding close to the south bank of the James River as you advance. Then, should the enemy be forced into his entrenchments in Richmond, the Army of the Potomac would follow, and by means of transports the two armies would become a unit.

" All the minor details of your advance are left entirely to your direction. If, however, you think it practicable to use your cavalry south of you so as to cut the railroad about Hicks' Ford, about the time of the general advance, it would be of immense advantage.

" You will please forward for my information at the earliest practicable day, all orders, details, and instructions you may give for the execution of this order.

" U. S. GRANT, Lieutenant-General.

" *Maj.-Gen. B. F. Butler.*"

From this exposition of Grant's designs upon the Confederate capital, it appears that he calculated to fight Lee between Culpepper and Richmond, and failing to defeat him away from his base, to make a junction with Butler's army on the James River, with the prospect that the latter would be able to invest Richmond on the south side, with its left resting on the James above the city.

But there was yet another part of Grant's ambitious and sweeping plan of operations in Virginia. He might take Richmond, without capturing the Government machinery, and without overthrowing Lee's army. In that view, further operations were necessary to isolate Richmond, and destroy its railroad communications. Gen. Sigel was therefore directed to organize all his available force into two expeditions, to move from Beverly to Charleston, under command of Gens. Ord and Crook, against the East Tennessee and Virginia Railroad. Subsequently, Gen. Ord, having been relieved at his own request, Gen. Sigel was instructed at his own suggestion, to give up the expedition by Beverly, and to form two columns, one under Gen. Crook, on the Kanawha, numbering about ten thousand men, and one on the Shenandoah, numbering about seven thousand men ; the one on the Shenandoah to assemble between Cumberland and the Shenau doah, and the infantry and artillery moved to Cedar Creek with such cavalry as could be made available at the moment, to threaten the enemy in the Shenandoah Valley, and advance as far as possible; while Gen. Crook would take possession of Lewisburg with part of his force, and move down the Tennessee Railroad, doing as much damage as he could.

Gen. Butler moved his main force up the James River, in pursuance of instructions, on the 4th May, Gillmore having joined him with the Tenth Corps. On the 5th he occupied, without opposition, both City Point and Bermuda Hundred. On the 6th he was in position with his main army, and commenced entrenching. On the 7th he made a reconnoissance against the Petersburg and Richmond Railroad, destroying a bridge seven miles from the former place, from which he took the conceit that he had now got well to the rear of the Confederate capital, and held " the key to the back-door of Richmond." He telegraphed to Washington : " We have landed here, entrenched ourselves, destroyed many miles of railroad, and got a position which, with proper supplies, we can hold out against the whole of Lee's army ! " This boast was to come to a singular conclusion.

In the month of April, the services and command of Gen. Beauregard had been called into requisition from Charleston to strengthen the defences around Richmond. On the 21st April, he passed through Wilmington with a large body of troops, and assumed command of the district on the south and east of Richmond. On the 16th May he attacked Butler in his advanced position in front of Drewry's Bluff. The action was sharp and decisive. Butler was forced back into his entrenchments between the forks of the James and Appomattox Rivers ; and Beauregard, entrenching strongly in his front, covered the railroads, the city, and all that was valuable to him. Butler's army was thus effectually cut off from all further operations against Richmond, as much so, wrote Gen. Grant, " as if his army had been in a bottle strongly corked."

OPERATIONS IN THE KANAWHA AND SHENANDOAH VALLEYS.

While Butler was thus neutralized, the movement in the Kanawha and Shenandoah Valleys, under Sigel, was to end in disaster. Gen. Crook, who had the immediate command of the Kanawha expedition, divided his forces into two columns, giving one, composed of cavalry, to Gen. Averill. They crossed the mountains by separate routes. Averill struck the Tennessee and Virginia Railroad, near Wytheville, on the 19th May, and, proceeding to New River and Christiansburg, destroyed the road, several important bridges and depots, including New River Bridge, forming a junction with Crook at Union. Gen. Sigel moved up the Shenandoah Valley, and on the 15th was encountered near Newmarket by Gen. Breck inridge, who drove the enemy across the Shenandoah, captured six pieces of artillery, and nearly one thousand stand of small arms, and inflicted upon him a heavy loss ; Sigel abandoning his hospitals and destroying the larger portion of his train. This signal defeat of Sigel was the occasion of his removal, and the appointment of Hunter to take command of the forces with a larger design, reaching to Lynchburg and Charlottesville, the operations of which, however, were reserved for another month.

The secondary parts of the operations of the month of May against Richmond having thus failed, Gen. Grant, despite his expressed determination to fight all summer on the line he held at Spottsylvania, proposed a movement to the North Anna River, by which he hoped to flank the little army of Lee, that he no longer could hope, even by the " hammering " process, to beat in the open field. Previous, however, to the commencement of this movement, he made an assault, on the 19th May, on Ewell's line, with the view of turning Lee's left ; but this failed, and the Federals returned to their camps after a heavy loss. On the night of the 21st the movement to the North Anna was commenced. Gen. Lee was thus necessarily obliged to evacuate his position on the Po, and, by an admirable movement, took up a new position between the North and South Anna Rivers before Grant's army had reached its new destination.

Foiled again, and finding his agile adversary again in his path, Grant found it necessary, on the 24th May, to make another flank movement, by recrossing the North Anna, and marching easterly towards the Pamunkey. To cover his plans, an attack was made on Lee's left, while a portion of Sheridan's cavalry tore up the Central Railroad. But the great Confederate was fully master of the situation, and could not be easily blinded. He comprehended Grant's tactics ; he was as prompt in his movements ; and he was far more skilful in his strategy than the Federal commander. Accordingly, no sooner did Grant's army, on the 28th, arrive at Hanovertown, on the Pamunkey, fifteen miles northeast of Richmond, than it was found the Confederates were in line of battle, from Atlee's Station, on the railroad, ten or eleven miles north of Richmond to Shady Grove, eight or nine miles north-northeast of the capital. The next day, Grant's forces were across the Pamunkey, marching towards Richmond ; and reinforcements from Butler's army, on the James River, were arriving at White House, which once formed the Federal base of supplies.

The singular fortune of war had again made the Peninsula a deadly battle-ground. One month had hardly elapsed since the campaign had begun ; and its record of carnage in this brief time was unsurpassed, while, on the other hand, never, in such a space, had such a sum of glory been achieved as that which now illuminated the arms of Lee. When he stood in array against Grant at the Rapidan, his force was not more than fifty thousand men. It was this force which had compelled Grant, after the fighting at the Wilderness and around Spottsylvania Court-house, to wait six days for reinforcements from Washington before he could move, and had baffled his favourite plan of reaching Richmond. Lee never received a single item of reinforcement until the 23d of May. At Hanover Junction, he was joined by Pickett's division of Longstreet's corps, one small brigade of Early's division of Ewell's corps, which had been in North Carolina with Hoke, and two small brigades, with a battalion of artillery under Breckinridge. The force under Breckinridge, which Grant estimated at fifteen thousand, did not exceed two thousand muskets. When he fell back to the lines immediately about Richmond, Gen. Lee was joined there by Hoke's division from Petersburg; but at the same time Breckinridge's force had to be sent back into the Shenandoah Valley, and Ewell's corps, with two battalions of artillery, had to be detached under Gen. Early's command to meet the demonstrations of Hunter upon Lynchburg. This counterbalanced all reinforcements. The foregoing statement shows, indeed, that the disparity of forces between the two armies in the beginning of the campaign was never lessened after they reached the vicinity of Richmond and Petersburg, but, on the contrary, was largely increased. It has well been asked, by a commentator on these remarkable facts: " *What would have been the result, if the resources in men and munitions of war of the two commanders had been reversed ?* "

The fact was that Grant, notwithstanding his immense preponderance of men and material, had, after losses almost equalling Lee's numbers, utterly failed in his design of defeating the heroic Army of Northern Virginia away from its base, and pushing the fragments before him down to Richmond, and had been forced to cover up his failure by adopting the derided Peninsular scheme of McClellan. The Northern public, however, professed to find occasion of exultation in the reflection that he was within a few miles from Richmond, without considering that Lee's army was as much a protection there as a hundred miles away, and that Grant had only by a monstrous circuit, reached a point, where, ascending the waters of Virginia, he might have landed at the very beginning of the campaign without loss or opposition. It was a remarkable exhibition of the gaseous nonsense of New York that a mob of twenty-five thousand persons should have assembled in that city " to render the thanks of the nation to Gen Grant " for a feat which was, simply and at once, absurd, disastrous, shocking, and contemptible.

CHAPTER XXXII.

THE first of June, 1864, found the position of the two armies around
Richmond as follows : Grant was between the Chickahominy and the Pamunkey, with his left thrown forward to Mechanicsville, his right withdrawn to White House, and his reserve massed in rear of his left, and Richmond somewhat behind his left flank. Lee was posted from Atlee's Station,
extending on his left to Gaines' Mill, with outposts as far as Coal Harbour.
His position conformed to that of 1862 ; and, indeed, the whole Confederate
line of battle was on ground occupied by both the armies at that time.

On falling back to Richmond it had been the first concern of Gen. Lee
to secure positions he knew, from the battles of 1862, to be good ones.

He, accordingly, sent forward to the right Kershaw's and Hoke's divisions of Anderson's corps, with orders to occupy the eminences around Gaines' Mill and Cold Harbour. This position had been previously carried by some Federal cavalry. But on arrival of Hoke's division, shortly afterwards reinforced by McLaws', the Confederates obtained possession of the desired posts. At the same time Breckinridge and Mahone, of Hill's corps, were equally successful in gaining certain advanced positions.

On the 2d June, as Grant continued to develop his left flank, the Confederates were put in motion on a parallel line, while Early, commanding Ewell's corps, swung round, late in the afternoon, and took the enemy in flank, drove him from two lines of entrenchments, and inflicted great loss. Meanwhile Breckinridge, supported by Wilcox, proceeded, under orders from Lee, to attack the advanced Federals, now on the extreme right at Turkey Hill, and there succeeded in driving them away. Thus another important position was obtained by Lee; this hill commanding the approaches from the north and east to the line of the Chickahominy. Meanwhile Grant was getting his troops into position for a decisive action. Early in the morning of June the 3d, his army, now extending from Tolopatomy Creek, across the road from Cold Harbour to the Chickahominy, advanced in full line of battle, upon the Confederates.

BATTLE OF COLD HARBOUR.

The Federal line of battle ran in the following order, from right to left: Burnside, Warren, Smith, Wright, and Hancock. The latter was opposed by Breckinridge's command on Lee's extreme right; Ewell's corps held the extreme left opposite Burnside; and Hill's corps was in reserve. The attack was led by Hancock, who momentarily carried the position held by Breckinridge's troops, but was severely repulsed, as this part of the line was reinforced by Milligan's Florida brigade, and the Maryland battalion. This was the only corps of the enemy that came in contact with the Confederate works. The two corps on the right of Hancock were repulsed; and Warren and Burnside staggered on the line of the rifle-pits. The fact was that Grant, in testing the question, whether Lee's army had or had not been demoralized by its experience from the Rapidan to the James, found his own army so incapable, that he was compelled to withdraw it in sheer despair. He "mounted his horse and rode along the lines to ascertain from the different commanders the actual state of things in their immediate front. He returned leisurely, absorbed in thought, and it was evident that the attempt would not be renewed." Of the results of the day, he wrote: "Our loss was heavy, while that of the enemy, I have reason to believe, was comparatively light." The fact was that the report of the adjutant-general at Washington showed a loss of seven thousand five hundred men in three days' operations on the Chickahominy, the greater portion of which occurred, of course, in the general action of the 3d of June.

For several days after the battle of Cold Harbour there was comparative quiet, and some unimportant skirmishes. During the night of the 5th Grant withdrew his right wing about two miles, and placed it behind a swamp, which protected both the flank and front of that portion of his army. The severe experience of the 3d satisfied him that Richmond could not be carried by a *coup de main,* and could no longer be approached with advantage from the north. On this side lay a difficult river and five miles of earthworks, stretched to the Confederate capital. Here, too, the enemy had to hold the Fredericksburg railroad, a long, vulnerable line, which would exhaust much of his strength to guard, and which would have to be protected to supply his army—a situation which would have left open to the Confederates all their lines of communication on the south side of the James. A full survey of all the ground satisfied Grant that he could not operate with advantage north and east of Richmond; he determined to make another movement by Lee's left flank, throw his army over James River, and seize Petersburg, hoping thus to cut off all the Confederate supplies, except by the canal; while his cavalry could be sent to Charlottesville and Gordonsville, to break up the railroad connection between Richmond and the Shenandoah Valley and Lynchburg.

On the 12th June, Grant completed his preparations to abandon the late field of operations about the Chickahominy, cross the James River, and occupy the south side towards Petersburg. To do this he had to make another movement round Lee's right, extending as far as Bottom's Bridge, and march down the Chickahominy as far as the next crossings at Long's and Jones' bridges. The movement was effected with skill. On June 13, the advance had reached Wilcox's landing on the James, near Charles' City Court-house, and the next day Grant's whole army was safely transferred to the opposite shore.

Gen. Lee did not attack Grant on his movement to the James. He was probably unable to do so. Richmond and Petersburg had both to be guarded, not only against the Army of the Potomac, but also that of Butler, who had come up the river in heavy force to co-operate with Grant; while an important detachment of Confederate force, as we shall see, had to be ready to move towards Lynchburg to meet the advance of a third army in that direction. It had been the expectation of Grant to make an easy capture of Petersburg, which Butler had previously failed to take, laying the blame of defeat on his subordinate, Gillmore. But he found that Lee had anticipated him in this new plan of operations; that Petersburg was well able to withstand a siege; that additional fortifications had been promptly erected around it and on the banks of the Appomattox, while Drewry's Bluff, also, afforded a good and strong point of defence.

BATTLES OF PETERSBURG.

Grant found it now necessary to "hammer" at Petersburg, which, properly regarded, was then a mere outpost of the Confederate capital, for even if he took the first, or rather the line of works that commanded it, similar works, around Richmond, twenty miles off, confronted him. Smith's corps, of Butler's command, having disembarked at Bermuda Hundred on the 14th June, moved rapidly upon Petersburg, and made an assault on the batteries covering the approaches to the town on the north-east. He got possession of this line of works, but was too timid to push his advantage, and waited the coming up of the Second Corps, under Hancock, two divisions of which arrived during the night, and relieved a part of Smith's line in the captured works. An attack was ordered in the evening of the next day, Burnside's corps having also come up and gone into position on the left. Three assaults were made with disastrous result; the Confederates assuming the aggressive, driving the enemy from his breast-works at Howlett's House, and opening upon him an enfilading fire, in which a large portion of a brigade that had sought shelter in a ravine was 'aptured by a Georgia regiment.

The next day the Fifth Corps was got up, and a third attack was made by the enemy four corps strong. It was repulsed at all parts of the line; and, again assuming the offensive, the Confederates made an attack on Burnside's line of advanced rifle-pits, drove the enemy back upon his supports, and remained in possession until day-light, when they retired to their own works.

Meanwhile Butler, taking advantage of the Confederates in his front having been withdrawn to Petersburg, sallied from behind his entrenchments and advanced towards the railroad, intending to tear it up. Lee promptly prepared for him. The lines necessarily vacated by Beauregard, when he had to fall back and defend Petersburg, had already been taken possession of by the Federals; but directly Butler made his attempt, Anderson was despatched with his corps from Richmond to repulse him. This was done most effectively—Pickett's division, the heroes of Gettysburg, again making here an impetuous charge, capturing the breastworks of the enemy. We may imagine how unfortunate Butler was in his official announcement of great victories, for on the very day that he despatched that he had destroyed the communication with Richmond, Gen. Lee was sending, by the railroad, troops from the capital for the defence of Petersburg.

The result of all these engagements, which had cost Grant, by an official calculation, 9,665 men, was that the Confederates were still in firm possession of their works covering Petersburg, and that Grant was left no other resource than to proceed to envelop the town as far as possible without attacking fortifications.

The immediate operations of his army appear now to have degenerated to an attempt upon the railroads. On the 22d an attempt was made by two divisions of cavalry to get possession of the Weldon railroad; but when a portion of the command had reached the Jerusalem plank-road, A. P. Hill's corps and Anderson's successfully encountered them, and drove them back with severe loss. Gen. Wilson, however, succeeded in reaching the railroad at Ream's station, below where the combatants were engaged, and tore up some of the track. Wilson, joined by Kautz, then struck across to the Southside railroad, doing some damage, and finally came upon the Danville track, having had a sharp engagement with a small Confederate force near Nottoway Court-house. Continuing along the Danville railroad to the southwest, they arrived at the covered bridge over the Staunton river, in the evening of the 24th. Here a body of Virginia and North Carolina militia met them, and after a brisk encounter Wilson and Kautz had to retire. This was the limit of their raid. They returned as rapidly as they could, but at Ream's station one thousand prisoners and all the enemy's artillery and trains were captured by a Confederate force under Hampton and Fitzhugh Lee. Kautz's knowledge of the country enabled him to escape. He, with his shattered command, reached camp on the 30th June, while Wilson, with his men in wretched condition, did not arrive till next day.

North of Richmond, Grant's designs on the railroads were no more successful, and the expedition of Sheridan already noticed as sent out to destroy the railroads between Richmond and the Shenandoah Valley and Lynchburg, had met with disaster, without accomplishing a single important result. He had been intercepted at Trevillian station while moving on the Gordonsville road; and reaching the latter place by a circuit, was twice repulsed by the infantry in the rifle-pits there, and pleading the "want of ammunition" was compelled to withdraw his command across the North Anna and retreat to the White House.

The month of June thus closed with Lee master of the situation around Richmond and Petersburg. In the same month there were other notable successes to strengthen the capital, and public attention was turned to events occurring in other parts of Virginia, the result of which was to open the Shenandoah Valley, that famous avenue into the territory of the North, and to afford Gen. Lee the opportunity of an important diversion. We shall see, indeed, that this ready and resourceful commander, with Grant fully occupied in the south of Virginia, was yet enabled quietly and skilfully to send another army of invasion into the Northern States.

OPERATIONS WEST OF THE BLUE RIDGE.

At the last reference to operations west of the Blue Ridge, Gen. Hunter—the same who had made himself famous by his *negrophilism* in the department of Beaufort, South Carolina—had taken command of the Federal forces there, and was about to enter upon an enlarged campaign. That campaign was dictated by Grant. It indicated the extension of the auxiliary movement against Richmond to as many points as Staunton, Lynchburg, Charlottesville and Gordonsville—the general design being to cut the communications of Richmond, in view of which Hunter was to move on the point that best invited attack.

West of the Blue Ridge the Confederate force was small, disarranged, and altogether unequal to meet these formidable enterprises of the enemy. It consisted of a few small brigades of inferiour cavalry, about two regiments of infantry, and a small brigade (Vaughan's) of dismounted troops acting as infantry. To supply the place of Breckinridge, who had gone to the Richmond and Petersburg lines, McCausland's little force, from Dublin, was sent to the front of Staunton, and Gen. William E. Jones was ordered to take all the troops he could move from Southwestern Virginia to the same position in the lower valley. Accordingly, Gen. Jones not only got together all the infantry west of the New River, but having dismounted Vaughan's brigade of cavalry also, took all to Staunton, leaving nothing in the extreme southwest but a few disjointed bodies of cavalry and Morgan's command to meet Burbridge, coming in from Kentucky.

Gen. Hunter, having received his instructions from Grant, immediately took up the offensive, and moving up the Shenandoah Valley, met Jones' little command, on the 5th June, at Piedmont. Here the Confederates were overpowered with the loss of more than one thousand prisoners, and of their commander, who, with hat in hand, was cheering his men when he fell, pierced through his head by a minié ball. On the 8th, Hunter formed a junction with Crook and Averill at Staunton, from which place he moved, by way of Lexington, direct on Lynchburg. He reached this place on the 16th June.

It now became necessary for Gen. Lee to detach a considerable portion of his force to meet this distant demonstration of the enemy, and to select a commander, the decision, energy and rapidity of whose movements might overthrow Hunter, and possibly make an opportunity to pass a column, however small, through the Valley of Virginia to threaten the Federal capital. For this work Gen. Early was selected. He had latterly commanded Ewell's corps, and with the great portion of this, he moved rapidly by the Orange and Alexandria railroad to Lynchburg.

On the 18th June Hunter made an attack on the south side of Lynchburg, which was easily repulsed. The next day the Confederates attacked, drove him in confusion, took thirteen of his guns, pursued him to Salem, and forced him to a line of retreat into the mountains of Western Virginia. Gen. Grant wrote: " Had Gen. Hunter moved by way of Charlottesville, instead of Lexington, as his instructions contemplated, he would have been in a position to have covered the Shenandoah Valley against the enemy, should the force he met have seemed to endanger it. If it did not, he would have been within easy distance of the James River canal, on the main line of communication between Lynchburg and the forces sent for its defence." As it was, no sooner did Gen. Early ascertain that Hunter was retreating by the way of the Kanawha River, thus laying the Shenandoah Valley open for an expedition into Maryland and Pennsylvania, than he returned northward and moved down that valley.

While the Shenandoah Valley was thus opened, Gen. John Morgan had done his part in breaking up the enemy's combination in Western Virginia. This adventurous cavalier—who had escaped from the Ohio Penitentiary, and returned to active service—was operating in Southwestern Virginia, when Gen. Jones, commanding there, was ordered, with all the troops he could transport, to Staunton, at the very time that Southwestern Virginia was about to be invaded by Burbridge. Having no force to meet Burbridge in front, it was resolved by Morgan to dash boldly into the heart of Kentucky, and thus draw the Federal commander away. This plan succeeded, but at the cost of the defeat of Morgan's command.

With a force of little more than two thousand cavalry, Gen. Morgan entered the State of Kentucky through Pound Gap. On the 11th June he attacked and captured Cynthiana, with its entire garrison. On the 12th he was overtaken by Burbridge, with a largely superiour force, and his command effectually dispersed, and finally driven from the State.

This was the last important expedition ever commanded by John Morgan; and we may add here some account of the tragical circumstances which suddenly and unexpectedly brought to a close the career of this extraordinary man, and which constitute a case of atrocious *murder*, unparalleled in the records of any events which assume the title of civilized war. Driven from Kentucky, Gen. Morgan attempted a smaller scale of operations in East Tennessee, and was next heard of near Greenville. He was here on the 3d September; the place lying on the great line of railroad from Virginia to Georgia by the way of Knoxville, and nineteen miles distant from Bull's Gap, where Gen. Gillem was encamped with a brigade of Federal cavalry. What now occurred, it is necessary to state with more particularity of detail than we have usually bestowed on the relation of single events, as the manner of Gen. Morgan's death has been variously questioned, the enemy claiming that he was killed in honourable combat.

The General established his headquarters at the house of a Mrs. Williams, in the town of Greenville. His own brigade was sent on the road leading to Rodgersville, for the purpose of getting forage, and a detachment of Tennessee cavalry, six hundred strong, was ordered under Col. Bradford, to encamp on the road leading to Bull's Gap, and to picket the road leading towards the enemy. The country between Greenville and the Gap is hilly, and wild, and very poor. Gen. Morgan's betrayal was at hand from a quarter he had least expected. He had no sooner retired to rest than a woman, the daughter-in-law of Mrs. Williams, mounted a horse, and, unnoticed, rode to the Federal commander, and informed him of the prize within his reach. Gillem immediately moved his command in the direction of Greenville; when about five miles from town he halted and sent a detachment through the woods, and succeeded in getting on the flank of Bradford's command, and driving him back from the road, leaving it open to Greenville. A detachment of four companies of the 13th Tennessee Cavalry was then sent forward to charge the town. They met with no resistance. The square on which Mrs. W.'s house was situated was surrounded immediately. The officers of Morgan's staff being aroused by the couriers, of whom there were three or four at the front gate, rushed out and were captured one by one. Gen. Morgan attempted to escape through the garden; finding exit in that direction cut off, he concealed himself among some grape vines. He had no weapon at all, Captain Rogers having one of his pistols, and one of his clerks the other. While the officers of his staff and couriers were together under guard within twenty yards of his concealment, he necessarily heard the questions asked them and the threats made against them.

Seeing that there was no hope of successful concealment, he came out and surrendered to Capt. Wilcox, of the 13th Tennessee Cavalry, who had already both of Morgan's pistols in his possession. This captain sat on his horse and conversed with the General for some time, and then rode off. A few minutes after he left, a man named Andrew Campbell, belonging to the Federal cavalry referred to, rode up and presented his gun at Gen. Morgan The General said: "For God's sake don't shoot me—I am a prisoner." The gun was fired and the General fell. The muzzle of the gun, a Colt's army rifle, was within two feet of Gen. Morgan's breast when it was discharged; his clothing and his body were blackened with powder. His murderer then dismounted and threw the General's body across his horse, in front of the saddle, and rode about town shouting, "Here's your horse thief." When permission was given to some of Gen. Morgan's officers to take possession of the body, they found it lying in the road.

about one mile from the place where he had been shot. It was so covered with mud that they could scarcely recognize it. The ball struck the centre of the breast, about three or four inches below its junction with the neck, and came out behind the hip bone. The brave commander met his death as he met his foes a thousand times before ; there was no shrinking—not a quiver of a nerve—though he saw murder in the brawny felon's eye. He fell, leaving to his countrymen a testimony of Kentucky chivalry—the record of a gallant, dashing life and a fearless death.

EARLY'S INVASION OF MARYLAND.

We left the situation in Virginia with Lee covering Richmond and Petersburg, and meditating a menace upon the Federal capital. No sooner was the defeat of Hunter known, than the rapidity of a new movement became imperative, and not a moment was lost in pushing Early's column towards Maryland. In spite of the prostrating heat, the troops made twenty miles a day, and the rumour of this determined advance came to the Federal authorities, at the time when Grant was supposed to be carrying everything before him. It was another illustration of Gen. Lee's wonderful enterprise, and showed this commander to be one of the most daring as well as the most skilful Generals of the age. That popular opinion which regarded Lee as a good slow, prudent commander without *dash* is one of the lowest and most imperfect estimates of his character. We see now that when Grant was hoping to suffocate him with numbers, he dared to detach a considerable portion of his army to threaten the capital of the enemy. He was left at Petersburg with only the corps of A. P. Hill, two divisions of Ewell's corps, and one division of Longstreet's. But Lee had rightly calculated that the diversion towards Washington, coupled with the panic it would occasion, would weaken Grant to a greater extent than himself, besides impressing him and the Northern public with the extent and activity of his resources, and obtaining an important moral effect.

It became necessary for Grant at once to find troops to meet the new movement. For this purpose the Sixth Corps was taken from the armies operating against Richmond and sent up the Chesapeake Bay to man the fortifications around Washington, while orders were sent to hurry forward the forces of Gen. Hunter from the Ohio. To the Sixth Corps was added the Nineteenth, which was under orders to proceed from the Gulf Department to the lines of Virginia, and which was already debarking in Hampton Roads. The garrisons of Baltimore and Washington were at this time made up of heavy artillery regiments, hundred-days' men, and detachments from the invalid corps; and the rapidity of reinforcements was the important and critical concern.

On the 3d July, Gen. Early approached Martinsburg, accompanied by a cavalry force under Ransom. Gen. Sigel, who was in command of the Federal forces there, retreated across the Potomac at Shephardstown; and Gen. Weber, commanding at Harper's Ferry, crossed the river, and occupied Hagerstown, moving a strong column towards Frederick City. Meanwhile Gen. "Lew." Wallace, a commander much akin in character to "Beast" Butler, and who had distinguished himself in Baltimore by a cowardly ferocity and an easy prowess in the arrest and persecution of citizens, pushed out from that city with Ricketts' division and his own command, and took a position at Monocacy Bridge.

BATTLE OF MONOCACY BRIDGE.

Gen. Early had pressed on, crossed the Potomac, and, advancing to Frederick City, found it evacuated by the Federal troops, and that the enemy had concentrated his forces at Monocacy Bridge, four miles distant. The Federals held the east bank of the river, which runs due north and south, and were drawn up along the railroad. Early, having crossed the river south of the bridge, sent forward Evans' brigade across an open field to develop the strength of the enemy. It moved steadily under a heavy fire of musketry until within fifty yards of the enemy's position, when another body of Federals emerged from the woods on its right, and took it in flank. The other forces of Early were rapidly moved to the critical point; a simultaneous charge was made; and the enemy broke in shameful confusion, leaving the railroad and national pike, and retreating in the direction of Gettysburg. His losses were more than a thousand killed and wounded, and seven hundred prisoners.

From Monocacy Gen. Early moved on Washington, his cavalry advance reaching Rockville on the evening of the 10th July. He was now within sight of Washington, and the fire of the skirmishers was heard at the "White House," and in the department buildings of the capital. The enormous march, however, had diminished his army. The five hundred miles of incessant advance, at twenty miles a day, left him only eight thousand infantry, about forty field pieces and two thousand cavalry with which to assault the works around Washington.

The most important of these works was Fort Stevens. On the 12th a severe skirmish, resulting from a reconnoissance, occurred in front of this fort; but Gen. Early declined to follow it up, and, by a decisive blow, attempt the capture of Washington. Reflecting that he was in the heart of the enemy's country, and not knowing what force defended the capital, he abandoned his design upon it, and in the night of the 12th commenced his retreat.

There has been much question as to the extent of the danger to which Washington was at this time exposed, and as to the merit of Early's declination of attack. Northern writers declare that if Early had made a vigorous attack when he first came up, and not lost a day in a fruitless reconnoissance, it would have resulted in the capture of the city, so feebly was it then defended. Fortunately we have some distinct evidence on this point. Gen. Grant has testified that two divisions of the Sixth Corps, and the advance of the Nineteenth Corps had reached Washington before Early got there. Whether it would have been prudent for Early to match this force, while Hunter was hastening from the West to strike his rear, and cut him off from his only avenue of retreat across the Potomac, is a question for the military critic to decide.

Gen. Early, having broke up his camp before Washington, retreated, and with little molestation recrossed the Potomac, and finally stood at bay on the Opequon to protect the Shenandoah Valley. The results of the expedition fell below public expectation at the South, where again had been indulged the fond imagination of the capture of Washington. But the movement was, on the whole, a success; Early brought off five thousand horses and twenty-five hundred beef cattle; and the primary object of the march had been accomplished when he retreated and posted himself in the Shenandoah Valley—a standing threat to repeat the enterprise upon Washington —for we shall see that it was no longer a mere detached column that opposed him, but an army of forty or fifty thousand men. To that extent Gen. Grant had been weakened, and the heavy weight upon Gen. Lee's shoulders lightened.

THE MINE FIASCO AT PETERSBURG.

While Early was detached from Lee's lines, Gen. Grant made what may be described as his last attempt to take Petersburg by a *coup de main*. There were three parts of the enterprise: an assault on the Federal position on Burnside's front; the explosion of a mine under an angle of the Confederate works, to open the way to the attack; and a feint of operations on the north side of the James, to deceive Lee into sending away a portion of his troops.

In June a plan had been suggested by one of Burnside's officers to excavate a tunnel under an angle of the Confederate works that was covered by a six-gun battery. On the 25th July the work was completed. Its length was about five hundred feet, and at the end of the tunnel the mine was formed, running parallel with and directly under the fort that was to be destroyed.   On the 27th, the enormous quantity of 12,000 lbs. of powder was placed in the mine, fuses were constructed and connected with the magazine, and everything was in readiness for the grand explosion.

The mine was exploded between four and five o'clock in the morning of the 30th July.   An immense mass of dull, red earth was thrown two hundred feet in the air ; human forms, gun-carriages, and small arms were mingled in what appeared to be a bank of clouds blazing with lightning ; a great shock smote the ear, and the ground trembled as if by an appalling convulsion of nature.   Instantly, before the rumble of the explosion had died away, every piece of siege artillery on the enemy's line, and all the field artillery that could be brought into position opened as with the grand chorus of death.   With such an infernal display to strike terrour into the Confederates and to demoralize men suddenly awakened from sleep, the Ninth Corps, fifteen thousand strong, marched out to attack, and complete what was thought to be an easy and certain victory.

But Lee's soldiers were not men who could be fought after the Chinese fashion of assailing the ears with terrible sounds.   They were quickly prepared to meet the enemy.   The assaulting column, on reaching the scene of explosion, found that there had been opened here a huge crater, one hundred and fifty feet long, sixty feet wide, and from twenty-five to thirty deep.   It did not advance beyond it ; instead of rushing forward and crowning the crest, the assailants made the most shameful exhibition of timidity ; they huddled into the crater, they sought shelter there, and no commands or persuasions could move them further.   A division of negro troops was thrown into the crater—this maw of death ; and for two hours the mingled mass of white and black troops, utterly demoralized, unable to pluck up courage to make a determined charge upon the crest, swayed to and fro in the hollow of the exploded earthworks, while the Confederates were rapidly bringing up their artillery on the right and left of the crater to destroy the enemy before he could extricate himself from the disgraceful coil.   Once a feeble charge, in which the black troops were put in advance, was made towards the crest.   It was encountered by Mahone's brigade.   His men were ordered not to fire until they could see the whites of the negroes' eyes.   At the first volley delivered at this distance, the blacks broke ; they were panic-stricken and past control ; they rushed through the troops in the crater back to the original lines, while into this slaughter-pen the Confederates now poured an incessant storm of bombs and shells.   Retreat across the open space in rear of it was to run the gauntlet of death.   The ground all around was dotted with the fallen ; while the sides and bottom of the crater were literally lined with dead, the bodies lying in every conceivable position.   Some had evidently been killed with the butts of muskets, as their crushed skulls and badly smashed faces too plainly indicated ; while the greater portion were shot, great pools of blood having flowed from their wounds and stained the ground. In a few short hours of morning the enemy had lost between four and five thousand men, and had accomplished nothing.

"This miserable affair," as Gen. Grant himself was forced to entitle it, appears to have been sufficient to satisfy him that he could not hope for the capture of Petersburg from expedients, partial efforts and *coups de main*, and that the task was one of magnitude far beyond his original comprehension. His last spasmodic effort went far to persuade the Northern public that his whole campaign was a failure, and that they had miscalculated the importance of his mere vicinity to the Confederate capital, when Gen. Lee had been able to hold Petersburg against an attack combining so many elements of success, and that too after he had detached an important column into the valley of Virginia, and sent five of his divisions to the north side of the James. The commentary of the New York *Times* was logical and significant. It said: "Under the most favourable circumstances, with the rebel force reduced by two great detachments, we failed to carry their lines. Will they not conclude that the twenty-five thousand men that held Grant in check are sufficient to garrison the works of Petersburg? Will they not conclude that, if they were able thus to hold their own with the force of from eighteen to twenty thousand men sent to the north side of the James River neutralized, this force is available for active operations elsewhere?"

CHAPTER XXXIII.

SHERMAN'S CAMPAIGN IN GEORGIA THE IMPORTANT CORRESPONDENT OF GRANT'S IN VIRGINIA.
—THE "ON-TO-RICHMOND," AND THE "ON-TO-ATLANTA," THE TWO IMPORTANT MOVE-
MENTS OF 1864.—SHERMAN'S DEMAND OF NUMBERS.—GEN. JOSEPH E. JOHNSTON'S COM-
MAND.—HE PROPOSES AN OFFENSIVE MOVEMENT.—IS BALKED BY BRAGG AT RICHMOND.
—STATEMENT OF JOHNSTON'S FORCES ON 1ST MAY.—JOHNSTON'S POLICY OF RETREAT.—
HE PROPOSES TO FIGHT AT CASSVILLE; BUT IS OVERRULED BY HOOD AND HARDEE.—HE
CROSSES THE ETOWAH—ENGAGEMENT AT NEW HOPE CHURCH.—BATTLE OF KENESAW
MOUNTAIN.—SHERMAN'S GHASTLY EXPERIMENT.—HE RESORTS TO MANŒUVRING.—JOHN-
STON RETIRES TO ATLANTA.—THE SITUATION AROUND ATLANTA.—DEFEAT OF STURGIS'
COLUMN IN NORTH MISSISSIPPI.—JOHNSTON MASTER OF THE SITUATION.—WONDERFUL
SUCCESS OF HIS RETREAT.—HE HOLDS SHERMAN SUSPENDED FOR DESTRUCTION.—NAVAL
FIGHT IN MOBILE BAY.—A MATCH OF 212 GUNS AGAINST 22.—HOW THE GUN-BOATS SELMA
AND MORGAN FOUGHT THE ENEMY.—GALLANT FIGHT OF THE IRON-CLAD TENNESSEE.—
—SURRENDER OF THE FORTS IN THE HARBOUR.—LITTLE VALUE OF FARRAGUT'S CONQUEST.
—EXCESSIVE LAUDATION OF HIM IN THE NORTH.—SINKING OF THE CONFEDERATE PRI-
VATEER ALABAMA.—REVIEW OF THE RESULT OF THE PRIVATEERING SERVICE OF THE CON-
FEDERATES.—A GLANCE AT BRITISH "NEUTRALITY."—HOW EARL RUSSELL WAS BULLIED
BY THE WASHINGTON GOVERNMENT.—THE STORY OF THE LAIRDS' RAMS.—CRUISE OF THE
ALABAMA.—WHY SHE FOUGHT THE KEARSARGE OFF THE FRENCH COAST.—CAPT. SEMMES'
MOTIVES FOR A NAVAL DUEL.—THE ALABAMA SINKING.—THE FEDERAL VESSEL SENDS
NO RELIEF.—MR. SEWARD'S LITTLE REMARK ABOUT "PIRATES."—DISCOVERY OF CON-
CEALED ARMOUR ON THE KEARSARGE.—HOW THE RICHMOND EDITORS WOULD HAVE
TREATED CAPT. WINSLOW.—A CURIOUS ANECDOTE OF ADMIRAL FARRAGUT.—CAPTURE OF
THE PRIVATEER FLORIDA.—THE EXPLOIT OF NAPOLEON COLLINS IN A NEUTRAL PORT.—
HE ATTEMPTS TO SINK AND THEN STEALS THE CONFEDERATE VESSEL.—THE NEW YORK
HERALD AND "THE PAGES OF HISTORY."—INVASION OF MISSOURI BY GEN. PRICE.—HOW
AND WHY IT FAILED.—THE TRANS-MISSISSIPPI SUNK OUT OF SIGHT IN THE WAR.

THE important correspondent of Grant's campaign in Virginia was
that of Sherman in Georgia; the great military effort of 1864 being resolved into two important movements: the "On-to-Richmond," and the
"On-to-Atlanta." These grand movements were on different sides of the
Alleghany mountains; a thousand miles of distance intervened between
them; but both concurred in the design of attempting deep operations in
the South, and reaching what were deemed vital points of the Confederacy.

Gen. Sherman demanded what Federal commanders invariably named as the condition of their success against the brave Confederate armies—vastly superiour numbers. Questions of generalship, skill and courage were concerns for the Confederates. Sherman did not discuss these; he wanted physical momentum; he demanded a hundred thousand men and two hundred and fifty pieces of artillery. The lavish government at Washington supplied the demand, minus twelve hundred men. Three armies were united under Sherman, viz.: the army of the Cumberland, Maj.-Gen. Thomas commanding; the army of the Tennessee, Maj.-Gen. McPherson commanding; and the army of the Ohio, Maj.-Gen. Schofield commanding. The effective strength of these three armies was 98,797 men, and two hundred and fifty-four guns.

Fortunately for the Confederacy the military genius of Gen. Joseph E. Johnston had been called again, although unwillingly, into service by President Davis, who had displaced Bragg from the Army of Tennessee only after he had accomplished a complete sum of disaster, and capped his career of misfortune on Missionary Ridge. On the 27th December, 1863, Gen. Johnston had assumed command of the army at Dalton, Georgia. In January he had fallen back from Dalton, and his advanced posts; on the 7th February he was encamped at Rome, Georgia; but he again advanced to Dalton shortly afterwards, and proposed then an offensive movement against the enemy, whose strength he knew would be greatly increased in the spring, and who, therefore, could be attacked with better advantage before such increase of the disproportion of numbers. Gen. Johnston knew very well that he could not expect reinforcements at pace with the enemy, and was, therefore, wisely determined to make at once a forward movement and try issues with him as soon as possible. But a most untimely controversy in Richmond defeated Johnston's just and promising plan of operations. Gen. Bragg had been removed from command of the army he had so disastrously led, to take the post, by the persistent partiality of President Davis, of " consulting or advising officer " to the Executive. The favourite in Richmond had his own plan of offensive operations differing from that of Johnston; President Davis agreed with him. Gen. Johnston, in vain, telegraphed to Richmond: " I expressly accept taking the offensive—I only differ with you as to details "; but the discussion of " details " lingered in Richmond, until, when in the month of April the President sent a messenger to Georgia to explain his plans, the opportunity of the offensive was past, the enemy was being reinforced to more than twice Johnston's number, and was only waiting for the signal from over the Alleghanies to commence the " On-to-Atlanta " movement.

On the 1st May, the effective artillery and infantry of the Army of Tennessee amounted to 40,900; the effective cavalry to about four thousand. Gen. Johnston was thus greatly overmatched in numbers; and he had no prospect of compensation, but in superiour skill and strategy. But the condition of his army was excellent in every respect, and had been made so by the admirable skill and inspiration he had brought to the work of its regeneration. It was well-fed, well-clad, in high and hopeful spirits ; and for the first time in its history there was no barefoot soldier in its ranks. Ninety days before, the army left by Bragg was dishearten-ed, despairing, and on the verge of dissolution. By judicious measures Gen. Johnston had restored confidence, re-established discipline, and exalted the hearts of his army. There was reason now to hope that the Army of Tennessee, the most ill-starred and successless of all our armies, had seen its worst days.

In the first days of May, simultaneous with the onward movement of Grant in Virginia, Sherman began his grand march into Georgia. The Federal advance was in three columns—Thomas moving in front, direct upon Johnston's centre at Dalton, with his advance at Ringgold and Tun-nel Hill ; Schofield from Cleveland thirty miles northeast of Chattanooga, *via* Red Clay, on the Georgia line, to unite with Thomas ; and McPher-son, by a flank movement of some forty or fifty miles upon Johnston's lines of communications at Resaca, a station on the Western and Atlantic railroad, at the crossing of the Oostanaula river, eighty-four miles from Atlanta, and fifteen miles south of Dalton.

The flank movement on Resaca forced Johnston to evacuate Dalton. On the 14th May, having moved to Resaca, he sustained, with perfect suc-cess, two attacks of the enemy on his breastworks, and drove him with a loss of two thousand men. But Johnston did not design to fight here ; he determined to fall back slowly until circumstances should put the chances of battle in his favour, and he hoped by taking advantage of posi-tions and opportunities to reduce the odds against him by partial engage-ments. In pursuance of this characteristic policy, he took up at leisure his line of retrograde movement in the direction of the Etowah River, pass-ing through Kingston and Cassville.

In rear of Cassville Gen. Johnston had proposed to deliver a decisive battle, taking position on a bold ridge with an open valley before it. Two of his corps commanders, however—Polk and Hood—questioned the value of the position against the enemy's artillery, flatly declared their distrust, and were for abandoning the ground immediately. " So unwill-ing were they," writes Gen. Johnston, " to depend on the ability of their corps to defend the ground, that I yielded, and the army crossed the Eto-wah on the 20th of May—*a step which I have regretted ever since.*" He had reason to regret it. While he retreated towards Allatoona Pass, a division of Thomas' army was sent to Rome, capturing it with its forts and artillery, and its valuable mills and foundries. Meanwhile Sherman pressed steadily on for Dallas with a view of turning the difficult pass at Allatoona.

On the 25th the Federal advance under Hooker struck Stewart's division at the New Hope Church, and a hot engagement of two hours ensued. The next two days there was constant skirmishing and fighting. Late in afternoon of the 27th, Cleburne's division assaulted McPherson at Dallas and left six hundred of the enemy's dead on the field. But these sharp encounters were of little significance ; for it was evidently not Sherman's intention to make a great battle, and risk dashing his army to pieces in trying to force the pass at Allatoona. He was merely developing his lines for a movement on Johnston's flank ; and when, on the 30th of May, his left had reached the railroad near Marietta, Johnston had no other choice than to abandon his position at New Hope Church, and retreat to the strong positions of Kenesaw, Pine and Lost Mountains.

BATTLE OF KENESAW MOUNTAIN.

These natural battlements covered the railroad back to the Chattahoochie river. On the 19th June the disposition of Johnston's forces was : Hood's corps with its right on the Marietta and Canton road, Loring's on the Kenesaw Mountain, and Hardee's, with its left extending across the Lost Mountain, and the Marietta road. Subsequently Cheatham's and Cleburne's divisions of Hardee's corps were moved up to Kenesaw Mountain, which was properly the apex of Johnston's lines.

On the 27th June Sherman attempted an assault by McPherson and Thomas on Johnston's left centre on Kenesaw Mountain. The battle was but the slaughter of thousands of his men. They never came in contact with the Confederate works ; they were swept by a fiery torrent of shot and shell ; and when the attack was withdrawn more than three thousand of the enemy were scattered over the rugged ground, dead or bleeding. On the Confederate side, Cheatham's division lost one hundred and ninety-five men, while two thousand of the enemy were killed and wounded in his front. In Cleburne's division the loss was eleven ; that in Loring's whole corps two hundred and thirty-six ; while on this part of the line the loss of the enemy was more than a thousand. Of this ghastly experiment Gen. Sherman was satisfied to write : " Failure as it was, and for which I assume the entire responsibility, I yet claim it produced great fruits, as it demonstrated to Gen. Johnston that I would assault, and that boldly."

After his repulse at Kenesaw Mountain, Sherman again resorted to manœuvring. On the night of the 2d July, he commenced moving his army by the left flank, and on the morning of the 3d found that Johnston, in consequence of this movement, had abandoned Kenesaw, and retreated across the Chattahoochie. He remained on the Chattahoochie to give his men rest and get up stores, until the 17th July, when he resumed operations, crossed the river, and established his lines within eight miles of Atlanta. Peach-Tree Creek and the river below its mouth was now taken by Johnston for his line of defence; the immediate fortifications of Atlanta were strengthened; and the two armies now confronted each other in what was unmistakably the crisis of the Georgia campaign.

To this point the incidents of the compaign had all been in favour of the Confederates. The engagements at Resaca, New Hope Church, and Kenesaw Mountain, had been all Confederate victories. In connection, too, with the campaign, Gen. Forrest had achieved a brilliant success in Northern Mississippi, and intercepting at Guntown, on the 10th June, an expedition under Sturgis on its way from Memphis to protect and operate in Sherman's rear, had driven it back in utter rout and confusion, and hotly pursued it a distance of a hundred miles, taking two thousand prisoners, and killing and wounding an equal number. This stroke uncovered Sherman's rear, and left him a hundred and thirty-five miles in the interiour of Georgia, in constant dread that cavalry might get upon his line, and destroy it beyond the possibility of further use. The situation was all that Gen. Johnston had anticipated; all that he wished for. He had performed all the conditions of the campaign he had proposed to himself; he had now " got the chances of battle in his favour;" he had " reduced the odds against him by partial engagements;" he had brought his army to Atlanta, after inflicting a loss upon the enemy five times as great as his own; and he had performed the almost marvellous feat of conducting a retreat through a difficult and mountainous country more than a hundred miles in extent, without the loss of *materiel* or of a single gun. Gen. Johnston held Atlanta more firmly than Lee held Richmond. Sherman was unable to invest the city, and to withdraw he would have to pass over a single road, one hundred and thirty-five miles long, traversing a wild and broken country. Johnston held him as it were suspended for destruction. The situation was brilliant for the Confederates. A pause had now been given to the parallel operations of the enemy in Virginia and Georgia—the one aimed at Richmond, the other at Atlanta;—both movements were now unmistakably in check; and intelligent men among the ranks of the enemy did not hesitate to declare that it was only necessary for the Confederates to maintain the situation at each point to put Northern patience to the last proof, and compel a peace.

In this interesting condition we must leave the great campaign of 1864 on the dominant lines in Virginia and Georgia, to make a rapid narrative of other events of the war, including certain successes of the enemy on the water, and some detached operations important enough to draw attention after them.

The naval events of 1864 may be briefly summed up as a battle in Mobile Bay; the destruction of the Confederate privateer Alabama, and the capture of her most efficient ally, the Florida. We shall discuss these in the order of their importance.

NAVAL FIGHT IN MOBILE BAY.

The enemy had long contemplated the possession of Mobile Bay guarded at its entrance by two imposing fortifications. Here was a diffi cult point to blockade; here was a nursery of the Confederate navy; and here vessels were already being constructed for raising the blockade.

In the latter part of July, Gen. Canby sent Maj.-Gen. Gordon Granger, with such forces as he could collect, to co-operate with Admiral Farragut against the defences of Mobile Bay. On the 5th August the Federal fleet, numbering fourteen steamers and four monitors, carrying in all more than two hundred guns, and manned by twenty-eight hundred men, moved steadily up the main ship-channel into Mobile Bay. Having once passed Fort Morgan, this huge armada had to encounter a Confederate naval force composed of one iron-clad—the ram Tennessee—and three wooden vessels.

The Brooklyn took the lead of the enemy's fleet in passing Fort Morgan, keeping up such a broadside fire on its batteries that the guns of the fort were almost silenced. But another danger had to be run; and as the fleet moved grandly on, a torpedo exploded beneath the iron-clad Tecumseh, and in a moment she had disappeared beneath the waves, carrying down with her her commander and nearly all her crew. As the fleet got past the fort, the ram Tennessee dashed out at the Hartford, Farragut's flag-ship, but finding her starboard side completely protected by the Monitors, was unable to reach her, and was content with an exchange of harmless fire.

The three Confederate gunboats, the Morgan, Gaines and Selma were ahead, the latter pouring a raking fire into the enemy's fleet. The ene-my passed up to a pocket of deep water, where he bore off somewhat to the westward, and appeared to be collecting his fleet. About this time the Gaines was disabled, and forced to retire in a sinking condition. The Morgan and Selma continued to fire into the Hartford and Brooklyn, the leading vessels of the enemy. The Metacomet, which had up to this time been lashed to the port-side of the Hartford, was now cast off, and steamed forward in the direction of the Selma and Morgan, the fire from the ene-my's fleet having ceased.

The Metacomet was a wooden gunboat, mounting ten heavy guns; and the Morgan and Selma were also wooden gunboats, the former carry-ing six and the latter four heavy guns. At this time the Confederate flag-ship Tennessee, with Admiral Buchanan on board, was in the neighbourhood of Fort Gaines, beyond signal distance of the Morgan and Selma. Shortly after the time when the Metacomet cast off, two other vessels of the enemy were also seen to be cast off and heading in the same general direction with the Metacomet, though distant from her about two and a half miles. Immediately on seeing the Metacomet cast off, the Selma, previously heading southwestwardly, changed her course and bore off up the Bay northwardly and eastwardly with as much steam as she could make, and continued on that general direction, using her after guns. Upon the Selma's turning off, the Metacomet bore down on the Morgan, which vessel engaged her as she came on for some minutes, when she also changed her course and steamed southeastwardly in the direction of shoal water, or Fort Morgan. The Metacomet now pursued the Morgan for some minutes, the latter still fighting her as she came, when a rain squall suddenly arose which temporarily obscured the vessels.

The obscurity of the squall lasted some fifteen minutes, and when it cleared off, the Metacomet was found to have abandoned the pursuit of the Morgan, and had gone in quest of the Selma, which was still pursuing her course up the Bay. The Metacomet was now distant from the Morgan some two miles, and was closely overhauling the Selma. The Morgan headed as if to go in the direction of the Metacomet and Selma, when the latter surrendered.

It appears from this statement that there was no combination of action or concert made or attempted between the Morgan and Selma at any time after the Metacomet cast loose from the Hartford. It is proper to explain that this statement is reduced from the findings of a naval court of inquiry called in the Confederacy to investigate the conduct of the naval battle in Mobile Bay; and that, while its authenticity is thus put beyond question, it is directly opposed to, and in utter variance with the official report of Admiral Buchanan, to the effect that the Morgan and Selma were engaged in fight, and at one and the same time, with the Metacomet, and that in the midst of that fight the Morgan withdrew and left the Selma to her fate. Indeed it was fortunate that the two vessels never at any time combined; for had such combination taken place it would have led to the concentration of the Federal gunboats and resulted in the loss of the Morgan as well as the Selma. There is no doubt that Commander Harrison of the first managed his vessel skilfully; and he ultimately saved her by a gallant run to Mobile. To estimate this feat it must be remembered that it took place after the severe action of the day; that it was undertaken in opposition to the unanimous opinion of a council of officers; that the enemy was between the Morgan and Mobile, his gunboats and iron-clads cruising about the Bay; that the night was calm and starlight, and the Confederate vessel high-pressure, and making black smoke which could be seen a long distance. Notwithstanding these adverse circumstances the Morgan succeeded in reaching the obstructions near the city, although pursued and shelled for the greater part of the way by three of the Federal vessels.

While the affair of the Metacomet and wooden gunboats was taking place the Confederate flag-ship Tennessee was three or four miles distant, slowly following up the rear of the enemy's column of ships, which, being of too great draught, were confined to a " pocket " of deep water of about five or six miles length and running in about a north-northwest direction. It was only the enemy's gunboats, being of light draught, that could go beyond these limits and pursue ours.

As the enemy's fleet, having passed the forts and dispersed the gunboats, was proceeding to cast anchor, the Tennessee at last gave sign of battle and made directly for the Hartford. It was a desperate enterprise, for although the vessel was protected by five and six inches of iron-plating, she was about to engage in a conflict in which she would be beset by a whole fleet. Farragut's orders to the Monitors were to attack the Tennessee, not only with their guns, but bows on at full speed. The doomed vessel was soon surrounded. The Monongahela, the Lackawanna and the Hartford, each struck her in turn; and the latter in rasping along her side poured a whole port broadside of nine-inch solid shot within ten feet of her casemate. The vessel still floated, but was unmanageable, as her steering chains were gone. A second and more terrible onset was prepared; the three vessels already mentioned again bore down upon her; a fourth, the Ossipee, was approaching her at full speed; and the Chickasaw was pounding away at her stern. As she was about being struck by the vessels converging upon her, a white flag was hoisted, and Admiral Buchanan surrendered his vessel only after she had been disabled, himself wounded, and his crew almost in a smothering condition. He might have anticipated the result of the unequal contest, and have declined it with honour.

The Federal success, however, was yet incomplete, as the forts still held out, although with little prospect of resisting a bombardment from the shore batteries of the enemy, and the Monitors and ships inside the Bay. On the 8th August Fort Gaines surrendered to the combined naval and land forces. Fort Powell was blown up and abandoned.

On the 9th Fort Morgan was invested, and after a severe bombardment surrendered on the 23d. The total captures amounted to 1,464 prisoners, and 104 pieces of artillery.

The enemy was thus in possession of Mobile Bay, and enabled to close the port to all ingress or egress of blockade runners. But this was the limit of his success; the city was still held by the Confederates, and months were to elapse before the enemy was to make any new demonstration upon it. The capture of the forts did not give the city of Mobile to the enemy, or even give him a practicable water basis for operations against it.

Yet Farragut's victory, so easily achieved and so little fruitful, was exclaimed over the North as one of the greatest naval achievements of the war, and was by Yankee hyperbole exalted above the deeds of Nelson at Trafalgar and the Nile. He who had by the most indifferent prowess— for the enemy's superiority on the water had always been a foregone conclusion—come to be the naval hero of the war, was immortalized after the modern New York fashion of big dinners and newspaper lyrics. A " poet " was employed to recite to him in public what the New York journals called " a masterly ballad," each stanza of which closed with the word " Farragut." A feast was prepared for him, where a plaster of ice-cream represented the American Eagle, and miniature ships, built of sticks of candy, loaded the table. The sober mind will turn from these coarse displays of New York enthusiasm, ridiculous to childishness, to look at facts. The naval fight in Mobile Bay was a match between eighteen Federal vessels, having two hundred and twelve guns, and four Confederate vessels, having twenty-two guns. The commentary of history will be taken from the words written at the time in the columns of the Richmond *Examiner :* " It was a most unequal contest in which our gallant little navy was engaged, and we lost the battle ; but our ensign went down in a blaze of glory."

We pass to other events of the naval service of 1864, to find a record of Federal success, coupled with peculiar circumstances of dishonour.

SINKING OF THE CONFEDERATE PRIVATEER ALABAMA.

The privateering service of the Confederate States had not accomplished all that the public had expected from it ; and yet the sum of its results was formidable, and amounted to a considerable weight in the war. From the time the pilot-boat Savannah and the little schooner Jeff. Davis sallied out in the first year of the war, terrour had been struck into the entire commercial marine of the enemy. The Sumter, carrying nine guns, under command of Capt. Raphael Semmes, was the first really formidable experiment of a Confederate privateer. After capturing a number of prizes, she was abandoned at Gibraltar, in January, 1862, as unseaworthy. Since then the two most famous Confederate privateers were the Alabama and the Florida, which scoured the seas from the East Indies to the Atlantic coast, inflicting on the Federal commerce and tonnage the most disastrous results.

A report was made to the Federal Congress of captures by Confederate cruisers up to the 30th of January, 1864. The list, which was not complete, footed up 193, with a tonnage of 89,704. At fifty dollars a ton, the vessels were valued at $4,485,200 ; the cargoes, at one hundred dollars a ton, were estimated at $8,970,400 ; total value, $13,455,500. Sixty-two were captured by the Alabama ; twenty-six by the Sumter, and twenty two by the Florida.

But the effect of the Confederate privateering on Federal tonnage was even more marked. The perils of capture were standing temptations to Northern ship-owners to transfer their vessels, and put them under the protection of foreign flags; and in the summer of 1864 it was officially reported at Washington that 478,665 tons of American shippage were flying other flags. This loss to the North, as a matter of course, involved a consequent increase of the tonnage and power of its commercial rivals, and was a bitter and humiliating infliction upon its pride.

The Alabama, the most formidable of the Confederate privateers or cruisers, had been built at Birkenhead, England, and left the Mersey, July 29, 1862. The construction of this vessel within the British dominions was long a theme of diplomatic accusations at Washington, in which it was charged that Great Britain had, in this circumstance, overstepped the limits and obligations of her neutrality in the war. To this foolish and insolent assertion the latter Government made a reply which should have been conclusive of the matter. On the 11th September, 1863, Earl Russell had written: "With regard to the general duties of a neutral, according to international law, the true doctrine has been laid down repeatedly by Presidents and judges of eminence of the United States and that doctrine is, that a neutral may sell to either or both of two belligerent parties any implements or munitions of war which such belligerents may wish to purchase from the subjects of the neutral, and it is difficult to find a reason why a ship that is to be used for warlike purposes is more an instrument or implement of war than cannon, muskets, swords, bayonets, gunpowder, and projectiles to be fired from cannon and muskets. A ship or musket may be sold to one belligerent or the other, and only ceases to be neutral when the ship is owned, manned, and employed in war, and the musket is held by a soldier, and used for the purpose of killing his enemy. In fact, the ship can never be expected to decide a war or a campaign, whereas the other things above mentioned may, by equipping a larger army, enable the belligerent which requires them to obtain decisive advantages in the war."

Here was a plain, comprehensive definition of neutrality, which the good sense of the world evidently accepted. It is a sad reflection upon the British Government that it should have been driven from a position so well fortified by reason and justice, and should have subsequently allowed itself to be bullied by the Washington Government into the seizure of two iron-clads (combining the ram and monitor principles), which were being built by the Messrs. Laird, at Birkenhead, as *alleged*, for the service of the Confederates. That seizure was made in 1863. The terms in which that outrage was demanded, and the mean and cowardly circuit by which the British Government ultimately conceded it, may be placed here as an example of the timidity of that Government, and a striking evidence that nothing had been further from its intentions during the war than the " recognition " of the Confederate States. The demand was made as follows

" LEGATION OF THE UNITED STATES, LONDON, *Sept.* 3, 1863.

" MY LORD : I have the honour to transmit copies of further depositions relating to the launching and other preparation of the second of the two vessels-of-war from the yard of Messrs. Laird, at Birkenhead, concerning which it has already been my disagreeable duty to make most serious representations to Her Majesty's Government.

" I believe there is not any reasonable ground for doubt that these vessels, if permitted to leave the port of Liverpool, will be at once devoted to the object of carrying on war against the United States of America. I have taken the necessary measures in the proper quarters to ascertain the truth of the respective statements current here, that they are intended both for the use of the Government of France or for the Pacha of Egypt, and have found both without foundation. At this moment, neither of those Powers appears to have occasion to use concealment or equivocation in regard to its intentions, had it any in obtaining such ships. In the notes which I had the honour to address to your Lordship on the 11th of July and the 14th of August, I believe I stated the importance attached by my Government to the decision involved in this case with sufficient distinctness. Since that date I have had the opportunity to receive from the United States a full approbation of its contents. At the same time, I feel it my painful duty to make known to your Lordship that, in some respects, it has fallen short in expressing the earnestness with which I have been in the interval directed to describe the grave nature of the situation in which both countries must be placed in the event of an act of aggression committed against the Government and people of the United States by either of these formidable vessels.

" I pray your Lordship to accept the assurances of the highest consideration with which I have the honour to be, my Lord, your most obedient servant,

" CHARLES FRANCIS ADAMS.

" Right Honourable Earl Russell, &c., &c."

The consequence of this menace was that the Messrs. Laird were forbidden to allow these vessels to leave their yard " without an ample explanation of their destination and a sustainable reference to the owner or owners for whom they are constructed." It was outrageously held by Lord Russell that " Messrs. Laird were bound to declare—and sustain on unimpeachable testimony such declaration—the Governments for whom the steam rams have been built." In other words, without an affidavit or other legal foundation for proceedings against them, these gentlemen were required to come forward and prove their innocence, a thing opposed to all the law of Coke and Blackstone, and practised for the first time in British dominions at the dictation of powers in Washington.

We return to a brief chronicle of the cruise of the Alabama. She arrived at Porto Praya on the 19th August. Shortly thereafter Capt. Raphael Semmes assumed command. Hoisting the Confederate flag, she cruised and captured several vessels in the vicinity of Flores. Cruising to the westward, and making several captures, she approached within two hundred miles of New York; thence going southward, arrived, on the

18th November at Port Royal, Martinique.   On the night of the 19th she escaped from the harbour and the Federal steamer San Jacinto, and on the 20th November was at Blanquilla.   On the 7th December she captured the steamer Ariel in the passage between Cuba and St. Domingo. On January 11th, 1863, she sunk the Federal gunboat Hatteras off Galveston, and on the 30th arrived at Jamaica.   Cruising to the eastward, and making many captures, she arrived, on the 10th April, at Fernando de Noronha, and on the 11th May at Bahia, where, on the 13th, she was joined by the Confederate steamer Georgia.   Cruising near the line, thence southward towards the Cape of Good Hope, numerous captures were made.   On the 29th July she anchored in Saldanha Bay, South Africa, and near there, on the 5th August, was joined by the Confederate bark Tuscaloosa, Commander Low.   In September, 1863, she was at St. Simon's Bay, and in October was in the Straits of Sunda, and up to January 20, 1864, cruised in the Bay of Bengal and vicinity, visiting Singapore, and making a number of very valuable captures, including the Highlander, Sonora, etc.   From this point she cruised on her homeward track via Cape of Good Hope, capturing the bark Tycoon and ship Rockingham, and arrived at Cherbourg, France, in June, 1864, where she repaired.

A Federal steamer, the Kearsarge, was lying off the harbour.   Capt. Semmes might easily have evaded this enemy; the business of his vessel was that of a privateer; and her value to the Confederacy was out of all comparison with a single vessel of the enemy, the loss of which would, of course, be but an unimportant subtraction from the immense superiority of the Federals on the water.   But Capt. Semmes had been twitted with the name of "pirate;" and he was easily persuaded to attempt an *éclat* for the Southern Confederacy by a naval fight within sight of the French coast, which contest, it was calculated, would prove the Alabama a legitimate war vessel, and give such an exhibition of Confederate belligerency as possibly to revive the question of "recognition" in Paris and London. These were the secret motives of the gratuitous fight with which Capt. Semmes obliged the enemy off the port of Cherbourg.

The Alabama carried one 7-inch Blakely rifled gun, one 8-inch smooth-bore pivot gun, and six 32-pounders, smooth-bore, in broadside; the Kearsarge carried four broadside 32-pounders, two 11-inch and one 28-pound rifle.   The two vessels were thus about equal in match and armament; and their tonnage was about the same.   On the morning of the 19th of June, the Alabama steamed out of the harbour of Cherbourg, for the purpose of engaging the Kearsarge, which had been lying off-and-on the port for several days previously.   She came up with the latter at a distance of about seven miles from the shore.   The vessels were about one mile from each other, when the Alabama opened with solid shot upon the enemy, to which he replied in a few minutes.

The two vessels, instead of coming to close quarters, resorted to a curious manœuvre—fighting in a circle, and steaming around a common centre. The distance between them varied from a quarter to half a mile. The Alabama fired alternately with shot and shell; her guns were admirably worked; but strange to say, the Kearsarge showed no sign of material damage, when, after more than an hour's fire, Capt. Semmes ascertained that his own vessel was in a sinking condition, large apertures having been made in her sides and between decks. He now turned his vessel towards the French coast, hoping to reach it under a full head of steam and a crowd of sail. It was too late; the ship was evidently doomed; the fires were extinguished in the furnaces; and when the Kearsarge, which pursued her, was four hundred yards distant, Capt. Semmes hauled down his colours, and prepared to surrender. His vessel was evidently settling under him, and he looked with anxiety to the Kearsarge for her boats to put out to receive the surrender and rescue her prisoners from the fate of drowning. No boat came. Instead of despatching relief, the Kearsarge fired five times upon the Alabama after her colours had been struck. "It is charitable to suppose," says Capt. Semmes, "that a ship of war of a Christian nation could not have done this intentionally." But there is another explanation of this act. It has since become known to the world that in a certain diplomatic letter from Secretary Seward on questions growing out of this battle, he has taken the position that the Federal vessel had choice of a capture of prisoners, or "of sinking the crew of the *pirate!*"

It appeared that nothing but a watery grave awaited the officers and crew of the Alabama. As the vessel was on the point of sinking, the unhappy and desperate men leaped overboard, and the waves were soon filled with drowning men. Happily an English yacht, the Deerhound, was upon the scene, and having been allowed by the Kearsarge to go to the rescue, steamed up in the midst of the drowning men, and rescued most of them from the water. Capt. Semmes was taken by the Deerhound's boat from the water, as he was sinking for the last time. He turned his face to the rescuing party, and said: "I am Capt. Semmes—save me." He was eagerly taken aboard when his rank was thus known, and, being covered with a tarpaulin, he was carried to the English yacht, directly under the guns of the Kearsarge, without attracting any attention from the vessel.

The loss of the Alabama, in killed and wounded, was thirty; and on the Kearsarge not a single life had been lost. But there was another inequality of results of much more curious interest. The hull of the Alabama had been fearfully opened by the enemy's shot and shell, and yet the Kearsarge, after the contest, showed such little evidence of serious damage, that it did not appear even necessary for her to come into port to repair.

The secret came out after the engagement. The Kearsarge had a *concealed armour*, that completely protected her from the thirteen or fourteen shots received in or about her hull. Her midship section, on both sides, was thoroughly iron-coated. This had been done with chain constructed for the purpose, placed perpendicularly from the rail to the water's edge, the whole covered over by a thin outer planking, which gave no indication of the armour beneath. This planking had been ripped off in every direction by the shot and shell of the Alabama, the chain broken and indented in many places, and forced partly into the ship's side. She was most effectually guarded, however, in this section from penetration; and in the hour's contest the Alabama little knew that she was fighting a mailed enemy, with scarcely a single chance in her favour.

In commenting on this discovery, the Richmond *Dispatch* referred to a certain custom of chivalry, that when a knight was discovered in concealed armour his spurs were hacked off by the public hangman. The Northern public, however, could scarcely be expected to take so fine a notion; and Capt. Winslow, the North Carolinian, who commanded the Kearsarge, easily entitled his exploit among the sensations of the day, reached the American coast to find himself famous, was overwhelmed with receptions and dinners in Boston, and had his physiognomy recorded on the first pages of the New York pictorials.

CAPTURE OF THE PRIVATEER FLORIDA.

A few weeks later another naval exploit of the enemy was practically to terminate the privateering service of the Confederates, and to give one of the most extraordinary illustrations of the enemy's utter disregard of means in obtaining any desirable result in the war. An account of this event is properly preceded by an anecdote told in the New York newspapers, of Admiral Farragut, the naval hero of the North. When the Russian Admiral, in 1863, wintered in New York with his fleet, it was an occasion of receptions and banquets, at one of which occurred the following conversation with Admiral Farragut. The latter was complaining of the American officer who did not capture a Confederate steamer in a neutral port. "Why, would you have done it?" asked the Russian. "Yes, sir," was the prompt reply. "But," said the Russian, "your Government would have broken you." "Of course it would," replied Admiral F.; "*but wouldn't I have had her!*" The New York journals reported this among the heroic anecdotes of their heroic men; when it was simply the brutal expression of advantage, the disowning of all international conscience, the characteristic Yankee bluster of might against right.

This curious exposition of international law by the Federal Admiral did not have to wait long for a practical illustration. After the capture of the Alabama, the enemy appears to have had an increased desire for the other important Confederate cruiser, the Florida, carrying eight guns. She had eluded the Kearsarge at Brest, and since then had ventured within sixty miles of New York, chasing the war steamer Ericsson, and capturing the steamer Electric Spark on the route to New Orleans. She was next heard from at Teneriffe, and subsequently entered the Bay of San Salvador, Brazil.

The Wachusett, a Federal steamer, was also in this neutral port; and her commander, Napoleon Collins, conceived the utterly outrageous and dastardly design of sinking the Confederate vessel at her anchorage, or capturing her by stealing upon her in an unguarded moment, and towing her out to sea. The circumstances of the outrage were of peculiar atrocity. A little past midnight of 6th October, the Wachusett slipped her cables, and bore down upon the Florida, when about one half the crew of the unsuspecting vessel were ashore. The Florida's officer on deck, when he saw the approach of the Wachusett, actually hailed her to avoid an accidental collision as he feared; little supposing that the Federal vessel was coming down under a full head of steam with the diabolical design of sinking a defenceless vessel with her crew asleep beneath her decks. The blow, however, was not well delivered, striking the Florida in the stern and not amidships as intended. As the Wachusett drew off, she demanded the surrender of the vessel, incapable of resistance, and having in a few moments boarded her, attached a hawser, and moving at the top of her speed. towed the Florida rapidly out to sea. The outrage was not discovered by the Brazilian fleet until the Wachusett with her prize had got out to sea, and then some harmless shots were fired, which passed over her pennant.

Of course Mr. Seward had to apologize to the Brazilian Government, and Capt. Collins had to go through certain forms of censure. But this was of no importance. The diplomatic apology did not prevent the Florida from being held as a prize, and afterwards being "accidentally" sunk in Hampton Roads. And the official affectation with Capt. Collins did not prevent the press from lauding him, and the New York *Herald* from saying: "Certainly, no page of history can show a more daring achievement"—another illustration, by the way, of how the North has measured glory in the war by the very degrees of wantonness and outrage.

INVASION OF MISSOURI BY GEN. PRICE.

In the close of this chapter and in the group of events of the war, in 1864, outside of the grand campaigns of Virginia and Georgia, we may properly place here a brief record of what was the most important of the detached military operations of 1864. This was a movement in the Trans-Mississippi, the invasion of Missouri by Gen. Price. It appears to have been altogether a detached operation, having no relation to the campaigns east of the Mississippi, and with but little effect on the general issues of the war. It is therefore narrated in a small space.

About the middle of September, Gen. Price entered Missouri, crossing the State line from Arkansas, by the way of Pocahontas and Poplar Bluff. He had about ten thousand men under the command of Gens. Shelby, Marmaduke, and Fagan. From Poplar Bluff, Price advanced, by the way of Bloomfield, to Pilot Knob, driving before him the various outpost garrisons, and threatening Cape Girardeau. Pilot Knob was evacuated, and Price thus obtained a strongly fortified position, eighty-six miles south of St. Louis, the terminus of the railroad, and the depot for supply of the lower outposts.

Gen. Rosecrans, the Federal commander in the Department of Missouri, was largely superiour in force to Price; but he appears to have been unable to concentrate or handle his troops, and the country was surprised to find Gen. Price moving almost without molestation through the large State of Missouri, doing incalculable mischief, and kindling the hopes of the Confederates with another campaign of wonders in this remote region of the war. From Pilot Knob Gen. Price moved north to the Missouri River, and continued up that river towards Kansas. Gen. Custis, commanding the Department of Kansas, immediately collected such forces as he could to repel the invasion; while four brigades of Federal cavalry, numbering about eight thousand men and eight rifled guns, were operating in Price's rear. On the 23d October, Gen. Price was brought to battle on the Big Blue, and defeated, Gens. Marmaduke and Cabell being taken prisoners, and the Confederates losing nearly all of their artillery. On the following day, Price was again attacked, near Fort Scott, and obliged hurriedly to retreat into Kansas. He then turned down to the south, and crossed the Arkansas River, above Fort Smith, into the Indian Territory. He subsequently went into winter quarters in the south of Arkansas, his men in worse plight than when they started from that State, and the conclusion of his campaign an undoubted failure.

The fact is that Gen. Price had retreated from Missouri, not so much under the stress of the enemy's arms as from inherent faults in his own enterprise. He had declared that his invasion was not a raid, that he came to possess Missouri; but the breadth of the excursion, its indefiniteness, and the failure to concentrate on important points, ruined him. While his command roamed through the State, his men, brought to the vicinity of their old homes, which they had not seen for several years, were exposed to unusual temptations to desert; and instead of being reinforced by recruits, his command was diminished by desertions at every step of the march, and almost ran through his fingers before he left the State. With this sad conclusion of Gen. Price's expedition, the last hope was banished from the Southern mind of possessing Missouri; and the operations of the Trans-Mississippi may be said now to have made their last figure of importance in the war.

CHAPTER XXXIV.

WE have already referred to the great consideration which attached to
the Presidential contest in the North which was now to take place; we
have stated that it gave a new hope for the South in 1864; and we have

indicated that the political campaign of this year was, in the minds of the Confederate leaders, scarcely less important than the military. Indeed, the two were indissolubly connected; and the calculation in Richmond was that if military matters could even be held in a negative condition, the Democratic party in the North would have the opportunity of appealing to the popular impatience of the war, and bringing it to a close on terms acceptable to the great mass of the Southern people.

For a thorough discussion of this political campaign it will be well to make a rapid review and analysis of parties in the North, even at the risk of some repetition to the reader.

Parties in the North were divided by very distinct lines. There were two questions upon which the division took place. One of these referred to the supremacy of the Constitution as opposed to military necessity—real or pretended. The other had reference to the relative powers of the Union and the States. On both these questions the party in power held loose and careless opinions, employing force wherever it would avail for military or partisan advantage. The opposition contended for a strict observance of the provisions of the Constitution and of the rights of the States. This was the general distinction.

But widely as the theories of these two parties separated them on questions touching the sanctity and scope of the Constitution, there was still a margin of difference left between the views of the Northern Democratic party and the Southern doctrines upon which the right of Secession was founded. The difference, however, concerned only the last alternative of Secession. According to the Northern view, the Union was inviolable and perpetual, and all grievances must be redressed within the Union by remedies which respected its integrity. According to the Southern view, Secession was a rightful remedy for evils otherwise incurable, sanctioned by the precedent and precepts of the men of 1776.

This latter doctrine had so limited a support at the North, however, that it was totally unknown in the controversies of parties. There, all, or nearly all, assumed that the Union was permanent and inviolable—differences of opinion turning upon the powers of the Union; the powers of the Federal Government; the rightfulness of extra-constitutional measures in time of war; and the expediency, and most judicious means of coercion.

The party in opposition to Mr. Lincoln's Administration—most properly designated as the Constitutional party—was composed chiefly of Democrats, but largely interspersed with Whigs of the stamp of Wm. B. Reed of Philadelphia, Robert C. Winthrop of Massachusetts, Reverdy Johnson of Maryland, Wm. B. Crittenden, and the like. In partisan parlance they were called "Copperheads," and they were reinforced in the debates, though generally opposed in the votes, by a class of men who had split away from the Democratic party, called "War Democrats."

It would be difficult to state in precise terms the political doctrines confessedly held by the Black Republican party. After a patient effort we have desisted from the attempt. The more responsible avowals and professions of its leaders cannot be reconciled with the fanatical utterances of its less conspicuous and more active representatives. Its policy as well as its professions were shaped to suit the hour; and changed with evey varying phase of the war. The party was conservative and apologetic in moments of distrust and apprehension; but always ready to overstep the limitations of the Constitution, and to burst through the restraints of law, in seasons of confidence and success. It was as unfaithful to its own promulgated schedules of faith, and programmes of policy, as to the laws of the land. It alike disregarded its oaths of fidelity to the Constitution and pledges of adherence to specific lines of policy. It would, therefore, be quite useless to quote from its several creeds and platforms, to ascertain its principles as a party; for it would be folly to judge of its character by its professions.

In sketching the career of one of the parties of the North, we necessarily present a history of that which constantly opposed it. The immediate subject of our review will, therefore, be the Black Republican party; which had absolute control of the war throughout, and which, in claiming the credit of its results, assumes the responsibility of its transactions.

As composed at the time of the election of Mr. Lincoln, this party was not precisely the same as it had been during the first years of its career. It was a party built up, as we have seen, through many years of effort, upon the agitation against slavery. In the beginning it was despised alike for its weakness in numbers and for its fanaticism. It received its ideas from the Anti-Slavery Society of England, and there is no doubt it was fostered during its early career by pecuniary subsidies from that same organization. After a few years, it began to acquire importance in the political contests of the country, as holding a balance of votes capable of turning the scales in several of the Northern States, where the great parties were nearly equipoised. Although it finally absorbed the great mass of the Northern Whig party, it was characterized in terms of severe reprobation by both Mr. Clay and Mr. Webster. The latter said, with prophetic truth: " If these fanatics and Abolitionists get power into their hands, they will override the Constitution, set the Supreme Court at defiance, change and make laws to suit themselves. Finally, they will bankrupt the country, and deluge it with blood."

Mr. Clay, in describing its purposes, said of it, in words well nigh verified already: " The ultras go for abolition and amalgamation, and their object is to unite in marriage the laboring white man and the black woman, and to reduce the white laboring man to the despised and degraded condition of the black man."

The proclaimed purpose of the war of the Black Republican party upon the Constitution, and of the organization which they proposed of the Union, was the abolition of slavery, and the securing of equal rights before the law to the African race. It is difficult to conceive how a party should meditate and plan a revolution of the Government and a radical revisal of the Constitution for such a purpose, without desiring to elevate the negro to a platform of social as well as political equality with the white man. Nor is proof wanting of the truth of Mr. Clay's grave imputation in this regard. The organs of the party have not been very reticent or secretive on this subject. From a vast multitude of similar utterances we quote a few. The New York *Tribune* often iterates the assertion that " if a white man pleases to marry a black woman, the mere fact that she is black gives no one a right to prevent or set aside such a marriage." The New York *Independent* is fond of a theory, that the German, Irish, negro, and other races have come to America, not for the purpose, each, of propagating its distinct species, " but each to join itself to each, till all together shall be built up into the monumental nation of the earth ; " " the negro of the South growing paler with every generation, till at last he completely hides his face under the snow." Enamoured with the character of Toussaint L'Ouverture, it says to those who cherish the prejudice of colour and caste, that " they must cease to call unclean those whom God has cleansed, that they must acknowledge genius whatever be the colour of the skin that enwraps it ; and that they must prepare themselves to welcome to the leadership of our armies and our senate, as Southern substitutes for Jeff Davis and his drunken Comus-like crew, that have so long bewitched and despoiled us, black Toussaints, who, by their superiour talents and principles, shall receive the grateful homage of an appreciative and admiring nation." Gen. Banks said, when in the House of Representatives, that " in regard to whether the white or black race was superiour, he proposed to wait till time should develop whether the white race should absorb the black, or the black the white." Wendell Phillips, the ablest and the boldest of them all, said, in 1863 : " Remember this, the youngest of you, that on the 4th day of July, 1863, you heard a man say, that in the light of all history, in virtue of every page he ever read, he was an amalgamationist to the utmost extent. I have no hope for the future, as this country has no past, but in that sublime mingling of races, which is God's own method of civilizing and elevating the world. God, by the events of His providence, is crushing out the hatred of race that has crippled this country until to-day." Theodore Tilton also said, that, " the history of the world's civilization is written in one word—which many are afraid to speak, and many more afraid to hear—and that is, amalgamation."

These citations are abundant to show the animus and purposes of the men in the front rank of the Republican party, who have always brought their colleagues, when necessary, up to their own standard and position. It is not pretended, however, to deny that there were milder phases of opinion in the Republican party. There were those who aimed only at the abolition of slavery ; on the idea expressed years before by Mr. Seward, and reiterated by Mr. Lincoln, that an irrepressible conflict existed in the Union between slave society and free society, which could only be allayed by making the Union all slave or all free. There were very few, if any, who were not determined to use the war as an instrument of abolition, and to prosecute it, not merely for restoring the authority of the Union, but also for securing the extinction of slavery in the South. No such purpose was responsibly avowed in the beginning ; but it was fully developed by the summer of 1864, when it became, as we shall see, very soon a leading issue between the Lincoln and M'Clellan parties.

Such were the antecedents, character, and composition of the party which had succeeded in the Presidential election of 1860. The shock which the announcement of the result gave to the country was very great ; but it was not greater than that which was felt by the successful party itself. Composed of extreme fanatical elements, and brought for the first time face to face with the serious and grave responsibilities of office, under that Union to which so many of them had avowed a bitter hostility, and under that Constitution to which they were obliged to swear support, and which they designed to subvert, they at once began to realize the serious difficulty of their position. That which most added to their embarrassment, however, was the fact that they had carried the election by only a plurality vote. They had received no support in one half of the Union ; and in the other half, they had triumphed by only a majority of suffrages. They could not command a majority in either House of Congress ; and they felt that if the election could be held over again, the classes which were esteemed to embrace the intelligence, worth, and patriotism of the country, would rally together, make common cause against them, and defeat their accession to power.

Thus circumstanced, it was the interest of the Republican party, as a party, that the secession movement should go on, and that the threatened dissolution of the Union should be consummated. We have already seen signs of their policy secretly to exasperate the feelings and confirm the purposes of the South ; and, with professions of conservatism and devotion to the Union, to secure to themselves in administering the Government the support of the classes who had opposed them at the North.

We might make here a large accumulation of proofs of the fact that the Black Republican party, on its accession to power, wanted dissolution and wanted war ; but we are not aware that it is now denied. It is a historical truth. It is a historical conviction, confirmed alike by the action the interests, and the avowals of the party. It is indeed a fact which they have taken no pains to conceal.

Although this party, after securing unrestrained command of the power and patronage of Government, shaped its policy at will throughout the war, and prosecuted their measures with haughty and arrogant indifference to the protests and resistance of the opposition, yet they had come into posesssion of office with alarm and humility. Not only were they in a minority of numbers, but they felt that they were hostile to the Constitution to which they were about to swear fidelity, and to the principles on which it had been administered from its foundation. They felt conscious that their success in the election had given a shock to the institutions of the country, and that both their capacity for administering the Government in the spirit of its institutions, and their fidelity to the Union and to the organic law were greatly, and with reason, distrusted. Mr. Lincoln's personal conduct in the emergency betrayed these instincts of unworthiness. His speeches during the progress from Springfield to Washington were a continual apology for his party and for his election; and his well-remembered inaugural address was an appeal to the country against being judged by the avowals and proclaimed tenets of the party which had elected him. It may be said that by the moderate declarations of the Republican party at the outset of the war, the suspicions of the conservative classes of the North were allayed, and the opposition party completely disarmed. Care had been taken to withhold these pacific utterances until too late for them to reclaim the South. The North placed entire faith in them; the South placed none at all. They failed to save Virginia, North Carolina, and Tennessee; and it required the most energetic employment of force, threat, and cajolery, even to retain Maryland and Kentucky. To reclaim the South, however, was not the object. The aim was to yoke the whole North into support of the measures which were meditated, and which it was intended gradually to develop. The scheme completely succeeded. The Constitutional peace party were silenced everywhere. The war feeling grew with astonishing rapidity. It carried away many of the more prominent men of the opposition. But it is to be admitted that from the reduction of Sumter down to the close of the war there was a Constitutional party in the North, which, although unable to do more than to make continual protest against the conduct of the ruling party, yet did make this protest with ability, manliness, consistency, and dignity. The difficulty was, it had not power during the war to put any check upon its career.

Those who have studied the characteristics and idiosyncracies of the Northern people, and have observed their fondness for an affected enthusiasm, and their proneness to give way to gregarious impulses, however absurd and reprehensible, were not surprised at the alacrity with which the masses of even moderate men rushed into the war movement, at the piping of the war party, and at the appeal of the drum and fife. So soon as individuals found the throng tending that way, they rushed enthusiastically into what seemed the popular current; and the very men who but yesterday were loud in condemnation of the aggressive and incendiary purposes of the Republicans, to-day made amends for their tardy Unionism, by a precipitate enlistment in the ranks of the Administration.

It is the first step which costs. The peace party was a peace party no longer. A few consistent men remained, but the party disappeared for a period. Conservatism underwent almost a total eclipse. Opposed to war; averse to the principle of coercion; believing in the superiour efficacy of pacific over belligerent measures for restoring the Union; regretting every blow that was struck and every drop of blood that was shed in the contest, the party of the Constitution, of fraternal Union, of law, of order, and of peace, found itself compelled, first in one step, then in another, then in all, to support the war, to vote men and means for its vigorous prosecution, for sixty days, for ninety days, for the first campaign, and then, on and on, to a successful conclusion. They thought to bide their time, and to employ every opportunity that should offer in the interests of peace; but the opportunity never came; the fury of the war-storm, increasing as it progressed, and engulfing and carrying away everything in its course, swept down all who talked of peace. The vast patronage brought to the Administration made it omnipotent, and enabled it to appeal with effect to the passions alike of the avaricious, the ambitious, the adventurous of all sorts and conditions of men. As the costliness of the war increased, and the number of offices and the profitableness of contracts augmented, so its power in the country grew and waxed more and more irresistible.

We are not inclined to judge the peace party of the North too harshly. The arguments which led them to sanction and sustain the first measures of the Administration were such as could not well be resisted by a party believing in the inviolability of the Union, and the duty of suppressing all attempt at disruption. They were beguiled into the first belligerent measures by the conservative tone and pledges of Mr. Lincoln and Mr. Seward: and they were, moreover, deceived into the belief that prompt and vigorous steps were the surest means of preventing a protracted, expensive, and bloody war. It was these first steps, taken under a sense of duty to the Union, taken, as they thought, really in the interests of peace, that involved them inextricably in the war. They ought to have remembered that all negotiation ends with the first blow and the flow of blood; that, then, it is a question of force, and no longer one of right and reason; that war is like that cave of bones and carcases in mythology into which led many tracks, but out of it, none.

Much of the apparent unanimity which prevailed in favour of the war was the result of terrour. The people of the North seem to have a peculiar dread of public opinion. The great majority will not only surrender their own convictions to what happens to be the popular caprice, but they will join the populace in persecuting those who entertain their own previous convictions. It was so in the crisis under consideration. But very effective measures were taken by the Government in aid of this spontaneous instinct of terrour. They revived the system of espionage and arrests which had been employed in France by Robespierre and Fouché. At first, it was pretended that the arrested persons held secret correspondence with the Southern authorities; but soon all disguise and hypocrisy were thrown off, and arrests were made on charges, even suspicion, of mere disloyalty. It was held that the safeguards which the Constitution threw around citizens, protecting them " in their persons, houses, papers, and effects against unreasonable searches and seizures; " guarantying them a speedy trial in open court of law, and giving them by the writ of *habeas corpus* the right to know at once the charge against them, and to have the validity of that charge examined by a judge having power to discharge;— it was held that these provisions were put in abeyance by the state of war, and that the liberty of the citizen was not to be considered when the nation's life was at stake.

At the South, where great armies were penetrating and beleaguering the country, where public and domestic danger were everywhere and at all hours present, and where disaffection could at any moment bring fearful calamity upon the community, these arrests by order of Government were rare. It was a constant complaint of Generals in the field, and of civil officers in the municipal service, that when dangerous persons guilty of overt acts of treason to the Confederacy, were arrested and sent to Richmond, they were, as a general rule, released on the most unsatisfactory explanations, and let loose again upon the country. Much has been said of the sufferings, humiliations, and spoliations inflicted upon " Union " men in the South; and infinite, ingenious, and unblushing falsehoods have been published on the subject; but when the period arrives for a dispassionate examination of real facts, the reader of the history will be amazed at the moderation which was observed by the Southern people, more especially by the Confederate Government, towards a class of persons capable of so much mischief in a society threatened by imminent and fearful peril from within and without.

But at the North, there was no necessity for arbitrary arrests. The country was not invaded. The war was at a distance; and was offensive, not defensive. Except in portions of the Border States, the public sentiment was unanimous as against the South; opinions only differing as to the best means of reducing the distant " rebellion." Yet a system of terrour was established, which could only have been warrantable at the South.

and was held to be unnecessary even there. No shadow of excuse existed for considering the North or any State of the North as disloyal; on the contrary, Democrats and Republicans poured out their money by millions, and sent their young men by hundreds of thousands to the support of the flag. Yet in the first weeks of the war, a system of arbitrary and despotic seizure and imprisonment was inaugurated, which continued even after the surrenders of Lee and Johnston. The number of arbitrary arrests that were made in the whole period of the war is variously estimated at from ten to thirty thousand. The great mass of arrested persons never had a trial, and knew nothing of the charges, if any at all, on which they were imprisoned. In the great majority of cases, not only was the writ of *habeas corpus* refused, but applications to be examined by officers selected by the Government itself were refused. Prisoners, suddenly arrested and dragged to prison, without an opportunity of seeing their families or arranging for the continuance of their business, after long incarcerations, were not only denied an examination of their cases, but they were officially informed that the employment of counsel was distasteful to the Government, and would prejudice their applications for trial and release. Though arrests were made at the suggestion of anonymous letters, yet letters from the persons imprisoned applying for release or for trial were left unopened, and often returned in that condition to their authors. Finally, it was determined, that not only should the ground of arrest be withheld from the imprisoned, but the fact of arrest be withheld from the public; detective officers being prohibited from reporting the cases of arrest to the press, or permitting an inspection of their books. Of course under this system, the number of denunciations against suspected persons became burdensome to the Central Government; and such paragraphs as the following began to appear in the official newspapers:

" Eight hundred names are now entered on the books of the secret police in New York city, of persons suspected of treason, and many arrests will be made."—*N. Y. Tribune*, Sept. 6, 1861.

" A large number of arrests are daily made at the North, the number averaging ten or twelve a day. These are made generally on complaints lodged with the departments at Washington. The Government is somewhat annoyed and astonished that petty cases of treason should be sent there for consideration. Any military commander can commit for treasonable acts, and the local officers should promptly act themselves."—*Hartford Courant*, Sept. 6, 1864.

The arrests soon became very flagrant in their manner and character. Clergymen were seized while at prayer at the altar on the sabbath-day. Judges were seized for judicial opinions rendered on the bench. Ladies were seized and imprisoned, subjected to nameless insults, forbidden the visits of friends. hurried from prison to prison, and indecently treated by officers. Mourners were seized at funerals, while burying their dead. Young children were arrested and imprisoned for months, in some cases for years. The victims of these proceedings were in many instances driven to lunacy and to suicide, some of them dying under their severe usage. The detective system took the feature of eaves-dropping, and domestic servants were enlisted in the pay of Government. Arrests were often made on the most frivolous and contemptible pretences. A father, hearing that his son was shot instantly dead in battle, exclaimed, "That is good," meaning to express his relief at the thought that he had escaped the agonies of a lingering, painful death; he was arrested for the "disloyal" expression, hurried precipitately to Camp Chase, and imprisoned for two months before the privilege of explanation was accorded him. Two ladies of undoubted loyalty were arrested in a carriage in the streets, for raising their handkerchiefs, and passing them several times over their mouths. They were suspected of making signs to prisoners; whereas they had been eating an orange. The system of terror was employed not only in the Border States, but was put in practice everywhere. In far interiour towns, where the idea of danger from the rebels was supremely ridiculous, it was as active as in Washington city or New Orleans. A single clergyman in Central New York, wrote thirty letters in two months, sending lists of his neighbours whose arrest he demanded. An order was issued by the President to all policemen in the country, commanding their services in these seizures. State machinery was thus brought to the help of this nefarious business. The system was vigorously employed for partisan purposes. "Democrat" was held to be synonymous with "traitor," and being a "Democrat" was often the only ground for arrest.

We make this recital to show how impossible it was, for a while, to maintain an opposition party at the North. The power of a Government, wielding a patronage of many hundred millions of dollars per annum, and supported by an army of more than a million of soldiers, half of them kept habitually in the North, and allowed to resolve themselves into a mob on the slightest pretence, was too great to be opposed by reason and argument, when brought to bear without scruple and with despotic ferocity upon a helpless and paralyzed opposition. Passive submission to despotic rule, being a necessity, became a temporary duty. We have no heart nor right to censure those who remained consistent though often silent opponents of the Administration, during such a period of force and terrourism. But there was a class of original conservatives, who did not remain passive; who went over heart and hand and soul to the Republican party; and who vied with the minions of power in intemperance of speech and violence of action. The principal authors of the enormities that were perpetrated will receive the due sentence of history; but what will be the ignominy that will attach to the names of men, who, in the character of

" War Democrats," deserted their political associations, apostatized from the principles which they had all their lives upheld; espoused the arbitrary doctrines, seconded the despotic practices, imbibed the truculent animosities of the ascendant party; and prosecuted the war in the vindictive spirit and for the revolutionary purposes avowed by the worst enemies of the Union and the Constitution!

In spite, however, of the ferocity of the Government and its minions, there was never a day during the war in which the conservative party failed to present a small phalanx in Congress to make opposition to the policy of the Government, and to raise a continual protest against its unconstitutional proceedings. Did space suffice, it would be interesting to recapitulate here the several votes which this small party gave upon successive measures considered by Congress. A very few instances must serve to illustrate their courage and fidelity to the Constitution.

Against the Confiscation Bill, the vote in the House of Representatives was 42; in the Senate, 13. Against the emancipation of the slaves of persons engaging in the rebellion, the vote in the House was 66; in the Senate, 11. Against striking out from the Confiscation Act the clause limiting the forfeiture to the offender's natural life, the vote in the House was 76; in the Senate, 13. The vote in the House against the resolution declaring that the United States ought to co-operate with any States in gradually abolishing slavery, was 36; in the Senate it was 10. Against the scheme of compensated emancipation in the District of Columbia, the vote in the Senate was 19, in the House 39. Against the proposition of enquiry into the practicability of inaugurating a scheme of compensated emancipation in the Border States, the vote in the House was 52. Against the bill repealing the Fugitive Slave Act, the vote in the House was 62; in the Senate, 12. Against the bill authorizing a suspension of the writ of *habeas corpus* the vote (March 3, 1863) was 45, in the House; in the Senate it would have been 13, but failed by accident to be taken by roll-call. This bill also indemnified the President and other officers of Government for arrests and seizures, not only in respect to subsequent but previous acts. An eloquent protest against the bill was signed by thirty-six members, who moved ineffectually to have it placed on the journal. The Government frequently suppressed newspapers; and the Postmaster-General forbade the transmission of journals characterized as disloyal through the mails. An effort to bring this subject before Congress was resisted by a majority of the House; the vote in favour of considering some action in favour of the liberty of the press, was 54. Against the resolution in favour of submitting the Amendments for the abolition of slavery in the United States, the final vote in the House (January 3, 1865), was 56; in the Senate, 6. Against the bill by which it was proposed to limit the action of the President in the readmission of insurgent States, overrun and subdued by the Federal power, and to subject these States to extra Constitutional conditions before readmission into the Union, the vote in the House was 66 ; in the Senate, 14.

These examples are sufficient to show how a small Constitutional party in the North held to their principles throughout the dark period of usurpation and despotism.   As the conservative party became less awed by terrourism, they became less restrained in speech and action.   In the progress of time, divisions began to arise in the Black Republican party, and protests to proceed from Black Republican politicians.   Democrats, who, absorbed in military operations in the distant fields of campaign, had for some time given no attention to internal and domestic concerns, having the indisputable right of soldiers to speak their sentiments, began to give expression to the disgust and alarm which the arbitrary proceedings of the Administration had naturally excited.   Thus the opposition grew formidable as the term of Mr. Lincoln drew towards a close ; and parties for and against the Administration began to be organized, and issues of principle to be evolved and defined, for the approaching Presidential canvass.

The party issues for 1864 turned in a measure upon the conditions of reconstruction ; and three sets of opinion on this subject were developed in the course of the canvass.   The Constitutional party held to the ground that the sole rightful object of the war had been the suppression of the rebellion ; and that, so soon as the power of the rebel authorities in any State was crushed, the State was by that fact already restored to the Union, from which it had never been legally separated ; and nothing remained to be done but the restoration of the lawful State Government. This position was afterwards compendiously expressed by their candidate, Gen. McClellan, in the declaration : " The Union is the sole condition of peace—we ask no more."

As will be seen in the sequel, the Administration or Government party went into the canvass on the issue of simple coercion ; proposing indeed to bring the insurgent States into the Union divested of slavery ; but divested by the expedient of an amendment of the Constitution.   But the pressure of the contest forced them into the necessity of adding to their platform a requirement, upon States returning to the Union, that they should themselves abolish slavery as a condition precedent to readmission.   They were, in other words, forced to abandon a Constitutional measure, and to substitute an extra-constitutional one in its stead.

The programme of the radical branch of the Black Republican party had been developed, some short time before, in the bill which passed Congress on the 3d of July, 1864, but which the President failed to sign, prescribing these three conditions as necessary preliminaries to the restoration of a seceded State to the Union : to wit, the disfranchisement by the States of the guilty leaders of the rebellion as to State officers ; the abolition of slavery by the act of the returning States themselves; and the repudiation of the rebel debt, also by the act of these States.

Another feature of this radical programme, but which had failed to be incorporated into the bill just mentioned, was, that no seceded State should vote in the Electoral College, nor be admitted to representation in Congress, until after proclamation by the President of its obedience to the laws of the United States, especially authorized by act of Congress passed expressly for the purpose. The project of requiring the admission of negroes to full citizenship and suffrage, had not then taken the form of a distinct, express additional exaction.

The National Convention of the Government party was held at Baltimore on the 7th of June, 1864. The votes were all given for Mr. Lincoln, except that of Missouri, which was cast for Gen. Grant. The ballot on the Vice-Presidency was nearly unanimous in favour of Mr. Andrew Johnson. A platform was unanimously adopted declaring in favour of maintaining the Union in its integrity and supreme authority against all enemies; of quelling the rebellion by force of arms and duly punishing traitors for their crimes; approving the determination of the Government not to compromise with rebels, and to refuse all terms except an unconditional submission to the Federal authority; promising bounties to maimed soldiers; upholding the acts and proclamations of the Executive in regard to slavery; calling for an amendment of the Constitution abolishing slavery; thanking the army and navy for gallant services; approving and applauding the acts of the President, especially his measures taken against open and secret foes; declaring none worthy of confidence but such as endorsed this platform; demanding the full protection of the laws of war for all men employed in the armies of the Union, without distinction of colour; welcoming foreign immigration; approving the National Pacific Railroad; pledging the national faith for the public debt; and denouncing all attempts of foreign powers to supplant republican institutions in the Republics of this continent.

The project of making the abolition of slavery by each revolted State a condition precedent to the readmission of the State into the Union was not incorporated into this platform. On the contrary, the language of the second resolution implied an intentional pretermission of that condition, in prohibiting, as it did, the offer of any terms to the rebels " except such as may be based upon an unconditional surrender of their hostility, and return to the Constitution and laws of the United States;" the Convention seeming to rely upon the proposed amendment of the Constitution for effecting that object. Mr. Lincoln, also, in the language which he employed in accepting the nomination of the Convention, took pains to exclude the idea of intending to require the abolition of slavery, as a condition of peace, by any other process than by means of an amendment to the Constitution. He said: "I approve the declaration in favour of st amending the Constitution as to prohibit slavery throughout the nation. When the people in revolt, with a hundred days of explicit notice that they could, within those days, resume their allegiance, without the overthrow of their institutions, and that they could not resume it afterwards, elected to stand out, such amendment to the Constitution as is now proposed, became a fitting and necessary conclusion to the final success of the Union cause. Such alone can meet and cover all cavils. Now, the unconditional Union men, North and South, perceive its importance, and embrace it. In the joint names of Liberty and Union, let us labour to give it legal form and practical effect." He thus clearly declared that abolition by an amendment of the Constitution was the "legal form" of procedure, which "alone can meet and cover all cavils." But the pressure of the canvass soon drove him away from this position; and forced him to propound a project for the abolition of slavery by unconstitutional proceeding. This project was interpolated by Mr. Lincoln into the platform of his party in his notable rescript of the 18th of July, dated from the Executive chamber, and addressed "*To whom it may concern.*" That extraordinary and unique partisan document was promulgated under the following circumstances :

Early in the summer of 1864, the Confederate Government had sent, as we have seen, a commission of intelligent persons to Canada, as a convenient and important theatre for the presence of a judicious agency. The commission held no specific authority themselves to participate directly in any conference with the Government at Washington looking to peace. In the action which they took, they went no further than to propose to confer on the expediency and preliminary conditions of such a meeting. The commissioners were Messrs. Clement C. Clay, James P. Holcombe, and Jacob Thompson. It is proper to observe that these persons were agents of the Confederate Executive; that their nominations to any mission were never communicated to the Congress at Richmond; and that they were paid out of the secret service fund. Using George N. Sanders and W. C. Jewett as intermediaries, they exchanged notes with Mr. Horace Greeley, with a view to obtain from President Lincoln, through the influence of that well-known politician, a safe-conduct to the city of Washington. This correspondence with Mr. Greeley commenced on the 12th July, 1864. By the 17th of the month, the President seemed to have consented to grant the safe-conduct; and Mr. Greeley had repaired to Niagara, apparently to deliver it to the commissioners. But it was soon developed in correspondence that the commissioners had no particular authority from their Government themselves to enter upon the subject of peace; and that Mr. Lincoln's passport, in terms, implied that its bearers should be expressly accredited to his Government on that subject. The commissioners could not therefore accept or make use of the paper. After various explanations, another paper finally came from Washington, addressed " To whom it might concern," and declaring, that any person or persons, having authority to control the armies then at war with the United States, bearing a proposition to treat, which should " embrace the restoration of peace, the integrity of the whole Union, and the *abandonment of slavery;* " should have safe-conduct both ways ; and their proposition would be received and considered by the Executive Government of the United States. This paper, alike with the others, was useless to the Confederate commissioners, who neither had authority to control the armies of the Confederate States, nor commission to treat directly on terms of peace, nor disposition to enter into conference with a power indecently and arrogantly assuming to dictate in advance the conditions of negotiation. This, Mr. Lincoln of course knew ; and it could not be pretended that his " passport " was offered in good faith. It was proposed in no expectation that it would be accepted. It bore the ear-marks of a mere partisan document. Those who concocted it felt that so rude a rejection as it gave to the overtures for a conference, would prejudice Mr. Lincoln with the country, which was earnestly desirous of peace ; and that it was necessary to interpose the popularity of abolition as an offset to the disfavour which the rejection of a peace conference must excite. In fact, it was not pretended that the paper was designed for any other than a campaign purpose ; and the frivolity of the President's proceeding was excused on the plea that the object of the commissioners in Canada, in opening the correspondence, was to make capital for the opposition party of the North. The personal surroundings of the commissioners in Canada were referred to by the Government press in confirmation of the truth of this imputation. Such is the history of this after-thought, of making abolition by the States in revolt a condition of their readmission into the Union ; such was the manner and occasion of interpolating this additional plank in the platform of the Government party. The party itself had pretermitted it at Baltimore in June. The radical spirits had supplied the omission in the bill for reconstructing the revolted States, which they had succeeded in carrying through Congress on the 3d of July. The President had virtually vetoed this bill, on the ground, taken in his speech accepting the nomination, that the only " legal form " of abolishing slavery was by means of the Constitutional amendment, called for by the Baltimore resolutions. What, therefore, the radical spirits of the party had failed to accomplish, the action of the Confederate commissioners and the reputation of George Sanders for political intrigue, had succeeded in achieving.

The National Convention of the Democratic party did not meet until after the appearance of this paper. It convened at Chicago on the 29th of August. Outside of the Convention there was a warm contest between the friends of Gen. McClellan and those who desired the nomination of a candidate less committed to the coercive policy, and less implicated in the war. This struggle did not turn upon a sufficiently tangible issue to give it importance. As a Union party, the great body of the opposition party was committed to the war as the only practicable means of preserving and restoring the Union. Gen. McClellan was known to be earnestly desirous of peace, and of peace on the single and simple basis of a restoration of the Union under the Constitution as it stood. This was the only ground on which the conservative party could go before the people in the canvass, and hope to succeed in the election. It would have been vain to expect success upon the principles of the very few Democrats and conservatives who believed, and believed correctly, that the war had been unrighteous and iniquitous in its leading object, no less than in the manner in which it had been conducted. The great body of the opposition concurred with Gen. McClellan in the opinion that secession was unwarrantable and iniquitous, and that it ought to be resisted by all the power of the Union. They considered, therefore, that the war was righteous in its object, and only iniquitous in the manner in which it had been prosecuted. Reflecting these views held by the mass of his party, and having no competitor for the nomination favoured by them, he was nominated with little if any opposition when the vote came on in the body of the Convention. Mr. George H. Pendleton was selected as the second candidate on the ticket, in a manner altogether flattering and creditable to that staunch and consistent defender of the Constitution.

The Convention unanimously adopted a platform declaring their unswerving fidelity to the Union; calling for a convention of all the States looking to the restoration of peace on the basis of a Federal Union of all the States; denouncing the military interference which had been practised in recent elections in the Border States; declaring that the aim and object of the Democratic party were to preserve the Federal Union and rights of the States unimpaired; reprobating the system of usurpation, tyranny, and despotism which the Administration had wantonly and systematically pursued throughout the war; reprehending the Government's cruel neglect of the Union prisoners of war; and tendering their sympathy and pledging their future protection to the soldiers and sailors of the army and navy of the United States.

Gen. McClellan's letter of acceptance soon after appeared, and by its pacific tone and conciliatory terms, removed much of the objection which the extreme peace men of his party had felt to his nomination. Affirming the necessity of preserving the Union entire in the most cogent terms; he declared, that its preservation " was the sole avowed object for which the war was commenced; " that " it should have been conducted for that object only; " that it should have been conducted on the principles of conciliation and compromise; that the re-establishment of the Union must be the indispensable condition in any settlement; and that " they should exhaust all the resources of statesmanship to secure such a peace, to re-establish the Union, and to secure for the future the constitutional rights of every State.'

Except in the important particular that the Government party proposed, in its amended platform, to abolish slavery by an extra-constitutional means, there was no great difference between the positions of these two parties in regard to slavery itself. The war had, by the summer of 1864, rendered the continuance of the institution impracticable; though Gen. Grant's declaration, made as early as August, 1862, that it was then dead and could not be resurrected, was certainly premature. By the summer of 1864, however, the fate of slavery had, in fact, been sealed. It probably could not have existed if the Confederacy had been established. It could not have survived a return to the Union, even if no objection had been made to its new incorporation there. Mr. Davis had acknowledged that it was no longer an issue between the North and South, several months before the rescript of Mr. Lincoln had transpired at Niagara. All thoughtful minds at the South were convinced that the institution had been too completely demoralized by the protracted duration of the war, and the long presence of liberating armies and negro brigades in the South, to be any longer a stable, a profitable, or a safe feature in the Southern economy.

There was, however, a grave constitutional point at issue on this subject between the conservative and the Government party, notwithstanding that practically the continuance of slavery was no longer in controversy. The conservatives denied the right to impose extra-constitutional conditions on the returning States; the Government party asserted this right, and asserted it wantonly. In that point of view the issue was vital. Why abolish what was already doomed to dissolution? Slavery had received its death-blow; why overleap the Constitution to cut its throat?

The Radical party did not insist upon thrusting its extreme demands as issues into the canvass. They held a convention at Cleveland, as early as May 31, and proposed a platform by way of preserving for its leading spirits a consistent record. They nominated John C. Fremont for the Presidency, and a very weak and rather obscure apostate from the Democratic party, John Cochrane, for the Vice-Presidency. All this, however, was for little more than mere form's sake. No effort was made to draw off voters from the body of the party, which supported the Government candidates; and none were drawn off. In his letter of acceptance, Gen. Fremont expressed his preference for supporting the candidate who should be nominated at Baltimore, if it could be done without violence to his sense of duty and consistency. The platform differed in no material particulars from that of Baltimore, excepting in the addition of a passage in the fifth resolution, hereafter to be noticed, and of the two following clauses, viz. :

"12. That the question of the reconstruction of the rebellious States belongs to the people through their representatives in Congress, and not to the Executive.

"13. That the confiscation of the lands of the rebels, and their distribution among the soldiers and actual settlers, is a measure of justice."

It is to be remarked, that even this radical platform omits the imposition of extra-constitutional conditions precedent upon the revolted States as requisite to their readmission into the Union even in respect to the institution of slavery; and that its fifth clause relies upon an amendment to the Constitution alone, as a means of accomplishing the object; that clause being in these words :

"5. That the rebellion has destroyed slavery, and the Constitution should be amended to prohibit its re-establishment, and *to secure to all men absolute equality before the law.*"

The reader will not fail to note how subordinate and obscure a position in this platform was assigned to the demand for negro suffrage and citizenship, which afterwards was made so prominent a feature in the policy of the Radicals.

Thus, if we look to the written terms in which the issues of parties were made up, they were as follows : The Conservatives demanded reconstruction on the sole, simple basis of the Constitution as it was. The Government party demanded a formal abolition of slavery by the revolted States as a condition precedent to restoration. The Radicals demanded— if we look to their legislation in Congress—the three conditions of the abolition of slavery by the States, the disfranchisement of the leading rebels, and the repudiation of the rebel debt; and if we look to their Cleveland platform, they demanded that the whole question of reconstruction should be left to the people of the North, through their representatives in the sectional Congress, that the lands of the rebels should be confiscated, and that " equality before the law " should be secured to all men.

On paper, the more ready and natural affiliation of parties would seem to have been between the Conservative and the Government parties; and the real antagonism to have been between the Radical party on one side, and the Government party and Conservatives, combined, on the other; and this might possibly have been the division, if the war had been already terminated. For it was apparent, even as early as the summer of 1864, that such would really become the dividing line of parties, when the questions of reconstruction should come immediately up for practical decision. But the election ante-dated reconstruction by more than a year; and the contest of parties turned, of course, upon the transactions of the war, rather than upon the conditions and results of a peace still unconquered.

The written issues of the canvass were therefore little considered. The debates hung and dwelt upon the usurpations of the Executive, and the revolutionary spirit, policy, and purposes of the party in power. These being the subject of respective assault and defence, the array of parties remained as during the war; the Conservatives and Democrats on one side; the Radical and Administration Republicans, on the other. The prosecution and defence proceeded upon the indictment embodied in the fourth resolution of the Democratic platform, "that the administrative usurpation of extraordinary and dangerous powers not granted by the Constitution; the subversion of the civil by military law in States not in insurrection; the arbitrary military arrests, imprisonment, trial and sentence of American citizens in States where civil law exists in full force; the suppression of freedom of speech and of the press; the denial of the right of asylum; the open and avowed disregard of State Rights; the employment of unusual test-oaths, and the interference with and denial of the right of the people to bear arms in their defence, are calculated to prevent a restoration of the Union, and the perpetuation of a government deriving its just powers from the consent of the governed."

The eloquence of the orators who made appeal against these high crimes, was worthy of the cause for which they stood. Some of the orations delivered on the inspiring theme equal, if they do not surpass, in power and pathos, any that were ever before delivered in vindication of human rights and in defence of constitutional liberty. No papers, in the political history of this country, exceed, in dignity of style, in power and cogency of argument, in thrilling interest of narration, in sternness of arraignment, in intensity of patriotic appeal and indignation, some of the papers that were put forth by the supporters of Gen. McClellan. But the weight of power and patronage proved sufficient to overbalance that of patriotism and reason.

It is not necessary to go further into the details of the canvass; and the reader will already anticipate its conclusion. The election of McClellan, of which there had been some probability in the midsummer of 1864, became impossible, in view of the rapid military successes of the North, which never failed to draw new adherents to Mr. Lincoln's Administration; illustrating how little there was of steadfast principle in party organizations in the North, and how much of political opposition gave way to the views of expediency and the persuasions of time-service. The "electoral necessity" at Washington for victories in the field was amply fulfilled. The canvass of 1864 concluded in the election of Abraham Lincoln by the vote of every Northern State, except Delaware, Kentucky, and New Jersey.

But in the analysis of the popular vote there was yet some encouragement. It stood twenty-two hundred thousand for Mr. Lincoln, eighteen hundred thousand for Gen. McClellan. Although too small for victory, the conservative vote was much larger than had been expected by reflecting men, after the fall of Atlanta, the reverses of Hood, and the success of Sherman. Under all the adverse circumstances under which the vote was given, it was creditable to the party which made the contest, and encouraging for the cause of constitutional liberty. It was given just after decisive reverses had befallen the Confederate cause, in the moments of victory and exultation, at a time the most propitious that could have been chosen by the war party, and the most unpropitious conceivable for the peace party. The election had occurred just at the time when the idea prevailed that a popular vote in favour of the war party would fall as a finishing blow upon the already exhausted and prostrate Confederacy; and that a vote in favour of the peace party would cheer the South to put forth renewed effort in the hope of securing the most favorable terms of peace. The adverse vote was not, therefore, a deliberate judgment of a majority of the Northern people against the principles of constitutional liberty. A large number of the men who helped to cast that majority vote were actuated by motives of expediency, thinking to save the Union first, and leaving it for a more eligible occasion to vindicate their attachment to constitutional principles. Thus, the victory of the Constitution was postponed; and its triumph reserved for another and uncertain time.

CHAPTER XXXV.

GEN. LEE had moved from the Rapidan to Richmond, with an increase
of reputation at each stage of the retreat. It is curious that when Gen.
Johnston moved from the Northern frontier of Georgia to Atlanta, even
with greater success, he should not have experienced similar tokens of approbation. The fact was that he was the subject of a deep intrigue in
Richmond, to displace him from the command of an army, whose affections and confidence he had never ceased to enjoy; and even while he was
moving in the march from Dalton, his removal from command was secretly
entertained in Richmond. There is a certain delicate evidence of this,
which the historian should not spare. While the march referred to was in

progress, a letter written by Gen. J. B. Hood to one who was supposed to have more than an ordinary concern, an affectionate interest in his career, declared then his confident anticipation of being soon elevated from the position of corps commander to the head of the Army of Tennessee. There was other evidence of the intrigue in Richmond. Gen. Bragg, the "military adviser" of President Davis, visited Johnston in his lines around Atlanta; never apprised him that his visit was of an official nature; put together everything he could to make a case against Johnston, and returned to Richmond with the alarming report that he was about to give up Atlanta to the enemy! Of this nonsense Gen. Johnston has written: "The proofs that I intended to hold Atlanta are, the fact that under my orders the work of strengthening its defences was going on vigorously, the communication on the subject made by me to Gen. Hood, and the fact that my family was in the town. That the public workshops were removed, and no large supplies deposited in the town, as alleged by Gen. Bragg, were measures of common prudence, and no more indicated the intention to abandon the place than the sending the wagons of an army to the rear, on a day of battle, proves a foregone determination to abandon the field."

But the Presidential fiat was to go forth in the face of all facts. On the night of the 17th July it was known in the Army of Tennessee, that a despatch had been received from Richmond, removing Johnston from command, and appointing in his place Gen. J. B. Hood. The news struck a chill in the army, such as no act or menace of the enemy had ever done. To Sherman it was the occasion of new spirit. When he heard that Hood was to be his future antagonist, he jumped to his feet, made a significant motion around his forefinger, and exclaimed: "I know that fellow."

Gen. J. B. Hood had been appointed by President Davis as "a fighting General," and was prompt to vindicate the cheap reputation that had procured for him such a command. With some reinforcements from the Southwest and levies of Georgia militia, Gen. Hood had now under his command an effective force of forty-one thousand infantry and artillery, and ten thousand cavalry. With reference to other Confederate forces in the field, his army was a large one, although it gave him but little margin for fanciful attacks and useless sacrifice of life.

THE BATTLES OF ATLANTA.

As Sherman approached Atlanta, two of his corps had swung around upon the Augusta road, destroying this line of communication, while Thomas took his command across Peach Tree Creek, directly in front of the Confederate entrenchments. While the enemy's right on the creek was in marching column, Hood, in the afternoon of the 20th July, directed an attack upon it, designing to take advantage of a gap between two of its divisions. The attack was led by Walker's and Bates' divisions of Hardee's corps ; and the massed troops, in admirable order, burst through the gap in the enemy's lines, and for a time appeared about to destroy his forces on the right. But a double fire was brought to bear upon their lines along the deep hollow they had penetrated ; and the attack was drawn off in good order, but after a half hour of deadly work, in which the killed and wounded were counted by thousands. The loss of the enemy was about two thousand ; that of the Confederates probably twice as large, as they were the assaulting party, and terribly exposed on the line of attack.

Next day, McPherson moved forward, and established a line east and south of Atlanta, and within three miles of the town. His command stretched beyond the Atlanta and Augusta Railroad, which he had torn up. Hood now hastily swung around Hardee's corps, followed by the others, and brought the bulk of his army against McPherson. Hardee moved against the enemy's extreme left, drove him from his works, and captured sixteen pieces of artillery. Gen. McPherson was shot dead as he rode along the line. Meanwhile, Cheatham attacked the enemy's centre with a portion of his command, and took six pieces of artillery. Affairs looked gloomy for the enemy ; he had been repulsed at several points, he had lost much artillery, and the stream of bleeding men going to the rear told how severely he suffered in the conflict. But about this time the enemy succeeded in concentrating his artillery, and Gen. Sherman sent word to Logan, who had succeeded McPherson, to mass his troops in the centre and charge. Exhausted, wasted, and bleeding, the Confederate columns gave way, abandoning most of the artillery they had captured in the early part of the day. The attack of the 22d was like that of the 20th—one of the most reckless, massive, and headlong charges of the war, where immense prices were paid for momentary successes, and the terrible recoil of numbers gave a lesson to the temerity of the Confederate commander.

Hood's attempt on the Federal left being frustrated, he fell back to his inner line of works. The intentions of Sherman appear now to have been to swing his army to Hood's extreme right, threatening the Macon road, and having in co-operation a great cavalry raid upon his rear. Stoneman was sent with five thousand cavalry, and McCook with four thousand men, to meet on the Macon road near Lovejoy's Station, where they were to destroy the rail, and also to attack and drive Wheeler's command. Stoneman requested permission to be allowed to proceed to Macon to release the Federal prisoners confined there. Sherman left this at his own discretion, in case he felt he was able to do so after the defeat of Wheeler's cavalry. But Stoneman did not fulfil the conditions He got down in front of

Macon, without going to Lovejoy's, and, in attempting to retreat, was hemmed in by Iverson, and was himself captured, together with one thousand of his men and two guns. McCook returned after losing five hundred men as prisoners. The cavalry raid was a decided failure, or as Sherman mildly expressed it, " not deemed a success."

On the 28th July Hood made a partial attack along the Lickskillet road, which he had occupied with Stewart's and Lee's corps. The conflict was desultory and without result on either side. After five hours of action, Hood retired with a loss of about fifteen hundred killed and wounded.

We have already noticed that Sherman did not have force enough to invest Atlanta completely. This was the great point in Johnston's calculations, when they were upset at Richmond; for Sherman, reduced to strategy, would have found his master in the cool and dexterous Johnston, whereas in Hood he had plainly his inferiour to deal with—a commander who had indeed abundant courage, but a scant brain with which to balance it. Sherman's army was not large enough to encircle Atlanta completely, without making his lines too thin and assailable. He never contemplated an assault upon its strong works. It was his great object to get possession of the Macon road, and thus sever Atlanta entirely from its supplies. It was not sufficient to cut the road by raids; it must be kept broken, and to accomplish this it was clearly necessary to plant a sufficient force south of Atlanta.

While Sherman meditated such a movement, Hood made the very mistake that would secure and facilitate it, and thrust into the hands of his adversary the opportunity he had waited for. He sent off his entire cavalry towards Chattanooga to raid on the enemy's line of communication— a most absurd excursion, since Sherman had enough provisions accumulated this side of that place to last him until he could restore his communications, and had also formed a second base at Allatoona.

Instantly, the Federal cavalry was on the Macon road. With his flanks easily protected, Sherman followed quickly with his main army. On the 31st August, Howard, on the right, had reached Jonesboro', on the Macon road, twenty miles southeast of Atlanta; Thomas, in the centre, was at Couch's; and Schofield, on the left, was near Rough-and-Ready, still closer to Atlanta.

Hood had no alternative now but to make a battle on or near the line of the Macon road, and there settle the fate of Atlanta. He might have moved out of the city on the north, and have overwhelmed what of Sherman's army—the Twentieth corps—was left there; but he would then have been in a country destitute of supplies. He determined to make the battle near Jonesboro', and the corps of Lee and Hardee were moved out to attempt to dislodge the enemy from the entrenched position he held across Flint River   The attack failed with the loss of more than two thousand men.   On the evening of the 1st September, the enemy's columns converged upon Jonesboro', and Hardee's corps, finding itself about to be flanked and overwhelmed, withdrew during the night, after having been cut up by two severe engagements, and with the loss of eight guns.

That night, finding his line of supply cut off, and the sum of his disasters complete, Hood determined to abandon Altanta.   He blew up his magazines, destroyed all his supplies that he could not remove, consisting of seven locomotives and eighty-one cars loaded with ammunition, and left the place by the turnpike roads.   He moved swiftly across the country towards Macon.   The next morning Sherman moved south to catch the retreating army, but at Lovejoy's, two miles beyond Jonesboro', he found Hood strongly entrenched, and, abandoning the pursuit, returned to Atlanta.

Sherman announced: " Atlanta is ours, and fairly won."   His army entered the city on the morning of the 2d September, and the successful commander rode through the streets to his headquarters without parade or ostentation.   He declared that his army, wearied by an arduous campaign, needed rest, and that he proposed to give it an interval of repose within the defences of Atlanta.   But the period of military inaction was to be employed in launching measures of the most extraordinary cruelty against the non-combatant people of Atlanta.   Gen. Sherman was the author of the sentiment, " War is cruelty, and you cannot refine it," which was caught up in the Northern newspapers as a bit of very sententious and elegant philosophy, when, in fact, denying, as it did, that war had any law of order or amelioration, it was a mere plagiarism from the bloody and detestable code of the savage.   This extraordinary doctrine Sherman at once proceeded to put in practice by depopulating Atlanta, and driving from their homes thousands of helpless women and children.   It was the most cruel and savage act of the war.   Butler, the tyrant of New Orleans, had only banished registered enemies.   Sherman issued a sweeping edict, covering all the inhabitants of a city, and driving them from their homes to wander as strangers, outcasts and exiles, and to subsist on charity. Gen. Hood, while he received the exiles within his lines, took occasion to protest, writing to Gen. Sherman himself of the measure his sinister mind had devised : " It transcends in studied and ingenious cruelty all acts ever before brought to my attention in the dark history of war."   But all protests were unavailing.   In vain the Mayor of Atlanta had pointed out to Gen. Sherman that the country south of the city was crowded already with refugees, and without houses to accommodate the people, and that many had no other shelter but what they might find in churches, and out-buildings ; that among the exiles were many poor women in an advanced state of pregnancy ; that the consequences would be woe, horrour, and suffering, which could not be described by words. Sherman was inexorable. He affected the belief that Atlanta might again be rendered formidable in the hands of the Confederates, and resolved, in his own words, " to wipe it out." The old and decrepit were hunted from their homes; they were packed into railroad cars; tottering old age and helpless youth were crowded together; wagons were filled with wrecks of household goods; and the trains having deposited their medley freight at Rough-and-Ready, the exiles were then left to shift for themselves.

The fall of Atlanta was a terrible blow to the Southern Confederacy; a reanimation of the North; the death of " the peace party " there; the date of a new hope of the enemy and of a new prospect of subjugation. " On that day," said the Richmond *Examiner*, " McClellan's nomination fell still-born, and an heir was born to the Abolition dynasty. On that day, peace waved those ' white wings,' and fled to the ends of the morning. On that day, calculations of the war's duration ceased to be the amusements even of the idle." President Davis had declared, when he removed Johnston, that " Atlanta must be held at all hazards." It was the most important manufacturing centre in the Confederacy; it was the key to the network of railroads extending to all portions of the Gulf States; it was " the Gate City " from the north and west to the southeast; it was an important depot of supplies, and commanded the richest granaries of the South. Such was the prize of the enemy.

The catastrophe moved President Davis in Richmond, and mortified the vanity that had so recently proclaimed the security of Atlanta under the command of Hood. He determined to visit Hood's new lines, to plan with him a new campaign, to compensate for the loss of Atlanta, and to take every possible occasion to raise the hopes and confidence of the people. It is remarkable that the visits of the Confederate President to the armies were always the occasions of some far-fetched and empirical plan of operations, and were always accompanied with vapours and boasts that unduly exalted the public mind. Mr. Davis never spoke of military matters without a certain ludicrous boastfulness, which he maintained to the last event of the war. It was not swagger or affectation; it was the sincere vagary of a mind intoxicated with conceit when occupied with a subject where it imagined it found its *forte*, but where in fact it had least aptitude. Mr. Davis, as a military commander or adviser, was weak, fanciful, to excess, and much too vain to keep his own counsels. As he travelled towards Hood's lines, he made excited speeches in South Carolina and Georgia. At Macon he declared that Atlanta would be recovered; that Sherman would be brought to grief; and that this Federal commmander " would meet the fate that befell Napoleon in the retreat from Moscow." These swollen assertions, so out of character, were open advertisements to the enemy of a new plan of operations. It appears that the unfortunate vanity of President Davis completely betrayed him. Referring to this period, Gen. Grant writes: "During this time Jefferson Davis made a speech in Macon, Georgia, which was reported in the papers of the South, and soon became known to the whole country, disclosing the plans of the enemy, *thus enabling Gen. Sherman to fully meet them.* He exhibited the weakness of supposing that an army that had been beaten and fearfully decimated in a vain attempt at the defensive could successfully undertake the offensive against the army that had so often defeated it."

The new offensive movement of Hood, advised by President Davis, was soon known to the country. Not satisfied with the revelation at Macon, President Davis addressed the army, and more plainly announced the direction of the new campaign. Turning to Cheatham's division of Tennesseeans, he said: "Be of good cheer, for within a short while your faces will be turned homeward, and your feet pressing Tennessee soil."

On the 24th September, Hood commenced the new movement to pass to Sherman's rear and to get on his line of communications as far as Tennessee. The first step was to transfer his army, by a flank movement, from Lovejoy's Station on the Macon Railroad, to near Newman on the West Point road. The significance of this might have escaped the enemy, but for the incautious language of President Davis at Macon, which at once gave rise to the supposition that this movement was preliminary to one more extensive. Sherman was instantly on the alert, sending his spare forces, wagons, and guns, to the rear, under Gen. Thomas, and, at the same time, sending Schofield, Newton, and Corse to take up different points in the rear of Atlanta.

On the 27th, Hood moved towards the Chattahoochee. On the 1st October, the enemy made a reconnoissance towards Newman, and discovered that Hood had crossed the Chattahoochee River on the 29th and 30th of September. Sherman immediately followed.

On the 5th October, when Hood's advance assaulted Allatoona, Sherman was on Kenesaw Mountain, signalling to the garrison at Allatoona, over the heads of the Confederates, to hold out until he relieved them. Hood moved westward, and, crossing the Etowah and Oostanaula Rivers by forced marches, attacked Dalton on the 12th, which was surrendered. Passing through the gap of Pigeon Mountain, he entered Lafayette on the 15th. From this place he suddenly moved south to Gadsden, Alabama, where he rejoined his trains, to make his fatal march towards Nashville.

Sherman waited some time at Gaylesville, until he became fully assured of the direction taken by Hood; and then abruptly prepared to abandon the pursuit, return to Atlanta, and mobilize his army for a march across the broad State of Georgia to the sea. His calculation was a plain and precise one. Gen. Thomas, at Nashville, could collect troops from the whole Department of the Mississippi; Rosecrans was able to send him reinforcements from Missouri; Sherman detached two corps—the Fourth and Twenty-third—to move, by the way of Chattanooga, to the relief of Thomas; and there was little doubt that with this force Thomas could ho d the line of the Tennessee, or if Hood forced it, would be able to concentrate and give a good battle. Sherman was left in command of four army corps, and two divisions of superb cavalry—a force of about sixty-thousand men. When Hood wandered off in the direction of Florence, Sherman was left free to complete his arrangements, and there was nothing to interfere with his grand projected march to the sea. In October, Gen. Grant, who was watching closely the development of the wretched Davis-Hood device to find some compensation for the loss of Atlanta, telegraphed Sherman : " If you were to cut loose, I do not believe you would meet Hood's army, but would be bushwhacked by all the old men, little boys, and such railroad guards as are still left at home." With nothing, of course, to fear from such an opposition, Sherman telegraphed his determination " to make a wreck of the road, and of the country from Chattanooga to Atlanta, including the latter city ; send back all his wounded and worthless, and with his effective army, move through Georgia, *smashing things*, to the sea."

The march would, indeed, have been a perilous enterprise, if there had been any considerable force in Sherman's front, or on his flanks. As it was, nothing opposed his march to the sea, and he had simply to pass through the gate-ways which the stupidity of the Davis-Hood campaign had left open. It is amusing to the student of history to have such a plain march entitled a grand exploit, when it was only a question of so many miles motion a day. Sherman knew very well that there was nothing to oppose him ; he knew that the Confederacy had been compelled to throw all its fighting power on its frontiers, for Grant had told him " it was but an egg-shell ; " he knew that the conscription had exhausted the interiour ; he knew that the country he would traverse was peopled with non-combatants, women, and children ; he knew that this country abounded with supplies, which the difficulties of transportation had withheld from Richmond. He simply proposed to take plain advantage of these circumstances, and march to the sea-board. There was no genius in this ; no daring ; it was merely looking the situation in the face. It is said that had Sherman failed he would have been put down as one of the greatest charlatans of the age. But there was no chance of failure when there was nothing to dispute the march. If, indeed, he had attempted the movement with a Confederate army in his front or on his flank, it is highly probable that the adventure would have taken rank with his movement in 1862 on Vicksburg, the greatest *fiasco* of the war, and his experiment with " the strategic triangle " in 1863, a piece of charlatanism and of disordered execution that should have decided his reputation.

It had been the original design of the enemy to hold Atlanta, and by getting through to the west, with a garrison left on the southern railroads leading east and west through Georgia, to effectually sever the east from the west. In other words it was proposed in the great campaign of 1864 to repeat the experiment of bisection of the Confederacy, first accomplished when the enemy gained possession of the Mississippi River. It was calculated of course to fight from Atlanta to the sea, and that the second stroke of bisection would be accomplished by cutting through a hostile array. In originating with Hood the movement north of Atlanta, President Davis simply saved the enemy all the trouble he had contemplated, cleared the way of opposition and opened a plain and unencumbered way to his original design, with an invitation to execute it without fear and at leisure.

We must leave here the story of Sherman's march to follow the erratic campaign of Hood. When the latter was ready to leave Florence, Sherman was far on his way on his march towards Savannah ; and the country beheld with amazement the singular spectacle of two antagonistic armies, both at once acting on the offensive, day after day marching away from each other, and moving diametrically apart. To appreciate what insanity must have inspired such a campaign on the Confederate side, we may remark the utter want of compensation in the two movements. Even throwing out of consideration the great fact that Hood's movement to the north uncovered Georgia and left her undefended to the sea, while itself encountered a second army of the enemy, yet even if Hood was successful, an invasion of Northern territory would be no possible equivalent for that of the South, where the ravage and loss of material resources might be vital ; and even in the least circumstance, the season of the year, the Confederate troops, badly clothed and shod, were put at the disadvantage of marching northward, while the enemy sought the genial clime of a Southern latitude.

HOOD'S TENNESSEE CAMPAIGN.

On the 20th November, Gen. Hood commenced to move his army from Northern Alabama to Tennessee. He pushed forward as if to cut off Schofield's retreat from Pulaski ; this Federal commander having taken position there, with the greater part of two army corps, and an aggregation of fort-garrisons from the surrounding country, while Thomas remained at Nashville. Schofield fearing that his position was about to be flanked, abandoned Pulaski, and attempted by a forced march to reach Columbia.

The want of a good map of the country, and the deep mud through which the army marched, prevented Hood overtaking the enemy before he reached Columbia ; but on the evening of the 27th of November the

Confederate army was placed in position in front of his works at that place. During the night, however, the enemy evacuated the town, taking position on the opposite side of the river, about a mile and a half from the town, which was considered quite strong in front. Late in the evening of the 28th November, Gen. Forrest, with most of his command, crossed Duck River, a few miles above Columbia, and Hood followed early on the morning of the 20th, with Stewart's and Cheatham's corps, and Johnson's division of Lee's corps, leaving the other divisions of Lee's corps in the enemy's front at Columbia. The troops moved in light marching order, the object being to turn the enemy's flank by marching rapidly on roads parallel to the Columbia and Franklin pike, at or near Spring Hill, and to cut off that portion of the enemy at or near Columbia.

The enemy, discovering the intentions of the Confederates, began to retreat on the pike towards Spring Hill. About 4 P. M., Hood's infantry forces, Cheatham in the advance, commenced to come in contact with the enemy, about two miles from Spring Hill, through which place the Columbia and Franklin pike runs. The enemy was at this time moving rapidly along the pike, with some of his troops on the flank of his column to protect it. Cheatham was ordered to attack the enemy at once, vigorously, and get possession of this pike. He made only a feeble and partial attack, failing to reach the point indicated. The great object of Gen. Hood was to possess himself of the road to Franklin, and thus cut off the enemy's retreat. Though owing to delays the signal opportunity to do this had passed at daylight, there was yet a chance of dealing the enemy a heavy blow. Stewart's corps and Johnson's division were arriving upon the field to support the attack. Stewart was ordered to move his corps beyond Cheatham's, and place it across the road beyond Spring Hill. He did not succeed in getting the position he desired, owing to some misunderstanding of orders, and, night falling, he went into bivouac. About midnight, ascertaining that the enemy was moving in great confusion—artillery wagons and troops intermixed—Gen. Hood sent instructions to Cheatham to advance a heavy line of skirmishers against him, and still further impede and confuse his march. This was not accomplished. The enemy continued to move along the road in hurry and confusion, within hearing, nearly all the night. Thus was lost a great opportunity of striking the enemy, and his line of retreat secured in the face of the Confederates without a battle.

Much of the disaster that was now to ensue in his campaign Gen. Hood attributed to the fact that "some of his Generals had failed him at Spring Hill." There was nothing left now but to pursue the enemy. At daylight Hood's army followed as fast as possible towards Franklin, Stewart in the advance, Cheatham following, and Lee with the trains, moving from Columbia on the same road. The Confederates pursued the enemy rapidly, and compelled him to burn a number of his wagons. He made a feint as if to give battle on the hills about four miles south of Franklin, but as soon as Hood's forces began to deploy for the attack, and to flank him on his left, he retired slowly to Franklin. Gen. Hood had learned from despatches captured at Spring Hill, from Thomas to Schofield, that the latter was instructed to hold that place till the position at Franklin could be made secure, indicating the intention of Thomas to hold Franklin and his strong works at Murfreesboro'. Thus Hood knew that it was all-important to attack Schofield before he could make himself strong, and that if he should escape at Franklin, he would gain his works about Nashville. The nature of the position was such as to render it inexpedient to attempt any further flank movement, and he therefore determined to attack the enemy in front, and without delay.

BATTLE OF FRANKLIN.

On the 30th November Stewart's corps was placed in position on the right, Cheatham's on the left, and the cavalry on either flank, the main body on the right under Forrest. Johnson's division of Lee's corps also became engaged on the left during the action. The line advanced at 4 P. M., with orders to drive the enemy, at the point of the bayonet, into or across the Big Harpeth River, while Gen. Forrest, if successful, was to cross the river and attack and destroy his trains and broken columns. The troops moved forward most gallantly to the attack. They carried the enemy's line of hastily-constructed works handsomely. They then advanced against his interiour line, and succeeded in carrying it also, in some places. Here the engagement was of the fiercest possible character. The Confederates came on with a desperation and disregard of death, such as had been shown on few battle-fields of the war. A Northern writer says: "More heroic valour was never exhibited by any troops than was shown here by the rebels." The devoted troops were mowed down by grape and canister. Many of them were killed entirely inside of the works. The brave men captured were taken inside the enemy's works on the edge of the town. The struggle lasted till near midnight, when the enemy abandoned his works and crossed the river, leaving his dead and wounded.

It is remarkable that in this hard-fought battle the Confederates used no artillery whatever; Gen. Hood's explanation being that he was restrained from using that terrible arm "on account of the women and children remaining in the town." Victory had been purchased at the price of a terrible slaughter. Hood's total loss in killed, wounded, and prisoners was 4,500. Among the killed was Maj.-Gen. P. R. Cleburne, Brig.-Gens. John Adams, Strahl and Granbury; while Maj.-Gen. Brown, Brig.-

Gens. Carter, Manigault, Quarles, Cockrell, and Scott were wounded, and Brig.-Gen. Gordon captured.

BATTLE OF NASHVILLE.

The next morning Gen. Hood advanced upon Nashville, where Scho-field had retreated, and where Thomas lay with his main force. He laid siege to the town on the 2d December, closely investing it for a fortnight. The opinion long prevailed in the Confederacy that in this pause and the operations of siege, Hood made the cardinal mistake of his campaign; and that if he had taken another course, and struck boldly across the Cumber-land, and settled himself in the enemy's communications, he would have forced Thomas to evacuate Nashville, and fall back towards Kentucky. This was the great fear of Gen. Grant. That high Federal officer, in his report of the operations of 1864, has written: " Before the battle of Nash-ville I grew very impatient over, as it appeared to me, the unnecessary delay. This impatience was increased upon learning that the enemy had sent a force of cavalry across the Cumberland into Kentucky. I feared Hood would cross his whole army and give us great trouble here. After urging upon Gen. Thomas the necessity of immediately assuming the offen-sive, I started west to superintend matters there in person. Reaching Washington city, I received Gen. Thomas's despatch announcing his attack upon the enemy, and the result as far as the battle had progressed. I was delighted. All fears and apprehensions were dispelled."

On the night of the 14th December, Thomas decided upon a plan of battle, which was to make a feint on Hood's right flank, while he massed his main force to crush in Hood's left, which rested on the Cumberland, and where the cover of the Federal gunboats might be made available. The brunt of the action did not fall until evening, when the enemy drove in the Confederate infantry outposts on the left flank. Hood, however, quickly ordered up troops from his right to stay the reversed tide of bat-tle; and the remainder of the day was occupied by the enemy in sweeping the Confederate entrenchments with artillery fire, while here and there his infantry attempted, in vain, to find a weak spot in their lines.

Under cover of the night Hood re-formed his line, and in the morning was found in position along the Overton Hills, some two miles or so to the rear of his original line. The new position was a strong one, running along the wooded crests of closely-connecting hills; while the two keys to it were the Granny White and Franklin pikes, leading to Franklin, Columbia, Pu-laski, and so down the country to the Tennessee River. Thomas' over-whelming numbers enabled him to throw heavy columns against Hood's left and centre. But every attack of the enemy was repulsed. It was four o'clock in the evening, and the day was thought to be decided for the Confederates, when there occurred one of the most extraordinary incidents of the war. It is said that Gen. Hood was about to publish a victory along his line, when Finney's Florida brigade in Bates' division, which was to the left of the Confederate centre, gave way before the *skirmish line* of the enemy! Instantly Bates' whole division took the panic, and broke in disorder. The moment a small breach was thus made in the Confederate lines, the whole of two corps unaccountably and instantly fled from their ditches, almost without firing a gun. It was a disgraceful panic; muskets were abandoned where they rested between the logs of the breastworks; and everything that could impede flight was thrown away as the fugitives passed down the Granny White and Franklin pikes, or fled wildly from the battle-field. Such an instance of sudden, unlooked-for, wild retreat, the abandonment of a victory almost won, could only have happened in an army where thorough demoralization, the consequence of long, heavy, weary work, and of tremendous efforts without result—in short, the reaction of great endeavours where success is not decided, already lurked in the minds of troops, and was likely to be developed at any time by the slightest and most unimportant circumstance.

Fifty pieces of artillery and nearly all of Hood's ordnance wagons were left to the enemy. His loss in killed and wounded was disgracefully small; and it was only through want of vigour in Thomas' pursuit that Hood's shattered and demoralized army effected its retreat. Forrest's command, and Walthal, with seven picked brigades, covered the retreat. The situation on the Tennessee River was desperate; Hood had no pontoon train, and if he had been pressed, would have been compelled to surrender; but as it was, Thomas' great error in resting upon his victory at Nashville enabled a defeated Confederate army to construct bridges of timber over the Tennessee River, while the Federal gunboats in the stream were actually kept at bay by batteries of 32-pounders.

Hood succeeded in escaping across the Tennessee, but only with a remnant of the brilliant force he had conducted across the river a few weeks before, having lost from various causes more than ten thousand men, half of his Generals, and nearly all of his artillery. Such was the disastrous issue of the Tennessee campaign, which put out of existence, as it were, the splendid army that Johnston had given up at Atlanta, and terminated forever the whole scheme of Confederate defence west of the Alleghanies.

CHAPTER XXXVI.

CAMPAIGN OF 1864 IN THE VALLEY OF VIRGINIA.—ITS GENERAL DESIGN AS A STRATEGIC
AUXILIARY TO RICHMOND.—THE NEW COMMAND OF THE ENEMY IN THE VALLEY.—GEN.
SHERIDAN AND HIS FORCES.—VIEWS OF GEN. LEE ABOUT THE RELIEF OF RICHMOND.—HE
DETACHES A FORCE UNDER GEN. ANDERSON TO CO-OPERATE WITH EARLY, AND " STIR UP "
THE ENEMY ACROSS THE POTOMAC.—ANDERSON AND FITZHUGH LEE FIND EARLY FALL-
ING BACK AND ASKING FOR REINFORCEMENTS.—THE ENEMY DECLINES A BATTLE AND
RETREATS TO HARPER'S FERRY.—STRENGTH AND DISPOSITION OF THE CONFEDERATE
FORCES ABOUT WINCHESTER.—NEARLY A MONTH CONSUMED IN MARCHING AND COUNTER-
MARCHING.—GEN. LEE ORDERS THE RETURN OF GEN. ANDERSON WITH KERSHAW'S DIVI-
SION.—BATTLE OF WINCHESTER.—GEN. GRANT ADVISES SHERIDAN TO " GO IN."—EARLY'S
SMALL FORCE.—HOW IT CAME TO BE SCATTERED OVER TWENTY-TWO MILES.—RAMSEUR'S
DIVISION SUSTAINS THE ATTACK UNTIL THE OTHER CONFEDERATE FORCES COME UP.—
GORDON DRIVES THE ENEMY.—HAPPY STROKE OF A CONFEDERATE BATTERY.—THE ENE-
MY'S INFANTRY ROUTED.—HIS CAVALRY GET ON THE CONFEDERATE LEFT AND REAR AND
CHANGE THE DAY.—RETREAT OF THE CONFEDERATES.—BATTLE OF FISHER'S HILL.—HOW
GEN. EARLY'S POSITION WAS DEFECTIVE HERE.—HE IS FLANKED ON THE LEFT, AND RE-
TREATS UP THE VALLEY.—THE ENEMY PURSUES TO STAUNTON.—SHERIDAN'S BARBAROUS
ORDER TO DEVASTATE THE VALLEY.—HE BURNS " TWO THOUSAND BARNS."—REFLECTIONS
UPON THIS OUTRAGE.—BATTLE OF CEDAR CREEK.—EARLY, REINFORCED, RESUMES THE
CAMPAIGN, AND DETERMINES TO MAKE A SURPRISE.—A FLANKING COLUMN OF CONFED-
ERATES CROSSES THE NORTH FORK OF THE SHENANDOAH.—TWO CORPS OF THE ENEMY
BROKEN AND PUT TO ROUT.—THE ENEMY PURSUED THROUGH MIDDLETOWN.—HOW THE
VIGOUR OF PURSUIT WAS LOST.—THE FOOLISH NEWSPAPER STORY ABOUT GEN. SHERIDAN'S
SUDDEN APPEARANCE ON THE FIELD.—THE CONFEDERATES DEMORALIZED BY PILLAGE.—
THE ENEMY MAKES A COUNTER-CHARGE, AND SWEEPS EVERYTHING BEFORE HIM.—GEN.
EARLY'S ATTEMPT TO PUT THE CENSURE OF THE DISASTER UPON HIS MEN.—HOW FAR HE
WAS RESPONSIBLE FOR IT.—TRUE EXPLANATION OF THE PAUSE IN HIS VICTORY.—REMOVAL
OF GEN. EARLY FROM COMMAND.—GEN. LEE'S GENEROUS LETTER TO HIM.—HOW THE
NEWSPAPERS BERATED HIM.—THE CHARGE OF HABITUAL INTOXICATION.—REVIEW OF THE
VALLEY CAMPAIGN.—ITS EFFECT DECISIVE UPON RICHMOND.—REMARK OF A CONFEDERATE
GENERAL.—SOME VIEWS OF THE MANAGEMENT AND DISPOSITION OF THE CONFEDERATE
CAVALRY FORCES IN VIRGINIA.

To Hood's unbroken series of disasters there was a companion-piece in
another part of the Confederacy : a small theatre of the war, but an important and a conspicuous one, associated with many heroic memories of

the Confederacy. This other chapter of misfortune was Early's campaign in the Valley of Virginia. In this campaign a Confederate General never won a victory; lost all of his artillery, and brought an army to practical annihilation. But, although like Hood's misadventure in these particulars, the campaign in the Valley is to be judged by another standard; while marked by some undoubted misconduct, it had much to excuse its impotent conclusion, and it was, in some respects, what its commander designated it—" a forlorn hope."

We have already pointed out the first object of Early's operations in the Valley as substantially the same which took Stonewall Jackson there in 1862—the diversion of a portion of the Federal forces from the great arena of combat in the lowlands. It was also important to save, as far as possible, the harvests of the Shenandoah and to protect the Gordonsville road; but the campaign was mainly a strategic auxiliary to the operations around Petersburg and Richmond.

In consequence of the threatening attitude of Early, who since he had moved across the Potomac, had been able to send a raiding party into Pennsylvania, which on the 30th July burned Chambersburg, Gen. Grant had been unable to return the Sixth and Nineteenth corps to the Army of the Potomac. On the contrary, he saw the necessity of an enlarged campaign to protect the frontiers of Maryland and Pennsylvania. What was called the Middle Department, and the Departments of West Virginia, Washington, and Susquehanna, were constituted into one under the command of Gen. Sheridan. The new commander was a man of a coarse, active nature, excessive animal spirits, and an intensely combative temperament—an antagonist not to be despised, although he had shown no distinct military genius, and was only remarkable in the war for the execution of single tasks indicated to him by his superiours. He had an amount of force which was all he could have asked for as a condition of success. In addition to the column of active operation under his command, consisting of the Sixth and Nineteenth corps, and the infantry and cavalry of West Virginia under Crook and Averill, there were assigned to him two divisions of cavalry from the Army of the Potomac under Torbert and Wilson. His effective infantry strength was about thirty-five thousand muskets; and his great superiority in cavalry was very advantageous to him, as the country was very open and admirably adapted to the operations of this arm.

Gen. Lee had long been persuaded that he was too weak to attack the enemy's works in his front at Petersburg. Information derived from trusty scouts and from reconnoissances pushed to the rear of the enemy's flanks, proved the impracticability of turning them. The only resource was strategy, and that obviously the renewal of the Valley campaign, to develop, if possible, a crisis in the situation about Petersburg and Richmond.

On the 4th August, 1864, an order was issued from the headquarters of Lee's army, dircting the march of Kershaw's division of Longstreet's corps, and Fitzhugh Lee's division of cavalry to Culpepper Court-house. Lieut.-Gen. R. H. Anderson was then commanding the troops of Gen. Longstreet (the latter being still incapacitated from duty by the wound received in the battles of the Wilderness), and was assigned to command the expedition. The force ordered for it was withdrawn from Grant's front on the south side of the James; Fitzhugh Lee's division being on the Confederate right in the vicinity of Ream's Station on the Weldon Railroad.

Gen. Lee's intentions, as explained to his officers, were to send the troops of Kershaw and Fitzhugh Lee to co-operate with Early in movements on the Maryland border, or even in the State itself. He wanted the enemy in Washington and vicinity " stirred up," as much as possible, and the impression produced that our force was a large one. Upon reaching Culpepper Court-House, Fitzhugh Lee was to go down towards Alexandria and make a demonstration in that vicinity, and if his information as to the disposition of the enemy's forces and strength warranted, Anderson and he were to cross the Potomac about Leesburg, Early crossing higher up, and all to act in concert against Washington or produce that impression. Gen. Anderson was sent on the expedition, though only one division of his corps was detached, because the enemy knew he commanded in Longstreet's place, and the idea might be taken that the whole corps was *en route*. It was possible, then, that Grant might send a corresponding force to counteract the movement, in which case the remainder of the corps could be sent, and the demonstration continued on a larger scale. In brief, Gen. Lee explained that he was going to try to manœuvre Grant from the front of Richmond. The other alternative which presented itself was that under the supposition that Lee had weakened himself by a whole corps, Grant might be induced to attack, which Gen. Lee conceived to be at that time a very desirable object.

No sooner had Anderson's and Fitzhugh Lee's troops reached Culpepper Court-House, than a despatch was received from Early, stating that, in consequence of the concentration of a large force in his front, whilst in the lower part of the Valley, he had been compelled to fall back to the strong position at Fisher's Hill, and asking for reinforcements. This necessitated the movement of Anderson and Lee at once to his support; and their march was at once directed to Front Royal, by the way of Chester Gap in the Blue Ridge. They arrived at Front Royal on the 15th August. Early was ascertained to be at Strasburg, some ten miles distant. The road connecting the two places and running to the base of the Massanutton or Fort Mountain, was in possession of the enemy, who was also in large force in Early's front.

Under orders from Gen. Anderson, Fitzhugh Lee started at daybreak on the morning of the 16th to communicate with Gen. Early and arrange a combined attack upon the enemy. The direct road being in possession of the enemy, he was obliged to cross the Massanutton Mountain, consisting at that point of three separate ranges in close proximity to each other, very precipitous and rough. He was accompanied by only one staff officer, and they were obliged to ride mules, so steep was the ascent. He arrived at Gen. Early's head-quarters that afternoon, arranged many details, and riding all night, was back with Gen. Anderson by daylight on the 17th. But the enemy had already commenced to retreat, and the opportunity for striking a blow was lost. He had discovered Gen. Anderson's position at Front Royal during the morning of the 16th, and had taken possession with a cavalry force of "Guard Hill," a commanding position on the north bank of the north fork of the Shenandoah River, opposite the town. Gen. Anderson, fearing that the force occupying it would be increased, and the position fortified, attacked the enemy during the afternoon of the 16th with Wickham's brigade of Lee's division, supported by Wofford's infantry brigade. After quite a spirited contest, the possession of the hill was secured by the Confederates. Early in the morning of the 17th, Anderson and Lee commenced their advance, and followed up the enemy's retreat. At Winchester they united with Gen. Early's column, driving the Federal troops through the town, capturing one piece of artillery and some prisoners. The pursuit was continued the next day, and the enemy driven to his stronghold at Harper's Ferry.

The Confederate force now consisted of the infantry divisions of Rodes, Ramseur, Gordon and Warton, and Lomax's division of Valley cavalry under Early and Breckinridge, and, under Anderson, Kershaw's division of infantry, and Fitzhugh Lee's division of cavalry. It happened that Anderson and Early had been both made lieutenant-generals the same day, though the former was the ranking officer in consequence of being the senior major-general. Their last commissions being of same date, and Anderson being in Early's department, he did not like to assume command of the whole force. Early being his junior, could not command it, and a very anomalous state of things resulted, producing much confusion and want of co-operation.

Instead of a campaign being inaugurated, which, from its offensive character and operations would compel more troops to be drawn from Grant's army to counteract it, and which was contemplated by Gen. Lee, nothing was done. Nearly a month elapsed in marching and counter-marching in the vicinity of Charlestown, productive of no results. Gen. Lee, perceiving at last that nothing was likely to be accomplished, directed Anderson, unless something of importance was in contemplation, to move back with Kershaw's division to Culpepper Court-House, where he would be in a position to be transported to him in case he decided to carry out a movement against the enemy in front of Petersburg, then under consideration.

Accordingly, on the 15th September Anderson moved off with Kershaw's division *en route* to Culpepper. Early was then in the vicinity of Winchester, having moved back for convenience of supplies, after the enemy had been driven to the river. Sheridan was between Charlestown and Berryville, with his advance covering the latter place. The cavalry pickets of the two armies were only a few miles apart.

BATTLE OF WINCHESTER.

The month of August and the fore part of September had been consumed in desultory and apparently uncertain operations. Notwithstanding his great superiority in force, the enemy appeared to be unwilling to risk a general engagement, the result of which might be to lay open to the Confederates the States of Maryland and Pennsylvania, before another army could be interposed to check them. But this excessive caution gradually wore off; the aggressive temper of Sheridan asserted itself against Grant's timidity; and the latter commander has since declared in an official paper, rather inelegantly, and with that taste for slang which seems to charactertize the military literature of the North: " Gen. Sheridan expressed such confidence of success, that I saw there were but two words of instruction necessary—' *Go in.*' "

But there appear to have been especial reasons for Sheridan's confidence. The effective strength of Gen. Early, reduced by the return of Kershaw's division to the Petersburg lines, was about eighty-five hundred muskets, three battalions of artillery and less than three thousand cavalry. The latter were mostly armed with Enfield rifles, without pistols or sabres, and were but a poor match for the brilliant cavalry of the enemy, whose arms and equipments were complete.

The day after Kershaw's departure, Early disposed his army as follows: Ramseur's division of infantry (a very small one, some fifteen hundred muskets), Lee's division of cavalry, under Wickham (Gen. Fitzhugh Lee having been placed in command of all the cavalry), were at Winchester. Wharton's division of infantry (a small one) and Lomax's cavalry were about Stephenson's Depot, some five miles from Winchester on the railroad. Rodes' and Gordon's divisions, in charge of Gen. Early himself, were marched to Martinsburg, for the purpose of breaking up again the Baltimore and Ohio Railroad, reported to have been repaired since the Confederates had last visited it. Martinsburg is about twenty-two miles from Winchester. From the situation of the two armies it will be seen that Sheridan, besides being in position almost on Early's flank, was, by the way of White Post, nearer the Valley turnpike, Early's line of communication, than a greater portion of the Confederate troops, with the advantage of coming out in rear of Early's right at Winchester. Sheridan saw the opportunity offered : Kershaw, with his large division gone, and the remaining troops stretched out for twenty-two miles. He decided, of course, to attack, and commenced moving up with the intention of seizing and occupying Winchester before Early could retrace his steps. On the afternoon and night of the 18th he began his movement from Berryville, eleven miles from Winchester.

Gen. Early left Martinsburg, though in ignorance of the enemy's movement, on the morning of the 18th, and encamped Gordon and Rodes' divisions that night in the vicinity of Bunker's Hill, some twelve miles from Winchester.

By daylight on the 19th the Confederate pickets had been driven in, and the enemy's cannon were thundering at Ramseur's little band, drawn up beyond the town of Winchester. Lee's cavalry division was soon in position on Ramseur's left, and the battle began. Never did men fight better, for they sustained the repeated and furious assaults of an enemy immensely their superiour, and alone maintained the contest until eleven o'clock in the morning, when the advance of Rodes' division made its appearance. Rodes' troops were hastily thrown into action, and their commander soon after killed. Gordon arrived next, and went in on our extreme left. Wharton, in command of Breckinridge's old division, arrived last, though nearer to Winchester than the other two. It had been holding in check two divisions of the enemy's cavalry under Torbert at Stephenson's depot, which had been sent around towards that place for the purpose of retarding the march of the troops hastening to the relief of Winchester.

A portion of Lomax's division arrived with Breckenridge, the remainder having previously come up ; and with the greater part of Lee's division of cavalry were transferred to the extreme right and placed opposite Wilson's cavalry to prevent it from swinging around and getting possession of the turnpike in rear of Winchester.

Gordon, previous to Breckenridge's arrival, had driven the enemy by a most gallant charge in line of battle, but going too far, had been driven back in turn. A battery of six guns, supported by a brigade of cavalry, had been placed on Gordon's extreme left. It allowed the enemy's advancing lines to pass it, their right almost brushing it, so close did it march to its position. The battery was concealed under the edge of a hill. Hardly had the Federal lines got beyond it than its intrepid, adventurous commander, Major Breathed,* ordered the guns to be placed in battery

* Of this officer, whose reputation for daring was known throughout the armies of Virginia, and of whom Gen. Fitzhugh Lee says, " he was the most recklessly brave man I ever knew," there is

upon the crest of the hill. In a few minutes, a most destructive and unexpected fire was poured into the enemy's ranks. It was something more than an enfilading fire. The Federal line of battle was soon broken by it. Gordon seized the opportunity, turned, and charged; and the retreat of the enemy soon degenerated into a rout. There appeared now but little doubt that the day was for the Confederates.

But at this time the enemy's reserve infantry, the greater part of Crook's Corps (the Eighth), made its appearance, prolonging their extreme right. Gordon's successful advance was stopped, for fear his flank was endangered. Breckinridge's troops, coming up at this time, were placed in opposition to Crook, and on Gordon's left; but his flank was very much overlapped by the superiour numbers of Crook.

The movement which placed Breckinridge in line of battle to confront Crook, freed the enemy's two cavalry divisions, Merritt's and Averill's, under Torbert. Their line was formed on Crook's right, in the shape of a semi-circle, and completely environed the Confederate left and rear. Every man on the Confederate side was closely engaged. A few hundred cavalry, and a small regiment of infantry, under Col. Patton, withdrawn from fighting in Crook's front, stayed for a little time the heavy movement of the enemy's cavalry. But it was impossible to hold it in check. The country was open; every movement of the enemy was discernible on the Confederate left; and yet there were no troops available to counteract what

an authentic incident, related by his commander, connected with Lee's early battles on the Rapidan.

Of this incident Fitzhugh Lee writes: " Maj. Jas. Breathed, commanding my horse artillery, by my order placed a single gun in position on a little knoll, as we were falling back, disputing the enemy's advance towards Spottsylvania Court-house. We knew the enemy's infantry were marching in column through a piece of woods, and the object was to fire upon the head of the column, as it debouched, to give the idea that their further advance would again be contested, and to compel them to develop a line of battle with skirmishers thrown out, &c. The delay which it was hoped to occasion by such demonstration was desirable in order to increase the chances of our infantry, then marching by another and parallel route to the Court-house. Under Maj. B's personal superintendence, shells were thrown, and burst exactly in the head of the column as it debouched. The desired effect was obtained; the head of the enemy's advance was scattered, and it was only with some difficulty a line of battle with skirmishers in its front was formed to continue the advance. I was sitting on my horse near Breathed, and directed him to withdraw his gun, but he was so much elated with his success that he begged to be allowed to give the enemy some more rounds. He fired until their line got so close that you could hear them calling out, " Surrender that gun, you rebel son of a b—h." Breathed's own horse had just been shot. The cannoneers jumped on their horses, expecting of course the gun to be captured, and retreated rapidly down the hill. B. was left alone. He limbered the gun up, and jumped on the lead horse. It was shot from under him. Quick as lightning he drew his knife, cut the leaders out of the harness, and sprang upon a swing horse. It was also shot from under him just as he was turning to get into the road. He then severed the harness of the swing horse, jumped upon one of the wheel horses, and again made the desperate trial for life. The ground was open between the piece and woods; the enemy had a full view of the exploit; and Breathed at last dashed off unharmed, almost miraculously escaping through a shower of bullets."

was now the decisive movement of the enemy's cavalry. The Confederate left was completely turned; the enemy was let in on the rear of the remainder of the line; and the Confederate infantry, which had so long withstood fourfold odds, now pressed heavily in front by the enemy's infantry, and on the right by his cavalry, was compelled to give way under the combined assault, and at last broke in confusion, retiring from the field and through Winchester, with the enemy in pursuit.

In this battle Gen. Early lost twenty-five hundred prisoners and five pieces of artillery. But in this battle there had been a surpassing display of courage in the men who had held their ground so long against the swarming forces of the enemy. It is quite certain that up to the moment when he put his cavalry in motion against the Confederate left, Sheridan had been virtually defeated. Not until the enemy's cavalry advanced on the Martinsburg road, attained the Confederate rear, and charged them in flank and rear, was there the least wavering. It is true that from that moment the action was lost. Early's line gave way in confusion; his artillery was fought to the muzzle of the guns, but could do nothing, and that night the Confederate forces were in full retreat up the Valley.

BATTLE OF FISHER'S HILL.

Gen. Early retired to Fisher's Hill, near Strasburg, a position overlooking the north branch of the Shenandoah River, and protected on the west by the North Mountain. This position has been described as a very defensible one, indeed the strongest in the Valley of Virginia. But a Confederate officer, who has ably reviewed the campaign, remarks: "When Early took up a position on the great range of hills above Strasburg, and waited to be attacked, he committed an error under the circumstances, which the General himself, at this day, would probably acknowledge. The ground there is unsuitable to receive an attack upon, unless the force standing on the defensive is strong enough to reach from mountain to mountain. Gen. Jackson is said to have expressed this opinion, and it is certain that he never made a stand there. Gen. Early did so, and was flanked on the left."

On the 22d October, Sheridan formed his force for a direct attack on Early's position, while Torbert's cavalry moved by the Luray Valley to gain Newmarket, twenty miles in Early's rear, to cut off his retreat. While making a feint of an attack in front, a corps of infantry was sent around to Early's left, resting on the North Mountain, flanked it, attacked it in rear, and drove it from its entrenchments. The whole Confederate line was easily disrupted, and Early retired in great disorder, losing eleven pieces of artillery. Happily his line of retreat was secured, as Torbert had been held in check at Milford by a small division of Confederate cavalry under Gen. Wickham.

The retreat was continued to the lower passes of the Blue Ridge. Gen. Early had lost half his army, and it was supposed that his career was now at an end. Sheridan pushed the pursuit to Staunton and the gaps of the Blue Ridge; but, before returning to Strasburg, and taking position on the north side of Cedar Creek, this Federal commander resolved upon an act of barbarism, competing with the worst reputations of the war. He determined to devastate the upper portion of the Valley as he abandoned it. This ruthless measure was not confined to the destruction of the crops, provisions, and forage; mills were burned, farming implements were destroyed, and a wanton vengeance was inflicted upon the country for many years to come. Gen. Sheridan wrote from Strasburg, as if he were commemorating a great deed, instead of writing down a record of imperishable infamy : " In moving back to this point, the whole country, from the Blue Ridge to the North Mountain, has been made entirely untenable for a rebel army. I have destroyed over two thousand barns filled with wheat and hay and farming implements; over seventy mills filled with flour and wheat; have driven in front of the army over four thousand head of stock, and have killed and issued to the troops not less than three thousand sheep This destruction embraces the Luray Valley and the Little Fort Valley, as well as the main valley."

Of this and other like atrocities of the enemy, there has been attempted a very weak excuse, to the effect that if the private property of the inhabitants of the Confederacy had not been destroyed, it might have been converted to the uses of the belligerent Government, and have helped to sustain it. Once for all, it may be said that this excuse excludes every sentiment of humanity in war, and may be logically carried to the last extremities of savage warfare. Some time ago a great indignation was awakened in Northern newspapers, when a Northern officer justified his putting to death some children belonging to a hostile Indian tribe on the ground that, if they had not been killed, they would have grown up to be men and chiefs, to fight the armies of the United States. But the logic of this was unimpeachable, quite as sound as that which justified the outrages of private property and deeds of devastation and horrour, committed by such men as Sheridan and Sherman. There are some things, even in war, which are to be done, or to be left undone, without regard to consequences. Modern war is not based upon logic; it is not merely a question of how much ruin may be done; it is not simple " cruelty," as Sherman defined it to the mayor of Atlanta; it recognizes certain claims of humanity and indicates a class of outrages for which no selfish reason is commensurate A writer of authority, treating of the law of nations, says : " When the French armies desolated, with fire and sword, the Palatinate in 1674, and again in 1689, there was a general outcry throughout Europe against such a mode of carrying on war ; and when the French minister Louvois alleged that the object in view was to cover the French frontier against the invasion of the enemy, the advantage which France derived from the act was universally held to be inadequate to the suffering inflicted, and the act itself to be therefore unjustifiable."

BATTLE OF CEDAR CREEK.

Having received reinforcements, Gen. Early returned to the Valley in October. These reinforcements consisted of one division of infantry (Kershaw's), numbering twenty-seven hundred muskets, one small battalion of artillery, and about six hundred cavalry, which about made up the Confederate losses at Winchester and Fisher's Hill. On the 9th October, Rosser's cavalry, which had hung on Sheridan's rear, was attacked on the Strasburg pike, while a division of cavalry, moving by a back road, took him in flank. In this affair the enemy took eleven pieces of artillery and several hundred prisoners. On the 18th October, Early was again at Cedar Creek, between Strasburg and Winchester. He had less than ten thousand men, and about forty pieces of artillery. His force was inadequate for open attack, and his only opportunity was to make a surprise. The enemy was posted on a line of low hills, the Eighth corps on the left, the Nineteenth corps in the centre, and the Sixth corps on the right, somewhat in rear and in reserve. Early's dispositions for attack were to make a feint with light artillery and cavalry against the enemy's right, while the bulk of his forces marched towards the left where the Sixth corps was posted.

The movement commenced a little past midnight. Whilst demonstrations were made against the Federal right, whence the sounds of musketry already announced a fight on the picket line, the flanking columns of the Confederates toiled along seven miles of rugged country, crossing the north fork of the Shenandoah by a ford about a mile to the east of the junction of Cedar Creek with that stream. The march was performed in profound silence. Many places had to be traversed by the men in single file, who occasionally had to cling to bushes on the precipitous sides of the mountain to assist their foothold. At dawn the flanking column was across the ford : Gordon's division in front, next Ramseur's, and Pegram's in reserve. A heavy fog yet favoured them. The enemy's pickets had not yet taken the alarm ; some of them had reported that they heard a heavy, muffled tramp and rustling through the underbrush, but no attention was paid to a supposed fancy, and no reconnoissance was sent out. Early had brought his column, unperceived. to the rear of the left flank of the Federal force ; and it remained now but to close in upon the enemy, and fight rapidly.

The surprise was complete. The Eighth corps was unable to form a line of battle, and in five minutes was a herd of fugitives. Many of the men awoke only to find themselves prisoners. The Nineteenth corps was soon involved in the rout. The valorous Confederates pressed on, driving the whole Federal left and centre, slaying many of the enemy in their camps, capturing eighteen pieces of artillery, fifteen hundred prisoners, small arms without number, wagons, camps, everything on the ground.

The retreat of the enemy was now a general one, the Sixth corps doing what it could to cover it. At Middletown an attempt was made to form a line of battle ; but the Confederates threatened a flank movement, got possession of the town, and put the enemy on what was supposed to be his final retreat to Winchester.

The vigour of the pursuit was lost here. The fire and flush of the valorous charge was quenched, as the men now betook themselves to plundering the Federal camps, taking no notice of the enemy in the distance beyond some skirmishing and desultory artillery fire. But the enemy had no idea of continuing his retreat to Winchester. At the first good ground between Middletown and Newtown the troops were rallied, a compact line formed, and the enemy soon put in a condition to resist further attack or take the offensive.

The Northern newspapers, with their relish for dramatic circumstance, had a singular story of how the sudden apparition of Gen. Sheridan on a black horse flecked with foam, which he had galloped from Winchester, where he had slept the previous night, reassured his fugitive army, and restored the battle. But the fact is that Sheridan did not appear on the field until the army had reorganized a new line of battle and made its dispositions for attack, which he did not change in any respect. The counter-charge was made at three o'clock in the afternoon. The Confederates were not prepared for it ; they had been demoralized by pillage ; when urged forward they had moved without enthusiasm ; and when in the afternoon Gen. Early decided to attempt an advance, he was compelled to move cautiously, feeling his way with artillery.

At the first contact with the enemy, Gordon's division broke ; Kershaw's and Ramseur's followed in retreat, and the field became covered with flying men. The artillery retired, firing slowly, and sustained only by Pegram's old brigade and Evan's brigade. Across Cedar Creek the enemy's cavalry charged in rear of the Confederate train without provoking a shot ; and a bridge on a narrow part of the road between the creek and Fisher's Hill having broken down, guns and wagons were abandoned. Many ordnance and medical stores, and twenty-three pieces of artillery, besides those taken in the morning by Early, were captured. About fif

teen hundred prisoners were taken, which fully made up for those
lost by the enemy in the morning.   The day was completely turned
against the Confederates and night closed with the enemy's infantry
occupying their old camps, and his cavalry pursuing the wreck of Early's
army.

With reference to the disaster of Cedar Creek, Gen. Early published an
address to his troops, ascribing to their misconduct the loss of the field,
and attemping to break the censure levelled at the commander.   He
wrote : " I had hoped to have congratulated you on the splendid victory
won by you on the morning of the 19th, at Belle Grove, on Cedar Creek,
when you surprised and routed two corps of Sheridan's army, and drove
back several miles the remaining corps, capturing eighteen pieces of artillery, one thousand five hundred prisoners, a number of colours, a large
quantity of small arms and many wagons and ambulances, with the entire
camps of the two routed corps ; but I have the mortification of announcing to you that, by your subsequent misconduct, all the benefits of that
victory were lost, and a serious disaster incurred.   Had you remained
steadfast to your duty and your colours, the victory would have been one
of the most brilliant and decisive of the war ; you would have gloriously
retrieved the reverses at Winchester and Fisher's Hill, and entitled yourselves to the admiration and gratitude of your country.   But many of you,
including some commissioned officers, yielding to a disgraceful propensity
for plunder, deserted your colours to appropriate to yourselves the abandoned property of the enemy ; and, subsequently, those who had previously remained at their posts, seeing their ranks thinned by the absence
of the plunderers, when the enemy, late in the afternoon, with his shattered columns made but a feeble effort to retrieve the fortunes of the day,
yielded to a needless panic, and fled the field in confusion, thereby converting a splendid victory into a disaster."

But this explanation of the conversion of a victory into a disaster, as a
personal defence of Gen. Early, is scarcely fair.   If soldiers resort to pillag-
ing on a field of victory the commander is the responsible party, unless
where it is shown that he resorted to the most extreme measures to restrain
a disorder so shameful and plainly deserving death on the spot, and that,
despite all efforts, the men had passed completely beyond his control.
The broad fact cannot be concealed that for four or five hours Gen. Early
was in the condition of a commander who had lost the vigour of pursuit
and was satisfied to put up with a half-way success.   This disposition to
pause in battle and be satisfied with a half victory was not the peculiar
story of Cedar Creek.   It was the curse of more than one Confederate
commander.   As Gen. Early counted his victory and paused in his career,
the refluent wave of the enemy overtook him, swept away his laurels, and
overwhelmed him with an unexpected disaster.   The story is not different

from that of other Confederate battle-fields where a mediocre commander has trifled with success.

Gen. Early had received a stunning defeat from which his army never recovered. The battle of Cedar Creek practically closed the campaign in the Valley, and most of Early's infantry were returned to Gen. Lee's lines. Breckinridge was detached and sent to command in the South-western Department. The three divisions (composing what was known as the Second Army Corps) formerly commanded by Rodes, Gordon, and Ramseur, were placed under the command of Gordon, the sole survivor of the three, and sent back to Gen. Lee. Nearly the whole of the cavalry were temporarily furloughed, the Government being unable to supply them with forage. Early was left with his headquarters at Staunton, and what remained of Wharton's division constituted the Army of the Valley.

The unfortunate commander continued for some time to move uneasily up and down the Valley, with his small force ; but all operations of moment had plainly ceased there ; there was not forage enough for any considerable body of cavalry ; and some weeks later we shall see the last appearance of Gen. Early on the military stage, at Waynesboro' ,where his command, consisting of about a thousand infantry, was captured, and the General with two staff officers escaped to Charlottesville, the melancholy remnant of an enterprise that had been planned to relieve Richmond and turn the scales of the war.

In consequence of the disastrous campaign we have narrated, but not until a very late period of the war, Gen. Early was removed from com-mand. Gen Lee wrote to his subordinate with characteristic generosity :

HEAD-QUARTERS C. S. ARMIES, *March 30,* 1865.

Lieut.-Gen. J. A. Early, Franklin C. H., Va. :

DEAR SIR: My telegram will have informed you that I deem a change of commanders in your department necessary, but it is due to your zealous and patriotic services that I should explain the reasons that prompted my action. The situation of affairs is such that we can neglect no means calculated to develop the resources we possess to the greatest extent, and make them as efficient as possible. To this end it is essential that we should have the cheerful and hearty support of the people and the full confidence of the soldiers, without which our efforts would be embarrassed, and our means of resis-tance weakened. I have reluctantly arrived at the conclusion that you cannot command the united and willing co-operation which is so essential to success. Your reverses in the Valley, of which the public and the army judge chiefly by the results, have, I fear, impaired your influence both with the people and the soldiers, and would add greatly to the difficulties which will, under any circumstances, attend our military operations in Southwestern Virginia. While my own confidence in your ability, zeal, and devotion to the cause is unimpaired, I have nevertheless felt that I could not oppose what seems to be the current of opinion without injustice to your reputation and injury to the service. I therefore felt constrained to endeavour to find a commander who would be more likely to develop the strength and resources of the country, and inspire the soldiers with confi-dence, and, to accomplish this purpose, thought it proper to yield my own opinion, and defer to that of those to whom alone we can look for support. I am sure that you will understand and appreciate my motives, and that no one will be more ready than yourself to acquiesce in any measures which the interests of the country may seem to require, regardless of all personal considerations. Thanking you for the fidelity and energy with which you have always supported my efforts, and for the courage and devotion you have ever manifested in the service of the country, I am, very respectfully and truly, your obedient servant,

R. E. LEE, *General.*

Censure in the newspapers ran high against Gen. Early; but it must be remembered that this was at a time when the temper of the Southern people was irritable and exacting, impatient to be refreshed with what was now the rare experience of a victory. Gen. Early was not a popular man; but he had had the reputation throughout the war of a hard, resolute fighter; and Gen. Lee's familiar designation of him as "his bad old man" suited the picture of a commander who garnished his speech with oaths, dressed in the careless, burly fashion of a stage-driver, and was famous for his hard, direct knocks in battle.* It was hinted in the newspapers that

---

* The following sketch of Gen. Early is from a graphic pen, and its fund of anecdote is amusing and characteristic:—

"He was a man past middle age, and of vigorous and athletic appearance. His stature approached if it did not reach six feet, and he seemed to be capable of undergoing great fatigue. His hair was black and curling, and just touched with gray; his eyes, dark and sparkling; his smile, ready and expressive, but somewhat sarcastic, as was the bent of his character. His dress was plain gray, with slight decoration. Long exposure had made the old coat which he wore quite dingy. A wide-brim hat overshadowed his sparkling eyes, his swarthy features, and grizzled hair. His face, set upon a short neck, joined to stooping shoulders, attracted attention from every one. In the dark eye you could read the resolute character of the man, as in his satirical smile you saw the evidence of that dry, trenchant, often mordant humour, for which he was famous. The keen glance drove home the sarcastic speech, and almost every one who ventured upon word combats with Lieut.-General Early sustained a 'palpable hit.' The soldiers of his army had a hundred jests and witticisms about him. They called him 'Old Jube,' sometimes 'Old Jubilee.' They delighted to relate how, after the defeat of Fisher's Hill, when the troops were in full retreat, their commander had checked his horse, raised his arms aloft, and exclaimed, 'My God! won't any of my men make a rally around Old Jubal?' To which a philosophic foot-soldier, calmly seeking the rear, replied: 'Nary rally, General.' A similar anecdote, which may or may not be true, is even yet immensely relished by Early's old soldiers. He is said to have exclaimed, when he heard of Lee's retreat, 'Now let Gabriel blow his horn. It is time to die.' Everything about the soldier was characteristic and marked. Speaking slowly and with a species of drawl in his voice, all that he said was pointed, direct and full of sarcastic force. These 'hits' he evidently enjoyed, and he delivered them with the coolness of a swordsman making a mortal lunge. All the army had laughed at one of them. While marching at the head of his column, dusty in his dingy, gray uniform, and with his faded old hat over his eyes, he had seen leaning over a fence and looking at the column as it passed, a former associate in the Virginia Convention, who had violently advocated secession. This gentleman was clad in citizens' clothes—black coat and irreproachable shirt bosom—and greeted Early as he passed. The reply of the General was given with his habitual smile and sarcastic drawl: 'How are you?' he said. 'I think you said the Whigs wouldn't fight!' The blow was rude, and made the whole army laugh. Of this peculiar humour a better instance still is given. After Fisher's Hill, when his whole army was in complete retreat, and the Federal forces were press-

much of Early's disaster in the Valley was due to his alleged intemperance, and that there had been too much " apple-jack " in the campaign But the charge of habitual intemperance was examined by a committee of the Confederate Congress, and disproved. It was not established indeed that Gen. Early was a believer in total abstinence—or as one of his Irish friends remarks, that the man was always " *beastly* sober "—but it was conclusively shown that in the line of his duty he was never under the influence of drink, and to no such imprudence could be attributed any misfortune of his military life.

The real character of Gen. Early's campaign appears in the narrative. Much of his disaster is to be fairly attributed to lack of numbers, his great disproportion to the enemy in this respect; but at the same time it is not to be denied that his loss of artillery was excessive and peculiar, and that in the field at Cedar Creek he had not shown the nerve and grasp of a great commander. His loss of artillery was so notorious, that wags in Richmond ticketed guns sent him " to Gen. Sheridan, care of Jubal Early." In a month he lost more than fifty guns. Briefly, it may be said that in the operations in the Valley Gen. Early committed no flagrant error, and did nothing to draw upon him a distinct and severe censure; yet, at the same time, he certainly did not display in this campaign the qualities of a great commander, never rose above mediocrity, and, with a superiour army upon him, went headlong to destruction.

The effect of the Valley campaign on the situation around Richmond may be almost said to have been decisive. The result of it, in this respect, was this : that it released a powerful force and made it available for Grant, while Gen. Lee could only make use of, as a corresponding force, the small remnant of a dispirited army. One of the highest and most intelligent Confederate Generals has not hesitated to express the opinion that " the battle of Winchester was the turning-point of the fortunes of the war in Virginia." The view is not unreasonable when we consider what was the object of Early's campaign. A battle fought in the Valley with decisive results might have relieved Richmond. Such was the idea of Gen. Lee. Battles were fought, but with decisive results for the enemy ; and Richmond fell.

ing him close, he was riding with Gen. Breckinridge. It might have been supposed that their conversation would relate to the disastrous events of the day, but Gen. Early did not seem to trouble himself upon that subject. In full retreat as they were, and followed by an enraged enemy, his companion was astounded to hear from Early the cool and nonchalant question : 'Well, Breckinridge, what do you think of the decision of the Supreme Court in the Dred Scott case, in its bearings upon the rights of the South in the Territories ? ' The man who could amuse himself with political discussions between Fisher's Hill and Woodstock on the 22d of September, 1864, must have been of hard stuff or peculiar humour. There were many persons in and out of the army who doubted the soundness of his judgment—there were none who ever called in question the tough fibre of his courage."

A general opinion prevalent at Richmond, and apparently strengthened by the experiences of the Valley campaign, was that the Confederate cavalry in Virginia had become very inefficient and unequal to its early reputation. The report is one of singular injustice, in view of the brilliant record of the cavalry for 1864, especially that part of it under the command of Gen. Fitzhugh Lee, the compeer and successor of Stuart, a model of chivalry and a leader whose star ascended to the highest realms of glory in the war. We have elsewhere referred generally to the operations of the cavalry in Grant's early combination against Richmond. It is a fact based upon official testimony, that Fitzhugh Lee's command fought nine consecutive days, commencing the day Grant crossed the Rapidan, and in that time lost one-half of its numbers in killed and wounded, its loss in prisoners in the same time being not more than thirty! His command was composed of Virginians, save one gallant company from Maryland. The simple inscription of the fact we have related is an undying title of glory for the cavalry of Virginia, testifying as it does to a courage and devotion, the parallels of which are scarcely to be found out of the pages of fabulous history.

It is to be remarked that the disasters of the Valley campaign were in a great measure due to the extreme numerical inferiority of the Confederate cavalry to that of the enemy. The distribution of our cavalry at this time in Virginia is a curious study and excites criticism. Only two brigades of cavalry were sent to the Valley by Gen. Lee. Gen. Grant sent two large divisions of three brigades each. At Petersburg and Richmond, the numbers of our cavalry exceeded those of the enemy. But unfortunately, the country in this vicinity (especially in Dinwiddie county) was but little adapted for this superiority to be displayed, it being very wooded and traversed only by narrow roads.

Grant had Gregg's division of two brigades on his left flank on the south side of the James—and four regiments under Kautz on the north side, guarding his right flank. Confronting Kautz, the Confederates had Gary's brigade, and opposite to Gregg, Bulter's division (Hampton's old command) of three brigades, W. H. F. Lee's division, of two brigades, and a detached brigade under Dearing. Rosser's brigade was afterwards sent to the Valley, but not until the battle of Winchester had been fought.

The Valley was especially adapted for the operations of cavalry. It is universally admitted that a preponderating force of cavalry gives immense advantages in a country suitable for its employment; for cavalry can live on the lines of communication of the army opposed to it, easily avoiding any infantry sent after it. In the Valley, where cavalry could be used to advantage, the Federal superiority was some six or seven thousand. Around Petersburg, where cavalry could only fight dismounted, our numbers were in excess of those of the enemy, but not, it is true, to the degree of the enemy's superiority in the other field of operations. If, however, the proportion had been to some extent reversed, and something like an equal match been made with the enemy's cavalry in the Valley, the result might have been different, or at least there have been one error and its consequences less in that campaign.

CHAPTER XXXVII.

IT is said that at the opening of the campaign on the Rapidan, Gen.
Meade, in conversation with Gen. Grant, was telling him that he proposed
to manœuvre thus and so; whereupon Gen. Grant stopped him at the
word "manœuvre," and said, "*Oh! I never manœuvre.*" We have seen
that the famous Federal commander, who thus despised manœuvring, had
failed to destroy Lee's army by "hammering continuously" at it; had
failed to take either Richmond or Petersburg by a *coup de main*. We shall
now see that he was no longer unwilling to avail himself of the resource
of manœuvring; and we shall observe that in this resource also, he was
overmatched by Lee, who showed himself his master in every art of war,

and indeed left Grant not a single branch of generalship in which he might assert his reputation.

For some time after the mine explosion, but little was done by the Federals in front of Petersburg. In the remaining months of summer and autumn, some manœuvres were executed with more or less breadth of design, which may be briefly stated here in the order of their occurrence.

On the 18th and 19th August, Grant's left under Warren, after a defeat on the first day, succeeded in holding the Weldon Railroad. This line of communication with the South was not of any great importance to Gen. Lee, as long as he held the road to Danville, the main avenue to the fertile grain districts of the South. A series of severe actions, however, ensued to break Warren's hold upon the road ; and he maintained his position only after a loss which he himself officially reports as 4,455 killed, wounded, and missing. Meanwhile Hancock's corps was brought in rear of the position held by Warren, and ordered to destroy a southward section of the road. On the 25th August, this force was encountered at Reams' station by A. P. Hill's corps under Wilcox, Heth, and Mahone. A vigorous attack of Heth broke the enemy's line, and drove a division which was in reserve, while one line of breastworks was carried by the Confederate cavalry under Gen. Hampton. The results of the day were, twelve stands of colours captured, and nine pieces of artillery, ten caissons, 2,150 prisoners, and 3,100 stand of small-arms. The Confederate loss was, in cavalry, artillery, and infantry, 720 men, killed, wounded, and missing. Warren, however, still continued to hold the Weldon railroad ; but after a sum of disaster, as we have seen, that was a very extravagant price, compared with the little real importance of the acquisition. The road was permanently retained by the enemy ; and he now proceeded to form a line of redoubts connecting the new position with the old left of the army on the Jerusalem plank road.

About the close of September, attention was again drawn to operations north of James River, and a movement on Gen. Butler's front resulted in a serious disaster to the Confederates, and, it must be confessed, accomplished one real success for this ill-stared General in the operations against Richmond. On the night of the 28th September, Butler crossed to the north side of the James, with the corps of Birney and Ord, and moved up the river with the design of attacking the very strong fortifications and entrenchments below Chapin's farm, known as Fort Harrison. A portion of Butler's force was moved on the Newmarket road, and while a severe engagement was occurring there, a column of the enemy made a flank movment on Fort Harrison, and practically succeeded in surprising this important work, which surrendered after a very feeble resistance on the part of the artillery, and while a force of Confederates was on the double-quick to reinforce it.

This fort occupied a commanding position below Drewry's Bluff, and constituted the main defence of that part of our lines. Its loss, with fifteen pieces of artillery, was a severe blow to the Confederates, attended with circumstances of mortification, and the resolution was quickly taken to attempt its recapture. Gen. Field was for attacking at once before the enemy could strengthen the position; but he was overruled, and the attack deferred until the afternoon of the next day. It was arranged that Anderson's, Bratton's, and Law's brigades of Field's division should make the assault in front, while Hoke was to attack on the other side, taking advantage of a ravine by which he was enabled to form his men within two or three hundred yards of the fort. The plan of attack miscarried by a singular circumstance. Anderson's men being put in motion merely to adjust the line, misunderstood the orders of their commander, leaped the breastworks of the enemy, rushed forward with a yell, and were soon past control. This necessitated rapid movement on the part of the other brigades. Gen. Hoke, awaiting the signal that had been agreed upon for action, did not move; and the enemy was thus enabled to concentrate his fire on the scattered assault of the brigades of Field's division. Law's brigade accomplished its object in retaking a redan to the left of the fort, thus protecting our left flank; but the main attack failed; and the general result was that the lodgment of Butler's army on the north side of the James was secured, and a position thus obtained very menacing to Richmond.

Before settling down to winter-quarters, Gen. Grant determined to make a last vigorous attempt to retrieve the campaign and to strike one more blow for the capture of Petersburg. The sequel of this enterprise was the occasion of the usual attempt to misrepresent it as a mere reconnoissance in force; but there can no longer be any doubt that Gen. Grant, in the movement of October, 1864, designed a real advance, and hoped to achieve a success which would influence the approaching Pesidential election, only a few days distant, and electrify the North with the news of a great victory.

He made every preparation to conduct the movement on the largest scale. Three days were occupied in the preparations. The hospitals were emptied of their sick and wounded, all of whom were sent to the rear. Five days rations were issued to the troops. All superfluous or unnecessary baggage was sent to the rear with the trains. The army was put in what is called light marching order. In fact, nothing was left undone to insure the success of the undertaking. During the night preceding the movement nearly all the Federal troops were withdrawn from the breastworks on both sides of the James and massed some distance in the rear, ready to march forward at daylight. Guns were mounted to cover Grant's communications with his base at City Point, in case the Confederates should take possession of the trenches he had evacuated, and every indication pointed to a design to abandon the line before Petersburg, and take possession of the Southside railroad.

The movement occupied three corps of the enemy, and commenced at daylight of the 27th October. The right of the Confederate entrenched line rested on the east bank of Hatcher's Run ; and it was hoped to turn this, and then march upon and lay hold of the Southside railroad, which was Lee's principal communication. As the advance of the enemy moved forward to the Boydton plank road, the Confederate pickets and skirmishers were encountered, and a lively fire of musketry was kept up all the morning. When the Boydton road was reached the Confederates were found strongly entrenched at every point. It was thought that by making a wide detour these intrenchments could be taken in flank and the Confederates forced back to Petersburg ; but when Hancock's corps reached a point below where the Confederate works were supposed to terminate, they were found to extend a considerable distance in the direction of Stony Creek, and their appearance was so formidable that it was deemed imprudent to attempt to carry them.

During Hancock's march towards what was supposed to be the extreme right of the Confederate line, a gap occurred between his right and the left of the Fifth corps. The Confederates were not slow to perceive the advantage. Gen. Heth had crossed Hatcher's Run to attack the enemy, and Mahone's division quickly assailed Hancock's right in its exposed situation, driving back Gibbon's division more than a mile, and inflicting upon it considerable loss. Meanwhile Hampton's cavalry fell upon the rear of Hancock, and increased the disorder. Mahone captured four hundred prisoners, three stand of colours, and six pieces of artillery. A subsequent effort of the enemy to recover his position was bravely resisted ; Gen. Mahone broke three lines of battle ; and night found him standing firmly on the Boydton road, and successfully resisting all efforts to drive him from it.

Finding the Confederates strongly fortified along the Boydton road, and also on both sides of Hatcher's Run, and seeing the hopelessness of attempting to break through works fully as formidable as those before Petersburg, Grant issued orders for the troops to withdraw to their original position,—that is, the entrenchments in front of Petersburg—and during the night they retraced their steps, and were settled back in their old camps. The design to turn the Confederate position and take possession of the Southside railroad, had been completely frustrated ; and thus failed, almost shamefully, Grant's ambitious movement of October, 1864.

While thus the Confederate lines around Richmond and Petersburg stood successful and defiant, the shadow of a great misfortune fell on another part of the country. In the last months of 1864, public attention was drawn unanimously and almost exclusively after the march of Sher-

man through the State of Georgia; and to this event, fraught with consequences and recriminations eventually fatal to the Confederacy, we must
now direct the course of our narrative.

SHERMAN'S MARCH TO THE SEA.

At last accounts of operations in Georgia, Gen. Sherman was meditating a march to the sea-board. Preparations were made to abandon all the
posts south of Dalton, and from Gaylesville and Rome orders were issued
concerning the new movement. In the latter place commenced the work
of destruction: a thousand bales of cotton, two flour mills, two tanneries,
foundries, machine-shops, depots, store-houses, and bridges were set on
fire; the torch was applied to private dwellings, and the whole town
wrapped in a fearful and indiscriminate conflagration. The march back
to Atlanta left a track of smoke and flame.

Having concentrated his troops at Atlanta by the 14th of November,
Sherman was ready to commence his march, threatening both Augusta and
Macon. On the night of the 15th the torch was applied to Atlanta; and
where the merciless commander had already created a solitude, he determined to make a second conflagration, by the light of which his marching
columns might commence their journey to the sea. The work was done
with terrible completeness; buildings covering two hundred acres were in
flames at one time; the heavens were an expanse of lurid fire; and amid
the wild and terrific scene the Federal bands played "John Brown's soul
goes marching on." The next morning Sherman's army moved from a
scene of desolation such as had occurred in no modern picture of civilized
war. From four to five thousand houses were reduced to ruins; and four
hundred left standing was the melancholy remnant of Atlanta. Nearly
all the shade trees in the park and city had been destroyed, and the sub-
urbs, stripped of timber, presented to the eye one vast, naked, ruined, deserted camp.

The main outline of Sherman's march was, that Howard, with the
right wing, should follow the Georgia Central road, running southeast
through Macon and Milledgeville to Savannah; while Slocum, commanding the left wing, was to march directly east, on the railroad leading from
Atlanta to Augusta, destroying it as he went. Two columns of cavalry—
one to the north of Slocum, and the other to the south of Howard—were
to protect their flanks, and conceal entirely from view the routes of the infantry. An order directed the army "to forage liberally on the march."

The country immediately around Atlanta had been foraged by Slocum's
corps when it held the city; but two days' march brought Sherman's
troops into regions of such abundance as were scarcely supposed to exist

within the limits of the Southern Confederacy. There were, indeed, many parts of the Confederacy which the difficulties of transportation had gorged with supplies, and none more so, perhaps, than that part of Georgia now traversed by Sherman's troops. There were pits of sweet potatoes, yards of poultry and hogs, and cellars of bacon and flour, offering abundance on every hand, and gratifying the soldiers with a change of diet. It is said "hard tack" was scarcely heard of in Sherman's army on its march through Georgia. The cattle trains soon became so large that it was difficult to drive them along; and they were turned nightly into the immense fields of ungathered corn to eat their fill, while the granaries were crowded to overflowing with both oats and corn.

Slocum continued to move out on the Augusta line, destroying the railroad as he advanced, until he reached Madison. This, a pretty town of two thousand inhabitants, was pillaged, the stores gutted, and the streets filled with furniture and household goods, broken and wrecked in mere wantonness. From Madison Slocum turned suddenly south towards Milledgeville, and on the 21st November entered the capital of Georgia. Meanwhile Howard, covered by a cloud of Kilpatrick's cavalry, had demonstrated on Macon, and crossing the Ocmulgee, had pressed on towards Milledgeville; Sherman's forces being thus rapidly concentrated at the capital of Georgia, after having threatened both Augusta and Macon, thus confounding the Confederates as to his intentions.

A part of Howard's command had been left at Griswoldsville, ten miles east of Macon, for demonstrative purposes merely. It was attacked by a force of Confederate militia, which marched out from Macon, and were severely repulsed by the enemy's artillery. This affair, small as it was, was the most serious fight of Sherman's campaign from Atlanta to the sea.

Having sufficiently rested at Milledgeville, Sherman resumed his march eastward; while Kilpatrick's cavalry continued to operate towards Augusta, advancing as far as Waynesboro', to create the impression of a heavy movement upon Augusta. There had been concentrated at this city some Confederate militia, two or three South Carolina regiments, and a portion of Hampton's command, sent there to remount. Even if the real movement of Sherman's army had been known, this force could not have interposed any serious obstacle to the advance of his main body, as long as his left wing was used as a strong arm thrust out in advance, ready to encounter any force which might attempt to bar the way. While Kilpatrick demonstrated savagely upon Augusta, Sherman marched rapidly on Millen, reaching it on the 2d December.

He had already penetrated and devastated the richest portion of Georgia, and was now on the line of the pine forests that sloped to the sea. For a hundred miles he had left behind him a wreck of railroads and a desolated country; he had consumed the fat of the land, and he had strewn every mile of his march with the evidences of savage warfare. His army had been permitted to do whatever crime could compass and cruelty invent. A Northern correspondent, who travelled with the army, thus relates its prowess in pillage and all provinces of cowardly violence : " Such little freaks as taking the last chicken, the last pound of meal, the last bit of bacon, and the only remaining scraggy cow, from a poor woman and her flock of children, black or white not considered, came under the order of legitimate business. Even crockery, bed-covering, or cloths, were fair spoils. As for plate, or jewelry, or watches, these were things rebels had no use for. Men with pockets plethoric with silver and gold coin ; soldiers sinking under the weight of plate and fine bedding materials ; lean mules and horses, with the richest trappings of Brussels carpets, and hangings of fine chenille ; negro wenches, particularly good-looking ones, decked in satin and silks, and sporting diamond ornaments ; officers with sparkling rings, that would set Tiffany in raptures—gave colour to the stories of hanging up or fleshing an ' old cuss,' to make him shell out. A planter's house was overrun in a jiffy ; boxes, drawers, and escritoires were ransacked with a laudable zeal, and emptied of their contents. If the spoils were ample, the depredators were satisfied, and went off in peace ; if not, everything was torn and destroyed, and most likely the owner was tickled with sharp bayonets into a confession where he had his treasures hid. If he escaped, and was hiding in a thicket, this was *prima facie* evidence that he was a skulking rebel ; and most likely some ruffian, in his zeal to get rid of such vipers, gave him a dose of lead, which cured him of his Secesh tendencies. Sorghum barrels were knocked open, bee-hives rifled, while their angry swarms rushed frantically about. Indeed, I have seen a soldier knock a planter down because a bee stung him. Should the house be deserted, the furniture is smashed in pieces, music is pounded out of four hundred dollar pianos with the ends of muskets. Mirrors were wonderfully multiplied, and rich cushions and carpets carried off to adorn teams and war-steeds. After all was cleared out, most likely some set of stragglers wanted to enjoy a good fire, and set the house, debris of furniture, and all the surroundings, in a blaze. This is the way Sherman's army lived on the country."

The sum of these villanies has passed into Northern history as a weight of martial glory. But the day will yet come when the hero of such a story, instead of enjoying as now the plaudits of ferocious and cowardly mobs, will obtain the execrations of civilized mankind. The facility of his progress was no achievement of genius to illuminate a record of villany It is clear enough, when it is known that there was nothing to oppose his march but some hasty levies of regular troops, and clans of scattered militia. It is melancholy to look over the map of this march, a region of swamp and thicket, and observe that in no portion of it could a field be found adequate to the display of ten thousand men, and reflect how small a Confederate force, put between Sherman and the sea, might have disputed his march, exacted a bloody toll at every defile, and brought him to grief and disaster. But there was no such force. The general story of the march is that the Confederates had no partisan fighting as in days past; that their levies of regular troops did not make their appearance in season for a concentration of strength at any one point; that Hardee, having a command of not more than ten thousand men, remained to cover Savannah; that the clans of militia and small detachments of Wheeler's cavalry were utterly unable to cope with the enemy, and were rather calculated to provoke his enterprise than to impede his march; and that the consequence was that the sum of opposition to Sherman's march was little more than a series of small skirmishes, without result on either side.

On the 2d December Sherman's army pivoted upon Millen, swung slowly round from its eastern course, and swept down in six parallel columns, by as many different roads, towards Savannah. About ten miles from the city his left wing struck the Charleston Railroad, and encountered some Confederate skirmishers, which indicated for the first time the presence of Hardee's army. Sherman's right wing was now thrown forward; his army closed gradually and steadily in upon Savannah; and on the 10th December it lay in line of battle, confronting the outer works about five miles distant from the city. His first task was to open communication with Dahlgren's fleet, which lay in Ossabaw Sound, and he therefore determined to capture Fort McAllister, at the mouth of the Ogeechee, which enters the ocean but a few miles south of the Savannah.

Fort McAllister was a large enclosure, with wide parapets, a deep ditch and thickly-planted palisades. There were twenty-one guns, large and small, in the fort, all mounted *en barbette*. It had resisted two or three bombardments of the enemy's iron-clads; and it appears that Gen. Hardee had overlooked the possibility of a land attack, and had neglected to strengthen the garrison. Anyhow the Confederate commander was not up to the quick decision of Sherman, who, instead of building entrenchments and rifle-pits, resolved to take the fort by assault. A whole division was ordered for the work, on the evening of the 30th December. The fort was commanded by Major Anderson; and its garrison, at the time of attack, was less than two hundred men. The fact that its guns were mounted *en barbette* exposed the gunners to the deadly aim of sharpshooters; and as the division of the enemy's troops commanded by Gen. Hazen advanced to the assault, it was found that the artillery of the fort did but little execution upon them. The Federals went easily over the parapet; but the little Confederate garrison, although desperately outnumbered, fought to the last. Many of these devoted men disdained quarter, and were bayoneted at their posts. Capt. Clinch, who commanded the artillery, refused to surrender until he was disabled by three sabre and two gun-shot wounds, and faint from loss of blood.

When Sherman saw the Federal flag raised upon Fort McAllister, he seized a slip of paper, and telegraphed to Washington: "I regard Savannah as already gained." The possession of the fort opened Ossabaw Sound, effected communication with Dahlgren's fleet, and indeed made the capture of Savannah, where Hardee appeared to be shut up with ten or twelve thousand men, but a question of time. But it was Sherman's hope to capture Hardee's army with the city; and movements were made to close up all avenues of escape, Sherman's army stretching from the Savannah to the Ogeechee River, while Foster's troops covered the railroad to Charleston. It was intended to place a division to operate with Foster by way of Broad River; but while Sherman's flank movement was in process of operation, Hardee outwitted him, and on the night following the enemy's demand for the surrender of the city, the Confederates had evacuated it, and were on the Carolina shore.

The evacuation was a complete surprise to Sherman. On the night of the 28th December, Hardee opened a fierce bombardment, expending his ammunition without stint. After dark, he threw his men on rafts and steamboats across the river to the South Carolina shore. The night was dark, with a fierce gust of wind deadening the sounds of the wagons and the tramp of the troops. As morning broke, the attention of the enemy was excited at last by unusual sounds, and his pickets were advanced on the extreme left of the line. Meeting no opposition, they pushed still further, crawled through the abatis, floundered through dikes and ditches, scaled the first line of works, and found it deserted. All the ordnance stores and supplies which Hardee could not transport, had been destroyed before the evacuation; he had burned the ship-yard and sunk two ironclads; but all the rest of the uninjured city fell into the hands of the enemy.

Sherman announced his success in a characteristic despatch. He wrote to President Lincoln: "I beg to present you, *as a Christmas gift,* the city of Savannah, with one hundred and fifty heavy guns and plenty of ammunition, and also about twenty-five thousand bales of cotton." And thus ended the story of the march to the sea. In his official report of his achievements, Gen. Sherman wrote: "We have consumed the corn and fodder in the region of country thirty miles on either side of a line from Atlanta to Savannah, as also the sweet potatoes, cattle, hogs, sheep, and poultry, and have carried away more than ten thousand horses and mules, as well as a countless number of their slaves. I estimate the damage done to the State of Georgia and its military resources at one hundred millions of dollars; at least twenty millions of which has inured to our advantage, and the remainder is *simple waste and destruction.*"

The North exhibited its characteristic measure of greatness by taking Sherman's "march from the mountains to the seas" as the greatest military exploit of modern times. It fitted the Northern idea of magnitude. It was, of course, "the Great March," as everything the North admired, from a patent-machine to an army, was "the great." But it is difficult for a sober historian to find in the easy marches of Sherman through Georgia, any great military merit, or to discover in the excessively vulgar character of this commander any of the elements of the hero. Where there is nothing to oppose an army, the mere accomplishment of distances is no great wonder or glory. From the time Sherman left Gaylesville to the day he encountered the lines around Savannah, he never had a thousand men on his front to dispute his advance; he had nothing to threaten his rear beyond a few bodies of Confederate horse; he moved through a country so full of supplies that his own commissariat was scarcely taxed to subsist his army; he himself telegraphed to Washington: "Our march was most agreeable," and compared it to "a pleasure-trip." And yet this pleasant excursion the North insisted upon amplifying as a great military exploit, to be compared with Napoleon's march to Moscow, and other splendid adventures of invasion, while the chief excursionist was raised to the dignity of a hero.

Sherman is an example of the reputation achieved in the North by intrepid charlatanism and self-assertion. He had elements of Northern popularity outside of the severe circle of military accomplishments. His swagger was almost irresistible; he wrote slang phrases in his official despatches; his style was a flash Fourth-of-July tangled oratory, that never fails to bring down the applause of a Northern mob. It is the office of history to reduce the reputations of the gazette. The man who is now known in Northern newspapers as a hero of the war and luminary of the military age will scarcely be known in future and just history, further than as the man who depopulated and destroyed Atlanta, essayed a new code of cruelty in war, marched so many miles, achieved much bad notoriety, and ended with a professional fame mediocre and insignificant, holding a place no longer conspicuous in the permanent records of the times.

CHAPTER XXXVIII.

THE exchange of prisoners taken during the war; their treatment in their places of confinement North and South; the incidents of the cartel, altogether, constitute so large and interesting a subject that we have reserved its treatment for a separate chapter. On the exposition of this intricate matter depends much of the good name of the Confederates and the contrary title of the enemy; and it may be remarked that no subject which tended to keep alive a feeling of bitterness and animosity between the

Northern and Southern people was more effective than recrimination about the cartel, and the alleged cruelty to prisoners of war on both sides. The exposition we propose to make is mainly by a chain of records, extending through the war, thus best securing authenticity of statement, and combining these documents in a unity of narrative, so as to place before the reader a complete view and a severe analysis of the whole subject.

In the first periods of the war, and with the prospect of its early termination, but little account was taken of prisoners captured on either side. Indeed, some time elapsed at Washington before any lists were kept of these captures; and after the first remarkable battle of the war, that of Manassas, in 1861, it was actually proposed (by Mr. Boyce of South Carolina), in the Provisional Congress at Richmond, to send back the Federal prisoners taken on that field without any formality whatever. The Fort Donelson capture, however, appeared to have developed for the first time the value and interest of the exchange question, and was the occasion of remarkable perfidy on the part of the Washington authorities.

Just previous to these important captures, Gen. Wool, on the Federal side, had declared, in a letter dated the 13th February, 1862 : "I am alone *clothed with full power*, for the purpose of arranging for the exchange of prisoners," and had invited a conference on the subject. Gen. Howell Cobb, on the part of the Confederacy, was appointed to negotiate with him ; and the two officers decided upon a cartel by which prisoners taken on either side should be paroled within ten days after their capture, and delivered on the frontier of their own country. The only point of tenacious difference between them was as to a provision requiring each party to pay the expense of transporting their prisoners to the frontier ; and this point Gen. Wool promised ·to refer to the decision of his Government. At a second interview on the 1st March, Gen. Wool declared that his Government would not consent to pay these expenses ; when Gen. Cobb promptly gave up the point, leaving the cartel free from all of Gen. Wool's objections, and just what he had proposed in his letter of the 13th February. Upon this, Gen. Wool informed Gen. Cobb that "his Government had changed his instructions," and abruptly broke off the negotiation. The occasion of this bad faith and dishonour on the part of the enemy was, that in the interval they had taken several thousand prisoners at Fort Donelson, which reversed the former state of things, and gave them a surplus of prisoners, who, instead of being returned on parole, were carried into the interiour, and incarcerated with every circumstance of indignity.

In the second year of the war a distinct understanding was obtained on the subject of the exchange of prisoners of war, and the following cartel was respectively signed and duly executed on the part of the two Governments. This important instrument of war invites a close examination of the reader, and is copied in full:

HAXALL'S LANDING, ON JAMES RIVER, July 22, 1862.

The undersigned, having been commissioned by the authorities they respectively represent, to make arrangements for a general exchange of prisoners of war, have agreed to the following articles:

ARTICLE I. It is hereby agreed and stipulated, that all prisoners of war held by either party, including those taken on private armed vessels, known as privateers, shall be exchanged upon the conditions and terms following:

Prisoners to be exchanged, man for man and officer for officer; privateers to be placed upon the footing of officers and men of the navy.

Men and officers of lower grades, may be exchanged for officers of a higher grade, and men and officers of different services may be exchanged according to the following scale of equivalents.

A general-commanding-in-chief, or an admiral, shall be exchanged for officers of equal rank or for sixty privates or common seamen.

A flag officer or major-general shall be exchanged for officers of equal rank or for forty privates or common seamen.

A commodore, carrying a broad pennant, or a brigadier-general shall be exchanged for officers of equal rank or twenty privates or common seamen.

A captain in the navy or a colonel shall be exchanged for officers of equal rank or for fifteen privates or common seamen.

A lieutenant-colonel, or commander in the navy, shall be exchanged for officers of equal rank or for ten privates or common seamen.

A lieutenant-commander or a major shall be exchanged for officers of equal rank or eight privates or common seamen.

A lieutenant or a master in the navy or a captain in the army or marines shall be exchanged for officers of equal rank or six privates or common seamen.

Master's mates in the navy, or lieutenants or ensigns in the army, shall be exchanged for officers of equal rank or four privates or common seamen.

Midshipmen, warrant officers in the navy, masters of merchant vessels and commanders of privateers, shall be exchanged for officers of equal rank or three privates or common seamen; second captains, lieutenants, or mates of merchant vessels or privateers, and all petty officers in the navy, and all non-commissioned officers in the army or marines, shall be severally exchanged for persons of equal rank or for two privates or common seamen; and private soldiers or common seamen, shall be exchanged for each other, man for man.

ARTICLE II. Local, State, civil, and militia rank held by persons not in actual military service, will not be recognized; the basis of exchange being the grade actually held in the naval and military service of the respective parties.

ARTICLE III. If citizens held by either party on charges of disloyalty for any alleged civil offence are exchanged, it shall only be for citizens. Captured sutlers, teamsters, and all civilians in the actual service of either party to be exchanged for persons in similar position.

ARTICLE IV. All prisoners of war to be discharged on parole in ten days after their capture, and the prisoners now held and those hereafter taken to be transported to the points mutually agreed upon, at the expense of the capturing party. The surplus prisoners, not exchanged, shall not be permitted to take up arms again, nor to serve as military police, or constabulary force in any fort, garrison, or field work, held by either of the respective parties, nor as guards of prisoners, deposit, or stores, nor to discharge any duty usually performed by soldiers, until exchanged under the provisions of this cartel. The exchange is not to be considered complete until the officer or soldier exchanged for has been actually restored to the lines to which he belongs.

ARTICLE V. Each party, upon the discharge of prisoners of the other party, is authorized to discharge an equal number of their own officers or men from parole, furnishing at the same time to the other party a list of their prisoners discharged, and of their own officers and men relieved from parole; thus enabling each party to relieve from parole such of their own officers and men as the party may choose. The lists thus mutually furnished will keep both parties advised of the true condition of the exchange of prisoners.

ARTICLE VI. The stipulations and provisions above mentioned to be of binding obligation during the continuance of the war, it matters not which party may have the surplus of prisoners, the great principles involved being : 1st. An equitable exchange of prisoners, man for man, officer for officer, or officers of higher grade, exchanged for officers of lower grade, or for privates, according to the scale of equivalents. 2d. That privates and officers and men of different services may be exchanged according to the same scale of equivalents. 3d. That all prisoners, of whatever arm of service, are to be exchanged or paroled in ten days from the time of their capture, if it be practicable to transfer them to their own lines in that time; if not, as soon thereafter as practicable. 4th. That no officer, soldier, employee in service of either party is to be considered as exchanged and absolved from his parole until his equivalent has actually reached the lines of his friends. 5th. That the parole forbids the performance of field, garrison, police, or guard, or constabulary duty.

JOHN A. DIX, *Major-General.*
D. H. HILL, *Major-General, C. S. A.*

SUPPLEMENTARY ARTICLES.

ARTICLE VII. All prisoners of war now held on either side, and all prisoners hereafter taken, shall be sent, with all reasonable despatch, to A. M. Aiken's, below Dutch Gap, on the James River, in Virginia, or to Vicksburg, on the Mississippi River, in the State of Mississippi, and there exchanged or paroled until such exchange can be effected, notice being previously given by each party of the number of prisoners it will send, and the time when they will be delivered at those points respectively; and in case the vicissitudes of war shall change the military relations of the places designated in this article to the contending parties, so as to render the same inconvenient for the delivery and exchange of prisoners, other places, bearing as nearly as may be the present local relations of said places to the lines of said parties, shall be, by mutual agreement, substituted. But nothing in this article contained shall prevent the commanders of two opposing armies from exchanging prisoners, or releasing them on parole, at other points mutually agreed on by said commanders.

ARTICLE VIII. For the purpose of carrying into effect the foregoing articles of agreement, each party will appoint two agents, to be called agents for the exchange of prisoners of war, whose duty it shall be to communicate with each other, by correspondence and otherwise; to prepare the lists of prisoners; to attend to the delivery of the prisoners at the places agreed on, and to carry out promptly, effectually, and in good faith, all the details and provisions of the said articles of agreement.

ARTICLE IX. And in case any misunderstanding shall arise in regard to any clause or stipulation in the foregoing articles, it is mutually agreed that such misunderstanding shall not interrupt the release of prisoners on parole, as herein provided, but shall be made the subject of friendly explanation, in order that the object of this agreement may neither be defeated nor posptoned.

JOHN A. DIX, *Major-General.*
D. H. HILL, *Major-General, C. S. A.*

Mr. Robert Ould was appointed agent of the Confederacy under this important text of the war. He was eminently qualified for the office. He was among the most accomplished jurists of the country; he had one of the most vigorous intellects in the Confederacy; he was a man of large humanity, dignified, and even lofty manners, and spotless personal honour. The record of his services in the cause of humanity and truth was one of the purest in either the public bureau or secret chamber of the Confederacy.

It will be seen that the chief, if not the only purpose, of the instrument copied above was to secure the release of all prisoners of war. To that end the fourth article provided that all prisoners of war should be discharged on parole in ten days after their capture, and that the prisoners then held and those thereafter taken should be transported to the points mutually agreed upon, at the expense of the capturing party. The sixth article also stipulated that " all prisoners of whatever arm of service are to be exchanged or paroled in ten days from the time of their capture, if it be practicable to transfer them to their own lines in that time; if not, as soon thereafter as practicable."

From the date of the cartel until July, 1863, the Confederate authorities held the excess of prisoners. During that interval deliveries were made as fast as the Federal Government furnished transportation. Indeed, upon more than one occasion, Commissioner Ould urged the Federal authorities to send increased means of transportation. As ready as the enemy always has been to bring false accusations against the Confederates, it has never been alleged that they failed or neglected to make prompt deliveries of prisoners who were not under charges when they held the excess. On the other hand, during the same time the cartel was openly and notoriously violated by the Federal authorities. Officers and men were kept in cruel confinement, sometimes in irons or doomed to cells, without charge or trial.

These facts were distinctly charged in the correspondence of Commissioner Ould. On the 26th July, 1863, he addressed a letter to Lieut.-Col. Ludlow, then acting as agent of exchange on the Federal side, in which he used the following impressive and vigorous language in vindication of himself and his Government: " Now that our official connection is being terminated, I say to you in the fear of God—and I appeal to Him for the truth of the declaration—that there has been no single moment, from the time we were first brought together in connection with the matter of exchange to the present hour, during which there has not been an open and notorious violation of the cartel, by your authorities. Officers and men, numbering over hundreds, have been, during your whole connection with the cartel, kept in cruel confinement, sometimes in irons, or doomed to cells, without charges or trial. They are in prison now, unless God, in His mercy, has released them. In our parting moments, let me do you the justice to say that I do not believe it is so much your fault as that of your authorities. Nay, more, I believe your removal from your position has been owing to the personal efforts you have made for a faithful observance, not only of the cartel, but of humanity, in the conduct of the war.

" Again and again have I importuned you to tell me of one officer or man now held in confinement by us, who was declared exchanged. You have, to those appeals, furnished one, Spencer Kellog. For him I have searched in vain. On the other hand, I appeal to your own records for the cases where your reports have shown that our officers and men have been held for long months and even years in violation of the cartel and our agreements. The last phase of the enormity, however, exceeds all others. Although you have many thousands of our soldiers now in confinement in your prisons, and especially in that horrible hold of death Fort Delaware, you have not, for several weeks, sent us any prisoners During those weeks you have despatched Capt. Mulford with the steamer New York to City Point, three or four times, without any prisoners. For the first two or three times some sort of an excuse was attempted. None is given at this present arrival. I do not mean to be offensive when I say that effrontery could not give one. I ask you with no purpose of disrespect, what can you think of this covert attempt to secure the delivery of all your prisoners in our hands, without the release of those of ours who are languishing in hopeless misery in your prisons and dungeons ? "

It is a fact beyond all controversy that officers and soldiers of the Confederacy entitled to delivery and exchange, were kept in confinement, in defiance of the cartel, some under charges, and some without. Many of these officers and soldiers were in confinement at the time of the adoption of the cartel, and continued to be so kept for months and years afterwards. In a few instances Commissioner Ould succeeded by persistent pressure in securing their release. In other cases, when from returned prisoners he would learn their place of confinement, and state it to the Federal agent, there would either be a denial of the fact that the party was confined there, or he would be removed to some other prison. Many of these prisoners were actually declared exchanged by the Federal Agent of Exchange, but yet still kept in prison, and all the others were entitled to delivery for exchange under the terms of the cartel.

To the serious allegation of a retention of prisoners in spite of the cartel and all the obligations of good faith, the Federal Government never attempted anything but a paltry counter-charge of the weakest and most disingenuous kind. During the period before mentioned the only complaints made by the Federal authorities of any breach of the cartel, were in the cases of such officers as were retained in consequence of President Davis' several proclamations, and in the case of Gen. Streight and his officers. In looking back over the prison records of the Confederacy, the author can find no instance of any officers or men who were kept in prison after the date of the cartel under the proclamations of Mr. Davis. In point of fact, nothing was ever done under them. No inquiry was ever made whether the prisoners led negro troops or not. Streight's men were detained for several months. The reasons for their detention were fully given. In a letter written by Commissioner Ould, August 1st, 1863, to Brig.-Gen. Meredith, he said: " In retaining Col. Streight and his command, the Confederate authorities have not gone as far as those of the United States have claimed for themselves the right to go ever since the establishment of the cartel. You have claimed and exercised the right to retain officers and men indefinitely, not only upon charges actually preferred, but upon mere suspicion. You have now in custody officers who were in confinement when the cartel was framed, and who have since been declared exchanged. Some of them have been tried, but most of them have languished in prison all the weary time without trial or charges. I stand prepared to prove these assertions. This course was pursued, too, in the face not only of notice, but of protest. Do you deny to us the right to detain officers and men for trial upon grave charges, while you claim the right to keep in confinement any who may be the object of your suspicion or special enmity ? "

Commissioner Ould also informed the Federal authorities, in 1863, that the charges against Streight and his command were not sustained, and that they were held as other prisoners. At the time, however, of this latter notification, other difficulties had supervened, which had almost entirely stopped exchanges.

Up to July, 1863, the Confederates had a large excess of prisoners. The larger number had been released upon parole after capture. Such paroles had been without question respected by both parties, until about the middle of 1863, when they were to be declared to be void (except under very special circumstances) by General Orders at Washington. The true reason of those General Orders was that the Federals had no lists of paroled prisoners (released on capture) to be charged against the Confederates. The latter had paid off all debts of that kind from their abundant stores. They, on the other hand, had many such lists which were unsatisfied, being principally captures in Kentucky, Tennessee, etc. Such being the state of affairs, on the 8th of April, 1863, Commisssioner Ould was informed that " exchanges will be confined to such equivalents as are held in confinement on either side." In other words, as all the paroles held by the Federals had been satisfied and paid for in equivalents, and as they then held none of such to be charged against the Confederates, they would no longer respect such as they held, and the latter must deliver men actually in captivity for such as they would send. The Confederates then had the outstanding paroles, but the Federals had the majority of prisoners in hand. The effect of all this would have been, after the Confederates had delivered all their prisoners, to leave a large balance of their people in prison, while they at the same time had in their possession the paroles of ten times as many prisoners as the enemy held in captivity. This arrangement Commissioner Ould refused with indignation. The officers and men, who gave the paroles referred to, were subsequently, in violation of their parole, and without being declared exchanged, ordered to duty, and served against the South. Thereupon, Commissioner Ould off-setted such paroles against similar paroles taken by our officers and men at Vicksburg, and declared a like number of the latter exchanged. That was the only way he had of " getting even " with the enemy ; and no one can say that the way was not fair and honourable.

From this time the provision of the cartel, that all prisoners, where practicable, were to be delivered within ten days was practically nullified, and was not respected during the remainder of the war. Such deliveries as were made afterwards, were in consequence of special agreements. The most strenuous efforts were made by Commissioner Ould to remedy this distressing state of things. The Confederate authorities only claimed that the provisions of the cartel should be fulfilled. They only asked the enemy to do what, without any hesitation, they had done during the first year of the operation of the cartel. Seeing a persistent purpose on the part of the Federal Government to violate its own agreement, the Confederate authorities, *moved by the sufferings of the men in the prisons of each belligerent*, determined to abate their fair demands, and accordingly, on the 10th of August, 1864, Commissioner Ould addressed the following communication to Major John E. Mulford, Assistant Agent of Exchange :

RICHMOND, VA., August 10th, 1864.

Maj. John E. Mulford, Asst. Agent of Exchange :

SIR : You have several times proposed to me to exchange the prisoners respectively held by the two belligerents, officer for officer, and man for man. The same offer has also been made by other officials having charge of matters connected with the exchange of prisoners. This proposal has heretofore been declined by the Confederate authorities, they insisting upon the terms of the cartel, which required the delivery of the excess on either side upon parole. In view, however, of the very large number of prisoners now held by each party, and the suffering consequent upon their continued confinement, I now consent to the above proposal and agree to deliver to you the prisoners held in captivity by the Confederate authorities, provided you agree to deliver an equal number of Confederate officers and men. As equal numbers are delivered from time to time, they will be declared exchanged. This proposal is made with the understanding that the officers and men on both sides, who have been longest in captivity, will be first delivered, where it is practicable. I shall be happy to hear from you as speedily as possible, whether this arrangement can be carried out.

Respectfully, your obedient servant,

R. OULD, *Agent of Exchange.*

The delivery of this letter was accompanied with a statement of the mortality which was hurrying so many Federal prisoners, at Andersonville to the grave.

On the 20th of the same month Major Mulford returned with the flag of truce steamer, but brought no answer to the letter of the 10th of August. In conversation with him, Commissioner Ould asked if he had any reply to make to the communication, and his answer was that he was not authorized to make any. So deep was the solicitude which Commissioner Ould felt in the fate of the captives in Northern prisons, that he determined to make another effort. In order to obviate any objection which technicality might raise as to the person to whom his communication was addressed, he wrote to Maj.-Gen. E. A. Hitchcock, the Federal Commissioner of Exchange, residing in Washington city, the following letter, and delivered the same to Major Mulford on the day of its date. Accompanying that letter was a copy of the communication which he had addressed to Major Mulford on the 10th of August :

RICHMOND, August 22, 1864.

Maj.-Gen. E. A. Hitchcock, U. S. Commissioner of Exchange:

SIR : Enclosed is a copy of a communication which, on the 10th inst., I addressed and delivered to Major Jno. E. Mulford, Assistant Agent of Exchange. Under the circumstances of the case, I deem it proper to forward this paper to you, in order that you may fully understand the position which is taken by the Confederate authorities. I shall be glad if the proposition therein made is accepted by your Government.

Respectfully your obedient servant,

Ro. OULD, *Agent of Exchange.*

On the afternoon of the 30th August, Commissioner Ould was notified that the flag of truce steamer had again appeared at Varina. On the following day he sent to Maj. Mulford the following note :

RICHMOND, August 31, 1864.

Maj. John E. Mulford, Assistant Agent of Exchange:

SIR : On the 10th of this month I addressed you a communication, to which I have received no answer. On the 22d inst. I also addressed a communication to Maj.-Gen. E. A. Hitchcock, U. S. Commissioner of Exchange, enclosing a copy of my letter to you of the 10th inst. I now respectfully ask you to state in writing whether you have any reply to either of said communications; and if not, whether you have any reason to give why no reply has been made ?

Respectfully, your obedient servant,

Ro. OULD, *Agent of Exchange.*

In a short time Commissioner Ould received the following response:

FLAG OF TRUCE STEAMER, "NEW YORK.'; }
VARINA, VA., August 31, 1864. }

Hon. R. Ould, Agent of Exchange:

SIR: I have the honour to acknowledge the receipt of your favour of to-day, requesting answer, etc., to your communication of the 10th inst., on the question of the exchange of prisoners. To which, in reply, I would say, I have no communication on the subject from our authorities, nor am I yet authorized to make answer.

I am, sir, very respectfully,
Your obedient servant,
JOHN E. MULFORD, *Ass't Agent of Exchange.*

This was the whole Federal reply to the humane proposition of the Confederacy—this the brief indication of their cruel purpose to let their prisoners rot and die in insufficient prisons, merely for the purpose of pointing a libel and colouring a story against the Southern Confederacy. The offer of Commissioner Ould was on the extreme of generosity. He proposed, when the enemy had a large excess of prisoners, to exchange officer for officer and man for man. This arrangement would have left the surplus in the enemy's hands. But the liberal offer, which would have instantly restored to life and freedom thousands of suffering captives, was never even heeded at Washington; it was brutally calculated there that such a delivery from the prison pens of Andersonville and elsewhere would put so many thousand Confederate muskets in the field, and cut off a chapter of horrours, from which it had been convenient to draw texts on the subject of "rebel barbarities." To keep that text before the world was the determined purpose at Washington. It had again and again been announced that the subsistence of the Confederacy had fallen so low—chiefly through the warfare of the enemy making it a point to destroy in all parts of the country supplies of every kind—that its own soldiers were compelled to subsist upon a third of a pound of meat and a pound of coarse corn meal or flour every day. With such reduced rations, Confederate soldiers themselves were often exposed with thin and tattered clothes to the freezing winter storms, without tents, overcoats, blankets or shoes. In these circumstances it was impossible to provide properly for many tens of thousands of prisoners at Andersonville, Salisbury, and other places south of Richmond, where crowded quarters, prepared only for smaller numbers, and frequent removals to prevent recapture, added to the discomfort of the prisoners, and swelled the list of mortality. The authorities at Washington refused to do their own part to relieve the sufferings of these unhappy men, and deliberately decreed the extension of their sufferings that they might put before the world false and plausible proofs of "rebel barbarity."

It is simply in opposition to all that is known of Southern generosity in the war to believe that the sufferings of Andersonville were the result of neglect, still less of design on the part of the Confederate Government. A single train of acts is not likely to be so opposed to the whole career and consistent character of a people in a four years' war. The site of the prison at Andersonville—a point on the Southwestern railway in Georgia had been selected under an official order having reference to the following points : " A healthy locality, plenty of pure good water, a running stream, and, if possible, shade trees, and in the immediate neighbourhood of grist and saw mills." The pressure was so great at Richmond, and the supplies so scant, that prisoners were sent forward while the stockade was only about half finished. When the first instalment of prisoners arrived, there was no guard at Andersonville, and the little squad which had charge of them in the cars had to remain ; and at no time did the guard, efficient and on duty, exceed fifteen hundred, to man the stockade, to guard, and do general duty, and afford relief and enforce discipline over thirty-four thousand prisoners.

In regard to the sufferings and mortality among the prisoners at Andersonville, none of it arose from the unhealthiness of the locality. The food, though the same as that used by the Confederate soldiers, the bread, too, being corn, was different from that to which they had been accustomed, did not agree with them, and scurvy and diarrhœa prevailed to a considerable extent ; neither disease, however, was the result of starvation. That some prisoners did not get their allowance, although a full supply was sent in, is true. But there not being a guard sufficient to attend to distribution, Federal prisoners were appointed, each having a certain number allotted to his charge, among whom it was his duty to see that every man got his portion, and, as an inducement, this prisoner had especial favours and advantages ; upon complaint by those under him, he was broke and another selected ; so that it only required good faith on the part of these head men, thus appointed, to insure to each man his share. But prisoners would often sell their rations for whiskey and tobacco, and would sell the clothes from their backs for either of them.

In regard to sanitary regulations, there were certain prescribed places and modes for the reception of all filth, and a sluice was made to carry it off ; but the most abominable disregard was manifested of all sanitary regulations, and to such a degree that if a conspiracy had been entered into by a large number of the prisoners to cause the utmost filth and stench, it could not have accomplished a more disgusting result. Besides which there was a large number of atrocious villains, whose outrages in robbing, beating and murdering their fellow-prisoners must have been the cause, directly or remotely, of very many deaths and of an inconceivable amount of suffering. We must recollect that among thirty-four thousand prisoners, who had encountered the hardships of the fields of many battles, and had had wounds, there were many of delicate physique—many of respectability, to whom such fellowship, such self-created filth, and such atrocious ruffianism, would of itself cause despondency, disease, and death; and when, in addition to this, was the conviction that the Federal War Department, perfectly cognizant of all this, had deliberately consigned them indefinitely to this condition, a consuming despair was superadded to all their other sufferings.

The merits of Andersonville may be summed up by saying that it was of unquestioned healthfulness; it was large enough and had water enough, and could have been made tolerable for the number originally intended for it. It appears that the increase of that number was apparently a matter of necessity for the time; that other sites were selected and prepared with all possible despatch; that the provisions were similar in amount and quality to those used by Confederate soldiers; that deficient means rendered a supply of clothing, tents, and medicines scanty; that the rules of discipline and sanitary regulations of the prison, *if complied with by the prisoners*, would have secured to each a supply of food, and have averted almost, if not altogether, the filth and the ruffianism, which two causes outside of unavoidable sickness, caused the great mass of suffering and mortality.

But the history of the extraordinary efforts of the Confederate authorities to relieve the sufferings of Andersonville, through some resumption of exchanges, does not end with the proposition referred to as made by Commissioner Ould to exchange man for man, and leave the surplus at the disposition of the enemy. It was followed by another more liberal and more extraordinary proposition. Acting under the direct instructions of the Secretary of War, and seeing plainly that there was no hope of any general or extended partial system of exchange, Commissioner Ould, in August, 1864, offered to the Federal agent of exchange, Gen. Mulford, to deliver to him all the sick and wounded Federal prisoners we had, *without insisting upon the delivery of an equivalent number of our prisoners in return*. He also informed Gen. Mulford of the terrible mortality among the Federal prisoners, urging him to be swift in sending transportation to the mouth of the Savannah River for the purpose of taking them away. The offer of Commissioner Ould included all the sick and wounded at Andersonville and other Confederate prisons. He further informed Gen. Mulford, in order to make his Government safe in sending transportation, that if the sick and wounded did not amount to ten or fifteen thousand men, the Confederate authorities would make up that number in well men. This offer, it will be recollected, was made early in August, 1864. Gen. Mulford informed Commissioner Ould it was directly communicated to his Government, yet no timely advantage was ever taken of it.

This interesting and important fact is for the first time authoritatively published in these pages. It contains volumes of significance. The question occurs, who was responsible for the sufferings of the sick and wounded and prisoners at Andersonville, from August to December, 1864? The world will ask with amazement, if it was possible that thousands of prisoners were left to die in inadequate places of confinement, merely to make a case against the South—merely for romance! The single fact gives the clue to the whole story of the deception and inhuman cruelty of the authorities at Washington with reference to their prisoners of war—the key to a chapter of horrours that even the hardy hand of History shakes to unlock. To blacken the reputation of an honourable enemy; to make a false appeal to the sensibilities of the world; to gratify an inhuman revenge, Mr. Stanton, the saturnine and malignant Secretary of War at Washington, did not hesitate to doom to death thousands of his countrymen, and then to smear their sentinels with accusing blood.

It was the purpose of Commissioner Ould to keep open the offer he had made, and deliver to the Federal authorities all their sick and wounded, from time to time, especially if the straits of war should deny the Confederates the means of providing for their comfort. To show how honest and earnest he was in his offer to Mulford, when the transportation did arrive, he did deliver to him at Savannah and Charleston thirteen thousand men, large numbers of whom were well, and was ready to deliver as many as his transportation could accommodate, and that too under the difficulties and pressure of Sherman's invasion of Georgia, when nothing but temporary shiftings were our expedients.

The transfer of the entire matter of the exchange of prisoners from the control of Secretary Stanton, who had been averse to all arguments of justice, and to all appeals on this subject, to that of Gen. Grant, offered to Commissioner Ould another oportunity to essay an effort of humanity. On the 11th February, 1865, he proposed to Gen. Grant, to deliver without delay all the prisoners on hand, upon receiving an assurance from him that he would deliver an equal number of Confederate prisoners, within a reasonable time. This was accepted, and every energy was used to send immediately through Wilmington, James River, and other practicable ways, all the prisoners we had. This was very speedily consummated, so far as all in prisons in Virginia, and North and South Carolina, were concerned. The presence of the enemy, and the cutting of our communications, only prevented the immediate execution elsewhere. Orders to that effect, and messengers to secure it, were sent to Georgia, Alabama, and the Trans-Mississippi. A return number of prisoners, to the amount of about five thousand per week, were sent to Richmond, until the fortunes of war closed all operations, even down to the matter of an adjustment of accounts. The adjustment has never been made.

The general subject of the condition and treatment of prisoners, on both sides, in the war, is involved in much we have already written of the history of the exchange question. But in order to make a proper case for posterity on a special and deeply interesting topic, Commissioner Ould urged and succeeded in raising a joint Congressional Committee at Richmond, to take the testimony of returned prisoners as to their treatment by the enemy. That Committee was raised, and a large mass of testimony was taken, which was unfortunately lost by fire. This Committee, however, made a report in February, 1865, a copy of which was preserved. It is a document which should be read with care; the space it occupies could scarcely be filled with a narrative more just and condensed; and we therefore annex it, in full:

REPORT OF THE JOINT SELECT COMMITTEE OF THE CONFEDERATE CONGRESS, APPOINTED TO INVESTIGATE THE CONDITION AND TREATMENT OF PRISONERS OF WAR.

The duties assigned to the committee under the several resolutions of Congress designating them, are " to investigate and report upon the condition and treatment of the prisoners of war respectively held by the Confederate and United States Governments, upon the causes of their detention, and the refusal to exchange; and also upon the violations by the enemy of the rules of civilized warfare in the conduct of the war." These subjects are broad in extent and importance; and in order fully to investigate and present them, the committee propose to continue their labours in obtaining evidence, and deducing from it a truthful report of facts illustrative of the spirit in which the war has been conducted.

But we deem it proper at this time to make a preliminary report, founded upon evidence recently taken, relating to the treatment of prisoners of war by both belligerents. This report is rendered especially important, by reason of persistent efforts lately made by the Government of the United States, and by associations and individuals connected or co-operating with it, to asperse the honour of the Confederate authorities, and to charge them with deliberate and wilful cruelty to prisoners of war. Two publications have been issued at the North within the past year, and have been circulated not only in the United States, but in some parts of the South, and in Europe. One of these is the report of the joint select committee of the Northern Congress on the conduct of the war, known as " Report No. 67." The other purports to be a " Narrative of the privations and sufferings of United States officers and soldiers while prisoners of war," and is issued as a report of a commission of enquiry appointed by " The United States Sanitary Commission."

This body is alleged to consist of Valentine Mott, M. D., Edward Delafield, M. D., Gouverneur Morris Wilkins, Esq., Ellerslie Wallace, M. D., Hon. J. J. Clarke Hare, and Rev. Treadwell Walden. Although these persons are not of sufficient public importance and weight to give authority to their publication, yet your committee have deemed it proper to notice it in connection with the " Report No. 67," before mentioned, because the Sanitary Commission has been understood to have acted to a greater extent under the control and by the authority of the United States Government, and because their report claims to be founded on evidence taken in solemn form.

A candid reader of these publications will not fail to discover that, whether the statements they make be true or not, their spirit is not adapted to promote a better feeling between the hostile powers. They are not intended for the humane purpose of ameliorating the condition of the unhappy prisoners held in captivity. They are designed to inflame the evil passions of the North; to keep up the war spirit among their own people; to represent the South as acting under the dominion of a spirit of cruelty, inhumanity, and interested malice, and thus to vilify her people in the eyes of all on whom these publications can work. They are justly characterized by the Hon. James M. Mason as belonging to that class of literature called the "sensational"—a style of writing prevalent for many years at the North, and which, beginning with the writers of newspaper narratives and cheap fiction, has gradually extended itself, until it is now the favoured mode adopted by medical professors, judges of courts, and reverend clergymen, and is even chosen as the proper style for a report by a committee of their Congress.

Nothing can better illustrate the truth of this view than the "Report No. 67," and its appendages. It is accompanied by eight pictures, or photographs, alleged to represent United States prisoners of war, returned from Richmond, in a sad state of emaciation and suffering. Concerning these cases, your committee will have other remarks, to be presently submitted. They are only alluded to now to show that this report does really belong to the "sensational" class of literature, and that, *prima facie*, it is open to the same criticism to which the yellow-covered novels, the "narratives of noted highwaymen," and the "awful beacons" of the Northern book-stalls should be subjected.

The intent and spirit of this report may be gathered from the following extract: "The evidence proves, beyond all manner of doubt, a determination on the part of the rebel authorities, deliberately and persistently practised, for a long time past, to subject those of our soldiers who have been so unfortunate as to fall into their hands, to a system of treatment which has resulted in reducing many of those who have survived and been permitted to return to us, to a condition, both physically and mentally, which no language we can use, can adequately describe."—Report, p. 1. And they give also a letter from Edwin M. Stanton, the Northern Secretary of War, from which the following is an extract: "The enormity of the crime committed by the rebels towards our prisoners for the last several months is not known or realized by our people, and cannot but fill with horrour the civilized world, when the facts are fully revealed. There appears to have been a deliberate system of savage and barbarous treatment and starvation, the result of which will be that few (if any) of the prisoners that have been in their hands during the past winter, will ever again be in a condition to render any service or even to enjoy life."—Report, p. 4. And the Sanitary Commission, in their pamphlet, after picturing many scenes of privations and suffering, and bringing many charges of cruelty against the Confederate authorities, declare as follows:—"The conclusion is unavoidable, therefore, that these privations and sufferings have been designedly inflicted by the military and other authorities of the rebel Goverment, and could not have been due to causes which such authorities could not control."—p. 95.

After examining these publications, your committee approached the subject with an earnest desire to ascertain the truth. If their investigation should result in ascertaining that these charges (or any of them) were true, the committee desired, as far as might be in their power, and as far as they could influence the Congress, to remove the evils complained of, and to conform to the most humane spirit of civilization: and if these charges were unfounded and false, they deemed it as a sacred duty, without delay, to present to the Confederate Congress and people, and to the public eye of the enlightened world, a vindication of their country, and to relieve her authorities from the injurious slanders brought against her by her enemies. With these views, we have taken a considerable amount of testimony bearing on the subject. We have sought to obtain witnesses whose position or duties made them familiar with the facts testified to, and whose characters entitled them to full credit. We have not hesitated to examine Northern prisoners of war upon points and experience specially within their knowledge. We now present the testimony taken by us, and submit a report of facts and inferences fairly deducible from the evidence, from the admissions of our enemies, and from public records of undoubted authority.

First in order, your committee will notice the charge contained both in "Report No. 67," and in the "sanitary" publication, founded on the appearance and condition of the sick prisoners sent from Richmond to Annapolis and Baltimore about the last of April, 1864. These are the men, some of whom form the subjects of the photographs with which the United States Congressional Committee have adorned their report. The disingenuous attempt is made in both these publications to produce the impression that these sick and emaciated men were fair representatives of the general state of the prisoners held by the South, and that all their prisoners were being rapidly reduced to the same state by starvation and cruelty, and by neglect, ill treatment, and denial of proper food, stimulants, and medicines in the Confederate hospitals. Your committee take pleasure in saying that not only is this charge proved to be wholly false, but the evidence ascertains facts as to the Confederate hospitals in which Northern prisoners of war are treated, highly creditable to the authorities which established them, and to the surgeons and their aids who have so humanely conducted them. The facts are simply these:

The Federal authorities, in violation of the cartel, having for a long time refused exchange of prisoners, finally consented to a partial exchange of the sick and wounded on both sides. Accordingly, a number of such prisoners were sent from the hospitals in Richmond. General directions had been given that none should be sent except those who might be expected to endure the removal and passage with safety to their lives; but in some cases the surgeons were induced to depart from this rule, by the entreaties of some officers and men in the last stages of emaciation, suffering not only with excessive debility, but with "nostalgia," or home-sickness, whose cases were regarded as desperate, and who could not live if they remained, and might possibly improve if carried home. Thus it happened that some very sick and emaciated men were carried to Annapolis, but their illness was not the result of ill treatment or neglect. Such cases might be found in any large hospital, North or South. They might even be found in private families, where the sufferer would be surrounded by every comfort that love could bestow. Yet these are the cases which, with hideous violation of decency, the Northern committee have paraded in pictures and photographs. They have taken their own sick and enfeebled soldiers, have stripped them naked; have exposed them before a daguerreian apparatus; have pictured every shrunken limb and muscle—and all for the purpose, not of relieving their sufferings, but of bringing a false and slanderous charge against the South.

The evidence is overwhelming that the illness of these [Federal] prisoners was not the result of ill treatment or neglect. The testimony of Surgeons Semple and Spence, of Assistant Surgeons Tinsley, Marriott, and Miller, and of the Federal prisoners, E. P. Dalrymple, George Henry Brown, and Freeman B. Teague, ascertains this to the satisfaction of every candid mind. But in refuting this charge, your committee are compelled, by the evidence, to bring a counter-charge against the Northern authorities, which they fear will not be so easily refuted. In exchange, a number of Confederate sick and wounded prisoners have been at various times delivered at Richmond and at Savannah. The mortality among these on the passage and their condition when delivered, were so deplorable as to justify the charge that they had been treated with inhuman neglect by the Northern authorities.

Assistant Surgeon Tinsley testifies: "I have seen many of our prisoners returned from the North, who were nothing but skin and bones. They were as emaciated as a man could be to retain life, and the photographs (appended to 'Report No. 67,') would not be exaggerated representations of our returned prisoners to whom I thus allude. I saw two hundred and fifty of our sick brought in on litters from the steamer at Rockett's. Thirteen dead bodies were brought off the steamer the same night. At least thirty died in one night after they were received."

Surgeon Spence testifies: "I was at Savannah, and saw rather over three thousand prisoners received. The list showed that a large number had died on the passage from Baltimore to Savannah. The number sent from the Federal prisons was three thousand five hundred, and out of that number they delivered only three thousand and twenty-eight, to the best of my recollection. Capt. Hatch can give you the exact number. Thus, about four hundred and seventy-two died on the passage. I was told that sixty-seven dead bodies had been taken from one train of cars between Elmira and Baltimore. After being received at Savannah, they had the best attention possible, yet many died in a few days." "In carrrying out the exchange of disabled, sick, and wounded men, we delivered at Savannah and Charleston about eleven thousand Federal prisoners, and their physical condition compared most favourably with those we received in exchange, although of course the worst cases among the Confederates had been removed by death during the passage."

Richard H. Dibrell, a merchant of Richmond, and a member of the "ambulance committee," whose labors in mitigating the sufferings of the wounded have been acknowledged both by Confederate and Northern men, thus testifies concerning our sick and wounded soldiers at Savannah, returned from Northern prisons and hospitals: "I have never seen a set of men in worse condition. They were so enfeebled and emaciated that we lifted them like little children. Many of them were like living skeletons. Indeed, there was one poor boy, about seventeen years old, who presented the most distressing and deplorable appearance I ever saw. He was nothing but skin and bone, and besides this, he was literally eaten up with vermin. He died in the hospital in a few days after being removed thither, notwithstanding the kindest treatment and the use of the most judicious nourishment. Our men were in so reduced a condition, that on more than one trip up on the short passage of ten miles from the transports to the city, as many as five died. The clothing of the privates was in a wretched state of tatters and filth." "The mortality on the passage from Maryland was very great, as well as that on the passage from the prisons to the port from which they started. I cannot state the exact number, but I think I heard that three thousand five hundred were started, and we only received about three thousand and twenty-seven." I have looked at the photographs appended to 'Report No. 67' of the committee of the Federal Congress, and do not hesitate to declare that several of our men were worse cases of emaciation and sickness than any represented in these photographs."

The testimony of Mr. Dibrell is confirmed by that of Andrew Johnston, also a merchant of Richmond, and a member of the "ambulance committee."

Thus it appears that the sick and wounded Federal prisoners at Annapolis whose condition has been made a subject of outcry and of widespread complaint by the Northern Congress, were not in a worse state than were the Confederate prisoners returned from Northern hospitals and prisons of which the humanity and superiour management are made subjects of special boasting by the United States Sanitary Commission!

In connection with this subject, your committee take pleasure in reporting the facts ascertained by their investigations concerning the Confederate hospitals for sick and wounded Federal prisoners. They have made personal examination, and have taken evidence specially in relation to "Hospital No. 21," in Richmond, because this has been made subject of distinct charge in the publication last mentioned. It has been shown, not only by the evidence of the surgeons and their assistants, but by that of Federal prisoners, that the treatment of the Northern prisoners in these hospitals has been everything that humanity could dictate; that their wards have been well ventilated and clean; their food the best that could be procured for them—and in fact, that no distinction had been made between their treatment and that of our own sick and wounded men. Moreover, it is proved that it has been the constant practice to supply to the patients, out of the hospital funds, such articles as milk, butter, eggs, tea, and other delicacies, when they were required by the condition of the patients. This is proved by the testimony of E. P. Dalrymple, of New York, George Henry Brown, of Pennsylvania, and Freeman B Teague, of New Hampshire, whose depositions accompany this report.

This humane and considerate usage was *not* adopted in the United States hospital on Johnson's Island, where Confederate sick and wounded officers were treated. Col. J. H. Holman thus testifies: "The Federal authorities did not furnish to the sick prisoners the nutriment and other articles which were prescribed by their own surgeons. All they would do was to permit the prisoners to buy the nutriment or stimulants needed; and if they had no money, they could not get them. I know this, for I was in the hospital sick myself, and I had to buy, myself, such articles as eggs, milk, flour, chickens, and butter, after their doctors had prescribed them. And I know this was generally the case, for we had to get up a fund among ourselves for this purpose, to aid those who were not well supplied with money." This statement is confirmed by the testimony of Acting-Assistant Surgeon John J. Miller, who was at Johnson's Island for more than eight months. When it is remembered that such articles as eggs, milk, and butter were very scarce and high-priced in Richmond, and plentiful and cheap at the North, the contrast thus presented may well put to shame the "Sanitary Commission," and dissipate the self-complacency with which they have boasted of the superiour humanity in the Northern prisons and hospitals.

Your committee now proceed to notice other charges in these publications. It is said that their prisoners were habitually stripped of blankets and other property, on being captured. What pillage may have been committed on the battle-field, after the excitement of combat, your committee cannot know. But they feel well assured that such pillage was never encouraged by the Confederate generals, and bore no comparison to the wholesale robbery and destruction to which the Federal armies have abandoned themselves, in possessing parts of our territory. It is certain that after the prisoners were brought to the Libby and other prisons in Richmond no such pillage was permitted. Only articles which came properly under the head of munitions of war, were taken from them.

The next charge noticed is, that the guards around the Libby prison were in the habit of recklessly and inhumanly shooting at the prisoners, upon the most frivolous pretexts, and that the Confederate officers, so far from forbidding this, rather encouraged it, and made it a subject of sportive remark. This charge is wholly false and baseless. The "Rules and Regulations," appended to the deposition of Major Thomas P. Turner, expressly provide, "Nor shall any prisoner be fired upon by a sentinel or other person, except in case of revolt or attempted escape." Five or six cases have occurred in which prisoners have been fired on and killed or hurt; but every case has been made the subject of careful investigation and report, as will appear by the evidence. As a proper comment on this charge, your committee report that the practice of firing on our prisoners by the guards in the Northern prisons appears to have been indulged in to a most brutal and atrocious extent. See the depositions of C. C. Herrington, Wm. F. Gordon,

Jr., J. B. McCreary, Dr. Thomas P. Holloway and John P. Fennell. At Fort Delaware, a cruel regulation as to the use of the "sinks," was made the pretext for firing on and murdering several of our men and officers—among them, Lieut.-Col. Jones, who was lame, and was shot down by the sentinel while helpless and feeble, and while seeking to explain his condition. Yet this sentinel was not only not punished, but was promoted for his act. At Camp Douglas, as many as eighteen of our men are reported to have been shot in a single month. These facts may well produce a conviction in the candid observer, that it is the North and not the South that is open to the charge of deliberately and wilfully destroying the lives of the prisoners held by her.

The next charge is, that the Libby and Belle Isle prisoners were habitually kept in a filthy condition, and that the officers and men confined there were prevented from keeping themselves sufficiently clean to avoid vermin and similar discomforts. The evidence clearly contradicts this charge. It is proved by the depositions of Maj. Turner, Lieut. Bossieux, Rev. Dr. McCabe, and others, that the prisons were kept constantly and systematically policed and cleansed; that in the Libby there was an ample supply of water conducted to each floor by the city pipes, and that the prisoners were not only not restricted in its use, but urged to keep themselves clean. At Belle Isle, for a brief season (about three weeks), in consequence of a sudden increase in the number of prisoners, the police was interrupted, but it was soon restored, and ample means for washing, both themselves and their clothes, were at all times furnished to the prisoners. It is doubtless true, that notwithstanding these facilities, many of the prisoners were lousy and filthy; but it was the result of their own habits, and not of neglect in the discipline or arrangements of the prison. Many of the prisoners were captured and brought in while in this condition. The Federal general, Neal Dow well expressed their character and habits. When he came to distribute clothing among them, he was met by profane abuse, and he said to the Confederate officer in charge, "You have here the scrapings and rakings of Europe." That such men should be filthy in their habits might be expected.

We next notice the charge that the boxes of provisions and clothing sent to the prisoners from the North, were not delivered to them, and were habitually robbed and plundered, by permission of the Confederate authorities. The evidence satisfies your committee that this charge is, in all substantial points, untrue. For a period of about one month there was a stoppage in the delivery of boxes, caused by a report that the Federal authorities were forbidding the delivery of similar supplies to our prisoners. But the boxes were put in a warehouse, and afterwards delivered. For some time no search was made of boxes from the "Sanitary Committee," intended for the prisoners' hospital. But a letter was intercepted, advising that money should be sent in these boxes, as they were never searched; which money was to be used in bribing the guard, and thus releasing the prisoners. After this, it was deemed necessary to search every box, which necessarily produced some delay. Your committee are satisfied that if these boxes or their contents were robbed, the prison officials are not responsible therefor. Beyond doubt, robberies were often committed by prisoners themselves, to whom the contents were delivered for distribution to their owners. Notwithstanding all this alleged pillage, the supplies seem to have been sufficient to keep the quarters of the prisons so well furnished that they frequently presented, in the language of a witness, "the appearance of a large grocery store."

In connection with this point, your committee refer to the testimony of a Federal officer, Col. James M. Sanderson, whose letter is annexed to the deposition of Major Turner. He testifies to the full delivery of the clothing and supplies from the North, and to the humanity and kindness of the Confederate officers—specially mentioning Lieut. Bossieux, commanding on Belle Isle. His letter was addressed to the President of the United States Sanitary Commission, and was beyond doubt received by them, having been forwarded by the regular flag of truce. Yet the scrupulous and honest gentlemen composing that commission, have not found it convenient for their purposes to insert this letter in their publication! Had they been really searching for the truth, this letter would have aided them in finding it.

Your committee proceed next to notice the allegation that the Confederate authorities had prepared a mine under the Libby prison, and placed in it a quantity of gunpowder for the purpose of blowing up the buildings with their inmates, in case of an attempt to rescue them. After ascertaining all the facts bearing on this subject, your committee believe that what was done under the circumstances, will meet a verdict of approval from all whose prejudices do not blind them to the truth. The state of things was unprecedented in history, and must be judged of according to the motives at work, and the result accomplished. A large body of Northern raiders, under one Col. Dahlgren, was approaching Richmond. It was ascertained, by the reports of prisoners captured from them, and other evidence, that their design was to enter the city, to set fire to the buildings, public and private, for which purpose turpentine balls in great number had been prepared; to murder the President of the Confederate States, and other prominent men; to release the prisoners of war, then numbering five or six thousand; to put arms into their hands, and to turn over the city to indiscriminate pillage, rape, and slaughter. At the same time a plot was discovered among the prisoners to co-operate in this scheme, and a large number of knives and slung-shot (made by putting stones into woollen stockings) were detected in places of concealment about their quarters. To defeat a plan so diabolical, assuredly the sternest means were justified. If it would have been right to put to death any one prisoner attempting to escape under such circumstances, it seems logically certain that it would have been equally right to put to death any number making such attempt. But in truth the means adopted were those of humanity and prevention, rather than of execution. The Confederate authorities felt able to meet and repulse Dahlgren and his raiders, if they could prevent the escape of the prisoners.

The real object was to save their lives, as well as those of our citizens. The guard force at the prisons was small, and all the local troops in and around Richmond were needed to meet the threatened attack. Had the prisoners escaped, the women and children of the city, as well as their homes, would have been at the mercy of five thousand outlaws. Humanity required that the most summary measures should be used to deter them from any attempt at escape.

A mine was prepared under the Libby prison; a sufficient quantity of gunpowder was put into it, and pains were taken to inform the prisoners that any attempt at escape made by them would be effectually defeated. The plan succeeded perfectly. The prisoners were awed and kept quiet. Dahlgren and his party were defeated and scattered. The danger passed away, and in a few weeks the gunpowder was removed. Such are the facts. Your committee do not hesitate to make them known, feeling assured that the conscience of the enlightened world and the great law of self-preservation will justify all that was done by our country and her officers.

We now proceed to notice, under one head, the last and gravest charge made in these publications. They assert that the Northern prisoners in the hands of the Confederate authorities have been starved, frozen, inhumanly punished, often confined in foul and loathsome quarters, deprived of fresh air and exercise, and neglected and maltreated in sickness—and that all this was done upon a deliberate, wilful, and long-conceived plan of the Confederate Government and officers, for the purpose of destroying the lives of these prisoners, or of rendering them forever incapable of military service. This charge accuses the Southern Government of a crime so horrible and unnatural that it could never have been made except by those ready to blacken with slander men whom **they** have long injured and hated.   Your committee feel bound to reply to it calmly but emphatically.   They pronounce it false in fact, and in design ; false in the basis on which it assumes to rest, and false in its estimate of the motives which have controlled the Southern authorities.

At an early period in the present contest the Confederate Government recognized their obligation to treat prisoners of war with humanity and consideration.   Before any laws were passed on the subject, the Executive Department provided such prisoners as fell into their hands, with proper quarters and barracks to shelter them, and with rations the same in quantity and quality as those furnished to the Confederate soldiers who guarded these prisoners.   They also showed an earnest wish to mitigate the sad condition of prisoners of war, by a system of fair and prompt exchange—and the Confederate Congress co-operated in these humane views.   By their act, approved on the 21st day of May, 1861, they provided that " all prisoners of war taken, whether on land or at sea, during the pending hostilities with the United States, shall be transferred by the captors from time to time, and as often as convenient, to the Department of War ; and it shall be the duty of the Secretary of War, with the approval of the President, to issue such instructions to the Quartermaster-General and his subordinates, as shall provide for the safe custody and sustenance of prisoners of war ; and the rations furnished prisoners of war shall be the same in quantity and quality as those furnished to enlisted men in the Army of the Confederacy."   Such were the declared purpose and policy of the Confederate Government towards prisoners of war—amid all the privations and losses to which their enemies have subjected them, they have sought to carry them into effect.

Our investigations for this preliminary report have been confined chiefly to the rations and treatment of the prisoners of war at the Libby and other prisons in Richmond and on Belle Isle.   This we have done, because the publications to which we have alluded chiefly refer to them, and because the " Report No. 67 " of the Northern Congress plainly intimates the belief that the treatment in and around Richmond was worse than it was farther South.   That report says : " It will be observed from the testimony that all the witnesses who testify upon that point state that the treatment they received while confined at Columbia, South Carolina, Dalton, Georgia, and other places, was far more humane than that they received at Richmond, where the authorities of the so-called Confederacy were congregated," Report, p. 3.

The evidence proves that the rations furnished to prisoners of war in Richmond and on Belle Isle, have been never less than those furnished to the Confederate soldiers who guarded them, and have at some seasons been larger in quantity and better in quality than those furnished to Confederate troops in the field.   This has been because, until February, 1864, the Quartermaster's Department furnished the prisoners, and often had provsions or funds, when the Commissary Department was not so well provided.   Once and only once, for a few weeks, the prisoners were without meat, but a larger quantity of bread and vegetable food was in consequence supplied to them.   How often the gallant men composing the Confederate Army, have been without meat, for even longer intervals, your committee do not deem it necessary to say.   Not less than sixteen ounces of bread and four ounces of bacon, or six ounces of beef, together with beans and soup, have been furnished per day to the prisoners.   During most of the time the quantity of meat furnished to them has been greater than these amounts ; and even in times of the greatest scarcity, they have received as much as the Southern soldiers who guarded them.   The scarcity of meat and of breadstuffs in the South, in certain places, has been the result of the savage policy of our enemies in burning barns filled with wheat or corn, destroying agricultural implements, and driving off or wantonly butchering hogs and cattle. Yet amid all these privations, we have given to their prisoners the rations above mentioned. It is well known that this quantity of food is sufficient to keep in health a man who does not labour hard. All the learned disquisitions of Dr. Ellerslie Wallace on the subject of starvation, might have been spared, for they are all founded on a false basis. It will be observed that few (if any) of the witnesses examined by the " Sanitary Commission " speak with any accuracy of the quantity (in weight) of the food actually furnished to them. Their statements are merely conjectural and comparative, and cannot weigh against the positive testimony of those who superintended the delivery of large quantities of food, cooked and distributed according to a fixed ratio, for the number of men to be fed.

The statements of the " Sanitary Commission " as to prisoners freezing to death on Belle Isle, are absurdly false. According to that statement, it was common, during a cold spell in winter, to see several prisoners frozen to death every morning in the places in which they had slept. This picture, if correct, might well excite our horrour; but unhappily for its sensational power, it is but a clumsy daub, founded on the fancy of the painter. The facts are, that tents were furnished sufficient to shelter all the prisoners; that the Confederate commandant and soldiers on the Island were lodged in similar tents; that a fire was furnished in each of them; that the prisoners fared as well as their guards; and that only one of them was ever frozen to death, and he was frozen by the cruelty of his own fellow-prisoners, who thrust him out of the tent in a freezing night, because he was infested with vermin. The proof as to the healthiness of the prisoners on Belle Isle, and the small amount of mortality, is remarkable, and presents a fit comment on the lugubrious pictures drawn by the " Sanitary Commission," either from their own fancies, or from the fictions put forth by their false witnesses. Lieut. Bossieux proves that from the establishment of the prison camp on Belle Isle in June, 1862, to the 10th of February, 1865, more than twenty thousand prisoners had been at various times there received, and yet that the whole number of deaths during this time, was only one hundred and sixty-four. And this is confirmed by the Federal colonel, Sanderson, who states that the average number of deaths per month on Belle Isle, was " from two to five; more frequently the lesser number." The sick were promptly removed from the Island to the hospitals in the city.

Doubtless the " Sanitary Commission " have been to some extent led astray by their own witnesses, whose character has been portrayed by Gen. Neal Dow, and also by the editor of the New York *Times*, who, in his issue of January 6th, 1865, describes the material for recruiting the Federal army as " wretched vagabonds, of depraved morals, decrepit in body, without courage, self-respect, or conscience. They are dirty, disorderly, thievish, and incapable."

In reviewing the charges of cruelty, harshness, and starvation to prisoners made by the North, your committee have taken testimony as to the treatment of our own officers and soldiers, in the hands of the enemy. It gives us no pleasure to be compelled to speak of the suffering inflicted upon our gallant men; but the self-laudatory style in which the " Sanitary Commission " have spoken of their prisons, makes it proper that the truth should be presented. Your committee gladly acknowledge that in many cases our prisoners experienced kind and considerate treatment; but we are equally assured that in nearly all the prison stations of the North—at Point Lookout, Fort McHenry, Fort Delaware, Johnson's Island, Elmira, Camp Chase, Camp Douglas, Alton, Camp Morton, the Ohio Penitentiary and the prisons of St. Louis, Missouri, our men have suffered from insufficient food, and have been subjected to ignominious, cruel, and barbarous practices, of which there is no parallel in anything that has occurred in the South. The witnesses who were at Point Lookout, Fort Delaware, Camp Morton and

Camp Douglas, testify that they have often seen our men picking up the scraps and refuse thrown out from the kitchens, with which to appease their hunger. Dr. Herrington proves that at Fort Delaware unwholesome bread and water produced diarrhœa in numberless cases among our prisoners, and that "their sufferings were greatly aggravated by the regulation of the camp, which forbade more than twenty men at a time at night to go to the sinks. I have seen as many as five hundred men in a row waiting their time. The consequence was that they were obliged to use the places where they were. This produced great want of cleanliness, and aggravated the disease." Our men were compelled to labour in unloading Federal vessels and in putting up buildings for Federal officers, and, if they refused, were driven to the work with clubs.

The treatment of Brig.-Gen. J. H. Morgan and his officers was brutal and ignominious in the extreme. It will be found stated in the depositions of Capt. M. D. Logan, Lieut. W. P. Crow, Lieut.-Col. James B. McCreary, and Capt. B. A. Tracey, that they were put in the Ohio Penitentiary, and compelled to submit to the treatment of felons. Their beards were shaved, and their hair was cut close to the head. They were confined in convicts' cells, and forbidden to speak to each other. For attempts to escape, and for other offences of a very light character, they were subjected to the horrible punishment of the dungeon. In midwinter, with the atmosphere many degrees below zero, without blanket or overcoat, they were confined in a cell, without fire or light, with a fetid and poisonous air to breathe—and here they were kept until life was nearly extinct. Their condition on coming out, was so deplorable as to draw tears from their comrades. The blood was oozing from their hands and faces. The treatment in the St. Louis prison was equally barbarous. Capt. William H. Sebring testifies: "Two of us, A. C. Grimes and myself, were carried out into the open air in the prison yard, on the 25th of December, 1863, and handcuffed to a post. Here we were kept all night in sleet, snow, and cold. We were relieved in the day-time, but again brought to the post and handcuffed to it in the evening—and thus we were kept all night until the 2d of January, 1864. I was badly frost-bitten and my health was much impaired. This cruel infliction was done by order of Capt. Byrnes, Commandant of Prisons in St. Louis. He was barbarous and insulting to the last degree."

But even a greater inhumanity than any we have mentioned was perpetrated upon our prisoners at Camp Douglas and Camp Chase. It is proved by the testimony of Thomas P. Holloway, John P. Fennell, H. H. Barlow, H. C. Barton, C. D. Bracken, and J. S. Barlow, that our prisoners in large numbers were put into "condemned camps," where small-pox was prevailing, and speedily contracted this loathsome disease, and that as many as forty new cases often appeared daily among them. Even the Federal officers who guarded them to the camp protested against this unnatural atrocity: yet it was done. The men who contracted the disease were removed to a hospital about a mile off, but the plague was already introduced, and continued to prevail. For a period of more than twelve months the disease was constantly in the camp, yet our prisoners during all this time were continually brought to it, and subjected to certain infection. Neither do we find evidences of amendment on the part of our enemies, notwithstanding the boasts of the "sanitary commission." At Nashville, prisoners recently captured from General Hood's army, even when sick and wounded, have been cruelly deprived of all nourishment suited to their condition; and other prisoners from he same army have been carried into the infected Camps Douglas and Chase.

Many of the soldiers of General Hood's army were frost-bitten by being kept day and night in an exposed condition before they were put into Camp Douglas. Their sufferings are truthfully depicted in the evidence. At Alton and Camp Morton the same inhuman practice of putting our prisoners into camps infected by small-pox, prevailed.

It was equivalent to murdering many of them by the torture of a contagious disease. The insufficient rations at Camp Morton forced our men to appease their hunger by pounding up and boiling bones, picking up scraps of meat and cabbage from the hospital slop tubs, and even eating rats and dogs. The depositions of Wm. Ayres and J. Chambers Brent prove these privations.

The punishments often inflicted on our men for slight offences, have been shameful and barbarous. They have been compelled to ride a plank only four inches wide, called "Morgan's horse;" to sit down with their naked bodies in the snow for ten or fifteen minutes, and have been subjected to the ignominy of stripes from the belts of their guards. The pretext has been used, that many of their acts of cruelty have been by way of retaliation. But no evidence has been found to prove such acts on the part of the Confederate authorities. It is remarkable that in the case of Colonel Streight and his officers, they were subjected only to the ordinary confinement of prisoners of war. No special punishment was used except for specific offences ; and then the greatest infliction was to confine Colonel Streight for a few weeks in a basement room of the Libby prison, with a window, a plank floor, a stove, a fire, and plenty of fuel.

We do not deem it necessary to dwell further on these subjects. Enough has been proved to show that great privations and sufferings have been borne by the prisoners on both sides.

WHY HAVE NOT PRISONERS OF WAR BEEN EXCHANGED ?

But the question forces itself upon us, why have these sufferings been so long continued ? Why have not the prisoners of war been exchanged, and thus some of the darkest pages of history spared to the world ? In the answer to this question must be found the test of responsibility for all the sufferings, sickness and heart-broken sorrow that have visited more than eighty thousand prisoners within the past two years. On this question, your committee can only say that the Confederate authorities have always desired a prompt and fair exchange of prisoners. Even before the establishment of a cartel they urged such exchange, but could never effect it by agreement until the large preponderance of prisoners in our hands made it the interest of the Federal authorities to consent to the cartel of July 22d, 1862. The 9th article of that agreement expressly provided, that in case any misunderstanding should arise, it *should not interrupt the release of prisoners on parole*, but should be made the subject of friendly explanation. Soon after this cartel was established, the policy of the enemy in seducing negro slaves from their masters, arming them and putting white officers over them to lead them against us, gave rise to a few cases in which questions of crime under the internal laws of the Southern States appeared. Whether men who encouraged insurrection and murder could be held entitled to the privileges of prisoners of war under the cartel, was a grave question. But these cases were few in number, and ought never to have interrupted the general exchange. We were always ready and anxious to carry out the cartel in its true meaning, and it is certain that the 9th article required that the prisoners on both sides should be released, and that the few cases as to which misunderstanding occurred should be left for final decision. Doubtless if the preponderance of prisoners had continued with us, exchanges would have continued. But the fortunes of war threw the larger number into the hands of our enemies. Then they refused further exchanges, and for twenty-two months this policy has continued. Our Commissioner of Exchange has made constant efforts to renew them. In August, 1864, he consented to a proposition which had been repeatedly made, to exchange officer for officer and man for man, leaving the surplus in captivity. Though this was a departure from the cartel, our anxiety for the exchange induced us to consent. Yet, the Federal authorities repudiated their previous offer, and refused even this partial compliance with the cartel. Secretary Stanton, who has unjustly charged the Confederate authorities with inhumanity, is open to the charge of having done all in his power to prevent a fair exchange, and thus to prolong the sufferings of which he speaks; and very recently, in a letter over his signature, Benjamin F Butler has declared that in April, 1864, the Federal Lieut.-Gen. Grant forbade him " to deliver to the rebels a single able-bodied man ;" and moreover, Gen. Butler acknowledges that in answer to Col. Ould's letter consenting to the exchange, officer for officer and man for man, he wrote a reply, "not diplomatically but obtrusively and demonstratively, *not for the purpose of furthering exchange* of prisoners, but for the purpose of preventing and stopping the exchange, and *furnishing a ground on which we could fairly stand*."

These facts abundantly show that the responsibility of refusing to exchange prisoners of war rests with the Government of the United States, and the people who have sustained that Government, and every sigh of captivity, every groan of suffering, every heart broken by hope deferred among these eighty thousand prisoners, will accuse them in the judgment of the just.

With regard to the prison stations at Andersonville, Salisbury, and other places south of Richmond, your committee have not made extended examination, for reasons which have already been stated. We are satisfied that privation, suffering and mortality, to an extent much to be regretted, did prevail among the prisoners there, but they were not the result of neglect, still less of design, on the part of the Confederate Government. Haste in preparation ; crowded quarters, prepared only for a smaller number ; frequent removals to prevent recapture ; want of transportation and scarcity of food, have all resulted from the pressure of the war, and the barbarous manner in which it has been conducted by our enemies. Upon these subjects your committee propose to take further evidence, and to report more fully hereafter.

But even now enough is known to vindicate the South, and to furnish an overwhelming answer to all complaints on the part of the U. S. Government or people, that their prisoners were stinted in food or supplies. Their own savage warfare has wrought all the evil. They have blockaded our ports; have excluded from us food, clothing and medicines; have even declared medicines contraband of war, and have repeatedly destroyed the contents of drug stores, and the supplies of private physicians in the country ; have ravaged our country ; burned our houses, and destroyed growing crops and farming implements. One of their officers (General Sheridan) has boasted in his official report, that, in the Shenandoah Valley alone, he burned two thousand barns filled with wheat and corn; that he burned all the mills in the whole tract of country ; destroyed all the factories of cloth, and killed or drove off every animal, even to the poultry, that could contribute to human sustenance. These desolations have been repeated again and again in different parts of the South. Thousands of our families have been driven from their homes, as helpless and destitute refugees. Our enemies have destroyed the railroads and other means of transportation, by which food could be supplied from abundant districts to those without it. While thus desolating our country, in violation of the usages of civilized warfare, they have refused to exchange prisoners; have forced us to keep fifty thousand of their men in captivity—and yet have attempted to attribute to us the sufferings and privations caused by their own acts. We cannot doubt that in the view of civilization we shall stand acquitted, while they must be condemned.

In concluding this preliminary report, we will notice the strange perversity of interpretation which has induced the "Sanitary Commission" to affix as a motto to their pamphlet, the words of the compassionate Redeemer of mankind:

"For I was anhungered and ye gave me no meat: I was thirsty and ye gave me no drink: I was a stranger and ye took me not in: naked, and ye clothed me not: sick and in prison and ye visited me not."

We have yet to learn on what principle the Federal soldiers sent with arms in their hands to destroy the lives of our people; to waste our land, burn our houses and barns, and drive us from our homes, can be regarded by us as the followers of the meek and lowly Redeemer, so as to claim the benefit of his words. Yet even these soldiers, when taken captive by us, have been treated with proper humanity. The cruelties inflicted on our prisoners at the North may well justify us in applying to the "Sanitary Commission" the stern words of the Divine Teacher: "Thou hypocrite, first cast out the beam out of thine own eye, and then shalt thou see clearly to cast out the mote out of thy brother's eye."

We believe that there are many thousands of just, honourable, and humane people in the United States, upon whom this subject, thus presented, will not be lost; that they will do all they can to mitigate the horrours of war; to complete the exchange of prisoners, now happily in progress, and to prevent the recurrence of such sufferings as have been narrated. And we repeat the words of the Confederate Congress, in their Manifesto of the 14th of June, 1864: "We commit our cause to the enlightened judgment of the world; to the sober reflections of our adversaries themselves, and to the solemn and righteous arbitrament of Heaven."

The general important fact of this report is, the declaration of the result of sworn investigations to the effect that from the necessity of the case, Federal prisoners suffered considerably in the South, but were not, unless exceptionally, treated with indignity, oppression or cruelty; and that the general rule was the other way as to our prisoners at the North— that the rule there was indignity, oppression and cruelty, and threatened, if not attempted, starvation in the midst of plenty. Where this fearful penalty was held over the victim was not in a land where the invader had proclaimed and carried out the policy of destroying every grain of wheat, and every ounce of meat, and everything that tended to its production; not in a land whose women and children were already perishing for bread, but starvation in a land that flowed with milk and honey, starvation in a land that had not only an abundance, but a superabundance even of the luxuries of life! *

* The author might make, from various memoranda he has personally collected of the experiences of Confederate prisoners, a very vast addition to the instances of suffering collected by the committee at Richmond. The following will suffice for examples. A Confederate officer, whose experience was at Johnson's Island, writes:

"No sugar, no coffee, no tea; only bread and salt beef, or salt pork, or salt fish, the latter as poor as poverty, and as unnutritious as pine shavings, varied occasionally with fresh beef, but never more than two-thirds enough of either. Occasionally, we would get one onion, or one potato each, and an ounce or so of hominy. Many would consume the whole at one meal; others thought it more wise to divide it into two or three meals; but all were hungry continually. Sir, it is a terrible thing to be hungry from day to day, from week to week, from month to month—to be always hungry! It is fearful to see three thousand men cooped up and undergoing such an ordeal! Should it be a matter of surprise that men dwindled from 200 to 140 and 100 pounds; that their eyes had a strange and eager expression; that they grew pale, cadaverous; that they walked with an

To the exposition made by the Richmond Congress of the humane endeavours of the Confederacy, with respect to prisoners of the war, there is yet an addition to be made. Impressed with the exaggerations of the newspapers on this subject, and desiring to secure the publication of the truth from time to time, Commissioner Ould, in January, 1864, wrote to Gen. Hitchcock the following letter :

CONFEDERATE STATES OF AMERICA,
WAR DEPARTMENT.
RICHMOND, VA., Jan. 24th, 1864·

MAJOR-GENERAL E. A. HITCHCOCK,
 Agent of Exchange ;

   SIR: In view of the present difficulties attending the exchange and release of prisoners, I propose that all such on each side shall be attended by a proper number of their own surgeons, who under rules to be established, shall be permitted to take charge of their health and comfort. I also propose that these surgeons shall act as commissaries, with power to receive and distribute such contributions of money, food, clothing and medicines as may be forwarded for the relief of the prisoners. I further propose that these surgeons shall be selected by their own Government, and that they shall have full liberty at any and all times through the Agents of Exchange, to make reports not only of their own acts, but of any matters relating to the welfare of the prisoners.

Respectfully your obedient servant,
RO. OULD, *Agent of Exchange.*

To this letter Commissioner Ould received no reply. In January, 1865, the proposition was renewed to Gen. Grant, with the following remarks : " It is true your prisoners are suffering. It is one of the calamities and

unsteady gait ; that all talked continually of ' something to eat '—of the good dinner, or breakfast, or supper they had had at times and places that seemed very long ago, and very far off; that they slept but to dream of sitting down to tables groaning with rich viands, where they ate, and ate, and still could not be satisfied ; that with miserly care they picked up every crumb ; that they pounded up old bones, and boiled them over and over, until they were as white as the driven snow; that they fished in the swill-barrel at the prison hospital ; that they greedily devoured rats and cats ; that they resorted to all manner of devices and tricks to cheat the surgeon out of a certificate ; that they became melancholy and dejected ; that they fell an easy prey to disease and death ! Ah ! there is many a poor fellow in his grave on Johnson's Island to-day, who would not be there had he been allowed wholesome food and enough of it."

 A personal friend of the author gives a long and painfully interesting account of his experience in a trans-shipment of prisoners from Hilton Head to Fort Delaware, the terrible facts of which rival all that is known of the horrours of the "middle passage." Of 420 prisoners shipped by sea, only sixty-two could walk when the vessel arrived at Fort Delaware ; the others were all down with sickness and exhaustion, and had to be taken to their cells on stretchers and ambulances. Many of them had lost their teeth by scurvy, and many were blind from disease. For months they had been subsisted on eight ounces of corn meal (ground in 1860) and one ounce of pickle (vitriol and salt), as a substitute for sorghum. Their rations were improved for a little while at Fort Delaware. But the regulations for cooking there allotted for such purpose to a company of 100 men every twenty-four hours, a log, 10 feet long and eight inches in diameter. There were no cooking utensils. Old pieces of tin were used over the fire. The men were locked up eighteen out of twenty-four hours, and only twenty at a time were allowed to pass out for the offices ofnature.

necessities of the war, made so not by our choice. We have done everything we can consistently with the duty we owe to ourselves. We intend to do the same in the future. But that great suffering must ensue if your prisoners remain in our hands, is very certain. For that reason, I propose that all of them be delivered to you in exchange, man for man, and officer for officer, according to grade, for those of ours whom you hold. Will not the cause of humanity be far more promoted by such a course, even if, as you suggest, the friends of prisoners, both North and South, are satisfied of the exaggeration of the reports of suffering so rife in both sections? If, however, prisoners are to remain in confinement, at least, let us mutually send to their relief and comfort stationary agents, whose official duty requires them to devote all their time and labour to their sacred mission."

Gen. Grant did not reply. Perhaps he thought matters were too near the end to entertain any new negotiations on the subject referred to. However this may be, whatever was to be the catastrophe, the conclusion is simply stated: it was to leave the Confederacy with a complete record of justice, a testimony of humanity, on the whole subject of the exchange and treatment of prisoners, which must ever remain among the noblest honours and purest souvenirs of a lost cause.

CHAPTER XXXIX.

HOW SHERMAN'S MARCH THROUGH GEORGIA DEVELOPED A CRISIS IN THE CONFEDERACY.—GEOGRAPHICAL IMPOSSIBILITY OF THE CONQUEST OF THE SOUTH.—ADDRESS OF THE CONFEDERATE CONGRESS.—A VULGAR AND FALSE ESTIMATE OF THE ENEMY'S SUCCESS.—MAPS OF CONQUEST AND COBWEB LINES OF OCCUPATION.—GENERAL DECAY OF PUBLIC SPIRIT IN THE CONFEDERACY.—POPULAR IMPATIENCE OF THE WAR.—WANT OF CONFIDENCE IN PRESIDENT DAVIS' ADMINISTRATION.—BEWILDERED ATTEMPTS AT COUNTER-REVOLUTION. —EXECUTIVE MISMANAGEMENT IN RICHMOND.—HOW THE CONSCRIPTION LAW WAS CHEATED.—DESERTERS IN THE CONFEDERATE ARMIES.—PECULIAR CAUSES FOR IT.—ITS FRIGHTFUL EXTENT.—HOW IT WAS NOT A SIGN OF INFIDELITY TO THE CONFEDERATE CAUSE.— CONDITION OF THE COMMISSARIAT.—BREAD TAKEN FROM GEN. LEE'S ARMY TO FEED PRISONERS.—ALARMING REDUCTION OF SUPPLIES.—MAJOR FRENCH'S LETTER.—LEE'S TROOPS BORDERING ON STARVATION.—EIGHT POINTS PRESENTED TO CONGRESS.—WHAT IT DID.—THE CONDITION OF THE CURRENCY.—CONGRESS CURTAILS THE CURRENCY ONE-THIRD.—ACT OF 17TH FEBRUARY, 1864.—SECRETARY SEDDON GIVES THE *coup de grace* TO THE CURRENCY.—HIS NEW STANDARD OF VALUE IN WHEAT AT FORTY DOLLARS A BUSHEL.—DISORDERS OF THE CURRENCY AND COMMISSARIAT AS CONTRIBUTING TO DESERTIONS.—IMPRACTICABILITY OF ALL REMEDIES FOR DESERTIONS.—NO DISAFFECTION IN THE CONFEDERACY, EXCEPT WITH REFERENCE TO FAULTS OF THE RICHMOND ADMINISTRATION. —PRESIDENT DAVIS AND THE CONFEDERATE CONGRESS, &C.—THREE PRINCIPAL MEASURES IN CONGRESS DIRECTED AGAINST THE PRESIDENT.—REMONSTRANCE OF THE VIRGINIA DELEGATION WITH REFERENCE TO THE CABINET.—RESIGNATION OF MR. SEDDON.—PERSONAL RELATIONS BETWEEN PRESIDENT DAVIS AND GEN. LEE.—WHY THE LATTER DECLINED TO TAKE COMMAND OF ALL THE ARMIES OF THE CONFEDERACY.—WANT OF SELF-ASSERTION IN GEN. LEE'S CHARACTER.—WHY HIS INFLUENCE IN THE GENERAL AFFAIRS OF THE CONFEDERACY WAS NEGATIVE.—RECRIMINATION BETWEEN PRESIDENT DAVIS AND CONGRESS.—A SINGULAR ITEM IN THE CONSCRIPTION BUREAU.—REMARK OF MRS. DAVIS TO A CONFEDERATE SENATOR.—THE OPPOSITION LED BY SENATOR WIGFALL.—HIS TERRIBLE AND ELOQUENT INVECTIVES.—A CHAPTER OF GREAT ORATORY LOST TO THE WORLD.—AN APPARENT CONTRADICTION IN THE PRESIDENT'S CHARACTER.—THE INFLUENCE OF " SMALL FAVOURITES."—JOHN M. DANIEL'S OPINION OF PRESIDENT DAVIS' TEARS.—INFLUENCE OF THE PRESIDENT ALMOST ENTIRELY GONE IN THE LAST PERIODS OF THE WAR.—THE VISIBLE WRECKS OF HIS ADMINISTRATION.—HISTORY OF " PEACE PROPOSITIONS " IN CONGRESS.— THEY WERE GENERALITIES.—ANALYSIS OF THE " UNION PARTY " IN THE SOUTH.—HOW GOV. BROWN, OF GEORGIA, WAS USED BY IT.—ITS PERSISTENT DESIGN UPON THE VIRGINIA LEGISLATURE.—HOW IT WAS REBUFFED.—HEROIC CHOICE OF VIRGINIA.—PRESIDENT

DAVIS' TRIBUTE TO THIS STATE.—WANT OF RESOLUTION IN OTHER PARTS OF THE CONFEDERACY.—SUMMARY EXPLANATION OF THE DECLINE AND FALL OF THE CONFEDERACY.—PROPOSITION TO ARM THE SLAVES OF THE SOUTH INDICATIVE OF A DESPERATE CONDITION.—HOW IT WAS IMPRACTICABLE AND ABSURD.—NOT FIVE THOUSAND SPARE MUSKETS IN THE CONFEDERACY.—PALTRY LEGISLATION OF CONGRESS.—GRASPING AT SHADOWS.

THERE was nothing fatal in a military point of view in Sherman's memorable march; and yet it dated the first chapter of the subjugation of the Confederacy. It brought the demoralization of the country to the surface; it had plainly originated in the pragmatic and excessive folly of President Davis; it furnished a striking occasion for recrimination, and was accompanied with a loss of confidence in his administration, that nothing but a miracle could repair.

We have already referred in another part of this work to the physical impossibility of the subjugation of the South at the hands of the North, as long as the integrity of the public resolution was maintained. This impossibility was clearly and distinctly stated, in an address of the Congress to the people of the Confederate States as late as the winter of 1864–5. That body then declared, with an intelligence that no just student of history will fail to appreciate: "The passage of hostile armies through our country, though productive of cruel suffering to our people, and great pecuniary loss, gives the enemy no permanent advantage or foothold. To subjugate a country, its civil government must be suppressed by a continuing military force, or supplanted by another, to which the inhabitants yield a voluntary or forced obedience. The passage of hostile armies through our territory cannot produce this result. Permanent garrisons would have to be stationed at a sufficient number of points to strangle all civil government before it could be pretended, even by the United States Government itself, that its authority was extended over these States. How many garrisons would it require? How many hundred thousand soldiers would suffice to suppress the civil government of all the States of the Confederacy, and to establish over them, even in name and form, the authority of the United States? In a geographical point of view, therefore, it may be asserted that the conquest of these Confederate States is impracticable."

The "geographical point of view" was decisive. The Confederacy was yet far from the extremity of subjugation, even after Sherman had marched from Northern Georgia to the sea-coast. He had left a long scar on the State; but he had not conquered the country; he had been unable to leave a garrison on his route since he left Dalton; and even if he passed into the Carolinas, to defeat him at any stage short of Richmond would be to re-open and recover all the country he had overrun. It was the fashion in the North to get up painted maps, in which all the territory of the South traversed by a Federal army, or over which there was a cob-web line of military occupation, was marked as conquest, and the other parts designated as the remnant of the Confederacy. This appeal to the vulgar eye was not without effect, but it was very absurd. Lines drawn upon paper alarmed the multitude; it was sufficient for them to know that the enemy was at such and such points; they never reflected that a title of occupation was worthless, without garrisons or footholds, that it often depended upon the issue of a single field, and that one or two defeats might put the whole of the enemy's forces back upon the frontiers of the Confederacy.

But the military condition of the Confederacy must be studied in connection with the general decay of public spirit that had taken place in the country, and the impatience of the hardships of the war, when the people had no longer confidence in its ultimate results. This impatience was manifested everywhere; it amounted to the feeling, that taking the war to be hopeless, the sooner it reached an adverse conclusion the better; that victories which merely amused the imagination and insured prolongation of the war, were rather to be deprecated than otherwise, and that to hurry the catastrophe would be mercy in the end. Unpopular as the administration of President Davis was, evident as was its failure, there were not nerve and elasticity enough in the country for a new experiment. The history of the last Confederate Congress is that of vacillating and bewildered attempts to reform and check the existing disorder and the evident tendency to ruin—weak, spasmodic action, showing the sense of necessity for effort, but the want of a certain plan and a sustained resolution.

In the last periods of the war, the demoralization of the Confederacy was painfully apparent. The popular resolution that had been equal to so long a contest, that had made so many proffers of devotion, that had given so many testimonies of sacrifice and endurance, had not perhaps inherently failed. But it had greatly declined in view of Executive mismanagement, in the utter loss of confidence in the Richmond Administration, and under the oppressive conviction that its sacrifices were wasted, its purposes thwarted, and its efforts brought to nought, by an incompetent government. This official mismanagement not only impaired the popular effort, but by the unequal distribution of burdens incident to weak and irregular governments, even where such is not designed, incurred the charge of corrupt favour, and exasperated large portions of the community. Rich and powerful citizens managed to escape the conscription—it was said in Richmond that it was "easier for a camel to go through the eye of a needle than for a rich man to enter Camp Lee;" but the rigour of the law did not spare the poor and helpless, and the complaint was made in the Confederate Congress that even destitute cripples had been taken from their homes, and confined in the conscription camps, without reference to physical disability so conspicuous and pitiful. It was not unusual to see at the railroad stations long lines of squalid men, with scraps of blankets in their hands, or small pine boxes of provisions, or whatever else they might snatch in their hurried departure from their homes, whence they had been taken almost without a moment's notice, and ticketed for the various camps of instruction in the Confederacy.

In armies thus recruited, desertions were the events of every day. There were other causes of desertion. Owing to the gross mismanagement of the commissariat, and a proper effort to mobilize the subsistence of the Confederacy, the armies were almost constantly on short rations, sometimes without a scrap of meat, and frequently in a condition bordering on absolute starvation. The Confederate soldier, almost starving himself, heard constantly of destitution at home, and was distressed with the suffering of his family, and was constantly plied with temptation to go to their protection and relief. A depreciated currency, which had been long abused by ignorant remedies and empirical treatment reduced nearly every home in the Confederacy to the straits of poverty. A loaf of bread was worth three dollars in Richmond. A soldier's monthly pay would scarcely buy a pair of socks; and paltry as this pay was, it was constantly in arrears, and there were thousands of soldiers who had not received a cent in the last two years of the war. In such a condition of affairs it was no wonder that desertions were numerous, where there was really no infidelity to the Confederate cause, and where the circumstances appealed so strongly to the senses of humanity, that it was impossible to deal harshly with the offence, and adopt for example the penalty of death. For every Confederate soldier who went over to the Federal lines, there were hundreds who dropped out from the rear and deserted to their homes. It was estimated in 1864, that the conscription would put more than four hundred thousand men in the field. Scarcely more than one-fourth of this number were found under arms when the close of the war tore the veil from the thin lines of Confederate defence.

CONDITION OF THE COMMISSARIAT.

We have elsewhere noticed the mismanagement of the Confederate commissariat, and the rapid diminution of supplies in the country. The close of the year 1864, was to find a general distress for food, and an actual prospect, even without victories of the enemy's arms, of starving the Confederacy into submission.

On the 2d May, two days before the battles of the last spring commenced, there were but two days' rations for Lee's army in Richmond. On the 23d June, when Wilson and Kautz cut the Danville Railroad, which was not repaired for twenty-three days, there were only thirteen days' rations on hand for Gen. Lee's army, and to feed it the Commissary General had to offer market rates for wheat, then uncut or shocked in the field—thereby incurring an excess of expenditure, which, if invested in corn and trans-portation, would have moved ten millions of bread rations from Augusta to Richmond.

At the opening of the campaign, Gen. Lee had urged the importance of having at least thirty days' reserves of provisions at Richmond and at Lynchburg. We have just seen how impossible it was to meet his views. It is a curious commentary on the alleged cruelty of Confederates to their prisoners, that in the winter of 1863-4, our entire reserve in Richmond of thirty thousand barrels of flour was consumed by Federal prisoners of war, and the bread taken from the mouths of our soldiers to feed them !

In the course of the campaign there had been the most serious reductions of supplies. The exhaustion of Virginia, the prevalence of drought and the desolation of the lower Valley and the contiguous Piedmont counties by the enemy, reduced her yield very considerably. The march of a Federal army through the heart of Georgia, and the possession of Savannah as a secure base for raids and other military operations, was, of course, calculated to reduce her yield. The amount of tithe had proved a very imperfect guide to the quantity of meat that might be obtained under its indications. Thus, in South Carolina, only two and one-half per cent. of the sum of the tithe was reported as purchased.

In Virginia the supply even of bread was practically exhausted, and but little more could be expected, even after the next wheat crop came in. The present corn crop was no better, probably worse, than the last. Add to this the destruction of whole districts by Federal armies, the effect of calling out the whole reserve force, and subsequently of revoking and putting into the field or in camp all detailed farmers at the period of seeding wheat, the absconding of numerous negroes under the fear of being placed in our armies, and it was apparent that no bread could be expected from Virginia.

In November, 1864, President Davis applied to the Commissary General to know if his magazines were increasing or diminishing. He sent back word that they were diminishing, and to give him more accurate information forwarded the following statement, made in the previous month, disclosing the alarming fact, that thirty million requisitions were unfilled.

Bureau of Subsistence. }
Richmond, October 18, 1864. }

Col. L. B. Northrop, Commissary-General of Subsistence :

Colonel : I have the honour to submit for your consideration the inclosed memorandum of meats on hand at the various depots and posts in the Confederate States, from which you will see at a glance the alarming condition of the commissariat. Georgia, Alabama, and Mississippi are the only States where we have an accumulation, and from these all the armies of the Confederacy are now subsisting, to say nothing of the prisoners. The Chief Commissary of Georgia telegraphs that he cannot send forward another pound. Alabama, under the most urgent call, has recently shipped 125,000 pounds, but cannot ship more. Mississippi is rendering all the aid possible to the command of Gen. Beauregard, in supplying beef. She is without bacon. Florida is exhausted, and can only respond to the local demand. South Carolina is scarcely able to subsist the troops at Charleston and the prisoners in the interiour of the State. During my late trip to North Carolina I visited every section of the State, for the purpose of ascertaining the true condition of affairs, and, under your orders, to send forward every pound of meat possible to the Army of Northern Virginia, and to supply the forts at Wilmington. After a thorough and careful examination I was unable (taking into consideration the local daily issues) to ship one pound to either Virgina or Wilmington; and but for the timely arrival of the steamer Banshee at Wilmington, Gen. Lee's order for thirty days' reserve at the forts could not have been furnished. From the enclosed memorandum you will notice that we have only on hand in the Confederate States 4,105,048 rations of fresh meat, and 3,426,519 rations of bacon and pork, which will subsist three hundred thousand men twenty-five days. We are now compelled to subsist, independent of the armies of the Confederacy, the prisoners of war, the Navy Department, and the different bureaus of the War Department.

Very respectfully, your obedient servant,

S. B. FRENCH, Major and C. S.

On the 5th December, the Commissary General brought the condition of things to the attention of the Secretary of War, coupling it with a statement of subsistence on hand, which showed nine days' rations on hand for Gen. Lee's army; and, quoting a letter from the commander, that day received, stating that his men were deserting on account of short rations, he urged prompt action. But none was taken. On the 14th December, nine days afterwards, Gen. Lee telegraphed President Davis that his army was without meat. This disaster was averted for the time by the timely arrival of several vessel loads of supplies at Wilmington.

In a secret session of the Confederate Congress in Richmond, the condition of the Confederacy, with respect to subsistence was thus enumerated:

First.—That there was not meat enough in the Southern Confederacy, for the armies it had in the field.

Second.—That there was not in Virginia either meat or bread enough for the armies within her limits.

Third.—That the bread supply from other places depended absolutely upon the keeping open the railroad connections of the South.

Fourth.—That the meat must be obtained from abroad through a seaport, and by a different system from that which prevailed.

Fifth.—That the bread could not be had by impressment, but must be paid for in market rates.

Sixth.—That the payment must be made in cash, which, so far, had not been furnished, and from present indications could not be, and, if possible, in a better medium than at present circulating.

Seventh.—That the transportation was not now adequate, from what-ever cause, to meet the necessary demands of the service.

Eighth.—That the supply of fresh meat to Gen. Lee's army was pre-carious, and if the army fell back from Richmond and Petersburg, there was every probability that it would cease altogether.

To meet these great necessities, nothing was done by the Government beyond a visionary scheme enacted in the last days of Congress, to raise three millions in specie to purchase supplies from those producers of the Confederacy, who were no longer willing to take scrip for their commodi-ties. Probably a tithe of the sum was raised, and the paltry scheme actu-ally executed in a few of the Western counties of Virginia.

THE CONDITION OF THE CURRENCY.

In 1864, the Confederate Government had given the finishing blow to the currency.

By the end of 1863, the policy of paying off all debts and making all purchases with money manufactured for the purpose as needed, had swollen the volume of the currency to more than six hundred millions of dollars. If we recollect that, before the war, fifty millions of bank notes, and twenty millions of specie, had sufficed for the currency of eleven States; and observe that about one-third of the area of these States was, in the beginning of 1864, under the control of the invader, we can appre-hend how excessively redundant a circulation exceeding six hundred mil-lions of dollars must have proved to be in the restricted territory remain-ing under the Confederate sway. Legislation was deemed to be absolutely necessary to bring down the bulk of this circulation, and to give greater value to the paper dollar. Accordingly, on the 17th February, 1864, an act of Congress was passed of a very sweeping character. The design of the law was, to call in from circulation, the whole outstanding six hundred millions of paper money; and to substitute for the old a new issue of greatly enhanced value. Its provisions were well calculated to effect this object. It provided that until the 1st day of April next succeeding the passage of the law, east of the Mississippi, and the 1st day of July west of this river, the holders of the outstanding currency above the denomination of five dollars, should be at liberty to exchange the same at par for four per cent. bonds of the government; which bonds should be receivable in the payment of all Confederate taxes. The law, however, did not exempt these bonds from taxation. It further provided that after the period first specified, this liberty of funding at par should cease, and that the entire body of the currency, except notes under the denomination of five dollars, should cease to be current, and should be exchangeable for the notes of a new issue at the rate of three dollars of the old issue for two dollars of the new ; and that non-interest-bearing notes of the denomination of one hundred dollars should be subject in addition to a further tax of ten per cent. per month, for the time they should remain outstanding after the 1st of April.   All the notes of the old issue were to be receivable in payment of taxes after the 1st of April, 1864, at the reduced rate at which they were exchangeable for the new issue.   But it was provided that notes of the denomination of one hundred dollars should not be exchangeable for notes of the new issue.   The privilege of exchanging should continue until the 1st day of January, 1865, and should then cease.   After that date, all treasury notes of the old issue remaining outstanding were to be subject to a tax of one hundred per cent.   Notes of the new issue, and notes of the old scaled to two-thirds of their full value, might be exchanged at the treasury for call certificates, bearing four per cent. interest and payable two years after the notification of a treaty of peace with the United States ; but notes of the old issue of the denomination of one hundred dollars were not to be thus exchangeable.

The effect of this measure was, to compel the conversion of all notes of the denomination of one hundred dollars into the four per cent. bonds.   It also presented to the holders of notes of the other denominations, the alternative of exchanging them at par for the four per cent. bonds, or of submitting to the tax of one-third, and converting them into notes of the new issue.   This latter course was preferred by a large majority of the note holders, under the conviction, that the reduction effected by the Act in this volume of the circulation, would so strengthen the value of the new issues, as to render the two new dollars which they received for the three old ones more valuable than the three.

The effect of the measure was, to produce a reduction in the mass of currency to the extent of rather less than three hundred millions of dollars ; and to leave, during the latter part of the year 1864, and the beginning of 1865, the amount of treasury notes in circulation in the Confederacy, at three hundred and twenty-five millions of dollars, an amount which was found to be perfectly manageable ; and which, indeed, under the depreciation of the new issue, which took place towards the close, was found to be inadequate to the wants of the country.   For, at the rate of sixty for one, at which the Confederate Government itself sold specie for several months in Richmond, this three hundred and twenty-five millions of currency represented only the value of five millions in specie and general property ; and the natural result was a very great stringency in the money market.

But the currency act of February signally failed in its object.   The new currency was not issued promptly.   The old currency remained in circulation, depreciated in value by the operation of causes which preceded the currency act, aided by the trenchant provisions of the Act itself.   The exchange of the new for the old money, was not effected in the country at large for many months; during which the worthlessness of the currency became an idea too firmly fixed in the public mind to be removed. One sad blunder, committed in the month of August, 1864, gave the money the *coup-de-grace*. The commissioners of the State of Virginia, charged with the duty of assessing the value of property taken by government, were directed by the Secretary of War, Mr. Seddon, to raise the price of wheat to forty dollars per bushel. At this rate the Secretary of War himself sold a large crop of wheat to the government, as did also a considerable number of his neighbours, who were large farmers on the James River. This action gave great dissatisfaction, and cheapened Confederate money to a degree from which it never recovered. Previously to this action, the people at large had for a long time received and paid the money at the rate of twenty for one. But when a prominent member of the Cabinet put down the value to forty for one, and authorized the commissioners of the government to shift the prices of commodities on this basis, the twenty dollar scale was discarded everywhere; and the public mind conceived a distrust of the money of which it never divested itself. The commissioners soon discovered their blunder, and re-established the old scale; but it was too late. From forty to one the price of the money went gradually down until, in February, it reached the low figure of sixty for one. For several months about this time, and until the evacuation of Richmond, the government steadily sold specie in Richmond at prices approximating that rate; and but for the value thus given, the money would have completely lost its purchasing power.

The statements of insufficiency of food in the army; the distress from the currency, the peculiar temptations which Confederate soldiers had to desert, not to the enemy, but to their own poverty-stricken homes; and the impracticability of executing the death penalty upon an offence which had so many circumstances to palliate it, sufficiently indicate how difficult to deal with was the question of desertions in the armies of the Southern Confederacy. The strong mind of Gen. Lee was long and painfully employed in devising a remedy for an evil which was eating into the vital parts of our resources, and which was indeed "*the army-worm*" of the Confederacy. But the evil was but little within the reach of any remedy and was logically uncontrollable. Appeals to patriotism were of but little avail, for in nine cases out of ten Confederate desertions had not happened from political disaffection, but from causes which had over-ridden and borne down public spirit. Attempts to reclaim deserters by force were equally unavailing, for whole regiments would have to be detached for the purpose, and there were unpleasant stories of the murder of enrolling officers in some parts of the Confederacy.

The fact is, the prime evil was behind desertions. In contemplating the decline of the Confederate armies, we must not rest on secondary causes, such as desertions; for these we have shown were almost entirely the consequence of a mismanaged commissariat, and a currency wrecked by mal-administration at Richmond. All the stories of Confederate decay are traced at last to one source: the misgovernment that had made make-shifts in every stage of the war, at last to the point of utter deprivation, and had finally broken down the spirit of its armies and the patience of its people. The disaffection in the Confederacy that was original, that was purely political, that did not proceed from some particular grievance of the administration in Richmond, was utterly inconsiderable, and was per-haps less than was ever known in any great popular commotion in the history of the world.

PRESIDENT DAVIS AND THE CONFEDERATE CONGRESS, &C.

There was a series of measures in the Confederate Congress directed against the administration of President Davis; it was the faint shadow of a counter-revolution; but as we have said, the disposition was not firm enough for a decisive experiment, and perhaps the public affairs of the Confederacy had lapsed too far to be reclaimed by legislative remedies. This series of measures was the appointment of Lee to a military dictator-ship; the restoration of Johnston to active command; and the reform of the Cabinet, so far at least as to secure a purer and better administration of the War office, then in the hands of Mr. Seddon, the wreck of a man, a walking skeleton, industrious, but facile, and at a period of life when the professional politician readily falls to the office of a tool in the hands of an arbitrary master. The two first measures were accomplished but im-perfectly. The command of all the Confederate armies was given to Gen. Lee, but this conscientious chieftain never practically asserted it. The restoration of Johnston was ungraciously conceded by President Davis; but he was not put in command of the forces south of Richmond until they had been swept by Sherman through two States into the forests of North Carolina, and were so broken and disorganized that the campaign may be said to have been already lost.

A delegation of the Virginia members of Congress, headed by Mr. Bo-cock, the speaker of the House, addressed to President Davis an earnest but most respectful paper, expressing their want of confidence in the ca-pacity and services of his Cabinet. The President resented the address as impertinent; and when Mr. Seddon, Secretary of War, recognizing the censure as particularly directed against himself, a Virginian, insisted upon resigning, President Davis took occasion to declare that the event of this resignation would in no manner change the policy or course of his administration, and made it very plain that the course of Mr. Seddon was to be ascribed to his punctilio, and to be taken in no manner as a triumph of the Opposition in Congress.

No man within the limits of the Southern Confederacy had such influence over its President as Gen. Lee. It was the only happy instance of well-bestowed confidence and merited deference on the part of President Davis; and to the last period of the war entire accord, and a warm personal friendship existed between himself and the commander of the Army of Northern Virginia. It will naturally be asked why, in such relations, Gen. Lee did not impose his views upon the President, varying as they did from the actual conduct of his administration, and inclined, as all the Confederacy knew, to a policy very different from that which President Davis actually pursued. Gen. Lee was in favour of enlisting negro troops, and he was anxious for the reorganization of the forces south of Richmond, and the restoration of Johnston to command. But for a long time Davis carried both points against him. Gen. Lee was offered the entire and exclusive conduct of the military affairs of the Confederacy; Congress made him commander-in-chief; the Legislature of Virginia passed a resolution declaring that "the appointment of Gen. Robert E. Lee to the command of all the armies of the Confederate States would promote their efficiency and operate powerfully to reanimate the spirits of the armies, as well as of the people of the several States, and to inspire increased confidence in the final success of our cause." Yet Gen. Lee did not accept the trust; he remained with his limited command in Virginia; he made no effort to carry out his views against the administration at Richmond. And what is most remarkable in all these differences between President Davis and Gen. Lee, there never was even a momentary disturbance of kindly relations, as between themselves, and of mutual compliments. Indeed, President Davis replied to the Legislature of Virginia, that he had desired to surrender all military affairs to Gen. Lee, but that the latter persisted in his refusal to accept a trust of such magnitude. He said: "The opinion expressed by the General Assembly in regard to Gen. R. E. Lee has my full concurrence. Virginia cannot have a higher regard for him, or greater confidence in his character and ability, than is entertained by me. When Gen. Lee took command of the Army of Northern Virginia, he was in command of all the armies of the Confederate States by my order of assignment. He continued in this general command, as well as in the immediate command of the Army of Northern Virginia, as long as I would resist his opinion that it was necessary for him to be relieved from one of these two duties. Ready as he has ever shown himself to be to perform any service that I desired him to render to his country, he left it for me to choose between his withdrawal from the command of the army in the field, and relieving him of the general command of all the armies of the Confederate States. It was only when satisfied of this necessity that I came to the conclusion to relieve him from the general command, believing that the safety of the capital and the success of our cause depended, in a great measure, on then retaining him in the command in the field of the Army of Northern Virginia. On several subsequent occasions, the desire on my part to enlarge the sphere of Gen. Lee's usefulness, has led to renewed consideration of the subject, and he has always expressed his inability to assume command of other armies than those now confided to him, unless relieved of the immediate command in the field of that now opposed to Gen. Grant."

The explanation of these differences between President Davis and Gen. Lee, without any issue ever being declared between them, is easy when the character of the latter is understood. No great actor in history had ever less self-assertion than Gen. Lee; outside of the limits of his particular command, he was one of those who never gave an opinion, except in the shape of a suggestion; his warm personal friendship resisted any attitude of hostility to the President; and although he differed from much of his policy, he went so far as to declare to several members of the Richmond Congress, that whatever might be Davis' errours he was yet *constitutionally* the President, and that nothing could tempt himself to encroach upon prerogatives which the Constitution had bestowed upon its designated head. The world will see in such conduct some pleasing traces of modesty and conscientiousness; although it is much to be regretted, in view of the circumstances and sequel of the Confederacy, that Gen. Lee was not an ambitious man, or did not possess more of that vigorous selfishness that puts the impressions of individuality on the pages of history. The fact was that, although many of Gen. Lee's views were sound, yet, outside of the limits of the Army of Northern Virginia, and with reference to the general affairs of the Confederacy, his influence was negative and accomplished absolutely nothing.

The last occupation of the Confederate Congress appears to have been a sharp recrimination between it and President Davis, as to the responsibility for the low condition of the public defences. A raging debate took place in secret session of the Senate. It was charged that the President had resisted all measures looking to the restoration of public confidence and the energetic administration of military affairs; that he had robbed the conscription of its legitimate fruits, by a weak and corrupt system of details; and the statistics of the conscription bureau were brought up to show that east of the Mississippi River, twenty-two thousand and thirty-five men had been detailed by executive authority, and so much subtracted from the strength of the Confederate armies by a single measure of the President's favour.

When in secret session, confidence in the President's military administration was put to the test, on the proposition to take the control and conduct of the armies from his hands, it was found that his party had dwindled down to an insignificant number, and that many who had previously supported him in much of evil report, now joined in recording the verdict of incompetency against him. When the vote came to be taken upon the proposition to put Lee in command of all the Confederate armies, Senator Henry of Kentucky, long the constant and intelligent friend of President Davis—indeed the leader of his party in the Confederate Senate—felt constrained to vote for this important change in the Administration of the Southern Confederacy. On the occasion of a social visit to the family of the President, he was called to task by Mrs. Davis, who bitterly inveighed against the purpose of Congress to diminish the power of her husband. She spoke with a spirit so extraordinary, that her words were well remembered. "If I were Mr. Davis," she said, "I would die or be hung before I would submit to the humiliation."

The man who was by general assent leader of the Congressional party against the President, was Senator Wigfall, of Texas. He had one of the largest brains in the Confederacy. He was a man of scarred face and fierce aspect, but with rare gifts of oratory; in argument he dealt blows like those of the sledge-hammer; he was bitter in his words, his delivery was careless and slovenly to affectation, but some of his sentences were models of classic force, and as clear-cut as the diamond. The terrible denunciations of this extraordinary man will be remembered by those who visited the halls of legislation in Richmond; but the newspapers were afraid to publish his speeches, beyond some softened and shallow sketches of the reporters. It is a pity that all of this splendid, fiery oratory, which might have matched whatever we know of historical invective, has been lost to the world. It is only now in the faint reflection of these censures of President Davis, we may study the character of the man who, while he did much to ornament the cause of the Confederacy, yet persisted to the last in a long course of practical errours, and was dead alike to censure and expostulation.

President Davis had a great reputation in the Confederacy for a certain sort of firmness. He was almost inaccessible to the advice and argument of those who might aspire to intellectual equality, and possibly dispute with him the credit of public measures. No man could receive a delegation of Congressmen, or any company of persons who had advice to give, or suggestions to make, with such a well-bred grace, with a politeness so studied as to be almost sarcastic, with a manner that so plainly gave the idea that his company talked to a post. But history furnishes numerous examples of men who, firm as flint in public estimation, and superiour to the common addresses of humanity, have yet been as wax in the hands of small and unworthy favourites. Severest tyrants have been governed by women and court-jesters. President Davis, firm, cold, severe to those who from position or merit should have been admitted into his counsels, was notoriously governed by his wife; had dismissed the Quarter-Master General of the Confederacy, on account of a woman's quarrel and a criticism of Mrs. Davis' figure; surrounded himself with and took into his housel old and intimate confidence men who had been "Jenkinses" and court-correspondents in Washington; was imposed upon by "travelled gentlemen" and obsequious adventurers; and frequently placed in the most important commands and positions in the Confederacy, men who had no other claim on his favour, than an acquaintance at West Point, or some social pleasantry in Washington. Those who knew Mr. Davis best testified that he was the weakest of men, on certain sides of his character, and that he had a romantic sentimentalism, which made him the prey of preachers and women. John M. Daniel, the editor of the Richmond *Examiner*—a single press so powerful in the Confederacy, that it was named "the fourth estate"—once remarked to Senator Wigfall, that the President was contemptibly weak; that his eyes often filled with tears on public occasions; and that a man who cried easily was unfit for a ruler. "I do not know about that," said the rugged Texas Senator; "there are times in every man's life, when it is better to take counsel of the heart than the head." "Well," replied Daniel, "I have only to say that any man whose tears lie shallow, is assuredly weak and unreliable. For myself, I admire the manner of the austere Romans: when they wept, the face was turned away and the head covered with the mantle."

It must be admitted that in the last periods of the war, the influence of President Davis was almost entirely gone, and that the party which supported him was scarcely anything more than that train of followers which always fawns on power and lives on patronage. There was a large party in the Confederacy, that now accepted its downfall as an inevitable result, in view of what stared them in the face, that all the public measures of Mr. Davis' administration had come to be wrecks. The foreign relations of the Confederacy were absurdities; its currency was almost worthless rags; its commissariat was almost empty; its system of conscription was almost like a sieve for water. Surely when all these wrecks of a great system of government lay before the eyes, it was no longer possible to dispute the question of maladminstration, debate the competency of President Davis, and give him a new lease of public confidence.

Much had been imagined in Richmond of propositions for peace negotiations, vaguely reported as pending in secret session of Congress. But this part of the secret history of the Confederacy is easily told; covers no very important facts; and will disappoint the reader, who may have expected from these chambers of mystery some startling revelations.

The propositions for pacification in the last Confederate Congress, never came to a practical point, and were loose efforts indicative of its weak and bewildered mind. None of these propositions ever originated in the Confederate Senate; no vote was ever taken there; they came from the House and were generalities.

Almost during the entire period of the war, there had been a certain Union party in some of the States of the Confederacy. Its sentiment was uniform during the term of its existence; but its designs varied at different stages of the war. Early in 1863, a party organization was secretly proposed in Georgia, to introduce negotiations with the enemy on the part of the States separately, without regard to their Confederate faith. It was supposed that the excessive vanity of Gov. Brown could be easily used in this matter; and he was weak enough to give his ear to the coarsest flattery and to believe what a charlatan told him, that "he (Gov. Brown) held the war in the hollow of his hand." The party of State negotiation obtained a certain hold in Georgia, in Northern Alabama, and in parts of North Carolina; but the great object was to secure the Legislature of Virginia, and for a long period an active and persistent influence was used to get the prestige of Virginia's name for this new project. But it failed. The intrigue caught such third-rate politicians as Wickham, and such chaff as James Lyons, and men who had balanced all their lives between North and South. But this was a low order of Virginians. In the last stages of the war, the Legislature of Virginia was besieged with every influence in favour of separate State negotiation with the Federal Government; propositions were made for embassies to Washington; but the representative body of the proudest State in the Confederacy was true to its great historical trust, and preferred that Virginia should go down to posterity proudly, starkly, with the title of a subjugated people, rather than a community which bartered its Confederate faith, its honour, and its true glory for the small measure of an enemy's mercy, and the pittance of his concessions. The deliberate choice of Virginia, in the very last period of the war, was to stand or fall by the fortune of the Confederate arms, holding her untarnished honour in her hands, and committing to history along with the record of success or of disaster the greatest and most spotless name of modern times.

In the month of January, 1865, Virginia raised her voice for the last time in the war, and gave official expression to her heroic choice. In a public letter of the two Houses of her Legislature to President Davis, it was then declared: "The General Assembly of Virginia desire in this critical period of our affairs, by such suggestions as occur to them, and by the dedication, if need be, of the entire resources of the Commonwealth to the common cause, to strengthen our hands, and to give success to our struggle for liberty and independence." The reply of President Davis was noble. Almost his last official writing was a tribute to the grand State of

Virginia. To the presiding officer of her Legislature, he wrote : " Your assurance is to me a source of the highest gratification ; and while conveying to you my thanks for the expression of the confidence of the General Assembly in my sincere devotion to my country and sacred cause, I must beg permission, in return, to bear witness to the uncalculating, unhesitating spirit with which Virginia has, from the moment when she first drew the sword, consecrated the blood of her children and all her material resources to the achievement of the object of our struggle."

If the spirit of Virginia had animated the entire Confederacy, a cause now prostrate might have been still erect and in arms, and perhaps triumphant. For after all, the main condition of the success of the Confederacy was simply *resolution*, the quality that endures ; and as long as the people were resolved to be free, there was no military power that could have been summoned by the enemy, to bring under subjection a country occupying so many square miles, and so wild and difficult as that of the South. The mind may easily discover many causes that concurred in the decline and downfall of the Southern Confederacy, and contributed something to the catastrophe ; but one rises uppermost, and, for the purposes of the explanation, is sufficient and conclusive—the general demoralization of the people, and that demoralization consequent upon such a want of confidence in the administration of President Davis, as was never before exhibited between a people and its rulers in a time of revolution. He who takes broad and enlightened views of great historical results, and is not satisfied to let his mind rest on secondary causes and partial explanations, will ascribe the downfall of the Southern Confederacy to a general breakng down of the public virtue, and the debasement of a people who, having utterly lost hope in their rulers, and having no heart for a new experiment, descend to tame and infamous submission to what they consider fortune.

We may properly add here some considerations of an extraordinary measure to restore the fortunes of the Confederacy, indicative, indeed, of the desperate condition of the country, and of the disposition of the government to catch at straws. Throughout the entire session of the last Congress in Richmond there was an ill-natured debate of a proposition to arm the slaves, and thus repair the strength and organization of the armies. The circumstances in which this proposition was discussed showed plainly enough that the yield of the conscription law had been practically exhausted, and were the occasion of prejudicial dissensions, which contributed to the overthrow of the Confederacy. It may easily be calculated that out of three million slaves, two hundred thousand might have been spared, and brought into the field. This addition, if made some time ago, might have turned the scale in favour of the South, considering how evenly the balance hung in the early campaigns of the war. But the time for this measure was past ; soldiers could not be improvised; there was no time to drill and perfect negro recruits before the resumption of the active and decisive campaign; and it is a striking evidence of the shiftlessness of the Confederate Government and the impracticability of the Congress, that there should have been debated a bill to put two hundred thousand negroes in the Confederate armies at a time when there were not five thousand spare arms in the Confederacy and our returned prisoners could not actually find muskets with which to resume their places in the field.

Whatever may have been the general merits of the question of enlisting the negro and competing with the enemy in this branch of the recruiting service, the time and circumstances in which the measure was actually discussed in Richmond rendered it impracticable and absurd, and gave occasion to a controversy which, however barren of proper results, created parties and drew lines of exasperated prejudice through different classes of the people. The country, in its exhausted state, could not half feed and clothe the few soldiers left in the ranks. Hence, under all possible circumstances, the negroes could but add to the painful embarrassments already existing. The policy of the government in this, as well as nearly all its measures, was lamentably weak and short-sighted. To suppose that it could accomplish with negro soldiers what it had totally failed to do with the white, who had a much greater interest in the issue, was supremely absurd. The actual results of the legislation of Congress on the subject were ridiculously small, and after the pattern of all its other productions in its last session—a pretence of doing something, yet so far below the necessities of the case, as to be to the last degree puerile, absurd, and contemptible. The proposition to arm negroes was made in November, 1864; it was debated until March, 1865; and the result was a weak compromise on the heel of the session by which the question of *emancipation* as a reward for the negroes' services was studiously excluded, and the President simply authorized to accept from their masters such slaves as they might choose to dedicate to the military service of the Confederacy.

Such paltry legislation indeed, may be taken as an indication of that vague desperation in the Confederacy which grasped at shadows; which conceived great measures, the actual results of which were yet insignificant; which showed its sense of insecurity—and yet, after all, had not nerve enough to make a practical and persistent effort at safety.

Eng.d by H.B.Hall.N.Y.

J. E. Johnston

GENL. JOE E. JOHNSTON

Engraved expressly for the Lost Cause by E. A. Pollard.

CHAPTER XL.

In capturing Savannah, Sherman not only obtained a great prize in
ordnance and cotton, which, after a fashion somewhat Oriental, he designated as a " Christmas gift " to his master in Washington. He also obtained a position of great military value. From the banks of the Savannah
River, he beheld opened before him all the avenues into and through
South Carolina, and discovered a new route, reaching to what had now
become the last and contracted theatre of war in the Confederacy. The
Northern newspapers declared that when Sherman's legions looked across
the Savannah to the shores of Carolina, they sent up a " howl of delight."
There was a terrible gladness in the realization of so many hopes and
wishes—in seeing the most hated State of the South almost prostrate, and
offering the prospect of outrage with impunity.

It had been the first idea of Gen. Grant, anticipating the arrival of
Sherman at Savannah, that, after establishing a base on the sea-coast, with
necessary garrison to include all his artillery and cavalry, he should come
by water to City Point with the remainder of his command, to ensure the
capture of Lee's army or to smother it with numbers. But this plan of
operations was changed. " On the 18th of December," writes Gen. Grant,
" having received information of the defeat and utter rout of Hood's army
by Gen. Thomas, and that, owing to the great difficulty of procuring ocean
transportation, it would take over two months to transport Sherman's
army, and doubting whether he might not contribute as much towards the
desired result by operating from where he was, I wrote to him to that
effect, and asked him for his views as to what would be best to do. A few
days after this I received a communication from Gen. Sherman, of date of
16th of December, acknowledging the receipt of my order of the 6th, and
informing me of his preparations to carry it into effect as soon as he could
get transportation. Also, that he had expected upon reducing Savannah,
instantly to march to Columbia, South Carolina, thence to Raleigh, and
thence to report to me; but that this would consume about six weeks'
time after the fall of Savannah, whereas by sea he could probably reach
me by the middle of January. The confidence he manifested in this letter
of being able to march up and join me, pleased me; and, without waiting
for a reply to my letter of the 18th, I directed him, on the 28th of December, to make preparations to start, as he proposed, without delay, to break
up the railroads in North and South Carolina, and join the armies operating against Richmond, as soon as he could."

The middle of January saw Sherman's troops actually in motion for
the Carolina campaign. His right wing, under Howard, was taken by

water to Beaufort, where it began to move up the Charleston Railroad; while the left wing, under Slocum, with Kilpatrick's cavalry, was to cross the Savannah at Sister's Ferry, and move up towards Augusta. The design of this disposition of forces was to confuse the Confederates as to Sherman's real objective point, and divide their forces at Augusta from those at Charleston and its vicinity, under the impression that each place was threatened; thus preventing their concentration, which might readily make the rivers successive lines of defence, and eluding any opposition until he had passed Columbia, which was really his first objective point.

Howard's movement on the right threatened Charleston and Branchville; and while one division remained at Pocotaligo to keep up the appearance of marching on Charleston by the railroad bridge near that point, the remainder of the command moved up the Salkahatchie River, crossed, almost without opposition, what might have been made a line of strong defence, and pushed on for the Augusta and Charleston Railroad. On the 6th February, Howard occupied two points on this railroad, at Ramburg and at Midway, and commenced destroying the track. Sherman's left wing had struck the road further up, towards Augusta, and had also commenced the work of destruction.

In reaching this important line of communication, Sherman's march had been tracked by fire. The well-known sight of columns of black smoke attested its progress. In Georgia not many dwelling-houses were burned; in South Carolina the rule was the other way, and positively everything was given to destruction and pillage. The country was converted into one vast bonfire. The pine forests were fired, the resin factories were fired, the public buildings and private dwellings were fired. The middle of the finest day looked black and gloomy, for a dense smoke arose on all sides, clouding the very heavens. At night the tall pine trees seemed so many pillars of fire.

The scenes of license and plunder which attended these conflagrations were even more terrible. Long trains of fugitives lined the roads, with women and children, and horses and stock and cattle, seeking refuge from the pursuers. Long lines of wagons covered the highways. Half-naked people cowered from the winter under bush-tents in the thickets, under the eaves of houses, under the railroad sheds, and in old cars left them along the route. Habitation after habitation, village after village, sent up its signal flames to the others, and lighted the sky with crimson horrours. Granaries were emptied, and where the grain was not carried off, it was strewn to waste under the feet of the cavalry, or consigned to the fire which consumed the dwelling. The roads were covered with butchered cattle, hogs, mules, and the costliest furniture. Valuable cabinets, rich pianos, were not only hewn to pieces, but bottles of ink, turpentine, oil, whatever could efface or destroy, was employed to defile and ruin. Horses were ridden into the houses. Beautiful homesteads of the parish gentry, with their wonderful tropical gardens, were ruined. Ancient dwellings of black cypress, one hundred years old, were given to the torch as recklessly as were the rude hovels. Choice pictures and works of art, from Europe, select and numerous libraries, objects of peace wholly, were all destroyed. The inhabitants were left to starve, compelled to feed only upon the garbage to be found in the abandoned camps of the soldiers. The corn scraped up from the spots where the horses fed, was the only means of life left to thousands lately in affluence.

Sherman had in his army a service which he seems proud to have exhibited as a novel and unique feature—that of so-called " bummers." The wretches thus curiously designated, were allowed as irregular foragers to eat up and plunder the country, often going twenty miles from the main columns to burn, to steal, to commit nameless crimes, always assured of welcome to the main body if they returned with horses embellished with strings of poultry or stolen vehicles laden with supplies. How far this worse than brigandish service was recognized by Gen. Sherman may be judged from the fact that, when at the close of the war, his army had a triumphal procession in Washington, the department of " bummers " was represented in the line ; and the crowd of admirers that pressed upon it was excessively entertained by men on scraggy mules, laden with broken furniture and household goods, representing the prowess of cut-throats and thieves.*

---

* A correspondent of the New York *Herald*, who accompanied Sherman's march through the Carolinas, gives the following definition of " the bummer :"

" Any man who has seen the object that the name applies to, will acknowledge that it was admirably selected. Fancy a ragged man, blackened by the smoke of many a pine-knot fire, mounted on a scraggy mule, without a saddle, with a gun, a knapsack, a butcher-knife, and a plug hat, stealing his way through the pine forests far out on the flanks of a column, keen on the scent of rebels, or bacon, or silver spoons, or corn, or anything valuable, and you have him in your mind. Think how you would admire him if you were a lone woman, with a family of small children, far from help, when he blandly inquired where you kept your valuables. Think how you would smile when he pried open your chests with his bayonet, or knocked to pieces your tables, pianos, and chairs, tore your bed-clothing in three-inch strips, and scattered them about the yard. The " bummers " say it takes too much time to use keys. Colour is no protection from these roughriders. They go through a negro cabin, in search of diamonds and gold watches, with just as much freedom and vivacity as they " loot " the dwelling of a wealthy planter. They appear to be possessed of a spirit of " pure cussedness." One incident of many will illustrate : A bummer stepped into a house and inquired for sorghum. The lady of the house presented a jug, which he said was too heavy ; so he merely filled his canteen. Then taking a huge wad of tobacco from his mouth, he thrust it into the jug. The lady inquired, in wonder, why he spoiled that which he did not want. ' Oh, some feller'll come along and taste that sorghum, and think you've poisoned him ; then he'll burn your d—d old house." There are hundreds of these mounted men with the column, and they go everywhere. Some of them are loaded down with silver-ware, gold coin, and other valuables. I hazard nothing in saying three-fifths (in value) of the personal property of the counties we have passed through were taken by Sherman's army."

At our last account of the stages of Sherman's march he had gained the peninsula formed by the Salkahatchie and Edisto Rivers, and had now the choice of going to Augusta or Charleston. He declined both places. In his official report, he says : " Without wasting time or labour on Branchville or Charleston, which I knew the enemy could no longer hold, I turned all the columns straight on Columbia." On the 16th February, his advance was drawn up on the banks of the Saluda in front of Columbia.

It had been hoped to the last by the people of Columbia that the town would be vigorously defended, and made a point of decisive contest in Sherman's pathway. But the old, wretched excuse of want of concentration of the Confederate forces was to apply here. Gen. Hardee was not the man to grasp the business of a large army, and he had never had his forces well in hand. The remnants of Hood's army, the corps of Cheatham and Stewart, had been brought to Augusta, to find that Sherman had given the cold shoulder to it, and moved down the railroad. On the lower part of the road, Hardee could not be persuaded that Charleston was not the chief object of Sherman's desires, and so lay behind his fortifications, at Branchville, to protect it. In this uncertainty of purpose there was no force afield sufficient to check Sherman's course. The only Confederate troops which contested his advance upon Columbia consisted of the mounted men of Hampton, Wheeler, Butler, etc., and, although they made stubborn head against the enemy, their opposition could not, of course, be more than that of severe skirmishing.

Yet, to the last moment, it was hoped Columbia might be saved. It was asserted that the corps of Cheatham and Stewart were making forced marches, with a view to a junction with the troops under Beauregard, and such was the spirit of the Confederate troops, and one of the Generals at least, that almost at the moment when Sherman's advance was entering the town, Hampton's cavalry was in order of battle, and only waiting the command to charge it. But the horrours of a street fight in a defenceless city, filled with women and children, were prudently avoided ; and the Confederate troops were drawn off from the scene at the very hour when the Federals were entering it. The gallant and chivalrous Hampton was eager to do battle to the last ; when it was proposed to display a white flag from the tower of the City Hall, he threatened to tear it down ; he reluctantly left the city, and so slowly that a portion of his command passed on the road to Winnsboro' in sight of the advance column of the enemy, giving it the idea of a flank movement of cavalry.

SACK AND DESTRUCTION OF COLUMBIA.

Columbia was surrendered to the enemy in the morning of the 17th

February, by the mayor, Mr. Goodwyn, who asked for the citizens " the
treatment accorded by the usages of civilized warfare." Sherman
promised this. As night approached, perceiving that the mayor was exhausted by his labours of the day, he counselled him to retire to rest, saying : "Not a finger's breadth, Mr. Mayor, of your city shall be harmed.
You may lie down to sleep, satisfied that your town shall be as safe in my
hands as if wholly in your own." Such was very nearly the language in
which he spoke ; such was the substance of it. He added : "It will become my duty to destroy some of the public or Government buildings ; but
I will reserve this performance to another day. It shall be done to-morrow, provided the day be calm." With this assurance the mayor retired.

But the work of pillage had begun when the Federal troops had first
reached the head of Main street. Stores were broken open, and the contents strewn on the side-walk ; citizens were robbed in the street ; no one
felt safe in his own dwelling.* Robbery was going on at every corner—

* We are indebted for many incidents of the sack and destruction of Columbia to a publication
in the Daily *Phœnix*. We group some of these incidents to make a partial picture of outrages innumerable and almost indescribable :

"At an early hour in the day, almost every house was visited by groups, averaging in number
from two to six persons. Some of these entered civilly enough, but pertinaciously entered, in some
cases, *begging* for milk, eggs, bread and meat—in most cases, demanding them. In the house,
parties less meek of temper than these pushed their way, and the first intimation of their presence,
as they were confronted at the entrance, was a pistol clapped at the head or bosom of the owner,
whether male or female.

"'Your watch!' 'Your money!' was the demand. Frequently, no demand was made. Rarely, indeed, was a word spoken, where the watch or chain, or ring or bracelet, presented itself con-
spicuously to the eye. It was incontinently plucked away from the neck, breast or bosom. Hundreds of women, still greater numbers of old men, were thus despoiled. The slightest show of resistance provoked violence to the person.

"The venerable Mr. Alfred Huger was thus robbed in the chamber and presence of his family,
and in the eyes of an almost dying wife. He offered resistance, and was collared and dispossessed
by violence.

"In the open streets the pickpockets were mostly active. A frequent mode of operating was
by first asking you the hour. If thoughtless enough to reply, producing the watch or indicating
its possession, it was quietly taken from hand or pocket, and transferred to the pocket of the ' other
gentleman,' with some such remark as this : 'A pretty little watch that. I'll take it myself ; it
just suits me.' And the appropriation followed ; and if you hinted any dislike to the proceeding,
a grasp was taken of your collar, and the muzzle of a revolver put to your ear.

        *   *   *   *   *   *   *   *   *

'· The venerable Mr. H— stood ready, with his *couteau de chasse* made bare in his bosom,
hovering around the persons of his innocent daughters. Mr. O——, on beholding some too familiar
approach to one of his daughters, bade the man stand off at the peril of his life ; saying that while
he submitted to be robbed of property, he would sacrifice life without reserve—his own and that of
the assailant—before his child's honour should be abused.

"Mr. James G. Gibbes with difficulty, pistol in hand, and only with the assistance of a Yankee
officer, rescued two young women from the clutches of as many ruffians."

        *   *   *   *   *   *   *   *   *   *

"A Mrs. J—— was but recently confined. Her condition was very helpless. Her life hung

in nearly every house. It was useless to complain. Crowds of escaped prisoners, soldiers, and negroes, intoxicated with their new-born liberty,

upon a hair. The men were apprised of all the facts in the case. They burst into the chamber—took the rings from the lady's fingers—plucked the watch from beneath her pillow, and so over-whelmed her with terrour, that she sunk under the treatment, surviving their departure but a day or two.

" In several instances parlours, articles of crockery, and even beds, were used by the soldiers as if they were water-closets. In one case, a party used vessels in this way, then put them on the bed, fired at and smashed them to pieces, emptying the filthy contents over the bedding.

" In several cases, newly made graves were opened, the coffins taken out, broken open, in search of buried treasure, and the corpses left exposed. Every spot in grave-yard or garden, which seemed to have been recently disturbed, was sounded with sword, or bayonet, or ramrod, in the desperate search after spoil."

*   *   *   *   *   *   *   *   *   *   *

A lady spoke indignantly to General Atkins, of Sherman's army, and said of that General, " He wars upon women ! "

" Yes," said Atkins, " and justly. It is the women of the South who keep up this cursed rebel-lion. It gave us the greatest satisfaction to see those proud Georgia women begging crumbs from Yankee leavings ; and this will soon be the fate of all you Carolina women."

Escorting a sad procession of fugitives from the burning dwellings, one of the soldiers said :

" What a glorious sight ! "

" Terribly so," said one of the ladies.

" Grand ! " said he.

" Very pitiful," was the reply.

The lady added :

" How, as men, you can behold the horrours of this scene, and behold the sufferings of these innocents, without terrible pangs of self-condemnation and self-loathing, it is difficult to con-ceive."

" We glory in it ! " was the answer. " I tell you, madam, that when the people of the North hear of the vengeance we have meted out to your city, there will be one universal shout of rejoic-ing from man, woman and child, from Maine to Maryland."

" You are, then, sir, only a fitting representative of your people."

Another, who had forced himself as an escort upon a party, on the morning of Saturday, said, pointing to the thousand stacks of chimneys, " You are a curious people here in house-building. You run up your chimneys before you build the house."

One who had been similarly impudent, said to a mother, who was bearing a child in her arms :

" Let me carry the baby, madam."

" Do not touch him for your life," was the reply. " I would sooner hurl him into the flames, and plunge in after him than that he should be polluted by your touch. Nor shall a child of mine ever have even the show of obligation to a Yankee ! "

" Well, that's going it strong, by ——; but I like your pluck. We like it d—e ; and you'll see us coming back after the war—every man of us—to get a Carolina wife. We hate your men like h—l, but we love your women ! "

" We much prefer your hate, even though it comes in fire. Will you leave us, sir ? "

It was not always, however, that our women were able to preserve their coolness and firmness under the assaults. We have quite an amusing story of a luckless wife, who was confronted by a stalwart soldier, with a horrid oath and a cocked revolver at her head.

" Your watch ! your money ! you d—d rebel b—h ! "

The horrid oaths, the sudden demand, fierce look and rapid action, so terrified her that she cried out, " Oh ! my G—d ! I have no watch, no money, except what's tied round my waist ! "

We need not say how deftly the Bowie-knife was applied to loose the stays of the lady.

which they looked upon as a license to do as they pleased, were parading the streets in groups. The reign of terrour did not fairly begin till night. In some instances, where parties complained of the misrule and robbery, Federal soldiers said to them, with a chuckle : " This is nothing. Wait till to-night, and you'll see h—ll."

In the town of Columbia was a Catholic convent, the Lady Superiour of which had educated Gen. Sherman's daughter, and now laid claim to his protection for the young women in her charge. A guard of eight or ten men were detailed for the institution. But a Catholic officer in Sherman's army visited the convent, warned the Lady Superiour of danger, and whispered to her, " I must tell you, my sister, Columbia is a doomed city."

A few moments later, while Mayor Goodwyn was conversing with a Federal soldier, three rockets were shot up by the enemy from the capitol square. As the soldier beheld these rockets, he cried out : " Alas ! alas ! for your poor city ! It is doomed. Those rockets are the signal. The town is to be fired." In less than twenty minutes after, the flames broke out in twenty distinct quarters.

Engines and hose were brought out by the firemen, but these were soon driven from their labours—which were indeed idle against such a storm of fire—by the pertinacious hostility of the soldiers ; the hose was hewn to pieces, and the firemen, dreading worse usage to themselves, left the field in despair. Meanwhile, the flames spread from side to side, from front to rear, from street to street. All the thoroughfares were quickly crowded with helpless women and children, some in their night-clothes. Agonized mothers, seeking their children, all affrighted and terrified, were rushing on all sides from the raging flames and falling houses. Invalids had to be dragged from their beds, and lay exposed to the flames and smoke that swept the streets, or to the cold of the open air in back yards.

The scene at the convent was a sad one. The flames were fast encompassing the convent, and the sisters, and about sixty terrified young ladies, huddled together on the streets. Some Christian people formed a guard around this agonized group of ladies, and conducted them to Sidney Park. Here they fancied to find security, as but few houses occupied the neighbourhood, and these not sufficiently high to lead to apprehension from the flames. But fire-balls were thrown from the heights into the deepest hollows of the park, and the wretched fugitives were forced to scatter, finding their way to other places of retreat, and finding none of them secure. Group after group, stream after stream of fugitives thus pursued their way through the paths of flaming and howling horrour, only too glad to fling themselves on the open ground, whither, in some cases, they had succeeded in conveying a feather-bed or mattress. The malls, or open squares, the centres of the wide streets, were thus strewn with piles of bed·

ding, on which lay exhausted figures, or crouched women and children wild with terrour. Every hour of the night was fraught with scenes of horrour such as we have described. By midnight, every large block in the business portion of the town was consumed. A lady said to an officer at her house, somewhere about four o'clock in the morning: "In the name of God, sir, when is this work of hell to be ended?" He replied: "You will hear the bugles at sunrise, when a guard will enter the town and withdraw these troops. It will then cease, and not before."

The sun rose with a wan countenance, peering dimly through the dense vapours whch seemed wholly to overspread the firmament. The best and most beautiful portion of Columbia lay in ruins. Eighty-four squares of buildings had been destroyed, with scarcely the exception of a single house. The capitol building, six churches, eleven banking establishments, the schools of learning, the shops of art and trade, of invention and manufacture, shrines equally of religion, benevolence, and industry were all buried together in one congregated ruin. Nothing remained but the tall, spectre-looking chimneys. The noble-looking trees that shaded the streets, the flower-gardens that graced them, were blasted and withered by fire. On every side there were ruins and smoking masses of blackened walls, and between, in desolate groups, reclining on mattress, or bed, or earth, were wretched women and children gazing vacantly on the site of what had been their homes. Roving detachments of the soldiers passed around and among them. There were those who looked and lingered nigh, with taunt and sarcasm. Others there were, in whom humanity did not seem wholly extinguished; and others again, to their credit be it said, who were truly sorrowful and sympathizing, who had labored for the safety of family and property, and who openly deplored the dreadful crime.

An attempt has been made to relieve Gen. Sherman of the terrible censure of having deliberately fired and destroyed Columbia, and to ascribe the calamity to accident or to carelessness resulting from an alleged order of Gen. Hampton to burn the cotton in the city. This explanation is a tardy one, and has come only after Gen. Sherman has observed the horrour which this crime has excited in the world, and realized some of its terrible consequences. To the imputation against Gen. Hampton, that chivalrous officer, whose word friend nor foe ever had reason to dispute, has replied in a public letter: "I deny emphatically that any cotton was fired in Columbia by my order. I deny that the citizens 'set fire to thousands of bales rolled out into the streets.' I deny that any cotton was on fire when the Federal troops entered the city. * * * I pledge myself to prove that I gave a positive order, by direction of Gen. Beauregard, that no cotton should be fired; that not one bale was on fire when Gen. Sherman's troops took possession of the city; that he promised protection to the city, and that, in spite of his solemn promise, he burned the city to the ground, deliberately, systematically and atrociously."

The facts are, as we have seen, that Columbia was fired in twenty different places at one time; that several hours before the commencement of the fire, a Federal officer had given warning at the Ursuline Convent that Columbia was doomed; and that just before the conflagration a Federal soldier, pointing to a signal of rockets, declared to the Mayor that the city was to be fired. There are living witnesses to attest these facts. But it has also been pertinently asked: Why did Sherman's soldiers prevent the firemen from extinguishing the fire as they strove to do? Why did they cut the hose as soon as it was brought into the streets? Why did they not assist in extinguishing the flames? Why, with twenty thousand men encamped in the streets, did they suffer mere stragglers, as the incendiaries were represented, to succeed in a work of such extent? Every circumstance shows that the conflagration was deliberately planned; that it was fed and protected by the soldiers; while the universal plundering simultaneous with it went unchecked, and was plainly part of the object attained through the means of fire.

The burning of Columbia was but of a piece with Sherman's record, and the attempt to exculpate him in this particular is but little consistent and plausible in view of his general conduct from the moment when he entered South Carolina. He had burned six out of every seven farm-houses on the route of his march. Before he reached Columbia, he had burned Blackville, Graham, Ramberg, Buford's Bridge, Lexington, and had not spared the humblest hamlet. After he left Columbia, he gave to the flames the villages of Allston, Pomaria, Winnsboro', Blackstock, Society Hill, and the towns of Camden and Cheraw. Surely when such was the fate of these places, the effort is ill-made to show that an exception was to be made in favour of the State capital of South Carolina, the especial and notorious object of the enemy's hate and revenge, and which, for days before the catastrophe, had been designated as "the promised boon of Sherman's army."

FALL OF CHARLESTON.

The march of Sherman, which traversed South Carolina, was decisive of the fate of Charleston. At Savannah, the Federal commander had been asked if he intended taking Charleston. He answered, "Yes; but I shall not sacrifice life in its capture. If I am able to reach certain vital points, Charleston will fall of itself. If the people remain there, they must starve, that's all."

The loss of Charleston was a severe trial to President Davis, who had a peculiar affection for the city. Even when Gen. Beauregard directed the evacuation of the city, so as to provide a force with which to fall upon Sherman, the President wrote such a despatch to Gen. Hardee, commanding in Charleston, as led him to suspend the evacuation, and obliged Beauregard to assume command, and to direct imperatively the measure to be completed.

Gen. Hardee completed the evacuation of the city on the 17th February. He destroyed the cotton warehouses, arsenals, two iron-clads, and some vessels in the ship-yard; but he was compelled to leave to the enemy all the heavy ordnance that could not be brought off, including two hundred pieces of artillery, which could only be spiked and temporarily disabled. A terrible incident of the evacuation, was an accidental explosion of powder in the large building at the depot of the Northwestern railroad, destroying several hundred lives. The building was blown into the air a whirling mass of ruins. From the depot the fire spread rapidly, and, communicating with the adjoining buildings, threatened destruction to that part of the city. Four squares, embracing the area bounded by Chapel, Alexander, Charlotte and Washington streets, were consumed before the conflagration was subdued.

Charleston came into the enemy's possession a scarred and mutilated city. It had made a heroic defence for nearly four years; for blocks not a building could be found that was exempt from the marks of shot and shell; what were once fine houses, presented great gaping holes in the sides and roof, or were blackened by fire; at almost every step were to be found evidences of destruction and ruin wrought by the enemy. After a display of heroism and sacrifice unexcelled in the war, this most famous city of the South fell, not by assault, or dramatic catastrophe, but in consequence of the stratagem of a march many miles away from it.

The evacuation of Charleston having been successfully accomplished, Hardee and Beauregard retired to Charlotte, whither Cheatham was making his way from Augusta to join them.

CAPTURE OF FORT FISHER—FALL OF WILMINGTON.

An important branch of Sherman's expedition through the Carolinas led from Wilmington. It was proposed by Gen. Grant to open still another base of operations towards Richmond, and with the capture of Wilmington, to effect an early communication with Sherman, and to sustain his march north by a co-operating column. Besides, it was important to get possession of Wilmington, as the most important sea-coast port left to the Confederates, through which to get supplies from abroad, and send cotton and other products out by blockade-runners. The Federal navy had been unable to seal the harbour, and Secretary Welles had been forced to confess, that fifty fast Federal steamers had been quite unable to maintain the blockade here. The theory of the enemy was that the nature of the outlet of Cape Fear River was such that it required watching for so great a distance, that without possession of the land north of New Inlet, or Fort Fisher, it was impossible for the navy to entirely close the harbour against the entrance of blockade runners.

An expedition directed by Gen. Grant, in the close of December, 1864, to capture Fort Fisher, had failed of success. For this expedition there had been assembled in Hampton Roads, under command of Admiral Porter, what Gen. Grant designated as " the most formidable armada ever collected for concentration upon one given point." The co-operating land force consisted of sixty-five hundred men, detached from Gen. Butler's command before Richmond. The expedition got off on the 13th December. Accompanying it was a vessel loaded with a large quantity of powder, to be exploded as near the fort as possible ; Gen. Butler having obtained the singular idea of levelling the fort, or demoralizing the garrison by the shock of the explosion. The boat was blown up in the night of the 24th December, and attracted such little attention that the Confederates supposed it to be nothing more than the bursting of one of the enemy's guns, and were never enlightened as to the object of the explosion until informed of it by Northern newspapers.

Porter's fleet had already commenced a bombardment of the fort ; and on the 25th December, under cover of this fire, a landing was effected by the enemy without opposition, and a reconnoissance pushed up towards the fort. The result of the reconnoissance was that Gen. Butler declined to attack, and very suddenly ordered the re-embarkation of the troops and the return of the expedition. This conduct of Butler was the occasion of his removal from command, and of a sharp recrimination which ran through official documents, newspapers, and even the lowest forms of personal controversy between himself and Gen. Grant. In a letter published in a Northern journal, Gen. Butler congratulated himelf that he had retired from command, without having on his skirts the blood of his soldiers needlessly sacrificed—referring to Grant's list of butcheries and utter disregard of life in the Virginia campaign ; and it could be said, if his powder ship had proved a ridiculous toy, it was at least not so expensive as Grant's experiment with the mine at Petersburg.

The fleet did not follow Butler's transports, and the persistence of Porter encouraged Grant to make another attempt to take Fort Fisher and secure Wilmington. He selected Gen. Terry to command the second expedition. The troops composing it consisted of the same that composed the former, with the addition of a small brigade numbering about fifteen hundred men, and a small siege train. The expedition sailed from Fortress

Monroe on the 6th January, 1865, but, owing to the difficulties of the weather, did not reach its destination until the 12th.

Gen. Braxton S. Bragg appeared again on the military stage, thrust there by President Davis, in the second defence of Wilmington. A Virginia newspaper announced the event irreverently, as follows: "Gen. Bragg has been appointed to command at Wilmington: Goodbye Wilmington!" There was no confidence in this Confederate commander; and although Fort Fisher had held out against a naval bombardment, and its garrison was largely increased when Bragg took command, it was very much feared that the enemy would obtain with him some new advantage, would effect some surprise, or succeed by some untoward event.

These fears were to be exactly realized. Fort Fisher consisted of two fronts—the first, or land front, running across the peninsula, at this point seven hundred yards wide, was four hundred and eighty yards in length, while the second, or sea front, ran from the right of the first parallel to the beach, to the Mound Battery—a distance of thirteen hundred yards. The land front was intended to resist any attack from the north; the sea front to prevent any of the enemy's vessels from running through New Inlet, or landing troops on Federal Point.

It was evidently the important concern to prevent a landing of the enemy's troops, or to dislodge them as soon as they got ashore; and Bragg's forces were disposed with that view, Gen. Hoke holding a line north of Fort Fisher. On the 13th January, Terry succeeded, under a heavy fire from the fleet, in landing several thousand troops on the sea-beach, some five or six miles above Fort Fisher. The place of landing was admirably selected; the troops being disembarked just above the neck of the sound, interposing a small surface of water between them and an attacking force, or compelling such force to work around the lower extreme of the sound—either of which movements would have to be executed under the fire of the whole fleet.

It was the purpose of Hoke to attack the enemy as soon as he advanced, and his cavalry was thrown out on his right flank, to observe the movements of the enemy, and report his first step towards establishing a line across the neck of land to the river. But it was found the next morning, that through the imperfect vigilance of the Confederates, the enemy had laid out a second line. During the night his troops, passing between Hoke's cavalry, and threading their way through the thick marshy undergrowth, made their way to the river, and next morning held an intrenched line on Hoke's right flank, extending nearly across the peninsula. Gen. Bragg at first gave the order to charge the enemy in his works, but after a close reconnoissance which discovered his force and position, determined to withdraw after reinforcing the fort, which was held by Gen. Whiting, with a garrison increased to about twenty-five hundred men. In the afternoon the enemy pushed a reconnoissance within five hundred yards of the fort. It seemed probable that troops could be got within two hundred yards of the work without serious loss; and it was a matter of doubt with the enemy, whether the necessary ammunition could be supplied by the open beach, if regular approaches were determined on. It was decided to assault the next day.

While these movements on land were taking place, the enemy's fleet had held Fort Fisher enveloped in a terrific fire for three days. More than four hundred guns poured torrents of shells and missiles on every spot. There were three divisions of the fleet—the first, led by the "Brooklyn," numbered one hundred and sixteen guns; the second, by the "Minnesota," one hundred and seventy-six guns; and the third, composed of gunboats, with one hundred and twenty-three guns. During the afternoon of the 15th January—the day appointed for the assault—this immense armament poured in a concentric fire upon the fort; and while the tossing clouds of smoke incessantly rolled up from the water, Terry organized his force for the assault—three deployed brigades following one another, at intervals of about three hundred yards, and each making its final rush for the west end of the land face of the fort.

The rapid fire from the water prevented the Confederates from using either artillery or musketry, on the advancing lines of the enemy, until they had got within sixty yards of the fort, when the fire of the fleet lifted so as not to involve the assaulting column. The Confederates were brought to the charge after having been packed in the bomb-proofs for fifty-six hours, many of them benumbed and exhausted. Capt. Braddy's company guarding the sally-port gave way. From seven to about ten o'clock at night, the fighting went on from traverse to traverse; it was a hand-to-hand fight, a heroic defence, in which bravery, endurance and devotion failed to overcome numbers. The enemy had not lost a man until he entered the fort, and the loss that he confessed to in the entire affair of seven or eight hundred killed and wounded, must have taken place within its inclosures. The garrison at last driven from the fort, retreated down the peninsula to the cover of some works near the inlet. But further resistance was useless; and about midnight, Gen. Whiting surrendered himself and men as prisoners of war, numbering over eighteen hundred, the remainder of his force being killed or wounded.

The fall of Fort Fisher ultimately decided the fate of Wilmington. It was followed by the blowing up of Fort Caswell, and the abandonment of the works on Smith's Island, which gave the enemy entire control of the mouth of the Cape Fear River. Fort Anderson, the main defence on the west bank of the river, was evacuated on the 19th February, on the appearance of Porter's fleet before it, in conjunction with a land force under

Schofield moving up both sides of the river. Wilmington was occupied without resistance; and the command of Gen. Bragg, which had remained idle there for more than a month (despite the earnest protest of Gen. Beauregard, who in vain had represented to President Davis that with the fall of Fort Fisher Wilmington became useless, and that the command there should be used at the earliest possible moment in the field against Sherman), was at last moved to what had now become the dominant theatre of hostilities in the Carolinas.

The new base which the enemy had now opened, was well defined by Gen. Grant as auxiliary to Sherman. The State of North Carolina, was constituted into a new military department, and Gen. Schofield, whose corps had been transferred here from the Tennessee lines, was assigned to command. The following instructions were given him by Gen. Grant:

"CITY POINT, VA., January 31, 1865.

General: Your movements are intended as co-operative with Sherman's through the States of South and North Carolina. The first point to be attained is to secure Wilmington. Goldsboro will then be your objective point, moving either from Wilmington or Newbern, or both, as you deem best. Should you not be able to reach Goldsboro, you will advance on the line or lines of railway connecting that place with the sea-coast—as near to it as you can, building the road behind you. The enterprise under you has two objects: the first is to give Gen. Sherman material aid, if needed, in his march north: the second, to open a base of suppiles for him on his line of march. As soon, therefore, as you can determine which of the two points, Wilmington or Newbern, you can best use for throwing supplies to the interior, you will commence the accumulation of twenty days' rations and forage for sixty thousand men and twenty thousand animals. You will get of these as many as you can house and protect to such point in the interiour as you may be able to occupy. * * * * * *

THE CAMPAIGN IN NORTH CAROLINA.

When Sherman left behind him the smoking ruins of Columbia, it was thought by the Confederates that he would move towards Charlotte, where all the rolling stock of the railroads destroyed had been run, and from which it could not be removed, on account of the railroad beyond that being of a different gauge. On the 21st February, Sherman passed through Winnsboro on the road to Charlotte; but on the 23d, his army suddenly swung on a grand right wheel, and moved rapidly off towards Fayetteville. On the 12th March, it reached Fayetteville. Meanwhile preparations had been made by the enemy on the coast, for a movement on Goldsboro in two columns—one from Wilmington, and the other from Newbern—and to repair the railroad leading there from each place, as well as to supply Sherman by Cape Fear River toward Fayetteville, if it became necessary. The column from Newbern was attacked on the 8th March, near Kinston, by Gen. Bragg, with his own troops and Hill's division of the Army of Tennessee. The enemy was completely routed, and fifteen hundred prisoners taken. On the 9th March, Gen. Bragg found the enemy several miles in rear strongly entrenched, and, after a faint attack, drew off.

On the 14th, this body of the enemy, under Schofield, crossed the Neuse River, occupied Kinston, and entered Goldsboro on the 21st. The column from Wilmington reached Cox's Bridge on the Neuse River, ten miles above Goldsboro, on the 22d.

It remained now for Sherman to keep the rendezvous and complete the combination. But to do so and make the last stage of his march, it was clear that he would have to do some more important and severe fighting than he had experienced since he and Johnston parted at Atlanta—the latter General having been put in command of the Confederate forces in the Carolinas. It appeared indeed that a formidable army was at last collecting in his pathway. Beauregard at Charlotte, had been reinforced by Cheatham and the garrison at Augusta, and had had ample time to move in the direction of Raleigh. Hardee had evacuated Charleston, in time to keep ahead of Sherman, and was moving to the same point. It was easy for Bragg and Hoke in North Carolina also to effect a junction with these forces, swelling them, it would be supposed, to a formidable army. But this army, which appeared so imposing in the enumeration of its parts, was no match for Sherman. When the enemy's campaign in South Carolina commenced, Hardee had eighteen thousand men. He reached Cheraw with eleven thousand, and Averysboro with about six thousand. Eleven hundred State troops left him between those places by order of Gov. Magrath of South Carolina; but the balance of his great loss was due, almost entirely, to *desertions*. These figures are from an official source, and show without the aid of commentary how low had fallen the military organization and spirit of the Confederacy.

On the 15th March Sherman put his army in motion from Fayetteville. In the narrow ground between Cape Fear River and Black Creek, which becomes Black River, and empties into the Cape Fear below Fayetteville, Gen. Hardee was posted, his force consisting of two small divisions under Maj.-Gens. McLaws and Taliaferro. He held his ground, without difficulty, on the 16th. But at night, finding that the Federal right had crossed Black River and moved towards Goldsboro, and that the left was crossing the creek as if to turn his position, he abandoned it before daybreak, and reached Elevation, on the road to Smithfield, at noon of the 17th.

On the 17th Gen. Bragg was encamped near Smithfield with Hoke's North Carolina division, four thousand seven hundred and seventy men. Lieut.-Gen. Stewart was in the same neighbourhood with nearly four thousand of the Army of Tennessee, under Maj.-Gens. Loring, D. H. Hill, and Stevenson.

At daybreak of the 18th a report was received from Gen. Hampton, to the effect that the Federal army was moving on Goldsboro in two columns: the 15th and 17th corps, on the direct road from Fayetteville to that place, and the 14th and 20th on that from Averysboro. By previous reports the former was nearly a day's march in advance of the latter, which would probably reach the point opposite Bentonsville early on the 19th. That place is about two miles north of the road, and sixteen miles from Smithfield. By the State map the roads followed by the Federal troops are twelve miles apart here, and Elevation twelve miles from Bentonsville. Orders were immediately given for concentration there that evening. Bragg's and Stewart's troops reached the ground easily. But Hardee's were unable to do so. Bentonsville is incorrectly placed on the map, and its distance from Elevation much greater than is indicated, and no direct road could be found. Consequently Hardee arrived not until the morning of the 19th. In the mean time the enemy came up, and attacked Hoke's division, which had been formed across the road, Stewart's corps on its right, its own much thrown forward. This attack was so vigorous that Gen. Bragg called for aid, and McLaw's division then arriving, was sent to him; the other, Taliaferro's, was placed on Stewart's right. Before these troops got into position, the attack on our left had been repulsed, as well as a subsequent one upon Loring's division. Hardee was then directed to charge with Stewart's troops and Taliaferro's division, the latter being thrown on the enemy's left flank. Bragg's troops were ordered to join in the movement successively, from right to left.

On the right, where the ground was open, the attack was perfectly successful, driving the 14th corps back at least a mile and a half into dense thickets; but the progress of the left was soon stopped in very thick woods by entrenchments. The fight began at three o'clock, and continued until dark. Wheeler's cavalry was to have fallen upon the rear of the Federal left; but a swollen creek which intervened kept it out of action. After burying the dead as far as practicable at night, and removing his wounded and many of those of the enemy, Gen. Johnston resumed his first position.

The battle—known as that of Bentonsville—although it had failed to fulfil what was probably Johnston's purpose, to cripple Sherman before he could effect a junction with Schofield, had been a most creditable affair for the Confederates. With fourteen thousand men they had encountered the 14th and 20th corps of the enemy and Kilpatrick's cavalry, an aggregate probably of forty thousand men.

On the 20th the whole Federal army was in Johnston's front, which was changed parallel to the road. The Confederates were compelled to hold their ground that day and the next, to cover the operation of carrying off their wounded. Sherman's whole army was before them, and made many partial attacks, all of which were repulsed. On the afternoon of the

21st, the 17th corps penetrated the thin line of cavalry which formed the Confederate left, and almost reached a bridge in rear of the centre, over which lay the only road left to Johnston. It was easily driven back by the reserve.

Before daybreak on the 22d Gen. Johnston moved towards Smithfield, leaving a few wounded who were too much injured to bear removal. His loss in the three days was two hundred and twenty-four killed, one thousand four hundred and ninety-nine wounded, and more than three hundred prisoners. That of the enemy must have been much greater, as the Confederates had the advantage in the fighting, and generally fought under cover. More than eight hundred prisoners were reported.

The junction of Sherman's and Schofield's forces was effected at Goldsboro' the next day. It made an army of more than one hundred thousand men within one hundred and fifty miles of the lines in Virginia. No sooner had Sherman disposed his army in camp about Goldsboro' than he hastened to City Point, where he had a conference with Gen. Grant, at which President Lincoln was present, and where was settled the final plan of combination against Richmond; it being intended that Sherman should move to the line of the Roanoke and thence on the Richmond and Danville road, or directly to the front of Petersburg. But this plan was never carried into operation; Grant saw reason to anticipate it; and the fate of Richmond was decided without any participation of Sherman in the catastrophe.

CHAPTER XLI.

IN the first months of 1865 Gen. Lee held both Richmond and Petersburg with not more than thirty-three thousand men. At this time Grant's
strength, as rated at the War Department in Washington, exceeded one
hundred and sixty-thousand men. Such was the disparity of force in the
final array of the contest for Richmond. Gen. Lee's lines stretched from
below Richmond on the north side of the James to Hatcher's Run away
beyond Petersburg on the south side. He had forty miles of defence; and
it may well be imagined that with his little force posted over such a dis-

tance, his line of battle was almost as thin as a skirmish line.   Duty was incessant; it was fatiguing in the greatest degree; the Confederates had no reserves, and when a brigade was taken to asssist at some threatened point, the position it left was endangered.   But even in this extreme situation, Gen. Lee had not yet despaired of the cause of the Confederacy. He was gravely sensible of the danger; in frequent conference with committees of the Congress at Richmond, he stated frankly his anxiety, but urged levies of negro troops, held out what hope he could, and expressly and firmly discountenanced any surrender of the Confederate cause by premature negotiations with Washington.   On one of these occasions he made the personal declaration for himself that he had rather die on the battle-field than surrender—a sentiment which provoked the sneer of a well-known " Union " man in Richmond, and the remark that " Gen. Lee talked like a school-girl."

The populace of Richmond was but little aware of the terrible decrease of Gen. Lee's army; and indeed the people of the Confederacy were studiously kept in the dark as to all details of the military situation.   So reticent had the Government become, that the newspapers were forbid publishing anything of military affairs beyond the scanty doles of information and the skeleton telegrams furnished to the reporters by an official authority, and copied at the desks of the War Department.   It thus happened that while there was a general despondency of the public mind, there were few outside the severe official circles of Richmond who knew the real extremities to which the arms and affairs of the Confederacy had fallen.   There was a dull expectation of what was next to happen; there was a vague condition of the public mind, in which, although not able to discover any substantial and well-defined ground of hope, it yet plodded on under the shadow of old convictions, and with a dim anticipation of something favourable in the future.   While every one affirmed that the affairs of the Confederacy were in a bad way, and while every one appeared to have a certain sense of approaching misfortune, there were very few who knew the real condition and numbers of the armies of the Confederacy, and realized how far had been undermined its system of defence. It was difficult indeed to believe that the Army of Northern Virginia— that army, whose name had been for four years as the blast of victory— had declined to a condition in which it was no longer capable of offensive operations.   It was difficult indeed to abandon altogether the idea that the happy accident of a victory somewhere in the Confederacy might not, after all, put a new aspect on affairs.   Even if the conclusion of subjugation had become probable, its day was at least uncertain, distant; and the opinion of Gen. Lee was quoted in the streets of Richmond that in any event the Southern Confederacy was likely to last another year's campaign.   Many lived in the circle of each day; the idea of Independence was yet in the loose conversations of the people ; and the favourite cantatrice of the Richmond Theatre sung to nightly plaudits, "Farewell forever to the star-spangled banner ! " Then there were those rumours of extravagant fortune, always indicative of a weak and despairing condition of the public mind ; among them endless stories of peace negotiations and European "recognition." A few weeks before Richmond fell, the report was credited for the space of three or four days by the most intelligent persons in the city, including some of the editors of the newspapers and President Davis' pastor, that a messenger from France had arrived on the coast of North Carolina, and was making his way overland to Richmond, with the news of the recognition of the Southern Confederacy by the Emperour Napoleon !

But in this dull condition of the public mind there came a well-defined rumour of "peace ; " an event in which another and last appeal was to be made to the resolution of the South.

THE FORTRESS MONROE CONFERENCE.

At different periods of the war the ambition of individuals on both sides had attempted certain propositions of peace, and sought to bring the parties at Richmond and Washington into such a position that they could not avoid negotiations, without subjecting themselves to the injurious imputation of preferring war. In pursuance of this diplomatic errantry, Mr. Francis P. Blair, a skilful politician, in January, 1865, obtained a passport from President Lincoln to go through the Federal lines, visited Richmond, and while disclaiming any official instructions or countenance from Washington, sought to prevail upon President Davis to send, or receive, commissioners to treat of peace between the contending parties. On the 19th January, Mr. Blair returned to Washington, taking with him a written assurance, addressed to himself, from President Davis, of his willingness to enter into negotiations for peace, to receive a commissioner whenever one should be sent, and of his readiness, whenever Mr. Blair could promise that he would be received, to appoint such a commissioner, minister, or other agent, and thus " renew the effort to enter into a conference with a view to secure peace between the *two countries*." The reply of Mr. Lincoln was no less diplomatic. He wrote that he was " ready to receive any agent whom Mr. Davis or any other influential person now resisting the national authority, may informally send me, with a view of securing peace to the people of *our common country*."

While the intermediation of Mr. Blair was taking place in Richmond, a number of Congressmen and leading politicians of the Confederacy had been exerting themselves to use the peculiar influence of the Vice-President, Alexander H. Stephens, in a negotiation with Washington, and for this purpose to bring him and President Davis to a friendly understanding. There had long been a coolness between these two high officers. Mr. Stephens had blown hot and cold in the war. At the beginning of the contest he opposed secession; after the great battles of 1862 around Richmond, he was intensely Southern, and thought the death of every individual in the Confederacy preferable to subjugation; at later periods of the war he squinted at "reconstruction," and dallied with the "Union" faction in the South. The reputation of this man is a striking example of how difficult it is in all parts of America for the people to distinguish between a real statesman and an elaborate demagogue. Mr. Stephens had a great idea of his personal consequence; he was touchy and exacting in his intercourse with other public men; and he refused to pass a word with President Davis until he had obtained from him the concession of a circuitous message that "the President would be glad to see Mr. Stephens." In the interview which took place, President Davis remarked graciously, but with a tinge of sarcasm in his tone, that he knew of "no one better calculated to conduct a peace negotiation with the North than Mr. Alexander H. Stephens." In the statement of his views the President was remarkably liberal. He allowed Mr. Stephens to name for himself the associate commissioners, who were R. M. T. Hunter of Virginia, and J. A. Campbell of Alabama; he burdened him with no detail of instructions; he said: "I give you a *carte-blanche*, only writing on it the one word, 'Independence.' "

The anxiously expected conference did not take place until the 3d of February. It was attended on the Federal side by President Lincoln himself, accompanied by his Secretary of State, Mr. Seward; the presence of the Northern President having been induced by an earnest telegram from Gen. Grant, expressing his personal belief that the Confederate commissioners, who had passed through his lines, were sincere in their desire for peace, and his strong conviction that a personal interview with them on the part of Mr. Lincoln was highly desirable. The Confederate commissioners were entertained on board of a steamer lying in Hampton Roads. The conference was studiously informal; there were no notes of it; there was no attendance of secretaries or clerks; there was an irregular conversation of four hours, enlivened by two anecdotes of Mr. Lincoln; but there being absolutely no basis of negotiation between the two parties, not even a single point of coincidence between them, they separated without effect. The Confederate commissioners obtained only from the interview the distinct, enlarged, and insolent demand of Mr Lincoln, that the South should submit unconditionally to the rule of the Union, and conform to the advanced position of the Federal Executive on the subject of slavery, which included an amendment to the Constitution abolishing this domestic institution of the South, a bill establishing a Freedmen's Bureau, and other measures looking to a new construction of relations between the black and white populations of the country.

The report of the conference and its results was made in the following message from President Davis, sent in to the Confederate Congress on the 5th February :

" *To the Senate and House of Representatives of the Confederate States of America :*

" Having recently received a written notification which satisfied me that the President of the United States was disposed to confer informally with unofficial agents that might be sent by me with a view to the restoration of peace, I requested Hon. Alexander H. Stephens, Hon. R. M. T. Hunter, and Hon. John A. Campbell, to proceed through our lines to hold a conference with Mr. Lincoln, or such persons as he might depute to represent him.

" I herewith submit, for the information of Congress, the report of the eminent citizens above named, showing that the enemy refuse to enter into negotiations with the Confederate States, or any one of them separately, or to give our people any other terms or guarantees than those which a conqueror may grant, or permit us to have peace on any other basis than our unconditional submission to their rule, coupled with the acceptance of their recent legislation, including an amendment to the Constitution for the emancipation of negro slaves, and with the right on the part of the Federal Congress to legislate on the subject of the relations between the white and black population of each State.

" Such is, as I understand, the effect of the amendment to the Constitution which has been adopted by the Congress of the United States.

" JEFFERSON DAVIS.

" Executive Office, Richmond, *February 5, 1865.*"

" Richmond, Virginia, *February 5, 1865.*
" *To the President of the Confederate States :*

" Sir : Under your letter of appointment of 28th ult., we proceeded to seek an informal conference with Abraham Lincoln, President of the United States, upon the subject mentioned in your letter.

" The conference was granted, and took place on the 3d inst., on board a steamer anchored in Hampton Roads, where we met President Lincoln and Hon. Mr. Seward, Secretary of State of the United States. It continued for several hours, and was both full and explicit.

" We learned from them that the message of President Lincoln to the Congress of the United States, in December last, explains clearly and distinctly his sentiments as to terms, conditions, and method of proceeding by which peace can be secured to the people, and we were not informed that they would be modified or altered to obtain that end. We understood from him that no terms or proposals of any treaty or agreement looking to an ultimate settlement would be entertained or made by him with the authorities of the Confederate States, because that would be a recognition of their existence as a separate power, which under no circumstances would be done ; and for like reasons, that no such terms would be entertained by him from States separately ; that no extended truce or armistice, as at present advised, would be granted or allowed without satisfactory assurances in advance of complete restoration of the authority of the Constitution and laws of the United States over all places within the States of the Confederacy ; that whatever consequences may follow from the re-establishment of that authority must be accepted, but the individuals subject to pains and penalties under the laws of the United States might rely upon a very liberal use of the power confided to him to remit those pains and penalties, if peace be restored.

" During the conference the proposed amendments to the Constitution of the United States, adopted by Congress on the 31st ult., were brought to our notice. These amendments provide that neither slavery nor involuntary servitude, except for crime, should exist within the United States, or any place within their jurisdiction, and that Congress should have the power to enforce this amendment by appropriate legislation.

" Of all the correspondence that preceded the conference herein mentioned and leading to the same, you have heretofore been informed.

" Very respectfully, your obedient servants,

" ALEX. H. STEPHENS,
" R. M. T. HUNTER,
" J. A. CAMPBELL."

It was doubtless calculated by President Davis that the issue of the Fortress Monroe Conference would give a flat answer to the party in the Confederacy that had been clamouring for peace negotiations, and make an opportunity to excite anew the spirit and indignation of the Southern people. It was indeed a powerful appeal to the heart of the South; it had displayed the real consequences of subjugation; it had declared what would be its pains and penalties and humiliation; it was the *ultimatum* of an enemy calculated to nerve the resolution of a people fighting for liberty, and to make them devote anew labour and life for the great cause of their redemption. It was thought in Richmond that the last attempt at negotiation would date a new era of resolution and devotion in the war. On the return of the commissioners a day was appointed for an imposing expression of public opinion on the event of the conference; all business was suspended in Richmond; at high noon processions were formed to the different places of meeting; and no less than twenty different orators, composed of the most effective speakers in Congress and the Cabinet, and the most eloquent divines of Richmond, took their stands in the halls of legislation, in the churches and the theatres, and swelled the eloquence of this last and grand appeal to the people and armies of the South. Two of the returned commissioners, Messrs. Hunter and Campbell, were among the orators of the day. Mr. Stephens had been urged to speak; but he had a demagogue's instinct of danger in the matter; it was an awkward occasion in which he might say too much or too little; and so he plead ill-health, and escaped to Georgia. It was an extraordinary day in Richmond; vast crowds huddled around the stands of the speakers or lined the streets; and the air was vocal with the efforts of the orator and the responses of his audience. It appeared indeed that the blood of the people had again been kindled. But it was only the sickly glare of an expiring flame; there was no steadiness in the excitement; there was no virtue in huzzas; the inspiration ended with the voices and ceremonies that invoked it; and it was found that the spirit of the people of the Confederacy was too weak, too much broken to react with effect, or assume the position of erect and desperate defiance.

A few days before this popular convocation in Richmond, and just on the return of the commissioners, President Davis himself had addressed a popular audience in the African Church. He was attended to the stand by the Governor of Virginia. He made a powerful and eloquent address; but in parts of it he fell into weak and bombastic speech, and betrayed that boastfulness characteristic of almost all his oral utterances in the war. As a writer, Mr. Davis was careful, meditative, and full of dignity; but as a speaker, he was imprudent, and in moments of passion, he frequently blurted out what first came into his mind. On this occasion he was boastful, almost to the point of grotesqueness. He declared that the march which Sherman was then making would be "his last," and would conduct him to ruin; he predicted that before the summer solstice fell upon the country it would be the North that would be soliciting peace; he affirmed that the military situation of the Confederacy was all that he could desire; and drawing up his figure, and in tones of scornful defiance, heard to the remotest parts of the building, he remarked that the Federal authorities who had so complacently conferred with the commissioners of the Confederacy, "little knew that they were talking to their *masters!*" Such swollen speeches of the President offended the sober sense of the Confederacy; and it was frequently said that he attempted to blind the people as to the actual condition of affairs, and never dealt with them in a proper spirit of candour. But this estimate of President Davis is probably a mistaken one. He was not insincere; in all his strange and extravagant utterances of confidence he probably believed what he spoke; and to the last he appears never to have apprehended the real situation. He was blinded by his own natural temper; in the last moment he was issuing edicts, playing with the baubles of authority, never realizing that he was not still the great tribune; he was sustained by a powerful self-conceit, and a sanguine temperament; and he went down to ruin with the fillet of vanity upon his eyes.

BATTLE OF HARE'S HILL.

In the last days of March, 1865, Gen. Lee made his last offensive demonstration, which ended in failure, and plainly and painfully revealed the condition of his troops. He determined to try Grant's lines south of the Appomattox; the attack being immediately directed by Gen. Gordon on the enemy's works at Hare's Hill. The project of assault was bold · its promises were large; one success might lead to another; and if the troops once got possession of a part of the enemy's line, in the flush of success they might be carried to the capture of the neighbouring works, and Gen. Lee might even venture on the great enterprise of getting possession of Grant's military road and cutting his entire right from its base at City Point and from the army north of the James.

The disposition of Gen. Lee's force was generally as follows: Longstreet commanded the Confederate left, across the James, and his right division extended to within a few miles of Petersburg. Gordon came next, with his three divisions, reduced by arduous and fatiguing marches and bloody battles in the Shenandoah Valley, to the dimensions of only respectable brigades. He commanded just in front of Petersburg, from the Appomattox to a small stream to the right of the city. It was along this line, almost its entire length, that a continuous struggle for months had been kept up, and in some places the opposing forces were but a few yards apart. A. P. Hill, with his three divisions, held the right, extending to Hatcher's Run, while the cavalry guarded either flank.

The assault of the 25th March was made two miles south of the Appomattox and just to the left of the Crater. Massing two divisions, Gordon, in the early light of the morning dashed on the Federal works. The enemy was surprised; the sharpshooters of Grimes' division, composing the advance, succeeded in driving the Federal troops from their works, and the Confederates occupied their breastworks for a distance of a quarter of a mile, with comparatively a slight loss and with the loss to the enemy of one principal fort (Steadman), and some five hundred prisoners. Had this opportunity been taken advantage of, there is no telling the result; but the troops could not be induced to leave the breastworks they had taken from the enemy, and to advance beyond them and seize the crest in rear of the line they had occupied. They hugged the works in disorder until the enemy recovered from his surprise; and soon the artillery in the forts to the right and left began their murderous fire on them. When fresh troops were brought up by the enemy, their advance was almost unresisted, and an easy recapture of the fort was obtained, the Confederates retiring under a severe fire into their old works. Nearly two thousand men took shelter under the breastworks they had captured, and surrendered when the enemy advanced, and the result was a Confederate loss much greater than that of the foe. This affair demonstrated to all that the day of offensive movements on the part of the Confederates was gone. The experiment had entailed a loss that could be ill afforded by Gen. Lee; and one more such disaster might have been irreparable.

THE LAST BATTLES AROUND PETERSBURG.

Gen. Grant had at first designed to await the junction of Sherman's forces for his final operations upon Richmond, so as to complete his assurance of victory. But he feared that if Sherman crossed the Roanoke river, Johnston would take the alarm, and move to Lee's lines; and as the circumspect Federal commander was careful to risk nothing, even approaching to an equal match of force, he determined to dispatch his final movement upon Richmond, and to make his experiment upon Lee's little army with no further occasions of delay. The area of critical operations in the Confederacy was now within close and narrow boundaries. Its fate was to be practically decided in operations taking place between the Roanoke and James Rivers in one direction, and the Atlantic Ocean and the Alleghany Mountains in the other. In this circumscribed space Richmond was the prominent figure, the critical point, and Lee's army the chief contestant.

The usual preliminary to a great action of the Federals—a movement of cavalry—was directed by Gen. Grant before the time assigned for a general movement of the armies operating against Richmond. The immediate object was to cut off all communications with the city north of James River; and on the 27th February, Sheridan moved from the Shenandoah Valley with two divisions of cavalry, numbering about ten thousand sabres. On the 1st March he secured the bridge across the middle fork of the Shenandoah, entered Staunton the next day, and thence pushed on towards Waynesboro', where Early, with less than twelve hundred men, disputed the *débouché* of the Blue Ridge. This force—a remnant of the Army of the Valley—was posted on the banks of a stream, with no way open for retreat; and Sheridan's magnificent cavalry easily ran over it, and took more than nine hundred prisoners. Gen. Early, with two of his staff officers, escaped by taking to the woods. The next day Charlottesville was surrendered; and here Sheridan paused to await the arrival of his trains, busy meanwhile in destroying the railroads towards Richmond and Lynchburg. His instructions prescribed that he should gain Lynchburg on the south bank of the James. From that point he was to effectually break up those main branches of Lee's communications, the Lynchburg railroads and James River Canal, after which he was to strike southward through Virginia to the westward of Danville and join Sherman. But moving towards the James River, between Richmond and Lynchburg, Sheridan found himself confronted by a swollen and impassable stream. He fell back, rounded the left wing of Lee's army, crossed the Pamunkey River at the White House, and on the 25th March joined Gen. Grant in the lines before Petersburg. He had not completed the circuit designed for him; but he had traversed thirteen counties, and done enormous damage. The damage to the canal was almost irreparable; every lock had been destroyed as far as Dugaldsville, twenty miles from Lynchburg; and as for the railroads radiating from Charlottesville to Waynesboro, Amherst Court-house and Louisa Court-house and extending from the South Anna to Chesterfield Station and the Chickahominy river, every bridge, nearly every culvert, and scores of miles of the rail itself had been completely destroyed.

Sheridan's cavalry, diverted back from its intended tour to North Carolina, proved a timely and important accession to Grant's strength in his final encounter. There were indications that that encounter was near at hand. There had been days of painful expectation along the Confederate line. In the vicinity of Petersburg the heavy booming of guns was occasionally heard away on the right sounding like distant thunder. Again sounds of conflict would open on the extreme left and the rattle of musketry and the beat of artillery would scarcely leave doubt of a battle in earnest; but after a few impulsive volleys strife would cease and a profound quiet prevail. The increasing signs of activity inside the enemy's lines indicated plainly enough preparations for attack or movement of some sort; but it was impossible to say where the blow would fall and how it would be delivered. In the words of one of their officers " each night the Confederates unfolded their blankets and unloosed their shoe-strings in uncertainty."

The movement designed by Gen. Grant may be briefly described as an attempt upon Lee's right and vulnerable flank by a turning column which contingently embraced his whole army and included a heavy operation of cavalry. On the day that Sheridan reached his lines, three divisions of what was called the Army of the James on the north side of the river, were withdrawn from Longstreet's front without attracting his attention, and were transferred to a position near Hatcher's Run. The Second and Fifth corps, which had held this part of the enemy's entrenched lines, were now foot-loose to manœuvre by the left; and co-operating with Sheridan's cavalry (about twenty-five thousand men in all), they were directed to move to the right of Lee's entrenched line, and threaten his communication by the Southside Railroad. The movement commenced on the 29th March.

To secure the defence of his right against this powerful column which Grant had thrust out by the left, was the immediate necessity that stared Gen. Lee in the face, for it was vitally important to secure the lines whereon his troops depended for their daily food; but it was at the same time indispensable that he should maintain the long entrenched line that covered Petersburg and Richmond. There was no resource but the desperate one of stripping his entrenchments to secure his menaced right and contest the prize of the Southside Railroad. In the night of the 29th, Gen. Lee, having perceived Grant's manœuvre, despatched Pickett's and Bushrod Johnson's divisions, Wise's and Ransom's brigade, Huger's battalion of infantry, and Fitzhugh Lee's division, in all about seventeen thousand men, to encounter the turning column of the enemy.

The right of the Confederate entrenched line crossed Hatcher's Run at the Boydton plank road, and extended some distance along the White Oak road. Four miles beyond the termination of this line there was a point where several roads from the north and south converged on the White Oak road, forming what is known as the Five Forks. It was an isolated position, but one of great value, as it held the strategic key that opened up the whole region which Lee was now seeking to cover. In the evening of the 29th, Sheridan occupied Dinwiddie Court-house, six miles southwest of where the two co-operating corps of infantry lay on their arms and about eight miles south of Five Forks.

A heavy rain the next day prevented further operations; but on the 31st Sheridan pushed forward to Five Forks, where he encountered two divisions of infantry under Pickett and Johnson. In the afternoon of the day this Confederate force, which had been moved down by the White Oak road, made a determined charge upon the whole cavalry line of the enemy, forced it back, and drove it to a point within two miles of Dinwiddie Court-house.

On the morning of the 1st April, Sheridan, now reinforced by the Fifth corps, commanded by Warren, advanced boldly again in the direction of Five Forks, having ascertained that the Confederates during the night had withdrawn all but a mask of force from his front. In the afternoon, Pickett and Johnson found themselves confined within their works at the Five Forks, and flanked by a part of the Fifth corps, which had moved down the White Oak road. The Confederate troops having got the idea that they were entrapped, and finding themselves pressed front, flank and rear, mostly threw down their arms. Five thousand men surrendered themselves as prisoners. The remnants of the divisions of Pickett and Johnson fled westward from Five Forks routed, demoralized, and past control; and Gen. Lee found that his right, wrenched violently from his centre, was turned almost without a battle, and that what he had counted as the bulk of his army was no longer of any use. It was the only occasion on which the Confederate commander ever exhibited anything like reproof in the field. He remarked that the next time the troops were to be taken into action, he would put himself at the head of them; and turning to one of his brigadiers, he ordered him, with singular emphasis and severity, to gather and put under guard "*all* the stragglers on the field," making a plain reference to the conduct of his officers.

But even if the shameful misfortune of Five Forks had not befallen

Gen. Lee, the result would not have been materially different; for the fate of Petersburg and Richmond was decided without this event. In massing upon his right, Gen. Lee had reduced the force defending Petersburg to two incomplete corps, Gordon's and Hill's; and these strung over nine miles of breastworks, made little more than sentinels. Before Longstreet, who commanded on the other side of the river, was made aware of the situation, and could obey Lee's orders for troops, Grant had descried the weakness of the Confederate lines before Petersburg, and determined the easy task of breaking them.

On the night of the 1st April, Grant celebrated the victory of Five Forks, and performed the prelude of what was yet to come by a fierce and continuous bombardment along his lines in front of Petersburg. Every piece of artillery in the thickly studded forts, batteries, and mortar-beds joined in the prodigious clamour; reports, savagely, terrifically crashing through the narrow streets and lanes of Petersburg, echoed upwards; it appeared as if fiends of the air were engaged in the sulphurous conflict. As dawn broke, Grant prepared for the attack, which was made in double column at different points on the Confederate line.

The assault was opened from the Appomattox to Hatcher's Run. The most determined effort was made on Gordon's lines, and here the enemy succeeded in taking a portion of the breastworks near the Appomattox. But they could not use the advantage which they had struggled so hard to obtain, the Confederates holding an inner cordon of works, and the position which the enemy had taken being exposed to a raking fire of artillery on the right and left. But while this contest was going on to the left of the "Crater," the enemy massed heavily against Hill's left opposite a position the weakest in the line, from which McGowan's brigade had been transferred the day previous, leaving only artillerists in the trenches and the picket in front. The Confederate skirmishers were driven with impunity, the batteries were carried in a moment, and a loud huzza that drowned the sound of battle on other parts of the line, proclaimed that the enemy had obtained an important success.

Just in rear, some two or three hundred yards, on many parts of the Confederate line, heavy forts had been erected to guard against just such results as had ensued. In rear of the line of works captured by the enemy were batteries Alexander and Gregg; and these two works were all that now prevented the enemy from completely cutting the Confederate lines in two to the Appomattox. After getting in order, the enemy moved on these works—on Fort Alexander first, taking it with a rush, although the gunners stood to their guns to the last, and fired their last shot while the Federal troops were on the ramparts.

In Fort Gregg there was a small and mixed garrison. Capt. Chew, of the 4th Maryland battery of artillery, was in command of the work. There was added to his battery of two 3-inch rifles and thirty men, a body of men known, in the vulgar parlance of soldiers, as "Walker's Mules," dismounted drivers to whom were given muskets. These men were Virginians and Louisianians who belonged to Walker's artillery brigade, and amounted in round numbers, to about one hundred. The remainder of the garrison, about one hundred and twenty, were some men from Harris' Mississippi brigade, and some North Carolinians. Both of these commands, the Mississippians and North Carolinians, had been driven back from the picket lines, and had fled into Fort Gregg for shelter.

Having run over Fort Alexander, the enemy moved on Fort Gregg with cheers. Confidently, in beautiful lines and in all the majesty of overpowering numbers, did the Federal troops advance upon the devoted work. They had got within fifty yards of it, and not the flash of a single rifle had yet defied them. The painful thought passed through the ranks of their comrades who watched in the distance that the garrison was about to surrender. But instead of a white flag, there was a white puff of smoke; and artillery and infantry simultaneously opened on the confident assailants, who, staggering and reeling under the death-dealing volley, at last gave way, and retreated in masses under cover. A loud and wild cheer rang out from the Confederate lines, and was answered in exultant tones by the heroic little garrison in Fort Gregg. But reinforcements were hastening from the lines of the enemy. There were none to send to the succour of the garrison; every Confederate soldier was needed at his post, and no reserves were at hand. As the enemy again came up in battle array, the troops moved forward in serried ranks, and soon the fort was canopied in smoke. It seemed by mutual consent that the conflict ceased on other parts of the line, while both sides stood silent and anxious spectators of the struggle at the fort. As the smoke lifts it is seen that the Federals have reached the ditch. Those in the distance could descry lines of blue uniforms swarming up the sides of the works; and as the foremost reached the top, they reeled and fell upon their comrades below. Once, twice, and thrice they reached the top, only to be repulsed; and yet they persevered while the guns in the embrasures continued to fire in rapid succession. Presently the sound of artillery ceased, and the Federals mounted the work, and poured a rapid fire on the defenders within. Many of the garrison, unwilling to surrender, used their bayonets, and clubbed their guns in an unequal struggle. But such resistance could be of short duration; and soon loud huzzas of the enemy told that the fort had been taken, and with it the Confederate army cut in two. But the event had been marked by a heroic self-immolation; of the two hundred and fifty men who defended the fort there were not more than thirty survivors; and to the illumined story of the Army of Northern Virginia, Fort Gregg gave a fitting conclusion, an ornament of glory that well clasped the record of its deeds.

As soon as the fort was captured, cannonading and sharpshooting were renewed on other parts of the line. In a moment heavy bodies of cavalry, emerging from the enemy's former lines, poured rapidly over the captured works, and galloped in squadrons towards the Appomattox, which was some four or five miles distant. Their track could be traced by the heavy columns of black smoke that rose from the various farm-houses on their route, which had been set on fire. The infantry, which had succeeded in capturing the fort, formed line fronting the Confederate right flank, and appeared as if they intended marching by the rear into Petersburg.

New dispositions were now made along the Confederate line. The protracted resistance offered by Fort Gregg enabled Gen. Lee to establish what of force remained to him in the manner best availing for the defence of Petersburg. Longstreet, accompanied by a small brigade (Benning's) of Fields' division, had arrived from the north side of the James in time to check the advance of the enemy long enough to enable fresh troops to hurry up in his rear, and to form a fresh line in front of Petersburg. Meanwhile Heth's division of A. P. Hill's corps regained some ground, and re-established their lines. But in the execution of the movement was lost the valuable life of Gen. Hill, who had seen his first service at the famous field of Manassas as Colonel of the Thirteenth Virginia regiment in Gen. Johnston's army, had passed rapidly through all the gradations of rank to Lieutenant-General, and had borne a constant and distinguished part in the four years' defence of the Confederate capital. Desiring to obtain a near view of a portion of the enemy's line, he had ridden forward, accompanied by a single orderly, when he unexpectedly came upon a party of six Federal soldiers concealed in a ravine. Gen. Hill wore only the stars of a colonel on a rough citizen's coat. He advanced upon the party, and commanded their surrender; they consented; but he neglected to disarm them, and reassured by finding there was no body of troops in the vicinity, they fired a treacherous volley, and shot him through the heart.

The line on which Gen. Lee had now closed around Petersburg was not intended for a renewal of battle, which was now hopeless, but merely to gain time for the execution of another purpose. A little while after the fall of Fort Gregg, ominous columns of smoke arose from numberless depots and warehouses of Petersburg. It was eleven o'clock in the morning when Gen. Lee wrote a hasty telegram to the War Department, advising that the authorities of Richmond should have everything in readiness to evacuate the capital at eight o'clock the coming night, unless before that time despatches should be received from him to a contrary effect!

EVACUATION OF RICHMOND.

A small slip of paper, sent up from the War Department to President Davis, as he was seated in his pew in St. Paul's Church, contained the news of the most momentous event of the war.

It is a most remarkable circumstance that the people of Richmond had remained in profound ignorance of the fighting which had been taking place for three days on Gen. Lee's lines. There was not a rumour of it in the air. Not a newspaper office in the city had any inkling of what was going on. Indeed for the past few days there had been visible reassurance in the Confederate capital; there were rumours that Johnston was moving to Lee's lines and a general idea that the combined force would take the offensive against the enemy. But a day before Grant had commenced his heavy movement a curious excitement had taken place in Richmond. The morning train had brought from Petersburg the wonderful rumour that Gen. Lee had made a night attack, in which he had crushed the enemy along his whole line. John M. Daniel, the editor of the Richmond *Examiner*, died the same day under the delusion that such a victory had been won; and John Mitchel, who wrote his obituary in the morning papers, expressed the regret that the great Virginian had passed away just as a decisive victory was likely to give the turning point to the success of the Southern Confederacy! The circumstance shows how little prepared the people of Richmond were on the bright Sabbath morning of the 2d of April for the news that fell upon them like a thunder-clap from clear skies, and smote the ear of the community as a knell of death.

The report of a great misfortune soon traverses a city without the aid of printed bulletins. But that of the evacuation of Richmond fell upon many incredulous ears. One could see the quiet streets stretching away, unmolested by one single sign of war; across the James the landscape glistened in the sun; everything which met the eye spoke of peace, and made it impossible to picture in imagination the scene which was to ensue. There were but few people in the streets; no vehicles disturbed the quiet of the Sabbath; the sound of the church-going bells rose into the cloudless sky, and floated on the blue tide of the beautiful day. How was it possible to imagine that in the next twenty-four hours, war, with its train of horrours, was to enter the scene; that this peaceful city, a secure possession for four years, was at last to succumb; that it was to be a prey to a great conflagration, and that all the hopes of the Southern Confederacy were to be consumed in one day, as a scroll in the fire!

As the day wore on, clatter and bustle in the streets denoted the progress of the evacuation, and convinced those who had been incredulous of its reality. The disorder increased each hour. The streets were thronged with fugitives making their way to the railroad depots; pale women and little shoeless children struggled in the crowd; oaths and blasphemous shouts smote the ear. Wagons were being hastily loaded at the Departments with boxes, trunks, etc., and driven to the Danville depot. In the afternoon a special train carried from Richmond President Davis and some of his Cabinet. At the Departments all was confusion; there was no system; there was no answer to inquiries; important officers were invisible, and every one felt like taking care of himself. Outside the mass of hurrying fugitives, there were collected here and there mean-visaged crowds, generally around the commissary depots; they had already scented prey; they were of that brutal and riotous element that revenges itself on all communities in a time of great public misfortune.

The only convocation, the only scene of council that marked the fall of Richmond, took place in a dingy room in a corner of the upper story of the Capitol Building. In this obscure chamber assembled the City Council of Richmond, to consult on the emergency, and to take measures to secure what of order was possible in the scenes about to ensue. It appeared to represent all that was left of deliberation in the Confederate capital. It was a painful contrast to look in upon this scene; to traverse the now almost silent Capitol House, so often vocal with oratory, and crowded with the busy scene of legislation; to hear the echo of the footstep; and at last to climb to the dismal show of councilmen in the remote room where half a dozen men sat at a rude table, and not so many vacant idlers listened to their proceedings. At the head of the board sat an illiterate grocer of the name of Saunders, who was making his last exhibition of Southern spirit, and twenty-four hours thereafter was subscribing himself to some very petty Federal officer, "*most* respectfully, your *most* obedient servant." Here and there, hurrying up with the latest news from the War Department, was Mayor Mayo, excited, incoherent, chewing tobacco defiantly, but yet full of pluck, having the mettle of the true Virginian gentleman, stern and watchful to the last in fidelity to the city that his ancestors had assisted in founding, and exhibiting, no matter in what comical aspects, a courage that no man ever doubted. When it was finally announced by the Mayor that those who had hoped for a despatch from Gen. Lee contrary to what he had telegraphed in the morning, had ceased to indulge such an expectation, and that the evacuation of Richmond was a foregone conclusion, it was proposed to maintain order in the city by two regiments of militia; to destroy every drop of liquor in the warehouses and stores; and to establish a patrol through the night. But the militia ran through the fingers of their officers; the patrols could not be found after a certain hour; and in a short while the whole city was plunged into mad confusion and indescribable horrours.

But the horrours of that night in the Confederate capital were to be studiously veiled from the eyes of the enemy. The Federal force on the north side of James River consisted of three divisions under the command of Gen. Weitzel; while Gen. Ewell covered this approach to the capital with a force about four thousand strong. The Confederates were silently withdrawn from Weitzel's front, their rear-guard traversing the city before daybreak. Weitzel had been instructed to push on, whenever satisfied of his ability to enter Richmond. During the whole day that Grant had been engaged in front of Petersburg, the entire lines north of the James were perfectly quiet. Weitzel's command had orders to make as great a show as possible. He fired no gun during the day, but as darkness came on, he set all his bands of music to work upon national airs. The Confederates vied with the musical entertainment; for many hours the night was filled with melodious strains. But about midnight a complete and absolute silence fell upon the lines. It was a dead quiet; a close mask to what was taking place in the doomed city; and not until the morning hours did the direful blazon in the sky proclaim to Weitzel that his hour had come and that Richmond was at his mercy.

There had been but little sleep for the people of Richmond in the night which preceded their great misfortune. It was an extraordinary night; disorder, pillage, shouts, mad revelry of confusion. In the now dimly-lighted city could be seen black masses of people, crowded around some object of excitement, besieging the commissary stores, destroying liquor, intent perhaps upon pillage, and swaying to and fro in whatever momentary passion possessed them. The gutters ran with a liquor freshet, and the fumes filled the air. Some of the straggling soldiers passing through the city, easily managed to get hold of quantities of the liquor. Confusion became worse confounded; the sidewalks were encumbered with broken glass; stores were entered at pleasure and stripped from top to bottom; yells of drunken men, shouts of roving pillagers, wild cries of distress filled the air, and made night hideous.

But a new horrour was to appear upon the scene and take possession of the community. To the rear-guard of the Confederate force on the north side of James River, under Gen. Ewell, had been left the duty of blowing up the iron-clad vessels in the James and destroying the bridges across that river. The Richmond, Virginia, and an iron ram, were blown to the winds; the little shipping at the wharves was fired; and the three bridges that spanned the river were wrapped in flames, as soon as the last troops had traversed them. The work of destruction might well have ended here. But Gen. Ewell, obeying the letter of his instructions, had issued orders to fire the four principal tobacco warehouses of the city; one of them—the Shockoe warehouse—situated near the centre of the city, side by side with the Gallego flour mills, just in a position and circumstances from which a conflagration might extend to the whole business portion of Richmond. In vain Mayor Mayo and a committee of citizens had remonstrated against this reckless military order. The warehouses were fired; the flames seized on the neighbouring buildings and soon involved a wide and widening area; the conflagration passed rapidly beyond control; and in this mad fire, this wild, unnecessary destruction of their property the citizens of Richmond had a fitting *souvenir* of the imprudence and recklessness of the departing Administration.

Morning broke on a scene never to be forgotten. It was a strange picture—impossible to describe—the smoke and glare of fire mingled with the golden beams of the rising sun. The great warehouse on the Basin was wrapped in flames; the fire was reaching to whole blocks of buildings; and as the sun rose majestically above the horizon, it burnished the fringe of smoke with lurid and golden glory. Curious crowds watched the fire. Its roar sounded in the ears; it leaped from street to street; pillagers were busy at their vocation, and in the hot breath of the fire were figures as of demons contending for prey.

The sun was an hour or more above the horizon, when suddenly there ran up the whole length of Main street the cry of "Yankees!" "Yankees!" The upper part of this street was choked with crowds of pillagers —men provided with drays, others rolling barrels up the street, or bending under heavy burdens, and intermixed with them women and children with smaller lots of plunder in bags, baskets, tubs, buckets, and tin-pans. As the cry of "Yankees" was raised, this motley crowd tore up the street, cursing, screaming, trampling upon each other, alarmed by an enemy not yet in sight, and madly seeking to extricate themselves from imaginary dangers. Presently, beyond this crowd, following up the tangled mass of plunderers, but not pressing or interfering with them, was seen a small body of Federal cavalry, riding steadily along. Forty Massachusetts troopers, despatched by Gen. Weitzel to investigate the condition of affairs, had ridden without let or hindrance into Richmond. At the corner of Eleventh street they broke into a trot for the public square, and in a few moments their guidons were planted on the Capitol, and fluttered there a strange spectacle in the early morning light.

A few hours thereafter, and Weitzel's troops were pouring through the streets of the city. A lady, who witnessed the grand Federal *entrée*, and has given a very graphic account of it, thus describes a portion of the scene: "Stretching from the Exchange Hotel to the slopes of Church Hill, down the hill, through the valley, up the ascent to the hotel, was the array, with its unbroken line of blue, fringed with bright bayonets. Strains of martial music, flushed countenances, waving swords, betokened the victorious army. As the line turned at the Exchange Hotel into the upper street, the movement was the signal for a wild burst of cheers from each regiment. Shouts from a few negroes were the only responses. Through throngs of sullen spectators ; along the line of fire ; in the midst of the horrours of a conflagration, increased by the explosion of shells left by the retreating army ; through curtains of smoke ; through the vast ærial auditorium convulsed with the commotion of frightful sounds, moved the garish procession of the grand army, with brave music, and bright banners and wild cheers. A regiment of negro cavalry swept by the hotel As they turned the street corner they drew their sabres with savage shouts, and the blood mounted even in my woman's heart with quick throbs of defiance." *

Meanwhile the fire raged with unchecked fury. The entire business part of the city was on fire ; stores, warehouses, manufactories, mills, depots, and bridges—all, covering acres ; the continuous thunder of exploding shells sounded in the sea of fire ; and in the midst of it was the long, threatening, hostile army entering to seize its prey. All during the forenoon, flame and smoke and burning brands and showers of blazing sparks filled the air, spreading still further the destruction, until it had swept before it every bank, every auction store, every insurance office, nearly every commission house, and most of the fashionable stores. The atmosphere was almost choking ; men, women, and children crowded into the square of the Capitol for a breath of pure air ; but it was not to be obtained even there, and one traversed the green slopes blinded by cinders and struggling for breath. Already piles of furniture had been collected here, dragged from the ruins of burning houses ; and in uncouth arrangements, made with broken tables and bureaus, were huddled women and children, with no other home, with no other resting place in Heaven's great hollowness.

Some tardy attempts were made to arrest the conflagration ; in the afternoon the military authorities organized the crowds of negroes as a fire corps ; but the few steam-engines that played upon the flames were not sufficient to check their progress. It was late in the evening when the fire had burned itself out. It had consumed the most important part of Richmond. Commencing at the Shockoe warehouse, the fire radiated front and rear, and on two wings, burning down Main street, half way between Fourteenth and Fifteenth streets, and back to the river, through Cary and all the intermediate streets. Westward, on Main, the fire was stayed at Ninth street, sweeping back to the river. On the north side of Main the flames were stayed between Thirteenth and Fourteenth streets. From this point the flames raged on the north side of Main up to Eighth street, and back to Bank street. The pencil of the surveyor could not have more distinctly marked out the business portion of the city.

The evening breezes had turned the course of the fire ; and as these

---

* "Nathalie, in *Norfolk Virginian*.

still continued, heavy mist-clouds hung upon the horizon, or streamed upwards on the varying current of the winds. As night came on, there was
a painful reaction after the day's terrible excitement; a strange quiet fell
upon the blackened city and its scenes of destruction. It was the quiet
of a great desolation. Groups of women and children crawled under shelters of broken furniture in the Capitol square; hundreds of homeless persons laid down to sleep in the shadows of the ruins of Richmond; and
worn out by excitement, exhausted as by the spasm of a great battle, men
watched for the morrow with the dull sense that the work of years had
been ruined, and that all they possessed on earth had been swept away.

While Richmond was filled with horrour and destruction, and the
smoke of its torment ascended to the skies, very different scenes were
taking place far away in the cities of the North. It was a strange reverse
to the picture we have been contemplating. With those fervours and
shows characteristic of the Northern mind, Washington and New York
were celebrating the downfall of the Confederate capital. Bells were rung;
wild and enthusiastic congratulations ran along the street; and vast crowds
collected, whose fantastic exhibitions of joy, not content with huzzas,
cheers, and dancing in the streets, broke out into a blasphemous singing
of hymns of the church. In New York twenty thousand persons in the
open air sung the doxology. There was, of course, an unlimited display
of flags; and as evidence of this characteristic exhibition it is said that
half an hour after the news of the fall of Richmond was known, not a
single large flag in the whole city of New York was left unpurchased.
These symbols of loyalty not only floated over houses, but were fastened
to carts, stages and wagons. The newspapers were mostly occupied with
spread-eagles and maps of Richmond. The *World* expressed the opinion
that the event of the day " more fully justified exuberant rejoicing than
any previous achievement in the history of the war." The New York
Herald—the organ *par excellence* of Yankee wind—went further, and declared that the taking of Richmond was " one of the *grandest triumphs
that had crowned human efforts for centuries.*"

Such stuff was characteristic of Northern newspapers. But looking to
facts we shall find a more precise language in which to describe the
achievement of Gen. Ulysses S. Grant in the fall of Richmond.

It was simply the consummation of the disgrace of this commander—
that he should have taken eleven months to capture a position at no time
held by more than one third of his forces, having lost in the enterprise in
killed and wounded more than double the numbers actually in arms
against him ! This sentence may grate on Northern pride; but it is
founded upon plain, unyielding figures; it is the inexorable statement of
the law of proportions; it can be no more contested than a mathematical
demonstration. As long as the intelligent of this world are persuaded of

the opinion that a great General is he who accomplishes his purposes with small, but admirably drilled armies ; who defeats large armies with small ones ; who accomplishes great military results by strategy, more than by fighting, who makes of war an intellectual exercise rather than a match of brute force, that title will be given to Robert E. Lee above all men in America, and the Confederate commander will be declared to have been much greater in defeat than Grant in his boasted victory.

The adulation of partisans has no permanent place in the records of glory. The office of the historian is to reduce the exaggerations of the present, and that without reference to the passionate criticisms of the times in which he lives. If the fact be that the North has produced no great General in this war ; that the exhibitions of generalship, chivalry, human- ity, and all that noble sentimentalism that properly belongs to the state of war have been more largely on the Confederate side ; that the Northern people have exhibited gross materialism in the war, have excluded that noble spirituality common to the great conflicts of civilized nations, and worshipped the grossest types of physical power, the fault is in themselves, and not in the pen that writes these things.

CHAPTER XLII.

THE Federal occupants of Richmond no doubt thought the people very submissive to the new authority. They saw no sign of violence, and they heard no expression of defiance. The population of Richmond moved mechanically before their new masters. But there was, for some days, an undercurrent of eager, excited thought which the Federals did not perceive; citizens whispered among themselves, and went around the street-corners to relate in low tones to each other some rumour eagerly grasped for the new hope it contained. Thus it was told in whispers that Gen. Lee had won a great victory on his retreat, that Johnston had struck Sherman a mortal blow, or that some other extravagant event had happened, some sudden relief of the falling fortunes of the Confederacy. It is not easy for men to descend at once to the condition of despair.

But even outside the circle of absurd rumours, there were intelligent minds in Richmond that still entertained lingering hopes of the cause of the Confederacy. The foundation of these hopes was small, but not altogether visionary. There was a chance that Lee might get off his army safely, and effect a successful retreat; he might unite with Johnston; and, although driven from Virginia, the armies of the Confederacy might reopen Georgia and the Carolinas, and place the Government nearer its resources of subsistence, with the control of a territory practically much larger than that in the Richmond jurisdiction.

These things were possibilities, very small and very remote. It was learned through Northern newspapers, circulated in Richmond, that President Davis, who had reached Danville, had issued there the following proclamation :

DANVILLE, VA., April 5, 1865.

The General-in-Chief found it necessary to make such movements of his troops as to uncover the capital. It would be unwise to conceal the moral and material injury to our cause resulting from the occupation of our capital by the enemy. It is equally unwise and unworthy of us to allow our own energies to falter, and our efforts to become relaxed under reverses, however calamitous they may be. For many months the largest and finest army of the Confederacy, under a leader whose presence inspires equal confidence in the troops and the people, has been greatly trammelled by the necessity of keeping constant watch over the approaches to the capital, and has thus been forced to forego more than one opportunity for promising enterprise. It is for us, my countrymen, to show by our bearing under reverses how wretched has been the self-deception of those who have believed us less able to endure misfortune with fortitude than to encounter dangers with courage.

We have now entered upon a new phase of the struggle. Relieved from the necessity of guarding particular points, our army will be free to move from point to point, to strike the enemy in detail far from his base. Let us but will it, and we are free.

Animated by that confidence in your spirit and fortitude which never yet failed me, I announce to you, fellow-countrymen, that it is my purpose to maintain your cause with my whole heart and soul; that I will never consent to abandon to the enemy one foot of the soil of any of the States of the Confederacy. That Virginia—noble State—whose ancient renown has been eclipsed by her still more glorious recent history; whose bosom has been bared to receive the main shock of this war; whose sons and daughters have exhibited heroism so sublime as to render her illustrious in all time to come—that Virginia, with the help of the people, and by the blessing of Providence, *shall be held and defended,* and no peace ever be made with the infamous invaders of her territory.

If by the stress of numbers we should ever be compelled to a temporary withdrawal from her limits, or those of any other border State, we will return until the baffled and exhausted enemy shall abandon in despair his endless and impossible task of making slaves of a people resolved to be free.

Let us, then, not despond, my countrymen, but, relying on God, meet the foe with fresh defiance, and with unconquered and unconquerable hearts.

JEFFERSON DAVIS.

This proclamation was the last effusion of the sanguine temperament of the Confederate President. It gave a new colour to the evacuation of Richmond. But the hopeful and ingenious minds which constructed the new theory of Confederate defence had failed to take in a most important element in the consideration—the moral effect of the fall of Richmond. They did not reflect that this city had been for four years the central object of all the plans and exertions of the war; they did not understand that it had become to the popular mind the symbol of the Confederacy; and they could not realize that when Richmond fell the cause lost in the estimation of the army and people the emblem and semblance of nationality and all appliances for supporting the popular faith and enthusiasm. But the sequel was to develop and demonstrate all these consequences, and the last hopes of the Confederacy were to be speedily extinguished.

RETREAT AND FINAL SURRENDER OF LEE'S ARMY.

In his last despatch from Petersburg, Gen. Lee had stated that some time during the night of the 2d April, he would fall back behind the Appomattox. He was then holding a semicircular line, the left resting on the Appomattox, narrowly including Petersburg; while his extreme right, which Sheridan was still pressing, was in the vicinity of the Southside Railroad, some fifteen miles west of the town. It appears that the enemy already imagined that he had cut off the troops on the right, supposing that they could not cross the river except through Petersburg; but in this he was mistaken. When night closed, the air was luminous with the steady glare of the burning warehouses in Petersburg. For several hours cannonading was kept up; but about midnight the Confederates began their retreat. By three o'clock in the morning, Gordon's whole corps, except a few pickets and stragglers, was safely across the river, and the bridge on fire.

As the troops from Petersburg got across the river, the heavily-charged magazine of Cummin's battery of siege guns blew up, lighting the deep darkness of the night with its fierce and vivid glare, and then shaking the earth like the shock of an earthquake. Fort Clifton's magazine in a moment followed, and then the explosion was taken up all along the line to Richmond. The scene was fierce and imposing. The retreating army left the light and pierced the midnight darkness. At each step some new explosion would sound in their ears. The whole heavens in their rear were lit up in lurid glare, and added intensity to the blackness before their eyes.

On leaving Petersburg, Gordon's corps took the river road; Mahone, with his division, and all other troops on the south side of the James, the middle road, and Ewell and Elzey, with the Richmond garrison, and other troops, the road nearest the James River. During the day following the evacuation of Petersburg, the Confederates made good progress, their route unimpeded by wagons and artillery. But after the junction of Gordon's corps with Mahone and Ewell, with thirty miles of wagons, containing the special plunder of the Richmond departments, they went at a rate so distressingly slow, that it was apparent that an enterprising enemy would have little trouble in overtaking them.

But the day passed without any attack of the enemy, and without the appearance of any considerable body of his forces. So far the retreat had been an occasion of reassurance; it had been effected safely; and with the additions made to the Petersburg section of troops from the Richmond lines and from Lee's extreme right, which had crossed the Appomattox above Petersburg, that resourceful commander had now well in hand more than twenty thousand troops. Gen. Lee had clearly seen that his retreat would put the enemy to the necessity of breaking up into bodies of one or two army corps, with a view to a vigorous pursuit. On the morning of the 3d, Grant commenced pursuit. Its order, calculated on the clear assumption that Lee would move for the Danville road, was as follows: Sheridan to push for the Danville road, keeping near the Appomattox; Meade to follow with the Second and Sixth corps; and Ord to move for Burkesville along the Southside road, the Ninth corps stretching along the road behind him. It was certainly a well-planned pursuit; but it involved the possibility that Lee might fall on the enemy in detail; it was a question of the rapidity of movements and combinations, in which, although Grant held the interiour line, his adversary was not in a hopeless situation; for Lee, even if forced from the Danville road, might take up an eccentric line, make a race to Farmville, there cross the Appomattox once more, and, by destroying the bridges after him, escape into the mountains beyond Lynchburg.

With spirits visibly reassured, the retreating army reached Amelia Court-house in the morning of the 4th. But a terrible disappointment awaited it there. Several days before, Gen. Lee had despatched most distinct and urgent orders that large supplies of commissary and quartermaster's stores should be sent forward from Danville to Amelia Court-house. But the authorities in Richmond bungled the command; and the train of cars loaded with these supplies ran through to relieve the evacuation of the capital, without unloading the stores at Amelia Court-house. Gen. Lee found there not a single ration for his army. It was a terrible revelation. To keep life in his army, he would have to break up half of it into foraging parties to get food; the country was scant of subsistence, a tract of straggling woods and pine barrens; and soon the pangs of hunger would tell upon the flagging spirits of his men, and consume the last hope. Meanwhile the forced delay of his army at Amelia Court-house gave

Sheridan, who was pursuing with his cavalry, and the Fifth corps, time to strike in upon the Confederate line of retreat. In the afternoon of the 4th he was reported at Jetersville, on the Danville Railroad, seven miles south west of Amelia Court-house. But it was no longer a question of battle with Gen. Lee; the concern was now simply to escape. His men were suffering from hunger; half of them had been sent or had straggled in quest of food; soldiers who had to assuage their craving by plucking the buds and twigs of trees, were scarcely to be blamed for courting capture; and thus with his army in loose order, in woful plight, diminishing at every step, Gen. Lee determined to try the last desperate chance of escape, and to penetrate the region of hills in the direction of Farmville, hoping to avail himself of these positions of defence.

On the 5th he took up this line of retreat; but the locomotion of his army was no longer what it had been. The troops went wearily along, averaging hardly half a mile an hour. It was with some satisfaction that they saw the wagons which had so effectually clogged their march begin to cast up their plunder. Jaded horses and mules refused to pull; de-moralized and badly-scared drivers, with straining eyes and perspiring bodies, plied their whips vigorously to no effect; difficult places in the road were choked with blazing wagons, fired to save their contents from the enemy; there were deafening reports from ammunition exploding and shells bursting, when touched by the flames; and on this line of terrible retreat, behind and on either flank, there was a running fight through every hour of the day. At every hill divisions would alternately halt, and form linse of battle and check the pursuers. As soon as proper disposition had been made on the next line of hills the rear division would move off and pass the others, only to form again at the next suitable defensive position. Thus toiled on the retreating army. Hundreds of men dropped from ex-haustion; thousands threw away their arms; the demoralization appeared at last to involve the officers; they did nothing to prevent straggling; and many of them seemed to shut their eyes on the hourly reduction of their commands, and rode in advance of their brigades in dogged indifference.

But in the jaded, famishing crowd there was yet left something of the old spirit which had made the Army of Northern Virginia famous through-out the world, and inscribed its banners with the most glorious names of the war. Its final retreat was not to be without its episodes of desperate and devoted courage.

On the 6th, the enemy having changed the order of pursuit to conform to Lee's new movement, Sheridan, with his cavalry, struck in upon the Confederate line of retreat just south of Sailors' Creek, a small tributary of the Appomattox. Ewell's corps, consisting of about four thousand two hundred men, was called upon to support Pickett, who, with his divi-sion reduced to about eight hundred men, was being sorely pressed by

Sheridan. On reaching the ground, and whilst deploying his troops into line of battle, it was discovered that Gordon's division, which formed the rear-guard of the army, had taken another road, following after the wagon train, and that the Federal forces had already occupied the high ground in Ewell's rear, opening upon his troops a rapid and deadly fire of artillery. A very brief time elapsed, when the appearance of a very heavy force of infantry, also in the rear, rendered it necessary to face about the Confederate line, and prepare for another conflict on the very ground over which it had just passed. The enemy advanced with spirit, and with the evident determination of bringing matters to a crisis, and thus, without being able to assist Pickett, Ewell, with his small force, was compelled to hold his ground against these overwhelming numbers in his (Pickett's) rear. At this critical juncture fresh troops were brought up against Pickett, and, charging impetuously on his line, it was easily broken, never again to be reformed, or restored to such order as to render it longer available. The enemy's forces, confident and exulting over the prospect of success, were now hurled upon the brave men of Ewell's corps. It, however, with an exhibition of valour never surpassed, continued to stand at bay. It kept up a most destructive fire, strewing the field with dead and wounded. But at last the unequal contest was terminated; Gen. Ewell was captured, and one of his division commanders, G. W. C. Lee; and the greater portion of the command surrendered, but not until they had given evidences of a pirit which the enemy had scarcely looked for in so small a portion of a ugitive army.

The retreat of what remained of the Confederate army was continued, until at last it had crossed the Appomattox and reached Farmville. Except Longstreet's command, it crossed the river during the night; Gordon's troops at the High Bridge going into bivouac on the opposite side, while Longstreet occupied the hills on the river near the town of Farmville. Here, on the morning of the 7th, the haversacks of many of the men were replenished for the first time since leaving Petersburg. It is said of these devoted men who yet clung to the great Confederate commander, that their suffering from the pangs of hunger " has not been approached in the military annals of the last fifty years."

At early dawn the enemy made an attack on Gordon at the bridge, and on Longstreet on the hills near Farmville. Firing the bridge, and leaving one brigade to check the enemy, the remainder of Gordon's corps took the railroad track to Farmville, leaving the brigade skirmishing sharply. On the high hills on the upper side of the Appomattox, just beyond Farmville, it appeared as if the Confederates intended to give battle. The artillery was placed in position, and active skirmishing had commenced with the Federal advance, which had crossed the river on the heels of the retreating rear-guard of the Confederates. The lines of infantry were formed in order of battle; but it was only done to cover the movement of the wagons, as the army took up its line of retreat. That portion of the Federal army which had crossed the river dashed on recklessly, and seemed to think they had only a demoralized mob to contend with. They drove the Confederate wagon guard in and cut the train in two, on the road the wagons were traversing; but Grimes' division advanced at a double-quick, attacked and charged the assailants, routed them, and captured two hundred prisoners.

During all day of the 7th, the Confederate army marched without molestation in the rear. Occasionally the enemy's cavalry would dash in on a portion of their wagon train, kill a few horses, frighten drivers and quartermasters, and then scamper away; but no serious impediment was offered to the march. The whole army had left the main road and were traversing dense thickets of oak and pine, through which ran rarely used and broken roads. On the 8th they continued to march steadily, and in the middle of the day struck a better road, and made rapid progress until dark, when the rear was within four miles of Appomattox Court-house. The head of the column had reached the Court-house. Lynchburg was but twenty-four miles off. Not a gun had been fired during the day. The troops went into camp without restraint. No enemy seemed near. The bands of the divisions enlivened the departing hours of day with martial music. The weary private soldiers prepared to sleep with a strange sense of relief and contentment.

But in this night of apparent security the general officers were consulting together; and their looks plainly indicated intense anxiety. Soon the rumble of distant cannon sounded in front. Presently came the ominous order for all the extra artillery to be cut down and the commands disbanded. The true situation was soon apparent to Gen. Lee. In pressing for Lynchburg he had to put himself in a dangerous predicament; he was on a strip of land not more than seven or eight miles broad between the James and Appomattox rivers; and the firing in front indicated that the outlet towards Lynchburg was closed by Sheridan, while Meade in the rear, and Ord south of the Court-house completed the environment and put Lee in a position from which it was impossible to extricate his army without a battle, which it was no longer capable of fighting.

Early in the morning of the 19th, Gordon's corps was ordered to move to the front through Apomattox Court-house, passing the entire wagon and artillery train of the army. Lee's army had at this time dwindled down to eight thousand men with muskets in their hands. Gordon was thrown out with about two thousand men in front; the wreck of Longstreet's command covered the rear; and between these thin lines was the remnant of the wagon train, and clinging to these thousands of unarmed stragglers, many of them famishing and too weak to carry their muskets.

Such was the condition and disposition of Gen. Lee's forces when Gordon attempted the last desperate task of cutting his way through Sheridan's lines.   The Confederate cavalry was drawn up in mass in the village.   The fields, gardens, and streets were strewn with troops bivouacking in line of battle.   In the early light of morning Gordon's corps marched through and to the west of the village.

After reconnoitring, it was discovered that the enemy in front was dismounted cavalry in heavy force.   Dispositions were made for attack, and about ten o'clock Gordon's line was ordered forward.   The enemy's cavalry was easily driven back; it seemed that an exit would be secured, until it was discovered that the cavalry was falling back upon large masses of infantry, which were hastening forward and just forming to advance.   It was the turn of the Confederates to fall back.   Gordon now sent word to Gen. Lee that the enemy was driving him back.   Just as his divisions had formed anew to resist a flank movement of Sheridan, while the skirmishers were engaged, while the Richmond Howitzers (who had fired the first gun at Bethel), having already discharged one volley, were loading for another, a flag of truce appeared upon the scene, and the action suddenly and strangely ceased.

The explanation of the cessation of hostilities was soon made known. While the pursuit of Lee's army by Grant's overwhelming forces was still in progress, the following correspondence, commenced at Farmville, had taken place between the two commanders, terminated by Lee's seeking the final interview, when he received the message referred to from Gordon :

April 7, 1865.

GEN. R. E. LEE, *Commanding C. S. A. :*

General : The result of last week must convince you of the hopelessness of further resistance on the part of the Army of Northern Virginia in this struggle.   I feel that it is so, and regard it as my duty to shift from myself the responsibility of any further effusion of blood, by asking of you the surrender of that portion of the Confederate Southern army, known as the Army of Northern Virginia.

Very respectfully,
Your obedient servant,
U. S. GRANT,
Lieutenant-General, commanding Armies of the United States.

April 7, 1865.

General : I have received your note of this day.   Though not entirely of the opinion you express of the hopelessness of further resistance on the part of the Army of Northern Virginia, I reciprocate your desire to avoid useless effusion of blood, and therefore, before considering your proposition, ask the terms you will offer on condition of its surrender.

R. E. LEE, *General.*

To LIEUT.-GEN. U. S. GRANT, Commanding Armies of the United States.

April 8, 1865.

To Gen. R. E. Lee, *Commanding C. S. A.:*

General: Your note of last evening, in reply to mine of the same date, asking the conditions on which I will accept the surrender of the Army of Northern Virginia is just received.

In reply, I would say, that peace being my first desire, there is but one condition that I insist upon, viz. :

That the men surrendered shall be disqualified for taking up arms again against the Government of the United States until properly exchanged.

I will meet you, or designate officers to meet any officers you may name for the purpose, at any point agreeable to you, for the purpose of arranging definitely the terms upon which the surrender of the Army of Northern Virginia will be received.

> Very respectfully,
> Your obedient servant,
> U. S. GRANT, *Lieutenant-General,*
> Commanding Armies of the United States.

April 8, 1865.

General: I received, at a late hour, your note of to-day in answer to mine of yesterday.

I did not intend to propose the surrender of the Army of Northern Virginia, but to ask the terms of your proposition. To be frank, I do not think the emergency has arisen to call for the surrender.

But as the restoration of peace should be the sole object of all, I desire to know whether your proposals would tend to that end.

I cannot, therefore, meet you with a view to surrender the Army of Northern Virginia; but so far as your proposition may affect the Confederate States forces under my command and tend to the restoration of peace, I should be pleased to meet you at 10 A. M. to-morrow, on the old stage-road to Richmond, between the picket-lines of the two armies.

> Very respectfully,
> Your obedient servant,
> R. E. LEE, *General C. S. A.*

To Lieut.-Gen. Grant, Commanding Armies of the United States.

April 9, 1865.

To Gen. R. E. Lee, *Commanding C. S. A.:*

General: Your note of yesterday is received. As I have no authority to treat on the subject of peace, the meeting proposed for 10 A. M. to-day could lead to no good. I will state, however, General, that I am equally anxious for peace with yourself; and the whole North entertain the same feeling. The terms upon which peace can be had are well understood. By the South laying down their arms they will hasten that most desirable event, save thousands of human lives, and hundreds of millions of property not yet destroyed.

Sincerely hoping that all our difficulties may be settled without the loss of another life, I subscribe myself,

Very respectfully,

Your obedient servant,

U. S. GRANT,

Lieutenant-General United States Army.

———

April 9, 1865.

General: I received your note of this morning on the picket-line, whither I had come to meet you and ascertain definitely what terms were embraced in your proposition of yesterday with reference to the surrender of this army.

I now request an interview in accordance with the offer contained in your letter of yesterday for that purpose.

Very respectfully,

Your obedient servant,

R. E. LEE, *General.*

To LIEUT.-GEN. GRANT, Commanding Armies of the United States.

———

April 9, 1865.

GEN. R. E. LEE, *Commanding C. S. A.:*

Your note of this date is but this moment, 11.59 A. M., received.

In consequence of my having passed from the Richmond and Lynchburg road to the Farmville and Lynchburg road, I am, at this writing, about four miles west of Walter's Church, and will push forward to the front for the purpose of meeting you.

Notice sent to me on this road where you wish the interview to take place, will meet me.

Very respectfully, your obedient servant,

U. S. GRANT, *Lieutenant-General.*

———

APPOMATTOX COURT-HOUSE, April 9, 1865.

GEN. R. E. LEE, *Commanding C. S. A.:*

In accordance with the substance of my letter to you of the 8th inst., I propose to receive the surrender of the Army of Northern Virginia on the following terms, to wit :

Rolls of all the officers and men to be made in duplicate, one copy to be given to an officer designated by me, the other to be retained by such officers as you may designate.

The officers to give their individual parole not to take arms against the Government of the United States until properly exchanged; and each company or regimental commander to sign a like parole for the men of their commands.

The arms, artillery, and public property to be parked and stacked, and turned over to the officers appointed by me to receive them.

This will not embrace the side-arms of the officers, nor their private horses or baggage.

This done, *each officer and man will be allowed to return to their homes, not to be disturbed by United States authority,* so long as they observe their parole and the laws in force where they may reside.

Very respectfully,

U. S. GRANT, *Lieutenant-General.*

LIEUT.-GEN. U. S. GRANT, *Commanding U. S. A.:*

General: I have received your letter of this date, containing the terms of surrender of the Army of Northern Virginia, as proposed by you. As they are susbtantially the same as those expressed in your letter of the 8th inst., they are accepted. I will proceed to designate the proper officers to carry the stipulations into effect.

Very respectfully, your obedient servant,

R. E. LEE, *General*

The interview of the two commanders took place at the house of Mr. Wilmer McLean. It was a great occasion; thrilling and wonderful memories must have crowded upon these two men as they stood face to face. But the interview was very simple; there was no theatrical circumstance; there was not a sentimental expression in what was said. No man abhorred anything melo-dramatic more than Gen. Lee. His manner with Grant bordered on taciturnity, but not so as to exhibit temper or mortification. "His demeanour," writes a Federal observer of the memorable scene, "was that of a thoroughly possessed gentleman who had a very disagreeable duty to perform, but was determined to get through it as well and as soon as he could."

He had come to the interview attended only by Col. Marshall, one of his aides. With courteous greeting the two commanders proceeded at once and simply to business; some explanations were required by Gen. Lee as to the meaning of certain phrases in the terms of surrender; and without other question or remark the act that was to put out of existence the Army of Northern Virginia was reduced to form at a deal table.

When Gen. Lee had been seen riding to the rear, the rumour of surrender flew like wild-fire through the Confederates. It might have been supposed that the worn and battered troops who watched on their arms for the result of the conference at McLean's house, would have been glad to welcome a termination of their sufferings, come in what form it might; that they would feel a certan joy when a long agony was over. But such was not the display, when about half past three o'clock in the evening Gen. Lee was seen thoughtfully riding back to his headquarters, and it was known that the surrender had been completed. His leading officers were assembled, anticipating the result and awaiting his return. When the terms of surrender were announced, they approached their great commander in turn, and shook hands, expressing satisfaction at his course, and regret at parting. The lines of battle that had awaited a possible renewal of the combat, were broken; but there were no huzzas, no scattering, not an indecent shout; but the men broke ranks to rush up to their beloved commander, struggling with each other to wring him once more by the hand. It was a most affecting scene. Rough and rugged men, familiar with hardship, danger, and death in a thousand shapes, had tears in their eyes, and choked with emotion as they thronged around their old chieftain, uttering words to lighten his burden and mitigate his pain. He had so often himself uttered such words to them, when they bled on the battle-field or toiled on the weary march. Now simple as ever, very serious but collected, with the marks of a Roman manhood yet about him, he turned to his soldiers, not to insult the occasion with a harangue or explanations or regrets, but merely to say, as the signs of tearless suffering gathered in his face : " Men, we have fought through the war together ; and I have done the best I could for you."

The day after the surrender Gen. Lee took formal leave of his army in the following plain and manly address :

HEADQUARTERS ARMY NORTHERN VIRGINIA, April 10, 1865.

After four years of arduous service, marked by unsurpassed courage and fortitude, the Army of Northern Virginia has been compelled to yield to overwhelming numbers and resources.

I need not tell the survivors of so many hard-fought battles, who have remained steadfast to the last, that I have consented to this result from no distrust of them ; but feeling that valour and devotion could accomplish nothing that could compensate for the loss that would have attended the continuation of the contest, I have determined to avoid the useless sacrifice of those whose past services have endeared them to their countrymen.

By the terms of agreement, officers and men can return to their homes, and remain there until exchanged.

You will take with you *the satisfaction that proceeds from the consciousness of duty faithfully performed ;* and I earnestly pray that a merciful God will extend to you His blessing and protection.

With an unceasing admiration of your constancy and devotion to your country, and a grateful remembrance of your kind and generous consideration of myself, I bid you an affectionate farewell.

R. E. LEE, *General.*

On the 12th April, the Army of Northern Virginia had its last parade. On that day, in pursuance of an arrangement of the commissioners of surrender, the troops marched by divisions to a spot in the neighbourhood of Appomattox Court-house, where they stacked arms and deposited accoutrements. About seventy-five hundred men laid down their arms ; but the capitulation included in addition some eighteen thousand stragglers who were unarmed, and who came up to claim the benefit of surrender and accept paroles. With remarkable delicacy, Gen. Grant was not present at the ceremony, and had not been visible since his interview of the 9th with Gen. Lee.

Indeed, this Federal commander had, in the closing scenes of the contest, behaved with a magnanimity and decorum that must ever be remembered to his credit even by those who disputed his reputation in other respects, and denied his claims to great generalship. He had with remarkable facility accorded honourable and liberal terms to the vanquished army. He did nothing to dramatize the surrender; he made no triumphal entry into Richmond; he avoided all those displays of triumph so dear to the Northern heart; he spared everything that might wound the feelings or imply the humiliation of a vanquished foe. There were no indecent exultations; no "sensations;" no shows; he received the surrender of his adversary with every courteous recognition due an honourable enemy, and conducted the closing scenes with as much simplicity as possible.

In the afternoon of the 12th April, Gen. Lee, attended by five members of his staff, rode into Richmond, and drew rein at his house on Franklin street. He passed on rapidly, as if to escape notice; blackened ruins threw their shadows across the way; strange faces were on the streets; but it was impossible for his commanding figure to pass without the challenge of curiosity, and there presently ran along the side-walks the shout, "It's Gen. Lee." Instantly there was a wild chase after the party of horsemen. The General simply raised his hat as he rode rapidly on; dismounting, he shook hands with some that pressed upon him; he showed an anxiety to enter his house, and in a few moments he had passed into the fondly-desired retirement of his simple home.

In Washington the surrender of Gen. Lee's army was taken as the close of the war. No sooner was it known than Secretary Stanton immediately telegraphed an order to the headquarters of every army and department, and to every fort and arsenal in the United States, to fire a salute of two hundred guns in celebration of the event. To Grant he despatched: "Thanks be to Almighty God for the great victory with which He has this day crowned you and the gallant armies under your command. The thanks of this department, and of the Government, and of the people of the United States—their reverence and honour have been deserved—will be rendered to you and the brave and gallant officers and soldiers of your army for all time."

A vast concourse of people assembled at the President's house to make the popular congratulations to Mr. Lincoln. There was music, illuminations; the ground was ablaze with triumphal lights; and the vast crowd called impatiently for a response from the President. It was a grand historical occasion; one of great thoughts and imposing circumstances; one for noble and memorable utterances. The President of the United States came forward, and called for the "rebel" song of "Dixie." He said:

" I have always thought that ' Dixie ' was one of the best songs I ever heard. Our adversaries over the way, I know, have attempted to appropriate it ; but I insist that on yesterday we fairly captured it. I referred the question to the attorney-general, and he gave it as his legal opinion that it is now our property. (Laughter and loud applause.) I now ask the band to give us a good turn upon it." It was the characteristic speech and last joke of Abraham Lincoln.

CHAPTER XLIII.

THE surrender of Gen. Lee was plainly the decisive event of the war,
and drew after it rapid and important consequences. The situation in the
Atlantic States south of Virginia, was weak; and that part of the Confederacy had been for some time thoroughly demoralized. The limits of
Johnston's command included North and South Carolina, Georgia and

LEIUT. GEN. E. KIRBY SMITH.

LEIUT. GEN. W. J. HARDEE.

MAJ. GEN. J. B. HOOD.

GEN. BRAXTON BRAGG.

GEN. JOHN H. MORGAN.

MAJ. GEN. FORREST.

LEIUT. GEN. L. POLK.

Eng⃰ by H.B. Hall, N.Y.

Engraved expressly for the 'Lost Cause' by E. A. Pollard.

Florida; and the fate of this extensive military territory depended upon an army whose effective force was less than twenty thousand men. Gen. Johnston's statement of the force at his command in the vicinity of Raleigh, was 18,578 total, infantry and artillery present for duty, of which not more than 14,179 were effective, with a cavalry force little over five thousand. Florida was destitute of troops, and South Carolina was pretty much in the condition of a conquered province, there being no known Confederate force in it beyond a division of cavalry less than one thousand. Gen. Johnston found himself by the disaster in Virginia, opposed to a combined force of alarming magnitude; there was great difficulty in supplying his troops; the enemy had already captured all workshops within the Confederacy for the preparation of ammunition and repairing of arms; and thus embarrassed, crippled and disheartened, what was accounted in point of importance the second army of the Confederacy, numbering on its rolls more than seventy thousand men, and yet reduced to less than one-third of this number by desertions and " absenteeism," abandoned the hope of successful war, and prepared to surrender.

SURRENDER OF JOHNSTON'S ARMY.

On the night of the 13th April, Sherman's army had halted some fourteen miles from Raleigh, when it received the news of the surrender of Lee. The next day it occupied Raleigh; Gen. Johnston having taken up a line of retreat by the railroad running by Hillsboro, Greensboro, Salisbury and Charlotte. Sherman commenced pursuit by crossing the curve of that road in the direction of Ashboro, and Charlotte; and after the head of his column had crossed the Cape Fear River at Avens Ferry, he received a communication from Gen. Johnston on the 15th April, asking if some arrangement could not be effected, which should prevent the further useless effusion of blood. It was eventually arranged that a personal interview should take place between the two commanders at a designated point; and on the 18th April, they met at a farm-house, five miles from Durham Station, under a flag of truce. In proposing a surrender, Gen. Johnston wanted some more general concessions than had been made in the case of Gen Lee; and the result was a military convention, which Gen. Johnston declared that he signed " to spare the blood of his gallant little army, to prevent further suffering of the people by the devastation and ruin inevitable from the marches of invading armies, and to avoid the crime of waging a hopeless war." This document, which we place here, was certainly an extraordinary one on Sherman's part.

MEMORANDUM, OR BASIS OF AGREEMENT, *made this eighteenth day of April, A. D. 1865, near Durham Station, in the State of North Carolina, by and between Gen. Joseph E. Johnston, commanding Confederate Army, and Maj.-Gen. W. T. Sherman, commanding Army of the United States, in North Carolina, both being present :*

1. The contending armies now in the field to maintain the *status quo*, until notice is given by the commanding general of any one to its opponent, and reasonable time, say forty-eight hours, allowed.

2. The Confederate armies now in existence to be disbanded, and conducted to their several State capitals, therein to deposit their arms and public property in the State arsenal, and each officer and man to execute and file an agreement to cease from acts of war, and to abide the action of both State and Federal authorities. The number of arms and munitions of war to be reported to the chief of ordnance at Washington City, subject to the future action of the Congress of the United States, and in the meantime to be used solely to maintain peace and order within the borders of the States respectively.

3. The recognition by the Executive of the United States of the several State governments, on their officers and legislatures taking the oath prescribed by the Constitution of the United States ; and where conflicting State governments have resulted from the war, the legitimacy of all shall be submitted to the Supreme Court of the United States.

4. The re-establishment of all Federal courts in the several States, with powers as defined by the Constitution and laws of Congress.

5. The people and inhabitants of all these States to be guarantied, so far as the Executive can, their political rights and franchises, as well as their rights of person and property, as defined by the Constitution of the United States and of the States respectively.

6. The Executive authority of the Government of the United States not to disturb any of the people by reason of the late war, so long as they live in peace and quiet and abstain from acts of armed hostility, and obey the laws in existence at the place of their residence.

7. In general terms, the war to cease—a general amnesty, so far as the Executive of the United States can command, on the condition of the disbandment of the Confederate armies, distribution of the arms, and the resumption of peaceable pursuits by the officers and men hitherto composing said armies.

Not being duly empowered by our respective principals to fulfil these terms, we individually and officially pledge ourselves to promptly obtain an answer thereto, and to carry out the above programme.

W. T. SHERMAN, *Major-General,*
Commanding Army U. S. in N. C.

J. E. JOHNSTON, *General,*
Commanding C. S. A. in N. C.

There was much surprise on the part of the Southern people, that a man of Sherman's furious antecedents and incendiary record in the war, should exhibit such a spirit of liberality as contained in the above paper. But further developments explained the apparent contradiction, and showed that Sherman intended the paper only as a snare ; that he was prepared to violate its spirit as soon as it was signed ; that he had made up his mind to disregard the paroles he took, and to refuse to protect them; and that he was performing a part of hypocrisy, the meanest it is possible to conceive. A few weeks after the conference at Durham Station, this man had the astounding hardihood to testify as follows before a committee of the Congress at Washington : " It then occurred to me that I might write off some general propositions, *meaning little, or meaning much*, according to the construction of parties—what I would term ' glittering generalities '—and send them to Washington, which I could do in four days. I therefore drew up the Memorandum (which has been published to the world) for the purpose of referring it to the proper Executive authority of the United States, and enabling him to define to me what I might promise, *simply to cover the pride of the Southern men*, who thereby became subordinate to the laws of the United States, civil and military. If any concessions were made in those general terms, they were made because I then believed, and now believe, they would have delivered into the hands of the United States *the absolute control* of every Confederate officer and soldier, all their muster-rolls, and all their arms. *I never designed to shelter a human being from any liability incurred in consequence of past acts* to the civil tribunals of our country, and I do not believe a fair and manly interpretation of my terms can so construe them, for the words, " United States courts," " United States authorities," " limitations of executive power," occur in every paragraph. And if they *seemingly* yield terms better than the public would desire to be given to the Southern people, *if studied closely and well, it will be found that there is an absolute submission* on their part to the Government of the United States, either through its executive, legislative, or judicial authorities."

It is almost impossible to find terms, within the decent vocabulary of history, to characterize the effrontery and self-complacency of this confession of a game of hypocrisy with a conquered honorable adversary, surrendering his arms with full faith in the promises of the conqueror! But even this record of double-dealing was to be surpassed. The man who affected so much generosity at Durham Station, and signed the name of " W. T. Sherman, Major-General, &c. " to the Memorandum quoted above, took occasion, after the surrender of Lee and Johnston, to make the following speech at a soldiers' festival in the State of Ohio :—

" When the rebels ventured their all in their efforts to destroy our Government, they pledged their lives, their fortunes, and their sacred honours to their cause. The Government accepted their wager of battle. Hence, when we conquered, *we, by conquest, gained all they had—their property became ours by conquest.* Thus they lost their slaves, their mules, their horses, their cotton, their all ; *and even their lives and personal liberty*, thrown by them into the issue, *were theirs only by our forbearance and clemency.* So, soldiers, when we marched through and conquered the country of the rebels, *we became owners of all they had*, and I don't want you to be troubled in your consciences for taking, while on our great march, the property of conquered rebels. They forfeited their rights to it, and I, being agent for the Government to which I belonged, gave you authority to keep all the quartermasters couldn't take possession of or didn't want.

Such an example of astounding inconsistency, such a record of un-blushing hypocrisy no public man could stand against for a day, except in that peculiar community of the North, where demagogueism and time-service are fair games, and "the *smart* man" gets the plaudits of the multitude, no matter in what line of conduct he asserts his ingenuity.

It may well be imagined that the truce of Durham Station was dis-regarded at Washington, and that no time was lost there in repudiating the propositions contained in Sherman's basis of agreement, which, in the extravagant language of that amateur diplomatist, was to restore "peace to the banks of the Rio Grande." Of course, no plan could be entertained at Washington that substituted the simple idea of a restored Union for that of subjugation. The Federal Government, as is already apparent in these pages, was not likely to be satisfied with anything short of the abo-lition of slavery in the South, the extinction of the State governments, or their reduction to provisional establishments, and the programme of a general confiscation of property. Sherman was censured and denounced in a way that shook his factitious military reputation; and it was said to be the madness of generosity to abolish the confiscation laws, and relieve "rebels" from all pains and penalties for their crimes. It was at once telegraphed from Washington throughout the country, that Sherman's truce was disregarded, and that Grant would go to North Carolina to compel Johnston's surrender on the same terms as Gen. Lee had accepted. On this basis, the surrender was eventually made; but Gen. Grant was generous enough to forbear taking control of Sherman's army, contenting himself with prompting that commander to what the Washington Gov-ernment had declared should be the text of the negotiations.

In following the logical chain of consequences of Gen. Lee's surrender, we are led to notice how each section of the Confederate defences gave way with this event. We have already seen how the cordon of the Atlantic States fell with Johnston's surrender; and we shall now see how the system of Confederate defence fell in the Southwest; and how, in a little time thereafter, the department of the Trans-Mississippi was pros-trated, completing the downfall of the Southern Confederacy.

OPERATIONS IN THE SOUTHWEST—CAPTURE OF MOBILE—WILSON'S EXPEDITION.

As part of the general design of the Federal arms in 1865, a move-ment was prepared early in that year against the city of Mobile and the interiour of Alabama. When Hood's ill-fated army was beaten and driven across the Tennessee River, the troops which Gen. Canby had sent to aid Thomas were returned, and, being heavily reinforced, prepared to undertake, with assured success, the capture of the city of Mobile—an enterprise which had not yet been ventured upon, unless very remotely, by any Federal army.

The works of Mobile were very strong, and the supplies of food were abundant for a siege. The heavy ordnance was excellent and well disposed. But the garrison was few in number, and the supply of ammunition was small. Other important interests of the Confederacy would admit of no more troops, nor of more ammunition being placed in Mobile.

A large Federal army was soon collected on the waters near Mobile, with a very great naval force and a fleet of transports adequate to all the requirements of so great an expedition. Early in March, the preparations for attack seemed complete. But the weather was bad and unfavourable to operations. On the 25th March, Gen. Canby commenced to move his forces to the attack. Two corps of infantry, respectively commanded by Gens. Granger and A. J. Smith, (the whole commanded by Canby in person) marched from their camp on and near Fish River, against the positions occupied by Gen Maury at Spanish Fort and Blakely.

The same day, a corps of infantry, with a strong force of cavalry, moved, under command of Gen. Steele, from Pensacola towards Salem, *via* Pollard. The whole of Canby's forces now in motion may be estimated at near sixty thousand effectives, being three corps of infantry, and about six thousand cavalry.

The whole artillery and infantry effective force holding Mobile, under Gen. Maury's command, numbered less than eight thousand. His cavalry numbered less than fifteen hundred, and were not available in the siege operations.

On the 26th March, Canby appeared in heavy force before Spanish Fort, and commmenced its siege. The same day, he threw a division as if against Fort Blakely, but did not yet take position for its siege. The position of Spanish Fort was about twelve miles from Mobile, on the eastern shore of Appalachie River, about two and a half miles above its mouth. The position was important as commanding the batteries, Huger and Tracey, which held the Appalachie River. The fortifications when the siege commenced, consisted of a battery on the water of six heavy guns and of three detached redoubts (open in the gorge) connected by a line of rifle-pits, with a line of abattis in front; the whole sweeping in a sort of semi-circle, and resting both flanks on the river. The whole length of coast was about a mile and a half. Gen. Randall Gibson, of Louisiana, commanded the forces and conducted the defence of Spanish Fort. The garrison of Spanish Fort was made up of the veteran Louisiana brigade of Gibson, (five hundred muskets), the veteran Alabama brigade, of Holtzclaw, (seven hundred muskets), and a brigade of Alabama *boys* under Brig.-Gen. Thomas, numbering about nine hundred effectives. There were besides, several companies of the Twenty-second Louisiana heavy artillery, and three companies of light artillery. Soon after the siege commenced, the brigade of boy-reserves was exchanged for Eaton's Texans and North Carolinians, which numbered only about five hundred muskets, and which made the whole infantry force about seventeen hundred muskets.

The enemy pressed his siege energetically, but cautiously. The defence was vigourous, bold and defiant. The little garrison, when manning their works, as they did incessantly for sixteen days and nights, stood in single rank, and several feet apart. The experience of defence soon showed that many things were lacking; but the troops vigourously applied themselves to remedy the defects, and in a few nights had constructed traverses and bomb-proofs, and chevaux-de-frise and rifle-pits, which proved amply sufficient for all their subsequent requirements. By energetic digging, the enemy managed to advance to within one hundred yards of portions of the main line of defence. He continually increased his batteries. He finally opened at close range, with a great number of wooden mortars; and although, in the early part of the operations, the skill and energy of Slocum's and Massenberg's, and Potter's artillerists could always silence the enemy's guns, they were quite ineffective now, and towards the close, every gun of the Confederates was easily silenced.

On the 8th April, Gen. Maury, after conference with Gen. Gibson, decided that the defence had been protracted long enough, and gave orders to commence that night to remove the surplus material, and stores, and men, so that by the night of the 11th, the whole force should be withdrawn. Early in the night of the 8th, the enemy made a forward movement on Gibson's left flank and established himself in such a position as would cut off further communications by the river with Mobile, and imperil the garrison. In pursuance of his general instructions, Gibson withdrew his garrison at once, and evacuated the position of Spanish Fort, necessarily leaving his guns and stores to the enemy. The garrison was immediately transferred to the city of Mobile, which, it was judged, would be soon attacked. Col. Patton tansferred his headquarters to Battery Huger, upon which, and Tracey, would depend the defence of the Appalachie River.

On the 31st March, Steele, who had marched with his corps from Pensacola, had dispersed the cavalry force, which, under Clauton, opposed his advance at Pine Barren Creek, and occupied Pollard; and now sudden'y appeared before Blakely and commenced to besiege it.

Gen. St. John Liddell, of Louisiana, commanded the forces at Blakely, which consisted of about 2,300 muskets, and three or four companies of artillery—in all about 2,600 effectives. The ground was better for defence than at Spanish Fort. The works were better placed ; and it was believed that the enemy would make but slow progress in its siege. The garrison consisted of the Missouri brigade, about four hundred and fifty muskets, under Gates ; a Mississippi brigade, eight hundred muskets ; the brigade of Alabama boy-reserves, under Thomas, nine hundred muskets ; a regiment of Mississippi dismounted light artillerists armed with muskets, and several companies of artillery.

Very little progress had been made in the siege of Blakely, when Spanish Fort was evacuated on the 8th April. During the following day, however, Canby was sending up his army from about Spanish Fort towards Blakely ; and in the evening, at five o'clock, he made a grand assault with a column of twenty-five thousand infantry. After being repulsed on many parts of the line, he succeeded in overwhelming the little garrison, and capturing it with the position.

Gen. Maury found his force now reduced to less than five thousand effective infantry and artillery ; his ammunition almost exhausted ; and the city of Mobile, with its population of more than thirty thousand non-combatants, exposed to the danger of assault and sack, by an army of more than fifty thousand men, ten thousand of whom were negroes. His instructions from his superiour officer were to save his garrison, and evacuate the city whenever he should find that judicious defence could no longer be made, and that an opportunity of withdrawing the garrison was still open to him.

On the night of the fall of Blakely, he resolved to evacuate Mobile, and save his army. On the morning of the 10th, the operations of the evacuation commenced. Many steamers were in the port prepared for this contingency ; upon them were hastily thrown such ordnance stores as remained fit for troops in the field, all of the light guns, and the best of the quartermaster's and commissary stores. The garrisons of the redoubts and batteries about the city were also embarked on these steamers, and sent up the Tombigbee river to Demopolis. The infantry forces accompanied the wagon train by the dirt road to Mendina or were sent up on the cars. The large depots of commissary stores were turned over to the mayor of Mobile, for the use of the people of the city.

In the morning of the 12th April, the evacuation was completed. Gen. Maury, with his staff, and the rear-guard of three hundred Louisianians, under Col. Lindsay, moved out of the city at daylight. Gen. Gibson remained to see to the execution of the orders, relative to the drawing in of the cavalry force of Col. Spence, which was to burn the cotton in the city, and then cover the rear of the army. After having seen to the execution of every order, Gen. Gibson directed the Mayor of the city to go out to the fleet with a white flag, and apprise the Federal authorities that Mobile had been entirely evacuated by the Confederate forces, and that no resistance would be offered to the enemy's entrance into the city. About two o'clock in the afternoon, Gen. Canby with his forces, marched into Mobile, and peaceably occupied it.

The Federal navy took but little part in the operations. Two monitors were sunk by torpedoes in an attempt to cross Appalachie Bar, when the fleet desisted from further action. During the progress of the evacuation, the little isolated garrisons of Tracey and Huger, under Col. Patton's command, restrained and returned with great effect the heavy fire of the enemy's batteries on the eastern shore. Here was fired the last cannon for the Confederacy in the war.

Whilst the operations against Mobile were in progress, a heavy movement of Federal cavalry was completing the plan of subjugation in the Southwest. An expedition, consisting of twelve thousand five hundred men, was placed under command of Gen. Wilson, who had been detailed from Thomas' army, and directed to make a demonstration, from Eastport, at the head of steamboat navigation on the Tennessee River upon Tuscaloosa and Selma, in favour of Canby's operations against Mobile and Central Alabama.

On the 22d March, all the arrangements having been perfected, and the order of march designated, the movement began. At this time Gen. Forrest's forces were near West Point, Mississippi, one hundred and fifty miles southwest of Eastport, while Gen. Roddy occupied Montevallo, on the Alabama and Tennessee River Railroad, nearly the same distance to the southeast. By starting on diverging roads, Wilson expected to leave the Confederates in doubt as to his real object, and compel their small bodies of cavalry to watch equally Columbus, Tuscaloosa and Selma.

The enemy in full strength approached Selma on the 2d April. Gen. Forrest, after an affair with his advance near Ebenezer Church, had fallen back to Selma. He had developed Wilson's force, and knew that he would not be able to save the city with the limited force under his command; but he determined to discharge what he considered to be his duty, and to make the best fight he could under the circumstances. The line of works was about four miles long. It was held by not more than three thousand men in all; fully one-half of whom were undrilled, untrained militia, with old-fashioned muskets in their hands, and so strung out over the ground they had to defend, that they were from five to ten feet apart. Skirmishing commenced in front of the works about noon. About four or five o'clock, a charge was made against that part of the line near the point where the Selma and Meridian Railroad crossed the works, and which was held by a Kentucky brigade, under the command of Gen. Buford. After an obstinate fight, the position was carried; the enemy came into possession of one of the most important depots in the southwest; and having occupied Selma, destroyed the arsenals, foundries, arms, stores and military munitions of every kind. Gen. Forrest escaped with a portion of his command. Having captured Selma, and communicated with Gen. Canby, Wilson determined to move by the way of Montgomery into Georgia, and after breaking up railroads, and destroying stores and army supplies, in that State, to march thence as rapidly as possible to the theatre of operations in North Carolina and Virginia. On the 12th April, his advance guard reached Montgomery and received the surrender of the city. Thence a force marched direct on Columbus, and another on West Point. Both of these places were assaulted and captured on the 16th; but at West Point, there was an episode of desperate Confederate valour in the dreary story of a country overrun almost without resistance.

Gen. R. C. Tyler, with an obstinate heroism, unsurpassed during the war, determined to hold West Pont, with less than three hundred men. He believed the maintenance of his post, and the delay of the opposing forces from crossing the Chattahoochie at that point, an essential aid to the defence of Columbus; and although his garrison was a feeble one, improvised, for the most part, from the citizens, he did not hesitate a moment in what he regarded the duty of a soldier, to hold his post at whatever sacrifice, to the last extremity. It was a hopeless defence, except for the purposes of delaying the enemy; and it was protracted until the brave and devoted commander had fallen dead with his sword in his hand.

This memorable defence of West Point was made in a small work— Fort Tyler—about half a mile from the centre of the town. Firing continuously with large cannon and rifles, the enemy slowly and cautiously approached the gallant little band of heroes until within about twenty steps of them. Then, with loud yells, they attempted to scale the works, but were repulsed and held at bay until all the ammunition in the fort had been exhausted; and then, when the Federals were in the ditch around the fort, the brave and gallant men inside of it, hurled stones, and even their unbayonetted guns, upon them. The Confederate flag was never hauled down, until by the Federals, nor any white flag hoisted until the enemy had leaped the parapet.

In referring to the affair of West Point, a Southern newspaper that yet dared to speak its mind, said: " A more gallant instance of devotion has never been known since the time of Charles, King of Sweden, when he, with his body-guard and a few house servants, in the heart of the enemy's country, defended himself against an entire army of Turks, until his place of retreat was burned to the ground by lighted arrows from the assaulting party."

On the 21st, Wilson, having united his forces, approached Macon, which was defended by Gen. Howell Cobb, with a small force, mostly militia. Within thirteen miles of the town, he was met by a flag of truce, bearing the following communication :

HEADQUARTERS DEPARTMENT TENNESSEE AND GEORGIA, }
MACON, April 20, 1865. }

To the Commanding General of the United States Forces :

GENERAL : I have just received from Gen. G. T. Beauregard, my immediate commander, a telegraphic dispatch of which the following is a copy :

"GREENSBORO', April 19, 1865. }
"Via COLUMBIA 19th, via AUGUSTA 20th. }

"MAJ.-GEN. H. COBB : Inform General commanding enemy's forces in your front, that a truce for the purpose of a final settlement was agreed upon yesterday between Gens. Johnston and Sherman applicable to all forces under their commands. A message to that effect from Gen. Sherman will be sent him as soon as practicable. The contending forces are to occupy their present position, forty-eight hours' notice being given of a resumption of hostilities. "G. T. BEAUREGARD,
"General Second in Command."

My force being a portion of Gen. Johnston's command, I proceed at once to execute the terms of the armistice, and have accordingly issued orders for the carrying out the same. I will meet you at any intermediate point between our respective lines, for the purpose of making the necessary arrangements for a more perfect enforcement of the armistice. This communication will be handed to you by Brig.-Gen. F. H. Robinson.
I am, General, very respectfully yours,
HOWELL COBB,
Major-General Commanding, etc.

This notice led to a correspondence, not necessary to be included here, and was ultimately followed by the final capitulation of the Confederate forces east of the Chattahoochie. The destruction of iron-works, foundries, arsenals, supplies, ammunition, and provisions in Alabama and Georgia was irreparable ; the Confederacy east of the Mississippi was evidently in a state of collapse ; and—the news of Johnston's surrender having traversed the country—Gen. Dick Taylor, on the 4th May, surrendered to Gen. Canby "the forces, munitions of war, etc., in the Department of Alabama, Mississippi, and East Louisiana." The terms of surrender were essentially the same as those accorded to Lee and Johnston : officers and men to be paroled until duly exchanged or otherwise released by the United States ; officers to give their individual paroles ; commanders of regiments and companies to sign paroles for their men ; arms and munitions to be given up to the United States ; officers and men to be allowed to return to their homes, and not to be molested so long as they kept their paroles and obeyed the laws where they resided, but persons resident in Northern States not to return without permission ; officers to be allowed to retain their side-arms, private horses, and baggage ; horses, the private property of enlisted men, not to be taken from them, but they be allowed to retain them for private purposes only. Thus, in the first days of May, all of the Confederate forces east of the Mississippi River had been surrendered.

THE TRANS-MISSISSIPPI—SURRENDER OF GEN. SMITH.

Although since the loss of Vicksburg, and with it the Confederate control of the Mississippi River, what was known as the Trans-Mississippi, had been to a great extent isolated, and but little able to contribute effectively to the Confederate cause, yet men remembered that it was a country of vast resources; and a general notion had long prevailed at Richmond that in the last extremity of fortune the Confederacy might here find a refuge. Even after the sum of disasters just narrated, it was hoped that the Trans-Mississippi would hold out, and the struggle be protracted until European interference might possibly occur to the relief of the Southern people; for throughout the war they had persisted in the belief that England and France had withheld recognition of the Confederacy only on the assumption that it would certainly accomplish its independence without involving them, and the conclusion was fair that on the failure of this assumption they would not hesitate to act.

In a general order of Gen. Kirby Smith, issued at Shreveport, on the news of the surrender of Lee, he declared to the Confederate troops of the Trans-Mississippi that if they held out, they would speedily and surely receive the aid of nations who already deeply sympathized with them. He added: "The great resources of the department, its vast extent, the numbers, discipline, and the efficiency of the army, will secure to our country terms that a proud people can with honour accept, and may, under the providence of God, be the means of checking the triumph of our enemy, and securing the final success of our cause."

But the last hope of the Confederacy was quickly to expire. To the lively and sanguine address of Gen. Smith there was but little response in the public mind. When the full extent of the disasters east of the Mississippi River was known; when the news came that a force of the enemy under Sheridan, had been put in motion for Texas; and when in the face of these announcements it was perceived that nothing but straggling reinforcements could be expected from the other side of the Mississippi, the consequence was that such demoralization ensued in Gen. Smith's army, and extended to the people of Texas, that that commander concluded to negotiate terms of surrender. On the 26th May, and before the arrival of Sheridan's forces, he surrendered what remained of his command to Gen. Canby. The last action of the war had been a skirmish near Brazos, in Texas. With the surrender of Gen. Smith the war ended, and from the Potomac to the Rio Grande there was no longer an armed soldier to resist the authority of the United States.

Most of the wars memorable in history have terminated with some momentous and splendid crisis of arms. Generally some large decisive battle closes the contest; a grand catastrophe mounts the stage; a great scene illuminates the last act of the tragedy. It was not so with the war of the Confederates. And yet there had been every reason to anticipate a dramatic termination of the contest. A war had been fought for four years; its scale of magnitude was unprecedented in modern times; its operations had extended from the silver thread of the Potomac to the black boundaries of the western deserts; its track of blood reached four thousands of miles; the ground of Virginia had been kneaded with human flesh; its monuments of carnage, its spectacles of desolation, its altars of sacrifice stood from the wheat-fields of Pennsylvania to the vales of New Mexico. It is true that the armies of the Confederacy had been dreadfully depleted by desertions; but in the winter of 1864–'5, the belligerent republic had yet more than a hundred thousand men in arms east of the Mississippi River. It was generally supposed in Richmond that if the Confederate cause was ever lost it would be only when this force had been massed, and a decisive field fixed for a grand, multitudinous battle. This idea had run through the whole period of the war; it was impossible in Richmond to imagine the close of the contest without an imposing and splendid catastrophe. In the very commencement of the war, when troops were gaily marching to the first line of battle in Virginia, President Davis had made an address in the camps at Rockett's, declaring that whatever misfortunes might befall the Confederate arms, they would rally for a final and desperate contest, to pluck victory at last. He said to the famous Hampton Legion: "When the last line of bayonets is levelled, I will be with you."

How far fell the facts below these dramatic anticipations! The contest decisive of the tenure of Richmond and the fate of the Confederacy was scarcely more than what may be termed an "affair," with reference to the extent of its casualties, and at other periods of the war its list of killed and wounded would not have come up to the dignity of a battle in the estimation of the newspapers. Gen. Lee's entire loss in killed and wounded, in the series of engagements that uncovered Richmond and put him on his final retreat, did not exceed two thousand men. The loss of two thousand men decided the fate of the Southern Confederacy! The sequence was surrender from the Potomac to the Rio Grande. The whole fabric of Confederate defence tumbled down at a stroke of arms that did not amount to a battle. There was no last great convulsion, such as usually marks the final struggles of a people's devotion or the expiring hours of their desperation. The word " surrender " travelled from Virginia to Texas. A four years' contest terminated with the smallest incident of blood-shed ; it lapsed ; it passed by a rapid and easy transition into a profound and abject submission.

There must be some explanation of this flat conclusion of the war. It is easily found. Such a condition could only take place in a thorough demoralization of the armies and people of the Confederacy ; there must have been a general decay of public spirit, a general rottenness of public affairs when a great war was thus terminated, and a contest was abandoned so short of positive defeat, and so far from the historical necessity of subjugation.

There has been a very superficial, and, to some people, a very pleasant way of accounting for the downfall of the Southern Confederacy, by simply ascribing it to the great superiourity of the North in numbers and resources. This argument has had a great career in the newspapers and in small publications ; and the vulgar mind is easily imposed upon by the statistical parallel and the arithmetical statement, inclined as it is to limit its comprehension of great historical problems to mere material views of the question. We shall give this argument the benefit of all it contains, and state it in its full force. Thus, it is correctly said that official reports in Washington show that there were called into the Federal service from the Northern States 2,656,553 men during the war, and that this number is quite one-third as many as all the white men, women, and children of the Southern States. Again, the figures in the War Department at Washington show that on the 1st of May, 1865, the military force of the North was 1,000,516 men of all arms ; while the paroles taken in the Confederacy officially and conclusively show that the whole number of men within its limits under arms was exactly 174,223. Thus, it is said, putting the number 1,000,516 against 174,223, and taking into account the superiourity of the North in war *materiel*, there is sufficient reason for the failure of the Confederate cause without looking for another.

This explanation of failure is of course agreeable to the Southern people. But the historical judgment rejects it, discovers the fallacy, and will not refuse to point it out. It is simply to be observed that the disparity of military force, as between North and South stated above, is not the natural one ; and that the fact of only 174,223 Confederates being under arms in the last period of the war was the result of mal-administration, the defective execution of the conscription law, the decay of the volunteer spirit, the unpopularity of the war, and that these are the causes which lie beyond this arithmetical inequality, which, in fact, produced the greater part of it, and which must be held responsible in the explanation. The fallacy consists in taking the very results of Confederate mal-administration, and putting them in comparison against a full exhibition of Northern power in the war.

The only just basis of comparison between the military forces of North and South is to be found in a careful parallel statement of the populations. This excludes all question of administration and political skill. Fortunately we have precise data for the estimate we propose. If we add to the Free States the four Slave States that followed their lead, under more or less compulsion, Delaware, Maryland, Missouri, and Kentucky, and to these the districts at Federal command from an early period of the war, say half of Tennessee and Louisiana and a third of Virginia, we have a population, by the census of 1860, of 23,485,722 on the Federal side. This leaves under the rule of the Confederacy 7,662,325. There is no doubt that this superiourity of the North in numbers had great weight; that it contributed much to the discomfiture of the Confederacy; that it must be taken largely into any explanation of the results of the war—but the great question, at last, remains, was this numerical inequality, of itself, sufficient to determine the war in favour of the North, considering the great compensation which the South had in superiour animation, in the circumstance of fighting on the defensive, and, above all, in the great extent of her territory. We fear that the lessons and examples of history are to the contrary, and we search in vain for one instance where a country of such extent as the Confederacy has been so thoroughly subdued by any amount of military force, *unless where popular demoralization has supervened*. If war was a contest on an open plain, where military forces fight a duel, of course that inferiour in numbers must go under. But war is an intricate game, and there are elements in it far more decisive than that of numbers. At the beginning of the war in America all intelligent men in the world and the Southern leaders themselves knew the disparity of population and consequently of military force as between the North and South; but they did not on that account determine that the defeat of the South was a foregone conclusion, and the argument comes with a bad grace from leaders of the Confederacy to ascribe now its failure to what stared them in the face at the commencement of the contest, and was then so lightly and even insolently dismissed from their calculation. The judgment of men who reflected, was that the South would be ultimately the victor, mainly because it was impossible to conquer *space;* that her subjection was a "geographical impossibility;" that three millions of men could not garrison her territory; that a country so vast and of such peculiar features—not open as the European countries, and traversed everywhere by practicable roads, but wild and difficult with river, mountain, and swamp, equivalent to successive lines of military fortifications, welted, as it were, with natural mounds and barriers—could never be brought under subjection to the military power of the North. And these views were severely just; they are true forever, now as formerly; but they proceeded on the supposition that the *morale* of the Confederacy would be preserved, and when the hypothesis fell (mainly through mal-administration in Richmond) the argument fell with it.

There is but one conclusion that remains for the dispassionate student of history. Whatever may be the partial explanations of the downfall of the Southern Confederacy, and whatever may be the various excuses that passion and false pride, and flattery of demagogues, may offer, the great and melancholy fact remains that the Confederates, with an abler Government and more resolute spirit, might have accomplished their independence.

This reflection irresistibly couples another. Civil wars, like private quarrels, are likely to repeat themselves, where the unsuccessful party has lost the contest only through accident or inadvertence. The Confederates have gone out of this war, with the proud, secret, deathless, *dangerous* consciousness that they are THE BETTER MEN, and that there was nothing wanting but a change in a set of circumstances and a firmer resolve to make them the victors. To deal with such a sentiment, to keep it whipped, to restrain it from a new experiment requires the highest efforts of intellect, the most delicate offices of magnanimity and kindness, and is the great task which the war has left to American statesmanship. Would it be strange, in a broad view of history, that the North, pursuing a policy contrary to what we have indicated, and venturing upon new exasperation and defiance, should realize that the South has abandoned the contest of the last four years, merely to resume it in a wider arena, and on a larger issue, and in a change of circumstances wherein may be asserted the profit of experience, and raised a new standard of Hope!

* The lapse of twelve pages after 729 is accounted for by the omission to number the steel plate pages in their order. See list of Illustrations.

CHAPTER XLIV.

THE record of the war closes exactly with the laying down of the Confederate arms. We do not design to transgress this limit of our narrative.
But it will not be out of place to regard generally the political consequences of the war, so far as they have been developed in a formation of
parties, involving the further destinies of the country, and in the light of
whose actions will probably be read many future pages of American
History.

The surrender of Gen. Lee's army was not the simple act of a defeated
and overpowered General; it was not the misfortune of an individual.
The public mind of the South was fully represented in that surrender.

The people had become convinced that the Confederate cause was lost; they saw that the exertions of four years, misdirected and abused, had not availed, and they submitted to what they conceived now to be the determined fortune of the war.

That war closed on a spectacle of ruin, the greatest of modern times. There were eleven great States lying prostrate; their capital all absorbed; their fields desolate; their towns and cities ruined; their public works torn to pieces by armies; their system of labour overturned; the fruits of the toil of generations all swept into a chaos of destruction; their slave property taken away by a stroke of the pen; a pecuniary loss of two thousand millions of dollars involved in one single measure of spoliation—a penalty embraced in one edict, in magnitude such as had seldom been exacted unless in wars synonymous with robberies.

As an evidence of the poverty of the South, produced by the war, we may cite the case of the State of South Carolina. By the census of 1860, the property of the State was value at $400,000,000. Of this, it has been estimated that the injury to the banks, private securities, railroads, cities, houses, plantations, stock, etc., amounted to $100,000,000. There were, by the same census, 400,000 slaves, valued at $200,000,000. This left only $100,000,000 for the value of all the property left in the State; and the principal portion of this consisted of lands, which had fallen in value immensely.

The close of the war presented the Government at Washington with the alternative of two distinct and opposite policies, with reference to the subdued Southern States. One was the policy of the restoration of the Union with reconciliation : the other the policy of restriction. The party that favoured the latter was not long in developing the full extent of its doctrine, which involved universal confiscation at the South, a general execution of prominent men, the disfranchisement of men who acted or sympathized with the Confederates, and the granting of the right of voting to the freed blacks. This hideous programme was announced not only as a just punishment of " rebels," but as a security for the future, and the indispensable condition of the public peace.

But to men who had read the lessons of history it was clearly apparent that this policy would be destructive of the very ends it proposed; that it would increase the acerbity of feeling at the South; that it would deliver the two races over to the most violent discord; and that it would be the occasion of immeasurable chaos and interminable anarchy. It was the immortal BURKE who uttered the great philosophical truth of history : that " liberty, and not despotism, was the cure of anarchy;" and who proposed as the speedy and sovereign remedy for the disorders of the Colonies, that they should be " admitted to a share in the British Constitution."

It was precisely this enlightened lesson which those who agreed in the sentiment of clemency, proposed to apply to the condition of the Southern States. It was this party which took its instruction from exalted schools of statesmanship ; which looked at the situation from the eminence of History ; and which desired to bind up with the Federal authority the rights, peace, and prosperity of all parts of the country.

Obviously the policy of this party, with reference to what was called " Reconstruction," was to consider the Southern States as in the Union, without any ceremonies or conditions other than what might be found in the common Constitution of the country. What may be designated generally as the Conservative party in the North, had long held the doctrine that, as the Union was inviolable and permanent, secession was illegal, revolutionary, null, and void ; that it had no legal validity or effect ; that it was the act of seditious individuals, and did not affect the *status* of the States purporting to secede. This branch of their doctrine was accepted by a large number of the Republican party ; among them Mr. Seward, the Secretary of State. President Lincoln had acted upon this theory when it became necessary to reorganize States overrun by Federal armies. It was held by the Conservative party, against all rational dispute, that the business of the Federal Government, with respect to the insurgent States, was simply to quell resistance, and to execute everywhere the Constitution and laws. Its contest was not with the States, but with the illegal powers within the States engaged in resisting its authority. When the resistance of these persons ceased, the work was done ; and the States were *eo instante, ipso facto*, as much within the Union as ever ; no act of re-admission being necessary. It only remained for the judiciary to proceed by indictment and legal trial, under the forms of law, against the individuals who had resisted the authority of the Union to test the fact of treason, and to vindicate the reputation of the Government. And this was the whole extent to which the policy of penalities could be insisted upon.

On this opinion there was soon to be a sharp and desperate array of parties at Washington. When, by the tragical death of President Lincoln, in a public theatre, at the hands of one of the most indefensible but courageous assassins that history has ever produced, the Executive office passed to the Vice-President, Andrew Johnson, the Southern people ignorantly deplored the change as one to their disadvantage, and the world indulged but small expectations from the coming man. The new President was sprung from a low order of life, and was what Southern gentlemen called a " scrub." In qualities of mind it was generally considered that he had the shallowness and fluency of the demagogue ; but in this there was a mistake. At any rate, it must be confessed, Mr. Johnson had no literature and but little education of any sort ; in his agrarian speeches in the Senate, he quoted "the Lays of Ancient Rome" as "*translated* by Macaulay;" and he was constantly making those mistakes in historical and literary allusions which never fail to characterize and betray self-educated men. Before his elevation to the Presidency, Mr. Johnson was considered a demagogue, who seldom ventured out of common-places, or attempted anything above the coarse sense of the multitude, successful, industrious, a clod-head, a "man of the people," that peculiar product of American politics. But there are familiar instances in history where characters apparently the most common-place and trifling, have been suddenly awakened and elevated as great responsibilities have been thrust upon them, and have risen to the demands of the new occasion. An example of such change was afforded by plain Andrew Johnson, when he stepped to the dignity of President of a restored Union, with all its great historical trusts for him to administer in sight of the world. From that hour the man changed. The eminence did not confound him; he saw before him a part in American history second only to that of George Washington; he left behind him the ambitions and resentments of mere party; he rose as the man who has been secretly, almost unconsciously, great—a common-place among his neighbour, the familiar fellow of the company—suddenly, completely to the full height and dignity of the new destiny that called him. The man who had been twitted as a tailor and condemned as a demagogue, proved a statesman, measuring his actions for the future, insensible to clamour and patient for results.

President Johnson belonged to an intermediate school of politics, standing between the doctrines of Mr. Calhoun and those of Alexander Hamilton. He was never an extreme State-Rights man; he had never recognized the right of nullification, or that of secession; but he was always disposed to recognize, in a liberal degree, the rights of the States, and to combat the theory that the Federal Government absorbed powers and privileges, which, from the foundation of the republic, had been conceded to the States.

It was fortunate that the Chief Magistrate of the country, who was to administer its affairs and determine its course on the close of the war, occupied this medium ground in politics—the one that suggested the practicability of compromise, and assured a conservative disposition in a time of violent and critical dispute. It was natural that on the close of hostilities the tide of public opinion should have set strongly in favour of Consolidation; and that men should apply the precedent of powers used in the war, to the condition of peace. The great question which the war had left, was as to the form and spirit of the Government that ensued upon it—in short, the determination of the question whether the experience of the past four years had been a Constitutional Revolution, or the mere decision of certain special and limited questions. This was the great historical issue. The

political controversies which figured in the newspapers were only its incidents; and the questions which agitated Congress all sounded in the great
dispute, whether the war had merely accomplished its express and particu
lar objects, or given the American people a change of polity, and dated
a new era in their Constitutional history.

At the time these pages are committed to the press, a series of measures has already been accomplished or introduced by the Radical party in
the Congress at Washington that would accomplish a revolution in the
American system of government, the most thorough and violent of modern
times. Propositions have been made so to amend the Constitution as to
deprive the States of the power to define the qualifications of electors;
propositions to regulate representation by the number of voters, and not of
population; propositions to declare what obligations assumed by the
States shall be binding on them, and what shall be the purposes of their
taxation. What is known as the Civil Rights Bill (passed over the President's veto) has not only established negro equality, but has practically
abolished, on one subject of jurisdiction at least, State laws and State
courts. In short, the extreme Black Republican party at Washington has
sought to disfranchise the whole Southern people, to force negro suffrage
upon the South, to prevent the South from being represented in Congress
so as to perpetuate the power of the Radicals, and afford them the means
of governing the Southern States as conquered and subjugated territories.

The practical fault of all Despotism is that it takes too little into account the sentimentalism which opposes it, and attempts to deal with men
as inanimate objects, to which the application of a certain amount of force
for a desired end is decisive. It never considers feelings and prejudices.
It does not understand that in the science of government there are elements to conciliate as well as forces to compel. The Northern radicals
look to the dragoon with his sword, the marshal with his process of confiscation, and the negro thrust into a false position as the pacificators of the
country and the appropriate sentinels of the South. They never reflect on
the results of such measures upon the feelings of the Southern people;
they do not estimate the loss in that estrangement which makes unprofit-
able companions; they do not imagine the resentments they will kindle;
they do not calculate the effect of a constant irritation that at last wears
into the hearts of a people, and makes them ready for all desperate enter
prises.

If on this subject the Northern people are best addressed in the language of their interests, they may be reminded that the policy of the Radicals is to detain and embarrass the South, not only in the restoration of
her political rights, but in her return to that material prosperity, in which
the North has a partnership interest, and the Government itself its most
important financial stake. The Southern people must be relieved from the

apprehension of confiscation, and other kindred measures of oppression, before they can be expected to go to work and improve their condition. They must be disabused of the idea that the new system of labour is to be demoralized by political theories, before giving it their confidence, and enlarging the experiment of it. The troubled sea of politics must be composed before the industry of the South can return to its wonted channels, and reach at last some point of approximation to former prosperity.

The financiers at Washington consider it of the utmost importance that the South should be able to bear its part of the burden of the national debt, and by its products for exchange contribute to the reduction of this debt to a specie basis. The whole edifice of Northern prosperity rests on the unstable foundation of paper credit. Every man in the North is intelligibly interested in the earliest development of the material prosperity of the South. It is not by political agitation that this interest is to be promoted; not under the hand of the Fanaticism that sows the wind that there are to grow up the fruits of industry. When the Southern people obtain political reassurance, and are able to lift the shield of the Constitution over their heads, they will be prepared for the fruitful works of peace; they will be ready then for the large and steady enterprises of industry. All history shows and all reason argues that where a people are threatened with political changes, and live in uncertainty of the future, capital will be timid, enterprise will be content with make-shifts, and labour itself, give but an unsteady hand to the common implements of industry.

He must be blind who does not perceive in the indications of Northern opinion and in the series of legislative measures consequent upon the war the sweeping and alarming tendency to Consolidation. It is not only the territorial unity of the States that is endangered by the fashionable dogma of the day, but the very cause of republican government itself. A war of opinions has ensued upon that of arms, far more dangerous to the American system of liberties than all the ordinances of Secession and all the armed hosts of the Confederates.

The State Rights put in question by the propositions we have referred to in Congress, are not those involved in the issue of Secession, and, therefore, decided against the South by the arbitration of the war. The Radical programme, which we have noted above, points the illustration that the war did not sacrifice the whole body of State Rights, and that there was an important *residuum* of them outside of the issue of Secession, which the people of the South were still entitled to assert, and to erect as new standards of party. It is precisely those rights of the States which a revoltionary party in Congress would deny, namely: to have their Constitutional representation, to decide their own obligations of debt, to have their own codes of crimes and penalties, and to deal with their own domestic concerns, that the Southern States claim have survived the war and are not subjects of surrender.

And it is just here that the people of the South challenge that medium doctrine of State Rights professed by President Johnson to make the necessary explanation, and to distribute the results of the war between North and South. They do not look at the propositions in Congress as involving a mere partisan dispute; they are not disposed to encounter them in a narrow circle of disputation, and make a particular question of what is one grand issue. They regard them in the broad and serious sense of a revolution against the Constitution; a rebellion against all the written and traditionary authority of American statesmanship; a war quite as distinct as that of bayonets and more comprehensive in its results than the armed contest that has just closed.

The following remarks of the President of the United States, do not magnify the occasion. They are historical:

"The present is regarded as a most critical juncture in the affairs of the nation, scarcely less so than when an armed and organized force sought to overthrow the Government. To attack and attempt the disruption of the Government by armed combination and military force, is no more dangerous to the life of the nation than an attempt to revolutionize and undermine it by a disregard and destruction of the safeguards thrown around the liberties of the people in the Constitution. My stand has been taken, my course is marked; I shall stand by and defend the Constitution against all who may attack it, from whatever quarter the attack may come. I shall take no step backward in this matter."

An intelligent foreigner, making his observations at Washington at this time, would be puzzled to determine whether the Americans had a Government, or not. There are the names: The Executive, the Congress, the Judiciary; but what is the executive question, what the congressional question, what the judicial queston, it appears impossible to decide. It is a remarkable fact that at Washington to-day, there is not a single well-defined department of political power! There are the paraphernalia and decorations of a government; an elaborate anarchy; but the well-defined distribution of power and the order necessary to administer public affairs appear to have been wholly lost, the charter of the government almost obliterated, and the Constitution overlaid with amendments, which, carried into effect, would hardly leave a vestige of the old instrument or a feature in which could be recognized the work of our forefathers, and the ancient creation of 1789. The controversy thus engendered is something more than a mere question of parties where there are points of coincidence between the contestants sufficient to confine opposition, and where both argue from the common premises of a written constitution. It is something more than the temporary rack and excitement of those partisan difficulties in which the American people have had so much experience of exaggerated dangers and foolish alarms that they are likely to give them attention no longer, but as ephemeral sensations. It is something vastly more than the usual vapours of the political cauldron. When a Congress, representing not much more than a moiety of the American States, and, therefore, in the condition of an unconstitutional authority and factious party, undertakes to absorb the power of the government; to determine Executive questions by its close "Committee of Reconstruction;" to put down the judiciary of the Southern States and by a Freedmen's Bureau, and other devices, erect an *imperium in imperio* in one part of the Union, it is obvious that the controversy is no narrow one of party, that it involves the traditions and spirit of the government, and goes to the ultimate contest of constitutional liberty in America. Regarding these issues, the question comes fearfully to the mind: *Has the past war merely laid the foundation of another?* The pregnant lesson of human experience is that few nations have had their first civil war without having their second; and that the only guaranty against the repetition is to be found in the policy of wise and liberal concessions gracefully made by the successful party. And such reconciliations have been rarest in the republican form of government; for, while generosity often resides in the breast of individual rulers, the history of mankind unhappily shows that it is a rare quality of political parties, where men act in feverish masses and under the dominion of peculiar passions.

To the division of parties in the North—Radicals and Conservatives—there has grown up to some extent a correspondent difference of opinions among the Southern people as to the consequences of the war. But only to a certain extent; for the party in the South that, corresponding to the theory of the Northern Radicals, account themselves entirely at the mercy of a conquering power and taking everything *ex gratia*, is only the detestable faction of time-servers and the servile coterie that attends all great changes in history, and courts the new authority whatever it may be.

There is a better judgment already read by the Southern people of what the war has decided as against themselves. The last memorable remark of Ex-President Davis, when a fugitive, and before the doors of a prison closed upon him, was: "The principle for which we contended is bound to reassert itself, though it may be at another time and in another form." It was a wise and noble utterance, to be placed to the credit of an unfortunate ruler. And so, too, the man, marked above all others as the orator of the South—Henry A. Wise, of Virginia, standing before his countrymen, with his gray hairs and luminous eyes, has recently proclaimed with trumpet-voice that all is not lost, that a great struggle of constitutional liberty yet remains, and that there are still missions of duty and glory for the South.

47

The people of the South have surrendered in the war what the war has conquered; but they cannot be expected to give up what was not involved in the war, and voluntarily abandon their political schools for the dogma of Consolidation. That dogma, the result has not properly imposed upon them; it has not "conquered ideas." The issues of the war were practical: the restoration of the Union and the abolition of slavery; and only so far as political formulas were necessarily involved in these have they been affected by the conclusion. The doctrine of secession was extinguished; and yet there is something left more than the shadow of State Rights, if we may believe President Johnson, who has recently and officially used these terms, and affirmed in them at least some substantial significance. Even if the States are to be firmly held in the Union; even if the authority of the Union is to be held supreme in *that respect*, it does not follow that it is to be supreme in all other respects; it does not follow that it is to legislate for the States; it does not follow that it is "a national Government over the States and people alike." It is for the South to preserve every remnant of her rights, and even, though parting with the doctrine of secession, to beware of the extremity of surrendering State Rights in gross, and consenting to a "National Government," with an unlimited power of legislation that will consider the States as divided only by imaginary lines of geography, and see in its subjects only "the one people of all the States."

But it is urged that the South should come to this understanding, so as to consolidate the peace of the country, and provide against a "war of ideas." Now a "war of ideas" is what the South wants and insists upon perpetrating. It may be a formidable phrase—"the war of ideas"—but after all, it is a harmless figure of rhetoric, and means only that we shall have parties in the country. We would not live in a country unless there were parties in it; for where there is no such combat, there is no liberty, no animation, no topics, no interest of the twenty-four hours, no theatres of intellectual activity, no objects of ambition. We do not desire the vacant unanimity of despotism. All that is left the South is "the war of ideas." She has thrown down the sword to take up the weapons of argument, not indeed under any banner of fanaticism, or to enforce a dogma, but simply to make the honourable conquest of reason and justice. In such a war there are noble victories to be won, memorable services to be performed, and grand results to be achieved. The Southern people stand by their principles. There is no occasion for dogmatic assertion, or fanatical declamation, or inflammatory discourse as long as they have a text on which they can make a sober exposition of their rights, and claim the verdict of the intelligent.

Outside the domain of party politics, the war has left another consideration for the people of the South. It is a remarkable fact that States reduced by war are apt to experience the extinction of their literature, the decay of mind, and the loss of their distinctive forms of thought. Nor is such a condition inconsistent with a gross material prosperity that often grows upon the bloody crust of war. When Greece fell under the Roman yoke, she experienced a prosperity she had never known before. It was an era rank with wealth and material improvement. But her literature became extinct or emasculated; the distinctive forms of her art disappeared; and her mind, once the peerless light of the world, waned into an obscurity from which it never emerged.

It is to be feared that in the present condition of the Southern States, losses will be experienced greater than the immediate inflictions of fire and sword. The danger is that they will lose their literature, their former habits of thought, their intellectual self-asssertion, while they are too intent upon recovering the mere *material* prosperity, ravaged and impaired by the war. There are certain coarse advisers who tell the Southern people that the great ends of their lives now are to repair their stock of national wealth; to bring in Northern capital and labour; to build mills and factories and hotels and gilded caravansaries; and to make themselves rivals in the clattering and garish enterprise of the North. This advice has its proper place. But there are higher objects than the Yankee *magna bona* of money and display, and loftier aspirations than the civilization of material things. In the life of nations, as in that of the individual, there is something better than pelf, and the coarse prosperity of dollars and cents. The lacerated, but proud and ambitious heart of the South will scarcely respond to the mean aspiration of the recusant Governor of South Carolina—Mr. Orr: "I am tired of South Carolina as she was. I court for her the material prosperity of New England. I would have her acres teem with life and vigour and intelligence, as do those of Massachusetts."

There are time-servers in every cause; there are men who fill their bellies with husks, and turn on their faces and die; but there are others who, in the midst of public calamities, and in their own scanty personal fortune, leave behind them the memory of noble deeds, and a deathless heritage of glory.

Defeat has not made "all our sacred things profane." The war has left the South its own memories, its own heroes, its own tears, its own dead. Under these traditions, sons will grow to manhood, and lessons sink deep that are learned from the lips of widowed mothers.

It would be immeasurably the worst consequence of defeat in this war that the South should lose its moral and intellectual distinctiveness as a people, and cease to assert its well-known superiourity in civilization, in political scholarship, and in all the standards of individual character over the people of the North. That superiourity has been recognized by every foreign observer, and by the intelligent everywhere; for it is the South that in the past produced four-fifths of the political literature of America, and presented in its public men that list of American names best known in the Christian world. That superiourity the war has not conquered or lowered; and the South will do right to claim and to cherish it.

The war has not swallowed up everything. There are great interests which stand out of the pale of the contest, which it is for the South still to cultivate and maintain. She must submit fairly and truthfully to *what the war has properly decided*. But the war properly decided only what was put in issue: the restoration of the Union and the excision of slavery; and to these two conditions the South submits. But the war did not decide negro equality; it did not decide negro suffrage; it did not decide State Rights, although it might have exploded their abuse; it did not decide the orthodoxy of the Democratic party; it did not decide the right of a people to show dignity in misfortune, and to maintain self-respect in the face of adversity. And these things which the war did not decide, the Southern people will still cling to, still claim, and still assert in them their rights and views.

This is not the language of insolence and faction. It is the stark letter of right, and the plain syllogism of common sense. It is not untimely or unreasonable to tell the South to cultivate her superiourity as a people; to maintain her old schools of literature and scholarship; to assert, in the forms of her thought, and in the style of her manners, her peculiar civilization, and to convince the North that, instead of subjugating an inferiour country, she has obtained the alliance of a noble and cultivated people, and secured a bond of association with those she may be proud to call brethren!

In such a condition there may possibly be a solid and honourable peace; and one in which the South may still preserve many things dear to her in the past. There may not be a political South. Yet there may be a social and intellectual South. But if, on the other hand, the South, mistaking the consequences of the war, accepts the position of the inferiour, and gives up what was never claimed or conquered in the war; surrenders her schools of intellect and thought, and is left only with the brutal desire of the conquered for "bread and games;" then indeed to her people may be applied what Tacitus wrote of those who existed under the Roman Empire: "We cannot be said to have lived, but rather to have crawled in silence, the young towards the decrepitude of age and the old to dishonourable graves."

THE END.